The Devil's Mortal Weapons

To many English Protestants, the centuries before the Reformation were an inseparable part of their own early modern cultural, religious, and textual present. However, it is not easy to discern the true scope of the Protestant engagement with the pre-Reformation past in texts in which no such engagement was openly signalled by the author or printer, and it is not always easy to distinguish the influences that shaped much of such textual output.

In order to address less obvious or straightforward influences, and map their place in the study of continuity and discontinuity between pre- and post-Reformation England, the present book contains a selection of texts that involve boundaries and their permeable nature, since boundaries reflect aspects of identity both openly acknowledged and unconsciously conveyed. Part 1 treats spiritual boundaries and moral peripheries (sin, emotion, spiritual health), and Part 2 physical boundaries and interactions (body, mind, physical health). Each deals directly or indirectly with religion, either through a discussion of explicitly religious problems or through the application of religious vocabulary or context to a work not overtly religious in nature, thus revealing religion as a culturally formative and significant force. Together they encompass a broad survey of English history, society, and science on the threshold of modernity.

Each late medieval text in this volume is paired with an early modern Protestant counterpart on the same topic; through this selection of primary sources, a history of engagement, hints of continuity, and evidence of discontinuity between these two periods can be traced. By investigating how boundaries and contrasts were contested and negotiated in pre-Reformation and early modern Protestant England, we can determine aspects of cultural identity prevalent in both periods, and thus reflect on how Protestants defined themselves and their world in relation to the past they inherited.

The Devil's Mortal Weapons

An Anthology of Late Medieval and Protestant Vernacular Theology and Popular Culture

JOANNA MILES

PONTIFICAL INSTITUTE OF MEDIAEVAL STUDIES

Acknowledgments

Project financed by the generous funding of the Polish National Science Centre (Narodowe Centrum Nauki, NCN), project no. 2013/09/N/HS2/02213, granted on the basis of decision DEC-2013/09/N/HS2/02213.

Library and Archives Canada Cataloguing in Publication

Miles, Joanna, 1986–, author

The devil's mortal weapons : an anthology of late medieval and Protestant vernacular theology and popular culture / Joanna Miles.

Includes bibliographical references.
Issued in print and electronic formats.
ISBN 978-0-88844-427-1 (softcover). – ISBN 978-1-77110-397-8 (PDF)

1. Reformation – England – Sources. 2. Protestantism – England – History – 16th century – Sources. 3. Protestantism – England – History – 17th century – Sources. 4. Christian literature, English – Sources. 5. England – Church history – 16th century – Sources. 6. England – Church history – 17th century – Sources. 7. England – Social life and customs – 16th century – Sources. 8. England – Social life and customs – 17th century – Sources. I. Pontifical Institute of Mediaeval Studies, issuing body II. Title.

BR375.M55 2018 274.206 C2018-904765-8 C2018-904766-6

Pontifical Institute of Mediaeval Studies
59 Queen's Park Crescent East
Toronto, Ontario, Canada M5S 2C4

www.pims.ca

MANUFACTURED IN CANADA

For Brent – for saving my life

Contents

Part 2

Acknowledgments

Work on this book was made possible by the generous funding of the Polish National Science Centre (Narodowe Centrum Nauki, NCN) for a project financed by the National Science Centre (Narodowe Centrum Nauki), no. 2013/09/N/HS2/02213, granted on the basis of decision DEC-2013/09/N/HS2/02213, entitled "Aspects of Otherness and Traces of Late Medieval Religiosity in the Literature of Seventeenth-Century Puritan Communities in England and America." I would like to express my gratitude to the National Science Centre for their support and funding of the entire project. I am also grateful to Adam Mickiewicz University in Poznan, and to the Faculty of English at Adam Mickiewicz University for hosting this grant and providing me with affiliation at the Faculty of English throughout the duration of the project. I would particularly like to thank the Dean of the Faculty, Prof. Katarzyna Dziubalska-Kołaczyk, for her help and support throughout the duration of this project. I would also like to thank the University of Toronto's Centre for Reformation and Renaissance Studies (CRRS) for allowing me to work with the CRRS's rare book collection, and for granting me access to University of Toronto library resources.

The sources for texts excerpted in the present anthology are of two kinds: ones I accessed directly in a number of libraries, and ones I accessed indirectly via facsimiles from rare book libraries available through *Early English Books Online* (*EEBO*).[1] In all cases, the excerpts are my own, original transcriptions from original primary sources. I wish to extend my sincere gratitude to The Centre for Reformation and Renaissance Studies Rare Book Library at Victoria University in the University of Toronto, the Thomas Fisher Rare Book Library, the Pontifical Institute of Mediaeval Studies Library, Houghton Rare Book Library at Harvard University, and the Rare Book and Special Collections Division, The Library of Congress, Washington, DC, for granting me access to their rare book collections.

1. *Early English Books Online*, Text Creation Partnership Phases I and II, Oxford, Oxfordshire; and Ann Arbor, Michigan. Full text is available by subscription at http://www.eebo.chadwyck.com.

Rare books stored in the British Library, the Bodleian Library, Cambridge University Library, Henry E. Huntington Library, and Folger Shakespeare Library I accessed through *EEBO*. I am very grateful to *EEBO*, which proved to be an invaluable source of research material. I am also grateful to all libraries whose resources I accessed, personally or via *EEBO*, in the process of writing this book, including the assistance their helpful staff offered during my work in their reading rooms, and via email, during the preparation of the manuscript. Particularly, I'd like to thank Emily Dourish of Cambridge Library who helped me with Cambridge Library classmarks.

I am also very grateful to Farhana Hoque, Senior Product Manager, ProQuest Information Solutions, for her help regarding the use of *EEBO*, and for answering my numerous questions.

I would also like to express my gratitude to the reviewers of this book, whose very helpful and constructive remarks and suggestions I included in its final version. Also, I extend my sincere gratitude to Fred Unwalla, Emily Reiner, and Megan Jones of PIMS, and the whole PIMS team for their support and patience during editorial work on this book. I would also like to thank Winston Black for his comments on the transcriptions and editorial conventions of this book.

I am also grateful to Richard Newhauser, Suzanne Akbari, Matt Kavaler, Herman Roodenburg, and Natalie Oeltjen for their suggestions and comments on various stages of this project.

I would like to also thank Małgorzata Kul and Karolina Rosiak for their friendship and support throughout the duration of this project.

Finally, I want to extend my deepest gratitude to my mother Ewa and my brother Szymon, for their unceasing support. Without their encouragement and help I would never have started this project. If it had not been for my husband, Brent, I would have never finished it, and I will be forever grateful to him for his support, patience, love, and for reading my work. You are my rock, and all I managed to achieve is thanks to you.

Joanna Miles (Ludwikowska)

Sources, Abbreviations, and Editorial Conventions

Many abbreviations and other scribal conventions typical of late medieval manuscripts are retained in the majority of early print versions of late medieval (pre-Reformation) texts as well as in a number of sixteenth- and seventeenth-century sources transcribed in this anthology. Such recurrence of scribal conventions in early printed texts was quite typical of the fifteenth and sixteenth centuries, when manuscript material served as a source for print versions of selected texts and many editors chose to retain, as closely as possible, the original spelling and overall appearance of the text they were printing. In the later sixteenth century, abbreviations gradually disappeared for a time from printed books, but were reintroduced in the seventeenth century. Abbreviations also remained in wide use throughout the early modern period in handwritten documents and letters, as well as in manuscript copies of printed books[1] (i.e., books copied from a printed original[2]). Thus, abbreviations and spelling conventions such as supertextual markers (e.g., p^{i}, y^{t}), tildes, brevigraphs (e.g., &, ſ), as well as, interestingly, manicules (in the early modern period often drawn by hand by readers of print-

1. Alpo Honkapohja, "Manuscript Abbreviations in Latin and English: History, Typologies and How to Tackle Them in Encoding," in *Principles and Practices for the Digital Editing and Annotation of Diachronic Data*, ed. Anneli Meurman-Solin and Jukka Tyrkkö, Studies in Variation, Contacts and Change in English 14 (Helsinki, 2013): http://www.helsinki.fi/varieng/series/volumes/14/honkapohja/, accessed 8 March 2017. See also Leonard Charles Hector, *The Handwriting of English Documents*, 2nd ed. (London, 1966); Michelle P. Brown, *A Guide to Western Historical Scripts from Antiquity to 1600* (London, 1990); and A.S.G. Edwards, "Representing the Middle English Manuscript," in *New Directions in Later Medieval Manuscript Studies: Essays from the 1998 Harvard Conference*, ed. Derek Pearsall (Woodbridge, Suffolk, 2000), 65–79.

2. In whole or excerpts; see the copy of John Ball's *Short treatise* (1637) in the Centre for Reformation and Renaissance Studies Rare Book Library at Victoria University in the University of Toronto, for an example of a hand-copied excerpt of a different treatise written into empty pages of a printed work.

ed texts[3]), frequently featured in early English print both before and after the Reformation.

For the sake of readability, and in order to make the texts more approachable to modern readers, the following changes and editorial conventions have been introduced to the original texts:

1. Scriptural citations have been transcribed and generally appear in the form used in the original texts. The conventional Latin abbreviations for books of the Bible have not been altered, but, in keeping with modern conventions, a colon has been introduced between chapter and verse.
2. The punctuation of the original texts has been modernized, as has been the paragraph layout of the texts (e.g., spaces between the heading and text, italicization of headings, paragraph markings, etc.). In some places, particularly in early modern texts, long sentences joined with semicolons or colons have been shortened. Forward slashes (/) used for punctuation in early modern printed editions of medieval texts have been omitted, and modern punctuation used instead, in places often not corresponding to where the original punctuation appeared. Contractions for saint (St.) in the texts have been replaced with St (no period). The early modern "long-s" (ſ) has been modernized to s.
3. Square brackets have been used to indicate a number of changes: to add editorial comments, primarily [*sic*], and to indicate that a marginal note from the source text was included in the transcription (these are predominantly Biblical quotations and dates), although in most cases such notes have been omitted from the transcriptions altogether.
4. Ellipses (...) indicate that elements of the excerpt have not been included in the transcription.
5. In pre-Reformation texts, Latin passages have been italicized, and titles of works have been transcribed as they appear in the text, whether italicized or not.
6. All abbreviations have been silently expanded in each text where they were encountered. The following conventions have been adopted:
   a. abbreviations signifying "and" have been expanded to and/And, apart from the et ligature used in et cetera (&c), which has been left in its original form,
   b. supertextual abbreviations such as yogh or y with superscript e or t; w

3. For hand-drawn manicules see, for instance, the 1477 copy of Peter Lombard's *Sententiarum libri IV* in Houghton Rare Book Library, Harvard University, or the 1678 copy of Richard Baxter's *Christian directory* in the Centre for Reformation and Renaissance Studies Rare Book Library at Victoria University in the University of Toronto.

with a superscript t, etc., have been expanded into their full form: y^t > that, w^t > with, y^e > the, y^u > thou, etc.,

c. macrons have been expanded into en, un, em, an, yon or ion and so on, as the logic of the text dictates (e.g., mā > man, etc.). Other abbreviations have also been expanded into their full form, e.g., th^9 > thus; d with a hook indicating the abbreviation for er has been expanded, e.g., fad > fader; ꝭ has been expanded as is or es; ꝑ expanded as per; ṫ expanded as ter; ṗ expanded as pri; p with a macron has been expanded into pre; etc.,
d. most contractions have been expanded, e.g., Ierl'm > Ierusalem, etc.

Apart from these changes, the original spelling in all transcribed texts, including certain special characters (such as yogh), and italicization in most post-Reformation texts, has been retained. Any other changes have been indicated in respective footnotes, or with the use of the conventions described above.

Unless otherwise noted, the place of publication for all early modern texts cited is London.

Early modern works consulted using *Early English Books Online* list *EEBO* in their citations; all other works were consulted in person and list only the library.

EEBO	*Early English Books Online*. Chadwyck-Healey. http://eebo.chadwyck.com/home.
MED	Online *Middle English Dictionary*. https://quod.lib.umich.edu/m/med/.
STC	A.W. Pollard and G.R. Redgrave, *A Short Title Catalogue of Books Printed in England, Scotland, and Ireland, 1475–1640*; 2nd ed. rev. and enlarged by W.A. Jackson, F.S. Ferguson, and Katherine F. Panzer, 3 vols. (London, 1986–1991).
Wing	*Wing Short-Title Catalogue 1641–1700 on CD-ROM* (Alexandria, VA: Chadwyck-Healey, 1996).
Wing, 2nd ed.	Donald Wing, *Short-Title Catalogue of Books Printed in England, Scotland, Ireland, Wales and British America and of English Books Printed in Other Countries, 1641–1700*, 2nd ed. rev. and enlarged by Timothy Crist, John J. Morrison, and Carolyn Nelson, 3 vols. (New York, 1972–1988); 3rd ed. of vol. 1 (New York, 1994).

Introduction

Peter Lake and Michael Questier, in their discussion of the religious landscape of early modern England, emphasize the merits of considering Protestantism in relation to the English pre-Reformation past. They argue that the reason why the Reformation in England ultimately took hold, through a complicated process characterized by enthusiasm from some, and reluctance from others, was because the question of religious reform was familiar to early modern audiences. The authors claim that

> even hot Protestantism may well have been less novel, less strange and off-putting, even to popular audiences, than it has been fashionable to of late assume. By thus stressing continuity with the late medieval past we can, paradoxically, strengthen the case for successful religious change by arguing that it was precisely these points of contact with existing pre-Reformation patterns of assumption and belief that gave even perfect Protestant and Puritan preachers an in with the people.[1]

Earlier, scholars such as Lynn Townsend White and Charles Hambrick-Stowe also argued that Protestantism and pre-Reformation England were connected in a number of ways, making Protestantism "the culmination ... of the most powerful religious tendencies of the late Middle Ages"[2] because "many Protestants recognized their kinship with medieval Roman Catholic devotional masters and with contemporary Anglican and even Catholic writers. ... [T]hey never isolated themselves from long-established devotional traditions. ... [E]xcerpts and phrases from medieval classics ... worked their way silently into Protestant devo-

1. Peter Lake and Michael Questier, *The Antichrist's Lewd Hat: Protestants, Papists, and Players in Post-Reformation England* (New Haven, CT, 2002), 316.

2. Lynn White, Jr, *Medieval Religion and Technology: Collected Essays* (Los Angeles, 1978), 105.

tional manuals, sermons, and treatises ... ."[3] Perry Miller states that Protestantism was

> a revolt against medieval thought, but only on a limited number of particulars; otherwise it was the same thought once more stabilized ... . At every turn we encounter ideas and themes which descend, by whatever stages, from medieval philosophy, while the forms of thinking, the terminology, the method of logic – though this was believed to have been drastically revolutionized in the sixteenth century – were still duplications of medieval habits, modified but not transformed.[4]

In the light of more recent scholarship it can perhaps be more accurately said that English Protestantism was not a revolt at all, and certainly not against "medieval thought." It was, rather, a movement opposed to particular elements of, predominantly, post-1215 church doctrine and aspects of pastoral praxis in England[5] which, while still impressive in its scope and implications, was not intended as a sweeping end of all things medieval. However, the exact nature of the relationship of English Protestants to their medieval past remains a complex subject.

The aims of this book are thus threefold. First, it wishes to provide a broad, varied, and slightly unconventional sample of primary sources in order to offer a selection of texts that illustrate how, in selected areas concerning pre- and post-Reformation England, many elements of cultural and textual history between the fourteenth and the seventeenth centuries outline both continuity and discontinuity, an engagement and disengagement with tradition, inspiration and opposition; to paraphrase Thomas Cartwright, "tradition not new but renewed."[6] Sec-

3. Charles E. Hambrick-Stowe, *The Practice of Piety: Puritan Devotional Disciplines in Seventeenth-Century New England* (Chapel Hill, 1982), 25, 28.

4. Perry Miller, *The New England Mind: The Seventeenth Century*, 3rd ed. (Cambridge, MA, 1982), 102, 104.

5. As John Foxe claimed in his *Actes and monuments,* Church doctrine was pure until the changes introduced by two popes, "Hildebrand called Gregory 7. which was nere about the yeare. 1080. And of Pope Innocentius 3. in the yeare 1215. By whome altogether was turned vpside downe, all order broken, dissipline dissolued, true doctrine defaced" (*Actes and monuments,* 1583, n. pag.).

6. In 1572, Thomas Cartwright wrote that Protestantism is not "innovation but renovation, and the doctrine not new but renewed" (*A Reply to an Answer Made of Master Doctor Whitgift Agaynst the Admonition to the Parliament,* 38).

ondly, the book aims to shed light on the intricacies of the relationship between early modern literature and its late medieval antecedent, for a better understanding of the origins of early modern English Protestantism. Thirdly, this book aims to illustrate areas of Protestant engagement with the English pre-Protestant past that have not traditionally been conceived as indicative of such an engagement, such as approaches to sin, emotions, or health.

In what follows, I discuss the complicated nature of Protestantism and Protestant identities. Then, the focus shifts to two popular and well-studied areas of Protestant interest in the late Middle Ages, namely vernacular theology and Chaucer, and then to the general Protestant familiarity with late medieval literature and religious and devotional texts, as certain trends and works that form the background for the present book are introduced. Through this brief examination of Protestant interest in the Middle Ages, the reader will recognize the broad scope of agendas and varied approaches to medieval literature among Protestant audiences, which deemed late medieval literature relevant, interesting, and engaging, at the same time as it was problematic in a number of ways. Finally, the historiographical context and specific thematic interests and elements of this book are presented in order to explain and justify some of the choices made in its composition and the selection of texts it contains. This, in turn, will lead the reader to the texts themselves.

Protestantism, Historiography, and Protestant Identities

The nature of Protestantism was inseparably connected to its understanding of its past. Therefore, it is necessary to consider what English Protestantism was exactly. The Reformation in England occurred at its own pace compared to the Reformation in continental Europe,[7] and within the English context and on

7. See, however, Diarmaid MacCulloch, "The Church of England and International Protestantism, 1530–1570," in *The Oxford History of Anglicanism*, vol. 1: *Reformation and Identity c.1520–1662*, ed. Anthony Milton (Oxford, 2017), 317–332; Eamon Duffy, *Reformation Divided: Catholics, Protestants and the Conversion of England* (London, 2017); and Ian Hazlett, *The Reformation in Britain and Ireland: An Introduction* (London, 2013), for more on the risks of considering the English Reformation as completely unique or separated from other Reformations in England and in continental Europe. As Anthony Milton puts it, "English religious exceptionalism thus appears nowadays to be more of a dictum on the European continent than it does in England itself" ("Reformation, Identity, and 'Anglicanism,' c.1520–1662," in *The Oxford History of Anglicanism*, 1: 1–28, at 24).

the English Reformation timeline "Protestant" meant a variety of things to different people, and at different times. Some scholars, in fact, choose not to use the word "Protestant" at all, wishing to avoid anachronism[8] or, in an attempt to avoid the intricacies and complexities of this vast group, choose to focus on particular Protestant groups instead. Nevertheless, as the term is often used as shorthand for a set of doctrines and beliefs shared by a number of specific groups, it is important to reflect on what "Protestant" means, or at least what it is understood to mean in this book.

The current scholarly norm regarding the Reformation itself maintains a nuanced approach that generally takes into account the important and enduring legacy of late medieval religious culture in early modern England, and the people's initial (apparent) lack of enthusiasm for reformist thought.[9] At the same time, contemporary scholarship acknowledges that religious change, on a spiritual as well as formal level, while gradual, was profound, and occurred alongside equally profound cultural changes in England of the sixteenth and seventeenth centuries.[10] A consideration of these changes, as well as of many areas of influence of pre-Reformation religion and culture, has resulted in a scholarly approach that prefers to speak of multiple reformations (or Reformations), or of a so-called long Reformation,[11] rather than of a singular event or process, which in turn extends these Reformations to any time between the fourteenth and the eighteenth centuries.[12] This approach greatly diversifies the understanding of "Protestantism," as it perceives conflicting currents in early modern approaches to "traditional religion," the devotional past, continental innovations to doctrine, political changes to Church organization, and various shifts in practical theology and pastoral care. How are we then to make any sense of what Protestantism meant

8. See, for example, Diarmaid MacCulloch, *Thomas Cranmer: A Life* (New Haven, CT, 1996), 3.

9. See, for example, Patrick Collinson, *The Birthpangs of Protestant England: Religious and Cultural Change in the Sixteenth and Seventeenth Centuries* (New York, 1988).

10. For a good discussion of Reformation historiography, see Peter Marshall, "(Re)defining the English Reformation," *Journal of British Studies* 49 (2009): 564–586.

11. See, for example, *England's Long Reformation, 1500–1800*, ed. Nicholas Tyacke (Oxford, 2003).

12. See, for example, *Cultural Reformations: Medieval and Renaissance in Literary History*, ed. Brian Cummings and James Simpson (Oxford, 2010); or Carter Lindberg, *The European Reformations* (London, 2011).

to Tudor and Stuart clergy and laity, if it seems they themselves were very much undecided?[13]

Early modern Protestantism, both historically and historiographically, is a spectrum rather than a singularity, and can include, depending on the viewpoint, any group of, for instance, anti-papists, evangelicals, conformists or nonconformists, Calvinists, Lutherans, Zwinglians, puritans, Anglicans,[14] Predestinarians, Anti-Calvinists, Independents, or Latitudinarians. The word "Protestant" itself had a bumpy and complex history and Protestants took a while to allow themselves to be associated with both the name and what it seemed to stand for.[15] "Protestant" was thus used variously to describe foreigners (namely Germans), English Reformers, heretics, or even Catholics by those unwilling to be seen as something other than "gospellers": "[early] Reformers spoke of themselves as brethren, as gospellers or evangelicals, or simply as true Christians. They were also unwilling to let go of the term 'Catholic,' although this was a battle which they eventually lost, just as their opponents were unwilling to relinquish their right to be considered evangelicals or gospellers. Those opponents instead labelled them as heretics; as new men; as Lollards; as Lutherans, Zwinglians, sacramentarians, Anabaptists or other."[16] In other words, there was

13. Anthony Milton's remark that "[t]here therefore seems to be a good deal of confusion, even schizophrenia, in the process of the English Reformation," captures this rather aptly ("Reformation, Identity, and 'Anglicanism,' c.1520–1662," 3).

14. See Milton, "Reformation, Identity, and 'Anglicanism,' c.1520–1662," for more on the ambiguities and challenges posed by the word "Anglicanism" in reference to early modern England. The term "Anglican" itself dates back to the late sixteenth century (Diarmaid MacCulloch, "The Latitude of the Church of England," in *Religious Politics in Post-Reformation England: Essays in Honour of Nicholas Tyacke*, ed. Kenneth Fincham and Peter Lake [Woodbridge, Suffolk, 2006], 41–59, at 42).

15. For a brilliant discussion of the history of the word "Protestant," see Peter Marshall, "The Naming of Protestant England," *Past and Present* 214 (2012): 87–128. See also *The Beginnings of English Protestantism*, ed. Peter Marshall and Alec Ryrie (Cambridge, 2002), particularly the introduction.

16. Peter Marshall and Alec Ryrie, "Protestantisms and Their Beginning," in *The Beginnings of English Protestantism*, ed. Marshall and Ryrie, 1–13, at 5. See also Peter Marshall's discussion of the uses of the word "Catholic" for polemical purposes by both "papists" and "reformers" in the sixteenth century in the chapter "Is the Pope a Catholic?" in his book, *Religious Identities in Henry VIII's England* (London, 2012), 169–198. On seventeenth-century approaches to Catholicism, see Anthony Milton, "A Qualified Intolerance: The Limits and Ambiguities of Early Stuart Anti-Catholicism," in *Catholicism and Anti-Catholicism in Early Modern English Texts*, ed. Arthur F. Marotti (London, 1999), 85–115.

no consensus on what Protestantism was in the sixteenth century, no more than in the seventeenth century. Regardless, most scholars would probably agree that "Protestant" in England meant something else than in a number of other Reformed Churches on the Continent, and that there were many unifying features of Protestantism in general[17] that in the long run made it distinct, from Roman Catholicism at least, very much as Protestants themselves insisted.

Indeed, what unites the majority of studies of Protestantism is the belief that "Protestant" meant "not Roman-Catholic," at least in England, where "it quickly clenched itself around a series of negatives and rejections: as it smashed the statues, whitewashed the churches and denounced the pope and the mass, Protestantism came to be constituted by its NO to Catholicism,"[18] making "popery an anti-religion."[19] And indeed, in early modern England, the nature of the initial Reformation of Henry VIII seems to have put the caesura there – the king, not the Pope, was the Head of Church of England, although Protestantism was also built on "noble affirmations – the sovereignty of the grace of God in salvation, the free availability of that grace to all who seek it, the self-revelation of God in his holy Word."[20] Throughout its seventeenth-century history, Protestantism was likewise characterised by anti-Catholicism fervently displayed not only by puritans but also by moderate members of the Church of England, all of whom perceived Catholicism and, more specifically, "popery," "'through a series of binary oppositions' in which 'every negative characteristic imputed to Rome implied a positive cultural, political or religious value which Protestants claimed as their own exclusive property.'"[21] However, what *was* the Church of England? That, it seems, was the question, and one which early modern Protestants often grappled with:[22] "the vast majority of intra-Protestant religious dispute was concerned with the promulgation of different versions of what the national Church was or should be rather than struggles between a stable Anglican essence and a number

17. See, for example, Alec Ryrie, *Being Protestant in Reformation Britain* (Oxford, 2013), 5–8.

18. Eamon Duffy, *Saints, Sacrilege and Sedition: Religion and Conflict in the Tudor Reformations* (London, 2012), 33.

19. Milton, "A Qualified Intolerance," 85. Peter Lake, "Anti-Popery: The Structure of Prejudice," in *Conflict in Early Stuart England: Studies in Religion and Politics 1603–1642*, ed. Richard Crust and Ann Hughes (Oxford, 1989), 72–106.

20. Duffy, *Saints, Sacrilege and Sedition*, 33.

21. Lake, "Anti-Popery: The Structure of Prejudice," 72–106, quoted by Milton, "A Qualified Intolerance," 85.

22. See, for example, Marshall, *Religious Identities in Henry VIII's England*, chapters 6 and 9, as well as the Introduction.

of puritan, sectarian or even Catholic oppositions."[23] In other words, what the Church of England was, was the principal problem.

Chronologically, Protestantism in England meant one thing in early Tudor times, something different during the reign of Elizabeth I, and something different yet again under Jacob I, Charles I, and Charles II, as well as during the Civil War, the Sectarian Crisis, and the Protectorate.[24] In each of these moments of English history various Protestant groups adhered to slightly different tenets of faith and approaches to Church polity and royal supremacy, depending on what one called "Protestant" – conforming, separatist, Calvinist, Laudian or, say, Congregationalist or Presbyterian.[25] Within these groups there were those who supported or opposed the establishment (or Established Church), were comfortable or uncomfortable with the Elizabethan Settlement[26] (or somewhere in between), supported or rejected the ceremonial revival, and so on. Political allegiance to a state-run body of the Church of England[27] divided Protestantism as well. As state policies on Church and religion changed, currents within spiritual

23. Peter Lake and Michael Questier, *Conformity and Orthodoxy in the English Church, c. 1560–1660*, ed. Peter Lake and Michael Questier (Woodbridge, Suffolk, 2000), xix.

24. See, for instance, Euan Cameron, *The European Reformation* (Oxford, 1991); *The Reformation World*, ed. Andrew Pettegree (London, 2000); C. Scott Dixon, *Protestants: A History from Wittenberg to Pennsylvania 1517–1740* (Oxford, 2010); Diarmaid MacCulloch, *Reformation: Europe's House Divided 1490–1700* (London, 2004); MacCulloch, *The Later Reformation in England, 1547–1603*, 2nd ed. (Basingstoke, 2001); MacCulloch, *Christianity: The First Three Thousand Years* (London, 2009); Carlos M.N. Eire, *Reformations: The Early Modern World, 1450–1650* (New Haven, CT, 2016).

25. See, for example, Diarmaid MacCulloch, "England," in *The Early Reformation in Europe*, ed. Andrew Pettegree (Cambridge, 1992), 166–187; Mathew Reynolds, *Godly Reformers and Their Opponents in Early Modern England: Religion in Norwich, c. 1560–1643* (Woodbridge, Suffolk, 2005); *The Beginnings of English Protestantism*, ed. Marshall and Ryrie; and *Conformity and Orthodoxy*, ed. Lake and Questier.

26. Particularly the 1559 Act of Uniformity which defined the form of worship and doctrine in the Church of England and re-enforced the Book of Common Prayer.

27. For more on the relationship between politics, national identity, and the state, see, for example, *The Monarchical Republic of Early Modern England: Essays in Response to Patrick Collinson*, ed. John F. McDiarmid (Oxford, 2007); Kevin Sharpe, *Remapping Early Modern England: The Culture of Seventeenth-Century Politics* (Cambridge, 2000); Leo Frank Solt, *Church and State in Early Modern England, 1509–1640* (Oxford, 1990); and Stephen A. Chavura, *Tudor Protestant Political Thought 1546–1603* (Leiden, 2011). See also Christopher Haigh on the "political" Reformation (as in governmental and state-related power plays) in his *English Reformations: Religion, Politics, and Society Under the Tudors* (Oxford, 1993); cf. a discussion of Haigh's idea in Ethan H. Shagan, *Popular Politics and the English Reformation* (Cambridge, 2003), 5.

and (non-)episcopal varieties of Protestantism changed also. Some groups disappeared, while others emerged, and differed both in how they responded to changes within the official body of the Church, and in how they proposed the Church should be organized. Such was the case with the puritans, who emerged as a distinct group after the introduction of the Elizabethan Settlement, sometime in the 1560s,[28] and with seventeenth-century sectarians (Antinomians, Anabaptists, or Quakers). Conformity to the Church of England divided Protestant groups, such as Presbyterians and Congregationalists, which theologically were to a large extent in agreement, and depending on circumstances blurred other categories of Protestantism as well. "Anti-Calvinists," for instance, such as Arminians or Laudians were conformists,[29] but so were some Calvinists, like moderate puritans. And if we consider the Church of England to be the Establishment, then Puritanism ceases to be non-conformist during the Cromwellian Protectorate (and thus becomes the Establishment),[30] whereas former episcopalians, due to adverse circumstances become, briefly, "Congregationalists" (meeting in secret and outside parish boundaries).[31]

The most divisive manner of defining Protestantism, however, is one that takes into account theological and devotional differences: adherence to specific aspects of Christian doctrine, particularly Reformed doctrine, mapped the English spiritual landscape with Calvinists, Lutherans, Zwinglians, Bezans, but also Antitrinitarians, Quakers, Predestinarians, Arminians, and overlapped with other categories, such as Presbyterians, conformists, or sectarians. In each theological

28. See, for example, Peter Lake, "Defining Puritanism – Again?" in *Puritanism: Transatlantic Perspectives on a Seventeenth-Century Anglo-American Faith*, ed. Francis J. Bremer (Boston, 1993), 3–29; and Brian H. Cosby, "Toward a Definition of 'Puritan' and 'Puritanism': A Study in Puritan Historiography," *Churchman* 122 (2008): 297–314. However, there is also strong evidence to suggest that there were also "puritans" within the Elizabethan Settlement, not necessarily directly opposed to it, who managed to pursue their reformist agendas in an (uncomfortably) conformist way. See Peter Lake, *Moderate Puritans and the Elizabethan Church* (Cambridge, 1982). For an interesting compendium of the theology of various divines that can be included under the umbrella term "puritan," see Joel R. Beeke and Mark Jones, *A Puritan Theology: Doctrine for Life* (Grand Rapids, 2012).

29. Laud himself, and most Laudians, saw themselves as heirs of the tradition of Thomas Cranmer and other sixteenth-century bishops (see Marcus Harmes, *Bishops and Power in Early Modern England* [London, 2013], 60, 78, 120 and throughout, particularly chapters 2 and 4).

30. Ann Hughes, "Cromwellian Church," in *The Oxford History of Anglicanism*, 1: 444–456.

31. Milton, "Reformation, Identity, and 'Anglicanism,' c.1520–1662," 20.

"camp" there was thus a considerable variety of approaches to Church polity and doctrine alike. For instance, not every conformist Elizabethan theologian was a Predestinarian, not all Calvinists were puritans, not all non-conformists were sectarians, not all separatists were Congregationalists, and so on.[32] The abundance of theological variety, in other words, is what forms the crux of the problem of defining Protestantism: each divine, each minister, and each theologian could be many things. Richard Baxter, for instance, can be variously described as puritan, Presbyterian, non-conformist, Calvinist, Arminian, "controversialist," or "proverbially moderate."[33] The central doctrines of the Reformation: justification by faith, predestination, or grace, divided English religious laity and clergy (ministry) as much as it unified them. They all agreed they were Christians, anti-papists, and not Roman Catholic, yet almost none agreed on the details of what that meant: "it was the way in which the synthesis was constructed, the relative stress or value placed on the constituent parts that tended to mark off one group from another."[34] Matters are complicated further by the fact that, since the revisionist work of Bossy,[35] Haigh,[36] and others, Catholicism is sometimes included in definitions of English non-conformism[37] (to which, for instance, Puritanism

32. Additionally, in many cases the way individual groups were labelled and defined in the early modern period was quite fluid (see, for example, Thomas Edwards' *Gangraena* [1646]).

33. Anthony Milton, *Laudian and Royalist Polemic in Seventeenth-Century England: The Career and Writings of Peter Heylyn* (Manchester, 2007), 1. On Baxter, see, for instance, Tim Cooper, *Fear and Polemic in Seventeenth-Century England: Richard Baxter and Antinomianism* (Aldershot, Hampshire; Burlington, VT, 2001); Cooper, *John Owen, Richard Baxter and the Formation of Nonconformity* (Oxford, 2011); Glen J. Segger, *Richard Baxter's Reformed Liturgy: A Puritan Alternative to the Book of Common Prayer* (Oxford, 2014); G.F. Nuttall, *Richard Baxter* (London, 1965); *Pietist Theologians: An Introduction to Theology in the Seventeenth and Eighteenth Centuries*, ed. Carl Lindberg (Oxford, 2005); Jordan J. Ballor, "The Shape of Reformed Orthodoxy in the Seventeenth Century: The Soteriological Debate Between George Kendall and Richard Baxter," in *Church and School in Early Modern Protestantism: Studies in Honor of Richard A. Muller on the Maturation of a Theological Tradition*, ed. Jordan J. Ballor, David Systma, and Jason Zuidema (Leiden, 2013), 665–678; John Coffey, *Persecution and Toleration in Protestant England 1558–1689* (London, 2000); and Paul Chang-Ha Lim, *In Pursuit of Purity, Unity, and Liberty: Richard Baxter's Puritan Ecclesiology in Its Seventeenth-Century Context* (Leiden, 2004).

34. Lake and Questier, *Conformity and Orthodoxy*, xix.

35. See, for instance, John Bossy, *The English Catholic Community, 1570–1850* (London, 1975).

36. See Haigh, *English Reformations.*

37. Particularly in the sixteenth century.

also belongs). In itself Catholicism is often imprecisely defined, meaning, for instance, all opposed to the Church of England who were Roman Catholic, or "the great mass of theologically unsophisticated semi- or reluctantly conforming churchgoers," or those who creatively interpreted the Book of Common Prayer to make it more traditional,[38] and whose beliefs can thus sometimes be seen as overlapping with Laudianism.[39]

Due to the complexities of the term outlined above, almost every book written on the subject of Protestantism tends to include a definition of what Protestantism is understood to mean in that given work: this book is no different. However, as I hope has been made evident from the above discussion, a precise definition is at the very least difficult, and also, perhaps, not entirely necessary. To have a good idea of what Protestantism means, it need not be rigidly defined as the Protestantism of a specific minister in a particular context in relation to a particular doctrine. Rather, at least in the case of this book, it should be enough to narrow down the vastness

38. *Catholics and the "Protestant Nation": Religious Politics and Identity in Early Modern England,* ed. Ethan Shagan (Manchester, 2005), 7.

39. "[T]he nature of Protestantism of those others who continued in the Church of England [i.e., Laudians] remains in some doubt" (Nicholas Tyacke, *Aspects of English Protestantism, c. 1530–1700* [Manchester, 2001], 207; see chapter 8 on Archbishop Laud). Peter Marshall, in contrast, calls this "the Tyackean model of Laudianism as the property of a radical clerical clique" and instead asks "could Laudianism have accomplished the decisive changes to parish worship and church fabrics that it did if it had been uniformly detested [?]" (*Reformation England 1480–1642* [London, 2012], 230). For various views on the Protestantism of Laudians see, for example, Kenneth Fincham, "The Restoration of the Altars," *The Historical Journal* 44 (2001): 919–940; J.F. Merritt, "Puritans, Laudians, and the Phenomenon of Church-Building in Jacobean London," *The Historical Journal* 41 (1998): 935–960; Peter Lake, "The Laudian Style," in *The Early Stuart Church, 1603–1642,* ed. Kenneth Fincham (Basingstoke, 1993), 161–185; Milton, *Laudian and Royalist Polemic in Seventeenth-Century England*; Marshall, *Reformation England 1480–1642*; Coffey, *Persecution and Toleration in Protestant England*; Leif Dixon, *Practical Predestinarians in England, c. 1590–1640* (Farnham, Surrey; Burlington, VT, 2014); Peter McCullough, "'Avant-Garde Conformity' in the 1590s," in *The Oxford History of Anglicanism,* 1: 381–393; Peter White, "The *Via Media* in the Early Stuart Church," in *The Early Stuart Church,* ed. Fincham, 211–230; and many more. Cf. Diarmaid MacCulloch's note that "[w]hite-hot protestants had generally been white-hot catholics, rather than springing fully-formed from the ranks of the religiously neuter" ("The Impact of the English Reformation," *The Historical Journal* 38 [1995]: 151–153, at 152). See Leif Dixon's definition of Laudianism (*Practical Predestinarians in England,* 211 n2), as well as Peter Lake's definition ("The Laudian Style," 162). See also the variety of approaches to Anglicanism in *The Oxford History of Anglicanism,* vol. 1.

of the term to make it operational.[40] This is what Alec Ryrie's definition of Protestantism does. Simply put, it is "the mainstream Protestant cultures of England."[41] But while I strongly and enthusiastically support Ryrie's claim that "early modern Protestantism was a *broad-based* religious culture," I do not entirely exclude Laudians or other conforming Protestants from the equation.[42] And, even though originally the project from which this book emerged was concerned with narrowly defined Puritanism only, I also do not wish to restrict my usage of the term "Protestant" to "Calvinists" or puritans, because there were many shades of interpretation of and adherence to Calvinism in England (with stronger or lesser impact of Predestinarianism and election ranging through the conforming and non-conforming groups of Protestants), and because there is plentiful evidence to suggest that throughout its history the Church of England was often closer to the theology of Bucer, Bullinger, or Vermigli than of Calvin.[43] Moreover, it was not approaches to Calvinism exclusively that drew the line between particular seventeenth-century Protestant groups. And indeed, as Ryrie notes, "the division between puritan and conformist Protestants, which has been so important in English historiography, almost fades from view when examined through the lens of devotion and lived expe-

40. "[A]s Kenneth Fincham has pointed out, 'bar a few separatists, all English Protestants were "Anglican" before 1642, members of an inclusive "national Church."' This is not to suggest that questions of where orthodoxy lay, or what was the authentic and representative voice of the Church of England, were not important issues to contemporaries. Rather, it is to suggest that it is the struggle between competing claims in this period that should itself be the object of historians' attention, with the historian's task being to understand the struggle itself, rather than to adjudicate between the different sides on the basis of a preconceived notion of what should be considered orthodox or authentic English Protestantism" (Milton, "Reformation, Identity, and 'Anglicanism,' c.1520–1662," 8, quoting Kenneth Fincham's introduction to *The Early Stuart Church*, ed. Fincham, 3–4).

41. Ryrie, *Being Protestant*, 6.

42. Ryrie excludes Laudianism although, as he notes, not because he "doubt[s] their Protestantism, but that it was different from wider Anglo-Scottish Protestant culture" (*Being Protestant*, 6). I agree that "[t]o try to exclude it [Laudianism] from English Protestantism is as unwarranted as to attempt to exclude puritanism itself" (Milton, "Reformation, Identity, and 'Anglicanism,' c.1520–1662," 10).

43. Stephen Hampton, "Confessional Identity," in *The Oxford History of Anglicanism*, 1: 210–227, at 226–227. See also MacCulloch, "The Church of England and International Protestantism, 1530–1570," in the same volume, on the decisive impact of Zürich divines on the development of English Reformation.

44. Ryrie, *Being Protestant*, 6. See also Peter Lake's remark about the risks of over-focusing on predestination when discussing the distinctiveness of various Protestant groups in the Church of England ("The Laudian Style," 162).

rience."[44] The same can be said of this division when examined through the lens of other aspects of religious culture gathered in this book. In other words, viewing Protestantism through the lens of approaches to practical devotion reveals that "the supposed distinction between puritan and conformist dissolves into a blurred spectrum in which even the extremes do not differ too starkly from one another," and that "the middle ground between Puritanism and conformity [or Calvinism or Anti-Calvinism] is so thickly populated that it hardly deserves its name," because "so many individuals ... resist easy categorization that the categories become suspect."[45]

Therefore, exploring various Protestant approaches to the pre-Protestant past in the context of a richly construed religious culture spanning from the late medieval period to the seventeenth century, I understand Protestantism to mean Reformed Protestants on the whole spectrum of conformism and non-conformism, with the exclusion of Catholics (for obvious reasons[46]) and of sectarians (for practical reasons[47]). In other words, "Protestants" here mean mainstream (seventeenth-century[48]) Protestants in the Church of England (including moderate puritans), "Anglicans," as well as non-conforming Protestants (some puritans and other non-sectarian Calvinists), and individuals that fall into a spectrum drawn by these points of reference. And, as Ryrie, I use the word Protestant "freely enough, but more as a tendency than a category"[49] partially because there is now a scholarly preference to avoid the term "Protestant" altogether,[50] and

45. Ryrie, *Being Protestant*, 7.

46. Though not without exceptions, including people such as Richard Carpenter, whose allegiance to Protestantism and/or Catholicism remains a knot almost impossible to untangle.

47. Primarily because seventeenth-century sectarianism as a phenomenon grew out of mainstream Protestantism and often these groups did not trouble themselves with establishing a relationship of succession with the pre-Reformation past. For this reason, in my view, sectarian groups should be treated separately, a treatment which largely surpasses the scope and interest of the present book.

48. Partially for reasons expounded on below, connected to the selection of texts in this book, but also because religious identities, and the form and shape of Protestantism in the sixteenth century, are very much their own entity, and the grandness and overwhelming nature of an attempt to chronologically trace all features of Protestantism throughout early modernity is beyond my reach, and is not my aim. The sensitive nature of sixteenth-century Protestantism in England can be very productively gleaned from Peter Marshall's *Religious Identities in Henry VIII's England*.

49. Ryrie, *Being Protestant*, 8.

50. See Marshall and Ryrie, "Protestantisms and Their Beginning," 5–6; Marshall, *Religious Identities in Henry VIII's England*, 5–7.

partially because it serves well the aim to draw a distinct contrast between late medieval texts included here (which often date from the early sixteenth century) and seventeenth-century texts of matured Protestantism in England. It is also enough for the purposes of this book to understand authors of texts gathered here as sitting comfortably somewhere on the Protestant spectrum rather than to try and attach a precise label to someone who would have not been able to label himself with any such precision: to narrowly select from the maze of confessions and identities is to impose rigid frames on fairly fluid positions. Thus, I use "Protestant" as a shorthand to distinguish from non-Protestants of pre-Reformation England rather than as an attempt at an overly generalized, or too rigidly specific, characterisation.[51] Religious and confessional identities do matter,[52] as various camps made claims about England's past for their own polemical purposes, but they matter almost exclusively in that context only (and most frequently only when such a claim is directly made which, as the reader will see, is rarely the case in texts anthologized here). Such claims need not be, and are not, superimposed on the contents of this volume.

In fact, even though many early modern polemicists made claims about their own relationship to the English past, as well as that of others, the true nature of this relationship is much less clear-cut, and is often conveyed unintentionally. Few would argue, however, that the past was entirely forgotten or rejected. Quite the opposite: the medieval English past participated and played an important part in the formation of Protestantism in the early modern period as "contemporary views of pre-Reformation Church" played a crucial part in "influencing

51. However, the particular confession or religious/group affiliation of individual authors, if known, is given in the introductions to the respective texts below.

52. In particular, the notion of confessionalization and Reformation identities comes to mind. Confessionalization, the early modern European process of aligning a given Church with the state, imposed by various rulers on their subjects, politicized religion and contributed to a large extent to conflicts and disagreements between various Protestant factions in England. This propelled the development of Reformed Protestant identities as largely political labels of belonging to a particular group that, in turn, placed itself in connection (or opposition) to the national Church endorsed by the state, and promoted by the state-appointed clergy. By the middle of the sixteenth century, however, these labels also became manifestations of more personal identities and devotional positions, variously inhabited by manifestly non-political lay people as much as more politically-pronounced polemicists. As Diarmaid MacCulloch writes, "ordinary people were beginning to own the religious labels that the officially agreed confessions and the decisions of Councils were creating: they found that they were Protestant, Catholic, Lutheran, Reformed" (*Reformation: Europe's House Divided*, 338).

and expressing more general perceptions of the Church of England."[53] The work of such scholars as Peter Marshall and Alec Ryrie, C. Scott Dixon, and William Bouwsma helps to further this argument.[54] Simply put, it is hard to imagine the people of England unanimously decided one day they were early modern and Protestant, and no longer "medieval." Therefore, it would be hard to understand why, even if this were so, they would choose, or would be able to choose, to forget all that their culture, history, society, tradition, and religion contributed to help them take such a "decision." Rather, it is perhaps more helpful to think of English Protestantism, with all its complexities, as something that developed *from* (or at least in connection to) pre-Reformation English culture, history, and religion, not *against* it. History is a "river full of debris" that through a "muddied, multilayered process" transmits culture and tradition by "preserv[ing] and pass[ing] along many bits and pieces of past systems,"[55] and it was through such a process that early modern Protestantism grew out of the English medieval tradition.

Early modern English Protestants were aware of, and did have an interest in, the English pre-Reformation past, one that human memory, family history, castles, cities, and churches constantly reminded them of.[56] Indeed, "all early modern Englishmen in a sense had Roman Catholic neighbours and kinsmen, in the form of their own ancestors,"[57] and this relationship fed both popular and more specialized interest in the past, such as the work of Protestant antiquarians Christopher Watson, Robert Hegge and, famously, Robert Cotton, who focused on continuities with the English Middle Ages[58] and actively collected remnants

53. Anthony Milton, "The Church of England, Rome, and the True Church: The Demise of a Jacobean Consensus," in *The Early Stuart Church*, ed. Fincham, 187–210, at 187.

54. Marshall and Ryrie, "Protestantisms and Their Beginning," 4; Marshall, *Reformation England 1480–1642*; C. Scott Dixon, *Contesting the Reformation* (London, 2012); William Bouwsma, *The Waning of the Renaissance* (New Haven, CT, 2002).

55. David Hall, *Worlds of Wonder, Days of Judgement* (Boston, 1989), 1.

56. See, for instance, Peter Marshall, *Belief and the Dead in Reformation England* (Oxford, 2002), especially the introduction and chapters 1–3 for more on memory and family history in the context of religious change of the fifteenth and sixteenth centuries.

57. Milton, "A Qualified Intolerance," 104.

58. Mervyn James, *Family, Lineage and Civil Society: A Study of Society, Politics and Mentality in the Durham Region, 1500–1640* (Oxford, 1974), 108–111, as cited by Oliver Harris, "'The Greatest Blow to Antiquities that ever England had': The Reformation and the Antiquarian Resistance," in *The Reformation Unsettled: British Literature and the Question of Religious Identity, 1560–1660*, ed. Jan Frans van Dijkhuizen and Richard Todd (Turnhout, 2008), 225–242, at 226.

of that past. Family tombs and family history records, arms and armour passed on from father to son, family residences, as well as local social relations, land arrangements within parishes, church-adjacent cemeteries, and multiple other elements of the pre-Reformation religious, cultural, local, and social historical landscape reminded Protestants that their lives were rooted in a culture within which they wished to introduce changes, but which they recognized as very much their own. In fact, such was the general recognition of connectedness to the medieval past that "[i]n response, English Protestant divines, and even those who were zealous in their anti-popery, were forced to develop a more positive picture of the pre-Reformation Latin Church … . The more that Protestant divines sought to 'Protestantize' the pre-Reformation Church, the more they reaffirmed the bonds between the present and the Catholic past."[59] In New England, likewise, the arriving Protestants wished to "re-create ancestral English culture, … restore an industrious, pastoral way of life that they associated with an idealized English past."[60] This past was not a classical one, as England did not have a Greco-Roman classical past, and it was not the past of pre-Norman conquest Britain which, while interesting to some early modern antiquarians, did not offer a tangible "Englishness" to Protestants. The past that they idealized was the English medieval past, one which they could glimpse from historical artifacts, cultural memory, and literature.

However, at the same time, the actual Protestant engagement with this heritage is in many ways a problematic subject: depending on the selection of sources one can arrive at very different conclusions about what early modern Protestants thought of the late Middle Ages. Even on classically Protestant issues such as justification by faith, election, or predestination, opinions can differ greatly. Berndt Hamm, for instance, concludes his work on Reformation theology and piety by stating that there were as many continuities as discontinuities between the late medieval and early modern periods in the context of justification, holiness, and election, and that only when considering the two periods together could one understand the process of religious transformation that occurred between the fourteenth and the seventeenth centuries.[61] While Hamm

59. Harris, "'The Greatest Blow to Antiquities,'" 226.

60. Joseph Conforti, *Imagining New England* (Chapel Hill, 2001), 13.

61. Berndt Hamm, "Why Did Faith Become for Luther the Central Concept of the Christian Life?" in *The Reformation of Faith in the Context of Late Medieval Theology and Piety: Essays by Berndt Hamm*, ed. Robert J. Bast (Leiden, 2004), 153–178; Hamm, "Volition and Inadequacy as a Topic in Late Medieval Pastoral Care of Penitents," in *The Reformation of Faith in the Context of Late Medieval Theology and Piety*, 88–127, at 126.

argues for the clearest differences in election and justification, scholars like Nicholas Watson argue the opposite on the same subjects. According to Watson, Protestant approaches to justification, election, predestination, as well as despair, which were important to early modern Protestants and followers of Calvin in particular, were strikingly similar to what they meant to late medieval audiences. Of these early Protestants, Watson observes that "[t]hose who seek to argue themselves or others out of despair in Protestant narratives use the same battery of energizing scriptural promises and point in the same way to the Christian obligation to hope as the medievals."[62] Early modern similarities with pre-Reformation culture, doctrine, or tradition were not surprising, and certainly not problematic to Reformers as long as they were congruent with what the Reformers thought was right. Watson also argues that an interchangeability of late medieval and Protestant approaches to these subjects "would not have surprised Calvin or his English followers, though [it] might surprise [some] scholars."[63] Peter Marshall, in turn, notes that "[w]e are rightly becoming more alert to the bridges and connections between late medieval and early reformist mentalities."[64]

Indeed, mentalities, or rather identities, in Protestant England were to a large extent negotiated and formulated in relation to the English past. While, as mentioned above, the interest of this book lies mostly in seventeenth-century Protestantism, the source for at least some aspects of Protestant identities lies in the process of earliest Reform, in the sixteenth century. As Marshall observes, "the early stages of the formulation of an English Protestant identity, the repudiation of 'man's traditions' for the high ground of *sola scriptura* proved to be a very rocky and unpredictable path" and "[t]he 'conversion-experience' of early English evangelicals was a dye finely compounded of social, cultural *and* theological pigments, and it made an indelible mark on the appearance of a distinctive Protestant identity."[65] It is beyond the scope of this book to discuss the English Reformation in the sixteenth century, particularly since Protestant identities in Tudor England were, it seems, more elusive than in the seventeenth century. However, the initial ways that people dealt with the seismic shifts in almost all aspects of life introduced by Henry VIII's Act of Supremacy, and the development of a revised

62. Nicholas Watson, "Despair," in *Cultural Reformations*, ed. Cummings and Simpson, 342–357, at 350.

63. Watson, "Despair," 351.

64. Marshall, *Religious Identities in Henry VIII's England*, 6.

65. Marshall, *Religious Identities in Henry VIII's England*, 82, 42.

approach to the past were what defined English Protestantism for the next century and a half. As people became divided by their allegiance or lack of allegiance to Henry and his new religion, they also reverted to some of the strategies of adaptation employed during the earlier religious controversies of the late Middle Ages. And as people then gradually developed a wide range of religious identities for themselves, so in Henrician England they began forming groups variously aligned in relation to politics, as well as in relation to theology (such as the conformist evangelicals at Henry's court who hoped for a state Reformation, the conformist and non-conformist Catholic bishops, and the general laity). For instance, those supportive of the doctrine of justification by faith (to which Henry was opposed) were forced to choose whether they stood by their beliefs, hid them, or changed them to fall in line with Henry's polity. The impact of pre-Reformation thinking and practice, mixed with a plethora of influences from the Continent and with the court politics of Henry, Edward, Mary, and Elizabeth, resulted in the emergence of identities that were, at the very least, fluid.

And indeed, "much modern scholarship on the early English Reformation has been keen to avoid ... confessional rigidity, anxious to recognise the fluidity of religious positions and the problematic nature of religious labels."[66] Religious identities in the Reformation in general

> were a product of the ways people chose, and were forced, to identify themselves relative to a number of competing external influences: inherited cultural resources, family and other forms of association, ecclesiastical and secular authority. In order to be a useful way of illuminating the past, "identities" need to be understood, not as stable, inherent or intrinsic, but as social personae fundamentally constituted by and through forms of engagement and self-representation, very often polemical and political ones.[67]

In other words, as sixteenth-century Reformation identities were polemical and polemically articulated (as they were also an expression of influences, ideas, and preferences of given individuals),[68] so also were the seventeenth-century identities that grew out of these Protestant "personae." And as the end result of the articulation of these identities in Tudor England was a set of overlapping, often

66. Marshall, *Religious Identities in Henry VIII's England,* 170.
67. Marshall, *Religious Identities in Henry VIII's England,* vi.
68. Marshall, *Religious Identities in Henry VIII's England,* vi.

conflicting and dynamic groups[69] that actively sought to define themselves through stating their positions on matters of doctrine and politics, as well as on the past (at least as far as theological tradition went), so also was this the result of the articulation of identities among Stuart Protestants. This, in turn, led to divisions in the seventeenth-century Church of England and to a rebranding of some groups: evangelical, for instance, gradually became an obsolete name and was variously replaced with Calvinist, Predestinarian, Presbyterian, Congregationalist, radical, or puritan.

The work of David Como on intra-Protestant approaches to predestination,[70] as an example of the elusive nature of Reformation identities, outlines a history of contention over the practical application of Calvinism in pre-Caroline England, and illustrates multiple problems many English Protestants had with adhering to this basic tenet of Calvinistic Protestantism within the Calvinist camp itself (including, among others, John Cotton). Como discusses the contentious nature of the practical application of Calvinism among non-Anglican English Protestants and outlines the painstaking development of a shaky "predestination consensus,"[71] achieved in order to provide for practical pastoral issues that were often seen as incongruous with Calvinistic theological theory. Como's work also brings to light the need in the new Protestant pastoral praxis for a reconciliation between Protestant ideas and a pre-Protestant connectedness to pastoral issues and communal needs, as many, particularly some Calvinist ministers, felt pre-Protestantism offered a more practical model that allowed for a better pastoral engagement within communities. Revealing fissures in the apparently uniform "Calvinism" of seventeenth-century England, Como's work proves Nancy

69. E.g., evangelicals, conformists, and Catholics; the latter includes the King himself who argued fervently that he remained a true Catholic after his Act of Supremacy (Marshall, *Religious Identities in Henry VIII's England*, 179).

70. David Como, "Puritans, Predestination and the Construction of Orthodoxy in Early Seventeenth-Century England," in *Conformity and Orthodoxy*, ed. Lake and Questier, 64–88.

71. A term first suggested by Nicholas Tyacke in *Anti-Calvinists: The Rise of English Arminianism c. 1590–1640* (Oxford, 1990). Peter Lake in his "Calvinism and the English Church," *Past and Present* 114 (1987): 32–76, David Wallace in *Puritans and Predestination: Grace in English Protestant Theology, 1525–1695* (Chapel Hill, 1982) and Patrick Collinson in *The Religion of Protestants: The Church in English Society, 1559–1625* (Oxford, 1982), propose similar ideas. See also Milton, "The Church of England, Rome, and the True Church." There is also a current of scholarship on Calvinism that opposes the idea of a consensus. See, for example, Peter White, *Predestination, Policy and Polemic: Conflict and Consensus in the English Church from the Reformation to the Civil War* (Cambridge, 1992).

Ammerman's observation that even "the most tightly bounded religious movement" possesses elements of "dissent and therefore complex versions of identity."[72] Religious identities, then, are extremely permeable: even as they can be fairly easily articulated by self-definitions of various groups along doctrinal, spiritual, sacramental, theological, or political lines, identity itself does not mean unity with such self-definition. In other words, "[w]hile church attendance and ceremony tend to portray clear lines of distinction between religious identities, cultural expressions of belief and practice can often produce hybrid forms that intersect and transcend these more rigid boundaries" because "[p]eople in the same church, sect, or religious movement often have varying opinions."[73]

Historiography on either side of the Reformation,[74] then, in combination with the extremely rich source material available on late medieval and early modern England alike, as well as the issues outlined above, prove that the study of Protestantism in early modern England and its relation to its pre-Reformation past can take multiple directions, and no one path will exhaustively answer the question of the impact this past had on the many shapes of English Protestantism. Even though it seems impossible to conduct an objectively conclusive study that would overcome all the complications that arise from studying the late medieval and the early modern together, as it is impossible to avoid making necessary concessions, inevitable generalizations, or choices that restrict a given study's source material and thus its conclusions, it is nevertheless important to try and do so: only through thinking about early modern Protestantism as connected to its late medieval past can we attempt to give justice to its complexity.

72. Nancy Ammerman, "Religious Identities and Religious Institutions," in *Handbook of the Sociology of Religion*, ed. Michele Dillon (Cambridge, 2002), 206 n6.

73. David J. Davis, *Seeing Faith, Printing Pictures: Religious Identity During the English Reformation* (Leiden, 2013), 6.

74. See, for instance, Lindberg, *The European Reformations*; Scott C. Hendrix, *Recultivating the Vineyard: The Reformation Agendas of Christianization* (Louisville, 2004); Heiko A. Oberman, "The Long Fifteenth Century: In Search of Its Profile," in *Die deutsche Reformation zwischen Spätmittelalter und früher Neuzeit*, ed. Thomas A. Brady (Munich, 2001), 1–18; Hamm, *The Reformation of Faith in the Context of Late Medieval Theology and Piety*; Alexandra Walsham, *Charitable Hatred: Tolerance and Intolerance in England 1500–1700* (Manchester, 2006); Lee Patterson, "On the Margin: Post-Modernism, Ironic History, and Medieval Studies," *Speculum* 65 (1990): 87–108, at 99; John Jeffries Martin, *Myths of Renaissance Individualism* (New York, 2004), 11–12; Christopher Hill, *The Century of Revolution, 1603–1714* (London, 1961), 4; Robert N. Swanson, *Religion and Devotion in Europe c. 1215–c.1515* (Cambridge, 1995); Swanson, *The Twelfth-Century Renaissance* (Manchester, 1999); and many more.

The Protestant Engagement with the English Medieval Past

In 1624 Thomas Bedford responded to a pamphlet that posed a question many Protestants were faced with since the beginning of the Reformation in England: "where was your church before Luther?" A number of works opposing Protestantism, particularly Calvinism,[75] pointed out this problem, and an apparent lack of evidence of the existence of a Protestant Church before the Reformation was given as proof of its heretical nature. Needless to say, the Protestants begged to differ. Bedford in particular took exception to the logic of such a question, arguing that it was likewise difficult for Roman Catholics to "prooue where their Church was before the *Trent* Councell; for it will asmuch trouble them to name a company of men in all points professing the *Trent* faith, as vs, to finde a company of men professing in all points the doctrine of the reformed religion."[76] Nonetheless, he devoted the remaining part of his work to list proof of the existence of Protestantism before Luther, focusing on England in particular, though he acknowledged that "to answer out of our own Chronicles" is to stumble over problems in producing evidence from before the fourteenth century "not that there were none, but that the Euidences are lost."[77] Due to this inability to produce proof from before Wycliffe, Bedford announced that he would focus on England between the fourteenth and the sixteenth centuries: as with many other Calvinists, he chose to trace the origins of Protestantism to medieval heretical groups. He started with

75. E.g., John Standish, *A discourse wherin is debated whether it be expedient that the scripture should be in English* (1554); Robert Parsons, *The warn-word to Sir Francis Hastinges wast-word* (1602); A.C., *An answer to a pamphlet, intituled: The Fisher catched in his owne net In which, by the way, is shewed, that the Protestant Church was not so visible, in al ages, as the true Church ought to be* (1623); and many more. The pre-Reformation origin of Protestantism was a matter of dispute both between Protestants and Catholics, and among various Protestant groups.

76. Thomas Bedford, *Luthers predecessours: or an answere to the question of the Papists: Where was your church before Luther?* (1624), 5. Many other writers wrote similar justifications of Protestantism, tracing it back to various stages in the history of religion: the early Church of late Antiquity, to Waldensians, Albigensians, Hussites, or the Greek or Russian Churches (Milton, "The Church of England, Rome, and the True Church," 191). See, for example, Simon Birkbeck, *The Protestants evidence* (1635), 150; and Anthony Cade, *A justification of the Church of England* (1630), throughout.

77. Bedford, *Luthers predecessours*, 3.

> the yeere of Grace 1370, in the time of *Edward* the third, King of England ... [when] *Iohn Wickliffe,* ... almost 200. yeeres before *Luther,* by the especiall prouidence of God, was raised vp here in England, to detect more fully and amply, the poison of the Popes doctrine, and to purge Religion from those dregs and filthinesse, with which it was defiled; a Professor of Diuinitie was he in Oxford, a man of note in his time, and of famous memory in the ages following: ... and [we] doe conclude, that our Church had a being, and the doctrine of the reformed Churches had professors, long before the dayes of *Luther.* ...
>
> But goe to, let vs goe on, and see what other can be named; one Swallow maketh no Summer, nor one professor a Church. ... Such were *Lau. Redman,* Master of Arts, *Dau. Sawtree,* Diuine, *Iohn Aschwarby,* Vicar of S. *Maries* Church in *Oxford, William Iones,* an excellent young-man well learned, *Th. Brightwell, Will. Haulam* a Ciuilian, *Ralph Grenhurst, Io. Scut, Ph. Norrice,* ... *Peter Paine,* Lord *Cobham,* with diuers others, ... About this time *W. Courtny* Archbishop, being in his Visitation at *Leicester,* conuented diuers before him, as *Dexter, Tailor, Wagstaffe, Scriuener, Smith, Henry, Parchmeanar, Goldsmith* .... There was also one *Matilda* an Anchoresse accused of the same opinions; all this happened in 1387. ...[78]

Bedford then enumerated others tried and convicted for heresy in England between 1389 and 1509, including William Swinderby, Walter Brute, William Thorpe, John Badly, John Oldcastle (Lord Cobham), John Browne, John Taylor, Ralph Mongin, Edmund Frith, William Smith, William Sweeting, as well as "many men and women ... persecuted in the Diocesse of Lincolne, vnder Bishop *Longland,* anno 1521. for opposing, or not consenting to ... Romish doctrine," and many other "Christians whom the common people called Lollards."[79] He concluded this impressive list by saying that

> duely considered, we may easily gather, what would haue bin the number of Professors, had the world looked friendly vpon them; For if when the Temporall Magistrate tooke hand with the Ecclesiasticall to suppresse them, and roote them out; if when all men of note and learning, either for hope of preferment, or feare of trouble, turned their studies otherwaies; if when the Scripture, and English bookes were forbidden; if when bookes were so rare,

78. Bedford, *Luthers predecessours,* 7–13.

79. Bedford, *Luthers predecessours,* 15.

and deare, and so hard to come by (as before the Science of printing was inuented they were) if notwithstanding all these hinderances, the Truth of God did so multiply amongst them, what would it haue done, had they had multitude of bookes, or those cheape, the Scripture in English, had they had learned men to guide them, had they liued in a peaceable time, had they had the Magistrate either for them, or at least not against them: for why was the increase of the Gospell in Bohemia by the preaching of *I. Husse,* more remarkable and further spred, then here in England, but that the Magistrate with his sword was not so seuere against them? Whence was it that *Luther* preuailed more then *Wickliffe,* but that hee had a supporter (the Duke of Saxony) which *Wickliffe* wanted? ... Wherefore all men may easily see, that they are much deceiued, who condemne this our doctrine of nouelty, and insultingly demand, *Where was your Church before Luther?* To whom wee answere out of this demonstration hitherto made, That euer since the dayes of *Wickliffe,* almost 200. yeeres before *Luther,* the doctrine of the reformed Churches, that is, those points wherein they differ from the church of Rome, and in which the reformation doth consist, these points (I say) were held and professed.[80]

Bedford's argument certainly seems persuasive and informative, and its main premise was familiar to many champions of Protestantism at the time, as the Protestants loved the Lollards. The conflict between English ecclesiastical power, represented first by William Courtenay (Bishop of London and, later, Archbishop of Canterbury) followed by his successor Thomas Arundel and other bishops, and John Wycliffe followed by the Lollards, served the Protestants in many ways. It provided a blueprint for their understanding of their place in English history, that of a persecuted minority.[81] It served as a self-legitimizing narra-

80. Bedford, *Luthers predecessours,* 8–28.

81. Foxe's *Book of martyrs* is primarily accountable for the persistence of the argument positing a Lollard proto-Protestant past even among groups that, in general, did not explicitly participate in the seventeenth-century dispute regarding the nature of the True Church before the Reformation (i.e., whether the medieval [and thus, symbolically, also contemporary] visible [conformist] or invisible [non-conformist] Church was the True Church). Lollardy served, if not as proof of a direct lineage, at least as proof that religious free-thinking and complex religious identities opposed to the Church of Rome existed before Luther (to whom English Protestants only rarely referred as their "ancestor").

tive to which many Protestants, particularly those who wished to trace their lineage back to sectarian medieval groups, could point and say "this is where we come from," indicating both a community of belief that they hailed from, and a succession, if indirect, of ideas and convictions from individuals, such as John Wycliffe, considered precursors of English Protestantism before its official emergence. For those who did not explicitly trace their origins from heretical groups of the past this was nevertheless useful as it revealed a community and continuity of generally Protestant belief over the previous centuries without a direct cultural succession from the Lollards or other groups. Finally, it was also a way to establish continuity with the English past that allowed Protestants to reconnect to their Englishness and establish themselves not as adherents to a foreign "heretical" influence, of Luther or Calvin, but as heirs to a well-established English tradition of religious reform, of Wycliffe.[82] A large number of Lollard texts were thus printed in the sixteenth century, both as evidence for the reformatory lineage of English Protestants, and as proof that they continued, rather than started, a trend.[83]

In other words, having history and tradition on their side gave the Protestants, in their view, the upper hand both in their conflict with the Roman Catholic Church, and also to some Protestant groups in intra-Protestant controversies. And the conflict was not for religious supremacy, not in 1624 when Bedford wrote his *Luthers predecessours*, and not even since the accession of Elizabeth I in 1558, but for a "superior hold on theological truth,"[84] for proof of who was right in matters of theology. These disputes over theological correctness extended both between Protestants and Catholics, and also between various Protestant groups in the seventeenth century: controversies over the real presence or ceremonial issues divided theologians and practitioners as much as matters concerning the covenant of grace and Church polity issues, such as the argument

82. Or, in the case of many non-Calvinist conformists, to the more or less orthodox medieval religious culture as a whole.

83. This was indeed what they always proposed was the case: "not innovation but renovation, and the doctrine not new but renewed" (Thomas Cartwright, *A Reply to an answer made of Master Doctor Whitgift agaynst the admonition to the Parliament* [1572], 38), later repeated by such theologians as Richard Hooker.

84. P.G. Maxwell-Stuart, "Rational Superstition: The Writings of Protestant Demonologists," in *Religion and Superstition in Early Modern Europe*, ed. Helen Parish and William G. Naphy (Manchester, 2002), 170–187, at 172.

between John Cotton and Roger Williams.[85] Due to ongoing polemical disagreements between Protestants and Roman Catholics, as well as intra-Protestant differences, the question of theological "correctness" and the legitimacy of the existence of various Protestant groups remained a pressing issue.[86]

For this reason, competing Protestant groups often defined themselves and others polemically by making claims about character, their own or of others, as well as about their affiliation to the past, be it to claim it, reject it, or wrench it away from a different group. Any religious identity "reflects associations with past tradition as well as the ideas of reform that reshape or remove aspects of that tradition,"[87] and many Protestant confessions attempted to use this tradition to their own advantage and to the disadvantage of other, competing groups. In general, the radical puritans preferred to emphasize their disconnectedness in principle from the Church of Rome.[88] Some, including moderate puritans, chose to narrate their origin story via the fortunes of heretical and separatist groups of the

85. See, for example, Roger Williams, *The bloudy tenent, of persecution, for cause of conscience, discussed, in a conference betweene truth and peace* (1644); John Cotton, *The bloudy tenent, washed and made white in the bloud of the Lambe* (1647); Williams, *The bloody tenent yet more bloody* (1652). See also, concerning issues of ceremonialism, the real presence, and controversies over tradition, for example, William Prynne, *A looking-glasse for all lordly prelates Wherein they may cleerely behold the true divine originall and laudable pedigree, whence they are descended; ... the first, betweene the Divell; the second, betweene the Iewish high-priests, and lordly prelates; and by their double dissimilitude from Christ, and his Apostles* (1636); Prynne, *The first-[third] tome of an exact chronological vindication and historical demonstration of our British, Roman, Saxon, Danish, Norman, English kings supreme ecclesiastical jurisdiction from the original planting, embracing of Christian religion therein, and reign of Lucius, our first Christian king, till the death of King Richard the First, Anno Domini 1199* (1655), and other works of Prynne; William Laud, *Seven sermons preached upon severall occasions* (1651), *The daily office of a Christian* (1683), and *The history of the troubles and tryal* (1695); and Lancelot Andrewes, *XCVI. sermons* (1628).

86. Especially in the light of newly emerging para-Protestant "sects" throughout the early modern period. During the "sectarian crisis" in particular many Protestants such as Thomas Edwards considered movements of this kind highly problematic (see his *Gangraena*, 1646).

87. Davis, *Seeing Faith, Printing Pictures*, 6.

88. This does not mean, however, that the puritans did not have a keen interest in the English past. William Prynne, for example, was a prominent member of the Society of Antiquaries. Other puritans, such as James Ussher, John Hooker, and Edward Dering were also enthusiastic antiquarians, and used their knowledge and study of the past to back up their claims that Protestantism was a return to the purity of the early apostolic Church (Harris, "'The Greatest Blow to Antiquities,'" 227–229).

Middle Ages, which they called the "invisible church." Thus, Bedford's argument that the only reason the Reformation did not take hold in England under the influence of Wycliffe was because he lacked the political support that could be compared to the support Luther received from the Duke of Saxony is highly persuasive. It also, to Bedford, provided irrefutable proof that it was England that was the true cradle of the Reformation, and thus any claims about the illegitimacy of Protestantism in England are inherently flawed.

Other puritans were not ashamed to rely on past theological traditions while at the same time condemning popish errors: there was a considerable amount of cherry-picking from scholastics and medieval theologians among such puritan writers as John Goodwin, Andrew Willet, or John Preston, who studied and admired many scholastics, including Duns Scotus, Thomas Aquinas, and William Ockham[89] (who was a great influence on Calvin as well[90]). Yet other Calvinists, such as Thomas Fairfax, displayed some sympathy to studies of the past that were considered "an apology for Catholicism" by some.[91] Laudians, on the other hand, tried to take a middle ground and claim the inheritance of the orthodox institutional medieval Church, the "visible church," as their own and at the same time aid their cause against puritans and Roman Catholics alike. They argued that non-episcopalian Calvinists (or at least puritans) had no tradition from before the Reformation and their claims to being the true Church were unjustified,[92] while

89. John Coffey, *John Goodwin and the Puritan Revolution: Religion and Intellectual Change in Seventeenth-Century England* (Woodbridge, Suffolk, 2006), 18; Darren M. Pollock, *Early Stuart Polemical Hermeneutics: Andrew Willet's 1611 Hexapla on Romans* (Göttingen, 2017), 280.

90. Catherine Gimelli Martin, *Milton Among the Puritans: The Case for Historical Revisionism* (Oxford, 2016), 178.

91. Harris, "'The Greatest Blow to Antiquities,'" 228.

92. See a variety of (predominantly puritan) responses to Laudian Church policies and Laud's decrees: Thomas Carwell, *Labyrinthvs cantuariensis* (1658), particularly on oral and unwritten traditions that hearkened back to sixteenth-century disputes; the two differing accounts of a "conference" between William Laud and "Mr. Fisher the Jesuite": Henry Burton, *A replie to a relation, of the conference between William Laude and Mr. Fisher the Jesuite* (1640), 9, and William Laud, *A relation of the conference between William Laud, late Lord Archbishop of Canterbury, and Mr. Fisher the Jesuite* (1673). See also William Prynne, *Canterburies doome* (1646); cf. accounts of Laud's opinions on the Church, Catholicism, and Roman Catholicism, Richard Baxter's warning about popery (*Fair warning, or, XX prophesies concerning the return of popery* [1663], [17], and Laud's answers to some of the charges laid against him (*The history of the troubles and tryal of the Most Reverend Father in God and blessed martyr, William Laud* [1695], 391).

they also refused to trace their own origin to explicitly proto-Protestant groups such as the Lollards. Instead, Laudians, and many conformists, preferred to view themselves as descended from the general conforming pre-Reformation godly,[93] and sought to justify their own policies through a selective interpretation of pre-Reformation Christianity and English religiosity that supported their vision of the national Church. "[I]n Laudian times, medieval piety was more likely to be held up for unqualified emulation,"[94] particularly since it was orthodox medieval religiosity that Stuart bishops pointed to as their origins "before Luther." Others, like the "via media"[95] supporter Richard Hooker, aimed to reconcile the medieval past and the Protestant present of the English Church by stating that the pre-Reformation Church was the True Church (choosing instead to define it simply as the outward or visible Church)[96] and the Church of England was its "reformed continuation."[97] He thus made explicit that the similarities to the pre-Reformation Church (displayed by episcopalian conformists and perhaps some episcopalian Calvinists, one might assume) and not the celebration of difference (as it was done by some Calvinists and radical puritans) were what made non-Calvinism (or at least non-Puritanism) the true heir of a venerable Christian tradition.[98]

Catholics, in their own right, developed yet a different manner of polemical engagement with their past as well as with the Protestant present in England, waging war on Protestantism in general, and on some writers and thinkers in par-

93. Milton, "The Church of England, Rome, and the True Church," 197.

94. Milton, "The Church of England, Rome, and the True Church," 197.

95. See White, "The *Via Media* in the Early Stuart Church"; and *The Oxford History of Anglicanism*, vol. 1, throughout.

96. Milton, "The Church of England, Rome, and the True Church," 206.

97. See Milton, "The Church of England, Rome, and the True Church," 206. See Richard Hooker, *The works of Mr. Richard Hooker ... vindicating the Church of England, as truly christian, and duly reformed in eight books of ecclesiastical polity: now compleated, as with the sixth and eighth, so with the seventh, touching episcopacy, as the primitive, catholick and apostolick government of the church, out of his own manuscripts, never before published: with an account of his holy life, and happy death, written by Dr. John Gauden* (1662).

98. For Laudians that tradition was particularly one of institutional and ceremonial succession. Also, "many Jacobeans took on Hooker's re-evaluation of the visible church, moderated through Field, by accepting both definitions, and applying them in different ways, using 'true church' definitions to attack Rome and 'visible church' definitions to attack separatist opponents." Milton, "The Church of England, Rome, and the True Church," 188, 204, 206–207.

ticular.[99] For instance, blows were exchanged between William Laud and the Jesuit John Fisher, and the pamphleteer Philip Woodward and the Protestants Andrew Willet and Mathew Sutcliffe.[100] Catholics tended to argue against the Protestant claims to the True Church of the medieval past by comparing Protestantism to heresy and by pointing out doctrinal and institutional discontinuities between medieval Catholicism and early modern Protestantism.[101]

With all that, the Protestant polemical use of the English past was not restricted to Lollardy[102] or the question of the True Church, particularly since many early Reformers hailed from orthodox backgrounds and from mostly anti-Lollard settings.[103] The writings of Chaucer also held high value in that department. In many ways, "the sixteenth and seventeenth centuries made Chaucer their own,"[104] and he became, much like the Lollards, a player in both the anti-Roman Catholic and intra-Protestant polemics of the early modern period. His works were thus as often used to justify claims penned by puritans made against

99. See, for example, Victor Houliston, *Catholic Resistance in Elizabethan England: Robert Persons's Jesuit Polemic, 1580–1610* (Aldershot, Hampshire; Burlington, VT, 2007); Duffy, *Reformation Divided*; Milton, "A Qualified Intolerance"; Alexandra Walsham, *Catholic Reformation in Protestant Britain* (Oxford, 2014); Walsham, *Church Papists: Catholicism, Conformity and Confessional Polemic in Early Modern England* (London, 1992); *Early Modern English Catholicism: Identity, Memory and Counter-Reformation*, ed. James E. Kelly and Susan Royal (Leiden, 2016). On sixteenth-century anti-Protestant polemics see, for example, *Catholic Renewal and Protestant Resistance in Marian England*, ed. Elizabeth Evenden and Vivienne Westbrook (Oxford, 2015).

100. See Phillip Woodward, *A detection, of diuers notable vntruthes, contradictions, corruptions, and falsifications Gathered out of Mr Sutcliffes newe challenge, and Mr Willets Synopsis papismi, and Tetrastilon papisticum* (1602).

101. See Milton, "The Church of England, Rome, and the True Church," 188–191 in particular. See also Michael Questier, *Conversion, Politics, and Religion in England, 1580–1625* (Cambridge, 1996), 23–39.

102. For more on the Protestant engagement with the English Lollard past see the work of Anne Hudson, especially *Lollards and Their Books* (Oxford, 1985), chapter 15; as well as her *The Premature Reformation: Wycliffite Texts and Lollard History* (Oxford, 1988), particularly chapters 7 to 10 and the conclusion; Margaret Aston, "Lollardy and the Reformation: Revival or Survival?" *History* 49 (1964): 149–170, and "John Wycliffe's Reformation Reputation," *Past and Present* 30 (1964): 23–51; *Texts and Controversy from Wyclif to Bale*, ed. Ann M. Hutchinson and Helen Barr (Turnhout, 2005).

103. Marshall, *Religious Identities in Henry VIII's England*, 5.

104. Mike Rodman Jones, "Chaucer the Puritan," in *Chaucer and Fame: Reputation and Reception*, ed. Isabel Davis and Catherine Nall (Woodbridge, Suffolk, 2015), 165–184, at 166.

episcopacy, as they were used by pro-Cromwellian apologists like Milton, while at the same time also being cited by many Anglicans, such as Stephen Harsenett, who opposed Roman Catholicism and Presbyterianism (and Puritanism) alike.[105] Thanks to Chaucer as much as Lollardy, Bedford and many others could claim that if England had a pre-Reformation past that was relevant to early modernity, that past was more relevant to early modern Protestantism as there *were* English "Protestants" in the fourteenth and fifteenth centuries, whereas there were no Catholics who would have identified themselves as post-tridentine Roman Catholics in England at all in that same past. Chaucer became a bridge between Protestant interests, with their drive to establish a proto-Protestant English tradition and engage and claim the English past as their own, and the more complex Protestant relationship with English culture and literature. This cultural heritage, not immediately tied to religious politics, formed both a means by which the Protestants understood who they were culturally, that is, English, and a vehicle by which they formulated their polemical arguments.

The 1602 edition of Chaucer[106] by the late Elizabethan Protestant moderate and conformist Thomas Speght,[107] for instance, provides an interesting study of such engagement. As did many other editions of Chaucer's works between 1532 and 1602, and much like our modern *Riverside Chaucer*, following an exhaustive account of Chaucer's genealogy, Speght's compilation contains all texts that, to the knowledge of the editor, were written by Chaucer, or fitted well with his style, including a few interesting additions to Chaucer's literary output. First, the anonymous *Plowman's Tale*, originally written ca. 1400, found its way into the 1602 edition, considered by Speght a good fit with other *Canterbury Tales* and placed between *The Manciple's Tale* and *The Parson's Tale*. It is an anticlerical Wycliffite text related to *Piers the Plowman's crede* (ca. 1395) and the wider Piers Plowman tradition. This tradition included texts both by Langland and by anonymous writers who were more or less pro-Lollard, like *Jack Upland*,

105. See Jones, "Chaucer the Puritan," throughout.

106. *The workes of our ancient and learned English poet, Geffrey Chaucer, newly printed*, ed. Thomas Speght (1602). See the copy at the Centre for Reformation and Renaissance Studies Rare Book Library, Victoria University at the University of Toronto.

107. Little is known of Speght, but his connection to Robert Cecil places him as a Protestant within the Elizabethan Settlement. See David Matthews, "Public Ambition, Private Desire and the Last Tudor Chaucer," in *Reading the Medieval in Early Modern England*, ed. Gordon McMullan and David Mathews (Cambridge, 2007), 74–89; Stephanie Trigg, "The Injuries of Time: Geoffrey Chaucer, Thomas Speght and Wade's Boat," *The La Trobe Journal* 81 (2008): 106–117; and Derek Pearsall, "Thomas Speght," in *Editing Chaucer: The Great Tradition*, ed. Paul G. Ruggiers (Norman, OK, 1984), 71–92.

as well as texts such as *Friar Daw's reply*, which was anti-Lollard. *The Plowman's Tale* and *Piers the Plowman's crede* were separately printed between 1533 and 1561 a number of times, the former going through at least two editions, in 1533 and 1548, and again later, in 1606. It was most likely because of these editions that John Foxe recognized the polemical potential of these works, and in his 1563 and 1570 *Actes and monuments* (as well as in its later editions up to 1610) praised *The Plowman's tale* (adding also *Jack Upland* to the Chaucer canon) as a clear sign of Chaucer's Protestantism, and promoted the "Chaucer the Protestant"[108] mythos among later editors of his works.[109] On this wave of popularity Speght also attached *Jack Upland* (ca. 1389) to his 1602 Chaucer compilation,[110] further promoting the Chaucer-Lollardy connection by suggesting that *Jack Upland* was "thought to bee that Crede which the Pellican speketh of in the Plowmans tale,"[111] so a text clearly, in Speght's view, related to "Chaucer's" *Plowman's tale.*

Speght's edition also contains other late medieval works, the majority of them non-polemical and non-religious, that he either attributed to Chaucer, like a selection of ballads and anonymous short texts, or acknowledged as written by other authors, such as Lydgate's *Siege of Thebes*, but still thought important enough to be included in his volume. Lydgate was well known to early modern audiences, but the inclusion of his works in pro-Protestant editions of the "ancient and learned English poet ... set out ... with a Coment in our tongue, as the Italians haue Petrarke" because of honour "he most worthily deseuereth,"[112] served the broader purpose of popularizing English literature of the late Middle

108. See Jones, "Chaucer the Puritan," throughout.

109. Mike Rodman Jones, "Early Modern Medievalism," in *The Cambridge Companion to Medievalism*, ed. Louise D'Arcens (Cambridge, 2016), 89–103, at 94.

110. For more on the Protestantisation of Chaucer and on *The Plowman's Tale*, see for instance, Andrew Wawn, "The Genesis of the Plowman's Tale," *The Yearbook of English Studies* 2 (1972): 21–40, and Wawn, "Chaucer, The Plowman's Tale And Reformation Propaganda: The Testimonies Of Thomas Godfray And I Playne Piers," *Bulletin of the John Rylands Library* 56 (1973): 174–192; Paul J. Patterson, "Reforming Chaucer: Margins and Religion in an Apocryphal 'Canterbury Tale,'" *Book History* 8 (2005): 11–36; Kathleen Forni, "The Chaucerian Apocrypha: Did Usk's 'Testament of Love' and the 'Plowman's Tale' Ruin Chaucer's Early Reputation?" *Neuphilologische Mitteilungen: Bulletin de la Société Neophilologique* 98 (1997): 261–272; J. B. Thorne, "Piers or Will: Confusion of Identity in the Early Reception of *Piers Plowman*," *Medieum Ævum* 60 (1991): 273–284; Mary Rhinelander McCarl, *The Plowman's Tale: The c. 1532 and 1606 Editions of a Spurious Canterbury Tale* (New York, 1997). See also *Protestant History and Identity in Sixteenth-Century Europe*, vol. 1: *Medieval Inheritance*, ed. Bruce Gordon (Aldershot, Hampshire; Brookfield, VT, 1996).

111. *The workes of our ancient and learned English poet*, ed. Speght, fol. 348.

112. *The workes of our ancient and learned English poet*, ed. Speght, [4], [7].

Ages, indeed much like Petrarch was popular in Italy. To be fair, perhaps late medieval literature did not necessarily need to be "popularized," as many texts were still known and read in the early modern period. Many medieval romances, *exempla*, and other works, point to an unswerving interest of early modern readers in "auncyent" literature: *The Seven sages of Rome*, printed a number of times between 1493 and 1688; *Apollonius of Tyre*, printed in 1510; *The Knight of the swan*, printed a few times in the early sixteenth century; *Guy of Warwick*, printed in 1553; Caxton's editions of *The Foure sons of Aimon* (1554); *Sir Eglamoure of Artois* (1555); *Valentine and Orson* (1555); and many Arthurian romances printed throughout the sixteenth century, as well as works like *A true tale of Robin Hood*, printed in 1686.[113] A number of Lydgate's works were also printed more than sixty times between 1476 and 1590, and from about 1600 to 1687, his selected works were included with editions of Chaucer.

In other words, Speght's volume not only testifies to the prevalent conviction about the rich proto-Protestantism of the fourteenth and fifteenth centuries in England, but also to the overall appeal and relevance of pre-Reformation literature to early modern audiences. Francis Beaumont, Speght's "very louing and assured good friend," said as much himself when he explained that he

> cannot forget to remember vnto you [Thomas], those ancient learned men of our time in Cambridge; whose diligence, in reading of [Chaucer's] workes themselues, and commending them to others of the younger sort, did first bring you and me in loue with him: and one of them at that time, &c all his life after, was (as you know) one of the rarest men for learning, in the whole world. The same may be said of that worthy learned man your good friend in Oxford,[114]

113. This text was also printed earlier, in the early sixteenth century, by Jan van Doesborch; E. Gordon Duff, *Printers, Stationers and Bookbinders of Westminster and London from 1476 to 1535* (Cambridge, 1906), 220.

114. This quotation makes reference to a divide sometimes posed between Oxford and Cambridge in regard to their approach to orthodoxy. Archbishop Cranmer, for instance, "tried to characterize religious reformers and conservatives as the parties of Cambridge and Oxford respectively" (Marshall and Ryrie, "Protestantisms and Their Beginning," 5–6). In texts that were less polemical, such as Speght's Chaucer volume (with the exception of the added Wycliffite content) or editions of romances, as Beaumont points out, both Cambridge and Oxford "agreed." According to Tudor biographers of Chaucer, he either attended Oxford and was a friend of Wycliffe, or attended Cambridge and was "mainstream"; according to Speght, Chaucer attended both.

> who with many other of like excellent iudgement haue euer had Chaucer in most high reputation.[115]

There was, then, not only continuity but also active readership, study, and promotion of late medieval literature carried throughout generations of scholars who passed their interests onto their students, and then by those scholars to their students who could subsequently, like Speght and Beaumont, "fall in love" with those authors again. The progression of scholarship on Chaucer outlined by Beaumont illustrates an active engagement of a few generations of readers with pre-Reformation literature in general: not a "rediscovery" of a lost past, but a continued interest that one generation passed onto another. The Prologue to the 1602 edition claims that all texts were copied from original manuscripts and, likewise, the majority of pre-Reformation texts compiled in this book come from early printed versions of works copied from medieval manuscripts by their early modern editors. Print editions of late medieval works are thus indicative of a more universal engagement with pre-Reformation literature and culture than merely the straightforward and standard proto-Protestant discourse regarding the past,[116] an engagement that made such texts accessible and appealing to a wider audience often uninterested in religious disputes.

Vernacular Theology and Protestantism

Pre-Reformation culture and texts were important to early modern Protestants for a variety of reasons apart from their potential as polemical tools. While also related to the developing methods of early modern historiogra-

115. *The workes of our ancient and learned English poet*, ed. Speght, [9].

116. Speght does draw his audience's attention to Chaucer's ideological "mistakes," in the *Parson's Tale* in particular, but he argues that they should be overlooked due to Chaucer's overall literary merit, which in turn possibly explains why he chose to add "Chaucer's" criticism of the clergy in the *Plowman's Tale* and in *Jack Upland* to his edition (*The workes of our ancient and learned English poet*, [25]). On the same page Speght also mentions the *Pilgrim's Tale*, written in the proto-Protestant semi-Lollard style as the *Plowman's Tale*, but most likely composed in the 1530s. Speght notices the differences in the language of the *Pilgrim's Tale* which seems to him more "modern" than that of the *Plowman's Tale*, and the difference in the intensity of the *Pilgrim's Tale*'s anti-clericalism, which he gives as the reason why he did not include it with Chaucer's works.

phy[117] which made the study of "auncyent" England a new pastime for some early modern scholars, the relevance of the late medieval English past to early modern Protestantism rested, in fact, largely on the nature of English religiosity in the two centuries preceding the Reformation. England of the fourteenth and fifteenth centuries was a religiously vibrant and complex place in which local community customs and religious observance mixed with a great interest in individual devotional reading, and an increase in individual devotional practices in general.[118] People of late medieval England were actively engaged in the religious and pastoral lives of their communities and parishes, participated in celebrations throughout the liturgical year, prayed, fasted, donated to churches and chantries, sang during services, and, most importantly, read religious and devotional works.[119] Even though a surge in individualistic and personal piety is typically associated with Protestantism, its origins should be traced to the affective piety of late medieval England.[120] It

117. For more on early modern historiography and understanding of history, see *The Uses of History in Early Modern England*, ed. Paulina Kewes (San Marino, CA, 2006), especially the essay by Daniel Woolf, "From Hystories to Historical: Five Transitions in Thinking about the Past, 1500–1700," 31–68. See also Alex Davis, *Chivalry and Romance in the English Renaissance* (Cambridge, 2003), and Davis, *Renaissance Historical Fiction: Sidney, Deloney, Nashe* (Cambridge, 2011), for a discussion of the role of medieval history and literature in the formation of the literary output of the Renaissance.

118. For more on this, see, for instance, Jennifer Bryan, *Looking Inward: Devotional Reading and the Private Self in Late Medieval England* (Philadelphia, 2008); Jessica Brantley, *Reading in the Wilderness: Private Devotion and Public Performance in Late Medieval England* (Chicago, 2007); and Nicole R. Rice, *Lay Piety and Religious Discipline in Middle English Literature* (Cambridge, 2008).

119. Multiple volumes have been written on the nature of the pre-Reformation English Church. For a survey, see, for example, Brantley, *Reading in the Wilderness*; Bryan, *Looking Inward*; Rice, *Lay Piety and Religious Discipline*; Miri Rubin, *Corpus Christi: The Eucharist in Late Medieval Culture* (Cambridge, 1991); Robert N. Swanson, *Church and Society in Late Medieval England* (London, 1993); G.W. Bernard, *The Late Medieval Church: Vitality and Vulnerability Before the Break with Rome* (New Haven, CT, 2012); Eamon Duffy, *The Stripping of the Altars: Traditional Religion in England, c. 1400–c. 1580* (New Haven, CT, 1992); Norman Tanner, *The Ages of Faith: Popular Religion in Late Medieval England and Western Europe* (London, 2009); Katherine L. French, *The People of the Parish: Community Life in a Late Medieval English Diocese* (Philadelphia, 2001); and many more.

120. More accurately, it should perhaps be said that issues of religious autonomy, individualism, and interiority were central to Christianity and its tradition throughout its history, shaping the affective and inward focus of late medieval English devotion. However, the form of devotional practice and spiritual interiority in fourteenth- and fifteenth-century England

was in such an atmosphere of omnipresent religiosity, increased devotional interests of the laity, and lay engagement in personal and communal piety that the religious consciousness and independence of the English flourished, and allowed for the development, as Protestants believed, of England's own "Reformation": Lollardy.[121]

While an exhaustive discussion of Lollardy would easily take up a separate volume, and is not the main focus of the present book, it is important at this point to highlight that Lollardy should not be seen simply as a heretical movement that strayed from the otherwise completely orthodox standards of religious life in late medieval England, nor merely as an ideological mutation or aberration that took hold over select individuals without connection to, or impact on, the rest of orthodox England. The highlights of Wycliffite "reform," such as the confiscation of clerical property, the ministry of all believers, the validity of vernacular Mass and Bible, and issues surrounding clerical "contamination" of doctrine and even Christianity in general were powerful ideas that caught the imaginations of many.[122] However, it remains largely a matter of debate whether Lollardy grew out of Wycliffe's ideas, or whether Wycliffe's ideas were so akin to the concerns and disputes circulating among the English faithful throughout the fourteenth century that they gradually became interchangeable, making Wycliffe stand as an inciter of change where he should perhaps more accurately be seen as one who simply voiced what was on the minds of many. If the latter was the case, then the laity of late medieval England in general, not just those who identified as Lollards, should be credited with being devotionally and religiously critical.[123]

---

has, it can be argued, a more immediate impact on sixteenth- and seventeenth-century religiosity which in itself, of course, tried to reinvent this inheritance as that of an early Christian tradition as much as that of a pre-Reformation influence.

121. See Hudson, *The Premature Reformation*, throughout. For a more traditionalist approach to the role of Lollardy in the development of English Protestantism, see also A.G. Dickens, *Lollards and Protestants in the Diocese of York 1509–1558* (Oxford, 1959).

122. See Hudson, *The Premature Reformation*, 60–119, where Hudson provides arguments for the existence of the familiarity of the early Lollards with Wycliffe's work. For a contrary point of view see, for example, J. Crompton, "John Wyclif: A Study in Mythology," *Transactions of the Leicestershire Archaeological and Historical Society* 42 (1966–1967): 6–34 and Crompton, "Leicestershire Lollards," *Transactions of the Leicestershire Archaeological and Historical Society* 44 (1968–1969): 11–44.

123. There has been an increasing scholarly trend towards dethroning Lollardy as the bastion of early Reformation in England, and to deny it any more than a minor role in enacting and encouraging the Reformation (see, for example, J.J. Scarisbrick, *The Reformation and the English People* [New York, 1984], 46; Richard Rex, *The Lollards* [Basingstoke, 2002], esp.

Therefore, a term that incorporates this complexity of approaches to religion and devotion in late medieval England, vernacular medieval theology, seems more appropriate than the narrow term "Lollardy" to denote the religious atmosphere of the time.

As Nicholas Watson suggests in his seminal essay on the subject,[124] a body of texts that can be described as popular, devotional, affective, or mystical is more accurately defined as vernacular theology as this term brings to attention the "intellectual content" and cultural significance of a wide array of works united by their focus on spiritual matters, rather than divided by their generic classification. Eliana Corbari further notes that "a broader application of the term vernacular theology to texts such as medieval sermons and hagiography, as well as plays, poetry, and some of the so-called 'mystical writings,' could lead to a more sustained study of these as theology, as well as literature and history."[125] Watson persuasively argues that the general intellectual ambience of late medieval England, and the emergence of Lollardy, as well as opposition to it, influenced the whole body of religious and devotional texts, and the spiritual lives of many people. This made popular, devotional, and theological writing of the fifteenth cen-

chapters 4 and 5, and Rex, "New Light on Tyndale and Lollardy," *Reformation* 8 [2003]: 143–171). The reader is advised to refer to the work of Richard Rex more broadly for more on this topic, particularly in regard to the impact Lollardy had on the pattern of religious change in late medieval and especially early modern England. However, while a direct causal relationship between Lollardy and Protestantism is impossible to trace and is considered nonexistent, the broader vernacular devotional culture of late medieval England that gave rise to Lollardy can and should, I think, be viewed as conducive to the birth of early Protestantism in England, not least because cases of Lollardy would have influenced some to rethink aspects of late medieval Catholicism. Likewise, reactions against Lollardy (such as Arundel's 1409 Constitutions) impacted the intellectual output of orthodox or semi-orthodox writers and thinkers, including their reactions to tightened Church censorship and control over belief and practice. In other words, a strong case can still be made for the indirect influence of Lollardy as well as reactions to Lollardy on the creation of an intellectual ambience that led directly to a reformist "awakening" of people like William Tyndale. For remarks on such a role of Lollardy in the onset of the English Reformation see, for example, Alec Ryrie, *Gospel and Henry VIII: Evangelicals in the Early English Reformation* (Cambridge, 2003), throughout, esp. chapter 7. See also MacCulloch, "England," 172–173.

124. Nicholas Watson, "Censorship and Cultural Change in Late-Medieval England: Vernacular Theology, the Oxford Translation Debate, and Arundel's Constitutions of 1409," *Speculum* 70 (1995): 822–864.

125. Eliana Corbari, *Vernacular Theology: Dominican Sermons and Audience in Late Medieval Italy* (Berlin, 2013), 63.

tury both distinctively different from previous such works, and indebted to the tradition it emerged from.[126] In other words, Lollardy can be seen as both the cause and effect of much of the emergent devotional individuality and independence of the late medieval laity and lay vernacular theology, which in turn gave rise to a vibrant culture of devotional plurality in England in the fourteenth and fifteenth centuries and which influenced ascendant Protestantism of the sixteenth century.

While, to an extent, many of the late medieval laity followed the patterns of religious life established as cultural habits, many also had their own opinions on individual aspects of devotion, had personal experiences with the clergy that formed the basis of their criticism, or displayed devotional curiosity that led them to seek beyond what was "prescriptively" available. In other words, there was a plethora of religious identities in pre-Reformation England, much as there was in the early modern period. Indeed, the "vernacular" of vernacular theology is a key word here: it was specifically texts in English that contributed to this curiosity and which served to satisfy it, and it was the insistence on the vernacular of the Lollards as well as those deemed to have Lollard sympathies (but who did not consider themselves to be among them) that led to the branding of Lollardy as heresy.[127]

126. Watson, "Censorship and Cultural Change in Late-Medieval England," 824–825. See the article throughout on the relationship between fourteenth- and fifteenth-century vernacular devotional texts, and part III on the debate over the relevance and risks of the use of the vernacular for religious education and reading at the time. See also Bernard McGinn, *Meister Eckhart and the Beguine Mystics: Hadewijch of Brabant, Mechthild of Magdeburg, and Marguerite Porete* (New York, 1994), 4–14, for more on vernacular theology.

127. As Watson puts it, citing J.A.F. Thomson, "Lollardy began life as a powerful expression of reformist tendencies inside the Church, whose status as a heresy was achieved as much by reactionary shifts within the definition of orthodoxy as by its own growing extremism. In its radical focus on interiority, Lollardy was and remained part of a larger European reaction in favor of personal simplicity and a focus on the word as well as the image, a reaction apparent not only in the Devotio moderna in the Low Countries but also, closer to home, in the works of Langland, Walter Hilton, and Julian of Norwich. ... For the Constitutions [a formidable reaction against Lollardy] were the peroration of an intense, approximately sixty-year cultural argument over the whole role of the vernacular in religious culture: an argument that took in larger questions about the intellectual capacities of the laity, the role of the clergy in ministering to them, and the suitability of vernacular language as a vehicle for religious truth ... [because] as lay interest in religious writing in English began its rapid rise, writing in the 'mother tongue' increasingly implied writing for an indeterminate and socially mixed group who had in common only the fact that they were not literati" (Watson, "Censorship and Cultural Change in Late-Medieval England," 826, 837, 838).

Measures introduced to stifle Lollardy, such as increased censorship and condemnation of vernacular theology, had the landslide effect of encouraging heterodoxy and para-orthodoxy in those who would perhaps never have given these matters any thought if these measures had not propelled them to do so. According to Nicholas Watson, Richard Rolle influenced lay religiosity in fourteenth-century England in a way that helped to "bring out the radical potential latent in pastoral theology's pedagogical programme, which cannot but risk emancipating people from dependence on ecclesiastical structures by letting them take responsibility for their own souls."[128] While such "emancipation" did not necessarily occur within all readers of Rolle, nor the whole of the literate laity in late medieval England, and was not at all entirely indebted to Lollardy either, its potential and appeal indicates an intellectually fertile ground for flexibly semi-orthodox approaches to emerge, with the vernacular, English, as the vehicle of this potential.

Jennifer Bryan notes that not only texts not normally considered heretical, like the *Seven poyntes of trewe love and everlastynge wysdom*, but also those with an official seal of orthodoxy, such as Nicolas Love's *Myrrour of the blessed lyf of Jesu Crist* (approved by Thomas Arundel himself), often discussed controversial issues of the time, such as real presence in the Eucharist, in ways that could be flexibly interpreted, and not always in favour of the established ecclesiastical drill on the matter.[129] The more such texts were available to the laity, the more approaches to devotional matters the laity developed, approaches that could be placed anywhere on the orthodoxy-heterodoxy spectrum (which is what Archbishop Arundel wanted to prevent with his 1409 Constitutions[130]). This variance of opinions and of levels of devotional consciousness and independence gave rise to a religious culture in which orthodoxy could mix with heterodoxy without clear-cut patterns of resistance and conflict: many thought of themselves as perfectly orthodox when they criticized their parish priest for greed or gluttony, while others perhaps considered a fellow parishioner in possession of a translation of the Bible the black sheep of the parish.

In such an ambience of variance, Lollardy as well as other versions of vernacular theology conducive to the emergence of individual religious identities not only flourished, but became integrated with many ideas and behaviours that

128. Nicholas Watson, "The Middle English Mystics," in *The Cambridge History of Medieval English Literature*, ed. David Wallace (Cambridge, 1999), 539–565, at 549–550, quoted by Bryan, *Looking Inward*, 43.

129. Bryan, *Looking Inward*, 53.

130. Watson, "Censorship and Cultural Change in Late-Medieval England," 836–840.

fitted into what might be called para-orthodoxy: not quite orthodox, but not completely heterodox either, from talking openly about the Gospel, which to some constituted preaching without a license, through privately reading the Bible in English or denying transubstantiation, to simply being unhappy with the pastoral performance of the parish priest. Whatever the local pattern of understanding what late medieval vernacular theology was, there were many who considered themselves Lollards, many that thought of themselves as orthodox but were considered heretics or eccentrics by others, and many that did not think of these things much at all, but simply carried on living how they thought was right.[131] In other words, Lollardy was one facet, or reflection, of the complexity and richness of the English pre-Reformation religious culture, one that illustrated, on the surface, the depth of approaches to religion in late medieval England. It was this devotional independence and curiosity of many pre-Reformation readers and churchgoers that allowed multiple versions of vernacular theology to take hold in England, a hold that lasted from the middle of the fourteenth century (if one assumes that the roots of para-orthodox ideas developed before Wycliffe penned his treatises) until the 1530s.[132] It was also this extremely large and rich body of para-orthodoxy, and not only narrow Lollardy, that the Protestants inherited and harkened back to in their own writings.

Why did Lollardy survive until as late as the 1530s, but then seems to have disappeared? After all, the official stance of the state Church in pre-Reformation England was that Lollardy was a heresy and was to be eradicated, and any outlets of vernacular theology that were too radical had to be stifled, and suspect texts banned. The answer to the question of the longevity of Lollardy lies in the widespread acceptance of many "Lollard," i.e., more broadly para-orthodox, ideas by many of the laity[133] who considered themselves fairly orthodox: it was very difficult to clearly say which ideas, apart from a handful, like denying transubstantiation, were straightforwardly heretical, at least to untrained parishioners. Additionally, the methods applied by the Church and state to root out heterodoxy

131. See Hudson, *The Premature Reformation*, 467–469, for an overview of the compliance of many Lollards with outward devotion (e.g., continuing to receive the host).

132. See Hudson, *The Premature Reformation*, 380–507, on the development of Lollardy throughout the fourteenth century until 1420, and on the pitfalls of its growth throughout the fifteenth century. See also Margaret Aston, *Lollards and Reformers: Images and Literacy in Late Medieval Religion* (London, 2003).

133. See, for example, Judy Ann Ford, *John Mirk's Festial: Orthodoxy, Lollardy and the Common People in Fourteenth-Century England* (Cambridge, 2006). See also Dickens, *Lollards and Protestants in the Diocese of York.*

were not always successful, and often much more lenient than those used against other heresies elsewhere in Europe. Many first-time English heretics interrogated by Church authorities were simply asked to recount their errors and swear they would not spread their heresy; only relapses were punished more severely and not all repeat offenders were punished with death.[134]

Notwithstanding the measures introduced by Thomas Arundel with his 1409 Constitutions combined with the efforts of his successors to ban anything with so much as a whiff of heresy, the ranks of para-orthodox laity and thinkers expanded steadily throughout the fourteenth, fifteenth,[135] and sixteenth centuries. It did not seem like heterodoxy was going to allow itself to be rooted out in England, but then in the 1530s it seems to have disappeared. This "disappearance," though, was not a waning of numbers, but in fact a change of label:[136] from 1534 onwards all who protested against the Pope and the sacraments could do so openly, and that included those who participated in religious disputes and interpretations of doctrine, as well as those who simply had their own take on religion and piety.[137] Additionally, the possibility of having the king support a reformatory movement, much like Luther's ideas were backed in Germany, encouraged many to unite despite their differences, and "stimulated a struggle to build a godly visible Church that tended to overshadow more abstract doctrinal

134. The number of Lollards punished by death depended on the county. Norwich, for instance, was infamous both for large numbers of Lollards, and large numbers of Lollard executions. See Hudson, *The Premature Reformation*, 446–507, for more on anti-Lollard state and Church measures.

135. Hudson, *The Premature Reformation*, 447–451, and throughout. See also the chapters "The Context of Vernacular Wycliffism" and "The Re-emergence of Reform," 390–507.

136. Revisionist historiography of the 1990s in particular supports this claim: "[h]istorians now agree that Lollardy still existed in England at the time of the Reformation, but it is uncertain how strong it was. On balance it seems that the surviving Lollards were attracted into the Reformers' camp, rather than that the first Reformers were affected by contemporary Lollardy" (Gerald Lewis Bray, *Documents of the English Reformation 1526–1701* [Cambridge, 1994], 17). Regardless, as can be surmised from what the Protestants themselves thought, Reformers were in fact influenced, by their own admittance, by Lollardy as well.

137. Particularly as those accused of heresy were not always necessarily Lollards, although given the fluidity of the term then and now, it is not always easy to categorize individual beliefs as straightforwardly Lollard or not. See, for instance, Marshall, *Reformation England 1480–1642*, chapter 2 throughout and pp. 33–39 in particular for a concise discussion of the historiography of pre-Reformation Lollardy and of continuities and discontinuities between Lollardy and early English Protestantism. See also the discussion of Lollardy by Wendy Scase in the *Cambridge Companion to Reformation Theology*, ed. David Bagchi and David C. Steinmetz (Cambridge, 2004), 15–21, for a concise articulation of Lollard belief.

speculation."[138] This explains why, even though many aspects of Henrician reform were considered unsatisfactory to some evangelicals and Lollards as well as other para-orthodox thinkers, they united in line with Henry's own beliefs (regarding the real presence, for instance, which Henry supported and Lollards tended to deny) and formed a front against those who threatened the possibility of an official sanction to reform, calling them "sacramentarians."[139]

In other words, the complex late medieval culture of vernacular theology gave rise to, and became, something else: Protestantism, from the onset internally divided into those conforming and not conforming with royal supremacy and state Reformation, but united in its drive to eradicate "popery."[140] The proto-Protestant argumentation of early modern writers in support of the existence of

138. Felicity Heal, *Reformation in Britain and Ireland* (Oxford, 2003), 317.

139. MacCulloch, *Thomas Cranmer: A Life*, 232–234, quoted by Marshall, *Religious Identities in Henry VIII's England*, 8. For more on the place of Catholicism in English nonconformity, see, for example, Bossy, *The English Catholic Community*; and Shagan, *Popular Politics and the English Reformation.*

140. See also Peter Marshall's discussion of the late medieval nature of the early Reformation in England: "As they emerged in the middle decades of the sixteenth century, Protestants were people with a group-narrative, a history they had had time to experience or invent. The evangelicals of the early years, almost by definition, were not. They were, in fact, late medieval Catholics, albeit ones who had become deeply unhappy with important aspects of medieval Catholic theology and devotion. Increasingly, historians are inclined to locate the origins of that unhappiness within the mainstream of medieval Catholicism itself, rather than to trace it back to a supposedly independent source, such as 'Lollardy' or 'humanism'" (*Religious Identities in Henry VIII's England*, 5; see also the first section throughout). It is also interesting to note that the views on Henrician Catholicism that Marshall mentions, one that suggests the emergence of a new version of Catholicism stimulated by Henrician policies (10), and one that criticizes it for not giving enough justice to the strong traditionalism and inspiration with medieval scholastic thought displayed by Catholics in early sixteenth-century England (11), can be at least partially reconciled if viewed through the lens of the legacy of late medieval para-orthodoxy. Those who seemed to have developed a "Henrician vision" of Catholicism as well as those who chose to seek reassurance in past and contemporary contrary thinkers were, perhaps, the very same people who a century earlier disagreed on how to enforce, obey, or disobey Arundel's Constitutions, and who made choices and arguments for their own versions of orthodoxy. In other words, it is worth considering that the Henrician evangelicals and the divided Catholic majority, conforming or not conforming with Henry's reforms, were continuations of reactive currents from before these reforms (with obvious new circumstances such as royal supremacy to adjust to), represented by people used to frequent and hearty religious dispute. Thus, by the end of the 1530s it was possible to have people in Henry's Reformed Church who argued for auricular confession, Latin mass and other traditions to be maintained, while claiming to be wholeheartedly Protestant (or rather, Reformed).

medieval antecedents to Protestantism (and thus in support of early modern Protestantism) was therefore quite reasonable, although what Protestant historical polemicists did not take into account was that "[h]yt is not al gold that glareth":[141] they overlooked the possibility that what they inherited as their Protestant identity was not just an openly Lollard culture with its conscious proto-Protestantism but, in fact, the complete cultural atmosphere in which such open Lollardy emerged and functioned, along with all its complexity, vagueness, and variance. In fact, many early Reformers came from perfectly orthodox and pious backgrounds,[142] and it seems that the significance of Lollardy for Protestants was blown out of proportion, whereas a consideration of para-orthodox late medieval vernacular theology was too frequently overlooked, although it most certainly found its way into many early modern texts, if inadvertently. In other words, what Protestant enthusiasts of pre-Reformation Lollardy did not realize was that they were influenced both by what was clearly seen as Lollard and by that which was much less clearly proto-Protestant, but rather simultaneously semi-orthodox and semi-heterodox: the vibrant English late medieval religious culture that brought Lollardy, as well as numerous other, individualistic approaches to theology and piety, to life. As Jan Frans van Dijkhuizen and Richard Todd note, "even after the Elizabethan Settlement of 1559, English religious culture was full of continuities with the past, with pre-Reformation religious culture only partially displaced."[143] In this, both conformists and non-conformists within the Church of England were united: those harkening back to Lollardy were as "correct" as those who preferred to look back to the general religious community of late medieval England.

Thus, many pre-Reformation texts were difficult to label as straightforwardly heretical or not (e.g., Thomas Wimbledon's famous *Redde rationem* sermon), as they remain difficult to label even today: the circulation of texts that often tested the boundary of orthodoxy was wide enough in late medieval England, and so mixed with works that theoretically remained completely orthodox (such as incomplete translations of the Bible that were allowed by the Church[144]), that the

141. Geoffrey Chaucer, *House of Fame*, line 272 (*The Riverside Chaucer*, ed. F.N. Robinson, 3rd ed. [Oxford, 1987], 351).

142. Marshall, *Religious Identities in Henry VIII's England*, 5.

143. Jan Frans van Dijkhuizen and Richard Todd, "Introduction," in *The Reformation Unsettled*, ed. van Dijkhuizen and Todd, 1–8, at 1.

144. See, for example, Wendy Larson, "Bible, English," in *Historical Dictionary of Late Medieval England 1272–1485*, ed. Ronald Fritze and William Robison (Westport, 2002), 54–55; and David Lawton, "Englishing the Bible, 1066–1549," in *The Cambridge History of Medieval English Literature*, ed. Wallace, 454–460.

English religious textual culture produced works which can be only categorized with any certainty as typically and so, complexly, "English." Such an inheritance suggests that, perhaps, the English were indeed in their own way "reformed" long before Luther,[145] and certainly more reformed in their own English way than they ever became after the influence of Lutheranism. While Luther's thought naturally had an impact on English Protestantism and translations of his works were staples of most Protestant libraries, it was rather short-lived in that what ultimately became English Protestantism was a very peculiar mix of other influences as well, and within it little was taken directly from Luther.[146]

This, in turn, in combination with the inheritance of Wycliffite, Lollard and para-orthodox influences from before the Reformation, partially accounts for the relative "reluctance" of the English to adhere to the Reformation after the Act of Supremacy. As Christopher Haigh has shown,[147] it took almost a century for England to become "truly" Protestant, and throughout the sixteenth century there were as many who called for further reform as there were those who were happy with not changing much. The sixteenth-century controversies over vestments and over aspects of worship including whether it was godly to pray for the dead or not, while not minor, were also perhaps not as major as we think: many of these controversies were well-established points of contention already in fourteenth-century England. The "reluctant Reformation," in other words, was reluctant not necessarily only because people were loath to be rid of their "traditional religion,"[148] although that certainly was an important aspect of the ambience of the time. It was reluctant also because it was, for many, simply unnecessary: some were either happy with the way things were, or were satisfied with the para-orthodox form of devotion within which they found room for heterodox ideas and behaviours they thought acceptable, while maintaining an avid participation in

145. As Anne Hudson points out, Luther "declared in the 1520s, 'We are all Hussites'; he might more accurately have declared, 'We are all Wycliffites,' as Hus himself in 1408 had stated his wish to be where Wyclif was" (*The Premature Reformation*, 60).

146. Paul D. Stegner, *Confession and Memory in Early Modern English Literature: Penitential Remains* (New York, 2016), 102. The question of the extent of the impact of Luther on the English Reformation, however, remains a complex one. While much scholarly work on the later Reformation agrees that the impact of Lutheranism was fairly short-lived in the English context, it was undeniably an impact not to be considered lightly. For a study of the Lutheran influence on English Protestantism focused on the early Reformation, see, for example, Michael S. Whiting, *Luther in English: The Influence of His Theology of Law and Gospel on Early English Evangelicals (1525–35)* (Eugene, OR, 2010); or C.R. Trueman, *Luther's Legacy: Salvation and the English Reformers, 1525–1556* (Oxford, 1994).

147. Haigh, *English Reformations*, throughout, especially Part I, III, and Conclusion.

148. Duffy, *The Stripping of the Altars*, throughout.

public popular piety. Yet others had such long-established ideas on what needed reformation that the Henrician reform was found lacking and insufficient.

These shades of reluctance were only a step beyond the "consensus" that functioned in England at least since Wycliffe, leading in turn to another consensus, developed during the reign of Elizabeth I. The pre-Reformation "consensus" was the occasionally uncomfortable coexistence of heterodoxy, orthodoxy, and para-orthodoxy within the English Church, parishes, and among pious individuals, within which, while not without tension, all could more or less comfortably find their place. The post-Reformation consensus, in turn, developed as an attempt to satisfy those for whom the initial Henrician Reformation was not "reformed" enough, while trying also to keep the majority, including the clergy, happy with the changes to church organization (largely, the issue of setting the English monarch as the head of the Church) via attempts to establish more crown control over parishes, while navigating also doctrinal changes that came as a consequence of becoming a Reformed Church,[149] with people "de-catholicized but un-protestantized."[150] That not everyone was happy with these changes was, of course, natural, and it was the tension between the adherents to these pre- and post-Reformation consensuses, and not so much between the pre- and post-Reformation religion and culture as a whole, that truly shaped early modern England and English Protestantism.

Medieval Catholicism, Devotional Literature, and Protestantism

Much like Lollardy and vernacular para-orthodox theology and devotion served early modern Reformers to establish themselves as heirs to an English-specific proto-Protestant heritage, and continued readership of late medieval texts and popular literature helped to maintain a sense of connectedness to this English tradition and culture, so pre-Reformation religion in general was a valuable source for many Protestants and Protestant groups. The Reformation, of course, was *about* religion and religious doctrine,[151] but that did not mean that it wished to abolish all that was written on the matter of religion since the establishment of

149. A similar description of a tense but functioning lay and vernacular para-orthodoxy (on the parish level) after the Reformation in England see, for example, Norman Jones, *The English Reformation* (Oxford, 2002); Christopher Marsh, *Popular Religion in Sixteenth Century England: Holding Their Peace* (New York, 1998).

150. Haigh, *English Reformations*, 290.

151. As it was also, for instance, about politics. See, for example, Duffy, *The Stripping of the Altars*; Haigh, *English Reformations*; and MacCulloch, *The Later Reformation in England.*

papacy. Rather, English Protestantism was a grouping of thinkers and believers within the large body of religion that actively re-evaluated its complex history and engaged with all that was deemed worthy and theologically sound, rejecting that which was "corrupt": "[t]he notion that the Church of England had undergone only a limited, qualified separation from Rome became increasingly fashionable," among conformists as much as puritans,[152] particularly in the seventeenth century. Through defining that which was deplorable and that which was praiseworthy (e.g., aspects of Augustinian piety for puritans, ceremonial worship to Laudians and some Anglicans, or a revisionist approach to free will and covenant of works for Arminians, etc.) a given group could define itself and other groups, and make their claim to theological correctness. This was particularly important, since "if Protestants wished to avoid the charge of schism, then it was vital that they resist the temptation to agree with Romanists that the Protestants had departed absolutely from Rome."[153] For this reason many Protestant writers "routinely denied that they were guilty of schism by stressing that they had been unwillingly forced to leave a tyrannical Church."[154]

Therefore, while there were many theological issues that many Protestant divines had with some writings of scholastic writers, such as Peter Abelard, their frequent approval and appropriation of selected writings of other thinkers such as Thomas Aquinas, Duns Scotus, Bonaventure, William Ockham, or even Peter Lombard, paved the way for Protestantism to embrace many aspects of pre-Reformation theology and religiosity, particularly devotional practices. In other areas of academic interest, medieval thinkers, likewise, ruled supreme: "[i]n logic, philosophy, philology and natural theology, Roman Catholic authors were still among the most important authorities cited by scholars across the doctrinal and confessional spectrum,"[155] as they were in Biblical commentary, casuistry, and other religious writing. In other words, medieval Catholicism and the English late medieval past were "familiar, even reassuring, ... from which a sense of estrangement had not necessarily been achieved."[156]

As Alec Ryrie points out, "while some Protestants were hostile to or embarrassed by their use of Catholic materials, others were unapologetic."[157] The

152. Milton, "A Qualified Intolerance," 89.

153. See, for example, Edmund Bunny, *A treatise tending to pacification* (1586) and Richard Bernard, *Looke beyond Luther* (1623); as cited in Milton, "A Qualified Intolerance," 89.

154. Milton, "A Qualified Intolerance," 89.

155. Milton, "A Qualified Intolerance," 91.

156. Milton, "A Qualified Intolerance," 92–93, 103.

157. Ryrie, *Being Protestant*, 287.

Protestant Richard Brathwaite, for example, in his anthology of devotional writing entitled *Spiritual spicerie* (1638), defended his choice to include a large number of medieval writers, from Bonaventure, through Henry Suso, Jacobus de Gruytrode, to Johannes Justus Lanspergius,[158] by saying that he wished to "reply to a rigid Precisian [i.e., puritan], objecting, that flowers from Romish authors extracted became lesse wholesome and divinely redolent."[159] Interestingly, Brathwaite was not a theologian, but a poet, and his familiarity with these pre-Reformation authors, as well as his choice to include them together with post-Reformation Protestant thinkers indicates that a recognition of the importance of medieval religious literature was not an exclusively academic or theological phenomenon, but something that occurred to a wider, lay, readership as much as to polemicists and theoreticians. In Brathwaite's view there was nothing to prevent an early modern reader from acquainting themselves with pre-Reformation works, or works of contemporary Roman Catholic authors if there was nothing theologically wrong with them, especially if they successfully led their readers to spiritual improvement. Theological appropriateness was, in fact, the only real criterion of evaluation of pre-Reformation religious scholarship, and made the majority of pre-Reformation scholasticism relevant to Protestant theology and self-fashioning strategies. Through an evaluation of "traditional" religious content and acceptance or appropriation of large chunks of pre-Reformation theological scholarship, Protestants established themselves firmly as Catholic,[160] while also determining their own, new takes on old issues, such as the sacraments.

Thus, disagreeing with the notion of more than two Biblically sanctioned sacraments, most Protestants did not think very highly of Peter Lombard's characterization of the sacraments (in which he lists seven) from his *Libri quattuor*

158. I am grateful to Suzanne Akbari for sharing her identification of, and thoughts on, Lanspergius and other authors in the *Spicerie* with me.

159. Richard Brathwaite, *Spiritual spicerie* (1638), 226.

160. This was very important to Protestants from the onset of the Reformation (arguing that it was they who were "truly" Catholic, as opposed to Roman Catholicism), and became increasingly important with the emergence of new heterodox movements within Protestantism, such as Arminianism, Quakerism, or Socinianism, in the seventeenth century (Richard Alfred Muller, *After Calvin: Studies in the Development of a Theological Tradition* [Oxford, 2003], 54). See also Marshall, *Religious Identities in Henry VIII's England*, 81–102 on disputes over "unwritten verities," and Milton, "A Qualified Intolerance," throughout.

sententiarum[161] but, at the same time, continued to use his *Sentences* as a foundation for theological teaching until at least the end of the sixteenth century (later replaced with the *Summa Theologica* of another scholastic thinker, Thomas Aquinas[162]). These thinkers counted Lombard, following Calvin's definition of *saniores scholastici*, among "trustworthy" scholastics, a group that also included Aquinas, Bonaventure, Duns Scotus, and many more.[163] Thomas Goodwin, a puritan minister and chaplain to Oliver Cromwell, referred to Bonaventure as his favourite and best of all scholastics.[164] The puritan William Ames noted that "[t]he Papists haue laboured much this way, to instruct their Confessors: and in a great deale of earth and dirt of Superstitions, they haue some veines of Silver: out of which, I suppose, I haue drawne some things that are not to be despised."[165] Richard Hooker thought of Calvin as their own Protestant Peter Lombard.[166] William Perkins, a renowned puritan theologian, often referred to a number of medieval scholastics, as he did in his Latin work on predestination, *De praedestinationis modo et ordine* (1599), where he wrote a "dialogue" between himself and Bernard of Clairvaux, Hugh of St Victor, Anselm, as well as Aquinas, Lombard, and others, "with whom he sometimes differs" but, just as often, did not differ.[167] In *A Reformed Catholike, or, A declaration shewing how neere we may come to the present Church of Rome in sundrie points of religion* (1597) Perkins summarized all points of controversy between the Roman Catholic Church and Protestantism and described what the Church of Rome and Protestantism held in common on each of these points (and then refuted all that Protestantism dis-

161. As well as many other doctrines and ideas Lombard set out in his *Sentences*. However, at the same time, Lombard was widely read and commented on throughout the Reformation, and many Reformation scholars were noted for being selectively supportive of some of the contents of the *Sentences* (Jean-Louis Quantin, *The Church of England and Christian Antiquity: The Construction of a Confessional Identity in the 17th Century* [Oxford, 2009], 86).

162. Quantin, *The Church of England and Christian Antiquity*, 86.

163. Muller, *After Calvin*, 54.

164. Thomas Goodwin, *Unregenerate man's guiltiness before God* (1692), 325.

165. William Ames, *Conscience with the power and cases thereof Devided into V. Books* (1639), "To the Reader," [5]; quoted by Milton, "A Qualified Intolerance," 92.

166. Richard Hooker, *Of the lawes of ecclesiastical politie* (1594), preface (quoted by Quantin, *The Church of England and Christian Antiquity*, 86). At the same time, Hooker is also often cited as the champion of "Anglicanism" (or the English "middle way") and an advocate of the ceremonial revival, which Calvinists in England were generally fervently opposed to.

167. W.B. Patterson, *William Perkins and the Making of Protestant England* (Oxford, 2014), 82.

agrees with).[168] Many other divines also "sought to locate Protestant doctrines in the medieval Church as a way of validating the search for institutional continuity and thereby reconciling these divergent tendencies," whereas others "increasingly sought to celebrate the devotional life and authority of the medieval Church, and to see the medieval centuries as models for contemporary emulation."[169] For this reason Jean Gerson, Saint Bernard, or Thomas Gascoigne "were all important protestant witnesses because they opposed popish abuses," even though all were perfectly orthodox medieval Catholics.[170]

Such active readership of pre-Reformation theology went hand in hand with interest and readership of pre-Reformation devotional works. For instance, the late medieval *Imitation of Christ* (ca. 1427) went through as many as forty print editions between 1567 and 1697, with numerous manuscript copies, and became an early modern bestseller. Other English works, from John Mirk's *Festial*, through Walter Hilton's *The Scale of perfection*, to sermons of Thomas Wimbledon and works of Richard Rolle and other mystics, were among the most frequently printed books in early modern England (for instance, *The Scale* was printed at least six times between 1494 and 1659; Wimbledon's *Redde rationem* at least fifteen times between 1540 and 1635). Works of Peter of Blois, and texts such as *The Clensyng of mannes sowle* and *The Pilgrimage of the life of man*, were likewise a printing success, and, combined with the sixteenth century's continued, though increasingly less frequent, hand-copying of manuscripts (with added marginal notes in places where a Protestant noticed a "popish" element but which was nevertheless faithfully copied[171]), illustrates that early modern audiences, includ-

168. Milton, "A Qualified Intolerance," 90. Perkins made sure to also note that, in the end, his purpose was to prove that the differences between the two made them irreconcilably different: "to confute all such Politikes as holde and maintaine, that our religion and that of the Romane Church differ not in substance, and consequently that they may be reconciled: yet my meaning is not here to condemne any Pacification that tends to perswade the Romane church to our religion"; *Reformed Catholike* (1597), [4]; see Milton, "A Qualified Intolerance," 90–91.

169. Milton, "Reformation, Identity, and 'Anglicanism,' c.1520–1662," 11.

170. Milton, "The Church of England, Rome, and the True Church," 192.

171. As was the case with, for example, London, British Library, Add. 17013, a manuscript copy of *The Book of vices and virtues* which contains numerous marginal notes in a sixteenth-century hand, some of which indicate Protestant readership with remarks such as "ye error of ye papiste" referring to passages on Purgatory, which the commentator "carefully censored ... by enclosing them within lines, and in some cases drawing fine lines across a whole passage, never, however, actually attempting to obliterate the text" (W. Nelson Francis, *The Book of Vices and Virtues: A Fourteenth Century English Translation of the* Somme Le Roi *of Lorens D'Orleans* [London, 1942], xlviii).

ing Protestants, had easy access to pre-Reformation religious texts, and not only could, but also most certainly did, read them.[172] Indeed, about forty to fifty percent of books printed by the 1540s were late medieval devotional and religious texts.[173] In other words, "early modern British Protestants had, for want of a better word, catholic tastes in devotional writing. Contemporary and medieval Catholic writers jostle with British and Continental Reformed Protestants on the lists of commercially successful religious books."[174] Furthermore, "[f]or all the occasional use of language of binary opposition between the forces of Protestantism and Catholicism, and alarmist talk of religious contagion, life in Protestant England was in fact littered with Roman Catholic ideas, books, images and people. English people did not suffer from a simple allergic reaction to all things popish."[175] In fact, medieval piety and vernacular devotion in particular were emulated and celebrated, particularly in the early Stuart Church, not only as evidence of the presence of true belief before the Reformation, but also for "its high standards of piety" and the "devotion and reverence which the medieval church ... had been able to instill."[176]

What needs to be pointed out, however, is that to Protestant audiences late medieval texts were not necessarily "Catholic," i.e., Roman Catholic. Before the Reformation, there was, it could be argued, no "Roman Catholicism" the way we understand it today, because the Roman Catholicism that Protestantism considered in opposition to itself was early modern (and largely post-tridentine), not pre-Reformation:[177] it was only "[b]etween 1545 and 1563, [that] the canons

172. For more on early modern Protestant readership of pre-Reformation texts, on their availability, and on the Protestant and Catholic printing of pre-Reformation texts see, for example, Duffy, *Reformation Divided*; *The Cambridge History of the Book in Britain*, ed. John Bernard, D.F. McKenzie, and Maureen Bell (Cambridge, 2003), esp. the sections "Religion and Politics" and "Vernacular Traditions"; Patrick Collinson, "Literature and the Church," in *The Cambridge History of Early Modern English Literature*, ed. David Loewenstein and Janel Mueller (Cambridge, 2002), 374–399.

173. Michael Alexander, *The Growth of English Education, 1340–1648: A Social and Cultural History* (University Park, PA, 1996), 94–96.

174. Ryrie, *Being Protestant*, 284. See also chapter 11, "Reading," throughout.

175. Milton, "A Qualified Intolerance," 86.

176. Milton, "The Church of England, Rome, and the True Church," 197.

177. While the initial Reformation was mostly concerned with such aspects of Church doctrine and practice as indulgences, purgatory, and justification, in England the majority of these issues were not considered by Henry VIII when signing his Act of Supremacy, and due to the upheavals that followed, of Reformation and Counter-Reformation under Mary Tudor, it was only in the reign of Edward VI (under the leadership of Thomas Cranmer) that Protes-

of the Council of Trent began the process of turning late medieval Catholic Christianity into early modern Roman Catholicism"[178] because "everyone consciously or unconsciously formed part of the same Catholic church structure."[179] The Protestant Richard Field argued, in fact, that it was only the Council of Trent that sealed Roman Catholicism as "heretical": "the Roman Church is not the same now that it was when Luther began" and "formerly, the Church of Rome was the true Church, but had in it a heretical faction: now the Church itself is heretical."[180] Likewise, other Protestants, including many puritans such as James Ussher, William Crashaw, and Richard Crakanthorpe, "searched medieval liturgies, prayers, councils and scholastic authors for proof that protestant doctrine still flourished well into the later medieval period and (in some cases) right up to the Council of Trent itself."[181]

In fact, many Protestants thought of themselves as "truly" Catholic[182] and as those who purified a corrupted Church rather than built a new one, as there were also writers who argued for a more "sectarian" descent from Lollards or Hussites.[183] As Thomas Bedford pointed out, "if they [the papists] meane the fun-

---

tantism began to slowly rise as the official religion of England. Finally, only under the Elizabethan Religious Settlement of 1559 was Protestantism implemented in England in a structured doctrinal manner. Because of Henry VIII's refusal to renounce Catholic ceremony and doctrine, and due to the time it took the English to reach (partial, at the very least) agreement on the form Protestantism was to take in England, the term "Roman Catholic" was not used in England to distinguish between those in communion with the Pope and Rome, and Protestants ("true Catholics") until at least the late 1550s. At the same time, those in opposition to the Pope and many Church practices and doctrines which gave rise to the Reformation in the first place did recognize, and associate, the "religion of Rome" with the ideas they were opposing. Nevertheless, the Protestants thought of Catholicism, including pre-Reformation religion, as their own, and the "corruptions" to this religion as the fault of the Church of Rome, and the legacy of Roman Catholicism which developed via contrast to the "true" Catholicism of the Protestants.

178. Marshall, *Religious Identities in Henry VIII's England*, 3.

179. MacCulloch, *Reformation: Europe's House Divided*, 38.

180. See Richard Field, *Of the Church fiue bookes. By Richard Feild, Doctor of Diuinitie* (1606), 175, cited in Milton, "The Church of England, Rome, and the True Church," 194.

181. See Richard Crakanthorpe, *Vigilius dormitans. Romes seer overseene* (1631), with Milton, "The Church of England, Rome, and the True Church," 194; see the whole section II for more on this subject.

182. Marshall and Ryrie, "Protestantisms and Their Beginning," 5; Muller, *After Calvin*, 54; Marshall, *Religious Identities in Henry VIII's England*, 179.

183. Milton, "The Church of England, Rome, and the True Church," 194.

damentall poynts of Religion, contained in the *Creed* for matters of faith, in the *Decalogue* for matter of practice, and in the *Lords Praier* for matter of praier, they themselues shall be our spokesmen, for they and wee hold these in common."[184] Likewise, the puritan theologian Richard Baxter said that "besides the Confession of the Enemies of the Church, Pagans, Infidels, Mahometans, Jews, and Hereticks; we have not one word that's part of our Religion, which yourselves confess not to be true,"[185] and the puritan Richard Bernard remarked that "wee doe not break off from her [the Church of Rome] simply, but in some respects, that is, as farre forth as she hath forsaken her former selfe: so that if shee would returne to the Catholike Faith and Religion[,] and forsake her Trentisme, Jesuitisme and Popery ... wee want ... to unite our selves unto her againe."[186] Many other Protestants, especially conformists, were of the opinion that there was no reason why Protestantism should not take, and benefit, from "whatever was not corrupt" and should "boldly claim it from Rome."[187]

It is thus unlikely that many Protestant writers or readers thought of pre-Reformation texts as *Roman* Catholic,[188] but rather as texts written in a time in which "proper" doctrine was, in places, contaminated by "popish" error, and needed clarification and correction. The distinction is subtle but crucial, because it explains why the Protestants treated both Church history and theology, and devotional pre-Reformation literature, as relevant to their, admittedly, complex, identity, and took from it freely whenever they could: pre-Reformation literature was not written off as fallacious or unworthy of reading by the sole virtue of being pre-Reformation. What *was* written off was that which various Protestant

184. Bedford, *Luthers predecessours*, 4.

185. Richard Baxter, *Naked popery* (1677), 24. It is also for this reason that Thomas Aquinas remained one of the most widely read and popular scholastics of the early modern period. The Protestants read his *Summa Theologica*, much like the works of many other pre-Reformation theologians, selectively, quite happily praising elements they deemed religiously correct, and criticizing what they deemed flawed. In particular, many appreciated the unifying quality of Aquinas' works. For this reason most Protestants "respected [Aquinas'] quest for unity, the technique of argument, and many of the basic Christian doctrines inherent in the *Summa Theologica*," but Calvinists "also recognized that the overall effect of the *Summa* was to justify the established Church" (Clarence J. Karier, *The Individual, Society, and Education: A History of American Educational Ideas* [Chicago, 1986], 4).

186. Bernard, *Looke beyond Luther*, 44, as quoted by Milton, "A Qualified Intolerance," 89.

187. Ryrie, *Being Protestant*, 287.

188. Instead, the words most commonly used to describe Roman Catholicism were "papists" (or, descriptively, "those in communion with Rome") or, as in John Bradford's *A sermon of repentaunce* (1553), "Latinistes" (n. pag.).

groups considered fallacious within any given text, without necessarily condemning the whole of it (unless, of course, it focused on a concept opposed to Protestantism in principle). There was an established polemical current of differentiating between the "outward" pre-Reformation Church contaminated by popish error and the true and "invisible" Church of pure believers and Christians that existed before the Reformation, particularly among more puritan-leaning writers. At the same time, some conformist Calvinists also stressed the continuity between conforming members of the pre-Reformation Catholic Church who were unhappy with some of its policies and the current Calvinist conformists (thus stressing also continuities within the "visible" Church).[189]

After all, many Protestants insisted, much like Brathwaite and Bedford, that there were *areas* of contention rather than a complete breakup between pre-Reformation religion and Protestantism.[190] Although, of course, these areas of contention in themselves made any reconciliation or complete agreement impossible, having them clearly and precisely defined helped many Protestants address frequently noticed similarities of interests, texts, subjects, and tastes that they shared both with other Protestant groups and with Roman Catholics, who likewise traced their lineage to pre-Reformation religion. By proving themselves as heirs to that tradition, the Protestants could claim it as their own, and further the cause for the erroneous nature of Roman Catholicism. At the same time, as Anthony Milton notes, many Protestants from various groups, including the puritans, preferred to stress the continuities and similarities between Protestantism and Roman Catholicism rather than to dismiss Roman Catholicism completely as the Whore of Babylon. Polemically, it made sense in order to justify Protestantism and make a case for it by admitting that the things shared by both religions were proof that both, and Protestantism in particular, were legitimate: "by pointing out how far the Church of England shared many of Rome's doctrines ... it could be concluded that Rome thereby granted the truth of Protestant doctrines."[191]

189. Milton, "The Church of England, Rome, and the True Church," 189, 192.

190. E.g., "those points wherein they differ from the church of Rome, and in which the reformation doth consist, these points (I say) were held and professed" (Bedford, *Luthers predecessours*, 8–28). What these points were, exactly, depended on the group: Calvinists objected to the real presence, ceremonialism and formal liturgy, as well as a number of other issues (such as seven sacraments); anti-Calvinists objected to some Roman Catholic interpretations of the Creed and Articles of Faith, as well as, obviously, the papacy; other groups opposed the idea of a formal or episcopalian Church (e.g., Quakers, Congregationalists, and so on).

191. Milton, "A Qualified Intolerance," 89.

Periodization

English Protestantism, then, was conscious and careful in evaluating its roots, and approached these roots as critically and as accurately as possible, trying to untangle what they deemed tangled. There was thus no reason for early modern Englishmen to reject or question the value of English pre-Reformation history or culture, the continuity of which they wished to highlight rather than stifle in their own writings, much like many wished to highlight continuity with England's religious past: it was not *Roman* Catholic but *English* Catholic. Similar to Bedford or Foxe, other early modern writers pointed out that the "200. yeeres before Luther" were an essential time in the history of English Protestantism.[192] These two hundred years before the Reformation were, by necessity, not seen as divided from the Protestant early modern present by the caesura of the Reformation. To many Protestants, culturally, religiously, and textually these two hundred years were an inseparable part of their own early modern present.

There is, therefore, no reason not to consider the late medieval and the early modern as connected, nor to refrain from a study of the early modern Protestant engagement with the English late medieval past, since early modern Protestants themselves actively argued for the validity of such a study. Likewise, many scholars point to the benefits of such an endeavour, while acknowledging certain problems connected to periodization that it inevitably encounters. Notwithstanding, Heiko Oberman and Charles Trinkhaus, for instance, state that it was "the later Middle Ages" that were "the beginnings of a new era"[193] because, as they claim, a view of the late Middle Ages as the cradle of early modernity whose "birthpangs" are visible in the fourteenth and fifteenth centuries, accounts for "the coexistence of continuity and discontinuity"[194] between the two periods. Throughout their book, Oberman and Trinkhaus gather essays collectively arguing that early modernity comes from the late Middle Ages and cannot be accurately studied in isolation from that period.

192. See, for example, John Bale, *The pageant of popes contayninge the lyues of all the bishops of Rome* (1547); John Carpenter, *A preparatiue to contentation* (1597); Francis Savage, *A conference betwixt a mother a devout recusant, and her sonne a zealous protestant* (1600); Thomas James, *An apologie for Iohn Wickliffe shewing his conformitie with the now Church of England* (1608); or Gilbert Burnet, *The history of the reformation of the Church of England* (1679).

193. Heiko Oberman and Charles Trinkhaus, "The Shape of Late Medieval Thought: the Birthpangs of the Modern Era," in *The Pursuit of Holiness in Late Medieval and Renaissance Religion*, ed. Heiko Oberman and Charles Trinkhaus (Leiden, 1974), 3–25, at 4.

194. Oberman and Trinkhaus, "The Shape of Late Medieval Thought," 4.

Oberman[195] also introduces the concept of the "Long Fifteenth Century" (ca.1350–1550) which accounts for the endurance of continuities with the late Middle Ages in sixteenth-century England and can serve to explain many other phenomena, such as the "reluctance" of the Reformation described by Haigh,[196] or the reluctance of the people of England to abandon their "traditional religion," as discussed by Duffy.[197]

These and other studies that multiplied evidence for the interconnectedness of late medieval and early modern England[198] led some scholars to move their demarcation of early modernity earlier than the previously agreed upon 1500, whereas others chose to move the end of the late Middle Ages later,[199] incorporating at least the first half of the sixteenth century as still very much "medieval." Louis Dupré, for example, estimates the existence of a "transition period" between the Middle Ages and the Renaissance and Reformation to span between

195. Oberman, "The Long Fifteenth Century."

196. Haigh, *English Reformations.*

197. Duffy, *The Stripping of the Altars.* Other historians of religion and the Reformation, such as Berndt Hamm (*The Reformation of Faith in the Context of Late Medieval Theology and Piety*); James F. White (*Protestant Worship: Traditions in Transition* [Louisville, 1989]), and Peter Lake and Michael Questier (*The Antichrist's Lewd Hat*) also stress the formative role of late medieval religiosity and culture on the development of early modernity and Protestantism. See also Patterson, "On the Margin," 99.

198. For example, *Bridging the Medieval-Modern Divide: Medieval Themes in the World of the Reformation*, ed. James Muldoon (Farnham, Surrey; Burlington, VT, 2013); *Reading the Medieval in Early Modern England*, ed. McMullan and Matthews; Jennifer Summit, *Medieval Books in Early Modern England* (Chicago, 2008); *The Five Senses in Medieval and Early Modern England*, ed. Annette Kern-Stähler, Beatrix Busse, and Wietse de Boer (Leiden, 2016); *Authority, Gender and Emotions in Late Medieval and Early Modern England*, ed. Susan Broomhall (New York, 2015); Alice Hunt, *The Drama of Coronation: Medieval Ceremony in Early Modern England* (Cambridge, 2008); and *Local Identities in Late Medieval and Early Modern England*, ed. Norman Jones and Daniel Woolf (New York, 2007).

199. This often falls in line with Ernst Troeltsch's now classic argument about the medieval nature of the Reformation ("Renaissance and the Reformation," trans. Lewis W. Spitz, *The Reformation: Material or Spiritual*? [Boston, 1962], 17–27). To quote Susan Schreiner, Troeltsch's well-established claim is that the Reformation was "basically the continuation of the Middle Ages" (Schreiner, *Are You Alone Wise? The Search for Certainty in the Early Modern Era* [Oxford, 2011], 9).

1400 and 1600,[200] taking the full emergence of the Reformation as the proper end of the Middle Ages, thus outlining the "late Middle Ages" as spanning those two centuries. Others within this revisionist movement also insist on different timeframes for the Reformation in England, and since it became associated almost inseparably with early modernity, such a delineation is also one that is understood to distinguish late medieval from early modern England. Christopher Hill,[201] for instance, suggests that the early modern period in England began only in 1604, with the ascension of James I, with the late medieval period ending in 1603 with the death of Elizabeth I, and Peter Marshall suggests that the English Reformation should be considered within the timeframe between 1480 and 1642.[202] In connection with even broader studies, such as Constantine Fasolt's work on the beginnings of the Reformation in the Carolingian period,[203] "the Reformation loses its uniqueness," much as the sixteenth-century Renaissance did in the face of the twelfth-century renaissance, "and represents a continuation of Europe's past."[204]

However, since both before and after the Reformation religion pervaded almost all aspects of life, including approaches to everything from society, gender, and travelling, to health, science, and commerce, it is useful to treat this moment of religious change (and continuity) as a point of reference in evaluating the similarities and differences between England before and after it occurred. In other words, as many early modern Protestants recognized themselves, the period between around 1350 and their own time (whether that may have been 1550 or 1650), was formative to their identity and culture, and belonged to their present in that it was immediately relevant to their immediate context and time. It is thus possible to think of the late medieval period in England as an "early" early modernity, just as more and more scholars consider the sixteenth century, and even the first half of the seventeenth century, as in many ways "late" late medieval. Following Brian Cummings and James Simpson in their excellent argument about the relative non-productivity of periodization, and the importance of

200. Louis Dupré, *Passage to Modernity: An Essay in the Hermeneutics of Nature and Culture* (New Haven, CT, 1995), 3, 41.

201. Hill, *The Century of Revolution, 1603–1714.*

202. Marshall, *Reformation England 1480–1642.*

203. Constantin Fasolt, "Europäische Geschichte, Zweiter Akt: Die Reformation," in *Die deutsche Reformation*, ed. Brady, 231–250, as cited in Schreiner, *Are You Alone Wise?*, 10.

204. Schreiner, *Are You Alone Wise?*, 10.

acknowledging the complexity of continuity and discontinuity between the late medieval and the early modern, it is thus perhaps best to read both periods as "period unbound" with "heterogeneous approaches to heterogeneous materials,"[205] that are simultaneously connected and unconnected, but always relevant to each other. This is how the Protestants themselves read their past.

The Structure of the Present Book

The Protestant dialogue with its cultural heritage, set within relatively fluid temporal and ideological distinctions, was, as can be surmised from the discussion above, complicated and certainly not always accommodating and approving of that past.[206] The difficulty in assessing and outlining this relationship increases when we consider that the Protestants might not always have been conscious of which aspects of English culture happened to originate in this crucial two hundred years before the Reformation, and so would not have signalled that a given author's understanding of a concept or issue was in fact influenced by something they read or heard that dates back to before the Reformation. Many pre-Reformation influences that did not pertain to Protestant problems with Roman Catholicism per se, as Bedford and many others articulated them, were less noticeable, problematic, and thus sometimes ignored by Protestant writers (and audiences) who were not always interested in reflecting on how they arrived at a conclusion unless it was in obvious and polemically important ways in opposition to the main points of contention with Roman Catholicism. It is thus not easy to discern the true scope of the Protestant engagement with the English pre-

205. Brian Cummings and James Simpson, introduction to *Cultural Reformations*, ed. Cummings and Simpson, 1–9, at 2.

206. Jones, "Chaucer the Puritan," 175–176. The complicated Protestant approaches to the Seven Deadly Sins are a good example: as many Protestants thought highly of the pre-Reformation inheritance of the heptad as disapproved of it, and even more were either unaware of this heritage or chose to use it in their own way, not adhering to any arbitrary numbering or list (which in itself is also a characteristic feature of the heptad). See, for instance, discussions of sin in Prynne's *A briefe svrvay and censvre of Mr Cozens* (1628), 23, cf. Richard Baxter, *Right method for a settled peace of conscience* (1653), 262–263. See also Richard Newhauser, "'These Seaven Devils': The Capital Vices on the Way to Modernity," in *Sin in Medieval and Early Modern Culture: The Tradition of the Seven Deadly Sins*, ed. Richard G. Newhauser and Susan J. Ridyard (Woodbridge, Suffolk, 2012), 157–188, esp. the section "The sins and religious polemics" for more on the afterlife of the Seven Deadly Sins in early modern England.

Reformation past in texts in which no such engagement was openly signalled by the author or printer, and it is not always easy to distinguish the influences that shaped much of such textual output. In other words, while the heritage of Lollardy, the religiously individualistic and increasingly independent devotional culture of vernacular theology in England, and Protestant writers' deep knowledge of their country's "reformatory" past did play a formative role in Protestant self-fashioning or various reformist groups, many other less obvious influences not straightforwardly connected to the above, while equally important, remain largely uncharted territory. This is largely because it is difficult to choose both the tools for such an analysis, and texts that could serve as its subject, without by necessity omitting others that would perhaps yield very different conclusions.

Nevertheless, the present book makes such choices by including a selection of texts that, by highlighting the development of selected concepts and trends, are intended to help to address these less obvious and straightforward influences, and map their place in the study of continuity and discontinuity between pre- and post-Reformation England. It thus adheres to the words of Heiko Oberman that the study of continuity between the late medieval and early modern is essential "in order to identify more accurately the innovative dimension of early modern Europe, including the Reformation,"[207] but it is also guided by the leitmotif of other studies, such as those by Susan Karant-Nunn,[208] Peter Lake,[209] and Peter Marshall and Alec Ryrie,[210] in which the study of continuity is directly connected to the study of change. The thematic interest of this book is broad, and spans a set of cultural subjects that I initially thought should be grouped together under the heading of "Otherness," understood as a notion influential to the formation of the cultural tradition of both periods, and in both periods tied to the notion of religion. However, while still inseparably connected to the question of "otherness," in the course of working on this book, boundaries and their permeable nature emerged as a more productive vantage point from which to consider what the texts grouped here explore. The concept of boundaries is vital as a characteristic feature of any given period or community, as the way boundaries (of behaviours, thoughts, actions, concepts, knowledge, or morality) were defined is a reflection of many aspects of identity subscribed to in a given period, culture,

207. Oberman, "The Long Fifteenth Century," 3.

208. Susan C. Karant-Nunn, *The Reformation of Ritual: An Interpretation of Early Modern Germany* (London, 1997).

209. Lake, *Moderate Puritans and the Elizabethan Church*; and Lake and Questier, *The Antichrist's Lewd Hat.*

210. *The Beginnings of English Protestantism*, ed. Marshall and Ryrie.

or community. It is also important as a recognizable carrier of tradition, because it comprises the essence of belonging to a culture through a shared conceptualization of that which is liminal, blurred, or rejected, feared, unfamiliar, that which strays from an accepted standard, or is simply unwelcome (and so, "Other"). Through investigating boundaries, in other words, one can learn a great deal about a given culture's or individual's identity, both openly acknowledged and unconsciously conveyed through normative and self-defining choices a culture and members of that culture make.

Identities, in other words, are formed through a variety of technologies of self-fashioning, many of them ingrained in an "othering" discourse of contrasts and boundaries, which can be both constraining or liberating, and always in flux. Both late medieval and early modern England were characterized by a mosaic of the acceptable and the aberrant, a culturally-specific English "self" and a culturally-specific English "other," both defined in accordance with religious, social, and political agendas of their time. There are thus boundaries, often blurred, between Protestantism and Roman Catholicism (or among various kinds of Protestantism), just like there were between the late medieval Church and vernacular para-orthodox theology (particularly in lay devotional works), between virtue and sin, men and women, reason and emotion, health and disease, and so on. By looking into what was recognized as different, evil, fearful, or incongruous, and by examining how this recognition was accommodated within an individual's and a culture's identity, we can get a glimpse of what that individual or culture thought of themselves and the surrounding world, and see patterns of engagement and disengagement with that culture's, and individual's, history. In other words, by investigating how boundaries and contrasts were contested and negotiated in pre-Reformation and early modern Protestant England, we can determine particular aspects of cultural identity subscribed to in both periods, and thus reflect on how Protestants defined themselves and their world in reliance on their inherited as much as newly developing cultural identity.

The fact that pre- and post-Reformation identities were to a large extent built on religious affiliation and belief made a unified identification particularly strong, and gave a sense of common cause, integrity, and shared values that connected people across time as well as across theological divisions. Pre-Reformation church-goers and post-Reformation Protestants differed in how they saw themselves in relation to a selection of religious doctrines, politics, the papacy, or aspects of worship, but on principle both late medieval and Protestant audiences saw themselves, and their cultural paradigm, as anchored in religion: modes of thinking and reasoning, dialectics, self-expression, private and public life were all immersed in paradigms framed by religion. Such a religiously-founded identity allowed English men and women both before and after the Reformation to develop spiritual and psychological inwardness,[211] and offered techniques of achieving spiritual maturity, but it also provided them with a sense a community and belonging, by forming foundations for personal and group behaviours, codes of conduct, and methods of understanding the world, and themselves.

Therefore, as both pre- and post-Reformation English communities shared the "self" of religious culture (i.e., a culture defined by religion and a culture of religion[212]) that pervaded the fabric of their existence, they also shared an understanding of the liminal sphere of internal (personal and spiritual) and communal (external, but shared by members of the community) "other." These were boundaries defined by that religious culture, even when they were not directly connected to religion: in both periods boundaries were created and policed in matters related, more or less closely, to religion as well as in matters of religion itself. Thus, reading texts in which pre- and post-Reformation writers deal with subjects they find controversial, foundational, or contestable, conveying what they deem the truth, illustrates what they thought about themselves, but also allows us as readers to draw other conclusions about the variety of approaches to problems these texts touch upon from the way they were formulated, described, and tackled, but not signalled explicitly.

An examination of how boundaries were contested and negotiated in pre- and post-Reformation England is thus an investigation both into self-fashioning, and into a constructed, blurred lineage of Protestant identity conveyed in a given text. Tracing engagement among cognitive, interpretive, ideological, moral, social, and intellectual aspects of pre- and post-Reformation identities, we can study how they shifted between pre-Reformation and Protestant works and how permeable the boundaries, and concepts of boundaries, within these identities were. That, in turn, leads to inferences about how early modern Protestants relied on a historically constructed English "self" to develop their own. The present book sets out from this approach and groups works that, through pairing different constructions of various kinds of contrasts ("otherness") in pre- and post-

211. I am indebted to my conversations with Matt Kavaler and Herman Roodenburg on the subject of affect and inwardness for ideas on how to productively include these concepts in my consideration of the source material of the present book.

212. Differentiated among particular Protestant confessions yet unified with shared Protestant values and doctrines.

Reformation texts, reflect a number of angles of the complicated pattern of the relationship between late medieval and Protestant England.

Through this selection of primary sources, a history of engagement, hints of continuity, and proof of discontinuity between these two periods can be traced, as primary sources can provide a glimpse into the intellectual, cultural, and religious milieu of the early modern period, contextualized by the specific agendas and politics of specific authors and texts. Reading works written and printed with particular audiences in mind allows us to understand the context, convictions, thoughts, desires, fears, and interests of their authors, printers, and readers better, bringing us closer to England in the early modern period. In other words, the difficulties of dealing with the study of Protestant engagement with the English late medieval past, if anything, encourage the task, as through reading source texts we can attempt to get closer to understanding what early modern Protestants thought of themselves, and how they connected to their past.

Texts chosen to be included in this anthology, however, rarely speak to one another in the way early modern editors prefaced their compilations of Chaucer, or religious polemicists cited Lollard writers. Instead, as the reader will see, they reveal a much subtler engagement, in which points of view, ideas, or arguments collide as often as agree with one another, indicating a shared root, belief, or concept rather than an explicitly signalled continuity, or discontinuity. In other instances, they are connected only indirectly, by their interest in a similar subject matter, an element of style, or genre they belong to, and are simply taken as representative of the variety or similarity of approaches to a given theme without a direct relation to each other. Still other texts were chosen for their individual stark contrast with other texts, or particularly striking similarities to some texts, and are not particularly representative of their genres. Such a variety of levels of engagement between texts, from direct to cursory, will hopefully open them up for more productive discussion than if they were all related in the same way. The texts were selected in order to open the floor for discussion, and to encourage the reader to challenge both what they know about pre- and post-Reformation England, and to reflect on what the works compiled here seem to indicate given how they work together.

The book is divided into two parts. Part 1 deals with "spiritual" boundaries and moral peripheries and gathers texts that describe issues related to the human self, namely various kinds of sin, emotions such as fear or grief, as well as, in section three, works that outline the modes of dealing with such fearful matters by maintaining spiritual "health." Part 2, in turn, deals with boundaries in the physical, or "external," realm, and focuses on issues related to the external world and interactions with others: the body as a defining boundary between self and another, the mind and reasoning as reflected in behaviours and, in section three, methods of dealing with disease as an externally perceived and communally consequential issue.[213] The unifying feature of both parts is that they both deal, directly or indirectly, with religion, either through a discussion of explicitly religious problems, such as sin, or through the application of religious vocabulary, or context, to a work much less religious in nature, e.g., on the plague, but one which reveals religion as a culturally significant and formative force.

In Part 1, the first section, on the soul, deals with the Seven Deadly Sins, and the sins of the tongue and the mouth, in order to illustrate approaches to sins inherited both by pre- and post-Reformation Christians from the larger body of Christian tradition, and to sins which developed as new additions or variations on the classic vices. This selection allows the reader to compare the understanding of what sin was, and of what its threats to the soul were to pre-Reformation and Protestant writers. Texts in this section speak on the heptad, on spatial imagery, as well as sin as evil speech, swearing, and drunkenness. The second section deals with emotions, i.e., feelings of fear, grief, and anxiety, and compiles works on the wrath of God, the End of Days, and the Devil, as well as death, dying, and loss that focus on the signs of the Apocalypse, pastoral uses of eschatological discourse, portraits of the Antichrist, the four last things, and the art of dying well. These important aspects of religious and devotional life of pre- and post-Reformation Christians provide a fascinating study of how Protestants relied on past models of verbalizing emotions in order to channel their own feelings concerning the Apocalypse or death. Finally, as the previous two sections deal with various kinds of spiritual threats and uncertainties, the third section illustrates strategies some authors recommended to their readers for the sake of maintaining their spiritual health, focusing on a selection of pastoral strategies for aiding troubled souls. This section is not intended to match the sins and emotions presented in the previous two sections, but is rather a compilation of pastoral guidance works on spiritual health measures in general, that is, a section on "tackling" the spiritual "other," and includes texts that speak on confession, repentance, divine love, doubt, despair, the general wellbeing of the soul, and sin as malady.

213. Some earlier works on boundaries understood as "otherness" can be of interest as background reading here. See, for example, Paul Ricoeur, *The Symbolism of Evil* (New York, 1969), *The Fallible Man* (New York, 1986), and *Oneself as Another* (Chicago, 1992); *Multicultural Dilemmas*, ed. Wojciech Kalaga and Marzena Kubisz (Frankfurt, 2009); *Cultural Otherness*, ed. Chandra Gupta and Debi Prasad Chattopadhyaya (Leiden, 1998).

The textual content of Part 1, due to its subject matter, is explicitly religious in nature. In contrast, the religious context of texts in Part 2 is much subtler as, while the subject matter of texts in Part 2 deals more with issues such as gender, race, the mind, and disease, the religious undertones of discourse in which these issues are framed, and the authorship or editorial provenance of some of them, will suggest a religious agenda even where one initially appears to be absent. Texts in this section, therefore, are indicative of the impact of religion on non-devotional aspects of pre-Reformation and Protestant life, and provide sources for a study of how an underlying religious affiliation of the author shapes (or does not shape) their approach to their chosen subject matter.

In section one of Part 2, then, the reader will encounter texts that deal with the body, the opposite of the soul, in which various descriptions of certain characteristics of both men and women outline a gender-related understanding of (non-)permeable contrasts. Then, perceptions of strangers and non-Christians (Muslims, "Kithayans," Pygmies, Tatars) will draw attention to approaches to physical and cultural boundaries, and reveal a culturally-specific self which late medieval and Protestant English men and women subscribed to (for instance via their appropriations of the legend of Prester John or other belief systems). In section two, texts dealing with the vices and virtues of the mind, as an opposite to emotions, are compiled to reflect what late medieval and early modern authors and audiences thought of the cognitive qualities of the mind and the appropriateness of certain behaviours. This section also explores the issue of the morality of wisdom and reason, as well as the "unreasonable" qualities of evil and sin, and groups texts that illustrate approaches to evil thoughts, ignorance, wisdom and folly, and broadly conceived human character. Finally, section three deals with various kinds of disease and with medicine, to illustrate approaches to physical health and measures against sickness, which reflect a holistic approach to human homeostasis anchored in a balance of God-given humours, and divinely governed elements and planets. Texts compiled here speak also on the moral duty of maintaining the health of the human body created in the image of God, with the use of medicines and wisdom revealed by God to theologically-versed physicians, and compiles texts dealing with proper exercise, the qualities and properties of medicines, the plague, fever, and general cures for various sicknesses.

There is a Further Reading section at the end of the volume that expands the historical and academic scope of texts compiled in Parts 1 and 2, and provides other examples of texts similar to those included in the anthology. Together, Parts 1 and 2 encompass a fairly broad survey of English culture, history, religion, society, and science, and each provides a glimpse into the rich world of late medieval and Protestant English literature, illustrating also the varied degrees and forms of the Protestant engagement with its pre-Reformation past.

Each section in Part 1 can be read in reference to its opposite in Part 2, but all sections can also be read one after the other. Although all texts within sections are paired, and sections are in turn paired with sections in the opposite Part, they need not be, and the reader will see that they also cannot be, read in one sequence only, because they are in conversation with one another on many levels, and none can be separated from the other. For instance, texts dealing with the body or spiritual health, as the reader will find, will be difficult to disconnect from texts on sin, and so on. Dealing thematically with broadly conceived "otherness," contrasts and boundaries, works included in these two parts were also selected to reflect areas of continuity and discontinuity between pre-Reformation England and Protestantism that are less frequently discussed, to shed new light on the study of broadly conceived English Protestantism. Consequently, texts excerpted here are, often, a bit more obscure and less read, perhaps less seminal, but thus indicative of a side of early modernity in England that could benefit from further inquiries into its less obvious and polemical characteristics.

The texts themselves were selected on the basis of their period of origin, subject matter, and their relative obscurity to modern readers. Writing itself into the debate about the temporal and cultural boundaries of the late medieval and the early modern in England, the present book contains late medieval texts paired in each Part, section, and subsection with an early modern Protestant text. While it is sometimes unclear whether a text should be labelled late medieval or "early" early modern, a choice was made to categorize texts that were printed before the Reformation in England, so before 1534, as "late medieval," but at the same time only texts that were printed, not manuscripts, were used, relying on the assumption that a printed text would have been more easily available to a wider early modern readership than a manuscript copy.[214] Protestant texts included in each pair all come from the seventeenth century, in order to provide a starker temporal contrast to the late medieval work in each pair, and to present the late medieval texts in comparison to works of matured

214. This is, of course, not to say that manuscript copies were not available – the majority of late medieval texts excerpted here were edited by their printers from manuscript sources. For more on early modern ownership of medieval manuscripts see, for example, Summit, *Medieval Books in Early Modern England*, throughout.

Protestantism in England.[215] The distinction, therefore, is pre-Reformation versus post-Reformation rather than medieval versus early modern. Although the Reformation as a religious phenomenon might not appear to be immediately relevant to some sections of the book, it can be considered as such if viewed as a larger cultural paradigm shift between the two periods. To readers who subscribe to a revisionist view of the Reformation as a culmination, not end, of medieval trends, this temporal distinction can nevertheless be useful as print in England flourished and the number of printed texts increased more or less around the same time as Henry VIII issued his Act of Supremacy,[216] making such a distinction simply practical: there are many more printed texts that are available to us today from the 1500s onwards than there are from the 1470s, even if their origin dates back to the fourteenth or fifteenth century.

Finally, texts excerpted in this book will, most likely, give rise to various interpretations of degrees of continuity and discontinuity, even (dis)connectedness, as they are, primarily, a selection of works that touch upon the select subject matter of this book only, and secondly, were chosen to illustrate both similarity and difference. The reader might notice, for instance, that Caxton's and Baxter's renderings of the Seven Deadly Sins seem to be similar, as are texts on women from both periods, but will see also that Protestant works on wisdom and the mind differ in their focus from late medieval works on the same subject (at least superficially, at any rate, as Baxter and Caxton can also be read as in stark opposition to their treatment of the vices, and so on). The reader is therefore invited to interpret all texts here as they will, and it is left to them to decide whether each pair

215. Also because confessionalization did not properly occur before the middle of the sixteenth century, both nominally and practically, and therefore there was no one in England at the time who would have been able to accurately (or willingly) describe themselves as Protestant, much less to point to a given Protestant confession or identity (Marshall, *Religious Identities in Henry VIII's England*, 3). This is not to say that sixteenth-century Protestantism was "immature," but simply to draw a clearer line between "old" identities and ideas of the late Middle Ages and the much-changed notions on similar subjects in the seventeenth century. Sixteenth-century texts often display easily discernible medieval influences whereas seventeenth-century works are much more challenging and their formative influences much subtler.

216. This does not, of course, undermine the success, integrity, and importance of print before the Reformation. For an excellent discussion of the cultural and ethical aspects of pre-Reformation printing that bridges the history of print from before and after the traditional 1500 divide, see Kathleen Tonry, *Agency and Intention in English Print, 1476–1526* (Turnhout, 2016).

illustrates continuity or discontinuity. All in all, the reader is cautioned to remember that the present book contains merely a selection, and does not purport to provide an exhaustive and conclusive sample of texts that decisively paint the picture of early modern Protestantism in England, or its relationship to the English late medieval past. Various readers may disagree on the exact nature of the relationship between pre- and post-Reformation ideas on any of the subjects touched upon by texts included in this volume, but its aim is not to produce definitive answers, but rather to demonstrate that there are questions to be asked. Many more texts could have been selected, or added, to this volume, but were not, for the sake of (relative) brevity, readability, and the above-described selection method. The Further Reading section suggests, apart from secondary literature, a selection of other primary texts that fit a given theme. If used in a classroom, the reading of this book will be productively expanded with sources suggested in that section.

Now, in the words of Richard Baxter, it is time to "crave your pardon for this long Apology: It is an Age where the Objections are not feigned, and where our greatest and most costly services of God are charged upon us as our greatest sins; and where at once I am accused of Conscience for doing no more, and of men for doing so much,"[217] and to pass on to the texts themselves.

217. Richard Baxter, *A Christian directory* (1678), n. pag. From the collection of the Centre for Reformation and Renaissance Studies at Victoria University in the University of Toronto.

PART 1

Soul

SEVEN DEADLY SINS

1a [Laurent d'Orléans,] *Le liure Royal that is to say the ryal book, or a book for a kyng ...*, trans. William Caxton (1485 or 1486). **1b** Richard Baxter, *A Ç̣hristian directory* (1678).

Introduction William Caxton, the first English printer and book retailer, is also known for his good instincts regarding the fifteenth- and sixteenth-century book market: he reached to medieval texts as print sources for material certain to become popular among his clientele, popularizing and disseminating works previously only available in manuscript copy. One such text was his rendering of a thirteenth-century *summa* by Laurent d'Orléans (*Le somme le roi*, ca. 1279). It also existed in other translations and editions before Caxton's,[1] including the fourteenth-century *Book of vices and virtues* (ca. 1375), though these were probably unknown to him, and did not have a wide circulation. The *Royal book*, as Caxton's version is known, is a more condensed version of d'Orléans' original, and contains a long set of directions on subjects like godly living, sins and temptations of the Devil, focusing also on a number of doctrinal and ethical issues.[2] It starts with an exposition on the commandments, followed by a detailed discussion of sins (ordered in accordance with the heads of the beast from the Book of Revelation) in which major and minor sins (the Seven Deadly Sins and their various branches) are discussed, with

1. Nine, including the Kentish 1340 *A enbite of inwit*.

2. See, for example, the introduction to the 1942 edition of *The book of vices and virtues* for more on the original text by Laurent D'Orléans and the changes introduced into Middle English translations of this text (*The Book of Vices and Virtues: A Fourteenth Century English Translation of the* Somme le Roi *of Lorens D'Orléans*, ed. W. Nelson Francis [London, 1942]). As the full title to the *Royal book* declares, Caxton's translation of the *Somme le Roi* was "reduced out of frensshe." See also Elaine Whitaker, "A Collaboration of Readers: Categorization of the Annotations in Copies of Caxton's *Royal Book*," *Text* 7 (1994): 233–242, for more on the later reception of Caxton's *Royal book*, including the post-Reformation censorship of words and expressions such as "the Roman church," or sections on purgatory in the twenty-two existing copies of the 1485 edition and in the 1507 editions by Richard Pynson and Wynkyn de Worde.

minor sins categorized according to the major sins they stem from. This is followed by a short discussion of "holy living" that leads to a good death, and a detailed section on a number of Christian virtues (nobility, prowess, etc.). The final part of the book is devoted first to the Pater Noster, then to the gifts of the Holy Spirit, and to the seven divine virtues, as well as the virtues of the Holy Ghost, followed by chapters offering instruction on how to avoid the Seven Deadly Sins and how to aspire to virtue. This, in turn, is followed by passages on specific virtues battling specific sins (e.g., humility battling pride, etc., adhering to the popular notion that contraries – virtues – can cure contraries – vices), and a description of the battles the soul fights against sins.[3] The text ends with passages on confession and good council, the virtues of mercy, chastity, and sapience, and on contemplative and active life. The excerpt below includes a discussion of the Seven Deadly Sins. Branches of each of the deadly sins, which are not included below, should also be of interest to the reader since they contain a singular degree of variation in the listing, ordering, and understanding of each of the sinful qualities represented by the described branch. The excerpt below is a selection of descriptions of major sins (all of the classic seven with the addition of one of the branches of sloth); to many of these Caxton provides matching remedies (virtues) in later parts of his text.

A Christian directory is a text in many ways similar to Caxton's, but it boasts a strong Protestant provenance. Richard Baxter was a renowned and prolific puritan minister and writer, and to many a controversial figure.[4] He was the author of over two hundred books on practical divinity, and an advocate of unification of Protestantism in England, while also being an unorthodox Presbyterian who promoted the necessity of repentance and faithfulness, and not faith only, as essential to salvation. One of his major works, the *Christian directory*, is a large compendium of Christian knowledge (for Protestants), and a set of instructions on leading a virtuous life. An extremely rich and long book, the *Directory* resembles a *summa* in that it contains essentials of Protestantism, and provides moral guidance on such subjects as how to interpret spiritual stirrings, how to recognize sin, how to lead a virtuous life, and many more. The book is divided into four parts: *Christian Ethicks, Christian Oeconomicks, Christian Ecclesiasticks,* and *Christian Politicks. Christian Oeconomicks* deals with relationships with others (family, marriage, children, servants, etc., as well as a good death), *Christian Ecclesiasticks* with worship, clergy, other religions (what to think of "Papists" in particular), and aspects of doctrine such as the Holy Spirit.

3. For more on these aspects of late medieval religious literature, see Morton Bloomfield, *The Seven Deadly Sins: An Introduction to the History of a Religious Concept, with Special Reference to Medieval English Literature* (East Lansing, MI, 1952), throughout.

4. See, for example, Paul Chang-Ha Lim, *In Pursuit of Purity, Unity, and Liberty: Richard Baxter's Puritan Ecclesiology in Its Seventeenth-Century Context* (Leiden, 2004), for more on Baxter and his religious views.

Christian Politicks deals with crimes (murder, theft, etc.), proper governance in civil communities, and relations with neighbours, as well as passages on the confession of sins and satisfaction (elements of the classic rite of penance). *Christian Ethicks* is of most interest here. Its chapters are devoted to a number of devotional issues, for the unconverted and converted alike, on regeneration and on avoiding the temptations of the devil (Chs. I–III). Chapters concerned with sins (IV, VI–X) deal with a variety of vices, presenting also counter-virtues (e.g., humility overcoming pride). There are sins categorized according to their "placement" in the soul: of the heart (Ch. IV), mind (Ch. VI), passions (Ch. VII), senses (Ch. VIII), mouth (Ch. IX), and body (Ch. X). Each of these parts of the soul include sets of vices: pride, hypocrisy, unbelief, covetousness, and flesh-pleasing belong to sins of the heart; evil thoughts and melancholy to sins of the mind, in which Baxter includes a discussion of contemplative and active life (Chap. VI Tit. 4); wrath, anger, and despair (doubting) belong to the sins of the passions; the unruliness of the eyes and ears, gluttony, and lust to the sins of the senses; swearing and idle talk to the sins of mouth (tongue); and sloth and idleness to the sins of the body.[5]

Both the *Royal book* and the *Christian directory* are large compilations of all deemed important to Christians: the major tenets of Christianity and Christian ethics, a description of worship and the sacraments, and, among other important subjects such as the Trinity and Holy Ghost, both texts focus on the notion of vices and virtues. Both, also, represent adaptations of the classic medieval genre of the *summa,* in both cases with important departures from the earlier, more classic texts such as those by John of Rupella, William of Auvergne, or William Peraldus. However, both texts retain some of the genre's original features, including long passages on sin and kinds of sin.[6] Because the genre of the *summa* was very popular in the Middle Ages, and its vernacular renderings particularly attractive to readers in the late Middle Ages, the genre had exceptional longevity, and persisted throughout the medieval period and smoothly entered early modern Protestant writing, albeit with some significant changes. While Protestant audiences were, as their ancestors, very much interested in learning "all that Christians need to know," their reading practices and expectations changed, as did the rhetoric of the authors of such texts. Also, some aspects of pre-Reformation Christianity present in Caxton's text (such as passages on Purgatory) could not find their way into a post-Reformation Protestant text,

5. I arranged the excerpts in a way that provides better symmetry with Caxton's text, but in the original text the order of the sections is different: lust is discussed after pride, followed by wrath, despair (sloth), evil eyes (a part of envy), and then gluttony, fornication and uncleanliness, sins of the tongue, ending with sloth and idleness. Envy is not discussed separately, but is referred to throughout the whole of *Christian Ethicks.*

6. See Richard Newhauser, *The Treatises of Vices and Virtues in Latin and the Vernacular* (Turnhout, 1993).

even though Baxter was of the opinion, like many other Protestants, that many doctrines, practices, and accomplishments of pre-Reformation Christianity were more than worthy to be included in Protestantism: for instance, Baxter advocated for the retaining of the concept of venial and mortal sins, rejected by most Calvinists.[7] Therefore, it is all the more fascinating to compare the presentation of those elements of belief that were retained by the Protestants with their pre-Reformation sources, and to read the pre- and post-Reformation understandings of sin together, the Seven Deadly Sins in particular, for contrast as much as comparison. The two excerpts below can thus be read as illustrating aspects of the development of the heptad between the fifteenth and the seventeenth centuries,[8] as well as of the changes in the medieval genre of the *summa.*

1a [Laurent d'Orléans,] *This book was compyled and made atte requeste of kyng Phelyp of Fraunce ... whyche book is callyd in frensshe, le liure Royal that is to say the ryal book, or a book for a kyng ...* , trans. William Caxton, Westminster, 1485 or 1486; unnumbered pages. *STC* 21429. **Source** The Library of Congress, Washington, DC (Incun. X. L33).

Herafter foloweth the deuysyon of the vij. dedely synnes, capitulo xiij

The fyrst heed of the beest is pryde, the second Enuye, the iij. yre or wrath, the iiij. slouthe, the v. auaryce, the vj. glotonnye, the vij. lecherye. Oute of these vij. synnes dedely descenden alle maner of synnes and therfore be they callyd chyef of vyces. For they ben chyef of al vyces and of alle synnes, be they dedely or venyal. Eueryche of these seuen dedely synnes is departed in many parties, and first we shal speke of the synne of pryde.

This was the first synne, and the begynnyng of al euyl, whan the angel lucyfer, for his grete beaute and his grete vnderstondyng, he wold haue ben aboue alle other angels and wold compare to god that so good and fayr had made hym, and by cause he took suche pryde in hym he fyl fro heuen in to helle and became a deuyll. And alle hys companye wyth hym.

Alle proude men resemble thys lucyfer whiche wyl be aboue the other and be more preysed, more allowed, and more enhaunced than the other whiche been better and of more valewe than they be. This synne of pryde is ouer perilous, for it blyndeth man and woman so that they knowe not ne see not the perylle wherin

7. As he did, for example, in his *Right method for a settled peace of conscience* (1653).

8. Both texts contain passages on the sins of the tongue and the sins of the tavern, both late medieval additions to the "classic" sins of the heptad; these were not included here, as there is a separate section devoted to the sins of the mouth and tongue below.

they be by synne. This is the right stronge wyn of the deuyl, and the moost especyal of which he enyureth or maketh dronke the grete lordes and ladyes, the bourgeyses, the ryche, the noble and valyaunte persones, and generally al maner of people. But in especyal the grete lordes and ladyes in suche maner that they knowe not them self, ne see not theyr defaultes, ne theyr folyes, ne theyr synnes.

Thys is the moost perylous maladye and sekenesse of al the other. Certeynly he is in grete peryl to whome alle tryacle torneth to venym, lyke as doctryne and chastysyng doth to the proude. For the more men chastyse and blame them of theyr defaultes, so moche more ben they angry and defende them. Pryde is the fyrst doughter of the deuyl, and she that hath moost grettest parte in his herytage. Pryde warreth ageynst god and his goodnes, and al graces, and ageyn al the good werkys that ben in the man, for pryde maketh of almesse synne and of vertu vyce. And thus is pryde a theef to god, and wyth the goodes that one ought gete heuen, he maketh hym wynne helle. This synne is the fyrst. For it assaulteth the knyghtes of our lord, and that laste leueth them. For whan the knyghtes of god haue ouercomen and vaynquysshed alle other vyces and synnes; Thenne assaulte them most strongly the synne of pride and of vayne glorye. ...

The ij heed of the beest of helle is enuye, capitulo xxiiij

The second heed of the beest of helle is enuye. This is the serpente that enuenymeth[9] alle. Enuye is moder of the dethe; And by the enuye of the deuyl came the dethe to the world. Thys is the synne that moost ryght maketh a man to resemble vnto the deuyl, hys fader. For the deuyl hateth nothyng more than the wele of another; And loueth no thynge but the harme of another. And by thys synne the enuyous man may not see the wele of another nomore than the oule may see the clerenesse of the sonne .... For thys synne poysenneth fyrst the hert of thenuyous[10] persone, and after the mouthe, and after that the werkys. The herte of the enuyous is so poysonned and ouertorned that it may not see the good of another but that it gryeue hys herte wythinforth, and Iudgeth euyl that which he seeth, or that he hereth. He taketh and demeth alwaye the werste, and in alle thys he dooth hys owen harme.

The hert of an enuyous persone hath so many venymous thoughtes and fals demynges and Iugementes that they may not be nombred. After thys, whan the enuyous persone dooth or hereth ony euyl of ony other what someuer he be, is hyt of harme of his body, as euyl of hys deth, or of hys sekenesse, or of euyl for-

9. Poisons: *MED* s.v. "envenimen".

10. The envious.

tune, as of pouerte or euyl spyrytuel, lyke as whan he hereth that somme whyche haue been holden for good men been blamed and deffamed of somme vyces and deffaultes. Of these thynges enioyeth the enuyuos persone in hys herte. After whan thenuyous persone hereth and seeth the wele of another; Thenne cometh to hym a sorowe and an heuynesse to his herte that he may not be eased ne make good chere ne fayr semblaunte. Now mayst thou see that the venemous herte of thenuyous persone synneth generally In malice, in gladness, and ioye of the harme of other, and in sorow of the wele of another. Thus synneth the enuyous by his mouth; For nedes must suche wyne come oute of the tappe as is wythin the vessel. And by cause that the herte is al ful of venym it byhoueth that suche yssue oute of the mouthe. Thenne by the mouthe of thenuyous persone yssue thre maners of venymous wordes, of whome dauyd spekyth in hys psaulter that the mouthe of thenuyous persone is ful of maledyctyon. For of the good and wele of another he myssayeth, appayreth, and lasseth as moche as he may.

Of hurtyng
For al the harme and deffaultes of another he secheth, and sercheth, and sheweth forth to hys power of Trayson; For alle that he seeth or hereth he peruerteth to hys power, and tourneth it to euyl and Iudgeth it falselye. After, the enuyous persone hath thre maners of venym in werke, lyke as he hath in his mouthe and in hys herte. For the nature of the enuyous is to quenche and to destroye to hys power alle goodnesses, be they lytyl, be they grete, or myddle, or perfyght. Thenne he is of the nature of a basylyke ... .

The iij heed of the beest of helle is Ire or wrath, capitulo xxv
The thyrd heed of the beest is Ire. But thou owest to knowe that there is an yre whyche is virtuous, that the good men haue ayenste thys synne, whyche geten the vertues ayenst the vyces. There is another Ire whyche is a moche grete vyce, that is felonnye of herte, oute of whome yssuen many braunches. And in especyal foure warres that the felons haue.

Of the fyrst warre of the synne of yre, which is suche, capitulo xxvj
The fyrst warre of the synne of yre is to hym self, for whan Ire surmounteth the man, she tormenteth the soule and the body soo moche that the man may not slepe ne reste. Somtyme yre taketh awaye the etyng and drynkyng, and maketh one to falle in a feuer or in so grete heuynesse, or malancolye, or despayr that he taketh the deth. This is a fyre that wasteth alle the goodes of the hows. The second warre that the felon hath that is to god. For yre and felonnye surmounte and

fyre somtyme alle the people by aduersyte temporalle, or by maladye and sekenesse, or by dethe of frendys. Or by ony manere of meschaunce that hys wylle is not doon, that he grutcheth and murmureth ayenst god our lord, and sayth maugre and in despyte of god and of alle hys Sayntes, and swereth and blasphemeth ayenst god and his blessyd sayntes. The thyrd warre of Ire that the felon hath that is vnto them that ben vnder hym, that is to his wyf, and to his meyne, and breketh pottes and cuppes lyke as he were oute of his wytte, and so is he. The fourth warre is withoutforth to his neyghbours and bydwellers aboute hym and of this braunche growe vj bowes. For whan Ire ryseth bytwene two men there is thenne stryf, dyscorde, words, vylonyes, wronges. And after rancour whyche dwellyth in the herte, after cometh hate, medlyng, and bataylle, after desyre for tauenge[11] hym, after otherwhyse homycyde, and manslaughter. After cometh ofte mortalle warre emonge the frendes, out of whiche yssuen ofte euyls in dyuers maners and many that may not be amended ... .

Of the synne of slouthe which is sayd accydye, capitulo xxvij

The fourth heed of the beest of helle is slouthe, whyche is callyd of clerkys accidye. This synne is greuous to doo wel. This synne is an ouer euyl rote and casteth oute many euyl braunches. For this synne causeth a man to come vnto euyl amendemente, and more euyl begynnyng, and ouer euyl endyng.

The fyrst vyce is fayntnes, that is whan a man loueth lytyl and fayntly our lord, whome he oweth to loue ardantly, and this happeth whan he is flawe, latchous, and slowful to do wel. The second vyce of slouthe is tendrenesse, that is the bedde wherin the deuyl resteth hym and sayth to the man or woman, Thou hast be euer tenderly nourysshed, thou arte of ouer feble complexion. Thou mayst not do grete penaunces, thou arte ouer tendre, thou sholdest anone be ded, and for this the caytyf suffreth to be cherysshed and to doo alle the eases and the delyte of his body. The thyrd vyce is ydlenesse. This is a synne of whome cometh many euyls, as the holy scrypture sayth. For whan the deuyl fyndeth a man ydle he putteth hym anone in his werkys, that is he maketh hym fyrst to thynke euyl, to desyre vylonyes, rybaudryes, lecheryes, to lose his tyme, and to leue to do moche good that he myght do by whyche he myght gete heuen. The fourth vyce of slouth is heuynesse, whan a man is so heuy that he secheth nothynge, ne loueth so moche as to lye doun, reste, and slepe. Somtyme, how wel he be slowe they been wakre and quycke ynough to the nedes of the world. But they be al slepy to the nedes and werkys of god, and for to do the werkys that shold be to

11. To avenge.

their sauacyon, and these maner men had leuer lose thre masses than a swete or a good slepe. The fyfthe vyce of slouthe is shrewdnes or cursydnes, that is whan a man lyeth in synne and feleth the temptacyons of the deuyl and of hys flesshe that assaylle hym. And for veray shrewdnesse he wyl not lyft vp his hede ne his herte to god by contrycyon, Ne crye to god deuoutelye by confession, Ne stratche vp his handes to god by satysfaccion. To suche slouthe resembleth the wycked man that had lyeuer rote in foule stynkyng pryson than to take vn hym the laboure to goo vp the steyer, or the degrees for tescape[12] and goo his waye.

Of pusyllanymyte, of delaye, and werynes, capitulo xxviij

The vj. vyce of slouthe is pucyllanymyte. In this vyce be they that haue fere and drede of nought, and dare not begynne to do wel for they haue drede that god shal fayle them. This is the fere and drede that som*me* peple haue of theyr dreme. They resemble hym that dare not entre in to the path or waye for fere of the snaylle that sheweth his hornes; And resemble also the chylde that dare not goo in the waye for gaglyng and syttyng of the ghees. Thyse ben the vj vyces that take aweye fro a man good begynyng. And for vj. other vyces the slowe persone may not haue good amendement. These been the vj. tatches or condycyons of euyl seruauntes that so do that noo good wyse man ought to receyue in to his seruyce; that is to wete whan he is delayeng, neclygent, forgeteful, slowe, latchous, and fayllyng to do wel. ...

Of the synne of auaryce or couetyse, capitulo xxxiiij

The fyfthe heed of the beest toforesayd is auaryce, whiche otherwyse is called couetyse, whiche is rote of al euylles lyke as saynt poule sayth. This is the maystresse whiche hath so grete a soole that al goon thyder for to studye, lyke as sayth the holy scripture. For alle maner of peple studye in auaryce: Prelate, Clerke, Laye man, and relygyous. Auaryce is a loue of dysordynate hauoyr[13] and rychesse. This dysordynaunce sheweth hym self in iij. maners generally. In getyng ardantly, in retaynyng straynably, and in despendyng scarcely. These been the thre braunches pryncypalle that growe oute of thys rote. But especyally and proprelye yssuen oute of this rote of auaryce many bowes whyche been moche grete dedely synne. The fyrst is vsure. The second thefte. The thyrd raueyne. The iiij. challenge. The fyfthe sacrilege. The vj. Symonye. The vij. malygnytees. The viij. marchandyse. The ix. in wycked craftes. The x. in euyl and wycked playes. ...

12. To escape.
13. Possession, from the French "avoir."

Of the synne of lecherye whiche is loue dysordynatly, capitulo xlvij

The vj. heed of the beest of helle is lecherye, which is oultrageous loue and dysordynate in flesshly delytes. Of this synne the deuyl deceyueth a man in vj. maners, lyke as sayth Saynt gregory. Fyrst in folysshe and false beholdynges. After in folysshe and lewde talkyng and wordes. After in false touchynges. After in fals kyssynges, after cometh the dede. For fro folysshe beholdyng cometh the commynycacyon and speche, and fro speche to touching, and fro touchyng to kyssyng, and fro kyssyng to the dede. Thus subtylly bryngeth the deuyl that one to that other. Fyrst this synne is deuyded in two maners, for there is lecherye of herte and lecherye of body. Lecherye of herte hath four degrees. For the spyryte of fornycacion which is the fyre of lecherye enbraceth the herte and maketh fyrst to come the thoughts, the figures, and the ymagynaciyon of synne in the hert and in consentynges; after the herte delyteth hym in folysshe thoughtes, and yet he delyteth how wel that, yet he wyl not do the dede and in this thought he abydeth, and thys delyte is the second degree, whiche may be a dedely synne, soo grete may be the delyte. The thyrd degree is the consentyng of the herte of reason and of wylle, and these consentynges coucluded been dedely synne in caas that the deed be dedely synne; after the consentyng cometh the desyre and the grete brennyng of the flessh that they haue to thys synne, and doon many synnes in the day, in seyng the ladyes and the damoysellys rychely and fresshly apparaylled, whyche ofte desgyse and araye them proudly for to make the fooles and musardes to muse and beholde theym. And certes they synne moche greuously for by theyr couetyse, by theyr pryde, and by theyr cause perysshen many soules and moche peple put to deth and to synne. For thus as sayth the prouerbe, dame dator is the arblast to the tour. For she hath not a membre in hyr body but it is a grynne of the deuyl. As salamon sayth, wherof must be gyuen acomptes at the day of Iugement of the soules, which by thoccasyn and cause of them be dampned. That is to vnderstonde whan they be occasyon and cause other to synne by theyr entysyng and labour. Lecherye of the body is departed in to the lecherye of the eyen, of the eerys, of the mouth, of the hands, and of al the fyue wyttes of the body, and in especyal of the vylaynnous dede and werke. To this synne apperteyneth al the thynges of the flesshe, that moeuen and desyre to do this synne. As doon these oultrages and the excesse of mete and drynke, of swete beddes and softe, of delycyous robes and in al maner of excesse of body without necessyte. ...

And it goeth mountyng fro degree to degree, and fro euyl in to werse. ...

Of the synne of glotonye, capitulo xlix

The seuenth heed of the beest of helle is the synne of the mouthe, otherwyse calyd glotonnye, which hath two offices, of whiche that one apperteyneth to the taste, as to ete and drynke, and that other is in spekyng. Therfore this vyce and this synne is deuyded in two partyes pryncypally, that is to wyte in the synne of glotonye whiche is in etyng and drynkyng, and in the synne of the shrewde tongue that is in foule and folysshe spekyng. And fyrst we shal saye of the synne of glotonye whiche is a vyce that moche pleaseth the deuyl, and dyspleaseth to god. By this synne hath the deuyl grete power in man, wherof we rede in the gospel that god gaf lycence to deuylles for to entre in to swyn, and whan they were entred they drowned them in the see. Thys sygnefyeth that the glotons that lede the lyf of hogges and of swyn, the deuyls haue leue to entre in to them and to drowne them in the see of helle. And maketh theym to ete so moche that they breste and drynke so moche that they be drowned. Whan the champyon hath ouerthrowen his felowe he holdeth hym by the gorge by cause he shold not relyeue. Ryght so is hyt of hym that the deuyl holdeth by hys synne; in his mete the deuyl renneth to hys gorge lyke as the wolf dooth to the sheep for to strangle hym, lyke as he dyd to Adam and Eue in paradys terrestre. Thys is the fysshar of helle whiche taketh the fysshes wyth the grynnes by the throte. This vyce dyspleseth moche, For the gloton doeth to hym grete shame whan he maketh his god of a sacke ful of dunge. That is his bely whyche he loueth more than god, and doubteth and serueth it. God commaundeth that he shold faste. The bely sayth nay, thou shat not but thou shalte eete longe and by leyzer. God commandeth to ryse erly, his god his bely sayth thou shalte not. I am ouer ful me lyst to slepe, the chirche is none hare he wyl not flee awaye, and it is not yet open. It shal wel abyde and tary for me. And whan the gloton aryseth he begynneth his matyns and his prayers and sayth O god what shal we ete this day, shal we not fynde that is ony thynge worthe. After these matyns comen the lawdes and sayth, A lord god how wel dranke we yester euyn the good wyn. and how good mete ete we. Thenne after this by wepeth the gloton his synnes and sayth, Alas, sayth he, I wende wel thys nyght to haue deyed. The wyne yestereuyn was ouer stronge myn heed aketh, I shal not be eased tyl I haue drunken. This god of the wombe, of glotonye, is ouer euyl, for fyrst he bycometh a tauern gooar and frequenteth tauernes, after he playeth at the dyse, and after he selleth his good awaye, after he bycometh a rybaulde, an holyer, and letchour, and at the laste he hangeth on the galowes. ...

1b Richard Baxter, *A Christian directory, or, A summ of practical theologie and cases of conscience directing Christians how to use their knowledge and faith, how to improve all helps and means, and to perform all duties, how to overcome temptations, and to escape or mortifie every sin: in four parts. I. Christian ethicks (or* *private duties.) II. Christian oeconomicks (or family duties.) III. Christian ecclesiasticks (or church duties) IV. Christian politicks (or duties to our rulers and neighbours)*, 1678, pp. 160–383.[14] *Wing* B1220. **Source** Centre for Reformation and Renaissance Studies Rare Book Library, University of Toronto (BV4500 .B37 1678).

[*Tome III. Cases of Conscience about Matters Ecclesiastical, Q. 113, Point 11.*] ... It is lawful to use Hieroglyphicks, or *Images* expressing *Virtues* and *Vices*; As men commonly make Images to decipher Prudence, Temperance, Charity, Fortitude, Justice, *&c.* and Envy, Sloth, Pride, Lust, *&c.* As they do of the five senses, and the four seasons of the year, and the several parts of mans age, and the several ranks and qualities of persons, *&c.* ... .

[*Tome I, Ch IV. Part V.*] *Directions against Pride, and for Humility*

§. 1. PRIDE, being reputed the great sin of the Devil by which he sell, is in the *name* and *general* notion of it, infamous and odious with allmost all,: but the *nature* of it is so much unknown, and the sin so undiscerned by the most, that it is commonly cherished, while it is commonly spoke against. Therefore the chief *Directions* for the conquering of it are those that are for the full *discovery* of it. For when it is *seen* it is *shamed*, and to *shame* it is to destroy it. ...

§. 3. I. *PRIDE is an inordinate self-exalting*: or *a lifting up our selves above the state or degree appointed us*. It is called ὑπερηφανία [hyperephania], because it is an appearing to our selves, and a desire to appear to others above what we are, or above others of our quality. It is a branch of SELFISHNESS, and containeth *man-pleasing* as before described, and produceth *Hypocrisie*, and is its original and life. It containeth in it these following acts or parts. 1. *A will to be higher or greater than God would have us be*. 2. *An overvaluing of our selves*, or *esteeming* our selves to be *Greater*, *Wiser*, or *Better* than indeed we are. 3. *A desire that others should think of us*, and *speak of us*, and *use us, as greater, or wiser, or better than we are*. 4. *An endeavour or seeking to rise above our appointed place*, or *to be overvalued by others*. 5. *An ostentation of our inordinate self-esteem in outward signs* of *speech or action*. Every one of these is an act of *Pride*. The three first are the *inward* acts of it in the *Mind* and *Will*, and the two last are its external acts.

§. 4. As the *Love of God* and *man* are the comprehensive duties of the Decalogue, expressed most in the *first* and *last Commandment*, but yet extending them-

14. Excerpts are arranged in an order not matching the page order of the book. Marginal notes in the original source were not included in the transcription. This source contains manicules.

selves to all the rest; so SELFISHNESS and PRIDE (which is a principal part of it) are the opposite sins, forbidden principally in the *first* and *last Commandment*, as contrary to the *Love* of *God* and *man*, but so as it is contrary to the rest. They are sins against the very *Relation* it self that *God* and *man* do stand in to us, and not only against a particular Law. They are against the very *constitution* of the Kingdom of God, and not only against the *Administration*. It is *Treason* or *Idolatry* against God, and a setting up our selves in some part of his prerogative. And it is a monstrous extuberancy in the Body, and a rising of one member *above* and so *against* the rest; either *superiours* (and so against the fifth command) or equals (against the rest).

§. 5. HUMILITY is contrary to pride; and therefore consisteth, 1. In a contentedness with that degree and state which God hath assigned us. 2. In mean thoughts of our selves, esteeming our selves no *Greater*, *Wiser*, or *Better* than we are. 3. In a willingness and desire that others should not *think* of us, or *speak of* us, or *use* us, as *greater*, or *wiser*, or *better* than we are; that they should give us no more honour, praise or Love than is our due; the redundancy being but a deceit or lye, and an abuse of us and them. 4. In the avoiding of all inordinate aspiring endeavors, and a contented exercise of our assigned offices, and doing the meanest works of our own places. 5. In the avoiding of all *ostentation* or *appearance* of that greatness, wisdom or goodness which we have not, and fitting our speeches, apparel, provisions, furniture and all our deportment and behaviour to the meanness of our parts, and place, and worth. This is the very *Nature* of *Humility*. ...

[*Tome I, Ch. VII. Directions for the Government of the Passions, Tit.* 7] *Directions against sinful Wrath or Anger*

§. 1. As *Anger* is against the *Love* of our neighbour, I shall speak of it afterwards. As it is against the *soul* itself, I shall speak of it in this place. *Anger* is the rising up of the heart in passionate displicency against an apprehended evil, which would cross or hinder us *of some* desired good. It is given us by God for Good, to stir us up to a vigorous resistance of those things which within us or without us do oppose his Glory or our salvation, or our own or our neighbour's real good.

§. 2. *Anger* is *Good* when it is thus used to its appointed end, in a right manner and measure. But, it is sinful 1. When it riseth up against God or any Good, as if it were evil to us. As wicked men are *angry* at those that would convert and save them, and that tell them of their sins, and hinder them from their desires. 2. When it disturbeth Reason, and hindereth our judging of things aright. 3. When it casteth us into any unseemly carriage, or causeth, or disposeth to any sinful words or actions: when it enclineth us to wrong another by word or deed, and to do as we would not be done by. 4. When it is mistaken, and without just cause. 5. When it is greater in measure than the cause alloweth. 6. When it unfitteth us for our duty to God or man. 7. When it tendeth to the abatement of Love and brotherly kindness, and the hindering of any good which we should do for others: Much more when it breedeth malice, and revenge, and contentions, and unpeaceableness in societies, oppression of inferiours, or dishonouring of superiours. 8. When it stayeth too long, and ceaseth not when its lawful work is done. 9. When it is *selfish* and *carnal,* stirred up upon the account of some carnal interest, and used but as a means to a *selfish* carnal sinful end: As to be angry with men only for crossing your *Pride,* or profit, or sports, or any other fleshly will: In all these it is sinful. ...

[*Tome I, Ch. X. Directions of the Government of the Body, Part I, Tit.* 2.] *Directions against Idleness and Sloth*

§. 1. Here I must shew you what *Idleness* and *Sloth* is, and what are the *Signs* of it: and then give you Directions how to conquer it. *Sloth* signifieth chiefly the *indisposition* of the *mind* and body; and *Idleness* signifieth the *actual neglect* or omission of our duties. *Sloth* is an *aversness to labour, through a carnal love of ease, or indulgence to the flesh.* This *averseness* to labour is *sinful, when it is a voluntary backwardness to that labour which is our duty. Sloth* sheweth it self 1. In *keeping us from our duty,* and causing us to *delay* it, or omit it; and 2. In making us to do it *slowly* and by the *halves.* And both these effects are called *Idleness,* which is the *omission or negligent performance of our duties through a flesh-pleasing backwardness to labour.* ...

§. 3. *Sloth* and *Idleness* thus described is *a sin* in all, but a far greater sin in some than in others. And you may thus know what *sloth* it is that is the most sinful. 1. The more sloth is *subjected* in the *mind it self,* and the less it is subjected in the *Body,* the greater is the sin. For the *mind* is the nobler part, and immediate seat of sin. 2. The smaller the *bodily distempers* or *temptations* are which seduce the *mind,* the greater is the *sin.* For it shews the *mind* to be the more corrupted and tainted with the disease of *sloth.* He that is under an *unresistible indisposition* of *body,* sinneth not at all (unless as he voluntarily contracted that disease). But if the *bodies indisposition* to *labour* be great, but yet not *unrefitable,* it is a sin to yield to it: but so much the *smaller sin* (*caeteris paribus*) as the bodily disease is greater. ... 3. He is most *sinfully slothful* who is most *voluntarily slothful.* As he that *endeavoureth* least against it; and he that most *loveth* it, and would not leave it; and he that is least troubled at it, and least repenteth and lamenteth it, and *contriveth to accommodate* his sloth. 4. The sloth is (*caeteris paribus*) the worst, which *most prevaileth* to the omission or negligent performance of our duty. But that *sloth* which doth but *indispose* us, but is so far conquered by our resistance, as not to keep us from *our duty*, or not *much* and *often*, is the smaller sin. 5. That is the most sinful sloth (*caeteris paribus*) which is against the *greatest duties*. To be backward to the most *holy* duties (as praying, and hearing, or reading the Word of God, *&c.*) or to *duties* of publick consequence, is a greater sin than to be lazily backward to a common toilsome work. 6. That is the most sinful *sloth* and *idleness* which is committed against the *greatest motives* to labour and diligence. Therefore (in that respect) a *poor man's* sloth is more sinful than a *rich man's*, because he is under the pressure of *Necessity*: And in another *respect* the *rich* mans sloth is worst, because he buryeth the greatest Talents, and is *idle* when he hath the greatest *wages*. ...

§. 4. *Sloth* is a thing that is easily discerned: The signs of it are 1. When the very *thought* of *labour* is troublesome and unpleasing, and *ease* seems sweet. 2. When duty is omitted hereby and left undone. 3. When the easie part of duty is culled out, and the harder part is cast aside. 4. When the *judgement* will not believe that laborious duty is a duty at all. 5. When that which you do, is done with an ill will, and with a constant weariness of mind, and there is no alacrity or pleasure in your work. 6. When you do no more in much time, than you might do in less, if you had a willing ready mind. 7. When the backward mind is shifting it off with excuses, or finding something else to do, or at least delaying it. 8. When you choose a condition of greater ease and smaller labour, before a laborious condition of life which in other respects is better for you. ... 9. When little impediments discourage or stop you: *The slothful saith, there is a Lyon in the way*, Prov. 22:13. His way is an *hedge of thorns*, Prov. 15:19. *He will not plow by reason of cold*, Prov. 20:4. 10. When you make a *great matter of a little business*: It cannot be done but with such preparation, and so much a do, that shews a slothful mind in the doer. Even the *putting his hand to his mouth*, and *pulling it out of his bosome* is a business with the sluggard: that is, he maketh a *great matter* of a little one, *Prov.* 26:15 and 19:24. 11. Lastly, The *fruits* of *slothfulness* use to detect it, in soul, and body, and estate: For it corrupteth, impoverisheth and ruineth all. The weeds of his *Field* or *Garden*, the *vices* of his soul, the sins of his life, the duties omitted or sleepily performed, the disorders of his family or charge, and usually, or oft, his poverty, do detect him, *Prov.* 24:30 and 12:24, 27.

[*Tome I, Ch. X, Part I, Tit.* 3.] *Directions against Sloth and Laziness in things spiritual: and for zeal and Diligence*

§. 1. *Zeal* in things spiritual is contrary to *sloth* and *coldness* and *remissness*; and *Diligence* is contrary to *Idleness*. *Zeal* is the fervour, or earnestness of the soul.

Its first subject is the *will* and *affections*, excited by the *judgement*; and thence it appeareth in the Practice. It is not a *distinct Grace* or Affection, but the vigor and liveliness of every grace, and their fervent operations. ...

[*Tome I, Ch. IV, Part VI.*] *Directions against Covetousness, or Love of Riches, and against worldly Cares*

§. 3. II. But *Worldliness* or *sinful Love of Riches* is, 1. When *Riches* are loved, and desired, and sought more for the *Flesh* than for *God* or our *Salvation*; even as the *matter* or *means* of our worldly prosperity, that the *flesh* may want nothing to please it and satisfie its desires. Or that *Pride* may have enough wherewith to support it self, by gratifying and obliging others, and living at those rates, and in that splendour, as may shew our Greatness, or further our Domination over others. 2. And when we therefore desire them in that proportion which we think most agreeable to these *carnal ends*, and are not contented with our *daily bread*, and that proportion which may sustain us as passengers to Heaven, and tend most to the securing of our souls, and to the service of God. So that it is the *end* by which a sinful Love of *Riches* is principally to be discerned, when they are loved for *pride* or *flesh-pleasing*, as they are the matter of a worldly corporal felicity; and not principally for God and his service, and servants, and our salvation. ...

§. 5. III. The *Malignity* or *Greatness* of this sin consisteth in these points, (especially when it is predominant). 1. The love of the *World*, or of Riches, is a sin of *Deliberation*, and not of meer temerity or sudden passion. Worldlings *contrive* the attaining of their ends. 2. It is a sin of *Interest, love* and *Choice*, set up against our chiefest *Interest*: It is the setting up of a *false end*, and *seeking that*; and not only a sin of error in the means, or a seeking the *right end* in a mistaken way. 3. It is *Idolatry*, or a denying God, and deposing him in our hearts, and setting up his creatures in his stead, in that measure as it prevaileth. The *worldling* giveth that *Love*, and that *Trust* unto the creature, which is due to God alone: He *delighteth* in it instead of God, and *seeketh* and holdeth it as his felicity instead of God. And therefore so far as any man *loveth the world, the love of the Father is not in him* 1 John 2:15. And *the friendship of the world is enmity to God.* 4. It is a contempt of *Heaven* when it must be neglected, and a miserable world preferred. 5. It sheweth that *unbelief* prevaileth at the heart, so far as worldliness prevaileth. For if men did practically believe the Heavenly Glory, and the promise thereof, they would be carried above these present things. 6. It is a debasing of the soul of man, and using it like the Brutes, while it is principally set upon the serving of the flesh, and on a temporal felicity, and neglecteth its eternal happiness and concernments. 7. It is a perverting of the very drift of a mans life, as employed in seeking a wrong end, and not only of some one faculty or act: It is a *habitual sin* of the *state* and *course* of mind and life, and not only a particular actual sin. 8. It is a perverting of Gods creatures to an End and Use clean contrary to that which they were made and given for ... .

§. 6. IV. The signs of Covetousness are these: 1. Not preferring God and our everlasting Happiness before the Prosperity and Pleasure of the flesh, but valuing and loving fleshly prosperity above its worth. 2. Esteeming and loving the creatures of God as provision for the flesh, and not to further us in the service of God. 3. Desiring *more* than is needful or useful to further us in our duty. 4. An inordinate *eagerness* in our desires after earthly things. 5. Distrustfulness, and carking cares, and contrivances for time to come. 6. Discontent, and trouble, and repining at a poor condition, when we have no more than our *daily bread*. 7. When the world taketh up our *thoughts* inordinately, when our *thoughts* will easilier run out upon the world, than upon better things. And when our thoughts of worldly plenty are more *pleasant* and *sweet* to us than our thoughts of Christ, and Grace, and Heaven, and our *thoughts* of want and poverty are more *bitter* and *grievous* to us than our thoughts of sin and Gods displeasure. 8. When our *speech* is *freer* and *sweeter* about prosperity in the world, than about the concernments of God and our souls. 9. When the world beareth sway in our *families* and *converse* and shutteth out all serious eadevours in the service of God, and for our own and others souls; Or, at least, doth *out short* Religious duties, and is preferred before them, and thrusteth them into a corner, and maketh us slightly huddle them over. 10. When we are dejected over much, and impatient under losses, and crosses, and worldly injuries from man. 11. When worldly matters seem sufficient to engage us in contentions, and to make us break peace, and we will by Law-suits seek our right, when greater hurt is liker to follow to our brothers soul, or greater wrong to the cause of Religion, or the honour of God, than our Right is worth. 12. When in our trouble and distress we fetch our comfort more from the thoughts of our provisions in the world, or our hopes of supply, than from our trust in God, and our hopes of Heaven. ... 15. When we are more careful to provide a *worldly* than a *heavenly* portion, for *children* and *friends*, and rejoyce more in their bodily than their spiritual prosperity, and are troubled more for their *poverty* than their ungodliness or sin. 16. When we can see our brother have need, and shut up the bowels of our compassion, or can part with no more than meer superfluities for his relief; when we cannot spare that which makes but for our *better* being, when it is necessary to preserve his *Being it self*; or when we give *unwillingly* or *sparingly*. 17. When we will venture upon *sinful means* for gain, as lying, over-reaching, deceiving, flattering or going against our Consciences, or the Commands of God. 18. When we are too much in *expecting liberality from others,* and think that all we buy of, should sell cheaper to us than they can afford, and consider not their *loss* or *want,* so that *we* have the gain; nor are contented if they be never *so bountiful to others,* if they be not for us. 19. When we make too *much ado* in the world for *riches,* taking too much upon us, or striving for preferment, and flattering great ones, and envying any that are preferred before us, or get that which we expected. 20. When we hold *our money* faster than our *innocency,* and cannot part with it for the sake of Christ, when he requireth it; but will stretch our consciences and sin against him or forsake his cause to save our estate. Or will not part with it for the service of his Church, or of our countrey, when we are called to it. 21. When the Riches which we have are used but for the pampering of our flesh, and superfluous provision for our posterity, and nothing but some inconsiderable crums or driblets are imployed for God and his servants, nor used to further us in his service, and towards the laying up of a treasure in Heaven. These are the *signs* of a *worldly covetous* wretch. ...

[*Ch. IV, Part VII.*] *Directions against the Master sin; SENSUALITY, FLESH-PLEASING or Voluptuousness*

§. 23. Direct. 2. *Be acquainted with the range of sensual desires, and follow them, and watch them in all their extravagancies.* Otherwise while you are stopping one gap, they will be running out at many more. I have given you many instances in my Treatise of *Self-denyal.* I will here briefly set some before your eyes:

1. Watch your *Appetites* as to meat and drink, both quantity and quality: Gluttony is a common unobserved sin: The flesh no way enslaves men more than by the appetite; As we see in Drunkards and Gluttons that can no more forbear than one that thirsteth in a burning Feavor.

2. Take heed of the Lust of uncleanness, and all degrees of it, and approaches to it: especially immodest embraces and behaviour.

3. Take heed of ribald filthy talk, and Love Songs, and of such incensing snares.

4. Take heed of too much sleep and Idleness.

5. Take heed of taking too much delight in your Riches, and lands, your buildings, and delectable conveniences.

6. Take heed lest Honours or worldly Greatness, or mens applause become your too great pleasure.

7. And lest you grow to make it your delight, to think on such things when you are alone, or talk idly of them in company with others.

8. And take heed lest the success and prosperity of your affairs do too much please you, as him, *Luke* 12:20.

9. Take not up any inordinate pleasure in your children, relations, or nearest friends.

10. Take heed of a delight in vain, unprofitable, sinful company.

11. Or in fineness of apparel, to set you out to the eyes of others.

12. Take heed of a delight in Romances, Play-books, feigned stories, useless news, which corrupt the mind, and waste your time.

13. Take heed of a delight in any recreations, which are excessive, needless, devouring time, discomposing the mind, enticing to further sin, hindring any duty, especially our delight in God. They are miserable souls that can delight themselves in no more safe or profitable things than Cards, and Dice, and Stage-plays, and immodest dancings. ...

[*Ch. VIII. Directions for the Government of the Senses, Part V, Tit. 1*]: *Directions against Fornication and all Uncleanness*

§. 2 1. There is no sin so odious, but *Love* to it, and *frequent using* it, will do much to reconcile the very *judgement* to it: either to think it *lawful* or *tolerable* and venial; to think it *no sin*, or but a *little sin*, and easily forgiven. And so with some brutish persons it doth in this. But I. It is Reason enough against any sin that it is *forbidden* by the most wise, infallible universal King of all the world. Thy *Makers will* is enough to condemn it, and shall be enough to condemn those that are the servants of it. He hath said, *Thou shalt not commit adultery*. I Cor. 6 9,10. *Be not deceived, neither fornicators, nor idolaters, nor adulterers, nor effeminate, nor abusers of themselves with mankind – shall inherit the Kingdom of God. ... The abominable – and whoremongers – shall have their part in the lake which burneth with fire and brimstone.* Rev. 22:15. *For without are dogs, and sorcerers, and whoremongers, and murderers* – Jude 7. *Even as* Sodom *and* Gomorrah *and the Cities about them in like manner, giving themselves over to fornication, and going after strange flesh, are set for an example suffering the vengeance of eternal fire.* I shall add no more lest I be tedious. ...

[*Ch. VIII, Part IV, Tit. 1, III.*] *The Greatness of the sin of Gluttony*

§. 16. 1. *Luxury* and *Gluttony* is a sin exceeding contrary to the *Love of God*. It is *Idolatry*. It hath the *Heart* which God should have. And therefore *Gluttons* are commonly and well called *Belly-Gods*, and *God-bellyes*, because that *Love*, that *care*, that *delight*, that *service* and *diligence* which *God* should have, is given by the *Glutton* to his *Belly* and his *throat*. He *Loveth* the pleasing of his Appetite better than the Pleasing of God: His *dishes* are more *delightful* to him than any holy exercise is. His *thoughts* are more *frequent* and *more sweet* of his *belly* than of God or Godliness: His *care* and *labour* is more that he may be pleased in meats and drinks, than that he may secure his salvation, and be *justified* and sanctified. And indeed the Scripture giveth them this name, Phil. 3:19, *whose end is destruction, whose God is their Belly, who glory in their shame, who mind earthly things,* being *enemies to the Cross of Christ,* that is, to *bearing the Cross for Christ, and to the Crucifying of the flesh,* and to the mortifying, suffering parts of Religion. Nay, such a *devouring Idol* is the *Belly* that it swalloweth up more by *Intemperance* and *excess* than all other Idols in the world do. And remember that the very *life* of the *sin* is in the *Appetite* and *Heart*: when a man's *Heart* is set upon his *Belly,* though he fare never so hardly through necessity, he is a *Glutton* in *Heart.* When you make a *Great matter* of it what you shall eat and drink as to the *delight,* and when you take it for a great loss or suffering if you fare hardly, and are troubled at it, and your thoughts and talk are of your *belly,* and you have not that *Indifferency* whether your fare be *course* or *pleasant* (so it be wholsome) as all *Temperate* persons have, this is the *Heart* of *Gluttony,* and is the *Hearts* forsaking of God, and making the *Appetite* its God.

§. 17. 2. *Gluttony is self-murder*: Though it kill not suddenly, it killeth surely. Like the dropsie which *killeth* as it *filleth,* by degrees. Very many of the wisest Physicions do believe that of those that over-live their Child-hood, there is scarce one of twenty, yea or of a hundred that dyeth, but *Gluttony* or *excess* in *eating* or drinking is a *principal cause* of their death, though not the most *immediate* cause. It is thought to kill a hundred to one of all that dye at Age. And it will not let them dye *easily* and quickly, but tormenteth them first, with manifold *diseases* while they live: You eat more than *nature* can perfectly concoct, and because you feel it not trouble you or make you sick, you think it hurts you not, whereas it doth by degrees; first, alter and vitiate the temperament of the blood and humours making it a crude unconcocted unnatural thing, unfit for the due nutrition of the parts; turning the nourishing mass into a burdensom excrementitious mixture, abounding with Saline or tartareous matter, and consisting more of a pituitous slime, or redundant serosity, than of that sweet nutrimental milk of nature, quickened with those *spirits* and well proportioned heat, which should make it fit to be the Oyle of life. ...

§. 18. 3. *Gluttony is* also a *deadly enemy to the mind,* and to *all* the noble employments of Reason both *Religious, Civil,* and *artificial.* It unfits men for any close and serious studies, and therefore tends to nourish ignorance, and keep men fools. It greatly unfits men for hearing Gods Word, or reading, or praying, or meditating, or any holy work; and makes them have more mind to sleep; or so undisposeth and dulleth them that they have no life or fitness for their duty ... .

§. 20. 5. *Gluttony* is the immediate symptome of a *carnal mind,* and of the damnable sin of *flesh-pleasing* before described. And a *carnal mind* is the very sum of iniquity, and the proper name of an unregenerate state. *It is enmity against God, and neither is nor can be subject to his Law:* so that they that are thus *in the flesh cannot please God: and they that walk after the flesh shall dye,* Rom. 8:6, 7, 8, 13. ...

§. 21. 6. *Gluttony* is the *breeder* and *feeder* of all other lusts ... . It pampereth the flesh to feed it, and make it a sacrifice for *lust.* As dunging the ground doth make it fruitful, especially of Weeds, so doth Gluttony fill the mind with the Weeds and Vermine of filthy thoughts, and filthy desires, and words, and deeds.

§. 22. 7. *Gluttony* is a *base* and *beastly kind of sin.* For a man to place his happiness in the pleasure of a *Swine* and to make his Reason serve his throat, or sink into his Guts, as if he were but a *Hogshead* to be filled and emptyed, or a Sink for Liquor to run through, into the chanel; or as if he were made only to carry meat from the Table to the Dunghill, how base a kind of life is this? yea, *many beasts* will not eat and drink excessively as the Gluttonous Epicure will do.

§. 23. 8. *Gluttony* is a *Prodigal consumer* and *devourer* of the creatures of God. What is he worthy of that would take meat and drink and cast it away into the chanel? nay, that would be at a great deal of cost and curiosity to get the pleasantest meat he could procure, to cast away. The Glutton doth worse: It were better of the two to throw all his *excesses* into the Sink or Ditch, for then they would not first hurt his body. And are the Creatures of God of no more worth? ...

§. 25. 10. *Gluttony* is a *sin* which turneth your own mercies, and wealth, and food, into your snare, and to your deadly ruine: Thou *pleases* thy *throat,* and *poysonest* thy soul. It were better for thee a thousand times that thou hadst lived on scraps, and in the poorest manner, than thus to have turned thy plenty to thy damnable sin ... .

§. 31. 16. *Luxury* is a *sin* most unseemly for men in so great misery, and incongruous to the state of the *Gluttonous* themselves. O man if thou hadst but a true sight of thy sin and misery, of death and judgement, and of the dreadful God whom thou dost offend, thou wouldst percieve that *fasting,* and *prayer,* and *tears* become one in thy condition much better than glutting thy devouring flesh. What a man, unpardoned, unsanctified, in the power of Satan, ready to be damned if thus thou dye (for so I must suppose of a Glutton) for such a man to be taking his fleshly pleasure! For a *Dives* to be faring sumptuously every day, that must shortly want a drop of water to cool his tongue, is as foolish as for a Thief to feast before he goeth to hanging: yea, and much more. For you might yet prevent your misery, and another posture doth better *beseem* you to that end: *Fasting* and *crying mightily to God* is fitter to your state. See *Ionah.* 3:8, *Ioel* 1:14, *Ioel* 2:15. ...

§. 35. 20. Lastly, It is a *spreading sin*, and therefore is become common, even the sin of Countreys, of *rich* and *poor*. For both sorts *love* their *bellies*, though both have not the like provision for them. And they are so far from taking warning one of another, that they are encouraged one by another: and the sin is scarce noted in one of a hundred that daily liveth in it. Nor is there almost any that reprove it, or help one another against it (unless by impoverishing each other) but most by perswasions and examples do encourage it (though some much more than others). So that by this time you may see that it is no *rare*, no venial little sin.

2a *The abbaye of the holy ghost* (1497?). **2b** John Moore, *A mappe of mans mortalitie* (1617).

Introduction Two manuscript versions of the *Abbaye* attribute the work to Richard Rolle or to John Alcock, bishop of Ely, and earlier printed versions (1496 and 1497) to John Alcock, but the 1500 printed copy does not attribute the text to anyone, leaving the authorship anonymous. Since its date of composition is probably somewhere around 1350[15] it is unlikely it was authored by Alcock, who lived in the late fifteenth century. While the English version of the *Abbaye*, as opposed to its French original, does emphasize Rolle-like affective aspects of piety, since its contents and style, in the end, are different from Rolle's, it is unlikely it was Rolle's either (though there was a late medieval tendency to attribute many anonymous devotional works to him).[16] The text was quite popular, today still extant in twenty-four fourteenth- and fifteenth-century English manuscripts, and three printed editions (all by Wynkyn de Worde). The *Abbaye*'s introduction reveals it was intended to provide an alternative to life in religious enclosure, presented to those who could not, for various reasons including poverty, take up such a life. The *Abbaye* was to provide such readers with ways of living contemplatively within their "active" life (i.e., regular lay life; the contemplative vs. active life was an important trope

15. V.M. Lagorio, "Abbey of the Holy Ghost," in *Lexikon des Mittelalters Online* (Stuttgart, 1999), via Brepolis, accessed 5 January 2017.

16. Boyda Johnstone, "Reading Images, Drawing Texts: The Illustrated *Abbey of the Holy Ghost* in British Library MS Stowe 39," in *Editing, Performance, Texts: New Practices in Medieval and Early Modern English Drama*, ed. Jacqueline Jenkins and Julie Sanders (New York, 2014), 27–47, at 47 n12; see also this chapter throughout.

in many late medieval devotional works). The *Abbaye* was thus akin to Walter Hilton's *Mixed life* (ca. 1390) or the anonymous *Fervor amoris* (ca. 1400), authored for the spiritual benefit of devout lay individuals who sought the most religiously profitable aspects of monastic life without having to enter the cloister.[17]

The *Abbaye* focuses on original sin and Christ's incarnation, as well as human conscience, virtues as contraries to sin, and as the soul's defences against the Seven Deadly Sins. Its organizing spatial allegory is that of an abbey (conscience), inhabited by virtues (nuns), such as Charity and Mercy, built by God and destroyed by the Seven Deadly Sins "let in" by the original sin of Adam and Eve; the ruin of the abbey scatters the nun-virtues around the world. After a period of chaos, Christ is sent to the world to seek out the nuns of the abbey and through his life and Passion he manages to locate and bring them together again, thus rebuilding the Abbey of the Holy Ghost for the future salvation of mankind. The Abbey is thus a spatial study of the human conscience before and after the Fall, describing its creation, destruction by sin, the period of loss before the coming of Christ, and finally, redemption and the rebuilding of the Abbey by Jesus' life and sacrifice. The excerpts below illustrate the mapping of conscience (in the abbey), of the Seven Deadly Sins (as assailants), and the journey of Christ in search for the lost virtues. The way in which he finds the lost virtues, with doubt, pain, and uncertainty highlighted in the text, underscores the humanity of the son of God, a trope typical of the late Middle Ages, and thus highlights also the grandeur of his sacrifice: divinity locked in a human body prone to sensations of fear, pain, and despair, subjected to torture for the sake of mankind.

A mappe of mans moralitie is a work different in many ways from the *Abbaye*, but there are many reasons why these texts can and should be read together. John Moore was rector of Knaptoft, and an ardent Protestant. His interests were primarily local, as he was opposed to enclosures in his county, and agitated against them; as rector he was transferred to Shearsby in 1610. He is known to have authored only two texts, one of them non-religious (*A target for tillage*, 1613), and the other, *A mappe of mans moralitie*, a religious piece on sin and human conscience.[18] The *Mappe*, noted primarily for its discussion of death, which places it among other Protestant works on death and original sin, also provides interesting insights on the Devil and sins as assailants attacking the human soul. The text is constructed as a "geographical" study of the human body before

17. Johnstone, "Reading Images, Drawing Texts," 28–29. See also Nicole R. Rice, *Lay Piety and Religious Discipline in Middle English Literature* (Cambridge, 2008), 2; and Rice, "Spiritual Ambition and the Translation of the Cloister: *The Abbey and Charter of the Holy Ghost*," *Viator* 33 (2002): 222–260.

18. William Albert Samuel Hewins, "Moore, John," *Dictionary of National Bibliography*, ed. Sidney Lee (London, 1894), 357–358.

and after the Fall, mapping the story of the Fall, discourse on sin, death, Satan, the power of God, and the redeeming sacrifice of Christ onto the imagery of the human body, its struggle against the threats of the Devil and his servants, its corrupt nature, and its redemption by Christ. The excerpts below illustrate the physical architecture of Moore's moral discussion, presenting Christ as a man, and the human body and soul as a direct likeness of God that Satan corrupted. In that respect, both the *Abbaye* and the *Mappe* share a number of important features: both present a "mapping" of human conscience and a "geographical" view of the soul and the soul's journey from innocence, through sin, to salvation; both present the violation of human conscience by sin as an assault of the Devil (thus applying a common late medieval motif of the Devil's attack on the human soul via sins, described as his arrows or army[19]); and both anchor the human soul and body as an image of God, the *Abbaye* by focusing on the humanity of Christ, and the *Mappe* by describing the human body and soul as created in the likeness of God. Finally, both describe the ideal state of man before the Fall, and the corruption and chaos that ensued after the Fall. In both texts sin is the ultimate corruption that stains the soul and destroys its symmetry (which in both texts is presented physically: either spatially or in terms of bodily appearance and congruity).

At the same time, many differences can be observed between the two texts, ranging from style to focus. The *Abbaye* is ultimately a tale of Christ's labour and suffering, whereas the Protestant *Mappe* bewails original sin more voluminously than the *Abbaye*, and only after a lengthy description of the warfare between the Devil and the human soul which the *Abbaye* lacks (having only the description of the siege of the abbey in the beginning) does the *Mappe* go on to present Christ as the Captain and Protector of the human soul, and talk about Christ's sacrifice for mankind, also spatially describing Heaven as City, and Hell as Prison. These two texts are thus connected by their presentation of sins as assailants of the Devil (with the *Abbey* focused more on the Seven Deadly Sins and the *Mappe* more on original sin, as well as the sins of the World, the Flesh, and the Devil[20]) and by their spatial framework of narrative and visual imagery. They differ in the emphasis they place on the aspects of the story (journey vs warfare), style, and other narrative elements, but their shared spatial understanding of the human soul, conscience, and the place of sin provide an interesting study of how devotional writers mapped out elements of Christianity for their readers.

19. See, for example, Bloomfield, *Seven Deadly Sins*, 110, 117, 118, 133, 221.

20. Another late medieval motif that developed in connection to the Seven Deadly Sins; "[i]t became common to range the Sins under these three classic divisions" (Bloomfield, *Seven Deadly Sins*, 394 n64).

2a *Here begynneth a matere spekynge of a place that is namid the abbaye of the holy ghost,* Westminster, 1497 (?); unnumbered pages. *STC* 13609. **Source** *EEBO*: British Library, London (IA.55232).

... Many men there be that wolde be in relygyon but they may not for dyuerse causes. Therfore they that may not be in bodyly relygyon they may be in ghostly relygyon yf they woll that is founded in a place that is called Conscyence. But fyrste the place muste be clensed with grace of the holy ghost. Two maydens that be called Loue and Ryghtwysnes shall cast awaye fro conscyence all maner of fylth. Thenne shal Mekenesse and Pouerte make the foundement therof and put awaye all worldely thought, that is though men haue worldely goodes, set they not theyr loue there vpon, and thenne may they well be called men poore in spyryte to whom Cryst gyueth his blessynge. This abbay must also be set vpon a ryuer, that is the ryuer of teeres on whiche ryuer was Mawdeleyne founded in sorowynge for her synnes. Therfor the grace of god and heuenly ryches came all to her wyl. Thenne shal Buxumnesse and mercy rere vp the walles in to heygth and make them stronge with almesdedes geuynge gladly to poore men after thy state is, thus saith Thobi,[21] *Si multum tibi fuerit habundanter tribue. Si tibi sit exiguum parum inpertire stude.* This is thus moche to meane. Yf thou be riche hauynge plenteeof wordly godes, gyue plenetuously thereof. Yf thou be poore be of good wyll to gyue gladly of suche thynge as thou hast. For saynt Poule sayth, *Hilarem datorem diligit deus.* That is to saye, god loueth the glad gyuer. Thus shall we buylde our hous in heuen with the loue of god and of our euencrysten. Thenne shall Pacyence and strength reyse vp all the pylars and vnderset them with botraces that no wynde of wordes of angre, ne of tempest of persecucyon, ne of temptacyon may cast them downe. Thenne we must make our cloystre in this maner that shall kepe vs ghostly, out of al worldly thought and syghtes, that is kepe we our eyen fro all euyll syghtes, our eeres fro euyll herynge, our mouth fro euyll spekynge, fro swerynge, and fro lyenge, and our hertes fro all euyll thoughtes. And yf we kepe thus this foure corners we shall buylde well our cloystre. A mayde, the hyght Confessyon shall make our chaptour hous. Predycacyon the fraytour, and Oryson the oratory, Contemplacyon the dortour. And yf thyse shalbe reysed vp to the worshyp of god they must stonde out fro worldly noyse, fro worldly besynesse and angre. Contemplacyon is not ellis but a deuoute herte with a brennynge loue to god to taste somdele of the blysse that is ordeyned for his chosen in heuen. Pyte shal be our fermour, Deuocyon cellarer, and holy

21. Thobias.

Medytacyon shall be garnetour. Whan all thyse offycers ben made the holy ghost is warden, with god fader founder, with god the sone wysdom of the fader. The worthy lady Charyte shal be abbesse of this hous, for all this other offycers shall obeye to Charyte. *Vnde omnia vestra in caritate fiant.* All thynge that ye do, saye or thynke, be they done in the love of god. Alas yf I durste saye full many be in relygyon but fewe be relygyous that do the byddynge of Poul to obeye to charyte, therefore lese they moche tyme and also ther mede. Now shall the worthy lady Wysedom be our Pryouresse. *Nam prior omnium est sapiencia.* The good lady Mekenesse that alwaye loueth herselfe shall be our suppryouresse. This abbay is of god blessyd that hath thyse gouernours, for all be blessyd that holde them in theyr scole. For they that kepe Charyte, Wysedom, and Mekenesse, the thre persones in trynyte shall gyue them heuen to mede. That soule is grete and hye in heuen that hath thyse thre within herself, Charyte, Wysdom, and Mekenesse. Dyscrecyon shal be tresorer and Oryson shal be chauntour .... Deuocyon is Celerer that kepeth all the wynes bothe whyte and redde. That ben all the worthy thankynges the whiche we all owe to do to god for the endeles goodnes that he hath done, dooth, and woll do to vs yf we woll ourself. ...

The goodnes that he doth to vs now is whyle we ben here in body and in soule, yeuynge vs al that we nede both bodyly and ghostly. Bodyly, as mete, drynke, and clothynge. Ghostly, as good thoughts, good words, and good dedes. And therto to them that ben good he graunteth a shelde of his grace and mynde of his passyon to kepe them fro the fende. And to theym that ben wycked and combred with synne he gyueth space and tyme to torne therfro and to amende yf they wol. ...

The goodnes that he woll doo to vs yf we woll dwelle and abyde styll in his seruyce, that is in good vertues. In herynge, seenge, spekynge, goynge, handlynge, and in all other dedes werkynge shall be to this. In tyme of dethe whan body and soule shall departe atweyne and the deuyl appere in his owne lykenesse before vs to make vs agast, and yf he may, to brynge vs in to mysbyleue, god wolde sende his owne angell and all our gode dedes that euer we here wrought wryten to shew vs and comforte vs, and dryue awaye the deuyll and lede our soules to blysse. The whiche blysse our lorde graunteth and gyueth to all his chosen and true seruaunt wha he sayth thus, *Venite benedicti patris mei percipite regnum quod vobis paratum est ab origine mundi.*

Penaunce shall be Keruer; the ryght well can make many good meetes, sufferynge many bytter sorowes for synne to make the soule mery and glad with god that before was clenge, for she had hym offended. Temperaunce shall serue in the fraytour and loke all aboute that mesure be had ouer all, that none haue to moche ne to lytell, neyther of etynge, drynkynge, ne of slepynge. Sobernes must nedes rede at the borde the lyfe of holy faders, what lyfe they lyued here in erthe to take of them example, to do as they dyde, and therby to wynne the mede that they haue. Pyte must be the Pytauncer that dooth that good that she may. Mercy must be Almener that gyueth to all and no thynge can holde to herself. The lady Drede, Porter that kepeth the cloystre of the hert that chacyth awaye all wycked vyces and called in good vertues, and closeth the gates of the cloystre that none euyl come not in to the herte, the eyen, the mouth, the eeres, ne in to other places by the fyue wyttes. Honeste is maystresse to teche nouyces curteysy, how thei shall haue them in ther dedes both to god and to man. Curteysy is Hostlere to calle in noble gyft, and Symplenes shall be her felowe that she be not to lyberall. Reason shall be Purueour that there be no defaute. Bounte shalbe Fermerer that seke men to serue. Her felawe shall be Largenesse to gyue eueryche that he nedeth. Medytacyon Garnetour for to gadre corne togyder that men haue theyr sustenaunce. Medytacyon is thought in god of his werkes, of his words, and of his creatures, and of his paynes that he loued vs with. For oft a good thought is better than many Indeuowte prayers. ...

Whan this abbaye was al well set and god therin serued, a tyraunt came and with grete power put in his foure doughters that were all of shrewed maners, the fende, fader of them all. The fyrste doughter, pryde, the other was enuye, the thyrde false demynge, the fourth flesshly lust. Thyse foure wenchis by counsell of the deuyll theyr fader came to noye this abbay, so nyght and daye in soule the worse rest they haue. Whan Charyte sawe this myscheyf and other ladyes of the house they range anone theyr chapytour bell and toke counsell of this thynge. And thenne sayd Dyscrecyon that they praye the holy ghost to come to helpe them with his grace. And thenne they kneled downe and sange, *Veni creator spiritus.* Thenne as it is sayd before came our lord Cryst Iesu in to his moder and restored this hous better than euer it was before. To hym glory and worshyp that lyueth without ende. ... We may vnderstonde that there was a fals tyraunt apostata that is named Sathanas that some tyme was pryour of the order of angels in the blysse of heuen, that for pryde ranne out of his blysful order in to sorowfull horrour of the payne of helle. He had soo grete enuy to this abbay of the holy ghost that it was so well with god and had so grete a lordship, He bethought hym how he myght distroye that noble hous and how he myght do to make the noble couente of vertues to renne out of theyr order, as he ranne out of his. He came in lykenes of a adder to thabbaye gate to come in, and the porter that was called Drede was not there redy, for without doubte yf Drede had be there the fende had not come in. And Eue sawe that he was there and as a grete fole she lete hym come in. ... And in the meane tyme that Adam and his wyf ete of the fruyte, the fals traytour with his thre knyghtes, that is is to saye Pryde, Couetyse, and Vaynglory, wente in this abbaye of the holy ghost and bare awaye al the good that there was, and bare awaye the chartour that god gaaf them to holde theyr place by. And therfore Adam ne his wyfe neyther theyr heyres from that daye vnto this daye had neuer right to chalenge ayen lordshyp of the blysse of heuen, but oonly by goddes mercy. And not onely thyse false theues brake the abbaye but also they bare awaye the godes, that is they draue awaye dyspytousely out of the abbaye all the noble couent of vertues ... .

God thenne sayd to Adam, For thou ete of that fruyte at thy wyues byddynge ayenste my forbyddynge, and for thou letest the abbay of the holy ghost to be so foule destroyed, and lete thabbesse and her couent to renne awaye fro theyr order, and knowest not whether, this shal be thy penaunce. Thou shalt be dryue out of paradyse in to the erthe acursed for thy synne. Therin shall thou dwelle with moche sorowe and woo all the dayes of thy lyfe ... . They lyued thenne in this worlde with moche woo and sorowe .ix. hondred yeres and .xxx. And sought the abbesse and her couent that were soo renne awaye. Also he wolde haue had somwhat wherwith he myght haue made agayn that abbaye of the holy ghost. ...

And in the meane tyme he fell seke for sorowe therof and deyed and his wyfe both. And theyr soules went to helle. Not onely they alone but al those that of them came by the space of .iiij. M. and .vi.C. yeres to helle they went eche one. For so longe was Adam in hell, and that was for thabbaye of the holy ghost that was theyr conscience was not made ayen as fayr ne as clene as it was before. Thus was Adam and his wyfe in helle many yeres in sorowe and care tyll almyghty god had pyte of theyr soules and sende downe his owne dere sone and bad hym go and seke the abbesse of the abbaye of the holy ghost and her couent. For he wyste better where they were than Adam wyst ... .

Whan god almyghty here thus thyse prophetes with many other good men to make moche moon with heuy chere many hundred yeres for the destruccyon of the abbaye of the holy ghost he had grete pyte of them that farid so. And that therefore mannes soule was in pryson and payne of helle and sholde haue be there without ende. He ordeyned a counseyle of the holy trynyte in the blysse of heuen, of the fader, sone, and holy ghost; ... they ordeyned that the seconde persone that is almyghty goddes sone sholde come in to this worlde and be borne of a mayde and become man, and make agayn the abbaye of the holy ghost and deye for loue of man on the rood tree, and so delyuer mannes soule fro the payne of helle. Thenne were there foure doughters of almyghty god whiche ben Mercy, Trouthe, Ryghtwysnes, and Peas, the whiche herde telle that mannes soule sholde be delyuered fro helle payne, and came all foure togyder before god almighty ... .

Thenne sayd Iesus, how is it that ye sought me, wyst ye not that I must be besy about my faders nedes. He sende me in to thys countre to seke up thabesse and the couent of thabbay of the holy ghost. And therfore I went amonge the maysters in to the temple and there founde I two ladyes of the couent, Ryghtwysnes and Wysdom; and so he fonde more than all they. Thenne went he home with Ioseph and his moder in to Nazareth and there he founde an other lady that was called Buxumnes. For he that is hyghest lorde was lowest of hert, and in al thynge buxome to his moder. Thenne went he forth xvij. yeres and an half, and euery daye at his borde he founde other two ladyes of that holy abbaye, and theyr names were Temporaunce and Sobrennes. He lad them with hym in to deserte to seke mo of her felowes. And there he founde other two ladyes that one hyght Penaunce and her felowe Strength ... .

Tho went Iesus in to the londe of Galyle and there he founde other two ladyes of that holy abbaye one hyght Shryfte and that other Predycacyon. For there preched Cryste fyrste and sayd to the people of the countree. *Penitemini et confitemini et credite euangelio*. Shryue ye you and do ye penaunce and be ye of good byleue the kyngdom nygheth faste. ... Thenne came he forth on a daye fro the mount of Olyuete in to the temple of Ierusalem to preche there, and whyle he was prechynge the Sarrasyns brought hym a woman take in auowtry, and sayd to hym, Lo mayster, this woman is now take in a spousebreche, what shal we now do with her. Moyses byddeth in our lawe that we sholde stone suche to deth. Cryste knewe theyr falshede that they dyde it to tempte hym, stowped downe, and wrote on the grounde with his fynger all theyr synnes, so that eche of them myght se how synfull other was. And thenne he sayde to them thus: Syth it is so that by your lawes this woman shalbe stoned to dethe, thenne whiche of you all that is without synne caste he on her the fyrste stone. Thenne all they were ashamed of themself and went out at the doore eche after other, and lete Cryste stonde allone with the woman. Thenne came two ladyes to hym of the abbaye of the holy ghost that were Mercy and Pyte ... . Thenne founde Cryste a lady of the couent that was called Reason and sayde, Gyue ye to themperour that longeth to hym and to god that longeth to hym, and that is reason.

One daye there as Cryste went by eth waye by hymselfe he remembred hym on mannes soule and on the abbaye of the holy ghost, and thenne he founde an other lady of the same house that men calle Gelousye . Thenne toke he his dyscyples preuyly and went towarde Ierusalem, and sayd to them thus: I haue al thyse xxxij. yeres and more be about to helpe mannes soule and to kepe vp the abbesse and the couent that wente out of thabbaye of the holy ghost, and I haue founde of them .xvi. And now I wol go to Ierusalem and be bounde, beten, hangen, and drawe, and I shal deye for loue of mannes soule, to fynde vp the other dele of the holy couent. This was a grete Ielousy and a grete loue. Thenn went they forth to Ierusalem to gader, and on a tyme as they were at theyr souper togyder Cryst founde two ladyes of that abbaye that men calle Curteysy and Honeste. For Cryst fed there at souper his dyscyples with his owne flesshe and blood. Whan he had so done he wysshe theyr fete and wiped them. At this offyce were foure ladyes: Curteysy and Buxumnes, Honeste and Mekenes .... As they went our lorde began to quake and drad, and thenne he sayd to them, Here I haue founde an other lady of the holy couent that is called Drede; I haue, he sayd, full moche drede ayen that I shall deye. Sytte ye downe, he sayd, and wake ye and byd your bedes tyll I come ayen to you. Thenne went he forth fro them as ferre as it were a stones caste, and there he founde other two ladyes, Medytacyon and Oryson ... .

Wake ye, he sayd, and praye that ye fall not in to temptacyon. Thenne went he ayen and founde Oryson and her syster Deuocyon and sayd, My fader syth it may none other be but that I must nedes suffre deth be it as you woll. Thenne came he ayen to his dyscyples and founde them slepynge as he dyde before. He went ayen the thyrde tyme and prayed as he dyde fyrste, and founde other ladyes of the holy abbay, Contemplacyon, Dalyance, and Iubylacyon. ... Thenne the Iewes toke Cryste and bounde hym as a theyf ful harde and sore. There he founde an other lady of that same hous and she was named Pacyence. ...

Thenne sayd Cayphas to our lorde, What sayst thou to thyse complaintes and trespasses that thyse men shewe ayenst the. Cryste founde there an other lady that is called Symplenesse. For he answered not to hym with one worde. ... Thenne they toke suche an other raggyd rough nayle and draue it thrugh both his fete with an hamour atones in to the harde tree, and whyle he was thus nayled on the crosse came many ladyes of the holy abbaye: Pouerte, Buxumnes, Penaunce, Symplenes, Pacyence, and Mekenes, to se how he dide. Thenne sayd Cryst to them, yf ye had your abbesse thenne had ye euerychone ... . The lady Pouerte was there all redy, for he hanged all naked, as he was born of his moder, on the crosse for mannes soule. And whyle he hangid there with his blody woundes al to hurlyd and all to rente, He founde the abbesse of the abbaye of the holy ghost that is callid Charyte, the whiche sayd, *Maiorem caritatem nemo habet ut animam suam ponat quis pro amicis suis.* More loue and charyte may noo man haue than to gyue his lyf for his frendes, as Cryst dyde for mannes soule. Whan Cryst had founde the holy abbesse Charyte and all her couent he was full glad in his herte, all though he felte moche wo of bodyly payne withoutforth. Thenne asked he a drynke to make with all thyse ladyes mery. And welcomed them and sayd (Scicio) I thurste. Thenne the false Jewes made hym to drynke of eysell and gall tempred togyder with myrre and put it to his mouth vppon a spounge. Whan our lorde had smellid the taste thereof he wolde no more thereof but he sayd thus. *Consummatum est.* That is to saye, I haue done all my faders message that he bad me doo on erthe. For I haue founde vp the abbesse and al the couent of the abbaye of the holy ghost and made ayen thabbay better than euer it was. Now he sayd, I woll go to Adam and to my frendes and delyuer them out of helle, and lede them ayen to the blysse of paradyse that neuer shall cesse. Whan he had sayd thus he gaaf vp the ghost and deyed in flesshe hangynge on the crosse all to russhyd and all to rent, so vnneth ony lymme henge by other bitwene two theuis for grete loue that he had to saue mannes soule. Thenne ghostly in his godhede he went down to helle and toke out Adam and Eve. ...

2b John Moore, *A mappe of mans mortalitie, Clearely manifesting the originall of death, with the nature, fruits, and effects thereof, both to the vnregenerate, and elect children of God. Diuided into three bookes; and published for the furtherance of the wise in practise, the humbling of the strong in conceit, and for the comfort and confirmation of weake Christians, against the combat of death, that they may wisely and seasonably be prepared against the same. Whereunto are annexed two consolatory sermons, for afflicted Christians, in their greatest conflicts. By Iohn Moore, minister of the word of God, at Shearsbie in Leicester-shire*, 1617, pp. 1–197.[22] *STC* 18057. **Source** Thomas Fisher Rare Book Library, University of Toronto (stc 00281).

[*Booke I, Ch. I, Sections 1–9*]

Ovr most gracious God, infinite in wisedome, and incomprehensible in loue towards mankinde, hauing before all worlds decreed to make himselfe most glorious in his Creation, did in his appointed time effect the same. For hauing made the world in wonderfull manner, and furnished it with all varietie of creatures, both for profit and pleasure, deuising in his wisedome and vnspeakable loue, a perfection of happinesse for man vpon the earth; at last, after a most exquisite manner consulted with himselfe for the shape of man, and finding no creature fit enough for a patterne of his portraiture, concluded with himselfe to make mankinde, as a Chrystall glasse of his glory, and a most liuely resemblance, after a sort, of his

22. Marginal notes in the original source were not included in the transcription.

Maiestie. And that not onely in the frame of his body, to be as it were a briefe Map and abridgement of the whole worlds perfection, which hee made as a most glorious Theatre, fully replenished with most admirable sights of all sorts, but (which is more) both in body and soule to represent his Creator, as his Vicegerent and petty Monarch on the earth, and seating him here as it were in his Throne, and putting his owne Scepter into his hand, and his Crowne of glory vpon his head, gaue him dominion and rule ouer all the workes of his hands; so that well may hte Prophet with wonder exlaime and cry out (*Psal. 8:4*) *Lord, what is man that thou art so mindefull of him? &c.* Now that this Image of God was liuely expressed in whole man (resembling his Maker both in his body, and in his soule) doth plainly appeare by the renuing of man in Christ, (Rom. 12:1–2; 2 Cor. 7:1) who is not onely sanctified in the one alone, but in the other. And first for mans Body: it did resemble God in that immortalitie wherein it was first created, as also in the seuerall members thereof, expressed the varietie of his perfections, and therefore (in respect of Gods diuers employments) in a borrowed speech are ascribed to him, as the hands and armes, to shew Gods omnipotencie and power; his eyes and eares, his piercing prouidence and sight, &c. I omit mans face and comely countenance (in which principally doth shine a certaine imperious maiestie and grace most conspicuous) causing all liuing creatures to stoupe vnto him; and besides the goodly order of all his outward parts (set and disposed in admirable sort) a glorious beauty spreading it selfe throughout, with wonderfull strength, agillitie, and nimblenesse of all his members, made him most famous, that very Naturalists and Pagans anatomizing his very body, not onely preferred the frame thereof before the worlds whole curious creation but (rauished in their senses with the consideration of the same) deified and preferred it aboue all measure.

Yet as waxe is more apt to receiue an impression then clay, so the soule, being a Spirit, commeth nearest to Gods nature. For first, the very substance of *Adams* soule did most liuely shadow out the diuine Essence, not onely in the simplicitie, inuisiblenesse and immortalitie thereof, but also in that power which it enioyed, to know and will. And as God is but one in the world, quickning, sustaining, and gouerning the same, so there is but one soule in the body, which (being whole in euery part thereof without augmentation or diminution) giueth vnto it both life, sense, and motion. Further, the soule is like vnto God in the faculties of the same. For as there is but one onely diuine Essence in the Godhead, and yet three distinct persons in respect of their externall actions, so the soule is but one, howsoeuer it consisteth of sundry essentiall qualities.

This Image of God in man consisted especially in the rule and dominion of the Creatures. *Let vs make man* (saith God) *in our owne image, that hee may rule the fowles of the ayre, fish of the sea, beasts of the earth.* Now, to rule well is required Knowledge, Memorie, Will, Vnderstanding and Iudgement; which are essentiall in God, and proper to our soules. Man had not onely giuen vnto him of God power and abilitie to vnderstand diuine and humane things, but was endued with other heauenly qualities, as Iustice, Wisedome, Temperance, Mercy, Loue, &c. Gods Image in man is righteousnesse, holinesse and knowledge. *Be renued* (saith the Apostle) *in the spirit of your minde,* [Ephe. 4:23–24] *and put on the new man, which after the Image of God is created vnto righteousnesse and true holinesse.* Whose qualities are necessarily inferred by the contrary, attributed to the olde man, where truth is opposed against lying, Christian anger against sinfull rage, iust dealing against falshood and wrong, holy and gracious speech against corrupt and filthy communication. And hee saith that this Image or new man is renued in knowledge after the image of him that created it; because the true knowledge of God transformeth man to the image of God his Maker, that is to say, to the true sinceritie and purenesse of the soule. Therefore presently following hee expresseth the qualities of this Image; to wit, *tender affection,* or bowels of compassion, *kindnesse, humblenesse of minde, meeknesse, long-suffering, forbearing, and forgiuing one another, Loue, Peace;* and these be the fruits of Gods Spirit, which renueth our hearts (as they are mustred by S. *Paul*) against which vertues (hee saith) there is no Law, which Image also is called a conformitie to Gods Sonne. ...

But that these things may appeare more plainly, wee are to know that the Image of a thing is the forme by which it is resembled, and a similitude is a qualitie of a thing, by which it is shadowed. Now man in his Image not onely resembled his Maker in knowledge and vnderstanding, but was also created in other celestiall conditions, as Iustice, Wisedome, Mercy, Loue, &c. (as before was declared) yet so as that Christ alone is the very ingrauen forme of his person, according to his Deitie, and in his Humanitie, so farre as it is capable of the same. And to this end hath God predestinated and elected vs, that we should be conformable to the Image of his Sonne, *Rom. 8:29.* Therefore God made vs of an vnderstanding nature, and capable of diuine perfection, when with these heauenly properties our soules were first endued, which now cannot be againe recouered but thorow the helpe of Christ, the true patterne and type of our first created Image. To conclude, how like we were made to God, appeareth by our proposed end of that selfe-same happinesse and blisse which wee feare to loose, and waite (through hope) to enioy with God himselfe, both in louing and knowing of him as hee is.

Mans soule by creation had Reason and Will, (as it were) for two wings: Reason to vnderstand and know, and Will to approue and elect things vnderstood and knowne. And these two wings did with equall force and sweet consent carry vp and support the soule, to guide it aright to God; that so it might sore aloft (with her affections) as the Eagle flying carryeth her young ones to inure them with the Sunne; so it might lift vp it selfe aloft from all infection whatsoeuer. A rectitude and vprightnesse was also added that it might beare the force and power (as it were) of a cleare and pleasant gale of winde to these two wings; which blast receiued into the braine did carry and freshly set forward the powers of the minde … .

[*Booke I, Ch. III, Sect. 1–12*]
Man, being thus created in so glorious an estate, raigning and ruling, not onely as a Prince, but (as it were) a petty God vpon the earth, all things being put in subiection vnder his feete, Sathan that olde serpent and enuious aduersary of mankinde, hauing fallen himselfe and his associates (by his and their owne transgression) into a most cursed and wretched estate, enuying at the blessednesse of our first parents, so happily planted vpon the earth, and placed in Paradise (possessing the body of the Serpent, and abusing his forme) drew *Enah* by his wiles to heare her God accused of vnkindnesse, and from hearing to suspition, and from suspition to plaine rebellion against his law; and so Sathan not contented, she was made his snare to catch her husband also. …

And now behold this vnkinde creature, this vngratefull wretch, and wicked man, forgetting God and his duetie, casting aside his blessings and graces (wherewith he abounded) most traiterously, villainously, and shamefully rebelling against his Lord, contemneth his Creatour, and setteth his God at naught; he listneth to the Diuell, and beleeueth his lies, and followeth (like a beast) his sensuall appetite, and euen in that one thing forbidden, spiteth his God, regardeth not his word, feareth not death that was threatned, but eateth of the forbidden tree, maugre the beard of God, and his iudgements.

… Notwithstanding Gods commanding and his threatning, he is most carelesse, and swiftly runnes headlong to sinne and wickednesse, and so entred into such a maze of miseries, from whence neither himselfe, nor his posteritie were euer able to vnwinde themselues; for so abusing his owne free will, he lost it, and was made a slaue to Sathan and himselfe. Gods image being by his fall defaced, he became like the diuell, and contemning life, he found out death, euen death eternall. This was the wages of his sinne, this was the hire of his labour, this profit reaped he for his paines.

God thrust him out of Paradise, and being expelled, he was kept out by the Cherubins, so presently he saw his shame, his figge leaues could not couer his nakednes; but God accursed him and his seede; he plagued the earth with barrennesse, and caused all the creatures to feele the smart of this his fall; and as he disobeyed God, so procured he the disobedience of all the creatures towards himselfe. Hereof comes the fiercenesse of Lyons, Beares, Tygers, Wolues, and all wilde beasts, hence ariseth all rebellions, and vprores, warres, seditions, scarcitie, dearth, and hunger, colde, and nakednesse; murther, plagues, and all kinde of calamities that are in the world, all which are forerunners of this eternall death, and ring-leaders to damnation. Thus Sathan suggesting a want of knowledge, because he knew not euill, and so corrupting his heart with a curious desire thereof (not able of himselfe to effect the ill that he suggesteth) procured man to the practise of ill, before he could obtaine to the knowledge thereof: euen as a man commeth to the knowledge of poyson by the dangerous taste thereof: so deare was the purchase of euils experience, that it sodainely procured mans ruine and fall. And so his passions were made to see, and his Reason blinde: in searching for knowledge, hee met with error. So Reason it selfe (the lampe of mans soule) which like the Sunne in the firmament, spreading her beames thorough mans little centre, is now become so dimme and darke, in his cloudy and ecclipsed skye, that the eye of the soule is as voide of light in things diuine, as the little sparkes of fire raked vp close in the ashes: which blindnes and ignorance of God and heauenly things, were not personall in *Adam* himselfe, but by possession entred into all his posteritie and of-spring. ...

[*Booke I, Ch. IIII, Sect. 4*]
God made *Adam* without corruption, and created him after his owne Image, yet thorow enuy of the Diuell came Death, and they that hold of his side proue it: so that the Father of Death is the Diuell; and as he is euill by nature, so likewise is Death in it selfe, issuing and proceeding from such a fountaine [Rom. 5:12 & 6:23]. The Diuell is the author of Sinne, and consequently of Death, for by Sinne Death entered, and Death is the wages thereof. [*1 Iohn 3:8*] *Hee that committeth sinne is of the Diuell, for the Diuell sinneth from the beginning; hee is a murtherer from the beginning; hee is both a lyer, and the father thereof*, not by creation, but by corruption. God made him an Angell, hee made himselfe a Diuell; so falling from God, hee fell from goodnesse, and became the father of sinne and wickednes. *Non stetit in veritate* [*Iohn 8:44*], he stood not in the truth. Hee that caused Sin, caused Death for sinne: *The third part of the waters became Wormewood [Apoc. 8:10–11], and many men dyed of the waters, because they were made bitter.* Bitternes caused death. ...

[*Booke II, Chapter IIII, Sect.1–4*]
... Our life is a warfare, and that most strange; for any other warre may haue an end [*Iob 7:1*], either by a conclusion of peace with the enemie, or by flying farre from him, or by ouercomming him in fight. But in this spirituall warre we cannot lawfully make any peace with these our enemies, the Diuell, World, and Flesh, &c. For so it would proue our ouerthrow and destruction; they being vnto vs so many traitours, and irreconcileable murtherers. It would be worse for vs, then for the silly Sheepe to make peace with the Wolues. Neither yet can we flee, and so get from them, for the Diuell will pursue vs into euery place, with his whole armies and huge hoasts of his olde tryed and trayned Souldiers to inuade vs: within vs are our corrupt affections, and couetous lusts, as his hirelings. And wheresoeuer we become in this life, these our enemies will finde vs out; therefore we must fight or be foyled, wee must ouercome, or be conquered ... .

And as the Diuill (with his armies) maketh war against all mankind, so especially he fighteth against Christ the head, and his faithfull members. ... The Diuell is a Peripateticke (saith one) alwaies walking and going about, seeking whom he may ensnare, and all is fish that comes to his net. Our hearts being as deepe riuers, and the Diuell being no more able to discerne the thoughts thereof, then the Angler can descry what fish is in the water (for the secrets of all hearts are onely knowne to God), hee baiteth a hooke for vs, and by the going downe of the line he knoweth we are sped. If he see any couetously giuen, he setteth riches before him; if any be ambitious, he offereth titles and preferments, &c. He hath manifold nets of temptations, sometimes besetting vs with vaine pleasures and sometimes incirkling vs with inordinate sorrow and care; now fetching vs in with feare, and anone pricking vs forward with pride and presumption. As he findeth vs affected, so he fitteth his baites, and by our ready and greedy apprehension of his temptations he effecteth our destruction. And as a cunning Fisher (knowing how to hold the fish he hath hooked) he will giue them line and libertie, but yet they shall walke no further then he list, that he may draw them backe againe at his pleasure: as the childe playeth with the bird tyed by the legge, not suffering her to flye but the length of the thread. Therefore the baite that he layeth for vs, being our bane, let vs not come within the length of his line, or within the compasse of his nets. Let Gods word rather be our baite and hooke to catch vs, which being taken, taketh vs, and happy is he that is taken therewith, no to his slaughter with the fish, but to the saluation of his soule with the faithfull. ...

[*Booke III, Ch. III, Sect. 1–5*]
Let vs now proceede to remoue such impediments (through the helpe of God) as lye in our way to hinder our speedie passage, in this our pilgrimage of death, which is (as wee haue heard) the true hauen of life, to all Gods children. Great and manifold are Sathans assaults in this our iourney, who still sheweth himselfe a professed aduersarie in all good proceedings. And here he commeth, not himselfe alone, but with a huge hoast and army of enemies, hauing the whole world, our flesh, and friends, to fight against vs. But of these things, in this place let it suffice to poynt at in generall, vntill wee come to a more particular discourse, as occasion shall be offered. And let vs first learne to arme our selues against these our deadly foes, that so being harnessed (as it were) with the armour of proofe, wee may strongly stand out, when wee shall be assailed, neuer yeelding to our foes, but following fast our Captaine Christ, to get the conquest in this our fight, which already is begunne, and shall most assuredly be gotten to all the faithfull.

Sathan first of all will thus be ready to assault vs. And art thou ready to dye O man? Why then behold the swarme of thy sinnes, the number of thy faults, and monstrous rebellions against thy God, both old and new, of age and youth, for which the wrath of God, the graue, and hell are ready to deuoure thee. The Law is thy Iudge, which doth condemne thee, thy God is iust and cannot but accurse thee, his sentence is passed, and will not cleare thee, &c. So that here (without Christ) no comfort can be found, hee onely must now protect vs, or else wee perish; his righteousnesse must be our roabe to hide our raggednesse, his merits the onely meanes to cloath our nakednesse; &c., Which things wee cannot possesse without a true and liuely Faith, which is the gift of God; and therefore wee must pray to haue it wrought in our hearts by the holy Ghost, and all good meanes. This, then, (as we haue heard already) will get vs the victory ouer the Diuell, and all assaults. It will oppose to this our deadly foe, life for death, holinesse for sinne, obedience for the Law; yea, all Christs satisfactions, to make the whole summe. But of this poynt wee haue sufficiently discoursed.

Then commeth the World, and will set abroach his baites. What wilt thou dye O man? I pray thee behold thy goodly buildings and stately roomes, thy lands and reuenues, thy rents and treasures, thy credit, wealth, and fame, thy pleasures and delights, and all that thy heart desireth. But alas, O World, this thy felicitie is fayned, thy loue is counterfeit, and thy promise is deceitfull. These things (I confesse) to be good in their kinde, and for my vse, so long as they stand with Gods fauour. Kept they may be, so that wee loose not God, who now doth call vs, and therefore may not keepe vs from him. Yet I know (O World) the vanitie of thy pleasures, the frailty of thy glory, and the ficklenesse of thy goods, and that all these are nothing in respect of the riches of heauen and happy life, which after death I am sure to haue; wherefore, *I desire to be dissolued, and to be with Christ*; in whom indeede are hid all the treasures of God; who also is the keeper of our true life [*Phil. 1:23, Col. 3:2*]: for this our wretched life which now we lead, is no life indeede, but a very death. For, *we are dead, and our life is hid with God in Christ*; wee walke by faith, and not by sight; yea, so long as wee are at home in this body, wee wander and goe astray from God our Lord [*2 Cor. 5:7*]. And thou, O World, which bewitchest so many to loue this life, what should I gaine, if I should serue thee? I am sure to be a foe to Christ who loues thee not, who prayeth not for thee, whose Kingdome is not of thee, and therefore to loue thee is to hate my God, which to doe is worse then death. Thy reward (I know) is nothing but nakednesse, for naked I came vnto thee, and naked I shall goe from thee: therefore I am willing to forgoe thee, and desire to be freed to dwell with Christ.

Lastly, comes the Flesh (with trembling and quaking) Why? wilt thou dye O man? see here thy friends and thy family, thy Wife and thy Children, thy Father, thy Mother weepe and waile, cry and call vnto thee, and wilt thou thus depart? wilt thou needes goe from them? It is good, no doubt, to tarry still among our friends with Gods good will; and there is nothing (vnder God) but it may be kept, so that God (being aboue all things which we haue) be not lost [*Math. 10:37*]: *For hee that loueth father or Mother, Wife, or Children, &c.* better then Christ, is not worthy of his presence. And though my friends lament the losse of my life, yet can they not redeeme it, for *what man is hee that liueth and shall not see death? and shall hee deliuer his soule from the hand of the graue?* [*Psal. 89:48.*] No, no, neyther riches nor strength, neyther power nor policie can preuaile in this poynt. Death neyther spareth pouerty, nor regardeth wealth, it esteemes neyther manners, age, nor time, but walketh in the gates of old men, and setteth snares continually for young men; no worldly practise can escape the bands of death. It alwayes pursueth vs, and wheresoeuer we goe, it layeth hands vpon vs. And though men labor to liue long, and desire that they might neuer come to the terme of their dayes; yet indeede it is no other thing to liue, then to make haste to death. Wherefore men doe walke whither they would not come, and willingly runne to the end of that course which euermore they haue abhorred; for death is the punishment of all men, the tribute of all men, the rule of all men, and the receiuer of all men: God hath set vs our bounds which wee cannot passe.

... And in going from you my earthly friends, I shall not yet be destitute of friends, but make a good exchange; for I goe to the Saints of heauen, to the liuing God, who is Iudge of all; to Iesus Christ my Redeemer, to the celestiall *Ierusalem*, to my abiding Citie, to the company of Angels, to the Congregation of the first borne, to the spirits of the righteous, and to ioyes vnspeakable beyond all mans conceit. Such be the comforts, the rewards, heritages, and exceeding priuiledges that God hath (before all worlds) prepared and alwayes had in store for his elect. And therefore still I desire to be freed from the flesh, to liue with Christ; *Wee haue here no continuing Citie, wee looke for one of God* [*Heb.* 13:13–14]; And I know that so long as I am in the flesh I cannot please God, and that if once this earthly house of this tabernacle were destroyed, I shall haue a *building giuen me of God, a house not made with hands, but euerlasting with God in the heauens* [2 *Cor.* 5:1] ... .

[*Booke II, Ch. I, Sec.* 1]
What our fearefull estate is without Christ we haue heard before, being holden in the shadow of death by the chaines of our sins, the weight and burthen whereof is the law of God laid vpon vs. Hell is our prison, and Death is our Gaolor to hold vs. See how fast we are locked from God and his Saints in the dungeon of Death, by the meanes of sinne which is a sword to the heart, a serpent in the bosome, poyson in the stomacke, a thiefe in the house. It woundeth Nature, stingeth the conscience, killeth charitie, and depriueth vs of Gods fauour, which is the worst of all. Now in this distresse, Christ came to visite vs in his due time, euen God and man (a right redeemer for vs) he tooke our cause vpon him, and wrestled with the Diuell that held vs by our sinnes in Death [*Heb.* 2:14–16; 17 *&c*]. This mighty Sauiour tooke flesh and blood to take our part, none could be our Mediatour but he alone, none amongst the Angels (for they are no men), not any amongst the Saints, for they were all sinners; neither any amongst the other creatures, for they were all corruptible; so that we can neither giue gold nor siluer for the redemption of our soules, neither can wee trust in the merits of Angels and Saints, who all want vertue for this worke; but onely in Christ the Sonne of God and man, a meete redeemer for vs, who is our Priest alone, abiding for euer, because he liueth for euer; neither can his Priesthood be translated to another; and as the sacrifice is his owne, so hee is Priest alone, to offer it to his Father; which he did once for all vpon the Crosse for all belieuers. ...

[*Booke II, Ch. II, Sec.* 5]
And where the Apostle saith that by death Christ ouercame him that had the power of death, it is clearely manifest what manner of death our Sauiour Christ sustayned, euen that ouer which the Diuell had his power, the same death which is the reward of sinne; by bearing it he ouercame it, and hee conquered no more then hee submitted himselfe vnto: for by death hee ouercame death, If hee suffered no more but a bodily death, hee ouercame also but a bodily death, and so

though wee all rise againe, yet should wee arise in the condemnation of the sinne of our soules; or if hee haue ouercome death and the power of it, both in our bodies and soules, then Christ hath suffered the paines of it both in body and soule, that wee might rise againe from the bands of death, and liue with him for euer: for hee hath broken the force of it no further then hee hath felt the sting of it himselfe. Therefore let vs beleeue that Christ, both body and soule, was made a sacrifice for our sinnes.

3a *Here begynneth a boke of a ghoostly fader that confesseth his ghoostly chylde* (1521?).
3b *The nine mortal weapons, or, So many deadly sins charged against poor mankind by Satan* (1650?).

Introduction The 1521 (?) *Boke of a ghoostly fader* is an example of a text akin to John Mirk's *Instructions for parish priests* (ca. 1400), a late medieval manual for priests touching upon a number of pastoral matters including confession, in that it contains what could be seen as a manual for pastoral evaluations of sin typically used during confession, except it is in verse and so it seems unlikely that it had a practical use for a priest in an actual pastoral situation (although its verse could have served as a mnemonic device to the priest). More likely, it was designed and used by lay readers who could perform such "confession" at home as an exercise in contemplation and meditation, its simple verse making it possible to memorize the passages with ease. The text is a guide to basic Christian knowledge, here regarding sin in particular although similar, longer works would also typically include information on the sacraments, gifts of the Holy Ghost, etc. It is a self-help book addressed to the reader, in which God the Holy Father, Jesus Christ, and Mercy participate in a kind of dialogue (although the notes indicating Mercy and Jesus Christ (JHS in the text) are placed only in the margins, and in an irregular pattern quite unlike a conversation). The text starts with an invocation to Jesus and God, followed by an introduction describing in brief the threat of hell and sin, among other things, and as part of the introduction (with no separate heading) swiftly passing on to the sin of pride as the primary of all sins, followed by envy, avarice, wrath, sloth, gluttony, and lust, and their descriptions. In a separate section the text describes the "circumstances" of the Seven Deadly Sins, focusing on the degrees of sin related to a sinner's circumstances, and talks about contrition.[23] The

23. This makes the text akin to a pastoral confession manual. See, for example, *Handling Sin: Confession in the Middle Ages*, ed. Peter Biller and A.J. Minnis (York, 1998); and Jonathan Hughes, "The Administration of Confession in the Diocese of York in the Fourteenth Century," in *Studies in Clergy and Ministry in Medieval England*, ed. David M. Smith (York, 1991), 87–154.

final part discusses the remedies to the deadly sins (meekness amending pride, etc.). There is also an interrogation of venial sins attached at the end, and these are connected to the five senses (seeing, hearing, smelling, tasting, and touching). This text is thus a reader-friendly self-examination manual and a devotional guide, reminiscent of both clerical manuals and works such as Walter Hilton's *Scale of perfection* (ca. 1380) and *The book of vices and virtues*, and harkens back to their tradition, though its versified form, while not unusual for such manuals, is nevertheless uncommon. Given its fairly late date of printing, it is an illustration of changes to the devotional manual genre, becoming a newer and "lighter," short versified work on the most important aspects of devotion. It is also indicative of the endurance of the Seven Deadly Sins, perhaps more than any other late medieval motif, as an important meditative aid.

The 1650 (?) *Nine mortal weapons* is significantly shorter than *The Boke of a ghoostly fader* but in principle focuses on a similar subject to *The Boke*'s first and third parts, which describe deadly sins. A one-page pamphlet that resembles many other works on moral subjects printed at the time, the *Nine mortal weapons* is also in many ways a stand-alone text in that it does not seem to contain any polemical content (as did many other short anonymous works[24]), but seems to be interested in the subject of sin exclusively, which was a topic typical to other genres such as puritan works on practical divinity. However, texts such as the *Ages of sin, or, sinnes birth & groweth with the stepps, and degrees of sin, from thought to finall impenitencie*, printed in 1635, indicate that some religiously-focused short anonymous texts were available to Protestant audiences. The *Nine mortal weapons* is a Protestant variation on the concept of the heptad (ordered as pride, avarice, lechery, envy, wrath, sloth, gluttony), described with the use of traditional Christian ideas on their qualities, with pride being the sin of the Devil, and avarice the root of all evil.[25] It adds two more sins to the seven, drunkenness and unbelief, as sins many Protestant ministers (e.g., Increase Mather) often preached against, though neither were absent from pre-Reformation works on sin: drunkenness in particular featured in later medieval works on sin as a branch of gluttony (e.g., Chaucer's *Parson's Tale*; *Jacob's well*, or in *Piers Plowman* where Gluttony, instead of going to church, goes to a tavern to drink).[26] The sins of the

24. Such as, for example, *A letter from a minister to a person of quality shewing some reasons for his nonconformity* (1662), *An Alarme for London to awake and mourne for sin, before God make her weepe for judgements ... : a subject very soasenable* [sic] *for these times, in a dialogue between Archippus a minister, and Philemon a godly Christian* (1643).

25. There was a lengthy dispute among theologians such as Gregory the Great, Augustine, and Thomas Aquinas on which sin should be treated as the root of all evil: pride, lust, or avarice, with various theologians leaning towards any of these three.

26. Another late medieval addition to categories of sin, deriving from Peraldus and the *Somme le roi* (Andrew Cowell, *At Play in the Tavern: Signs, Coins, and Bodies in the Middle Age* [Ann Arbor, 1999], 114).

tavern as a whole (gambling, drinking, swearing, etc.) were a late medieval addition to the heptad. Nevertheless, drunkenness and unbelief as separate "deadly" sins are a Protestant contribution to the tradition of the heptad. The text thus retains the concept of deadly sins, using the word to denote not a doctrine or theological truth, but the gravity of each sin. The fact that this text retains the concept of the heptad is a reflection of the endurance of the conviction about the graver nature of these sins above others, even if most Protestants would agree that on a certain level all sins were "deadly." In other words, the Seven Deadly Sins are here highlighted as an important and culturally and religiously evocative concept, to which sins are *added* rather than removed, drunkenness and unbelief being considered as deadly as pride or avarice.[27]

The second part of *The Nine mortal weapons*, like the third section of *The Boke of a ghoostly fader*, lists remedies for each of the deadly sins, including humbleness as a remedy to pride, and so on. The verse form of *The Nine mortal weapons* is even simpler and more concise than that of the *Boke*, capturing the gist of every sin in no more than four lines, and providing much less contemplative material due to its lack of discussion of penance or contrition, and no specification of circumstance, which further suggests the Protestant provenance of this text. Pre-Reformation works such as the *Boke* relied on an existing tradition of confession which expected the priest to take into consideration the circumstances of each sin, whereas by the seventeenth century, traces of such confessional culture were almost invisible in Protestant texts. It is thus interesting that while the confessional application of the Seven Deadly Sins became almost entirely obsolete in the Protestant tradition,[28] the heptad itself did not, and remained an important self-study framework, even if shortened and made more user-friendly than before, a "shorthand for designating sinfulness per se."[29] *The Nine mortal weapons* can thus be read as a later iteration of the issues treated in the 1521 *Boke of a ghoostly fader*, where verse indicates lay popular rather than confessional use, while still being anchored in the pastoral tradition of the late Middle Ages.

27. Adding sins to the traditional heptad was not uncommon for pre-Reformation preachers and texts as well: the Seven were adjusted to preaching purposes and as often as not were shrunk or extended to include fewer or more than seven sins (Newhauser, *The Treatises of Vices and Virtues*, 88; Bloomfield, *Seven Deadly Sins*, 212, 430; Siegfried Wenzel, *The Sin of Sloth: Acedia in Medieval Thought and Literature* [Chapel Hill, 1968], 12).

28. See also John Bossy, "Moral Arithmetic: Seven Sins Into Ten Commandments," in *Conscience and Casuistry in Early Modern Europe*, ed. Edmund Leites (Paris, 1988), 214–234.

29. Richard Newhauser, "Introduction: Understanding Sin: Recent Scholarship and the Capital Vices," in *Sin in Medieval and Early Modern Culture: The Tradition of the Seven Deadly Sins*, ed. Richard G. Newhauser and Susan J. Ridyard (Woodbridge, Suffolk, 2012), 1–18, at 11.

3a *Here begynneth a boke of a ghoostly fader that confesseth his ghoostly chylde, the whiche speketh fyrst of the. vii. deedly synnes, and after of the cyrcumstaunce that to them belongeth*, 1521 (?); unnumbered pages. *STC* 3288. **Source** *EEBO*: Cambridge University Library (Sel.5.35(10)).

... Of pryd tothe I will begyn
Haste thou sone synned therin
Haste thou ony tyme wyttyngly
Wrathed thy god greuously
Haste thou ben inobedyente
Agaynst goddes commaundements
Haste thou by pryde set at naught
Hym that hathe the good taught
Haste thou ony tyme boost made
Of ony thynge thou haste hade
Of vertue, of connynge or of wyt
Whiche god hymselfe sende the hyt. ...
Haste thou thyne owne gylte forsaken
And to another the blame taken
Haste thou fayned thyselfe holy
To hypocrysy and to foly
In trust that is sholde be hyde.
Thy foule synne and thy foule pryde
Haste thou ony tyme by vayn glory
Thought thyselfe so good and holy
That thou hast had grete dysdane
Of thy neyghbours that thou has sayne
Hast thou ben proude my sone I saye
Bycause thou hast ben stedfast in the faye. ...

Of Enuye
The seconde synne in ordre veryly
Is the foule synne of Enuy.
Hast thou ben euermore grutchynge
Agaynst god for ony thynge
Hast thou ben in herte glad,
When thy neyghboure hathe harme had
Hast thou had in herte grefe

Of his good and his relefe
Hast thou be glad and mery
When he hath ben seke and sory
Or has thou ben sory and madde
When he hathe ben mery and gladde. ...

Of Couetyse
Mercy
The thyrde synne without myse
Is the the synne of Couetyse.
Hast thou man in ony wyse

Ihesu
By wronge and couetyse
Begyle thy neyghboure fre or bonde

Mercy
Of thys house good or londe
And by strength and extorcyon kepeth possessyon
And mayketh thereof no maner restytucyon
O mortall man remebre this chaunce
Before god it asketh vengeaunce. ...

Of the synne of wrathe
Mercy
Wrathe than ys the fourth synne
And grete Jeoperdy to slepe therin
Hast thou ony tyme in thy desyre
In thy malice and in thy yre
That at thy pleasure and for thy sake
Vengeaunce upon man or beest sholde be take.
Hast thou in thy malice, yre, and werke
Layde vyolent hande on preest or clerke
Or on thy neyghboure in cyte or shyre
Otherwyse then good ordre wyll requyre
On wyfe, chylde, or seruaunte
Beynge with the in seruyce or conanunte
Sofore peraduenture thou dydest them streke. ...

Of the synne of Slowthe
The .v. synne then is Slowthe
Euen as the boke showthe
Haste thou ben slowe and take no hede
To teche thy godchildren Pater noster and Crede
Hast thou ben slowe for to here
Goddis seruyce when tyme were.
Haste thou come to chyrche late
And speke of synne by the gate
Haste thou ben slowe in goddes seruyce
Or trouble it by ony vyce.
Haste thou letted ony mon
That to chyrche wolde haue gone
Hast thou spoken ony rybawdy
Wythin the chyrche or sentwary
Hathe thyne herte ben wrathe and greate
When goddess seruyce was sayd or treate.
Haste thou herde it to the ende
Or thou out of the chyrche wende ...
I truste sone by my talkynge
Unto thy mynde call some thynge.
And I charge the be not a drede
But shewe it me in goddes stede,
I will the helpe by our sauyours sygne
And thereto I laye my soule for thyne.

Of the synne of Glotony
Cristus
The syxte synne then is Glotony
A trewe promyter vnto Lechery
And bycause the synne of glotony
Is in experyence nowe dayly
Of it I will but a lytell spell
For of it many man can tell
The vse is nowe in cyte and dale
Unreasonably to drynke wyne and ale
With hey howe fyll the pot by the eye
And this is called euery good company

And to make of other as they arne
Of goddes chyldren the deuyls barne
Haste thou fasted as thou sholdest do ...
Dayes that thou were Joyned vnto
Haste thou broken ony fastynge daye
If thou haue thou must saye.
Haste thou also for Glotony
Etynge or drynkynge to fyersly
Haste thou eten or dronken more
Then thy need asketh fore ...
Haste thou cherysshed thy body ofte
In swete metes and clothes softe
Arte thou wonte to go to the nale[30]
There to fyll thy foule male[31]
And to drawe other with the
To bere the company in the degre ...
If thou haue ony more nowe in thy herte
Shewe it good sone breuely and smerte
And be thou chylde, wyfe, or mon
I wyll gyue the thyne absolucyon.

Of the synne of Lechery
The vii. synne is Lechery, last of all
Of it somwhat I aske I shall
Haste thou synned in Lechery
Tell me sonne hardely.
And as sure as god made Peter and Poule
I haue auctoryte to saue thy soule.
Whether it were with wyf or mayde
With kynne or alyaunce that thou by laye
And yf she were kynne to the
Howe nye kynne thou must tell me
Or whether she were ancres or nonne
Wedowe or wyfe tell yf thou conne
Or ony that vowed chastyte

30. Go to a tavern: *MED* s.v. "āle".
31. Belly: *MED* s.v. "māl(e".

Or common woman if she be
Or whether thou dydest by strengthe so
Or by the assente of her also
Haste thou ony tyme wrought or do
And styred thy flesshe the more therto
As clyppynge or kyssynge there they byth
That thy body hath be tempted therwith ...
And yf thou be a woman
Tell me doughter yf thou can
Of what degree this man was
That synned with the in that case
Kynne, or syngle, or ony spouse
Or what degree of relygyous
Whether it were for couetys
Of golde, or syluere, or ought of his
Then the synne doubled it were
And nedeth penaunce moche the more

... Bethynke ye nowe in euery degre
What more in thought cometh to the
For that thou doost hyde frome me
The deuyll truely wyll shewe the
At the Iugement before echon[32]
Unto thy shame and confusion
And that thou shewest in confessyon me before
Of it thou shalte neuer here more
But for thy good wyll and obedyence
Thou shalte be had in to our sauyours presence
And there to be in Ioye and blysse
With blessyd company and not to mys
Et magis gaudium in celo there is
More Ioye of a synner that hathe done amys
And forsaketh synne or synne forsake hym
Ye and more made of heuen within
Then of many one that neuer synne knewe
These be the wordes of our sauyoure full trewe.

32. Each one.

Thus of the .vii. deedly synnes I make an ende
All thynges amysse god maye amende
I beseche the swete Iesu so it maye be
Amen amen of charyte.

3b *The nine mortal weapons, or, So many deadly sins charged against poor mankind by Satan, our grand enemy for our everlasting destruction,* 1650 (?); text consists of one page only. *Wing* N1158B. **Source** *EEBO*: British Library, London (C.121.g.9(42)).

O People all now here mark well
Which I to you do plainly tell,
Your time doth pass and fade away,
Your body soon must turn to clay.

...

Nine Weapons charg'd against us be
By Satan our grand Enemie,
The which are Nine most deadly sins
That many souls to ruine brings.

I./II.
The First is Pride came from the Devil,
The second Covetousness the root of evil.
They are the Grand and horrid Crimes,
That most do use in these sad times.

III.
The third is Lechery, or lust most Vile
That Soul and Body doth defile.
The lustful whore with greedy mind,
Longs for a Knave where she may find.

IV.
The Fourth is Envy, Like the Serpent Snake.
Unhappy thing would all unhappy make.

And hates that we should happy be,
And therefore seeks our miserie.

V.
The Fifth is Wrath Like firie-Hell,
Executing Mischief sad and fell.
Wrath will be Cruel in his mood,
Not sparing for to spill Man's Blood.

VI.
The Sixth is Sloath, will take no pain,
His Soul to save, sweet Christ to gain.
Sloath will not labour, but be Idle,
The Devil hath him in his bridle.

VII.
The Seventh is gluttonie, a monstrous thing,
Which doth in Hell with *Dives* bring.
More happy *Lazarus* that Crumbs did eat,
Than *Dives* with his sumptuous meat.

VIII.
The Eighth is Druknenness, a beastly sin,
Which men dead all foaming in.
Their Drunken Gore makes them to reel,
And down they tumble into Hell.

IX.
The Ninth is Unbelief, the worst of all,
The most damning sin that can befall.
It robs God of his Honour, and his Crown,
And in Hell's deepest Torments throws us down. ...

SINS OF THE TONGUE AND MOUTH

4a *The example of euyll tongues* (1525?). **4b** William Gearing *A bridle for the tongue* (1663).

Introduction Medieval interest in the sins of the tongue peaked in the thirteenth century with William Peraldus[33] and his *Summa of vices and virtues* (*Summa de virtutibus et vitiis*) (ca. 1250). Peraldus' text, in contrast to earlier texts which included only short passages on the sins of the tongue, treats evil speech as a separate theological unit and problem, adding a section on the sins of the tongue to his discussion of the Seven Deadly Sins. This gave rise to the later medieval inclusion of the sins of the tongue among the deadly sins. Peraldus' *Summa* was an extremely popular text, circulating in over fifty manuscripts and then in a number of printed editions in both the sixteenth and the seventeenth centuries.[34] The tradition started by Peraldus found its way to later medieval pastoral manuals such as *The book of vices and virtues* (ca. 1375). Other works inspired by the *Somme le roi* (1279), a popular theological and devotional *summa* which itself was based on Peraldus' *Summa*, include Caxton's 1485 translation, and works such as *A myrour to lewed men and wymmen* (ca.1350), the *Aȝenbite of inwit* (akin to but different from the *Prick of conscience*, ca. 1340), and many others. The sins of the tongue were greatly popularized in the fourteenth and fifteenth centuries and become commonly recognized as a cardinal vice. *The example of euyll tongues*, which was possibly composed as early as 1510, according to the *STC*, but printed in 1525, embodies this legacy, though as in the case of the *Boke of the ghoosly fader*, it is a more condensed, and versified, work that reflects popular interest in the subject rather than theological attention to a spiritual problem. Often considered one of the vices of tavern, the sins of the tongue were from the beginning of theologians' interest in them regarded as vices predominantly social in context, as problems of society and human interaction much more than other sins. Blasphemy, slander, and rebellious speech were also often prosecuted in local courts. *The example of euyll tongues* is an example of a text that focuses on social issues behind the sins of the tongue rather than on their theological origin or consequences, and there is little in it that makes reference to sin apart from the remark that even the most sincere confession can be ruined by an evil tongue.

33. Richard Newhauser, "Introduction: Cultural Construction and the Vices", in *The Seven Deadly Sins: From Communities to Individuals*, ed. Richard Newhauser (Leiden, 2007), 1–17, at 10.

34. Bettina Lindorfer, "*Peccatum Linguae* and the Punishment of Speech Violations in the Middle Ages and Early Modern Times," in *Speaking in the Early Modern World*, ed. Jean E. Godsall-Myers (Leiden, 2003), 23–42, at 26–27. See also Edwin D. Craun, *Lies, Slander, and Obscenity in Medieval English Literature: Pastoral Rhetoric and the Deviant Speaker* (Cambridge, 1997), esp. 14–16, for a discussion of Peraldus' contribution to making the sins of the tongue a capital sin.

A bridle for the tongue (1663), on the other hand, reverts back to the more religious side of the problem of the sins of the tongue, providing an interesting illustration of a return to an earlier tradition. As Bettina Lindorfer puts it,

> "[f]rom the fourteenth through the seventeenth century, the medieval systems of speech abuse are taken over with no substantive changes in their theoretical underpinnings .... Instead, treatises from this era continue, sometimes copying verbatim, medieval treatises on speech abuse without any great innovations. ... [E]arly modern period treatises on the government of the tongue ... are intimately connected with the various medieval systems of the sins of the tongue."[35]

As exemplified by the Calvinist Protestant minister William Gearing, the medieval model of understanding uncontrolled speech as sin did indeed survive, but the early modern period took the discourse of the sins of the tongue to another level: they were now a subject of texts directed at these sins alone, unlike most pre-Reformation works where the sins of the tongue were usually considered in relation to other sins. Works such as Thomas Adams' *The taming of the tongue* (1619) indicate that the Protestants understood unruly speech as both a social and a spiritual vice. They raised the sins of the tongue to the rank of a problem worthy of being considered separately from other sins such as drunkenness or avarice. The sins of the tavern were also not alien to Protestant writers, who condemned playing dice and drinking, but their focus on the sins of the tongue is conspicuous.[36] Gearing's work is thus a very traditional take on the subject, as he discusses all of Peraldus' sins in detail, but it is also part of the post-Reformation innovation, as he discusses these sins separately from the sins of the heptad, though of course the relationship between sins like slander and sins like murder, or envy, was recognized. *A bridle for the tongue* is thus simultaneously similar to and different from *The example of euyll tongues* which, while also focusing exclusively on evil speech does not consider it from a religious but from a social perspective only.

4a *The example of euyll tongues*, 1525 (?); unnumbered pages. *STC* 10608. **Source** *EEBO*: British Library, London (IA.55266.(1)).

With pyte moued to my payne I dyde me dres
To shew the people what doth them most greuans
I saye yll tonges full of bytter crewelnes

35. Lindorfer, "*Peccatum Linguae*," 24.

36. For more on this subject, see Susan Juster, *Sacred Violence in Early America* (Philadelphia, 2016), 127.

In this worlde may be no greter penaunce
Thes be the clappers of sorowe, the skorges of vengans
These preuy morderers these comberous hell wedes
Because of grete meschefe and dystroyers of good dedys.

Yf there were in the worlde none other punyshement
But yll tonges onely in especyall
Of very ryght it were suffycyent
Seyenge how euery creature nowe ouer all
Is sodeynly smyten with this venemous spere mortall
Of comberous tonges that god ne man dredys
By cause of myschefe and dystroyers of good dedys.
Bothe ryche and poore be brought in torment
By this cursed slo worme that swelleth worse than a tode
I mene the yll tonge that venymous serpent
Whiche many good doer destroyed with a worde
Who ledeth theyr lyfe now in peasyble concorde
Full fewe for yll tonges so moche sorowe bredys
They be cause of myschefe and dystroyed good dedys.

No enemy so lytell we out hym to doute
Ne none so grete rome but remedy may be founde
If it in tyme be perceyued and brought oute
Than to a good ende it may rebounde
But an yll tonge so brode renrieth the sounde
Fro bad to worse and so myschefe spedys
Whiche caused many a man to withdrawe good dedys

The tonge is instrument of lyes, treason, and treachery
And causeth warre, morther, myschefe without ende
Grete multytude of other wich ypocrysy,
Rebellyons, thefte, dyscorde full yll to defende
Fyghtynge, chydynge to stryfe euer Intende
With shame and sclaunder to yll fortune all ledes
Lo how the tonge caused myschefe and dystroyed good dedes.

... A false tonge wyll euer Imagyne and saye
That neuer by creature was sayd ne thought
And this hath be sene and is euery daye

The fader and mother betraye and in sorowe brought
Many good folke hath sclaunder dere bought
As loste theyr goodes and theyr lyues also
For by an yll tonge the good name is soone a go.

Many there be that neuer dyde offende
Whiche by an euyll tonge is brought to dysshonoure
And in to an euyll name sone they be comptende
That a .M.[37] to theyr good name cannot them restore
The claterers condycyon is to grose[38] vp more and more
Maydens by them is blamed, wedowes, and other mo
For by an euyll tonge the name is soone go.

There is many one blamed and accused for nought
And many gyltles theyr lyues fro them is take
The and a thousande into pouerte brought
That dayly goth a begynge and prayed for goddes sake
And all thorowe tale tellers his scrowe[39] doth wake
Whiche caused many one theyr selfe to slo
Where by an euyll tonge theyr good name is a go.

Full many be brought to dyseas and captyuyte
In euery regyon that man can trauayll
The tonge is causer of this wofull aduersyte
Full lytell or nought now dooth trouth auayll
True heyers be dysheryte without ony fayll
With wepynge and waylynge some waxeth blynde
And all causeth euyll tonges, moost enemy to mankynde.

37. Unclear. Typically, the abbreviation .M. (or any other Roman numeral between two full stops) indicates a numeral (e.g., a .C. men = a hundred men), but in this case the numeral is not followed by a noun, making it difficult to discern what was intended here. Perhaps the abbreviation refers to "Magister" (teacher) for which the abbreviation M. was commonly used.

38. Assemble, bring together: *MED* s.v. "grōsen".

39. An error for "sorowe" according to the note for line 68 in the transcription of *The Example of Evil Tongues* (London, 1525) available at the Textbase of Early Tudor English website: https://www.otago.ac.nz/english-linguistics/tudor/euyll_tongues10608.html, accessed 15 June 2018.

Thoughe some preestes now be neuer so pacyent
And in towne and cyte be pease ouer all
Or though the relygyous be neuer so obedyent
Yet an euyll tonge wyll trouble them all
Multyplyenge of lesynges by hym aryse shall
To trouble good people in soule and mynde
This is euyll tonges moost enemy to mankynde

Yf ony man wolde begynne his synnes to reny[40]
Or ony good people that fro vyce dyde refrayne
What so euer he were that to vertue wolde applye
But an yll tonge wyll all ouerthrowe agayne
Lo by whome is raysed all this grete payne
Of sorowefull sclaunder that flyeth as the wynde;
These yll tonges be moost enemy to mankynde.

I saye not but warre is grete abusyon
Yet is there not so many as is with yll tonges slayne
And though honger be neuer so sharpe for the season
Yet for all that god some people doth sustayne
Of frostes grete some people be not fayne
But so sore grefe no where may we fynde
As it the yll tonge, moost enemy to mankynge.

Though sodayne deth be neuer so rigorous
Yet by preestes it seaseth at the laste
But where all yll tonges lyste to be malycyous
There is neuer remedy whan the worde is past
To lye and saye wronge they be neuer agast
Of heuen and hell they haue lytell mynde
I meane yll tonges, moost enemy to mankynde.

Speke of salpeter, arsnek, or ony poyson mortall
The fyre of hell, the blood of serpentes venymmous
Ye fynde none sone so peryllous amonge all
As is the yll tonge to them that be virtuous

40. Cleanse spiritually, renounce: *MED* s.v. "reneien" v.(1), v.(2).

They be of malyce so full and rygorous
For they that lyste to do well and ther o do theyr payne
By the euyll tongue all is ouerthrowe agayne.

Therfore euery creature take hede what ye saye
For yf the worde be escaped at any throwe
It wyll not be called agayne though thou wolde laye
Bothe lyfe and goodes and on it bestowe
I wolde wete how we a good tongue sholde knowe
It wyll not be for by the subtyll trayne
Of the yll tongue whiche all ouerthroweth agayne.

... All people beware of these yll tonges most peryllous
And eschewe them where euer you go
Tonge breketh bone he is so malycyous
And none hath hymselfe all knoweth it is so
Sclander cometh lyghtly whiche causeth grete wo
For though thou be in name I tell the playne
By an yll tonge all is ouerthrowen agayne.

These comberose clamores in euery towne
That thynge whiche the deuyll can not brynge about
An yll tonge wyll performe by vnkynde perolysene[41]
Yf a thousande fendes were to gyder in a route
Coude not by theyr malyce suche falshede vter oute
To brynge the people to grete dessensyon
As doth these yll tonges, mannes moost confusion.

O enuyous tonges destroyers of hye and lowe degree
Thy wycked sedes thou doest sowe downe
Here and elles where ouer euery countre
Bothe in cyte, borowe, village, and towne
Sease thy rorynge thou fendly lyon
In the coffer of scyence hyde the full soone
For yll tonges is mannes most confusyon

41. This might be a printer's error; perhaps the original word read "perolys" (perilous) followed by a noun. For a plausible explanation, see the note for line 143 in the transcription of *The Example of Evil Tongues* available online; see n39 above.

He that can kepe his tonge and beware
Laude vnto hym shall euer encrease
And where that euer he go he nede not to care
For he is sure of reste and pease.
More of this mater I need not reherse
For take these wordes for a conclusion
That yll tonges is euer mannes confusyon.
Amen

4b William Gearing, *A bridle for the tongue, or, A treatise of ten sins of the tongue ... shewing the nature of these sins ... with the causes and aggravations of them, and remedyes against them: together with many considerations, rules, and helps for the right ordering of the tongue: divers common places succinctly handled, and divers cases cleered,* 1663, pp. 18–28.[42] *Wing* G432. **Source** *EEBO*: British Library, London (151-304q).

CHAP. IV. *Sheweth in divers particulars how much men fail in this point.*
This then may inform us how great a number of men there are whose seeming shews of Religion will be found to be but vain, because of their unbridled tongues; consider how common this sin is, and how many that profess themselves Christians are guilty of these sinnes in an high degree; and let us hence see what great cause we have to lament the great decay of Religion with the Prophet, *Psal.* 12:1, 2. *Help Lord, for the Godly man ceaseth, for the faithful fail from among the children of men:* and He proveth it is by this; *They speak vanity every one with his Neighbour; with flattering lips, and with a double heart do they speak*; and mark how general it is: *every one speaks vanity to his Neighbour*: and if this be so bad, joyned with a seeming shew of Religion, what is open prophaness? The Prophet *Jeremiah* complaineth also, wishing his eyes were a fountain of tears, that he might weep day and night for his people, and bewaile the misery that is coming upon them, and all because of this sin: *they bend their tongues like their bowe for lyes. Jer.* 9:3 *they will not speak truth, they have taught their tongues to speak lyes* ver. 5 *their tongue is as an arrow shot out, it speaketh deceit; one speaketh peaceably to his neighbour, but in his heart he lieth in wait.* ver. 8 shall I not visit for these things, saith the Lord? So St *Paul, Rom.* 3, when he insisteth upon the general corruption of nature, he quickly passeth it over, but he spends two verses, *viz.* the 13 and 14 upon the sins of the tongue; speaking of wicked men, he saith, *their throat is an open Sepulcher,*

42. Marginal notes in the original source were not included in the transcription.

with their tongues ther have used decit, the poison of Asps is under their lips, whose mouth is full of cursing and bitterness; the poyson of Asps is under the tongues of such persons; now, Naturalists observe of the Asp that it poisoneth a man secretly, with a kind of delight, and it is such a poison as is incurable, killing a man in four hours; very fitly representing the poison of the tongue, for such a one woundeth his brother in secret, and he knoweth not who hurteth him; and he hardly admits of cure again. We have great cause to bewail the commonnesse of this sin in these Gospel-times; a sin so rife, even among those that seem to be Religious, that we may lay it to heart, and beware thereof; and so much the rather, because the sins of the tongue are a special cause of procuring misery upon a Land, and People. Consider therefore:

1. That when men come to the publike worship of God, to hear the word of God, *&c.* and yet take no care of their tongues, God esteems them more like unto poisonous creatures then to men that have his Image upon them; more like to Asps or venemous serpents then men; of such the Prophet speaketh, saying, *They have sharpned their tongues like a serpent.* Psal. 140:3 and his case when he was among them, was as bad as *Daniels* in the Lions Den: *My soul*, saith he, *is among Lions, and I lie even among them that are set on fire; even the sons of men, whose teeth are spears and arrows, and their tongue a sharp sword*. Psal. 57:4 and the Lord tells the Prophet *Ezekiel, that briars and thorns were with him*, such as scratch and tear all that come near them; *ond that he dwelt among Scorpions*, the most poisonful of all other creatures. *Ezek.* 2:6.

2. The Lord compareth men of evil tongues to all kind of deadly instruments; *to a maul, to a sword, to a sharp arrow*. Prov. 25:18; the one is sufficient to knock a man on the head, the other to run thorow his body, and the other to pierce him to the heart; to signifie to us that while a man may goe about to avoid one, he may yet be in danger of being hurt by another before he is aware of it.

3. By these sins of the tongue, men break no less then three commands of God at once. 1. The sixth Commandement, *Thou shalt do no Murder*; men are apt to think if they lay not violent hands upon their neighbour, it is nothing; but our Saviour, *Mat.* 5:21, 22, sets down three sins as breaches of this command: 1. causeless and unadvised anger, though it break not out into words. 2. rash and inconsiderate words. 3. railing and reviling speeches; and these shall be in danger of Hell-fire: and how many poor souls have run this hazard, and yet never considered this!; and besides this, I shall add further, there is yet a fourfold murder of the tongue.

1. By commanding any to be unjustly slain and executed, as *Saul* commanded *Doeg* to fall upon the Priests of the Lord, who slew fourscore and five

persons. 1 *Sam.* 22:17, 18. Thus *David* contrived the death of *Uriah*, and commanded *Joab* to set him in the front of the battle against the children of *Ammon*, where he was slain. 2 *Sam.* 11:15. Thus *Absalon* gave charge to his servants to kill *Amnon.* 2 *Sam.* 13:28 and *Ahab* and *Jezebel* to the Nobles and Elders of the City to put *Naboth* to death. 1 *Kings.* 21:10.

2. By giving counsel to any to procure the death of any one; thus *Herodias* taught her daughter *to aske the head of John Baptist in a Charger of Herod. Mar.* 6:24.

3. By giving ill language, and reviling words, whereupon a fray is occasioned, and murder ensueth.

4. By bearing false witness against any one, in case of life.

2. By the sins of the tongue men break the eighth Commandement, which is, *Thou shalt not steal.* Though many men rob not their Neighbors of their Goods, yet of their good names; and this is a sin of an higher nature than stealing their Goods; for the loss of Goods may be valued, but the loss of a mans good name cannot: *a good name is better then precious ointment*, Eccles. 7:1. Costy ointments are reckoned among the treasures and happiness of Princes; and he that robs a man of that, robs him of his choicest Jewels; *the death thereof is an en evil death; the grave were better then it*, saith the son of *Syrach. Eccles.* 28:21.

3. There is a plain breach of the ninth Commandement, *Thou shalt not bear false witness against thy neighbour.* Now a false witness sins, 1. Directly against God, robbing him of his honour by speaking an untruth, breaking his Law that forbids it. 2. He doth injury to the Judge whom he deceiveth by lying. ... 3. To an Innocent whom he betrayeth by bearing a false Testimony.

4. These sins of the tongue, are of such a nature that without Grace to repent of them, and forsake them, they will exclude a man out of Heaven; the Apostle mentioneth a Reviler to be one that shall be shut out of Heaven. 1 *Cor.* 6:9, 10. And *chap.* 5 he saith that private familiarity with such must be cast off; and that men may see the danger of it, *David* proposeth the question, *What shall be given unto thee, or what shall be done unto thee thou false tongue?* and himself maketh answer by the spirit of God: *Sharp arrows of the mighty, with coals of Juniper. Psal.* 120:3, 4, that as they shoot at God, and his people, so God shall shoot at them; he shall give them *coals of Juniper*, because it is observed to be the most hot and lasting fire; this shall be their punishment: expositors think this war spoken of *Doeg*, when *David* was at *Nob*, he was there under a pretence of worshiping the Lord, for it was the Sabbath day, and *Doeg* would seem Religious; but, as soon as he is gone to *Saul* see what becometh of his seeming shew of Religion: he reporteth the matter concerning *David* and *Ahimelech* unto another end then

they did intend it; wresting their words to make *Saul* think there was a plot against him, when they intended no such thing. And though for the matter it was the truth he did relate, as we may see in the story, yet for this it is that the spirit of God calls him a false tongue. See his sin and his doom. *Psal.* 52 his sin, *ver.* 1, 2, 3, 4 *he boasted himself in mischief, his tongue devised mischief, like a sharp razor, working deceitfully, loving lying rather than to speak Righteousnesse: Thou lov'st all devouring words, O thou deceitful tongue.* See his doom. *ver.* 5: *God shall likewise destroy thee for ever. He shall take take thee away, and pluck thee out of thy dwelling place, and root thee out of the Land of the living:* and this shall be his *Epitaph.* ver. 7 *Lo, this is the man that made not God his strength, &c. but strengthned himself in his wickedness.*

These things being so, what reason then have we to be the more careful to avoid these sins! there being more sins in a disorderly tongue then men are aware of; for even those that take some care of othe sins, yet fail much herein; there needs a great deal of grace to keep the tongue within compass; much power may be gotten over other sins, when yet we may not seriously think of this, but let us carefully take heed hereof; for as far as this remains in any man, and is not watcht against, and pray'd against, and a man brought to be humbled under the sight of it; so much vanity and emptiness is in the Religion of that man; his Religion is but an outward appearance; there's little truth of Religion in such a mans heart.

5a Stephen Hawes, *The conuercyon of swerers* (1509). **5b** Richard Younge *A hopefull way to cure that horrid sinne of swearing* (1652).

Introduction Much like the sins of the tongue gradually became a part of the deadly sins, and then the sins of the tavern, so did swearing find its way to the attention of many moralists as a "deadly" sin. Swearing (making oaths or cursing) was the use of God's name in vain, blasphemy, and in such late medieval texts as that of Stephen Hawes, was inseparably connected to other deadly sins such as pride or envy. *The conuercyon of swerers*, composed as a divine message narrated through the voice of a humble author, is comprised of an apology, a description of divine mercy saving sinners from hell, and then a complaint (in the voice of Christ) to those rejecting that mercy, repeatedly wounding Christ with their sins, the sin of swearing in particular. The passage below focuses on swearing in the context of the Seven Deadly Sins, as well as on the enemies of mankind: the devil, the world, and the flesh; it presents swearing as one of the snares of the Devil.

Richard Younge, a puritan minister, focuses in *A hopefull way to cure that horrid sinne of swearing* (1652) on swearing and cursing as an offence to God, and likewise talks about the sin of rejecting God's mercy. The text is framed as a dialogue with a Messenger and a Swearer, the Messenger being the voice of God, and the Swearer the personification of sinners. The piece begins by a recounting of the mercy of God showered upon sinners through the sacrifice of his son, and an apology by the Messenger for talking in the voice of God. The following excerpt is a selection of statements on swearing (omitting the dialogue sequence) as sin, as ingratitude, and as a mortal threat to salvation. Younge's, much like Hawes' text, presents swearing as a trap set for sinners by the Devil.

Both texts are thus a take on the sin of swearing as separate from other sins of the tongue, while not being separate from other (deadly) sins: as Hawes considers swearing in relation to the sins of the heptad, so Younge considers it in connection to blasphemy, or murder. What the texts share is an understanding of swearing as a sin and a social problem; these texts are also connected by references they make to the medieval concept of the enemies of mankind: the world, the flesh, and the devil.[43] Both Hawes' and Younge's works are thus interesting studies of the development of the sin of swearing, and an illustration of the endurance of the motif of the three enemies of mankind. At the same time, these texts differ in their poetics and style, with *The conuercyon of swerers* as a text of social criticism first, and a moral critique of swearing second, whereas Younge's *A hopefull way to cure that horrid sinne of swearing* is a primarily a pastoral text condemning the ungodliness of swearing, and providing criticism of it as a social vice only secondarily.

5a Stephen Hawes, *The conuercyon of swerers*, 1509; unnumbered pages. *STC* 12943. **Source** *EEBO*: British Library, London (61308).

I lytell or nought expert in poetrye
Remembrynge my youth so lyght and frayle
Purpose to compyle here full breuyatly
A lytell treatyse wofull to bewayle
The cruell swerers whiche do god assayle
On euery syde his swete body to tere
With terryble othes as often as they swere.
But also for drede plonged in neclygence

43. Bloomfield, *Seven Deadly Sins*, 163. The understanding that sins originate in the world, the flesh, and the Devil found its way into many Protestant texts. For instance, Cotton Mather wrote that unless a woman is virtuous, she "will not stop to be the servant of the world, or of the flesh, or of the Devil" (*Ornaments for the daughters of Zion*, 1692, 20). A similar passage can be found in, for example, *A fair warning for the murders of infants* (1691), a record of the trial and execution of Mary Goodenough (p. 4), and many other texts.

My penne doth quake to presume to endyte
But hope at laste to recure this scyence
Exorteth me ryght hardely to wryte
To deuoyde ydlenesse by good appetyte
For ydlenesse the grete moder of synne
Euery vyce is redy to lette ynne.

I with the same ryght gretely infecte
Lykely to deye tyll grace by medecyne
Recured my sekenes, my payne to abiecte
Commaundynge me by her hye power deuyne
To drawe this treatyse for to enlumyne
The reders therof by penytencyall pyte
And to pardon me of theyr benygnyte. ...

Christ:
They newe agayne do hange me on the rode
They tere my sydes and are nothynge dysmayde
My woundes they open and deuoure my blode
I, god and man moost wofully arayde
To you complayne, it maye not be denayde
ye nowe to tug me, ye tere me at the roote
yet I to you am chefe refuyte and boote.[44]

Wherfore the kynges reygnynge in renowne
Refourme your seruauntes in your courte abused
To good example of euery maner towne
So that theyr othes whiche they longe haue vsed
On payne and punysshement be holly refused
Meke as a Lambe I suffre theyr grete wronge
I maye take vengeaunce thoughe I tary longe.

I do forbere I wolde haue you amende
And graunte you mercy and ye wyll it take
O my swete brederne why do ye offende
Agayne to tere me whiche deyed for your sake

44. Deliverance: *MED* s.v. "bōte" n.(1).

Lose my kyndenes and frome synne awake
I dyde redeme you frome the deuylles chayne
And spyte of me ye wyll to hym agayne. ...

Vnto me dere broder my loue and my herte
Tourmente me no more with thy othes grete
Come vnto my Ioye and agayne reuerte
Frome the deuylles snare and his subtyll net
Beware of the worlde all aboute the set
Thy flesshe is redy by concupyscence
To burne thy herte with cursed vyolence.

Thoughe these thre enmyes[45] do sore the assayle
Upon euery syde with daungerous iniquite
But yf thou lyst they may nothynge preuayle
Nor yet subdue the with all theyr extremyte
To do good or yll, all is at thy lyberte
I do graunte the grace thyn enemyes to subdue
Swete broder accepte it, theyr power to extue.

And ye kynges and prynces of hye noblenes
With dukes and lordes of euery dygnyte
Indued with manhode wysoome and ryches
Ouer the comons hauynge the souerayntе
Correcte them whiche so do tere me
y cruell othes without repentaunce
Amende by tyme lest I take vengeaunce
Exodi vicesimo. Non accipies nomen dei cui in vanum.

Unto the man I gaue commaundement
Not to take the name of thy god vaynfully
As not to swere but at tyme conuenyent
Before a Iuge to bere recorde truely
Namynge my name with reuerence mekely
Unto the Iuge than there in presence
By my name to gyue to the good credence.

45. This is a reference to the late medieval idea of the three enemies of mankind: the world, the devil, and the flesh.

A, my brederne yf that I be wrothe
It is for cause ye falsly by me swere
Ye knowe your selfe that I am very trothe
Yet wrongfully ye do me rente and tere
ye neyther loue me nor my Justyce fere
And yf ye dyde ye wolde full gentylly
Obeye my byddynge well and perfytely.

The worldly kynges hauynge the soueraynte
ye do well obey without resystence
ye dare not take theyr names in vanyte
But with grete honoure and eke reuerence
Than my name more hye of magnyfycence
ye ought more to drede whiche am kynge of all
Bothe god, and man, and reygne celestyall. ...

Than why do ye in euery maner of place
With cruell othes tere my body and herte
My sydes and woundes it is a pyteous cace
Alas swete brederne I wolde you conuerte
For to take vengeaunce ye do me coherte
From the hous of swerers shall not be absent
The plage of Justyce to take punysshement.

Unde. Ecclesiastici xxxiii. *Vir multum iurans implebitur iniquitate et non descendet a domo plaga*

A man moche swerynge with grete iniquite
Shall be replete and from his mancyon
The plage of vengeaunce shall not cessed be
Wherfore ye brederne full of abusyon
Take good hede to this dyscrypcyon
Come nowe to me and axe forgyuenes
And be penytente and haue it douteles. ...

Wo worthe your hartes so planted in pryde
Wo worthe your wrath and mortall enuye
Wo worthe slouth that dothe with you abyde

Wo worthe also in mesurable glotony
Wo worthe your tedyus synne of lechery
Wo worthe you whome I gaue free wyll
Wo worthe couetyse that dothe your soules spyll. ...

Wo worthe you whiche do me forsake
Wo worthe you whiche wyllyngely offende
Wo worthe your swerynge whiche dothe not aslake
Wo worthe you whiche wyll nothynge amende
Wo worthe vyce that dothe on you attende
Wo worthe your grete vnkyndenes to me
Wo worthe your hertes withouten pyte. ...

Blessyd be ye leuynge yll company
Blessyd be ye hauntynge the vertuous
Blessyd be ye that my name magnefy
Blessyd be ye techynge the vycyous
Blessyd be ye good and relygyous
Blessyd be ye in the lyfe temperall
Whiche applye yourselfe to Ioye celestyall. ...

With my blody woundes I dyde your chartre seale
Why do you tere it, why do ye breke it so
Syth it to you is the eternall heale
And the releace of euerlastynge wo.
Beholde this lettre with the prynte also
Of myn owne seale by perfyte portrayture
Prynte it in mynde and ye shall helthe recure.

And ye kynges and lordes of renowne
Exhorte your seruauntes theyr swerynge to cease
Come vnto me and cast your synne adowne
And I my vengeaunce shall truely releace
With grace and plente I shall you encreace
And brynge you whiche reuolue inwardly
This my complaynt, to eternall glory.
Amen.

5b Richard Younge, *A hopefull way to cure that horrid sinne of swearing: or, An help to save swearers, if willing to be saved. Being an offer or message from him whom they so daringly and audaciously provoke. Also a curb against cursing*, 1652, pp. 1–15. *Wing* Y161. **Source** *EEBO*: British Library, London (4412.l.36(3)).

MEMB. 1.

... §. 2. Think me not too bold, or over harsh, for I speak to you both *for* and *from* my *Maker* and *Redeemer*. Yea, be perswaded to hearken a while unto me, as you would have *God* another day hearken unto you. Are you *Christians*, as you call your selves? if you be, you have at least heard what *God* and *Christ* hath done for us. How when we were in a sad *condition*; when by sin we had forfeited our selves and all we had, and wilfully plunged our *souls* and *bodyes* into eternall torments: When neither *heaven, earth*, nor *hell* could have yeelded any satisfactory thing besides *Christ*, that could have satisfied *Gods* justice, and merited *heaven* for us; then, O then! The *eternall God* would dye, *viz.* so far as was possible or necessary, that we might not dye eternally, *Iohn* 3:16. A mercy bestowed, and a way found out, that may astonish all the sons of *men* on earth, and *Angels* in *heaven*. And all this even against our wils, when we were his enemies, mortally hating him, and to our utmost fighting against him, and taking part with his only enemies (*Sin* and *Satan*) as now you doe, not having the least thought or desire of reconcilement, but a perverse and obstinate will to resist all means tending thereunto.

§. 3. O my brethren! bethink your selves; It is his *maintenance* we take, and live on. The *air* we breath, the *earth* we tread on, the *fire* that warms us, the *water* that cools and cleanseth us, the *cloaths* that cover us, the *food* that does nourish us, the *delights* that cheer us, the *beasts* that serve us, the *Angels* that attend us, even all are his. That we are not at this present in *hell*, there to fry in flames, never to be freed. That we have the free offer of *grace* here, and everlasting *glory* in heaven hereafter, we are only beholding to him. And shall we deny this *Lord* that hath bought us? shall we most spightfully and maliciously fight on *Satans* side against him with all our might, and that against *knowledge* and *conscience*? I wish you would a little think of it.

§. 4. For favours bestowed, and deliverances from danger, bind to gratitude: or else the more bonds of duty, the more plagues for neglect. The contribution of blessings, requires retribution of thanks; or will bring distribution of judgments. And certainly, if a *friend* had given us but a thousand part of what *God* hath, we should heartily love him all our lives, and think no thanks sufficient. And in reason, Hath *God* done so much for us, and shall we denye him any thing he requireth of us? though it were our lives, yea our souls; much more our *sins,* most of all this sottish and damnable sin, in which there is neither *profit,* nor *pleasure,* nor *credit,* nor any thing else to provoke or intice us unto it, as in other sins; for all you can expect by it is the suspicion of common *Lyers,* by being common *Swearers;* Or that you shall vex others and they shal hate you.

... *Wherefore I beseech you by the mercies of God* (who hath removed so many evils, and conferred so many good things upon you, that they are beyond thought or imagination) to leave it, especially after this *warning,* which in case you doe not, will be a sore witnesse, and *rise up in judgment against you another day.*

MEMB. 2.

... §. 6. And as to swear by the *creature* makes the sin far more *heinous,* so the more mean and vile the thing is which you swear by (be it by my fay, by cock and pie, hares foot, by this cheese, and such like childish oaths, which are so much in use with the ignorant and superstitious swarm) the greater is your sin in swearing such an Oath, because you ascribe that unto these basest of creatures, which is only proper to God, namely, to know your heart, and to be a discerner of secret things. Why else should you call that creature as a witnesse unto your conscience that you speak the truth, and lye not, which only belongeth to God? And therefore, the Lord cals it a forsaking of him; as mark well what he saith, *Jer.* 5:7, *How shall I spare thee for this? thy children have forsaken me and sworn by them that are no Gods.* And do you make it a small matter to forsake God, and make a God of the creature? ...

§. 7. *Messeng.* You must not *measure all others by your own bushell,* for although ill Dispositions cause ill Suspicions; even as the *eye* that is bloudshood sees all things red, or as they that have the *Jaundies* see all things yellow; yet know that there be thousands who can say truly through Gods mercie that they had rather choose to have their souls passe from their bodies, then a wilfull premeditated *lie,* or a wicked *oath,* from their mouths; wherefore, when you want experience, think the best as charitie bids you, and leave what you know not to the *searcher* of hearts.

§. 8. As for the number of Swearers, it cannot be denyed, but the sin is a most universall, and this is it which hath incensed Gods wrath and almost brought an universall destruction upon our whole *Nation;* but is not this excuse [*That others do so*] a most reasonlesse plea, and only becoming a *fool*? when our Saviour Christ hath plainly told us, that the *greatest number go the broad way to destruct on, and but a few the narrow way which leadeth unto life,* Mat. 7:13, 14. And *S. Iohn,* that *the whole world lyeth in wickednesse,* 1 John 5:19. And that *the number of those whom Satan shall deceive is as the sand of the sea,* Rev. 20:8 & 13:16, Isa. 10:22, Rom. 9:27. And tell me, Were it a good plea to commit a *Felonie,* and say that others do so? Or Wilt thou leap into Hell and cast away thy soul, because others do so? A sorry comfort it will be to have a numerous multitude accompanie us into *that lake of fire that never shall be quenched.* ...

MEMB. 4.

... §. 14. Well may they beleeve what the *World,* the *Flesh,* and the *Devill* suggests unto them. As *Satan* (that he may make smooth their way to perdition) will perswade the most *impudent* and *insolent* sinners, *Drunkards, Adulterers, Blasphemers, Sabbath-breakers, Bloodthirsty Murtherers, Persecuters of the Godly,* and *contemners of Religion,* that they may take liberty to continue their sensuall lusts by a *testimony of Scripture,* and apply *Christs passion* as a *warrant* for their licentiousnesse; his *death* as a *licence* to sin, his *crosse* as a *Letters patent* to do mischief. And hereupon, as if a *Malefactor* should *head his drum of Rebellion with his pardon*: they live as if the *Gospell* were quite contrary to the rule of the *Law,* or as if God were neither to be *feared* nor cared for. Hence they exercise their saucie wits in prophane *scoffs at Religion,* and disgrace that *bloud* whereof hereafter they would give a *thousand worlds for one drop*; hence they tear *heaven* with their *blasphemies,* and bandie the dreadfull name of God in their impure and polluted mouths, by their bloody oaths and execrations; hence they are so *witlesse, gracelesse,* and *shamelesse* as to swear and curse even as *dogs bark.* Yea, they have so sworn away all grace that they count it a grace to swear; and are so far from beleeving what God threatens in his Word against sin, and what is affirmed of his justice and severity in punishing all wilfull and impenitent sinners with eternall destruction of *body* and *soul,* that they presume to have part in that merit which in every part they have so abused; to be purged by that *bloud* which now they take all occasions to disgrace, to be saved by the same *wounds* and *bloud* which they *swear by,* and so often *swear away*; to have *Christ* an *Advocate* for them in the next life, when they are *Advocates* against *Christ* in this. ...

6a *Here begynneth a lytyll new treatyse or mater intytuled and called the .ix. drunkardes* (1523). **6b** *A timely warning to drunkards* (1673).

Introduction The sin of drunkenness does not become a sin discussed as distinct from gluttony until the fourteenth century. An increase in the number of alehouses in England led to a more widespread tavern attendance and, in turn, to increased moral concerns about drinking. As the number of alehouses continued to grow throughout the early modern period, moralist interest in drunkenness did, too.[46] But as most late medieval texts treated drunkenness as an aspect of gluttony and considered it often as a part of the "sins of the tavern," so Protestant writers increasingly wrote separate sermons or treatises about drunkenness as a sin of its own (such as Increase Mather's 1673 *Wo to drunkards*).

Thus, the anonymous 1523 *Lytyll new treatyse or mater intytuled and called the .ix. drunkardes* is one of the very few pre-Reformation texts focusing on drunkenness exclusively (and not, like William Dunbar's 1507 *Dance of the seven deadly sins*, or the *Scale of perfection* (ca. 1380), in passing or as an aspect of gluttony). Its subject matter is biblical. It recounts examples of how drunkenness brought death or woe to drunkards, relying on the Bible as a recognizable and trustworthy source of its argument, which is that drunkenness is a sin condemned, and punished, by God. However, at the same time the text does not discuss the sin in detail nor with any theological pastoral commentary, letting its source material speak for itself. The excerpt below is the most "spectacular" of the examples given in the *Lytyll new treatyse* and is the story of Holophernes beheaded by Judith, as the text suggests, due to his untamed love for drink. This work is thus an interesting take on the biblical story of Judith because it focuses less on her heroic feat, or the divine nature of her power given to free her people, but on the foolishness and repulsiveness of the vice of drunkenness which brings Holophernes' demise.

Similarly, the anonymous *Timely warning to drunkards* also recounts examples of drunkenness causing death or pain to the drunkard, but the author of this text chose to focus on real life examples rather than on biblical sources. The aim was perhaps to add more realism to their text, or perhaps in the view of the author, examples of drunkenness abounded so much in society that recourse to anything other than real life was neither necessary nor instructive enough. Nevertheless, the text does retain a religious bent conveyed in its initial passage on the sinfulness of drunkenness which draws the soul away from God, a thought not unfamiliar to readers of *Piers Plowman*, nor to many early modern Protestants. The *Timely warning to drunkards* belongs, much like the *Nine mortal weapons*, to the genre of popular short moralizing anonymous texts, along with a few other texts such as the earlier *Looking-glass for drunkards, or, The good-fellows folly moderately reproving all such as practise as the beastly sin of inordinate and excessive tippling* (1641?) and *A statute against drunkennesse, viz. 4. Jacobus 5. The penaltie of a drunkard* (1644). At the same time as the *Nine mortal weapons* is thematically related to devotional treatises, so the *Timely warning to drunkards* is related to explicitly religious works such as sermons, with Increase Mather's *Wo to drunkards. Two sermons testifying against the*

46. Richard W. Unger, *Beer in the Middle Ages and the Renaissance* (Philadelphia, 2004), 38–41, 141.

sin of drunkenness: wherein the wofulness of that evil, and the mistery of all that are addicted to it, is discovered from the word of God as a prominent example. Both texts are short and to the point, and do not dwell on theological aspects of the sin, but instead attempt to illustrate the trouble it can get the drunkard into in this life much more so than in the next, both were thus placed against each other to illustrate how texts 150 years apart understand the immorality of the sin of excessive dringking, and how they present the social ramifications of drunkenness, while presenting it in a way that appeals to popular audiences.

6a *Here begynneth a lytyll new treatyse or mater intytuled and called the .ix. drunkardes whyche tratythe of dyuerse and goodly storyes ryght plesaunte and frutefull for all parsones for to pastyme with*, 1523; unnumbered pages. *STC* 7260. **Source** *EEBO*: Bodleian Library, Oxford (016420317).

Howe Olophernes becam drunke.
This done, Olophernes commaunded to caray Iudith into his tabernacle were his ryches lay and commaunded also that mete shulde be brought unto hyr fro hys owne tabyll. Than sayd Iudyth, I may nat ete of your mete leste our lord shulde be angre with me, butt I shall ete of the mete that I haue brought with me. Than sayd Olophernes, whan thy mete is etyn what wyll ye than doo. Than sayd Iudith, I haue mete anoughe untyll the tyme that our lord gyueth me understandyng that is to my purpose; and so is Iudith brought unto the tabernacle of the day to pray to our lorde, whiche Olophernes graunted hyr to goo and cum when she wolde to pray to hyr lord, by the space of .iii. dayes longe. As nyght cam so went she to the vallay of the Cytte of Betulie and washed hyr in the sayd fountayne, and than assendynge unto the mountayne She prayed to hyr lorde, god of Israel, that he wolde derecte and lede hyr from hyr enemyes; on the forthe daye Olophernes made a great feste whereat was all his lords and all o he commaunded his chamberlayne to goo for Judyth, sayng it were great reprofe and shame vnto vs that all eryons that suche a fayre woman shulde goo fre fro vs. Than went Uaago untyll Iudyth sayng, my lorde Olyfernes prayeth you to cum and drynke a cuppe of wyne with hym. She herynge thys denyed nat the message and sayd, I will neuer whyle I lyfe ageste saye my soueraygne lords commaundement. And so she arose and dressed hyr to goo toward Olyfernes. And as sone as she cumme afore hym he was greatly take with the loue of hyr, saynge, drynke wyth me, whom she thanked saynge, nowe shall I bothe ete and drynke wyth you. Than toke she suche vytalles as hyr mayde Abre had dressed for hir and satte downe and eate and dranke wyth hym. And Olyfernus for great ioy dronke

so much wyne that neuer all the dayes of his lyfe was he so gretly ouersene as he was at that tym.

Howe Iudyth smote of the hed of Olyfernes
As nyghte cam euery man drewe to his lodgynge and Uaago[47] his chamberlayne shytte the dore of the chamber of Olophernes and departed; and Iudyth was alone in the chamber and Olophernes as owerseen with drynke laye slepyng in his bed in the same chamber. Iudyth commaundyd hyr mayde the she shulde stande withoute to kepe the dore. And she approchyng nere the bedd of Olophernes prayd secretely saying, O my lorde god of Israhel comforte and strength me in this howre, and loke vpon me handy works that by the helpe of the I may brynge my purpose to passe. Than went she vntyll a pyller of the bed where honge the sworde of Olophernes, whyche she drewed out. And as she had the naked sworde in hyr hand she toke hym by the here of the hed saying, conforte me good lorde in this howre; And she smote tweyse and with the seconde stroke she smote of his hed. That done she gaue the hed vntyll hyr mayde whyche put it in a satchyll or baggage. ...

And as Uaago harde these tydynges he wente into the chamber to the bed of Olyphrenes and as he cam to the beddes syde where he smote bothe his handes to gyther to the entente to haue waked hym the more softly and esely as he was wonte for to do, and whan he sawe that he aude nat awake, he drewe the curtyn where he sawe Olyphrenes lyinge with his hed smytten of. Than cryed he with a hye voyce vnto the pepyll saynge, A woman of Heb[48] hathe done a mysteuous dede, beholde here lyethe Olophernes ded and his hed caryed a waye. ... and thus by drunnkynnes this prynce Olyphernes lyke a wretch was slayin.

6b *A timely warning to drunkards: or, the drunkards looking-glass in which is set forth the great and beastly sin of drunkenness: with one and twenty examples of Gods judgments upon several drunkards. Necessary to be set up in all houses:*

47. This is Bagoas (Bagao) from the Judith story; cf., for example, Judith 12:10: "et factum est quarto die Holofernis fecit cenam servis suis et dixit ad Bagao eunuchum vade et suade Hebraeam illam ut sponte consentiat habitare mecum," and Judith 12:12: "tunc introivit Bagao ad Iudith et dixit non vereatur bona puella introire ad dominum meum ut honorificetur ante faciem eius et manducet cum eo et bibat vinum in iucunditate," cited from *The Vulgate Bible,* Volume 2B: *The Historical Books: Douay-Rheims Translation,* ed. Swift Edgar, Dumbarton Oaks Medieval Library 5 (Cambridge, MA, 2011), 1877.

48. Cf. "una mulier hebraea" in the matching fragment of the Vulgate Bible on which this text relies for its contents. I am grateful to Brent Miles for helping me with this.

being a caution to young and old, 1673; pamphlet consisting of one page only. *Wing* T1284. **Source** *EEBO*: British Library (816.m.22[49]).

... 3. Drunkenness steals the heart away from God and all Goodness, and of a Man, metamorphoseth him into a Beast. How uncapable is a drunken man to pray, or to perform any thing that is good, but is then fit to do all manner of wickedness that the Devil or his own bad Heart shall prompt him to, as Murder, Whoredom, Incest, Theft, or any other grevious sin, as you may read in the following Examples, which are too true. Some of them I had of Ministers of good credit, and the other I have observed and seen. And God grant that thou mayst take warning by them, lest a worse thing fall upon thee.

I. The first Example is of one in *Northamptonshire*, living not many years since at *Desborough* in that County, which I saw with my eyes. As I was walking along, there rides by me on the Road a man very much in drink, but as he rid he fell off his Horse, and never spake more, but being carried to the next Town, he lay in a sad condition for a day or two, and so died. ...

III. Not so long since a Soldier in *Salisbury* in the midst of his Healths, drinking and carousing in a Tavern, drank a Health to the Devil, saying *That if the Devil would not come and pledge him, he would not believe there was either God or Devil*; whereupon his Companions, stricken with horror, hastened out of the Room; and presently after, hearing hideous noise and smelling a stinking favour, the Vintner ran up into the Chamber, and coming in, missed his guest, and found the Window broken, the Iron Bar in it bowed and all bloody, but the man was never heard of afterwards.

IV. Two Servants of a Brewer in *Ipswich* drank themselves drunk for the Rump of a Turkey; and afterwards, as they were struggling for it, they fell backwards into a Cauldron of scalding Liquor, whereof one died presently, and the other lingering died with greater pain. ...

XI. On the tenth day of August 1629, one *Thomas Wilson*, a Labourer, a known Blasphemer of Gods Name by Oaths and Curses and given much to drinking and excess, upon a slight occasion moved to displeasure against his Wife, and not daring to do much violence unto her, turned it upon himself, and with his knife stabbed himself, many of his Friends and Neighbours being present, and so he died.

XII. A young Gentleman being drunk, as he rode homewards was thrown by his Horse, and had his Brains dashed out by the Pomel of his Sword. ...

We shall conclude all with the words of the Apostle Paul, in *Gal.* 5:21. *Envyings, murders, drunkenness, revellings and such like, of which I tell you before, as also I have told you in time past, that they that do such things shall not inherit the Kingdom of God.*

Emotion

FEAR OF THE WRATH OF GOD, THE END OF DAYS, AND THE DEVIL

7a *Here beginneth a lytel treatyse the whiche speketh of the xv. tokens the whiche shullen bee shewed afore that drefull daye of judgement* (1505?). **7b** *The doome warning all men to the Iudgemente* (1581).

Introduction The end of the world and the Final Judgment were some of the most widespread motifs in religious treatises in both pre- and post-Reformation England. Texts dealing with subjects that caused fear in their audiences, such as hell, damnation, death, or the wrath of God, were popular, and numerous, because they objectified the fear and uncertainty of the End, as the set scenario of the Apocalypse made it easier to imagine and prepare for. At the same time, such texts satisfied human curiosity about the future, the cognitive need to know and understand the world and its cycles, and served as a reminder of mortality and the inescapable nature of divine power which, in the end, held ultimate control over human life and afterlife. Many texts on the Apocalypse contributed to an ever-increasing spread of millennialism that, while not invented in the Middle Ages, evolved in the twelfth and thirteenth centuries with the works of such thinkers as Joachim of Fiore and Hildegard of Bingen into a form that persisted throughout the late medieval and early modern periods. These texts served as (biblical) commentary on history (the ages of the world) and the present (particularly for Protestants), and for making prognoses for the future.[1] Pre-Reformation England in the time of Wycliffe was a time of heightened apocalyptical mood due to events that made many think the End of Days was near: the Black Death, the Great Schism, the Peasant Revolt and Lollardy, the English conflict with the Papacy, even an earthquake in London in 1382, all made many sure that the Apocalypse was coming. Apocalyptycism was thus on the rise in this period, as visible in many texts, such as the Wycliffite *Last age of the Church* (1356) and, according to

1. Marjorie Reeves, "The Development of Apocalyptic Thought: Medieval Attitudes," in *The Apocalypse in English Renaissance Thought and Literature*, ed. C.A. Patrides and Joseph Wittreich (Manchester, 1984), 40–73, at 53–59.

some, even *Piers Plowman.*[2] This was reinforced by the Reformation which, in many ways, brought another set of uncertainties to the world: religious conflicts on a national and international scale, and personal crises that pushed many Protestants into despair over the uncertainty of their own salvation. Many sixteenth-century texts, such as Robert Crowley's 1550 edition of *Piers Plowman,* looked to fourteenth- and fifteenth-century works for millenarian insights into the nature of the world and its future.[3] Later Protestantism likewise used apocalyptic discourse for polemical purposes, as much as a means of periodization,[4] remaining in line with the apocalyptic and millenarian tradition of the twelfth century and its later developments. But like in pre-Reformation literature, apocalyptic texts served also to objectify fear by submitting its source to a methodical analysis, a detailed description, and a formula (based on The Book of Revelation, but also apocryphal texts) that made the fear itself easier to deal with.

The anonymous *Lytel treatyse the whiche speketh of the xv. tokens the whiche shullen bee shewed afore that drefull daye of judgement* (1505) is an example of just such a text. It was most likely translated into English from Dutch by the printer, Jan van Doesborch, who sometime in the early sixteenth century branched out onto the English market and established a considerable reputation for himself and his texts.[5] Around 1523 he was recorded as living in London under the name Johanne of Dwysborow (also under variant spellings), supplying new books to the English market in cooperation with Wynkyn de Worde. De Worde took over the position of major English printer after Caxton's death around 1492, and was looking for new books to sell to his English audience; often these works came from other countries, the Netherlands among them. As a printer, Doesborch was interested in innovative texts on subjects he believed his audience would find engaging,[6] and his choice of an apocalyptic text drawing heavily on the Bible suggests an ongoing interest in such subject matter.

2. Morton W. Bloomfield, "Piers Plowman as a Fourteenth-Century Apocalypse," *Centennial Review* 5 (1961): 281–295.

3. Larry Scanlon, "Langland, Apocalypse, and the Early Modern Editor," in *Reading the Medieval in Early Modern England,* ed. Gordon McMullan and David Matthews (Cambridge, 2007), 51–73. See also John Aberth, *From the Brink of the Apocalypse: Confronting Famine, War, Plague, and Death in the Later Middle Ages* (New York, 2009), 5, for the argument that in terms of apocalypticism the late medieval and the early modern eras should be read as one period.

4. See Jaroslav Pelikan, "Some Uses of Apocalypse in the Magisterial Reformers," in *The Apocalypse in English Renaissance Thought and Literature,* ed. Patrides and Wittreich, 74–92; and Bernard Capp, "The Political Dimension of Apocalyptic Thought," in *The Apocalypse in English Renaissance Thought and Literature,* ed. Patrides and Wittreich, 93–124.

5. P.J.A. Franssen and A.E.C. Simoni, "Jan van Doesborch (?–1536), Printer of English Texts," *Quaerendo* 16 (1986): 259–280.

6. Franssen and Simoni, "Jan van Doesborch (?–1536)"; I am grateful to Matt Kavaler for his help in investigating the history of Jan van Doesborch.

The *Lytel treatyse the whiche speketh of the xv. tokens* consists of three parts. The first one, excerpted here, describes the signs of the impending Apocalypse. The following two parts focus on the Passion, with the second describing "who that oure lorde shall shewe the blyssed tokens of his passyon to theym tho that be dampned to grete payne, and to them that bee saued to grete myrthe and glorie," and the third "the nombre of the fote stappes of oure lorde the whiche hy wente in his passion and also other deuote maters" which the author authenticates by saying "yf ther bee ony person that wolde saye it were not authentic. Lete hem therfore not bee trobbled in his mynde. for it hath hondred tymes bee more and gretter than men there of can writte &c." (n. pag.). The text is thus about two different, and yet connected events: the Apocalypse, and the Passion of Christ. Reading about both encouraged the audience's active intellectual engagement, as both the Passion and the end of the world were often recommended as subjects of contemplation. In other words, Doesborch's choice of connecting the two was logical and fit into a trend contemporary to the publication of his text, in which millenarian fears mixed with the guilt for sin that brought on the Passion of Christ, sin that would be judged during the Final Day. The *Lytel treatyse the whiche speketh of the xv. tokens* induced a thoughtful evaluation of the audience's world as well as their deeds, and then led the audience further into introspection by discussing the role of the Passion, and thus their own sins, in the beginning, progress, and final outcome of the Apocalypse. In other words, the text discusses human fears and uncertainties by giving them form, and encourages the reader to deal with them by eliciting a reflective and introspective response.

The *Doome warning all men to the Iudgemente* (1581) is a text in many ways similar to the *Lytel treatyse the whiche speketh of the xv. tokens*: it also provides a detailed description of the signs that the Apocalypse is near, and connects them to the life (and death) of Christ. At the same time, the *Doome* is in a way more personal, because it describes events in human history, in specific locations, and, interestingly, in the past rather than future, unlike Doesborch's text. It thus creates an even more pressing sense of threat because it indicates that many of the signs of the impending Apocalypse have already been noted many years before its publication. It implies that the End of Days not only can happen, but most likely indeed will happen any day, by painstakingly recounting, year by year, the tokens of doom that people apparently missed. Relying on its audience's knowledge of the Book of Revelation, and so of the signs of the Apocalypse, of prophesies of the Antichrist, the Antipope, and the Tyrant, the author conveys his message in a clear way, but allows his audience to arrive at the dreadful conclusion that the Apocalypse is near themselves. The way this text manages fear, then, is by engaging the audience's knowledge of the Book of Revelation and anxiety about salvation, and leading it through a lesson in history by treating the Apocalypse as historiography, after Joachim of Fiore. In other words, it not only objectifies the fear of the End of the World and the Final Judgment through the familiar discourse of natural disasters (much like the 1505 text), but also through inviting the audience to draw their own, much less contemplative but much more fearful (because disempowering) conclusions about the inevitability, and nearness, of the End.

Stephen Batman (or Bateman), a Protestant preacher and clergyman (and chaplain to Mathew Parker, the Archbishop of Canterbury),[7] was known as an author and translator as well, not least for his translation and edition of the thirteenth-century encyclopedic work by Bartholomeus Anglicus, *De proprietatibus rerum*. His *Doome warning all men to the Iudgemente* is his translation of Konrad Lycosthenes' *Prodigiorum ac ostentorum chronicon* (1557), a compendium of strange occurrences in the world, "wonders," monsters, and "providences," but Batman made a few changes to the original text by drawing both on the history of England for additional examples, and on English ballads for additional sources of wonders and supernatural occurrences. Most importantly, however, he added the theological, apocalyptic agenda that Lycosthenes' original did not possess. His *Doome* thus became a vernacular text of warning, an elaborate and highly visual work with the pastoral purpose of a lengthy and highly imaginative sermon, and a lesson in "dreadful" history at the same time. These two texts thus work well together, as both focus on signs of the impending Apocalypse and both are representative of the widespread presence of apocalyptic texts on the medieval and early modern book market alike. At the same time, both are each other's mirror image, one forecasting the future and the other delving into the past. Both retain also the connection between signs of the end of the world and their meaning with regard to the Second Coming by connecting the Apocalypse to Christ and his death. The excerpt of Batman's text below illustrates his approach to the signs of the Apocalypse in particular, in contrast to those chosen by the author of the 1505 *Lytel treatyse.*

7a *Here beginneth a lytel treatyse the whiche speketh of the xv. tokens the whiche shullen bee shewed afore that drefull daye of Judgement. And who that our lorde shall aske rekenyng of euery body of his wordis, workis and thoughtes. And who oure lorde wyll shewe us other xv. tokens. of his passion, to theym that been deyeth in dedely synne*, Antwerp, 1505 (?); unnumbered pages. *STC* 793.3. **Source** *EEBO:* British Library, London (C.25.e.10).

In this begynnyng so wyl I writte of the xv. tokens they whiche shullen be shewed afore the drefull daye off dome of our lorde Jesus Christus and there shal we shewe oureself Ionge and olde &c.

7. Alan W. Bates, *Emblematic Monsters: Unnatural Conceptions and Deformed Births in Early Modern Europe* (Amsterdam, 2005), 66–70.

And our lorde wyll that there shal be shewed iiij. tokens, after doctours sayng. For oure lorde is so mercyful that hy wyl not punisshe vs but hy wyl shewe somme tokes[8] afore. And that we maye be sory off our synnes and do penaunce. And after thise forsaide iiij. tokens shullen yet bee xv. other tokens bee shewed. ...

And that firste token of the iiij. shalbe that the myght of Sathan thorugh the passune[9] of our lorde was made lasser, and was bounden, and shalbe onbonden. All be it that he by the myght of the passie[10] be bonden, and may not do so moche harme to the menshen as hy was wonte to do. But the deuyl is bonden at certen tymes, and hi shalbe onbonden, that hi maye do the more harme to the people wyth temptacien and tribulacien, for to assaye theym tho that bee chosen. But in the last tyme of the worlde shullen the goode bee very goode, and the euyll shullen bee very badde. Lyke the holy writters shewen in the laste chaptre of apocaliosis,[11] *Tempus prope est qui nocet, noceat adhuc, et qui in sordibus est sordescat adhuc, et iustus iustificetur adhuc, et qui sanctus est sanctificetur adhuc.* ...

That thyrde token shalbe as all maner of euil and synnes shalbe in this worlde, and the fere of god be put done and haue none thinkyng on hym. And whan faythfull and pacience shal not besette be, but al maner of eueyll shalbe vsed, and whan the menschen shullen louen with a secretely loue and care of none man but for her owne profit. And also we shalbe a fore the eynde of the worlde be prowde, and hy shal make moche of hemself and shall blasphemeren the name of our lorde, and they shullen not care of there fader or moder, and than they shullen loue flesly natur more than god, as the apostel in the ij. epistle ad thymoteum. Therfor latte euery body remembre in hem self what people nowe a daye be lyuinge in this worlde and loke wel yf this aforesayde thinges not be nowe a dayes shewed and done, and serve none synne. For it is not well possible that ony body myght writte the grete synnes the noweadayes be done praye to god that he wyll torne hys people that the maye do penaunce afore there deth.

That forthe token that shall be fore the eynde of the worlde and fore the other .xv. tokens and afore that grete ordil, afore the daye of dome, and than shal there be grete peruerten and warre, and there shal be warre in many dyuers landes of the worlde and also amonge al creatours in this world lyuing. For as matheus sayde in. xiiij. chapitre, Fyghtyng and warres shalbe amonge vs, and also one body shal aryse ayenst thother, and also one kynge ayenst onother, and also trayson shalbe amoge[12]

8. A macron is probably missing in the print; "tokens" is meant here.

9. Passion.

10. Passion.

11. "Apocalypsis" is meant here.

12. "Amonge" intended here; macron missing.

townes; all haue they made pays, and pays shalbe oute the world, and layed done and also the prinshe ayenst his comen, and his comen ayenst hem. And also ther shalbe none closter of monkes nor of nonnes, it shalbe full of peruertes or contrary one that other. And than shal it be as as Jheremias writted in his .x. chaptre, *Unusquisque se a suo proximo custodiat.* That is to saye, Euery man kepe hem of his neygbour or frinde, and troste not his broder for one shal shewe an other a fayre face but in herte of hym is fulle fals; and also one broder shal mocke that other, and hy shal laye snares and gynes[13] for hem to begyle yf he maye. ... And whan al thise thinges and peruerten shalbe thorughout of all the worlde, than shal it be an token of the laste termyn, or eynde of this worlde ... .

But wee knowe not yff these. xv. tokens shullen be shewed one after on other, or yf ther ony other token shalbe shewed betwene. Therof sayde saint hyronimus none certen, nor none doctour but they putte it in the wyl of oure lord, but our lord maye therwyth do hys wyll but hy is almyghty.

Of that forthe token

That forthe token shalbe that the see and all see and all other waters and ryuers shullen bernen of the fyre, that whiche shall Come oute of heuen, and shal punysshe theym that haue lyued lecherously in this worlde, after there lustisnes of the fleshe, and haue lyued ayenst the commaundement of our lorde Iesu. And suche folke shal berne in the fyre made of brymstone. Lyke ye fynde in Apocalipsi in his xxi chaptre. *Erit pars eorum in igne et sulphure.* And also for there plesure the whiche they haue hadden in there lecherousnes shullen haue a sonder peyne in euerlastyng fyre, Lyke ye fynde in apocalipsi, in his xviij. chaptre. *Quantum in delicijs fuit tantum date tormentum et luctum.* Gyue theym payne after that they haue deserued, the whiche haue lyued lecherously, and hauen kepte other mennes wyues, and hauen lyued after there owne plesure and flesely luste. Therefore shall this token be shewed that the see and alle Ryuers shullen bernen as ye here maye see portred &c. ...

Of that x. token

That .x. token shalbe that al men and wymmen, they that had hydde them in the erth shullen come ayen out of ther holes like as madde folke. And shullen so sore bee aferde that one shal not mowe speke to that other. And this shall god shewe in one token, that whan god shall gyue Iugement ouer the good and badde Shal hy no man excuse, whiche Iugement them is shewed wyth many tokens yf they wolde nott torne theym fro their synnes and doo penaunce. ...

13. Device, machine, contraption; also cleverness, ingenuity: *MED* s.v. "ğinne".

Of that xiij. token:
That .xiij. token shalbe that all men, wymmen, and children they than bee alyue op[14] the worlde, shullen deye wythout ony remedy. And hy shall this done for that they shullen aryse ayenst the day of dome wyth them that haue ben dede in the begynning of the worlde to that daye to aforesayde. And certeynly this shal bee a pytuosly worke that all people tho that ben alyue, goyng, sytting, standing, liggyng, etyng, or drynking shullen be hurt so shortly wyth the lancie of deth sudenly. Ọ ye wretched people ye wene to lyue euer, but thinke that ye shal deye, and you knowe nor daye nor houre. And also you thinke not on your synnes. O ye men and wymmen what shal ye do whan ye haue none tyme for to amende your synnes.

7b [Konrad Lykosthenes,] *The doome warning all men to the Iudgemente: Wherein are contayned for the most parte all the straunge Prodigies hapned in the Worlde, with diuers secrete figures of Reuelations tending to mannes stayed conuersion towardes God: In maner of a generall Chronicle, gathered out of sundrie approued authors by St. Batman professor in Diuinite*, trans. Stephen Batman, 1581; unnumbered pages. *STC* 1582. **Source** *EEBO*: The Huntington Library, San Marino, CA (59456).

The second part of the Cronicle, warning to the general iudgement, and comming of our Lorde Iesus, beginning from the byrth of Christ, vntill this present yeare of our Lord God. *1581.*
... [3.4.5.6.] There were great Earthquakes at *Rome*; a great flood ouerthrew the Bridge of *Tiber* by which ouerflowing men mighte haue rowed thorowe the Cittie for seuen dayes; when *Herod* was dead of the dropsie, hauing his body full of Lyce, his priuie members rotted, from whence scrauled fylthie Vermine, the Crampe benummed all the Sinowes of his bodye. Such was the Tragicall end of *Herod,* suffering iust punishment for the Babes destroyed in *Bethleem,* practiced purposely for our Sauiours sake.

... [7.8.9.10.] There was an Eclipse of the Sunne the tenth yere. Immediately following, *Augustus* banished *Archelaus* king of the Jewes, to *Vienna,* a Citie of *Fraunce. Iudea* is committed to foure Rulers. So cruell a famine inuaded *Rome,* that the Emperour commaunded the families of fencers, and all Straungers, and a great number of Seruants, sauing Phisitions and teachers, to bee thrust out of the Citie. ... This yeare among diuers prodigies there appeared a Comet. *Quin-*

14. Probably "of" intended here.

tilius Varrus was slayne by the *Germanes, Arminius* being their Captayne: For after that *Manilius* in his first Boke hath shewed that Comets doe portend insurrection and wars both abrode and at home ... .

A briefe rehearsal of the signes foreshewing the wares

A Comet like a sworde enduring the space of a whole yeare ouer the city, then followed a tumult or bloudie mischiefe among themselues.

A light in the Temple in the night time, the space of halfe an houre.

A Cowe calued a Lambe, in the middest of the temple.

A greate Gate opening it selfe, of Brasse, in the Inner Temple, that twentie men could scarce shut, about the first houre.

The one and twentieth daye of Maye a Diuell in the forme of a man appeared, after whyche Monstruous actes, cruell murtherings ensued.

An army of souldiours in the cloudes. A commotion in the ayre.

A voice was hearde in the Temple that sayde, *Lette vs goe hence.*

One Iesus the sonne of Ananias, foure yeres before the warres, cried continually *wo, wo,* al about *Iersusalem.* ...

The Holy figure

... [1415] The Diuell alleaged scripture, but error hath mistaken the Truth.

There was a notable eclipse of the Sunne the sixth Popish *Feria* after *Corpus Christi* day. *Ion Hus* comming out of *Boemia* (a maintayner of the truth against the Pope), contrarie to his safe conduit and faith given him by *Sigismondus* kyng of *Hungarie,* was burned at *Constance,* after he had made confession of his faith the first day of July, and his scholler *Ierome* of *Prage* was made a Martyre in the same place the thirtith day of May. *Lewes* the *Dolphin* departed this life, after whom his brother *Iohn* succeeded.

The one and twentith day of July whych was *Saint Magdalens* day, *Basil* was shaken with a very sore earthquake, in so much that a great part of the inhabitants flying out of the Citie got themselues to the mountains, as it were to a place of saftie, and some into the woods and fields. ...

[1419] In *Englande* Sir Iohn Oldcastle knighte Lorde *Cobham* was hanged in chaines, and after brente as an Hereticke, in the Monuments of Martyres sayde to be hanged and brent in thickets fielde, besides *Sainte Gils,* as sayeth D. Cooper.

The fourthe of December the Riuer of *Rhene* did ouerflow so much with abundance of rayne, that it ouerthrewe with violence the Bridges of *Lafenburge* and *Brisig,* and in *Hollande* it rente asunder thirtie Cities and Villages, to the greate destruction of men and beastes.

The Romaine Empire made war against the *Boemians* as heretickes, hauing the *Tigurians* and some other Cities in *Switzerland* theyr helpers. The thirteenth of the Calendes of December, in the night, the Occean sodainely ouerflowed, the windes raysing the surges and stormes; it couered all South *Holand* with water: beasts and men perished, there were drowned aboue seuen hundred villages and parishes, with Churches, Colledges, Monasteries, Priestes, and Monkes. ...

[1425] The seauen and twentith day of September, aboute midnight, was a terrible Earthquake, which continued the space of two hours. The Duke of *Brytaine* forsoke the Englishmen and alied him with the *Dolphin*, Lanquet. Cooper. ...

[1427] In *Englande* was very vnseasonable weather, for by continuall rayning from Easter to Michaelmasse tide the haruest of corne was greatelye hindered; it followed that the Englishmen besieged the Citie of *Orleance* continuing the time of whiche siege, the noble and valiaunt *Sir Thomas Montague* was slaine by a great misfortune, whose death was the begynning of all miserie to the Englishemenne, for after thys misshape, they lost by little and little all theyr possessions in *France*. ...

[1433] ... In *Poland* a bright Comet appeared in the night, more than three months vending his flame towards the Weast, and that yere king *Vratislaus* dyed. In *Germany* there folowed scarcity of Corne for four yeres. ...

Moreouer this yere there appeared a wonder whyche Aeneas Siluius writeth of in his *Europe*. In the territorie of *Bononia* verye many small Antes climbed vp vpon a dry Peare tree to feede; there came after them no small number of greater Antes whiche partlye slue them, and partlye caste them downe; almoste two hours after there arose so greate a number of small Antes, that all the field seemed to be couered with a blacke hoste; they came all beset in companies, and enuironing the stemme of the tree on eury side, beganne by little and little creepe vp, when the greater Antes perceyued that theyr enemies were at hande, they clustering togither aboue, awaited the fighte; the armies met togither and ioyned in battayle, the greater with sharpe nipping slue the lesser on euerye side, and in short space they slue them, that there grew vnderneath vpon the ground, at the roote of the Peare tree, no small heape of them falling downe and dying, but when the lesser Antes stucke stiffely vnto it, twentie or more dydde togither beset one of theyr enimies, and fighting before and behind, struck him through with their stinges euery where; at length, the greater being ouercome and all slaine, they were worthilye punished for their rashe battalye whyche they firste beganne. These were done in the sighte of manye of the Romishe Churche, when Pope

Eugenius the fourth helde Peter Chaire, who being *Venetian* borne stirred great vprore in *Rome* by persecuting the predecessors of Pope Martin, hoping thereby to haue gotten great summes of money, by meanes of whiche his lewdenesse hee was driuen to flye *Rome* for a tyme vnto *Florence*; and, at hys returne, he ... caused Thomas Redonius, a white frier, a famous preacher to be burned at *Rome*, 1436, bicause he earnestly reproued the pride, riot, and vniust cursings of the Pope.[15]

8a Thomas Wimbledon, *A sermon no lesse fruiteful then famous* (1599). **8b** Increase Mather, *Heaven's alarm to the world* (1682).

Introduction Apocalyptic fears were most persuasively induced, as well as manipulated, in sermons, as the anxiety over salvation and the Final Judgement allowed preachers to personally engage their listeners in a reckoning of their deeds, personalizing the message of a given sermon. The two texts below both were originally preached as sermons. Thomas Wimbledon's 1388 *Redde rationem vilicationis tue*, preached on the occasion of the renewal of royal vows by Richard II, is a *sermo ad status*,[16] that is, a sermon in which audiences were addressed according to the social (or professional) group they belonged to; it was written with a political as much as pastoral purpose in mind.[17] At the same time, however, the author, Thomas Wimbledon, who was possibly chaplain to John Sanders and a licensed preacher in Winchester, though little is known about him,[18] made sure to also broaden the pastoral agenda of his sermon. By making the sermon about good leadership and kingship it was also relevant to the rest of the audience as it drew attention to the reckoning of the Final Judgment as a general reckoning of all human action, narrowing in from the "vineyard" understood as the kingdom to each person's own "vineyard."

15. The passage about the ants was, most likely, to serve as a parable.

16. Carolyn Muessig, *Preacher, Sermon and Audience in the Middle Ages* (Leiden, 2002), 255–257.

17. Wimbledon makes references to the biblical king Rehoboam and his misrule of his country as a warning for Richard, whose reign was evaluated critically at the time (Anne Middleton, "Acts of Vagrancy: the C Version 'Autobiography' and the Statute of 1388," in *Written Work: Langland, Labor and Authorship* ed. Steven Justice and Kathryn Kerby-Fulton [Philadelphia, 1997], 208–318, at 308).

18. Gerald Robert Owst, *Preaching in Medieval England: An Introduction to Sermon Manuscripts of the Period c. 1350–1450* (New York, 2010), 360. It is possible that there may have been some suspicion of heterodoxy against Wimbledon as the license that he obtained in 1385 (licensing preachers was common practice at the time and was to serve to prevent the spread of Lollardy) forbade him to preach anything that smacked of heresy or heterodoxy, although the sermon itself is perfectly orthodox (Siegfried Wenzel, *Latin Sermon Collections from Later Medieval England* [Cambridge, 2005], 171–174).

The sermon is comprised of two parts, first directed at *oratores, bellatores* and *laboratores* (understood to comprise all society in the Middle Ages[19]) and their role in society (the three estates producing a healthy society when in agreement and cooperation). The second part speaks of two judgments the soul is subjected to: immediately after death, and at the End of Days. Fear of judgment is thus amplified by this sermon: it first warns about the importance of proper conduct of each member of each social group, passing on to the first reckoning after death, and then focuses on the fearful final reckoning after which the world will be at its end. It speaks of moral and personal considerations that every person listening to the sermon should take heed of, such as spiritual readiness for death and, while contextualized by current catastrophic events (particularly the Peasants' Revolt of 1381 and earthquake of 1382) and predicting the end of the world would come in 1400, the sermon contains also a more general call for the moral self-evaluation of all in both their social and private lives. This powerful piece was extremely popular in the early modern period. John Foxe included it in his *Actes and monuments* (1563), and thus disseminated it among Protestant audiences. Throughout the early modern period the sermon was widely read, and was printed a number of times in the sixteenth, seventeenth, and eighteenth centuries, and later.[20] The copy used here dates to 1599, but the sermon itself was preached in 1388, copied in at least 15 manuscript editions which subsequently were printed, first in 1540 (the earliest traceable edition), and was extant already in three editions (1540, 1550, and 1561) before being included in Foxe's text.

Increase Mather's *Heaven's alarm to the world* is, likewise, a sermon firmly ingrained in its context, and speaks of the need for reform of the second generation of citizens of New England, whom Mather saw as spiritually slack and lacking in the religious zeal of their fathers. Natural disasters that were raging in New England, such as the droughts of 1662 and 1666, bad crops of 1664, 1665, and 1668, as well as other calamities such as wars with Native Americans (1675) and "fearful signs" such as comets all made Mather, a popular and respected puritan preacher, convinced that God was angry with his chosen people.[21] Mather thus called his audience to consider all supernatural occurrences (such as the 1666 comet which to him looked like a spear aimed at the heart of New England, Boston) and natural disasters as signs of God's wrath with the corruption, sinfulness, and moral decay of New England. He was deeply concerned that God would punish New Englanders by destroying their colony, bringing an end to the puritan cause (as it was brought to an end in England by the end of the Protectorate, the Restoration of 1660, and

19. Muessig, *Preacher, Sermon and Audience*, 255–257.

20. Lynn Staley, "Susanna's Voice," in *Sacred and Profane in Chaucer and Late Medieval Literature*, ed. Robert Epstein and William Robins (Toronto, 2010), 46–67, at 57–58.

21. Emory Elliott, *Power and the Pulpit in Puritan New England* (Princeton, 1975), 89–91, 113.

the Great Ejection in 1662). His *Heaven's alarm* thus calls for moral reform of all Protestants in New England; it does have a fairly narrow focus on Boston and Massachusetts, but at the same time the sermon is Mather's cry to all who would listen about the need for moral improvement, repentance, and the need to come back to the godly behaviour of the past. In Mather's prognosis, the end of the world was to come in 1694. Both sermons, then, discuss the image of God as Judge, and God as an angry father chastising his children. Both sermons are rebukes and reminders of the need for godliness and obedience to God, and both are contextualized by current events that made both authors predict a precise date of the end of the world frighteningly close to the date of each sermon (12 years in both cases). At the same time, these two texts differ in their contexts, audiences, styles, sequences, and visions of God's wrath, providing an interesting comparison of approaches to the Apocalypse and the Final Judgment in pre- and post-Reformation pastoral use, as well as of the clerical manipulations of their audience's fears, tailored to achieve moralizing purposes.

8a Thomas Wimbledon, *A sermon no lesse fruitefull then famous: preached at Paules Crosse, on the Sunday of quinquagesima, by R. Wimbledon, in the raigne of King Henry the fourth* [sic], *in the yeere of our Lord, 1388, and found out hid in a wall. Which sermon is heere set forth by the old coppy, without adding or diminishing, saue the olde and rude English, heere and there amended*, 1593 [i.e., 1599]; unnumbered pages. *STC* 25834. **Source** The Library of Congress, Washington, DC (BX890 .W48 1599).

To the Christian Reader.

... Read therefore diligently thys little Sermon, so long since written, and thou shalt perceiue the same quick spirit in the Authour therof that thou now merueilest at in other men of oure time. He sharply, ernestly and wittingly rebuketh the sinnes of all sorts of men, and speaketh as one haunge authorite, and not as the Scribes and Pharisies, which with theyr leaden and blunt dart, could neuer touch the quick, though they haue occupied and worne the Pulpit of many yeares. The word of God is liuely and mighty in operation, and sharper then any two-edged sword, and cutteth euen vnto the diuision of the soule, and of the Spirit, and of the ioyntures, and marrow, &c. Wherfore eftsoones I exhorte thee, to read thys little Treatise diligently, and not onely to reuerence authoritie, and the liuely spirit, and word of God therin, but also to lerne both to acknowledge, and moreouer to amend the wickednes of thy life, which God grant for his beloued sonne Christ Iesus his sake. Amen.

The second part of this Sermon

... For the first yee shal know that ther be two iudgements: the first, anon after the departing of the body and soule, which is a particular doome, whereof Luke speaketh in his Gospell. The second doome shall bee anon after the general resurrection, and that shal be vniuersall, and of this speaketh S. Mathew. To the first shall euerie man be called one after an other, as the worlde passeth. To the second shall wee come altogether in the twinckling of an eye. To the first, men shall bee called by three Sumners or Seriants; the first is Sicknes, the second Age, the third Death. The first warneth, the second threatneth, and the thirde taketh. ... I say also that there shal be another day of iudgment, to the which all men shall come together in the twinkling of an eie, and this shal be vniuersall. And like as to the other, euery man shalbe called by these 3. Sumners, so to this iudgement all the world shalbe called with three general Sumners. And right as the other three messengers shew a mans end, so do these messengers tel the end of the world. The first is the worlds sickness, the second is his age and feeblenes, and the third is his end. The sickness of the world thou shalt know by charity wexing cold, and his age and feeblenes thou shalt knowe by tokens fulfilled, and his ende thou shalt know by Antichrists pursuing. First, I sayd, thou shalt know the worldly sicknes by Charity wexing cold. Clarkes that doo write on naturall thinges say that the body is sick when that his kindly heate is too little, or when it is too much. Then sithence vnderstand as thus, that al men is as one body, whose kindly and naturall heate is Charity, that is, loue to God, and loue to thy neighbor; vnnaturall or vnkindly heate is lustfull loue to other creatures. When therfore thou seest that the loue of men to Godward, and to their neighbours is colde, little, and faint, and the loue of worldly things, and lusts of the flesh, is great and feruent, then know thou wel that vnkindly heat is too great, and kindly heat is too little. That this is knowledge if this sicknes I may proue by Christs authority, for he himselfe gaue this as a signe, drawing to the ende of the world, for that wickedness shall be plenteous, Charity shall wexe colde. Therefore when thou seest Charity thus little sette by of the world, and wickednes increase because that worldly things be most set by and loued: know wel that the world and his wealth passeth, and that this Somner is come. ...

The second Sumner that shal warne all the world is the age of the world and his feeblenes, and sheweth tokens fulfilled: but I know well that we be not sufficient to know the times that the Father hath put in his own power to shew certainly the day, the yeere, or the howre of iudgement. This knowledge was hyd from the very Apostles of Christ, and also from Christes manhood, as to shew it to us. Neuerthelesse, we may by authority of Scriptures, with reasons and expositions of holy men, wel and openly shew that this day of wrath is nie. ... I shall shew you that this day is at hand, but howe nie, I cannot say, nor will not. For if Paul sayd a thousand, three hundred yeres and more past, we be those on whom the endes of the world be come: much more may we say the same that be so much neerer the end then he was. Also, S. Chrisostome sayth: Thou seest darknes ouer all, and why doubtest thou that the day is at end? First on the vallies is darknes when the day draweth downward. When therefore thou seest the valleyes darke, why doubtest thou whether it be neere night or no? But if thou see the Sunne, so low that darknes be vppon the hils, thou wilt say doubtlesse that it is night. Right so, if thou see in the secular men that darknes of sinne beginneth to haue the maistrie, it is a token that the worlde endeth. But when thou seest Priestes that bee put in the toppe of suffrancie of Spirituall dignite, that should bee as hyls among the common people, in perfect liuing, that darknes of sinne hath got the vpper hand of them who doubteth but that the worlde is at an end. Also, Abbot Ioachim in the exposition of Ieremie, saith: That from the yeere of our Lord 1300, all times be to bee suspected by me, and we be past this suspect time nie one 100. yeres. ...

But if we leane to the Gospell of Mathew, we shal find that the Disciples of Christ asked three questions. First, what time the Cittie of Jerusalem should be destroyed. The second, what tokens were of his comming to iudgment, and the third, what signe should be of the end of the world. And Christ gaue no certiane time of these thinges when they should fall, but he gaue them tokens, by the which they might know when they drew neere. To the first question of the destruction of Jerusalem, he said, When the Romans come to besiedge the citty, then soone after it shalbe destroyed. And as to the second and third, he gaue them many things, as were these: That Realme shall rise against Realme, and people against people, and that there should bee pestilence and earthquakes, the which wee haue seene in our daies. But the last token that hee gaue was thys: When yee see the abhomination of holines spoken of by Daniell, standing in the Sanctuarie, then who so readeth, let him vnderstand. Upon which text argueth a Doctor in a booke that hee maketh of the end of the world. ... And this abhomination, as Doctors say, shall be in the great Antichtists daies, a thousand two hundred and ninty daies. Now proueth this Doctor that a day must be taken for a yere both by authority of the Scripture in the same place, and in other, and also by reason. And so it is thought to this Clarke that the greatest member of Antichrist shall come and appeare more in the 14. hundreth yeere from the byrth of Christ then any time els before, which number of yeeres is now fulfilled, not fully xij. yeres wanting. ...

But take wee heede to the fourth part of the seconde vision of S. Iohn in the booke of Reuelations, in the which vnder the opening of vii. Seales is declared the state of the Church from the time of Christ to the end of the worlde. ...

I said also in my second principal part, that it was to be knowne before what Judge we must reckon, that is, God him selfe, he that seeth all our deedes, and all our thoughts, from the beginning of our life to the end, and he shal shew there the hid things of our harts, opening to all the world the righteousnes of his iudgment, so that by the power of God euery mans deeds shalbe shewed to al the world. And so it seemeth by the words of S. Iohn in the Apocalips, where hee did see dead men great and little, standing to the figure of the throne. And books were opened, and another booke was opened that was of life, and dead men were iudged after the things that were written in these books after their owne dooings. These bookes be mens consciences that now be closed, but then shalbe opened to al the world to read therin, both their deeds and thoughts. And the booke of life is Christes lyuing and doctrine, that is hid now to them that shal be damned thorow their own malice, that counsaile men to followe the world, rather then God. In the first booke shall be written all that we haue done, in the other, all that we shold haue done. And then shal dead men be iudged after those things that be written in the books. And if the deeds that we haue done, that be written in the bookes of our consciences, be according to the book of Christes teaching and liuing, the which is the booke of life, we shal be saued, or else wee shall be damned, for the iudgements shall be giuen after our works. Looke therefore now what is written in the Booke of thy conscience while thou art heere, and if thou find any thing contrary to Christes life and teaching, scrape it out with the knife of repentance, and write it better, euermore thinking that thou shalt giue a reckoning .... Then shall those false seruaunts goe with the deuil, whom they haue serued in the earth, swallowing them into the endlesse fire. But the rightful men shal goe into euerlasting life. Then shall be fulfilled that is written in the booke of the priuities: Wo wo, wo shal be vnto them that dwell on earth .... Also woe shall be to the sinne of thought, to thee that hast shut out of thy heart the meine God .... As thou here hast shut god out of thine hart, so shal he shut thee out of heauen. ...

Or if thou hast beene lecherous, a glutton or a couetous man, know saith Paule: That neyther adulterer, nor vncleane person, that is a glutton, or a couetous person, shal euer haue entrance into the kingdom of heauen, but fire and brimstone and the spirit of tempests, that is, the fiend of hell, shall be part of their paine as it is written in the Psalter. When these damned men be in this woe, they shall sing this ruful song, written in the book of mourning: The ioy of our harts is gone, our mirth is turned to woe and sorrow, the crownes of our head is fallen from vs. Alas for the sinne that wee haue doone. But ioy, ioy, and ioy, shal be vnto them that be saued. Ioy in God, ioy among themselues, and ioy in other that be saued … . Oh how happy are they for that their trauailes be finished thorow Christ, which brought them to so gracious an ende. Then they are happy for that they be escaped the perils of the world and the paine of hell.

8b Increase Mather, *Heaven's alarm to the world, or A sermon wherein is shewed that fearful sights and signs in heaven are the presages of great calamities at hand, preached at the lecture of Boston in New-England, January 20, 1680*, Boston, 1682, pp. 1–38.[22] *Wing* 1218/1219. **Source** *EEBO*: The Library of Congress, Washington, DC (M1218).

Luk. 21:11 – Fearful Sights, and great Signs shall there be from Heaven.
The Lord Jesus Christ, having told his Disciples that great Calamityes were hastning upon Jerusalem and upon the Jewish Nation; they enquire when those things should come to pass, and what *Signs* should precede and presage the Judgements predicted. This we see in the 7th Verse of this Chapter, *They asked Him, saying, Master, but when shall these things be: and what* Sign *will there be when things shall come to pass?* In Answer unto which Enquiry, the Lord Christ doth in this Context mention several things, some of which were to be more remote, and others more immediate *Signs* of that miserable Destruction, which the sacred and unerring lips of Christ had foretold. 1. False Christs would arise, V. 8. *Many shall come in my Name, saying, I am Christ*, &c. … . 2. Another Sign mentioned, is that of Warres, and Commotions, V. 9. *When you shall hear of Wars and Commotions, be not terrified: for these things must first come to pass; but the end is not by and by.* … 3. Another Sign is that mentioned in the 10th V. *Nation shall rise up against Nation, and Kingdom against Kingdom.* … 4. There were to be *great Earth-Quakes in divers Places;* In the beginning of this Verse. Such things are usually signs of Divine Anger, and so portentous of great Changes and Calamityes: the Intimations of State-Quakes, yea of Nation-Quakes. Historians speak of very tremendose Earthquakes which hapned in diverse places, whereby several famous Cities perished, not long before *Jerusalem* was destroyed. 5. *Famines.* … 6. *Pestilences.* These two Judgements (*Limoi kai Loimoi*, as in the *Greek* it is elegantly expressed) of *Famine, and Pestilence,* do often go together, the latter following at the heels of the former, and being occasioned thereby. 7. *Fearful Sights and great*

22. Marginal notes in the original source were not included in the transcription.

Signs in Heaven: which are the words now before us to consider of. Fearful Sights, *Gr. Phobetra, Terriculamenta.* Such Sights as strike a terror into the hearts of men that are the Spectators of them ... .

Doct. *That Prodigious awful Sights and Signs in Heaven, are oftentimes, the Presages of great Calamity coming upon the World.*

For the further clearing of this Doctrine, three things may be enquired into. 1. What Sights and Signs are the Presages of Calamity? 2. How it doth appear that they are so? 3. What Calamityes such Signs do commonly presage?

Q. 1. *What Sights and Signs in Heaven are Presages of Calamity?*
Ans. 1. There are Signs in the *starry Heaven.* The great God, when he made the World, placed the Stars in Heaven, to be for Signs as to Events that in the ordinary Course of Nature should come to pass. *Gen.* 1:14. *God said, Let there be lights in the Firmament of heaven, and let them be for Signs.* They are for Signs of Heat and Cold, wet and dry Seasons, and the like. Hence the Lord spake to *Job,* as in Ch. 38:31. *Canst thou bind the sweet Influences of* Pleiades, *or loose the bands of* Orion? ... And hence the Stars are called by the name of the *Signs of heaven,* Jer. 10:2. *Learn not the way of the heathen, and be not dismayed at the Signs of heaven.* Which words may well be understood concerning the Stars and Constellations in the heavens. For the Heathen, the *Chaldeans* especially (among whom the *Jews* were then going to dwell) superstitiously imagin'd that the Stars were Rulers of the World, and did therefore stand in fear of them, and worship them; which heathenish Idolatry the Lord doth caution and charge his People against. The Stars of Heaven are for natural Signs. Their Motions and Appearances are significations that such and such things, will according to that Course of Nature which God hath setled, come to pass in the World. There are also *extraordinary Stars,* sometimes appearing in the Heavens. God in his Providence doth so order, as that sometimes, *Blazing Stars* are seen in heaven. Such *Stars* are called *Comets,* from the stream like long Hair, which useth to attend them. Such a Star is *Prodigious,* and a *Fearful Sight.* And of this may the words of the Text be understood. The *Jewish* Historian reports, that not long before the destruction of *Jerusalem,* there was a *Blazing Starre* in form of a Sword, which seemed to impend over the City, for a Year together: This now was a *fearful Sight,* and a *great Sign from Heaven.*

2. There are fearful Sights and Signs appearing in the *Air,* sometimes in the lower heaven, which we move and breathe in. Prodigious Meteors are sometimes seen there. And strange Appearances, which are either seen, or heard speaking. Of these fearful sights and signs, is the Text likewise to be interpreted.

Josephus relates that before the *Romane* Army destroyed *Jerusalem*, there were seen in the Air, Iron Chariots, and Souldiers in battel aray; and in the night time, a great Light appeared in the Temple, for half an hour together, with as much brightness as if it had been noon day; and a Voice was heard saying, *Let us be gone from hence.*

Qu. *How doth it appear that such Fearful Sights are Presages of Calamityes coming upon the World?*
Ans. 1. The Scripture is clear for this. The Text before us doth expresly declare no less. And the Prophet *Joel* foretelling the same Calamityes which this Text hath reference unto, saith also, that prodigious Signs in heaven should presage and portend them. *Joel*, 2:30, 31. *I will shew Wonders in the heaven.* Truly, Blazing Stars are Wonders in the heaven. *And in the Earth, blood, and fire, and pillars of smoke before the great and the terrible Day of the Lord come.* When *Jerusalem* was destroyed, and the *Jewish* state dissolved, that was a great and notable Day of the Lord, a Type of the great Day of Judgement. *Wonders*, even prodigious and amazing Signs should precede it. ... Yea, the Scripture informs us, that *Fearful Sights and Signs in heaven*, shall precede the Great and General Day of Judgement, as Presages thereof. *Luk.* 21:25. *There shall be Signs in the starres*, meaning that such things should be observed among the Stars in heaven, as would be a Sign that Christ's coming to Judge the World, did approach. Wherefore in Verse 28. it is said, *When these things come to pass, then look up, and lift up your heads, for your Redemption draweth nigh.* The Day of *Judgement*, is a Day of *Redemption*, and is so called in other Scriptures, *Ephes.* 4:30. Then shall the Bodies of the Saints be redeemed from the power of the Grave; and both Bodies and Souls, redeemed from all Evils of sin and of suffering. *Rom.* 8:23, 1 *Cor.* 1:30. At the Resurrection, in the last Day, will the great Redemption be to the Saints of God, and the greatest Miseryes to the Wicked that ever were thought of. And Signs in heaven shall precede them. And hence it is, that *Fearful Sights* are called *Signs* in the Scripture; it is partly on this account, in that they are *Signs* that the Lord is coming forth out of his holy habitation, to punish the World for their Iniquityes. ...

3. Many times such fearful Sights are tokens of God's Anger; which is another Reason why they are called *Signs*, as being Signs of the Anger of God. Signs that flaming Vengeance is kindled, and burning in Heaven against a sinful World. Now when God is angry, then Publick Judgements come, as Testimonyes of Divine Displeasure. *Personal* Afflictions are not alwayes Evidences of God's Anger, as we see in *Job*: but *Publick* Judgements are ever wont to be so. 'Tis thought that the

ninetieth Psalm was penned by *Moses* on occasion of a publick Judgement, the Plague which broke in upon the Children of *Israel*, and swept away many Thousands of them: And saith he, *We are consumed by thy Anger, and by thy Wrath are we troubled*, V. 7. So that if Publick Judgements come, God is angry, and his Wrath kindled: He doth by them testify, and power down his righteous Displeasure from Heaven. Inasmuch then as fearful Sights are Tokens of God's Anger, they are Presages of great and publick Calamities. As the *Rainbow* (though a natural Sign) is a token of Divine *Favour*; so are prodigious Sights Tokens of Divine *Anger*.

4. These fearful Sights are many times Presages of those things which make way for great Changes and Calamityes to come upon the World. They are oftentimes (Blazing Stars in a more special manner are so) the Presages of the death of great; yea, and of worthy Men. Is not the fatal downfal of *Augustulus* (the last *Roman* Emperour) in the Scripture emblematically set forth, by that of a *Blazing-Star* falling to the ground? *Rev.* 8:10. *There fell a great star from heaven, burning as it were a lamp.* It is conceived, that the ruine of *Augustulus*, dethroned by *Odoacer* the *Herulian*, was signified by those words, and that he is resembled to that sort of *Comets*, which is called *Lampadias*. And when there is a Star burning and blazing in heaven, commonly it proves fatal to some *Augustulus*; whence great Changes and miseryes ensue. Yea, the Death of *worthy* (as well as *great*) Personages is sometimes portended by such Signs. A little before great *Constantine's* death, a blazing Star appeared, and infinite miseryes followed. In the Year 1556. a Comet (then vulgarly called a *fiery Beesom*) was seen; and soon after, many learned, useful, worthy Men dyed; whose death was an unspeakable loss and misery to the places where they had lived.

Quest. 3. *What Calamityes do such fearful Sights and Signs in heaven presage?*
Ans. We must not be particular and positive in Interpretations of things of this nature. When a fearful Sight appears in heaven, which the whole World cannot but take notice of, now to make a particular and absolute determination that such a Place, or such a Person, such a Judgement, is certainly intended thereby, is too much boldness. In general, we may safely say, that there is just cause to expect that great Calamityes are at hand: but what Persons or Places shall more eminently fall under those Judgements, is not for us to determine; but we must leave that with God, who best knows what himself intends to do.

This being premised, we proceed in Answering the Enquiry before us.

1. Sometimes such Signs are Presages of great Persecutions coming upon the Church of God. The Lord in mercy to his People, giveth them such Warn-

ings, that so they may prepare for what's a coming, or make haste to enter into the Chambers of safety, as it were for a little moment, till the Indignation be overpast. *Nero*'s bloudy Persecution had a *Blazing Star* to precede it. The same is true concerning the *Arian* Heresy and persecution, that flood spoken of in the *Revelation*, which the Dragon cast out of his mouth, and whereby the Woman, the Church, fled into the Wilderness, was in eminent danger of being swallowed up and devoured. *Rev.* 12:15.

2. Sometimes such Signs in heaven are Presages of miserable Dearths and Scarcity. That Blazing Star impending over *Jerusalem*, which the Text hath reference unto, was attended with a terrible. Famine, whereby multitudes perished. And therefore such Signs are frequently portentous of those Judgements, which cause Want and scarcity. ...

3. Lamentable Deaths and Destructions amongst Men, have been oftentimes presaged by such Sights in heaven. Sudden and amazing Ruines, by *Earthquakes*, by *Inundations*, by *Fire*, and the like awful Visitations, have been thereby portended. Especially destructions by mortal and contagious Diseases. That strange Disease, known by the name of *Sudor Anglicanus*, which in a peculiar manner pursued those of the *English* Nation, even when in strange Lands; whence they were dreaded in all places where they came, there was a *Blazing Star* that did precede it. Especially that which is, of all Diseases miserable Mortals are subject unto, the most terrible, I mean the *Plague* of *Pestilence*, it is frequently thus presaged. Such Sights are *Heaven*'s *Alarm* to a sinful World, to give notice that God hath bent his Bow, and made his Arrows ready, and that if Sinners turn not, the Arrows of Pestilence and Death shall fall down upon them speedily. This might be confirmed by a multitude of Instances; but it needs not. Our own Experience is enough. We cannot but remember the *Blazing Star* that was seen but 16 Years agoe, and a terrible *Plague* followed; so that in our own Nation, near upon an *hundred thousand* were swept away in one City, and in one Year. And it is reported, that immediately after that great *Blazing Starre*, which appeared above threescore years ago, God sent the *Plague* amongst the Natives in this Land, which swept them away in such multitudes, as that the living were not enough to bury the dead. So did the Lord cast out the Heathen before this his People, that the way might thereby be prepared unto our more peaceable settlement here, The Lord in mercy grant, that we may never, by becoming like unto the Heathen in Profaneness and Irreligion, provoke Him to do unto us, as He hath done unto them.

4. Such fearful Sights and Signs in heaven, are usual Presages of War among the Nations, and so of those Devastations and Desolations which the Sword

leaveth behind it. Prodigyes on the *Earth* doe sometimes betoken War and Bloodshed, 2 *King.* 3:22. And Signs in *Heaven* do no less. ... And are there not some alive, and here before the Lord this day, that can remember the *blazing Star* which appeared in the 9*th.* and in the 10*th.* Moneths, in the Year 1618. and the next Year began that unhappy War in *Germany,* which proved so fatal to the *Protestant* Interest there.

Thus have we seen what Judgements and Calamityes, *Fearful Sights in heaven* are commonly the Presages of. As for that *SIGN* in heaven, now appearing, (which hath occasioned me to speak this Word at this time) what Calamityes may be portended thereby, which of the Judgements mentioned, or whether all of them be not thereby presaged, I shall not say; but leave it unto God and Time to discover. Only, in general we have cause to fear that sweeping Judgements are thereby signified; that the Lord is coming down from Heaven with a long Beesom of Destruction, which shall sweep away a world of Sinners before it.

I conclude with a word of *Application:* Nor would I speak any thing, but the words of Truth and soberness, as becometh a Messenger of Christ to doe, when speaking in His Name.

Use: *Let us hence be Exhorted to approve our selves as those that are under the solemn, awful Warnings of God, ought to do.* I need not say (for every one knows it) that there is a Fearful Sight and Sign appearing in the heavens. Such a formidable *Blazing-star,* as that the like hath seldom been observed. It concerns us then to hearken to the voice of the Lord therein; who by such tremendous Sights is speaking awfully to the children of Men. Hear then *Heaven's Alarm* this day. You will say, But what should we now do? *What doth the Lord expect from us, when there are such dreadful Presages of Evils coming upon the World?*

Answ. I. It now concerns us to be *awakened out of all Security.* That's one of God's ends (his declared end) in causing such *Fearful Sights* to be taken notice of, that so he might awaken a secure sleeping World. And indeed the Lord manifests his Goodness and Compassion towards sinful Creatures therein. It was a pious Speech of that Emperour, who beeing somewhat terrified at the sight of a *Blazing-starre* said to those about him, *Let us admire the Clemency of that God, who before He smites us, causeth such Signs in heaven, that so He might awaken us out of our Security.* O let us beware of crying Peace, Peace, when the Day of Destruction is at hand. O take heed of sleeping, and dreaming of nothing but worldly Prosperity at such a Time as this. When the Lord Jesus Christ had told his Disciples that calamitous Times were a coming, and mentioned the Signs and Presages thereof, He bids them *Watch therefore,* Luk. 21:36. Let us not then please our selves with imagining that such Fearful Sights are Signs of *Mercy* only, and not of *Judgement*. ... Such fearful Sights are usually Signs that those Judgements, which are (as *Tertullian* speaks) *Tonsurae humani generis*, God's sharp Razors on Mankind, whereby He doth poll, his Sythe, whereby He doth shear down multitudes of sinful Creatures, doe draw near. In which respect, there is no doubt to be made of it, but that God by this *Blazing-star* is speaking to other Places, and not to New-England onely. And it may be, He is declaring to that generation of hairy Scalps who go on still in their Trespasses, that the day of their Calamity is at hand, and that the things which shal come upon them make haste. *A strange Sight* doth betoken *strange Punishment* coming upon those that have been prodigious workers of Iniquity. Yet let not us promise to our selves nothing but Prosperity in the doleful and the bitter Day, when there shall be Lamentation generally. I am perswaded that the floods of great water are coming. I am perswaded that God is about to open the windows of heaven, and to pour down the Cataracts of his Wrath, ere this Generation (wherein *Atheism* and *Profaneness* are come to such a prodigious height) I say, ere this Generation is passed away. But what reason have we to think that no drops of the fatal Storm shall come near to us? If we so conclude, we may provoke the Lord to say, *The Sinners of my People shall dye by the Sword, who say, The Evil shall not overtake us nor prevent us*. To be awakened out of Security, and tremblingly to wait for the good Pleasure of God, whatever it may be, is the most likely way to find Rest in the day of Trouble.

2. *This should put us upon preparing for another Day of Trouble*. And this should we do the rather, since the Changes portended by this *Comet*, are like to come *speedily* as well as *certainly*. ... Let us then prepare for Trouble. We should not onely expect it; but so expect it, as to prepare for it. Certainly we have reason so to do. If there had been no *Blazing-star*, yet upon other accounts, we have cause to expect and prepare for *another Day of Trouble*, which seems to be hastning upon thee O *NEW-ENGLAND*, and upon thee, O *BOSTON*! The *Sins* which are amongst us, are surer and blacker Signs of Judgement than any *Signs in heaven* that we may think of. I say the Sins, the *Pride*, the *Profaneness*, the *Worldliness*, the general *Security* and *Iniquity* that prevaileth amongst us. ... And now know for certain that if destroying Judgements and Death overtake any in their Sins, and sweep them away to Hell, their blood shall be upon their own heads. For the Lord hath fired his Beacon in the heavens, among the Stars of God there; the *Fearful Sight* is not yet out of sight. The *Warning-piece* in heaven is going off, now then if the Lord discharge his *Murdering-pieces* from on high, and men be found

in their Sins, unfit for Death, their blood shall be upon them. They had Warning given them that the Sword was a coming: Lo, the Lord himself gave them the warning; but they would not take warning, their blood shall be upon them. Moreover, if Troubles should not come, yet it will be wisdom to prepare for them. If the Lord, after Hee hath sent his Angel to stand with a drawn Sword over *Jerusalem*, should be entreated to spare us, yet it will never do us hurt to prepare for the most deadly Arrows of Affliction that may light upon us, whilst in this Vale of Tears.

3. *We should do what in us lyes to divert those Judgements, which seem to be impending, and blazing over our heads.* This word of Comfort, I may safely speak, *The Lord's Threatenings are not absolute, but conditional.* So far as we in these ends of the Earth, these goings down of the Sun, are spoken unto, by this Sign in the heavens, it is possible we may escape the Evils threatened thereby, if we duely hearken to the Voice of God therein. *Jer.* 18:7, 8. *At what time I speak concerning a Nation and concerning a Kingdome, to pluck up, and to pull down, and to destroy it: if that Nation against whom I have pronounced, turn from their Evil, I will repent of the Evil that I thought to doe unto them.* So that when desolating Judgements are threatned, either by the Word, or by the awful Works of God, those denunciations of Wrath are not *absolute*, but *conditional.* If Repentance intervene, the Evils which otherwise must be looked for, may be diverted. See therefore *Jer.* 36 3, 7. *It may be the house of* Judah *will hear all the Evil which I purpose to do unto them, that they may return every man from his evil way.* Ay, a general Repentance is that which will do, if every man turn from his evil way, *that I may forgive their Iniquity and their sin. It may be they will present their Supplication before the Lord, &c.* … . *Pray alwayes that you may be accounted worthy to escape all these things that shall come to pass.* Prayer may do much toward the averting of wrathful Judgements and Desolations. …

If we be found a praying, an humble, a reforming People, wee need not doubt but that *Under the shadow of His Wings, we shall make our Refuge, untill the Calamity be overpast.*[23]

23. This word is unclear in the copy used, but "overpast" is the final word in the transcription of a different copy of Increase Mather's *Heaven's alarm to the world* (Boston, 1680) available at the Evans Early American Imprint Collection website: https://quod.lib.umich.edu/e/evans/N00252.0001.001?view=toc, accessed 11 June 2018.

9a *Here begynneth the byrthe and lyfe of the moost false and deceytfull Antechryst* (1525?).
9b *A true and plaine genealogy or pedigree of Antichrist* (1634).

Introduction The figure of the Antichrist is an inseparable part of most Apocalyptic narratives, modeled on the Book of Revelation. Many religious and polemical texts of the fourteenth and fifteenth centuries also used the subject of the Antichrist to convey opinions about the Church of Rome, priests, or heretics. With the advent of print, stories about the Antichrist became increasingly popular, and via that popularity lost some of their religious meaning. Instead, many such texts became works of para-religious imagination that focused on the character of the Devil and Antichrist in relation to the religious narrative of the Apocalypse, but narrowing in on the Antichrist in particular. Such a text is the *Byrthe and lyfe of the moost false and deceytfull Antechryst*, a work that is fairly rare in that most medieval vernacular texts contained discussions of Satan's devices against Christians, or apocalyptic visions of the Antichrist, but few works were about the Devil, or Antichrist, only, with the exception of the *Robert the Devil* tales.[24] The text is incomplete, missing chapters three through five, but it is not difficult to infer their contents: as the title suggests, the text recounts the story of Antichrist from his birth throughout his reign, chapter one being entitled "how the fader shall lye with his doughter and shall engedre on her the chylde of perdycon that is Antechryst," with subsequent chapters describing the life and deeds of the "cursed chylde." In that, the text recounts the life of the Antichrist as parallel to the life of Christ, offering, for each event in Christ's birth and life, a mirror image of the Antichrist: as Christ was born during the night in Bethlehem, so the Antichrist was born during the day in Babylon; as Christ performed miracles, so the Antichrist would perform false miracles, and so on. The *Byrthe and lyfe of the moost false and deceytfull Antechryst* awakens an emotional, fearful response in its readers via the realism with which it constructs the character of the Antichrist, in reference to well-known stories of Christ's life and nativity: the more the readers knew about Christ, the more they learned about the Antichrist, the enemy of mankind, and the more frightening the Devil became.[25]

The 1634 *True and plaine genealogy or pedigree of Antichrist* is a text on exactly the same subject, the birth and life of the Antichrist, but with significant changes, as it was written after the Reformation in England. As opposed to providing the genealogy of

24. For example, *Here beginneth the lyf of the moste myscheuoust Robert the deuyll whiche was afterwarde called the seruaunt of god* (1500) is an edition of the medieval legend originating sometime in the thirteenth century. However, neither the Robert the Devil stories nor similar works (such as *Sir Gowther*, ca. 1400) talk about the Devil in an apocalyptic context.

25. Jean Elizabeth MacFarlane, "Antichrist in English Literature, 1380–1680" (PhD diss., University of Florida, 1980), 167–170.

Antichrist as coming from imaginary parents, such as Schalcus and Ulcas, or providing other imaginary genealogies through compiling existing narratives of the life of the Antichrist, as done by Adso of Montier-en-Der in his *De Antichristo*, ca. 950,[26] this text traces the pedigree of the Antichrist to the Pope, much like Wycliffe did in the 1380s.[27] It is thus representative of its genre, in which both anonymous texts and well-known writers such as William Prynne[28] accused Roman Catholic priests and the Pope (and in Prynne's case, also Laudians) of being directly descended from the Antichrist. An anonymous pamphlet against the papacy, the *True and plaine genealogy or pedigree of Antichrist* follows, in places, the pre-Reformation genre it originates from, in which relative freedom from religious doctrine "reflect[s] popular legends: strong, longstanding influences, whatever the religious establishment may have thought of them."[29] The *True and plaine genealogy* is wholeheartedly focused on polemics, and drawing associations between the Roman Catholic Church and the life and activities of the Antichrist, in contrast to the *Byrthe and lyfe of the moost false and deceytfull Antechryst*, which is directed at neither heretics nor the established Church. Both texts thus offer a glimpse into the plethora of objectifications of the Antichrist in both periods, and indicate the complex textual uses of religiously orthodox stories (such as the nativity and the Book of Revelation) to weave stories of their own. They belong to different genres, one being a para-religious tale of the coming of the Antichrist at the end of days, the other a polemical work contextualizing this coming with contemporary conflicts between religious groups; they were also written for different audiences, but these differences lend themselves to illustrating how the discourse of the origins of the Devil as Antichrist could serve both moralizing, and polemical purposes, and how these purposes evolved over time, particularly since the *True and plaine genealogy or pedigree of Antichrist* harkens back to Wycliffite polemic.

9a *Here begynneth the byrthe and lyfe of the moost false and deceytfull Antechryst, the whiche shall come into the worlde as the prophesy of many prophetes recorde, and is taken out of sondry bokes, with the tokens and sygnes that shall falle before the comynge of oure lorde Jesu cryst to the generall Jugement*, 1525 (?); unnum-

26. See, for example, Curtis V. Bostick, *The Antichrist and the Lollards: Apocalypticism in Late Medieval and Reformation England* (Leiden, 1998).

27. For example, see the fourteenth-century Wycliffite *Epistola Luciferi ad cleros.*

28. William Prynne, *A looking-glasse for all lordly prelates. Wherein they may cleerely behold the true divine originall and laudable pedigree, whence they are descended; together with their holy lives and actions laid open in a double parallel, the first, betweene the Divell; the second, betweene the Iewish high-priests, and lordly prelates; and by their double dissimilitude from Christ, and his Apostles* (1636).

29. Richard H. Hardin, "Apocalypse Then: Tamburaline and the Pleasures of Religious Fear," *Baylor Journal of Theatre and Performance* 3 (2006): 31–41, at 35.

bered pages. *STC* 670. **Source** *EEBO:* Cambridge University Library (Syn. 7.52.17).

At this present tyme shall be wryten of the ferefull sygnes that shall happen before the comynge of oure lorde Jesu cryst to the Jugement, at the dredefull daye of dome with the forth comynge of the moost false heretyke, Antechryste, as is sygnyfyed by the mouthe of oure sauyoure Jesu cryst in the xxi. chapytre of saynt Luke saynge thus. *Erunt signa in sole et luna: et in terris pressura gentium.* That is to say. Tokens shall be in the sonne, in the mone, and sterres, and in the erthe grete oppressyon of people, thrughe the confusyon of the noyse and cryenge of the see and flodes. The people shall waxe dry and waste awaye thrughe the ferefull curse that shall come ouer all the worlde. ...

The viii. chapytre sheweth vs how Antechryst shall gete many kyngdomes and londes vnder his domynacyon and subgeccyon and also he shall put vnto dethe many kynges and grete lordes that wyll not beleue in his cursed lawe.

As it is wryten in the Appocalyps. *Ad trahet ad se magnam partem stellarum.* Antechryst shall drawe vnto him a grete parte of the sterres, that is for to knowe hyghe prynces reignynge on erthe. For some he shal gete to himwarde by force and some by dowayres and gyftes. In lykewyse it is wryten in the Appocalyps in the thyrde chapytre. Unto hym is gyuen myghte in all the generacyon or kynred of people. But after the prophetysynge of Danyell and of saynt Johan in the Appocalyps in his xiii. chapytre and Johannes[30] camestor in scolastica historia, Antechryst shall caste thre kynges out of the oryente. That is to wete the kynge of Affryke, the kynge of Egipt, and the kynge of Ethyope, the whyche he shall put to dethe, And vii. other kynges shal become subiect to hym. And other kynges of the erthe he shall subdewe by stronge hande. But the kynge of Lybye shall not come to the beleue of the false Antechryst, vnto the tyme that he shall reuyue his fader the olde kynge of Lybye, and his moder. And than shall Antechryst with arte magycke or with the deuilles crafte make to aryse the forsayd kynge and queen fro dethe to lyfe. And than shall they gyue vnto Antechryste lawde and prayse as yf he were god. And whan that is achyeued and done, the kynge of Lybye shall beleue on that false Antechryste and all his people. And than shall all his people be marked with the token of Antechryste on theyr foreheedes, and vpon theyr ryght handes, and with this marke Antechryst shall subdue the worlde to hym and his

30. Word crossed out by a reader.

myserable credence, as it is wryten in (compendio theologie)[31] in the .vii. boke and .ix chapytre.

... The xvij. chapytre sheweth how Antechryst shall persecute the good people with grete tourmentes and afflyccyons that he shall do to theym. As saynt Gregory sayth in the .xxxii. moralyte.

So whan Antechrist shall sytte in his pryde and tryumphant magest,[32] reysed vpryght as a Cedre tree he shal make his men and satilytes to dyuyse many grete paynes and tourmentes as the martyrs in tymes past were payned with. With the whiche paynes this most false Antechryst shal persecute the good people. For some he shall put to dethe with the swerde, of some he shall cut away the hands and fete, and of some to drawe the guttes out of theyr belyes al quycke, and some he shall cast amonge furyous beestes to be deuouered and slayne, and some he shall make to be rosted all quycke, and some he shall brenne to pouder, and some with other meruaylous paynes whiche were ouer longe to tell, for he shall fynde other tyrannous engyns that neuer were seen a fore.

And oure lord shall shewe dyuers myracles for the good people in theyr tourmentes and anguysshes. Then shall the seruauntes of that false Antechryst, whiche punysshe the good people, doo many myracles by the operacyon and myght of the deuyll. And in the presence of the sayd martyrs they shall make the crucyfyxe of our lorde and the ymages of our lady and of other sayntes to falle, the whiche ymages they wyll make to speke and saye that all the worshyp and honoure the whiche ye haue done to vs is false and vayne, this is the veraye Messyas vnto whome ye ought to doo reuerence. And they shall make deed bodyes to reuyue in the presence of them, and they shall say tourne to hym for your beleue is false, this is the veray messyas. And this Antechryst shall make to roste the good people, as Saynt Laurence was. And thenne shall he make to ryse fro dethe to lyfe the fader and moder of them that thus is rosted. And they shall say, Good chyldren ye ben out of the right way for ye beleue not well ne right wysly, this is the veray messyas that was promysed in the lawe, and therefore torne agayne to hym and saue your lyfe. O good lorde what trybulacyon and vehement calamyte shall be then in the worlde, than shall be the tyme of heuynes. Of the whiche dayes the holy man Job was affrayed and he desyred ententyfly of our lorde that he myght not lyue those dayes. In lyke wyse Saynt Poule desyred also of our lorde not to lyue vnto the dayes of the regne of Antechryst. Alas who shall than be sted-

31. Parentheses in the original text.

32. Original text has "magest" here; an emendation was made by a reader adding the final "e" by hand.

fast and sure syth these holy men were abasshed and dredde, how shal we poore wretched and myserable sinners than doo. We ought than to be sore esmayed[33] and troubled. For many of the good people shal hyde theym in caues and holes amonge the cragged roches for fere of the paynes and tourmentes of Antechryst, but hunger and thyrst shall constrayne them to come out agayne. For than shall neyther meet ne drynke be solde vnto them. For than shall Antechryst do maken generall proclamacyon and commaundement throughout all the worlde that no man ne woman shall be so hardy to selle to ony persone meet or drynke but that he haue the token of Antechryst both in the forheed and also on the ryght hande vpon payne to forseyke bothe body and goodes. ...

9b *A true and plaine genealogy or pedigree of Antichrist, wherein is cleerely discouered that hee is lineally descend from the diuell,* 1634; text consists of one page only. *STC* 674. **Source** *EEBO*: British Library, London (C.40.m.11.(2)).

... My rusticke Muse declares his very name,
His pedigree, and of what house he came.
There was a braue heroicke Gentleman,
... One deadly-*Darkenesse* was his eldest sonne;
And thus (in truth) this royall race begun
And then that *Darknesse* did beget by chance,
A son, an heire, and cald him *Ignorance*;
Of his true byrth ther's no man need enquire,
You see the sonne is fully like the Sire.
This *Ignorance* liued a while, and then
He begot *Error* and his bretheren,
Error begot *Freewill* and *Selfe-conceit,*
Freewill got *Merit,* that deceiuing bait,
Merit begot *Forgetfullnesse of Grace*;
And then his sonne *Trangression* tooke his place:
And that *Transgression* did beget *Distrust,*
Who deeming God lesse mercifull then Iust:
Maugre his justice to maintaine his action,
Begot a sonne and call'd him *Satisfaction.*
This *Satisfaction,* e're his father dide,
Being excessiuely possest with pride,

33. Frightened: *MED* s.v. "esmaien".

Reiected quite Christs bloody sacrifice,
Which once for all he offered in such wise
That he for all his peoples sinnes thereby,
Did God's pure justice fully satisfie.
The cause why *Satisfaction* did this thing,
Was that thereby he might to credit bring
His onely sonne, *the sacrifice o'th Masse,*
As proud a Knaue as e're his father was.
For if to him come any one or other,
Desiring helpe for some deceased brother,
Vpon condition of a golden fee,
Hee'l contradict the mighty God's decree,
And disanull his judgements past also,
And bring to weale whom God hath plac'd in woe,
For if you'll trust him, this man doth excell,
Hee'l hunt the place where all the Furies dwell,
And search the *Lymboes;* nay, hee'l not be sory
To search throughout the furious Purgatory,
And euery nooke and secret corner there,
Bee't in the Fier, Water, Earth, or Aire,
(For though that he hath fetched thousands thence,
And did withall their deadly sinnes dispence,
Has quite forgot, his wits are so decay'd,
Whereof, wherein, and when that place was made),
But hauing found him, then he will surpasse,
And bring the man from where he neuer was,
Vnto a place of myrth and melody,
Where, if he were not, he can neuer be.
The *Priests annoynting* his successor was,
And *Superstition* thereon came to passe.
This *Superstition* was a royall thing,
For he begot *Hypocrisie* the King.
Hypocrisie got *Gaine by offering,*
And of that *Gaine* did *Purgatory* spring,
Then *Purgatory* passing reasons bounder,
Was certainely, *Anniuersarie's* founder:
He by a stranger without Matrimony,
Did then beget the *Churches Patrimony,*

Then *Mammon, of Iniquity* his sonne,
Begot a Child, as his Father had done:
A worthy sparke, *Abundance* was his name,
And of *Abundance, Ease,* (a gallant) came.
Ease begot *Cruelty*, and he *Dominion*;
Dominion, Pompe; and *Pompe, Ambition,*
And of this man old *Simony* did grow,
A bribing Knaue, how cleere soeuer he show,
This man of issue was not without hope,
For why he liu'd to see his sonne the *Pope,*
Who in this world doth beare a great renowne,
And on his head doth weare a triple Crowne,
Whose charity if it were to his power,
He could clense Purgatory in an hower,
And send the soules that in that place do dwell,
Straight vp to Heaven from that smoky Cell.
He thinkes perhaps his power hereon is grounded
The former place his predecessors founded,
And for the latter none can him withstand,
He beares the Keyes of heauen in his hand.
But here's a griefe that to a mischiefe grew,
Because his *Holinesse* let in so few,
Or else iust none, which is a grieuous thing,
His Keyes haue lost theyr vse of opening.
And as the Keyes oth[34] *Pharisees* his brothers
Shut heauens gate against themselues and others.
... Now Christ his Parson, openly did show
His Kingdome was not of this world below.
But Pope his Vicar commands all estates,
Kings, Emperors, and greatest Potentates,
And turnes his power to furious tyranny,
Against that Christ and all his company:
And by his rage they now abide affliction,
He's *Antichrist* without all contradiction. ...

34. "O'th" intended here.

DEATH, ANXIETY, AND SORROW

10a [Denis the Carthusian (?),] *Here after foloweth the prologue of the foure last thynges* (1479/1480). **10b** Simon Birckbek, *A treatise of the four last things, death, judgement, hell and heaven, commonly called the Quatuor novissima* (1655).

Introduction The genre of texts about the four last things, or *quattuor novissima*, death, judgement, hell, and heaven, dates back to late medieval Christian eschatology and to the events of the late Middle Ages such as the aftermath of the Black Plague, various social upheavals, the Great Schism, and proto-Reformatory heresies; these are often seen as the genesis of heightened devotional and meditative interests in death, judgement, heaven, and hell in the late medieval period. The death of the body, followed by Judgement Day, and then subsequent condemnation in hell, or reward in heaven, occupied the thoughts of late medieval theologians, preachers, and laity alike. Death, judgement, and hell in particular, being sources of anxiety (about the certainty of salvation), guilt (for sin), and fear of death, punishment, and the torments of hell stimulated many to meditate on mortality, their conscience, and the transience of life, throughout their lives as much as in the hour of their deaths. Fear and anxiety over death and judgement allowed preachers to deliver their pastoral message of caution, and death's irrevocability and disconnectedness from the controversies of the Reformation, along with the unwavering desire of many to die a good death, ensured the popularity of such texts in the early modern period as well. Thomas More, for instance, was of the opinion that meditation on death was of great "profit and commodity."[35]

The genre of writing about the four last things is usually dated back to the fifteenth-century thinkers Denis the Carthusian, in his *Quattuor Novissima*, and Gerard de Vliederhoven, in his *Cordiale*, which set the tone for "a genre of moral treatises on the Four Last Things and established a tradition for later eschatological iconography"; both were widely available throughout the fifteenth and sixteenth centuries.[36] Both were also printed many times, and gave rise to other works on the subject in the early modern period (between

35. Margaret Aston, "Death," in *Fifteenth-Century Attitudes: Perceptions of Society in Late Medieval England*, ed. Rosemary Horrox (Cambridge, 1994), 202–228, at 202–204. See also Thomas More's unfinished *The Four Last Things* (1522), envisioned to discuss the four last things in connection to the Seven Deadly Sins (with a meditation on each of the four aiding to counteract a given sin).

36. Jacek Kowzan, "*Memorare Novissima Tua*: The Iconography of the Four Last Things as a Representation of Religious Identity," in *Art and Identity: Visual Culture, Politics, and Religion in the Middle Ages and Renaissance*, ed. Sandra Cardelli, Emily Jane Anderson, and John Richards (Cambridge, 2012), 97–127, at 99.

1479 and 1691) by such Protestant authors as Robert Bolton, William Sheppard, and William Bates. Protestants found the genre very appealing as it touched upon both individual death, in line with the pre- and post-Reformation interest in personal spirituality, and the general judgement of all souls on Judgement Day, which persisted as an important element of religious dialectics. A meticulous guide in self-study impressed on the audience the remembrance of mortality and divine power over the soul. Spiritual introspection made this genre popular both among pastoral writers, who often made references to the four last things (even if a given work was not devoted to this subject alone), and audiences for whom such works provided consolation, instruction, and a theoretical and theological explanation of what awaited the soul after death, as well as a guide on how to prepare for what was, inevitably, coming.

The 1479/1480 *Here after foloweth the prologue of the foure last thynges* is Caxton's edition of Denis the Carthusian's *Quattuor novissima*, translated from French by Anthony Woodville, but has clear references to Gerard de Vliederhoven's text as well, as the subtitle of this 1479/1480 copy reads "The Cordial, or a booke de Quatuor Novissimus." The work itself is divided into four parts regarding death, judgement, hell, and heaven (subdivided into chapters with prologues), preceded by a general prologue and concluded by an epilogue by the translator and editor. *A treatise of the four last things, death, judgement, hell and heaven, commonly called the Quatuor novissima* (1655) by the Protestant clergyman Simon Birckbek,[37] as the title itself suggests, firmly writes itself into the same tradition as Caxton's edition of Denis the Carthusian's text and is a good example of the perseverance of the genre in the early modern period. Just as many other early modern works on the four last things which display "at times a surprising degree of homogeneity across denominational borders," Birckbek's text is likewise in principle no different from its pre-Reformation antecedents; the concept of the four last things was not only devotionally flexible and appealing, but also easily reconcilable with Protestantism.[38] At the same time, Brickbek's text illustrates the stylistic changes that the genre underwent in the course of its development in England. While in regard to content it is faithful to the tradition of Denis the Carthusian and de Vliederhoven (minus references to Purgatory, of course, which were incompatible with Protestantism), in respect to style it is very clearly a Protestant text. Both these works are adaptations of the original genre, and both illustrate the characteristics of editorial and content-related choices applied in the compilation of such a work before and after the Reformation, providing insight into similarities and differences of approaches to the pastoral aspects of teaching on the four last things.

37. Best known for *The Protestant's evidence, showing that for 1,500 years after Christ divers Guides of God's Church have in sundry Points of Religion taught as the Church of England now doth* (1635).

38. Kowzan, "*Memorare Novissima Tua*," 110.

10a [Denis the Carthusian (?),] *Here after foloweth the prologue of the foure last thynges*, ed. William Caxton, trans. Anthony Woodville, Westminster, 1479/1480, pp. i–x.[39] *STC* 5759. **Source** *EEBO*: Bodleian Library, Oxford (016417168).

Here after foloweth the prologue of the foure last thynges

Memorare nouissima et in eternum non pecabis, Ecclesiastici septimo capitulo. Ecclesiasticus sayth in his seuenth Capitre these wordes folowynge. Bere well in thy mynde the last thynges and thou shalt neuer falle in synne. ... It is to be noted that after the sayeng of sayntes, men saye comynly ther be foure the last thynges. And whiche they be it appereth clerely by the wordes of Saynt Bernard in a sermon, where he sayth in all thy werkes haue remembraunce of thy laste thynges, whiche be four. That is to wyte fyrste: Bodely dethe. Seconde, The daye of Iugement.

39. Every second page is numbered in this copy. The date suggested by *EEBO* is 1496 but no copy printed by de Worde from 1496 seems to exist. The copy of this text has the date 1478 written onto its title page, and the epilogue by William Caxton describes in detail how he came to possess this translation of a text originally in French (which was a translation from Latin) and gives the date of 1479 or 1480 as the end of his work on the edition: "Whiche werke presente I began the morne aiter the sayd Puryfycacyon of oure blyssed Lady. Whiche was the daye of Saynt Blase Bysshop and Martyr And fynysshed on the euen of the Annuncyacyon of oure sayde blessyd Lady fallyng on the wennesdaye the four and twenty daye of Marche. In the .xix. yere of kynge Edwarde the fourthe." The final page of the copy gives Caxton's W&C logo as the printer without the later addition of de Worde's name; after he inherited the press and the logo in 1492 (taking until 1496 for de Worde to settle issues surrounding Caxton's will), the logo then contained "W&C and Wynkyn de Worde," printed beneath it. Although occasionally only the W&C was used without de Worde's name, it is distinctively different from de Worde's later translation. For this reason I assume the date to be 1479 (which is also the generally accepted dating of Caxton's edition of this work) rather than 1496, and Caxton and not de Worde as the printer for this copy. As to the text Anthony Woodville, Earl Rivers, translated from, the French *Quatre Dernierres Choses* by Jean Mielot (translator from the Latin), it is unclear whether it is a translation of Denis the Carthusian's text, or Gerard de Vliederhoven's work. Possibly it is a mix of both, as there is confusion as to the contributions of both authors to the genre (see for instance James Willoughby, "The Provision of Books in the English Secular College," in *The Late Medieval English College and Its Context*, ed. Clive Burgess and Martin Heale [Woodbridge, Suffolk; Rochester, NY, 2008], 154–179, at 166). It seems some scholars attribute the original from which Mielot and then Woodville translated to either Denis the Carthusian or Gerard de Vliederhoven (and both are considered equally important to the genre), though judging by River's translation it seems to be a mix of both, or perhaps Woodville's choice of "Cordiall" is merely a reference to de Vliederhoven's work while providing a fairly faithful adaptation of Denis' text only. See Kowzan, "*Memorare Novissima Tua*," 99–102, for more on the contrast between Denis the Carthusian's and Gerard de Vliederhoven's works as well as for more on de Vliederhoven's text. Both pieces were very popular works on the four last things, and both were reprinted a number of times, surviving also in many manuscripts.

Thyrde, The paynes of helle. Fourth, The glorie of heuen. O what thyng is more horrible than dethe. What thyng is more dredefull and terryble than the day of Jugement. What thyng is more Importable to be suffred than the gehenne and paynes of helle. And what is a more Joye full blysse than celestyall glorye. Saynt Bernard sayd in the same sermon, These ben the four wheles of the chare wherof the Remembraunce bryngeth mannes soule to the euerlastyng glorye of paradyse. These ben also iiii. moeuynges that awake the spiryte of man to that ende that he disprayse alle worldly thynges and retorne vnto his creatour and maker. ...

Thus endeth the prologue of this booke named Cordyall. Whiche treateth of the four last and fynall thynges that ben to come. And here begynneth the fyrste parte of the sayd four last thynges

The fyrst parte of the four last thynges. Whereof the remembraunce withdraweth a man fro synne is deth present or temporell. And therefore seyth saynt Bernard in a bok called the Myrour of monkes. The most souerayn phylosophye is to thynke all way on deth. And he that beryth it in his mynde in what place so euer he go shall neuer synne. Saynt Austin sayth in his boke of exortacyons. There is noo thyng that soo well reuoketh and calleth a man from synne as often Remembraunce of dethe; Certayn it is that thynge whiche causeth a man to be humble, to dysprayse hymselfe and to do penaunce.

How Remembraunce of dethe maketh a man to be humble and meke

The first chapitre of the fyrst parte pryncypal

I Say that recordyng the Remembraunce of deth maketh a man to be meke and humble hym selfe. And therfor sayth Saynt Austyn in the book that he made of our lord. A man knowyng himselfe to be mortall. It shal put from hym all maner of pryde. In very trouthe all our other thynges, as well good as badde, be incerteyne. But of deth oonly we maye be well ensured. And how be it that the hour therof to vs is hydde and incerteyn. Yet alway she is approchyng and shal surely come without longe taryeng. And to this purpose sayth Ecclesiastis in his .xiiii. chapitre, Bere well in remembrance that deth shal not tarye. It is also wryten in Thoby[40] that dest hasteth and that there may no fleeng auayle. Also by the comune lawe of nature euery man must paye his mortall trybute. Saynt Bernarde sayth in a sermon, O wretched man why doost thou not dyspose thy selfe to be redy at all houres, thynke that thou arte now dede syns thou knowest well that necessaryly it behoueth the to dye.

40. Thobias.

Remembre wel how thyn eyen shall tourne in thy hede, and the veynes breke in thy body, and thyn herte shal deuyde in two partes by the righte sharpe anguysshe and payne of deth. Who is he thenne that ought not to drede and make hymselfe humble, whan he knoweth certaynely that he must retourne and become erthe. Now truly there shall be none excepcyon of persones. But al shall passe that waye for as it is wryten in the seconde books of kynges. Whe[41] shall all dye and the erthe shall swolowe vs, as it dooth water cast therupon whiche neuer retourneth. We rede also that this worde (Mors) in latyn maye well so be called. For it is a bytter morsell vnto all men in soo moche that no creature maye escape it. And therfore it is sayd in the boke of dyspraysyng of the worlde, Dethe cutteth doun and dystroyeth all thynges create and made in fleshe. She bothe beteth doun the hye men and lowe, for she hath domynacion vpon worldly lyuyng thynges. She regneth Imperyally ouer the nobles and dredeth no lyuyng creature, for her power is comyn ouer prynces and dukes. She taketh aswell the yonge as the olde. And whan she smyteth she hath mercy of no creature. Alle thynges create in flesshe peryssheth vnder her honde. Nor ther be none so stronge but that she beteth them doun without rescuse. And ther is no thynge beryng lyfe but that she destroyeth and wasteth it without onÿ escape. And she neyther taketh mede, allyaunce, ne frendshyp. What shall I more saye, euydently dethe spareth no body. For neyther poore ne ryche shall mowe escape out of her cheyne. Certaynly I vnderstande now that dethe is thende of all worldely lyuynge thynges. And therfore it is wryten in Ietha the Poete. That deth taketh away and dooth anyntyse[42] all quycke thynges. Lo, it is[43] not sayde that the wyse Cathon and the good Socrates ben dede. Whiche gyueth example that there is neyther scyence ne doctryne that may preserue one fro the ruynouse darte of deth. It is writen in Ecclesiastes in the seconde chapitre. As well dyeth the wyse man as the fole. It is wryten in Isaye in the .xxxiii. chapitre. Were are now become the lettred men. Where ben the prechers of the worde of god. Where be they that were wont to teche the childern. These questions implyed as moche as to saye they lyue not and be goon and paste in the comyn course with other and dede of this worlde. Now, by cause Ietha named but only the two afore specyfyed. I praye the tell me, Where is now Hector of Troye, where is become Iulius Cesar, where is Alexander the grete, where is Iudas Machabeus, where is the myghty Sampson. Where is Crassus the riche, where to[44] the fayre Absolon, where is Galyen the physy-

41. "When" is meant here.
42. Expel, destroy, eliminate: *MED* s.v. "anientishen".
43. "Is it" would make more sense here.
44. "Where is" would make more sense here.

cyen and Auycenne his felowe, where is the wyse Salomon, where is Arystocle[45] the phylosopher, and where is Virgyle the right experte poete, be not all these dede and passed out of this worlde as pylgryms and gestes, and departed hens in a right short space; yes, certaynly ther is not one lefte a lyue of them. Al their Ioyes were but vanytees and are fayled, and theyr dayes be consumed and passed. And as the Psalter seyth, man passed his dayes resemblyng a shadowe, and one tyme he is hole and stronge of all his members, and on the morow seke and leyde in the erthe. ... Man is subget vnto deth, oost[46] of the place where he is a voyager passyng, semblably vnto a pece of snowe. Also lyke a reed bery and lyke a newe apple by whiche thynge is euydently shewed how frayle, how sleder,[47] and also how lytyll endurynge is the lyfe of a man. And not oonly the lyf of poure people, But also the lyfe of alle humane creatures, be they neuer so ryche or puyssaunt. For deth is a comyne thynge and spared noo body. And alle be it she is cruwell and peruerse, yet she kepeth egally one lawe in takyng as wel kynges and prynces as poure folkes. ... And where ben the lordes and tyrauntes, Ben not they all consumed and brought to powdreyes of theyr days. And so shall be of oures. Is not theffecte of lyfe altered in to wormes. Beholde and loke in to theyr graues whether thou canste knowe there whiche is the lorde, whiche is the seruaunt, whiche was the poure, whiche was the riche. Dysceuere yf thou can by knowleche the prysoner from the kyng, the stronge from the weke, the fayre from the fowle, Crysostome seyth, what hathe hit auayled them that haue lyued in lechery, and in the voluptuousnesse of this presente lyfe tyll theyr laste dayes. Auyse you now and beholde in theyr sepulcres and see yf thou canste aspye therin ony sygne of pryde, yf thou canste haue ony knowleche of theyr rychesse, or of theyr lecherye. Axe where is become theyr ryche araye and theyr straunge dysguysed garmentes with theyr voluptuous and theyr nyce lookes. And where be also now theyr grette companyes and grete nombre of seruauntes that folowen them. Where be now theyr laughynges, theyr playnges. And theyr outrageous gladnesses out of mesurable temperaunce, where is all this become, and whether is it passed. Beholde dylygently fyrste the ende of one thynge and then of that other, and drawe the nere theyr sepultures. And thou shalt fynde nothynge therin but oonly asshes, and the remanaunte stynkyng and fulle of wormes.

A, remembre thy selfe what is thende of all mortall men, be it so that they haue passed the cours of theyr lyues in delectable pleasures, or elles in labour or in contynence of theyr flesshe yet alll must dye. (Saynt Bernarde) sayth in his

45. Aristotle.
46. Host: *MED* s.v. "hōst(e" n.(2) or "ost(e".
47. "Slender" was most likely intended here.

meditacyons. Tell me nowe where be the Amerouse people of this worlde that late were amonge us. In trouthe there is nothyng lefte of them but asshes and wormes. Thynke thenne and remembre often tymes what thyng they be, and what they haue ben here tofore. Parde,[48] they haue ben men as thou arte, they haue eten and dronken, lawhed and made grete chere in theyr tymes. And after, in a momente they descended in to helle. And after in a momente they descended in to helle. And theyr flesshe delyuered for wormes mete, and theyr soule geuen in to helle; There to be tormented by fyre vnto that the body shall come and Ioyne ageyn there vnto. And to be plonged togyder in thembrachementes[49] or paynfull Iehennes sempyternall[50] with them that haue ben there felawes in doyng synnes and commyttyng vyces withoute repentaunce, penaunce, and satysfaccyon. O, what hath it prouffyted theyr vayne glorye, theyr short Ioye and the puyssaunce of this worlde, the voluptuousnes of the flesshe, the dysceyuable rychesse, the grete nombre of theyr seruauntes, the vnhappy concupyscens; where be theyr playes and, where is theyr bostynge and theyr worldly pryde. The more they had theyr delectacyon and Ioyed ther in here, the more shall be theyr payne and sorowe there. And so after a grete voluptuous pleasyre they shall haue a myserable and a perpetuell paynfull sorowe. And theyr beyng shall tourne them to ruyne and harde tourmentes. Loo, all that is comyn vnto them may happen vnto you. ... O ye myserable synners that suffre the wretchednesse of this presente lyfe to retorne and lede you from the ryghte waye. And the meane tyme ye passe your dayes in makynge good chere ye are descendyng to hell beyng on lyue. And thenne eueryche of you maye saye, the anguysshes of sorowfull dethe haue enuyronned me. And I haue founde my selfe in the peryll of hell. These ben myserable creatures that this presente lyf dysceueth. Of whome is wryten in (Job) the xxi. chapytre. These felowes whoos lyfe is inhaunsed in pompe and pryde and be comforted by theyr rychesse, They thynke that theyr seed shall abyde alwaye by the multytue of theyr frendes and of theyr neyghbours, theyr houses to be alwaye assured and in peas. The rodde of god not to come vpon them, theyr kyen to conceyue and not to be bareyn .... Sothly the riche man that by synne hath deserued the paynes of helle had ben better to haue lyued vertuously in grete nede and pouerte all his lyfe than to haue gret habondaunce of riches and atte laste for his synfull lyfe to be dampned. Alas what proufyteth it thenne the grete tresours and hepes of golde and syluer whan synners shall be sente in to lowe tenebres of helle, there to be payned and tormented euer lastyngly without

48. By God; indeed, in truth; without a doubt, of course: *MED* s.v. "pardẹ̄".

49. Bonds or snares: *MED* s.v."embrăcen".

50. Everlasting, eternal: *MED* s.v. "sempiternăl".

seasynge. My ryght dere broder and frende, what sayst thou of the riche and myghty people of this worlde. Dye they not as well as other; in good fayth me semeth they be noe thynge priuyleged for, as it is wryten in the book of sapience the .vii. chapytre, the entre of this lyfe is one and comune to all, and semblably soo is the Issue. Iob sayth in his .xx. chapytre, This man dyeth stronge, lusty, and riche, his bowelles be full of greece,[51] and his bones full of mery. And this other dyeth lene and feble full of sorowe and withoute ony riches, that notwithstondyng they shall slepe both in powdre, and wormes shall ete them. Loo how the riche and puyssaunt men of this world haue theyr deth comune and egall with the poore people. And therfore it is wryten in (Ecclesiaste) in the .x. chapytre, The lyfe of al puyssant lordship is righte breyf. For this day this man is a kyng and tomorow he is dede; of suche a kyng is red in the seconde chapytre of the fyrst boke of Machabees, how his glory is a foule dounghyll and as vyle as a worme, he is to day enhaunsed and to morowe ther is nothyng to be founde of hym … . Certeynly thenne I now knowe that the yeres that passe taketh from vs all thynges; wherfore, then, yf thou be ryche, stronge, or fayre, what vayleth it yf thou be a bysshop, a priour, or an abbot, what vayleth it yf thou be a grete excellente myghty lord, yf thou be a kynge or a pope, what vayleth it. All passeth right hastly without longe taryeng. And here resteth but oonly the merytes wherof the good shall cause vs to be gloryfyed.

And therfore sayd Isydore in an omely,[52] my right welbeloued bretheren, we oughte to thynke how breef and short is the worldely felycyte, how lytyll is the glorye of this worlde, and how frayle and faylynge is the temporall myght therof. And therfore euery man maye saye where be the kynges, where be the prynces, where be the emperours, where be the riche and myghty men of this worlde; they be all past lyke a shadow, and vanysshed lyke a dreme of the nyght; for though one wolde seke them they wyll not be founde here; what shall I more say; the kynges be passed and the prynces be dede, neuerthelesse there be many that wenen to lyue long and neuer to dye, But alwayes to rest in this present lyfe. Certeynly they be foles. For it shall not be so, But they shall dye as other prynces and men haue done. For as Seneca seyth in his epistles to Lucyll.

The yssue of this present lyfe is deth. It is writen by a poete named Ieta, The deth vndothe all lyuyng thyng, and euery lyfe fynysseth by dethe. Certayn the worldly deth concludeth all the vayn felycytees of men. For yf thou dyde preche the fayth of Abraham, the pyte of Ioseph, The charyte of Moyses, The strengthe of Samson, The swetnesse of Dauyd, The myracles of Elyzeus, The richesse and

51. Melted fat, lard: *MED* s.v. "grēse".

52. Homily.

prudence of kyng Salomon, the beaute of Absolon; And in wepynf[53] occupyed the extremytees of all these in declaryng theyr endes, the hystoryes wolde shewe that there is but one conclusyon. That is to say, deth. Here it appereth righte manyfestly by the thyng a fore sayd that beaute, linage, condycions, wytte, richesse, nor worshyp can not kepe a man but that he must stumble and fall and rotourne to asshes; for all thyng that is engendred renneth alway towarde his deth. Ouyde[54] sayth that all thyng that is engendred asketh and requyreh to come agayne to theyr vnyuersall modre, That is to saye the erthe. For all that hath ben and paste afore maye be resembled to a rennyng ryuer. ... The lyfe of the flesshe is laboure. The concepcyon of the flesshe is but fylthe. The ende therof is rotennesse. And the byrthe is but vyle. ... Consyder than the begynnyng of thy lyfe, the myddle and also the last ende. And thou shalte fynde therin a ryghte grete occasyon and cause to meke and humble thy selfe. Nowe what sayst thou, what thynkest thou, what rekenynge makest thou of thy selfe, arte thou ought but powder of the erth. It is wryten in the .xii. chapytre but more playnly in the .iii. chapytre of the same Ecclesiastes, The powdre recometh to the erthe that it come fro, that is to wete to right a fowle, roten erth full of wormes. And therfore wryteth. Iob in his .xvii. chapytre. I haue sayd to rotennesse, thou art my fader and my moder; and I haue sayd to the wormes, ye be my brethern and my sustres. It is redde in Ecclesiasticus in the xvii chapytre that euery man is erth and asshes, and therof haue take theyr beyng. And also it was sayd to a man, Thou arte but powdre and to powdre shalt retorne. And as Aleyn[55] amonysseth and warneth, the when thou shalte lye in the colde erth, thou shalt torne to powdre and wormes mete, and from thensforth there shall no creature be in wyll to loke vpon the. For thy flesshe shall be more ranke in stynche than the flesshe of a roten hounde. To this purpose sayth the holy man Saynt Bernarde, what is a more vyle and stynkyng thynge than the careyne of man. And what is a more odeous thynge to beholde than a dede man The more delectable he hath been in his lyffe, to the contrarye his loke shalbe horryble after his dethe; what shall it proufyte vs richesses, delectacyons, and worldely worshyppes. The richesse defende vs not from dethe, nor delectacyons from the wormes, nor the worshippes from foule stynkynges. O myghty god eternall, in how myserable chaunce is man inclosed. Certeyne, my righte dere frende, yf thou thoughtest dylygently of the thynges afore sayd, thou sholdest therby fynde a right grete occasyon to meke and humble thyselfe. For Remembraunce of dethe causeth humylyte in man. ... Righte thus passeth the

53. "Wepyng" possibly intended here.

54. Ovid.

55. Possibly Alain de Lille.

vayne glorye of this worlde. Lyke to saye, that as the fyre brenneth lyghtly the flaxe and counerteth hit to asshes. Semblably, the glorye of this worlde fayleth and passeth. ...

10b Simon Birckbek, *A treatise of the four last things, death, judgement, hell and heaven, commonly called the Quatuor novissima. By Simon Birckbek Bachelor in Divinity, sometime fellow of Queens College in Oxford, and now minister of Gods word at Gilling in Richmondshire*, 1655, pp. 6–7, 14–20.[56] *Wing*, 2nd ed. B2946. **Source** *EEBO*: British Library, London (E.1460[2]).

Section I
Of Death, and the large extent thereof
... Here we are differenced, as it were, by divers Liveries, some high, some low, some rich, some poor, some private, some common men, some Patricians, some Plebeians; there's no such Heraldry in the Grave, in the Land of silence whether we are going, all these Titles are quite forgotten. Chessemen are distinguished upon the boord whilest the game is playing, but being done, they are tumbled into the bagge without order. In the grave, there, great and small meet together, and there (as *Job* speaks) *the servant is free from his master*, free among the dead, as free as his master. Plowmen there are full Compeers to Princes, and the Spade there may challenge precedence to the Scepter.

And this according to *Job's* drawing up of our Pedigree; *we may say to corruption, thou art my father, and to the Worm, thou art my mother, and my sister*. In the grave the rich and the poor meet together, and within a few years after, a man shall not be able to discern between the shoulder blade of the one and the other.

The *Saladine* on his death-bed, gave charge, that his inner garment should be fastned to a spear, and born Ensign-wise, at his Funerall, and a Herald to proclaim, *This shroud is all that Saladine Conqueror of the East carries away with him*. We brought nothing hither, and we must carry nothing with us but our winding sheet, yea, rather that must carry us.

Death and diseases know no faces, or rather dicern all faces, whatsoever mask or vizour they put on. There was one turned grey, and to seem young and fresh coloured his hair black; but Death told him she would not be so cousned.[57] *Non omnes fallis, scit te Proserpina canum*.[58] Death commands in chief, is master of the

56. Marginal notes in the original source were not included in the transcription.
57. Tricked or deceived (a spelling of "cozen").
58. A quotation from Martial's *Epigrams*.

field, admits no parley, gives no quarter, takes no truce. There was an old souldier had done good service to his Lord; and falling sick, his Lord coming to visit him, asked him, what he would have him do for him. Nothing, Sir (said he) but to take truce for me with Death for a day or two. Alas (said he), that's not in my power. Why then, said the sick-man, I do vow and promise to him who is able to do this for me, that if he free me at this time from the stroak of Death, I will henceforth serve him alone, all my life long; and so he did.

Death commands all Arts and Sciences, there's no Grammar can rule it, no Physick cure it, no Rhetoric perswade it.

St Hierom saith, *Aristotelis argumenta non proderunt,* it is not *Platoes* Ideas, nor *Aristotles* Eleuchs, or Topick places can void the common Plea of Death, or stay Judgment; there's a Writ of *Diem claufit extremum,* and another *Ad audiendum Judicium,* will be returned upon all flesh; and there's no Sophistry can elude their process. ...

Sect. III

Our mortality must be minded, and means and helps used to minde us of it. And the great benefit thereby.

It were fit we took Death into consideration, inasmuch as not Christians only but the wiser Heathen did so. They had their Remembrancers who called on them in their beds, at their boards, in the midst of their Feasts, in their greatest jollities, to put them in minde of their mortality. *Philip of Macedon* had a Page who came to him every morning with this *memento, Philip, remember thy self that thou art a mortall man.* The old *Romans* whilest they rode through the streets in triumph, had one who bad them look behind them, and remember that they were but men. The *Aegyptians* at their Feasts and Banquets caused the Anatomy of a dead man to be brought before them; *Hierom* set a dead mans skull before himself daily. The old Anchorites and Recluses scraped daily some part of their graves with their nails, they tell us, that *Sancta Francisca* of *Rome* made her a cup of a dead mans skull to drink in, to allay the pleasure of the liquor, and to minde her Death. *Joseph of Arimathea* made his Tomb in his Garden, to put him (in all likelihood) in minde of Death even in the midst of his pleasures and delights. And some at this day wear a Seal Ring with a Deaths Head cut in it, with the Motto of *Memento mori.* And there is a Story of one that gave a young Prodigall a Ring with a Deaths head carved thereon, upon condition that he should every day for the space of an hour, seven daies together, look thereon, and think upon it, and this bred a strange alteration in his life.

Some may (haply[59]) think it a melancholy Subject to muse and meditate on Death and Mortality. But, there's great benefit thereby if we hold on out thoughts upon our ending day. The flight of a Bird is directed by her train, the course of a Ship is steered by the Helm, and our life is better ordered by the serious apprehension of our end.

There is much evil prevented thereby, and much good gotten thereby.

The serious thoughts of Death tyes a man to good behaviour. When *Job* presents to himself the thought of his Death, it made him husht and quiet, he durst not contest with an underling and inferionr.[60] But when that is out of a mans thoughts, he is like an evil Servant in the Parable, when he thought his Master was gone far off, then he laies about him, distempers himself, and beats his fellow-servants, like the lewd woman in the *Proverbs,* when the good man is not at home but gone a long journey, she grows wanton and secure; so fares it with such as put farre away the evil day, such as make (in their own conceit) a League or a Covenant with death, whereas if they thought seriously of death, it would fright them out of a sinfull course of life; then would the Swearer think, Death may seize on me whilst the Oath is in my mouth. The drunkard would fear lest Death should come between the cup and the Lip, as it did to *Belshazzar,* and then what shal become of my poor soul?

The thought of Death weans us from doting on the world, we use it as though we used it not, and for then we see we must part with it, and Death takes all away, friends and acquaintance, houses, Lands, and possessions, honours and Offices, the pleasures and comforts of this life, that when the soul departs it carriers nothing away with it but grace, Gods favour, and a good conscience, so as now we become *mundo mortui, We are crucified to the World and the World to us.* We are no more affected therewith then a dead man is taken with the pleasures of this life.

The frequent thoughts of mortality acquaints us with death. They say that he which sees the Basilisk before he ben seen of it, prevents and avoids the poison of that Serpent. He that minds death often is forewarned, and forewarned forearmed. Prævision is the best prevention, and præmonition the best præmunitioa, Death steals not on such at unawares. He that manages an horse at an armed stake fits him to rush into the main battle without fear. He that with *Joseph of Arimathea* walks every day a turn or two with Death in his Garden, he grows acquainted with it. We see that savage Beasts, as Lions and Bears are not terrible to such as converse with them, no more is death to such as can protest with *St Paul* that they *die daily,* they daily prepare themselves for it. ...

59. The "a" is printed upside down.

60. Inferiour.

The thought of Death serves to patient a mans heart in the midst of his pressures, for then he thinks with himself, I shall be shortly called hence, I am troubled and wronged here, I shall be righted and quiet there; I am ill at ease now, I shall be well anon, *Nubecula est, cito transivit,* as Athanasius said of his troubles, this Cloud will soon be overblown. I am now drawing on a pace to my dissolution, hold out faith and patience, your work will speedily be at an end. ...

Let us consider how Death steals on us too. *Solomon* tells us, that *evil daies will come,* and cloud will follow upon cloud, and then the keepers of the House (the hands) will wax feeble; The pillars of the house (the legges and thighs) will wax faint and weak; Those that look out at the windows (the eyes) will be dark and duskish. Then all the daughters of musick (the ears) they will begin to wax thick too heavy, and so of the rest. Then reflect upon thy self, and say, Death is already in mine eye, in mine ear, I begin to be dim-sighted, and thick of hearing, in my limbs and joynts, they begin to be lazy, stiff and cold. Let the whitenesse of our hairs, the weaknesse of our joints, and the wrinkles in our face be as *Job* speaks, as so many witnesses of our approaching mortality.

Well then, if thou hast received the Advertisements and Summons of Death, fliegh them not, but take special notice thereof. For when these Harbingers and forerunners appear, the King of terrours is not far off. When those Messengers appear, the sound of their Masters feet (as *Elijah* said) is behind them. Prepare thy self too meet these Ushers of Death, but be not afraid of this King of terrours, this King of Fear, as *Lewis* the eleventh was, who straightly charged his servants that when they saw him sick they should never once dare to name that bitter word Death in his ears. But do thou think about Death, think of it by thy self alone, think what it is to die, think what treads on the heels of it when thou art gone. A judgement and doom, and that judgement so straight as the righteous shall scarce escape it, so heavy as the mightiest shall not endure it. Consider I say by thy self, what it is to die, consider with other folk, be ready to speak of it, and to minde both thy self and others of mortality. Lord teach us by the short span of our life to number our daies, that thereby in the reminder thereof we may apply our hearts unto wisedom.

11a *Here begynneth a lityll treatise shorte and abredged spekynge of the arte and crafte to knowe well to dye,* trans. William Caxton (1490). **11b** Nicolas Bernard, *The penitent death of a woefull sinner* (1642).

Introduction Books on *ars moriendi,* the art of dying well, were a popular late medieval genre that remained widely read in the early modern period. While related to texts on the four last things and the work of Denis the Carthusian,[61] the genesis of this genre dates back to Jean Gerson's early fifteenth-century *Ars Moriendi* which focused on the deathbed struggle between good and evil for the soul of the dying, with the Devil (or devils) tempting the dying soul into submission to a final sin, and angels, or saints, or the Virgin Mary trying to save the dying person's soul. Gerson's original work, considered to be the founding text of this genre, was printed by William Caxton in translation in 1490, and gave rise to a large number of other texts either directly inspired by Gerson's work, or only loosely based on it, printed throughout the late Middle Ages and after the Reformation.[62] Many of these works, apart from narrating the battle between the devils and the forces of good for the soul of the dying sinner, also contained often lengthy descriptions of how to prepare oneself for death in a way that would prevent yielding to the temptations of fear and the devil in the final hour, how to meditate on one's mortality, how to find consolation in death, and how to navigate fear so as to benefit from it, not giving in to despair. Hope, stalwartness, contemplation, and patience were recommended as wards against despair and ungodly anxiety, and along with directions on how to "die well," i.e., how to prepare oneself for death, were popular and recurring features of post-Reformation *ars moriendi* manuals.[63] The tradition flourished well into the seventeenth century, finding a receptive Protestant audience, with numerous texts on dying well circulating both among Protestants and non-Protestants of early modern England, with such works as Thomas Becon's *Sick mannes salve* (1561), Christopher Sutton's *Disce Mori* (1600) or Jeremy Taylor's *Holy living and holy dying* (1650) among many others.

Caxton's translation of Gerson's work, the *Lityll treatise shorte and abredged spekynge of the arte and crafte to knowe well to dye* (1490), while it belongs to the *ars moriendi* genre and provides prescriptions on how to die well, has also a distinctive focus on death itself, and the fear and anxiety that it gives rise to. It focuses on guiding its reader through the process of death in order to have a well-planned passing that would benefit the soul in the afterlife. It is primarily concerned with arranging the soul's smooth participation in what the text describes as an elaborate spectacle and performance of dying, involving not only the person about to pass but also their family, priest, and possibly also friends or members of their community, as well as, of course, angels and devils. It is also a manual of prayers and considerations that will appease the fear of dying and, as the text vouches, when all the offered directions are performed as suggested, the reader is guaranteed to be

61. Carlos M.N. Eire, "Early Modern Catholic Piety in Translation," in *Cultural Translation in Early Modern Europe*, ed. Peter Burke and R. Po-chia Hsia (Cambridge, 2007), 83–100, at 87.

62. Peter Marshall, "Angels Around the Deathbed," in *Angels in the Early Modern World*, ed. Peter Marshall and Alexandra Walsham (Cambridge, 2006), 83–103, at 86.

63. Helen Cooper, "The Afterlife of Personification," in *Medieval Shakespeare: Pasts and Presents*, ed. Ruth Morse, Helen Cooper, and Peter Holland (Cambridge, 2013), 113–116.

able to "tame" death, or at least the fear of death, and to pass so smoothly as to awe the gathered audience. The *Lityll treatise* is divided into six parts, first focusing on the praise of death and on dying gladly, the second on temptations awaiting the dying, the third on questions to be considered when dying, the fourth giving instructions and teachings on what to remember on the deathbed, the fifth providing a remembrance of the Passion, with the sixth containing a set of prayers to be said to, and by, the dying. All in all, it is a concise manual resembling a script that provides both instructions on how to deal with each stage of dying, and methods of achieving consolation in its commendation of dying gladly, as well as various prayers and considerations that are to elevate the spirit.

The Protestant Nicolas Bernard's *The penitent death of a woefull sinner* (1642) is as much a work on death as it is a political pro-episcopalian work attempting to redeem a bit of the reputation of John Atherton, a bishop in the Church of Ireland convicted and executed for "buggery" (homosexuality), whose "sins of the flesh" provided opponents of episcopacy with arguments against it.[64] For this reason, Bernard's text is on the one hand a very thorough and spectacular description of a good death, as it is through such a death that he believed Atherton could be redeemed (and so also the cause of episcopacy could be as well); on the other it is also an interesting example of a criminal conversion narrative.[65] In such narratives, a convicted criminal not only confessed his sins and returned in his heart and soul to Christ, but also converted to the specific branch of Protestantism that was, most often, the denomination of those who either convicted him, or wished to use his execution for polemical purposes (in this case, Bernard and his pro-episcopacy camp).[66] *The penitent death of a woefull sinner* is therefore a work which, relying on the staples of traditional *ars moriendi*, provides also a polemical twist on the importance of dying gladly and remorsefully, drawing particular attention to tears and weeping as a sign of true remorse, and providing consolation to its readers in that it indicates that even the most horrendous sinner can die a good death. Thus, both Caxton's *Lityll treatise* and Nicolas Bernard's *The penitent death of a woefull sinner* treat a good death as a kind of a performance, in which adherence to the rules of the performance has beneficial effects on both the dying, and those witnessing the death. However, Caxton's text is con-

64. John McCafferty, "Irish Bishops, Their Biographers and the Experience of Revolution, 1656–1686," in *The Experience of Revolution in Stuart Britain and Ireland*, ed. Michael J. Braddick and David L. Smith (Cambridge, 2011), 253–269, at 261.

65. For more on this subject see, for example, Peter Lake and Michael Questier, *The Antichrist's Lewd Hat: Protestants, Papists, and Players in Post-Reformation England* (New Haven, CT, 2002), throughout, esp. Section II. See also Katherine Royer, *English Execution Narrative 1200–1700* (London, 2014).

66. For more on Nicolas Bernard's text, see Peter Marshall, *Mother Leakey and the Bishop: A Ghost Story* (Oxford, 2007), Chapter 5.

fined to the private sphere of home in which the dying person is surrounded by family, friends, and neighbours, whereas Bernard's work is an example of a good public death, one beneficial to a particular confession, or cause, and so does not focus on the internal peace of the dying soul but rather on the highlights of the performance as it was seen from the outside, by its audience.

11a *Here begynneth a lityll treatise shorte and abredged spekynge of the arte and crafte to knowe well to dye*, trans. William Caxton, Westminster, 1490; unnumbered pages. *STC* 789. **Source** *EEBO*: British Library, London (C.11.C.8.).

Whan it ys soo that what a man maketh or doeth, it is made to come to some ende. And yf the thynge be goode and well made, it muste nedes come to goode ende. Thenne by better and gretter reason euery man oughte to entende in suche wyse to lyue in this worlde in kepynge the commaundementes of god, that he may come to a goode ende. And that oute of this worlde full of wretchedness and tribulacyons he may goo to heuen vnto god and his seyntes, in to Joye perdurable. ...

Of the allowynge or praysynge of the dethe and how[67] *one ought gladly for to deye*
As thenne the bodyli deth is the most ferfull thing of all other thinges, soo yet is the deth of the soule of as moche more terryble and reprouchable, as the soule is more noble and more precyous than the body. And the deth of synners is ryghte cursyd and euyll, but the deth of iuste and true people is precious to fore god, for the ded men ben well happy that dye in our lorde. To this purpose sayth Plato, the contynuell remembraunce of the deth is souerayn wysedom. Also for trouth, the bodyli deth of good people alleweye is none other thinge but the yssue or goynge oute of pryson, ande of exyle and dyschargynge of a ryghte greuouse burthen. that is to wyte of the body fynisshynge of all thinges, and ende of all maladyes and sekenesses, and also of all other stryues mortall. Is it thauoydynge[68] of this present wretchidnesse, it is consumpcyon of all euyllis, and the breakynge of all bondes of this cursid and euyll worlde. It is the payment of the dette of

67. Part of the title between "dethe" and "one" is illegible under the stamp, but a 1972 Oxford University PhD dissertation by G.R. Morgan ("A Critical Edition of Caxton's *The art and craft to know well to die* and *Ars moriendi* Together with the Antecedent Manuscript Material," https://ora.ox.ac.uk/objects/uuid:ba4eb789-b9cc-49c5-8bcc-f22542 1fc77c), which includes a transcription of this text from a copy at the British Library, reads "and how" in the illegible part of this *EEBO* copy.

68. Perhaps "the voiding"? I am grateful to Winston Black for the suggestion.

nature, retourne in to the countree, and entree in to ioye and glorye. Therfore sayth the wyseman that the daye of the deth is better than the daye of the byrthe. But this worde oughte to be vnderstande for theym that be goode onely.

And therefore euery goode crysten man and also eueryche synner verily contrite oughte not to be sorowfull ne trouble hym of the temporall or bodyly deth, ne he oughte not to fere ne doubte hit. For what some euer mater or cause be layd to hym, but he oughte to suffre and receyue it pacyently, and in thankis, and gladly in confermyng him selfe playnli; And in comyttynge hooly his proper wyll to goddys wylle, like as he is bounden to hym.

For well to deye is gladly to deye: and to conne dye is to haue in all tymes his herte redy and appareysed to thynges heuenly and supernall. And that at euery houre whan the deth shall come to the persone that he be founde redy and that he receyue it with out ony contradiccyon, but also ioyully as he shold abide the comynge of his good frende. To this purpose sayth the philosopher that naturel reason well conseyllyd iudgeth that the goode deth ought better to be chosen that the euyl lyfe. And that one ought sonner to chose the bodily deth that doo ony thyng ayenst the wele of vertue. Thus then it appereth of the praysing of the deth. And that euery good persone and religyous ought to desire departyng of the body and the soule. For to be wyth our lord Iesu cryste, and for to leue this present worlde for the better to lyue in the world to come.

11b Nicolas Bernard, *The penitent death of a woefull sinner. Or, the penitent death of John Atherton, Late Bishop of Waterford in Ireland. Who was executed at Dublin the 5. of December. 1640. With some Annotations upon severall passages in it. As also the sermon, with some further Enlargements, preached at his Buriall. The Second Edition. By Nicholas Barnard Deane of Ardagh in Ireland*, 1642, pp. 171–179.[69] *Wing*, 2nd ed. B2015. **Source** Thomas Fisher Rare Book Library, University of Toronto (B13 05376).

... To conclude, how can it be, but a joyfull estate, when a Man is assured his sinnes are forgiven. If we consider it in these three things: *Hee hath peace with God*. Peace of *Conscience*. Peace with *Death*. The two latter are consequences of the first. ...

2. Hee hath peace of *Conscience*. The *Earth* no outward weight can moove, yet the stirring of a few unruly vapours within, will make some parts to *quake*. There are some men no *outward* Crosses can trouble, but the guilt of some *secret*

69. Marginal notes in the original source were not included in the transcription.

sinnes within hath made them tremble. The soule of a wicked man is often like *a troubled Sea,* or like *the Ship in a storme* the Disciples were tossed in, but as soone as Christ entred, there was *a calme.* So as soone as the Conscience is possest of Christ, there is peace. Some when they are *disquieted* in their mindes doe as *David* wished he could doe (Psalm. 55:7) *When fearefulnesse and horrour overwhelmed* him, *Oh, that I had wings like a dove, then would flie away and be at rest,* Goe travell, as if they would out ride the crie of Conscience which they carry with them. Some send for *Musicke,* as *Saul* for a *Harper* when his *evill spirit* came upon him. Others deale with their Consciences, that thus arrest them in Gods name, as some have done with the *Serjeant,* make him *Drunke,* and so escape him. These wayes and the like had this our *Brother* tryed formealy, but found no found [*sic*] peace, till he thus turned to Christ, *the Prince* of it. The *Marriners* in that mighty tempest rowed hard to get the Ship to land, but no means would doe, till *Ionas was cast out,* and then presently *the Sea ceased from her raging.* I have beene a witnesse of *strong tempests* raysed within his Conscience when he first grew sensible, but after he had *disburdn'd it,* and out with those *pressing* sins in such salt and overflowing teares, in Confession and Repentance, he soone found the fruit of *that* call of our Saviour: *Come unto me you that are weary and heavy laden, and I will give you rest.* Having like *Noah's* Dove *strayed* from the *Arke* of Christ, hee found no rest for the feete of his Soule, till he returned to Christ againe. 'Tis a usuall division of these foure sorts of Consciences, *a quiet but not a good, neyther good nor quiet, a good but not a quiet, both good and quiet.* The two former he had experience of in his life, the two latter neere his death, the *misery* of the one, and the *happinesse* of the other (which he had so lately exchanged); how sensibly have I heard him expresse, apprehending in the *deepest* degree of his humiliation, more true content, than in the height of all his sinfull pleasures. *Chrysostome* cals the Conscience *Gods Coine,* wherein as the Kings *Image* is in his, so is *Gods* instamped in this. And therefore as we give that which *is Cesars to Cesar,* so hee exhorts, to give this which *is Gods to God*: and a *good Conscience before God and man,* 'tis the richest pearle, the most invalueable treasure under Heaven. *S. Pauls glory* and *joy* (1 Cor 1:12, Act. 23:1).

3. *Thirdly,* he hath peace *with Death*; a *Bee* without her *sting* is more feared than hurtfull. 'Tis so with this, once freed from the guilt of sinne, *the sting* of it. Hee that knowes he owes nothing, flies not the aproach of the Bayliffe. He that is assured of the *blotting out of the handwriting that was against him* needs not to shun the arrest of death. Be it *sudden,* yet 'tis no *untimely* to him. What a *measure* of this Christian valour was found in this our *Brother* after this spirituall sealing, hath been manifested *before many witnesses,* and needs not any repetition here.

Onely observe what this blessed change *in him* had wrought in others *of him*. Hee once wept much by himself *in private*, when the tongues of men with good cause were open against him in *publike*. Now *teares* of all sorts are shed for him *publikely*, when hee had *Comforts* within himself *secretly*. Hee that was *hated* at his *Condemnation*, is *lov'd* at his *Execution*. Such as were *griev'd* at his *life*, are *comforted* at his *Death*. He *began* with his *owne* teares, he *departs* with the *sobs of others*. And I doubt not, but what hee *sowed* in teares, hee *reapes* in joy, what was *seal'd* here on Earth, is *ratified* in Heaven. From a *Death* temporall hee is passed to a *life* eternall, Vnto which God of his mercie bring us all, for the merites of *his deare Sonne. To whom with the Father and the holy Spirit be all honour, and glory now and evermore. Amen.*

Spiritual Health

CONFESSION AND CONTRITION

12a William Lichfield, *The remors of conscience* (1510). **12b** Christopher Love, *The penitent pardoned* (1657).

Introduction Contrition and confession were some of the most important and widely covered subjects related to Christian penance and penitence in the Middle Ages. Numerous theological texts explored the intricacies of penance, and the requirement of auricular confession brought penitence into the foreground of lay devotional experiences. In the vernacular, texts such as the fourteenth-century *Prick of conscience* made individual meditation on sin and personal experiences of contrition one of the main interests of lay readers: musing on one's sinfulness evoked true contrition, which texts such as the *Weye of paradis* (ca. 1400) argued were indispensible to obtaining God's forgiveness.

William Lichfield, a poet and clergyman, was a famous London preacher who, according to Thomas Gascoigne, left behind over three thousand English sermons after his death in 1448.[1] Apart from his pastoral prowess, he was also noted for his poetry, as his verse *The complaynt of God to sinful man and the answer of man* and *Dialogue of the Passion between God and the penitent soul* were not only copied a number of times in manuscript form[2] but were also later printed at least three times by Wynkyn de Worde, in 1510, 1515, and 1534, although the printed editions are deficient, lacking a few leaves.[3]

1. R.M. Ball, "Lichefeld, William (d. 1448), preacher and author," in *Oxford Dictionary of National Biography* online (Oxford, 2004), https://doi.org/10.1093/ref:odnb/16638, last updated 25 September 2014.

2. Now Cambridge, Gonville and Caius College, 174, ff. 469–482. Lambeth Palace Library holds two fifteenth-century copies: London, Lambeth Palace Library, 306 and 853; see *Political, Religious, and Love Poems*, ed. F.J. Furnivall (London, 1866), 169–203.

3. See also Dennis Everard Rhodes, "The Remorse of Conscience," *Library* 13 (1958): 199–200, for more on this text. For an edition of London, Lambeth Palace 306 and 853, *The Complaynt of God* as *Christ's Own Complaint, "Man Make Amendis or Þou Die" (Otherwise Called the Remorse of Conscience)*, see *Political, Religious, and Love Poems*, ed. Furnivall, 169–203; this text is considerably longer than the early print version used here.

The text below, from de Worde's first printed edition of *The remors of conscience*, is most likely a printed version of *The complaynt of God*, although the title de Worde chose suggests also some affinity with the *Dialogue of the Passion between God and the penitent soul*, and bears also a clear resemblance to the *Prick of conscience*. The 1510 text, just as its fifteenth-century original version, is also related to *ars moriendi* texts in that it narrates a dialogue between a dying sinner and God, with the sinner asking for mercy and God calling on the sinner to repent. The sinner mourns the sins committed in his lifetime and appeals to Christ and his Passion as a source of mercy in order to beg forgiveness and attain salvation in the face of sudden death, for which the sinner could not prepare properly.[4] What the sinner is offered in return, however, is neither a simple assurance of mercy and salvation, nor straightforward forgiveness. In the dialogue, *Deus* rebukes the sinner for his sins and omissions, and is rather more of an angry God than the sinner would have perhaps wished to encounter; *Deus* is offended and angered with the sins of the dying soul. Captured within a moment not unlike the plot of the morality play *Everyman*, *The remors of conscience* follows this conversation until the sinner seems to understand the need for virtue and remorse, and God seems appeased, leading to the consoling conclusion that even though death may be sudden and unexpected there is always time to repent and make amends for sin. The dialogue is thus reminiscent also of confession in that it is a dialogue of chastisement and apology for sin, between the highest confessor of the soul, God, and the sinner, in accordance with the late medieval conviction that confession should be made to God in the heart and spirit (and only then verbalized in front of a priest).[5] *The remors of conscience*, then, leads its readers through a meditative dialogue with God that provides a recipe for reconciliation and comfort.

In the early modern period, with penance deprived of its sacramental status, contrition and confession became much more complicated, and there was no longer any guarantee that even the most genuine contrition would persuade God to forgive the sinner's misdoings, at least to Calvinists. Nevertheless, multiple Protestant texts explored the

4. Cecilia A. Hatt, *English Works of John Fisher, Bishop of Rochester: Sermons and Other Writings 1520 to 1535* (Oxford, 2002), 353–354.

5. Penance and confession were complicated subjects in late medieval England, with generally two approaches as often clashing as coexisting: the lenient approach represented by, for example, John Burgh, or John Mirk, which encouraged the deepening of the private dimensions of penance and minimized recommendations for clerical severity; and the assumption that penance should be harsh and the priest punishing, as suggested by, for example, Jean Gerson, or William Lyndwood, which encouraged the interrogative, inquisitional role of the priest during confession. For more on the subject of late medieval confession, see, for instance, *The New History of Penance*, ed. Abigail Firey (Leiden, 2008); *Handling Sin: Confession in the Middle Ages*, ed. Peter Biller and A.J. Minnis (York, 1998); Jonathan Hughes, "The Administration of Confession in the Diocese of York in the Fourteenth Century," in *Studies in Clergy and Ministry in Medieval England*, ed. David M. Smith (York, 1991), 87–154.

issues of contrition and confession, both theologically and practically, not necessarily to persuade their readers about the efficacy of penance in absolving sin (which to most Protestants was a despicable and popish hope), but for consolation. The Presbyterian Christopher Love's *The penitent pardoned* (1657, orig. 1649) is, indeed, focused on confession as a means of achieving spiritual consolation. In particular, much like Lichfield's text, though for different reasons and in a different style, Love's text is interested in private confession to God which he discusses in contrast to the Roman Catholic version of confession, clearly distinguishing his Protestant approach by frequently comparing it to what he deems "popish." Thus, carefully navigating doctrinal complexities, Love's text assures the sinner that confession to God leads to peace of mind and heart. At the same time, though, in his echo of approaches to confession by John Calvin, Richard Baxter, and Thomas Hooker, Love does not avoid the problem of repeating many pre-Reformation directions on confession.

This includes William of Auvergne's rather memorable metaphor of the purging effects of confession as "vomit," (from his *De Sacramentis*, ca. 1228) used by many Protestants, such as Richard Baxter. Indeed, William of Auvergne's apt statement that confession "is a vomiting of necessary and healthy purgation, and spiritual emptying. If anyone asks why this vomiting should happen, I answer that it comes from the filth in which you wallow,"[6] found its way almost literally to Baxter's *Right method for a settled peace of conscience* (1653). There, Baxter writes that "The Vomit of Confession must work to the bottom and fetch up that hidden sin, which is it that continueth your Calamity. Read Mr, T. Hooker ... who shews you the danger of not going to the bottom" (*Method*, 512).[7] Thomas Brooks' 1652 *Precious remedies against Satan's devices* also speaks of repentance as "the vomit of the soul; and of all purgatives, none so difficult and hard as it is to vomit" (*Precious remedies*, 36); similarly, Love uses the metaphor of confession as vomit on page 6 of his work (see below). Other examples of pre-Reformation directions and practices on confession also made their way to Protestant texts, including Love's. In his discussion of private confession, Love, like many other Protestant divines (including Calvin himself in later editions of his *Institutes*), ultimately defends confessing to a clergyman "if need be," and gives proof of the inheritance of "earlier and recurrent debates over the role of confessors and penitents, the place of the rite in Christian life, and the nature of Christian penitential theology,"[8] including debates from before the Reformation, which esca-

6. Lesley Smith, "William of Auvergne on Confession," in *Handling Sin*, ed. Biller and Minnis, 95–109, at 96.

7. Similarly, Thomas Adams advises vomit of repentance for usury (*The Soul's Sickness*, 1629, 23).

8. Paul D. Steigner, *Confession and Memory in Early Modern English Literature: Penitential Remains* (New York, 2015), 174–175.

lated after 1517. In other words, Love's careful Protestantism allowed him to weave an admirable defence of Protestant ideas on confession, but also revealed the underlying old uncertainties about the role of the clergyman and the merits of confessing to another, apart from the internal confession to God, that troubled Christian theologians at least since the twelfth century. *The penitent pardoned* contains instructions on proper confession and, while not focusing on an angry God, impresses on its readers that only a genuine reckoning of one's conscience leads to true reconciliation with God. Thus differing in many respects, these two texts are a good comparison of approaches to private confession to God and consolation that the sinner should draw from their dialogue with God, each text contextualized by contemporary pastoral and confessional polemics.

12a William Lichfield, *The remors of conscyence. Here begynneth certayne demonstracyons by our lorde to all synfull persones with the remors of mannes conscynce to the regarde of the bounte of our lorde*, 1510; unnumbered pages. *STC* 20881.3. **Source** *EEBO:* Cambridge University Library (Sel. 5.6).

Deus.
Our gracyous god moost in magnyfycence
His mercyfull eyen casteth from heuen on hy
Seynge his creatures in deedly vyolence
Hymselfe complayneth by pyte full ruthfully
Saynge, o man deuoyde of intellygence
Open thyn eeres vnto my call and cry
And tell me yf I haue done to the offence
That thou forsakest my wyllyngly
Man suche a loue to the I dyde take
This world in seuen dayes whan I it wrought
Thou was the last thynge that I dyd make
Bycausė I wolde thou wanted nought
... But vnto this takest thou none entente
Thou tournest fro me full vnkyndly
On loues vnlefull thy loue is lente
Thy herte beholdeth not heuen so hye
For all the goodes I haue the sente
The lysteth not ones to saye gramercye
In tyme to come or thou repente
Man make amendes or that thou dye.

Homo.
A crysten soule conceyued in synne
Receyued in conscyence thus complaynynge
He fell downe flatte with dolefull dynne
And sayd lorde mercy souerayne kynge
I moost vnkynde wretche of man kynne
I knowe I am thy traytour vntrue in my lyuynge
This wycked lyfe that I lyue in
I may it nought hyde from thy knowynge
I want wordes and also wytte
Of thy kyndnesse to speke a clause
That I haue thou gaue me it
Of thy goodnes withouten cause
Though I haue greued the and do yet
Thy benefaytes thou nought withdrawse
I haue deserued to haue hell pytte
So haue I lyued ayenst thy lawse
But lorde thou knowest mannes feblenesse
How frayle it is and hath ben aye
For though the soule haue thy lykenesse
Man is but fulsome erth and claye
In synne conceyued and wretchednesse
And to the soule rebell alwaye
Fyrst a man groweth as dooth gresse
And he wasteth after as floures or haye
Syth man is than so frayle a thynge
And thy power so grete in kynde
This worlde is but a twynkelynge
Thou mayst destroye the myght of the fynde
With thy ryght lorde mercy mynge
And to my sore salue thou fende
Sore me repenteth of my myslyuynge
Mercy lorde I wyll amende.

Deus.
Man I gaue the bodyly hele
That thou sholde it spende in my seruyce
Fayrenes also and fetures fele

Man what doost thou with all thyse
Thou with delytes of the deuyll doost dele
Whiche is to me a grete despyse
Thou lyuest a lecherous lyfe vnlele
Fro yere to yere thou lyst not ryse
Thou studyest after nyce araye
And makest grete cost on thy clothynge
To make the semely as who sholde saye
Thou coudest amende my makynge
Thou purposest the daye by daye
To set my people in synnynge
Thy wretched wyll thou folowest alwaye
What ende synne hathe thou thynkest no thynge
In Noes tyme bycause of synne
And for lecherye in especyall
What vengeaunce came than to mannes kynne
Saue .viii. persones drowned were all
On sodome and gomor and the men within
How I made fyre and brymstone fall
Fro heuen on them that bode therin
For synne were destroyed bothe grete and small
Man wenest thou my myght be lesse
Than it was than or that elles I
Thou hast no as moche wyckdnesse
As whan I smote the moost pyteously
But yf thou wyll thy fautes redresse
Though I now spare for my mercy
Man thynke on my ryghtwysnesse
And make amendes or that thou dye.

Homo.
I wote well lorde ryghtfull thou arte
And that synne must be punysshed nede
But one thynge holdeth in hope my herte
Thy mercy passeth my mysdede
I know well that I may not sterte
I haue so done me ought to drede
With beaute and with bodely quarte

To serue the I haue taken no hede.
I haue myspended my yonge age
In synne and wantonnesse also
To serue god slowe and loued to rage
A gloton, a lechour I was bothe two
I am worth none other wage
But for to dwell in endlesse woo
... And through thy grace I am not agast
What sore and sekenesse on me sene
To suffre whyle my lyfe may last
For vtterly I wyll attende
To punysshe that I haue trespast
Mercy Ihesu I wyll amende.

Deus.
Man I haue sente the syluer and golde
And all thy welth within thy wone
To susteyne the and thy housholde
And also other many one
Thou myght haue holpen yonge and olde
That ben deseased and woo begone
My seruauntes suffred bothe hungre and colde
Relefe of the yet haue they none
If thou gyue for my loue a farthynge
Thou doost it with an heuy herte
In almesse thou gyuest no thynge
For drede thou fall in pouerte
In flesshely lust and worldly lykynge
What euer thou wastest, mery thou arte
Of suche I wyll haue a rekenynge
... A clene conscyence shall that daye
More profyte the and more set by
Than all the goodes or the monaye
Than euer was vnder heuen or skye.
It wyll neuer helpe to plete[9] nor praye
For as ryghtwyse than deme wyll I

9. Plead a cause: *MED* s.v. "plēten".

And therfore man whyles thou maye
Make amendes or that thou dye.

Homo.
I wote well lorde fro yere to yere
Full greatly greued I the haue
That I wolde nor they mercy were
My mothers wombe had be my graue
For what profyteth my lyuynge here
But afterwarde I sholde be saue
But Ihesu as thou bought me dere
Leue not my soule in hell caue
My waste expense I wyll withdrawe
For waste well called maye it be
For it was spended my boost to lawe.
... Had I it spente in goddes seruyce
But thorugh they grace lorde I am in drede
As men that lyeth and may not ryse
For haue I and myn all our nede
With the remenaunt lorde at thy deuyse
The poore and naked with cloth and fere
Seke men that lyen in goddes bandes
That haue no syluer for to spende
And prysoners bounde bothe fete and handes
Ofte to vysyte and them attende
Whan I se them that in nede standes
Suche as I haue I shall them sende
Lorde let these werkes lesse my bande
And mercy Ihesu I wyll amende.

Deus.
Man yf thou amendes wylte make
Gyue thyne almesse of thyn owne goodes
And se thou werkes no man to wrake
To venge ony other mennes modes
If thou vntruely from ony take
And therwith fynde forty theyr fodes
Suche sacryfyce I forsake

They be to me as souer as wormewode
The pore people thou doost oppresse
With sleyghtes and wyles many one
Thou makest chyrches and do synge messe
Thou mendest wayes where men ouer gone
And some men curse and some men blesse
Whiche shall I hereof these two
If thou wylte haue grace as I gesse
Let all falsenes be fledde the fro
The mothes that thy clothes ete
And thou lettest pore men go bare
Thy drynke soureth and mouleth thy mere
Wherwith the poore man myght well fare
The rust that thy syluer dooth frete
Thy goodes that euyll goten are
They crye on the vengeaunce grete
The for to spyll but yet I spare
With holdest here ayenst the ryght
Frome thy seruauntes vpon the crye
Man oftentymes thou hast me hyght
Thou wolde amende and leue foly
Thou spekest full fayre bothe daye and nyght
Thou brekest my commaundementes contynually
Yet is me lothe with the to fyght
But make amendes or that thou dye.

Homo.
Swete lorde I may not agaynst saye
I haue not holden that I the hyght
I greue the gretely euery daye
I do not as I had the plyght
I wolde do well but, welawaye,[10]
with enemyes I am euer beset
whan my soule fayne wolde the paye
My flesshe is fyrst that wyll me let
And euer the fatter that I it fede

10. Alas, woe: *MED* s.v. "weilāwei".

Euer the fressher it is my foo
Yet bere it aboute I must nede
Full feble it is it wyll me sloo
The worlde, the fende, the flesshe they bede
Some with well and some with woo
what may I do with a wycked wede
To fyght ayenst thre enemyes soo
whan I enforce me other whyles
And thynke I wyll lyue a true lyue
And forsake all batayles and gyles
The worlde byddeth me batayle belyue
... But now I thynke withstondynge this
To forfake falnesse withouten ende
And restore that I toke amys
And paye my dettes fayre and hende
And to rewarde eche man his
As reason is than wyll I spende
And gyue myne almesse there nede is
Mercy Iesu I wyll amende.

Deus.
Man I haue sente the kyndly syght
And vnderstandynge, skyll, and wytte
To rule thy selfe by reason ryght
As reherseth holy wryte
That clerely sheweth the godly lyght
How thou sholde deedly synne forsake
And on that maner thou please me myght
What ayleth the thus fro me to shake
Worlde rychesse royall repayre
In welth and thynges of Iolyte
... Foule spekynge is to the a feest
I comforte the, I make the chere
And thou inwardly louest me leest
I call the vnto me yere by yere
Thou wylte not come at my request
As fro thy foo thou fro me feles
I folowe the fast and on the crye

Thou wrappest the with all vanytes
And thynke my speche to the but folye
And a thynge that nought is thou wylte lese
My Ioye that lasteth endlesly
Man yet vyce leue and vertue chese
And make amendes or that thou dye.

Homo.
Swete Iesu none answere I can
But ofte crye mercy with herte stable
Alas for woo why is a man
Worse than a beest vnreasonable
All beestes sythen the worlde began
In kyndely werkynge ben durable
Saue onely I of wyll wan
That do full many dedes dampnable
I was made to knowe my maker
And to loue hym ouer all thynge
And I a sleper and neuer waker
To take kynde knowynge of my kynge
To tryfles haue I ben a great hede taker
A songe of sorowe maye I synge
For had I ben of synne a forsaker
Of cryste sholde I haue had some knowynge
My ghoostly eyen ben full of duste
Cursed couetyse hath blynded me
They ben blodeshotten with flesshly luste
That heuenly kynge maye I not se
But lorde though I haue ben vniuste
Through helpe of thy benygnyte
I hope to rube awaye the ruste
With repentaunce and grace of the
And where that I haue afore this
My wyll in worldly thynge haue spend
From hens forwarde my purpose is
Thy lawe to lerne to my lyues ende
Thy .x. commaundementes truly ywys

Them to kepe I wyll me mende bende
And there as I haue done amys
Mercy, Ihesu, I wyll amende.

12b Christopher Love, *The penitent pardoned. A treatise: wherein is handled the duty of confession of sin and the priviledge of the pardon of sin. Together with a discourse of Christs ascension into heaven and of his coming again from heaven. Wherein the opinion of the Chiliasts is considered and solidly confuted. Being the sum and substance of several sermons preached by that faithful servant of Christ, Mr. Christopher Love, late minister of the Gospel at Lawrence Jury, London,* 1657, pp. 5–33.[11] *Wing* L3171. **Source** The Library of Congress, Washington, DC (BX9318. L57 Pre 1801 Col).

Sermon 1. [Febr. 24. 1649][12]
Epigraph:
Text, PSALM 32. latter part of Vers. 5.
I said, I will confesse my transgressions to the Lord, and thou forgavest the iniquity of my sin.

... Forgivenesse of sin is not laid down as an effect flowing from a cause, but as a consequent flowing from an antecedent. ... A man is sick at the heart when meat doth not digest; the vomiting of the load off of the stomach doth ease the stomach; when the conscience is burdened, when a mans spirit is troubled, pouring out of complaints and confession to God doth ease the mind. A sinner is like a vessel of new wine filled and stopt up close; till it hath vent it is ready to burst; so is a godly man filled with sin, till he can vent by confession to God, his heart is ready to burst. *Psal. 119. vers. 25. My soul cleaveth unto the dust, quicken thou me according to thy word. Vers. 26. I have declared my waies, and thou heardest me, teach me thy Statutes.* As if he should have said, My soul cleaves to the dust, I am in a very low and sad condition, but *I* have declared my waies, *I* have confest my sins; then God heard me, then *I* had peace, then *I* had quiet, then *I* had comfort: that is the first Reason, secret confession to God, it doth give a great deal of ease and holy quiet to the minde. A second Reason why justified persons must confess sin is because God loves to hear the complaints and confessions of his own people;

11. Marginal notes in the original source were not included in the transcription, apart from the date of the sermon.

12. A note in the text.

lying on the face the best gesture, and the mourning weed the best garment that God is well pleased with. *Jer. 31. vers. 18. I have surely heard* Ephraim *bemoaning himselfe, &c.* (that is) confessing his sin unto God.

Cant. 2. vers. 14. O my Dove, that art in the clefts of the rock, in the secret places of the staires; let me see thy countenance, let me hear thy voice: for sweet is thy voice, and thy countenance is comely. God delights to see and hear the complaints and the confessions of his servants unto him: *so* David *speaks, I declared my waies, and thou heardest me with pity and complacency.* God had rather see men come with ropes about their necks, and with sackcloth about their loins by a humble confession, as the servants of *Benhadad* did, then to see ornaments about their necks by a self-justification. Christ loves to hear and see the mourning condition of a justified person. A third Reason why justified persons must confesse sin to God is because confession of sin doth help to quicken the heart to strong and earnest supplication to God. *Psal. 32. vers. 6.* For this shall every one that is godly pray unto thee in a time when thou mayest be found, surely in the floods of great waters they shall not come nigh unto him. Confession quickens supplication, in *Dan. 9. vers. 20.* And whiles I was speaking and praying, and confession my sin, and the sin of my people Israel, and presenting my supplication before the Lord my God, for the holy mountain of my God. &c. that Gabriel came and touched him. &c.

Confession is to the soul as the whet-stone is to the knife, that sharpens it and puts an edge upon it; so doth confession of sin; confessing thy evils to God doth sharpen and put an edge on thy supplications: that man will pray but faintly, that doth confesse sin but slightly. Solemn and secret confession of thy evils unto God doth greatly help to quicken strong supplications unto God. A fourth Reason why justified persons must confesse sin unto God is because confession of sin will worke a holy contrition and a godly sorrow in the heart. *Psal. 38.* vers. 18. *For I will declare mine iniquities, I will be sorry for my sin.* Declaration doth work compunction; confession of sin, is but the causing of sin to recoyle on the conscience; which causeth blushing and shame of face, and grief of heart.

A fifth Reason why justified persons must confesse sin unto God is because their secret confession of sin doth give a great deal of glory to God, it gives glory to God's Justice. I do confesse sin, and do confesse God in justice may damn me for my sin: it gives glory to Gods mercy. I confesse sin, yet mercy may save me: it gives glory to Gods omnisciency; in confessing sin I do acknowledge that God knoweth my sin: confession of sin gives glory to God. *Josh. 7.* vers. 19. *And* Joshua *said unto* Achan, *My son, give I pray thee, glory to the Lord God of Israel, and make confession unto him, and tell me now what thou hast done, hide it not from me.* It is *a giving glory unto God.* A sixt Reason why justified persons must confesse sin unto God is because holy confession of sin will imbitter sin, and indear Christ to them, when a man shall let sin recoyle on his conscience by a confession. These after reflexions, and these after recollections of sin, do greatly imbitter sin, and do indear Jesus Christ; the stronger desires that a sinner hath after Jesus Christ, the more he doth inhaunce the price of Jesus Christ ... .

When God doth bring a beleever under some grievous outward affliction, then is a fit time for him to confesse sin to God. It is a saying of *Gregory*, Sins do blinde the eyes of men when they sin, yet those eyes come to be opened by the punishment, the punishment openeth those eyes which the fact hath shut. ... It may be now thou art in health, thou dost not now confesse thy uncleannesse, and thy drunkennesse, and thy pride, and thy prophanenesse; but what wilt thou do when God brings thee on a death-bed? when God hedges in thy waies with thornes, the conscience will reflect on thee, and suggest guilt to thee, and draw out confession from thee, it is a fit season; when God doth bring a man under any outward affliction, then he is in good plight to confesse sin ... .

A second Season wherein a man is in a good plight to confesse sin, is when the conscience of a man is set in office by God to persue him with clear and with strong accusations. When God puts the conscience of a man in office to persue him with strong accusations, touching evils he hath omitted; then that man is in a fit plight, if he will take hold of it. Even *Judas* himselfe when conscience awakened him, went and confessed to the High Priest and the Scribes; and said, I have sinned in betraying innocent blood. If *Judas* took advantage so much upon the awakening of conscience to confesse sin, then a beleever hath much more helpe. Beloved, the main use of conscience in man is to bring him upon his knees, to make him humble in the confession of his waies; conscience serves to excuse me when I do well, but the main use of conscience is to accuse me when I do ill, and so to put me on confession to God, therefore mark, saith *David, I roared all the day;* there was the noyse of *Davids* conscience for his Adultery, *then I said I will confesse my transgressions;* when conscience roars by accusation, then let the heart confesse to God: I do earnestly beg you to take these fit Seasons: you are in a good plight to confesse sin when God doth lay you under afflictions, when God doth make conscience accuse you, that you do deceive in your trades, that you are ingulphed under lust. O, then pursue these accusations of conscience, then you are in a fit plight to confesse sin to God.

... First see hence that not only wicked men must confesse sin; but regenerate men, pardoned men. It is no servile, no slavish, no legal work. Though the lowest Beleever be above the power of sin, yet the highest Beleever is not above the confession of sin, because not above the practice of sin. As long as men continue acting of sinne, men must never leave confessing of sin; as long as sinne leaks into thy soule, thou must so long be pumping; confession is to the soule as a pump to the ship. O, what leaks into thy heart by heedlesnesse and carelesness, pump out by confession. Till thou art above the actings of sinne, thou art not above the confessing of sinne: as long as the body natural doth gather corrupt humours, so long there must be Purges and Vomits; if the body should still be gathering corrupt humours, nature wouldb bestfled[13] by these humours, thou art gathering sin to sin, thou art adding iniquity to iniquity: confession is a spiritual Purge, it doth cleanse and purge the heart; see therefore the great need that even pardoned men have to confesse their faults.

... First Rule in *confession of sin unto God is this;* single out some bosome and master lust that doth most frequently enslave thee, and make confession and complaints against that to God; do not onely confesse sin in the lump and general, but single out the most beloved lust, those sins which for the present do most subject and enslave thy spirit, which do most overcome thee and prevail over thee in thy Christian course; against those thou shouldest bend most of thy complaints and confessions: this wisedome God's people of old did expresse ... .

A second rule to guide thee in the matter of confession of sin to God is this: Make conscience to confesse your small and secret evils as well as your open and grosser sins. Our secret sins, saith the Prophet, are in the light of thy countenance ... . When you confesse and acknowledge secretly your sins unto God, labour to greaten your sins with all the heinous circumstances and heart-humbling aggravations you can imagin. Thus the servants of God used to do, when they confest sin unto God, they would confesse sin with all the heinous circumstances. ... Here *Paul* comes to aggravate his sin: there are eight aggravations that here *Paul* doth lay down of his sinne, wherby he would greaten sin unto himself that he might be the more humble.

1. First of all, they were not ordinary men that he cast into prison, but they were *Saints,* and to wrong them is a sacriledge, *the Saints have I cast into prison.*

2. Secondly, To cast a man into prison for debt is no injustice if the man be able to pay: *but many have I cast into prison,* why? *for professing the name of Jesus of Nazareth,* meerly for professing *Christ.*

3. Thirdly, If it had been but one or two Saints it were not much, but they were a greater number, *Many of the Saints did* I *cast into prison.*

13. Meaning "would be stifled"; possibly a printing error.

4. Fourthly, he aggravates his sin further: to cast them into prison and give them in prison liberty, is not much, but he *shut them up in prison,* and kept them close prisoners.

5. Fifthly, If he had rested there, it had not been much, but *he gave his voyce against them to put them to death.* Nay,

6. Sixthly, He goeth higher, for he did wrong to their souls too, for *he compelled them to blaspheme God.*

7. Seventhly, To aggravate it further, he was mad against them, *and* I *was exceedingly mad against them;* hee was mad with rage, and with passion, and with fury against the Saints of God.

8. Eighthly, I *did persecute them to strange Cities;* them I did not kill, I made them leave their Wives and Children, and made them run and shift for their lives into strange corners. This is the nature of a true penitent, not to confesse sin slightly and carelesly, but in confession of sin to cloath his sins with all aggravations that can be. In confession of sin we should aggravate it that we have sinned against mercies, correction, warnings, resolutions, checks of conscience, motions of the Spirit, *&c.* and this is a good Rule if you will follow it .... .

A fourth Rule in confession of sin is this: In your confessions look not discouragingly on God as an angry Judge, but hopefully, as on a displeased Father; to confesse sin to God as an angry Judge, is to make you but condemned Malefactors in your confessions; therefore make confession to God only as a displeased Father; converted men do confesse sin to God as a Father, whilest you have an eye of sorrow upon sin you are to have an eye of hope upon pardon, thus Gods people did in their confessions. To confesse sin to God as a Judge is to howl like dogs because you shall be beaten; but to confesse sin to God as an angry Father, is child-like with a fiducial confidence of pardon. ... In confession you are to go to God hopefully, as to a displeased father: confessions when they come to God as a Judge, create fear, horrour, and amazement on the conscience, but when confessions are mingled with hope, and come to God as a Father, they work a holy brokennesse of heart, a holy tendernesse and remorse on the conscience. We should confesse our sins to God as a Patient confesseth his disease and bodily distemper to his Physician in hope of Cure. ...

Leave not confessing of sin until shame hath filled your face, and sorrow hath filled your heart; it is a great fault in many people if they confesse their sin in crying God mercy in a general way, they think they have made God a compensation for all the injuries they have done him, though they never have any godly sorrow for their sins, but, beloved, you are not to content your selves with such confession. ...

A sixt Rule in confession of sin is this, If thou findest thy heart straitned in confessing present guilt and present sins upon thee, then labour to review and recollect ancient guilt and ancient sins: This is a very useful thing in a mans Christian course. It may be a man or woman professing Christianity, may not know the sins he, or she hath done this last week; for want of heedfulnesse and observation of their waies, in that case let them recollect what they have done many years agoe, recollect old sins, when new sins do not come to remembrance, and be humbled for them ... .

Lastly take this Rule, take more freedom in confession of sin in secret before God, then in publick before men.

... Holy confession in godly men makes the soul to be more active and inquisitive after cure, remedy, and pardon for sin; holy confession makes the soul industrious. I confesse sin, but how shall I subdue sin? I acknowledge sin, but how shall I get pardon for sin? It makes it enquire how to get cure and remedy for the evils which before were confest. *Job. 7:20. I have sinned, What shall I do unto thee, O thou preserver of men? &c. I have sinned,* there is his confession: *Lord what shall I do?* there is his industry. Thus the Jewes they were convinced by *Peter* of their great sin, insomuch as they cryed out, *What shall we do to be saved?* But false confession leaves men idle, and careless; confesse they do, but they are not inquisitive how to get pardon for those sins they do confesse.

Secondly, Holy confession of sin unto God in godly men is attended with remorse of conscience, and with grief of heart; ... there is confession and sorrow joyned together. ... Whilest confessions are in the mouth, there will be either tears in the eye, or sorrow in the heart, if confession be true. The wicked confesse sin, but they never grieve for the sins they have committed, they are not ashamed, neither can they blush, in the Prophets language.

Thirdly, A godly man in confession of sin hath more freedom of spirit to confesse his particular sins in secret then he hath in publick: *I have powred out my soul before God,* saith the Psalmist; confession of sin is a pouring out of the soul *before God*; he that can pour forth complaints against sin in secret more then in publick is a grecious man. The wicked are only for confession of sin before men, and not before God. ... Thus a godly man in confessing sin, his belly is as ready to burst with new wine, he must needs have vent, else he is broken, he must needs confesse sin; his sin drives him to God. But confession is extorted and wrested from wicked men. ... A godly man is conscious to confesse secret and small sins, as well as grosse wickednesse. ... Godly men confesse sin out of a sight and sense of sin, as it is dishonourable to God, rather then as it is a shame and reproach unto themselves. Confess thy sin rather for the foul nature of it, that it doth dis-honour God, then for the evil consequence of it, that it deserves damnation to the sinner. ... Holy confession of sin in godly men leaves a holy awe, and a dread upon the heart, making them afraid to commit the sin after they have confest it, making them afraid to come into the occasion of that sin which they have confest. ... A godly man may commit a sin which he hath confest, but yet he retains a fear and awe upon his heart, that it shall not prevail over him in his practice. Wicked men confess sin they have committed, yet they are bold and adventurous to commit the same sin again which they have confest.

... A second reproof, is to those of the Popish Religion, who in stead of secret confession of sin to God in prayer doe presse vehemently Auricular confession in the ear of the Priest. Touching this Auricular confession, they spend many volumes to make good the divine right of it; the Councel of Trent do lay an *Anathema* on any that shall not count Auricular confession to be necessary to salvation.

There are these several mistakes and errours in the Popish Doctrine of Auricular confession.

First, They urge the necessity of it, that you must not expect salvation without it.

Secondly, Confession against whom, and when you did it, all the circumstances of your sins you must acknowledge to the Priest.

Thirdly, That the Priest upon your confession hath power from Christ to give you pardon, and to give you absolution; these goe currant with them about Auricular confession. ...

There is one Use more of this Point, and that is for lamentation and humiliation; to humble you in the presence of God, that seeing God calls you to confesse sin to him, you have so many palpable and manifest defects in secret confessing of your sins to God. ...

> The first Defect in confession of sin unso[14] God is this, that when men come to confesse sin to God, they have such a barrennesse and confusion on their spirits, that they cannot call to remembrance their particular sins to confesse them. ...
>
> A second Defect in the confession of sin to God is this, when men in prayer do confesse many sins to God, yet do leave out their master and predominant sins: many men are large in confession, yet do leave out their master sins. ...

14. Probably "unto" was intended here.

A third Defect in confession of sin to God is this, to have the heart to hanker after the committing of those sins you do confesse. ...

A fourth Defect in confession of sin to God is this, to confesse to God the sins of your life, but not the sins of your nature: many men will be large in confessing the sins of their life, but seldom or never bewail the sins of nature, that vicious inclination in the heart to sin ... .

A fifth defect is this, to confesse grosse and open sins, but not to confesse small and secret evils: we are commanded to keep the Law as the apple of our eye ... . Now you know, a man that keeps his eye will not only keep his eye from great blowes, but from small motes, which may put out the eye as well as a great blow; men should not only take heed of great blowes, great transgressions, but they should take heed of lesser motes, small sins. Now, beloved, good men many times commit those sins that are infamous, that the natural light of conscience can control them for, why those evils are complained of, and confest; but secret evils, wandring thoughts in duties, vanity of minde, the deadnesse of the heart, emptinesse of spiritual meditations, inward distrust; these evils are seldome bewailed and confest; this is many times a Defect found in good men, good men are not so apt to confesse omission of good, as commission of evil.

A sixt Defect in confession of sin to God is this, to confesse sin more because of its guilt, then of its spot: my meaning is, more because sin hath a damning power, then a defiling nature; more because sin damns thy soul, then defiles thy conscience. ...

A seventh defect in confession of sins to God, is this, to confesse those sins to God, which if men should charge us with, we should deny and be angry. ...

The eighth defect in confession of sin unto God is this, not to have the heart sensibly affected with those sins that are confessed to God; many confesse as if they were telling stories rather what other men did, then what themselves did. ...

The looking-glasse will shew you the blemishes in the face, which the eye cannot else discern: beloved, get a knowledge of the spiritualnesse of God's Law, of the extent of God's Law, that the Law doth reach the inward man, that God's law reacheth to those very first motions of the soul, those very inclinations to sin that are in thine heart, be acquainted with the Law, and by that thou wilt come to the knowledge of sin. Physicians have used this remedy to their Patients. In a Convulsion Fit they would wish them at that time to look their face in a glasse, that when the Patient doth see what an ugly countenance he hath, and what an ugly posture he is in at that time, he might strive the more against it. So doe you look your face in a looking-glasse to see those deformities that are within you, this will make you confesse, and this will bring you on your knees. Secondly, If you would confesse sin aright, observe diligently your own waies and hearts. ... Thirdly, Keep fresh in your remembrance some particular sin or other, when you come to prayer it will help you in confession; it is barrennesse as I told you that you do not see what matter you have to confesse, that makes you so scanted in you confession; would you but present some particular sin when you come to God, you would be in better plight to confesse sin to God. this the Psalmist doth, *51. vers.* 3. For I acknowledg my transgessions, and my sin is ever before me. He means the sin of Adultetery. When *David* came to prayer, he would put before his eyes the sin of adultery: now set sin before thine eyes when thou commest to prayer, and that is the way to feed thy spirits with confessions to God in a prayer. ...

A word of Use further for direction.
If it be so, that Justified persons are bound to make secret confessions unto God: then,

First, Christians keep a heedfulnesse over your hearts, that you may not let sin go unconfest; make conscience and be heedful that sin committed by you may not be unconfest; a sin unconfest as to the apprehension may be unpardoned; a sin unconfest cannot be mourned for, cannot be actually repented of. ... A second Direction is this, Depend not upon the most inlarged and the most sensible confessions that ever you have made to God, suppose thou hast poured out thy soul to God, thou art never the better; thou, O man, when thou doest confesse sin, thou doest but like a begger shew God thy sores, thy botches, and scabs, do not depend upon your confessions; as you must not depend upon your righteousnesse, so not upon confession of your sinfulnesse. ... Observe this further, the manner of the expression, the *confession* was in purpose and intention, but the *forgivenesse* is actuall: observe from hence this note, That God doth recompence the very gracious purposes as well as performances of his own servants. God forgave, but *David* did but purpose to confesse; *I said I will confesse, and thou forgavest.* O beloved what a God doe yee serve! your masters are not pleased with your purposes to work, if you doe no labour with your hands; you serve a God which takes will for work; God takes purposes if they be reall, for performances. The Lord doth recompense not onely gracious performances, but also gracious purposes in his owne servants. ... God doth not onely look on wicked mens purposes, to punish them for them, and good men's purposes to reward them for them; but God doth looke on the purposes of devils to doe hurt, for to prevent them. A notable passage, *Luk. 21. Peter, Peter* saith Christ, *Satan hath desired to winnow thee like Wheat. I have* (actually) *prayed*; the hurt was only the devils purpose, and the devils desire; but when the temptation was but in the desire, then saith Christ, *I have* actually *prayed for thee.* O fall down and admire the condescension of Christ, he doth crown your purposes and endeavours, and desires: *I said I will confesse my transgression, and thou hast forgiven the iniquity of my sin. From the connexion of confession and forgivenesse of sinne*; And thou forgavest, *which is by way of connextion not causation, with an* et *not an* ergo. *The Doctrine I hence observe is this,* That there is a necessary connexion between a penitentiall confession of sinne, and forgivenesse of sinne: I confessed, and God forgave. ... He that covereth his sinnes, shall not prosper; but whoso confesseth and forsaketh them shall have mercy.

13a John Goodale, *Here begynneth a lytell treatyse called the myrrour or lokyng glasse of lyfe for comfortyng of the soule* (1532?). **13b** John Ball, *A short treatise* (1637).

Introduction Little is known of the author of the *Lytell treatyse called the myrrour or lokyng glasse of lyfe* (1532?) and it is uncertain if he was John Goodale or Goodall, or perhaps the text had a different author all together. The text itself is a rich work on spiritual self-discovery and is considered by some as the first evangelical autobiography due to its prologue in which the author discusses his pre-conversion life with sincere repentance.[15] Repentance is, in fact, the leitmotif of this work, lauding contrition and honest confession resulting from self-knowledge, recommending to fear God with love, and love Him with fear. It focuses on instructions for prayers and meditations that can produce self-knowledge, result in brokenness of heart, and lead to repentance for sin. Being thus proto-Reformatory in its approbation of self-discovery and spiritual conversion, the text is at the same time firmly anchored in the late medieval genres of *summa* and *speculum* literature ("mirrors," or compendia of various fields of knowledge), with sections on the Deadly Sins, other 'social' sins such as drunkenness or adultery, the pains of hell awaiting unrepentant sinners, a compilation of quotations from Church Fathers and scholastic thinkers such as St Bernard of Clairvaux, as well as a long exposition on mercy and the works of mercy, the five wits, and so on. One of its functions was, typically of its genre, to provide a summary of Christian knowledge and doctrine necessary for every Christian to know and use in everyday life, making it also an example of a link between *summae* and later

15. Peter Marshall, *Religious Identities in Henry VIII's England* (London, 2012), 34.

works of "practical divinity," a popular Protestant genre (with Richard Baxter as one of its most influential and popular authors). The focus of the excerpt below is on promoting self-examination, prayer, and confession to achieve spiritual health and comfort, and appeasing the fear of divine wrath through a performance of piety, introspection, and sincere and unconditional repentance for all sin and corruption.

Much like the *Lytell treatise* is a good example of the *summa* and *speculum* genres, so John Ball's *A short treatise* is a perfectly and straightforwardly Protestant catechism of the basic tenets of (Protestant) Christianity, with a puritan bent, as Ball was a student of William Perkins and a puritan divine himself.[16] It went through as many as fourteen editions before 1632, and has the form of questions and answers, much like in a classroom setting (and Ball was, indeed, also a teacher). Among basic Christian tenets, the *Short treatise* provides instruction also on the spiritual benefits of being Christian (or, more specifically, Protestant) in that adherence to God and his law helps to battle the miseries of life and death, and can provide consolation as much as strength to all Christians grappling with doubt and uncertainty. It also recommends meekness, compliance and, above all, repentance. Through that, as Ball asserts, the true meaning of being Christian, and the true feeling of election can be discovered, as can the "Loue and delight in that which is good, ioyned with a sincere desire, purpose, and endeauour, dayly to amend whatsoeuer is amisse, and to lead a life according to the lawe of God."[17] It recommends contrition and brokenness of heart as well as shame and hatred of sin as the proper attitude to confession. This specific copy of John Ball's *Short treatise,* located in the Centre for Reformation and Renaissance Studies Rare Book Library at Victoria University in the University of Toronto also contains (due to a printing error leaving a number of pages originally blank) extensive marginalia continuing Ball's work with further questions and answers about the sacraments. Both Goodale's and Ball's texts are instructive, and both contain summaries of doctrines deemed appropriate and necessary to their Christian audiences; both also speak of such basic aspects of Christianity as the Scripture, sin, confession, divine mercy, and self-examination. Both texts also recommend contrition and repentance as means of achieving spiritual comfort, at the same time as each approaches these recommendations differently, and for different reasons. Read together, these texts illustrate the multiple approaches to repentance and contrition in both periods, since both texts are very representative of their genre.

16. David Zaret, "The Use and Abuse of Textual Data," in *Weber's Protestant Ethic: Origins, Evidence, Contexts,* ed. Hartmut Lehman and Guenther Roth (Cambridge, 1987), 245–272, at 253.

17. Ball, *A short treatise,* 174.

13a John Goodale, *Here begynneth a lytell treatyse called the myrrour or lokyng glasse of lyfe for comfortyng of the soule*, 1532 (?); unnumbered pages. *STC* 11499. **Source** *EEBO*: Cambridge University Library (Syn. 8. 53. 108 (3)).

... *Charyte causeth or moneth vs to the loue god through fayth. The .ix. Chapytre*

... *An ordre of Crysten lyuynge.*
Fere god with loue
And loue god with fere
Desyre a way to be with hym
Serue hym dayly with some prayer.
Brydle the affeccyons of thy mynde
Subdue thy sensuall appetytes and desyres
Thruste downe all prowde affeccyons
Coldly refrayne thy wrath
Byleue and truste surely in cryste Ihesu.
Worshyp hym and his mother mary
Call often for the grace of the holy ghost
Loue alway peas and equyte
Thynke often of deth
Drede or fere the Iugement of god.
Alway truste suerly in goddes mercy
Be alway well occupyed
Beware of losse of tyme
Forget trespaces done to the
Forgyue them gladly
Chastyse thy carnall body
Be sober of thy mouthe
In meates and drynkes
Be sober of thy talkynge
Use no fowle language
Loue clennesse with chastyte
Use alway honest company
Also beware of ryot
Dyspende mesurably
Be trewe in thy worde and dede
Reuerence thou thyne elders

And obey thy superyors
Be felowe and assocyat to thy equallys
Be also benynge and louyng vnto thyne inferyors
Loue all people in god
Stande faste and truste in grace
In fallynge downe dyspayre not
And euer take a fresshe good new purpose.
Perseuer constantly
Use ofte clene confessyon
And wasshe clene with repentaunce
And therwith sorowe for thy synnes
And aske often for mercy
In no wyse be no slouggarde
But awake quyckely.
Enryche the with vertue
Lerne dylyently
And teche that thou hast lerned louyngly. ...

Of prayer and of effycacy and vertue therof. The. x. Chapytre.
Accordyng to the mynde of saynt Austyn, prayer is the helpe and remedy for the soule, and comforte, and consolacyon, and subdewynge of the deuyll and voydynge of all synnes. There is nothynge of more vertue or excellency in the syght of god here then is pure deuocyon or prayer .... Furthermore they that wyll pray must be hole affeccionat in the promyse of cryst. And truste suerly in the wyl of god as he wytnesseth in the euangelyst. Mat. 7. (axe and ye shall fynde, knocke and it hall be openyd, as who sayth axe for mercy and it shall be gyuen);[18] you seke the meanes and helpe your selfe, and god wyl helpe you, and ye shall fynde, knocke at the dore of your harde herte or conscyence with repentaunce, and the vertue of god shall open the dore of your herte for to receyue grace, for he wold haue wytnesse of hym selfe here amonge vs in strengthynge of our faythe; thus we maye euydently proue and perceyue the wyll of the father in heuen to warde vs here in erth. ...

Saynt Austyn saythe there is no greffe so paynfull as is the greffe of ones conscyence, wherfore except thy conscyence be pure and clene of god nor of no saynt can thy prayer be harde nor acceptable, and specyally yf thou be in deedly synne.

18. "Shall" was intended in place of "hall." The bracket seems to end after "mercy" in the original copy; it was moved here to include the whole expression.

Dauit cormundum crea in me deus. Psal. 50. Saynt Bernarde sayth when thou entrest in to prayer in thy chambre closet, churche or elswhere, Fyrste seperat and expell out of thy mynde all mondanytes and worldly thoughtes or busynesse and elyuat thy herte and mynde, all hole vnto god onely, our father in heuen, and pray vnto hym in thy herte purely and syncerly, and in so doynge thou pleasest god more then yf thou shuldest say ouer all the bedys that be in the worlde, otherwyse in vaynglory hauynge thy mynde ruffled in worldly busynesse. ...

The vertue of confessyon and to knowlege thy selfe. The. xi. Chapytre.
Saynt Austyn[19] de penitentia sayth that confession is a sacrament whiche is the helthe of man and the saluacyon of the soule, and the restorynge of vertue and the sperklynge abrode or castynge away of vyces and synnes, and the deuyll and his werkes. And shytteth vs out of the gates of helle and openeth vs the gates of paradyse. Saynt Austyn sayth that person that is a synner and offendeth god dayly and wyll not be knowen of his synnes, but with a stoborne herte lyueth in his carnall pleasure and obstynat to warde god in knowlege of his synnes and offences dothe to the deuyll great pleasure, and gyueth his soule to eternall dampnacyon. And in contrary wyse he that confesseth hym and knowlegeth hym self therof. And no more wyllynge to offende god doth please god and so through god he possesseth his soule with grace eternall, for he that wyl hyde his synnes from god hydeth hym self from god, wherfore knowlege thy offences and thou shalt fynde alway mercy in hym. ...

13b John Ball, *A short treatise, contayning all the principall grounds of Christian religion. By way of questions and answers, very profitable for all men, but especially for housholders*, 1637, pp. 1–226.[20] *STC* 1318.5. **Source** Centre for Reformation and Renaissance Studies Rare Book Library, University of Toronto (BT1030 .B34 1637).

Q. What are the spirituall miseries?
An. Blindnes of minde, the spirit of slumber and giddines, horrour of conscience, hardnesse of heart, a reprobate sense, and strong delusions ... .

Expos. 25. To be blinde in minde, is to be utterly destitute of the true knowledge of God, and of the life to come, and to be hastening to endlesse woes, and yet not understand it.

19. "In" seems to be missing here.

20. A number of the biblical citations, including those in the notes on the margins of the printed copy, were not included in the transcription.

26. The Spirit of slumber is that which through a vaine perswasion of a mans good and safe estate, lulleth him a sleepe in security. Deut. 29:19.

27. Horrour of conscience is when the conscience awakened filleth the soule with deepe doubts, hellish and unrecoverable desperation, and remedilesse feares of everlasting damnation. ...

28. Hardnesse of heart is a fearfull judgement of God, whereby the heart is past all feeling and remorse, shut fast up that neither the Word, nor works of God can kindly work upon it. Esa. 48:4, Zach. 7:11–12.

29. A reprobate sense or minde, is a minde destitute of judgement, and voyd of common reason, taking evill for good, and good for evill, neither fearing God, or reverencing Man, regarding neither right nor wrong, Luke 18:4.

30. Strong delusions are when men are given over to take pleasure in beleeving lies, and idle fancies of vaine heads. To these wee may adde phrensie, madnes, Deut. 28:28, to be given over to vile affections; God with-drawing from men his grace, and in his secret but just and dreadfull judgement giving them over to most sordide, and loathsome, unnaturall, and inordinate lusts, Psalme 81:12, Gen. 19:5. ...

Q. After a man doth know his miserie, what must he learne in the next place?
An. The true means how he may escape the foresaide misery, and be restored to hapinesse. ...

Expos. 1. God in justice passed by the Angels who fell without the enticement of any other, 2 Pet. 2:4, Iude. 6, Matth. 25:41, but of his infinite love, free grace and mercy, Esa. 43:25, Ier. 31:3, Hos. 14:4, Iohn 3:16, Rom. 5:8, 9, Ephes. 1:5, 6, 1 Iohn 5:19, he hath prescribed meanes whereby man might escape misery, and be restored to happinesse, Acts 2:37, 38, 39, 40. ...

Q. How doth the Word worke faith in us?
An. By shewing us our miserie, and the true meanes of our recouerie, encouraging us being humbled, to receiue the promises of the Gospel ... .

Expos. 6. The word commaundeth the humbled to beleeue, promiseth them comfort, Math. 9:13, Luke 15:32, setteth forth the necessity, and exellency of faith, Iohn 3:18, 36, the danger of unbeliefe, Mark 16:15, Iohn 12:48, Act. 13:46, the tender mercies and compassions of the Lord, Psa. 103:8–12, and how he inviteth, perswadeth, and intreateth him to beleeve, 2 Cor. 5:20.

Q. How doth the Spirit worke by the word?
An. It doth teach us wisedome to apply things generally spoken, particularly to our selves, secretly upholdeth against despaire, stirreth up in us good desires,

doth soften the heart, and draw us to call upon Christ for salvation, before we haue the feeling of comfort ... .

Q. Ought we not in prayer to make particular confession of our sinnes?
A. Yes, so farre as we can come to the knowledge of them, and this we must doe with griefe, hatred, and shame, freely accusing and condemning our selves before God, with broken and contrite hearts. ...

Expos. 4. Sorrow for sinne must bee hearty and continuall, and as much as may be particular, Psal. 102:4, especially for the sinnes which have made great breaches in the soule, Psal. 51:1, 2, 4, yea, sinne should be our chiefe sorrow.

5. The soule should abhorre sinne, especially for the loathsomnesse of it, Psal. 97:10, Psal. 119:163, Iob 42:6, Amos 5:15, darkning Gods glory, Gen. 39:9, breaking his law, soiling all it toucheth, 2 Cor. 7:1, Iam. 1:21, Hag. 2:12, 13.

6. God is infinite in Majestie, Psa. 86:10, and of pure eyes, Hab. 1:13, a man therefore should blush at the remembrance and confession of sinnes before God, Ezra 9:6 and Dan. 9:7, seeing his face would be covered with shame, if a man should know them. ...

Q. What is the principall worke of faith?
An. It purifieth the heart. ...

Expos. 20. To purifie the heart is to abate and crucifie the power of sinne in the believers, and by little and little to renew them in holinesse and righteousnesse ... . The spirit of God is the author of sanctification, ... faith is the instrument of the holy Ghost, whereby the heart is cleansed. ...

Q. What followeth thereupon?
An. A fighting and combating against sinne and corruption. Gal. 5:17.

Expos. 21. Those that are sanctified, are sanctified in every part, ... and yet but in part, ... so that grace and corruption are mingled together in the best, Rom. 6:13 and 7:25, whence followeth a spirituall combate, not of the mind with the will, or the will with the affections onely, ... nor of divers desires onely, in respect of sundry and different considerations, but of the part regenerate with the part unregenerate, ... as of the minde regenerate, with the mind unregenerate, and so of the will, &c. This cumbat is continuall, against the first motions to sinne, not onely against outward grosse evill. ... The effect hereof is, that a man sanctified cannot doe what he would, Gal. 5:17; sometimes he is grievously foiled by the flesh, Matth. 26:40, 41, but in the end the spirit shall get the victorie. ...

Q. What is a third thing that followeth hence?
A. Love and delight in that which is good, ioyned with a sincere desire, purpose, and endeavour, daily to amend whatsoever is amisse, and to lead a life according to the lawe of God. ...

Expos. 24. The same spirit which wrought the grace of faith and cleanseth the heart, doth sweetly incline it both to long after, and to cleave with ioy to that which is good. ...

25. The true beleever hath laid aside the practise and desire of all sinne, Psal. 119:113, 128, 163, not onely out of a foresight of the ill consequences and fearefull evills that may fall, 1 King. 8:47, Ezek. 18:28, Luk. 15:17, but even out of love to the chiefest good, and all goodnesse, 2 Cor. 5:14, and that with a true purpose, Psal. 119:106, Act. 11:23, and well advised deliberation, Ruth. 1:16; therefore, hee is willing to espie out, and reforme whatsoeuer is out of order, Psal. 119:59. But note heere, that all have not the like measure of grace, Rom. 12:3, neither can with like victorie overcome their corruption .... The strong should not waxe proud, Rom. 11:20, Gal. 1:1, Rom. 14:3, nor the weake be dismayed overmuch, Rom. 14:4, Mar. 4:31, 32.

26. The redeemed of the Lord doe see that many waies they are bound to obey, ... and also that it is a blessed thing to beare the yoke, ... and so they resolve to deny their owne will, and follow the Lord. ...

Q. How should a man bridle and reforme these unruly passions?
A. Let him highly esteeme a Christian life, pray earnestly, set himselfe most against the corruptions that bee strongest in him, shun the occasions of sinne, hide the commandement in his heart, and apply the death of Christ for the killing of corruption. ...

COMFORT AND CONSOLATION

14a John Ryckes, *The ymage of loue* (1525). **14b** John Duncon, *The returnes of spiritual comfort and grief in a devout soul* (1648).

Introduction Little is known about John Ryckes, apart from the fact that he was an observant Franciscan friar in late medieval Tudor England. As is evident from his most well-known text, *The ymage of loue* (originally written in Latin and translated by John Gough[21]) he was interested in reforming the Church from within, actively participating in the late medieval debate over images in particular. His work is thus aligned with such pre-Reformation writers as Walter Hilton, John Mirk, Nicolas Love, and the preacher Thomas Wimbledon in that Ryckes tried to reconcile a subtle critique of the Church, particularly regarding the material affluence of some of the clergy, with an overall orthodox approach to the Church. His view of the Church and its doctrine was, indeed, orthodox, but due to the critical undertones of *The ymage of loue*, the text was placed under investigation for heresy, and was criticized by Thomas More and Bishop of London Cuthbert Tunstall. It is perhaps more accurate to say that the book was submitted for review before being printed, and it was approved, with such eminent Church figures of the time as Bishop of Rochester John Fisher (who also wrote extensively against Luther), Syon Abbey's confessor-general, and abbess of Denny Elizabeth Throckmorton all in favour of reading Ryckes' work, placing it comfortably in the "realm of orthodoxy."[22]

Ryckes wrote *The ymage of loue* as a gift to the community of nuns at Syon Abbey, the work itself focusing primarily on the kinds of human love and its outward and inward signs which reflect (or obscure) the image of the true love of God. It was popular among its contemporary pre-Reformation audience (with sixty copies alone purchased by the nuns of Syon Abbey), but it was likewise found interesting by Protestants after 1534 with an expanded edition with Protestant commentary printed in 1587.[23] Interestingly, however, the text had a bumpy history between 1525 and 1534 as, due to the controversies of the early Reformation (particularly Luther's criticism of images), de Worde was forced

21. Jennifer Bryan, *Looking Inward: Devotional Reading and the Private Self in Late Medieval England* (Philadelphia, 2008), 218 n74.

22. David J. Davis, *From Icons to Idols: Documents on the Image Debate in Reformation England* (Cambridge, UK, 2016), 19.

23. Mary C. Erler, *Reading and Writing During the Dissolution: Monks, Friars, and Nuns 1530–1558* (Cambridge, 2012), 3–4; Davis, *From Icons to Idols*, 19–20; Mary C. Erler, *Women, Reading, and Piety in Late Medieval England* (Cambridge, 2002), 107; Alan Stewart, "The Trouble with English Humanism: Tyndale, More, and Darling Erasmus," in *Reassessing Tudor Humanism*, ed. Jonathan Woolfson (New York, 2002), 83.

to withdraw all the copies he sold the Syon Abbey under pressure from Syon's supervising bishop.[24] While the text devotes considerable space to the notion of images and cautiously navigates the controversy surrounding religious iconography at the time, it is, it needs to be remembered, a devotional text written for a religious community, in that it focuses also on God's mercy, the soul's qualities of compassion and charity, as well as meekness and genuine contrition as the path that leads the soul towards the true image of divine love. It recommends repentance and offers spiritual comfort in the seeking and finding of God's mercy and love, its "true image," through charity. The text argues that outward devotion and elaborate piety are meaningless if they do not stem from true and genuine affection towards Christ and Christian values, and in order to find solace, spiritual "homeostasis," one needs to focus not on the physical signs of devotion, but on inward feeling of connectedness to God, meekness towards Christ, and an openness to others and their needs. Rycke's texts belongs to the older genre of mystical writings (such as Richard Rolle's *Incendium amoris*, ca. 1343, or Hugh of St Victor's *De arca Noe morali et mystica*, ca. 1125–1130, which Ryckes invokes towards the end of his work) in that it places emphasis on heart and "thinking" with the heart, but also writes itself into later fourteenth- and fifteenth-century debates over images, and in that tends to agree, albeit loosely, with John Mirk's *Festial*, (ca. 1400), in which the notion of the primacy of image over text is qualified but, ultimately, supported.

John Duncon was a Laudian minister and a proponent of "softer" Protestantism, advocating for doing away with the apparent sternness of Calvinistic English Protestantism, so as not to lose too many faithful to Roman Catholicism which, by contrast, seemed more comforting and joyful, and was gaining Protestant converts throughout the early seventeenth century.[25] Accordingly, Duncon's *Returnes of spiritual comfort and grief in a devout soul* is a text emitting pastoral warmth, offering spiritual comfort and consolation stemming from true self-knowledge and a strong relationship with God. In that, while generically it is an "epistolary" text, it places itself firmly within other Laudian works that furthered their cause against Calvinist "sternness." Written in the form of letters and answers, the text is a dialogue between a soul and its comforter. The soul at first seems happy and content with its spirituality, but its joy is soon overshadowed by doubt, self-loathing, and a sense of loss of assurance, and comfort. The sender of letters, Lady Lettice (Cary), to whom John Duncon was chaplain (and later also biographer), appears lost in the meanders of understanding true election and assurance, can no longer feel justified in Christ, and speaks of losing her way. The answers that come to these letters first affirm the necessity of outward devotion, of which the sender is rightly proud, but draw

24. Bryan, *Looking Inward*, 56.

25. Alec Ryrie, *Being Protestant in Reformation Britain* (Oxford, 2013), 79.

attention to the deeper layers of faith, inward devotion, that the sender seems to lack. Throughout the exchange the sender begins to doubt herself and the genuine nature of her inward piety, to which a reply comes with instructions for the doubting soul to look deeper into herself, identify and name her inner feelings, repent, and find which of these feelings are in fact temptations and lies of the Devil. Thus the addressee of the letters, perhaps a minister, maybe Duncon himself, guides the sender of the letters through a process of self-discovery that leads, through doubt, to spiritual comfort and assurance, an understanding of the superficiality of outward devotion only, and to a deeper awareness of the Devil's devices aimed to prevent the soul from finding the true meaning of God's love and mercy.

Both texts here excerpted thus focus on divine love, speak about outward and inward devotion, repentance, and observance of worship that can only be true if it is genuine and comes from inner conviction. The message of each text is likewise similar: doubt is the first step on a path to discovering true faith, true assurance, and true devotion, and only through genuine and contrite introspection, and "searching" with the heart, can a soul achieve spiritual illumination. The texts also differ in many ways, particularly in regard to the means of achieving this illumination of which they speak, and in Ryckes' clear focus on images and the word play he uses distinguishing false, physical images and genuine, spiritual images of love, which Duncon does not do. Both texts are thus differently constructed guides through meditative self-study, and together are an example of the development of the genre of manuals for "practical" contemplation through self-examination and repentance.

14a John Ryckes, *The ymage of loue. Here foloweth a goostly pamphlete or mater compendyously extract of holy scrypture, and doctours of ye chyrche, called ye ymage of loue, very necessary for all vertuous persones to loke vpon*, 1525; unnumbered pages. *STC* 21471.5. **Source** *EEBO*: The Huntington Library, San Marino, CA (69192).

Where the treu ymage is founde and what it is. Capi. v.

Than as I stode coniecturynge what I myght do scripture spake vnto me and sayd, *luc. xxiiij*, O folysshe man why doest thou seke a lyuynge thynge amonge deed thynges; lyght in derkenes, a ghostly thyng amonge erthely thynges, incorruptyble amonge corruptible; it is not there, it is meruaylous, goodly, and wonderfull to be holde; the ymage that thou sekest it can not be seen of the bodely eyes but onely with Aungelles eyes and pure with them that be deed frome this worlde leuynge with cryst; and he sayd also all that euer I had was nothynge to the pryce therof. Neuerthelesse I wolde fayne haue had it, *sapi. vij*, for thoughe I sawe it neuer I remembre that a shadowe I sawe therof in a glasse whiche passed by me sodeynly without ony taryenge and delited me so that euer syns I haue suche a desyre to it that I wold be glade to gyue all that I haue for a lytyll syght of it; but consyderynge myne vnworthynes and inhabylyte to come therby I stode in a stody whether I myght seke ony more for it in scrypture or not. Than met with me the prophete and shewed that it was vayne for me to gyue corruptyble ymages to suche persones; *pm. xliiij, Quia omnis gloria eius filie reges abintus.* For all the glory and pleasure of a kynges doughter is inwarde ghostly in the soule; ye be the doughters of the heuenly kynge espoused to his sone Iesu, your father, I suppose, dyde gyue you this liuely ymage whan he spake to you by grace and sayd, *Audi filia et vide.* &c. Heere my doughter and se. Inclyne thyn eere and be obedyente, forgete thy contrary men, forgete thy fathers howsholde, that is, forsake thy naturall loue, thy worldely loue, thy flesshely loue, forsake all vanytees and make the naked of all erthly thynges by pouerte and chastyte, and than the kynge my sone shall couete the beaute, and apparell the with clothes of verteu. Thus I doubte not he that hath called you from derkenes vnto so grete lyght of grace and hath now taken you vnto his spouses, he hathe nowe shewed you this ymage and gyuen it vnto you moche more goodly than I can dyscryue it as it is, for it is infinyte and incomprehensible yet it pleaseth hym to shewe it vnto all meke soules after theyr capacite, callynge them his daughters, sayenge, *Audi filia,* Heere my doughter in treu fayth and meke obedyence. *Et vide.* And se what I haue do and do dayly for you, se what ye do agayn or haue doo for me, se also what I do prepare for you. The beholdyng of these thre thynges I thynshold leaue some prynte of this ymage in our soules, but moche more in you that be his specyall spouses. And of this prynted ymage at the leest I wolde shewe you somwhat in parte to performe myne entent, and yet I fere me of presumpcion in enterprisynge for to shewe that I neuer knewe, or that ye knowe better than I; yet a blynde man maye shewe that he can not se yf it be put in to his handes.

Saynt Paule put a glasse in to my hande, holy scrypture, and bade me come out of derkenes in to lyght, for yf thou wyll se this ymage thou must loke besely vpon this glasse, for it can be shewed none other wyse here but by a glasse in a derke symylytude which do not shewe the thynge expressely as it is, but the tyme shall come, I trust, that we shal se the very selfe thynge in dede. I loked vpon this glasse and I coude se nothynge but my owne face fouly deformed with many foule spottes; I was bydden for to go wasshe me and make me clene and get me vnto the lyght, so I dyde and yet my eyes were so dymme with duste and humour of vanyte and carnalite that I coude not yet perceyue this ymage. I wente to a place of relygyon and toke a ghostly father, shewynge hym myne entente that I came fore to clarifye my syght that I myght at the leest ones se this ymage. There me thought it sholde be, for there were the moost goodly aparyld aulters with tabernacles subtelly caruen and costly gylte, there was the moost swetest Harmony of songes and organs and goodly deuout obseruaunce that euer I sawe or herde, in so moche that it moued me for a tyme vnto relygyon, there wherin I asked counsell of my ghostly fader; but he perswaded me the contray, sayenge it is not all golde that sheneth as gold, there is one thynge that dystroyeth moche goodness, the in ordynate loue to our selfe whiche is cause of moche yll .... Thus I perceyued that charyte myght lacke for all this gay outwarde thynges and obseruaunces, for all the gaye syngynge and playenge or multyplyenge of orysons nor yet they be not euident profes of loue and charite, but som time some of them letteth or hyndereth charyte and contemplacyon, sterynge the mynde to elacion and vainglory; but charyte, sayth saynt Paule, is to edyfy our neyghboure, to thynke our selfe membres of one body, and so to vse our selfe one to an other as the membres naturally do in the body, and so to vse our selfe one to another consyderynge our selfe as one body in cryste, to be as gladde of our neyghbours profyte as of our owne to helpe them in theyr distresse, as they wolde be holpen in theyr owne, louyngely to reforme and correcte them that do a misse, to helpe and releue them that be fallen in decaye, bodely or ghostly, to conforte the heuy, to helpe the seke, to socoure the nedy.

And as to saye in fewe wordes, to referre all our ryches, laboure, studies, and care to this ende that we myght profyte and do good vnto many in our sauyour cryste, that as he was not borne for his owne profyte, nor lyued here for his owne pleasure, nor dyed for his owne greter pleasure, ne for to come the rather to Ioye but he gaue hym selfe all hole to our vse and profyte, so sholde we applye our selfe to the commodytees and profytes of our euen crysten, and not to our synguler profyte, onely the more we profite vnto many the more is our auayle and meryte; yf it were thus, sayd a good relygeouse man to me, the lyfe of relygeous sholde be moche more Ioyous, pleasaunt, and easy than it is where nowe we se it is contrary, heuy, paynfull, laborious, full of supersticyons, obseruaunces, and vayne customes leauynge fro them the treu waye of lyfe, the folowynge of cryste the olde maner of lyuynge that was vsed, taught, and shewed by our holy fore fathers. ...

How it sholde be honoured. Capi. x.

Our lorde consyder the inwarde thynges of man. *Non secundum visionem iudicabit, neque secundum auditum aurium arguet, &c.* And he shall Iudge not after the outwarde seynge of mans eyes nor after the heeryngem of the eeres, but after the very ryght, and after the thought and the entent of man. Therfore yf a man take hede and is ware what he do in the syght of man, moche more let hym be ware what he do in the syght of god. The body is cladde in a relygeous vesture, it is well, but what auayleth that yf the mynde bere a seculer habyte after the worlde. They kepe scylence without forth, moche more take hede that the mynde inwarde be at rest from vayne thoughtes, not clateringe with worldely ymagynacions. In the materyall temple we kneele and go lowe to the grounde: what profyte is that yf in the inwarde temple of our soule we stonde sturdely ryght vp aeynst god, or our superyoures by dysobeynge theyr commaundementes; some fast and abstayne frome many thinges that do not defyle man as of them selfe, but shall they not rather absteyn them frome suspeccyon, detraccyon, and frome all ylle sayenge of other whiche polluteth and defyleth bothe other persones conscyence, and theyr owne; many do adourne and make gaye the materyall chyrche and hath grete reuerence to it, but what is that, where the temple of there soule, as Ezechiell sayd, is ful of serpentes, Idolles, and abomynacyons of egepte, that is yll and vnclene thoughtes worthy to be suspended;we syng and pray god with our tonge, let vs se that we do so also with our hert and mynde; we speke fayre and deuoutly with our mouth, let vs meane aswel in our soules or els it is not well. ... It is very well done oftentymes to accuse our self before a preest of our synnes; it is treuth yf it be also afore god; whan do we vtterly accuse our selfe before god, whan we vtterly hate our synnes and forsake them with inwarde contrycyon, for the treu loue and feere of god for an inwarde wounde must haue an inwarde medsyn; yf ye heere the worde of god which is moost necessary for the soule, heere it inwardely lest it be sayd. *Math. xiij. Audientes non audiunt.* They heere and heere not, but heere so goddes wordes outwarde that ye may saye with the prophete, I shall heere what my lorde speketh in me with feruent desyre to accomplysshe in dede that is shewed in worde, that it maye be sayd to you, blyssed be they that heere the worde of god, that is with the eere of obedience, whiche eere Dauyd exhorted the kynges doughter to enclyne, she whose beaute is withinforth in golden hemmes as we spake of before. This I haue spoken that we sholde not leene ne trust to moche vnto outwarde obseruaunces and cerymonyes, more otherwyse than the treuth doeth assygne, sayenge that also they be lytyl acceptable but yf ghostly and inwarde workynge goeth that all we maye not leue of the honourable and deuoute customes and holy ordynaunces of the chyrche. ... These it behoueth not to omyt ne to leue of, but to obserue them the other, that is the ghostly and inwarde obseruaunce is necessary and must nedes be do, yf we wyll haue ony profyte of them. Saynt Iohn therfore sayth in his gospel, *John xiij. Spiritus est deus,* God is a spyrytuall thynge, therfore sayth he, he must be serued with spyrytuall sacryfyce; remembre he knewe not the folysshe vyrgyns that had lampes of goodly workes outwarde but they lacked that they sholde haue had withinforth the oyle of grace, wherfore they were excluded from the maryage. Therfore rere vp an aulter in your temples that is your selfe, that be the lyuynge temples of god. There set vp lyghtes, gete you lernynge bothe by doctryne and grace, wherby ye maye worke, teche, and shewe examples of light, make there your oblacyons of a meke and a contryte herte, there sence our lorde with brennynge cooles of loue and swete ensence of deuocyon, there kneele mekely with reuerent inclinacyons, there make prostracyons with lowly feere and compuccyons, there fyxe vp your ymages of loue, there vse your medytacyons and contemplacions, there beholde these two ymages that I spake of before.

That one is a gret ymage increate and incomprehensyble, that is god hymsefe. *Deus charitas est, j. John iiij.* The other is our lytyll ymage, our lytyll loue created and caused by te ymage of god, as a lytyl ymage in a glasse, but yet it is very precyouse and good by meanes wherof the soule hath lyfe and the ghostly sences that I spake of. And thoughe it be very lytyll and nothynge in comparyson to the other ymage that is infynyte and without comparison excedynge all thynges create, yet he wyll haue it vnto the lykenes of his loue saying, *John xv., Hoc mando vobis vt diligatis inuicem sicut dilexi vos.* This I commaunde you, that ye loue togyther as I haue loued you ... .

14b John Duncon, *The returnes of spiritual comfort and grief in a devout soul. Represented (by entercourse of letters) to the right honourable, the Lady Letice, Vi-Countess Falkland, in her life time. And exemplified in the holy life and death of the said honorable lady. Published for the benefit and ease of all who labour under spiritual affliction*, 1648, pp. 1–7, 48–53. *Wing* D2605. **Source** Pontifical Institute of Mediaeval Studies Library, University of Toronto (BV4812 .D86 1648 IMSR).

The First Letter.
Upon the Souls constancy and frequency in holy Duties, her comforts in them are represented.
... Your Spiritual directions I have observed, as punctually as I could: I am present at all publicke Assemblies, in the house of God, and bear my part constantly in that solemn worship of his Name. And to these publicke devotions I adde private Prayers with my family, Morning and Evening, and to them, Secret, in my Closet, and these duties I perform constantly; for I remember you told me that that strict precept of the Apostle, *Pray continually*, hath not ordinarily a

more qualified sense then this, Observe your set-times of Prayer, constantly, without intermission.

Neither am I lesse constant at Sermons, and Catechisings, and at the holy Sacrament of our most blessed Lords body and blood; though I cannot be so frequent at these duties, Those I can hear but once a week, this I can receive, but once a moneth. And on daies of Humiliation, I labour to intermix more earnest, as wel as more frequent Prayers, for the publick necessities, and for mine own private wants; endeavouring to observe the ordinary and extraordinary Fasts of the Church, as strictly as my weak body, and my weaker flesh will give me leave. ...

Now and then I compare the former pleasures and delights I had in worldly things, at Court, with these I now I enjoy, and I account them all as drosse and dung in comparison of these. And if it were Capital in the Judicial Law for any one to have a perfume in his house like to that of the Tabernacle, *Exod. 30.*, surely he is not guiltles who fancies any true sweetnesse or delight any where but in the Tabernacle: no perfume can be made, nor ought to be thought so sweet, so fragrant, so excellent as this; no delights, or comforts in our own houses, or the Kings Court either, comparable to these of the *Tabernacle*, and the *Temple* of God. ...

And now upon the *sense* and *feeling* of these *joys* and *comforts* in the service of God, I am confirmed in hope that neither Life, nor Death, nor Angels, nor Principalities, nor Powers, nor things present, nor things to come, shall be able to separate me from the *Love of God*, and of his service, and worship; but as I have begun, so I shall (by Gods grace) persevere in it, to my lives end. ...

The Answer.
Sheweth the special favour of God, affording at the first beginning of a Devout life, both sensible and spiritual Consolations.
Sir,
Yours I received and rejoyce with you, for the *Comforts* and *joys* you find in the *service* of God, and for your diligence in holy duties, and exercises of Devotion: you now taste, and see the goodnesse of the Lord, that in keeping of his Commandments there is exceeding *delight* and *joy*; *Psal. 19*, not onely *comfort* layed up for it hereafter, but also *comfort* in it here; even such as ey hath not seen, nor ear heard of man to conceive what God hath prepared, even in this world ... for such as love him; *Cor. 2:9*, so that vertue and piety is an excellent reward to it selfe. ...

For you confesse your self a great gainer already, haveing in possession *Gold* in stead of *Brasse*, *Sliver* for *Lead*, *Spiritual* delights and pleasures for *worldly* and

Carnall. Instead of husks (fit onely for swine) in a *strange* Country, you have *goodly provision* (a fatted Calf) and this attended with mirth and music, in your *fathers* house. ... I must tell you, that all such comfort and delight (as you seeme to speak of) is not spiritual, nor lasting. In these holy exercises (of fasting, praying, meditating, hearing Sermons, and receiving the blessed Sacrament, and such like) there is an outward and sensible comfort, as well as an inward, and spiritual comfort; and those sensible consolations (as they are called) not so lasting, and permanent, as these inward comforts are; consider this, I pray, and examine whether your comforts be inward, and spiritual, or outward and sensible comforts onely, or whether you abound with both ... .

The Seventh Letter.

The soul feeleth (as he conceives) a partial privation of grace, and growing suspicious of the sincerity of his faith and repentance, feareth a total privation of grace, in her.

... I lament ... a *privation* of that *grace* of Fervor and zeal; My soul is not filled with it now, as formerly.

Neither may I dissemble it, sometimes I fear *worse,* even a *total* privation of this, and of all other *graces,* and vertues. Either that God hath withdrawn his holy graces from me, or else that I was never truly partaker of them; that I flattered and deceived my self, when I hoped that God hath accepted my *Faith* in Christ, and my *Repentance* to my justification.

The other day while I was judging my self for my sins, an *allegation* was cast in, against my *Repentance* also, and that was accused of *unsincerity,* and *hypcrosie.* And proof was brought of it: My *grief* and sorrow for my *sins* was compared with my *sorrow* for *other* things. The small bottle of my penitential tears was brought forth, and set by the bottle of my tears for worldly crosses; and when it appeared how enlarged I had been in these, and how straitned in those, that I have wept far more for the loss of a friend, or of a pension for some yeares, then for the invaluable loss of my Lord God, eternally. This plea was prosecuted against me, with a great deal of importunity, and though I my self was both the advocate and the judg in the case, yet I could not be so partial either in pleading, or in determining, as to acquit my self, but upon this *proof* and evidence was forced to condemn that *repentance* (mine own though it were) as feigned and unsincere, or incomplete at least, and therefore *unacceptable* in the sigh of God. ...

The Answer.
Prescribeth a strict examination of her Faith and Repentance; and sheweth these fears and jealousies may be the Temptations of the Divel.
Sir,
Whether you will take part with *Fear*, or *Hope*, you your self must resolve: yet somewhat I shal say concerning the *fears* which arise in you, that you are not justified before God, nor reconciled to him.

It is good to *fear* alway; it keeps us low, lest *pride* enter, and it keeps us active, lest *sloth* seize upon us; and so we humbly labour to make our *Calling* and *Election* sure; and when I sadly consider how many miscarry through Spiritual *security*, not at all suffering themselves to mistrust their condition towards God, I am not forward to cast out fear. Yet there is *torment* in fear, and a firm *hope*, we grounded (if it ejects not fear it self) wil wholly allay the torment of it. ... if your faith were lively, with love, and trust in God, and your repentance unfeigned, assure your self, it was no other spirit but the holy Spirit of God (who can neither deceive us, not can be deceived) who said unto your soul, *Christus est justitia tua and salus tua* Christ is thy justification, and thy salvation. ...

And if upon *examination* you find that your heart hath been, and is truely humbled for your sins, and afflicted at the remembrance of them; and doth also firmly resolve against them for the time to come; if you be sorely displeased, both with the sinner, and with the sin, abhorring your self, and your transgression, you may cherish and confirm your hopes that God is reconciled to you, through Christ.

15a [William Flete,] *The remedy ayenst the troubles of temptacyons* (1508). **15b** Obadiah Sedgwick, *The doubting beleever* (1641).

Introduction William Flete was an English Augustinian friar, mystic, writer, and (having left for Italy about 1359) spiritual advisor to Catherine of Siena. His *De remediis contra temptaciones*[26] was a powerful influence on Walter Hilton's *Scale of perfection* (ca. 1380) and on Julian of Norwich's *Revelations of divine love* (ca. 1395) and was probably

26. For a translation of one of the original Latin manuscripts, see Edmund Colledge and Noel Chadwick, "Remedies Against Temptations: The Third English Version of William Flete," *Archivio Italiano per la Storia della Pietà* 5 (1968): 201–240. For a study of the impact of the Latin and English versions of Flete's work see Michael Benedict Hackett, "William Flete's 'De Remediis contra temptationes' in its Latin and English Recensions: The Growth of a Text," *Mediaeval Studies* 26 (1964): 210–230.

known to the author of the *Cloud of Unknowing* (ca. 1390?). It was translated into Middle English sometime in the latter half of the fourteenth century (most likely around 1380). One of these translations was *The remedy ayenst the troubles of temptacyons*,[27] which expanded the fairly brief *De remediis* substantially, becoming also the source of the first printed edition of Flete's work. A few of the Latin manuscripts, and Wynkyn de Worde (who must have relied on a Middle English manuscript of *The remedy ayenst the troubles of temptacyons*), wrongly attributed the text to Richard Rolle, and so de Worde's three printed editions give Rolle as the author (occasionally, Walter Hilton was also considered as a probable author).[28]

The text is divided into two parts. The first, in ten chapters, speaks of despair, its sources, and remedies against it. Each chapter focuses on a different aspect of despair or its causes. The overall focus of the text is on despair that stems from spiritual doubt of assurance and that attacks the soul through the reading of the "wrong" texts, through disputing aspects of faith, through devoting too much thought to fear, or through the lies and tricks of the Devil (which the soul is exposed to when immersing itself in these activities). Flete's work recommends faith and hope in God's mercy to counter fear and despair, and warns that excessive reading, particularly of difficult theological works that are easily misunderstood by lay persons, may lead to confusion and loss of assurance because an unprepared soul is not able to argue (with the Devil) about the fine points of faith, and will allow itself to be forced into doubt. Instead, much like the author of the *Cloud of unknowing, The remedy ayenst the troubles of temptacyons* recommends simplicity in faith, trust, and hope for divine mercy as well as justification[29] and good deeds, and cautions to avoid thoughts that lead to spiritual torment.[30] The second part of this text (an addition to the Middle English manuscript de Worde took the text from, not in the original *De remediis*) gives instructions on saying the Rosary, a "deuoute medytacyon in sayenge deuoutly the psalter of our lady withdyuers ensamples" and refers to "the moost blessyd Domynyck the noble fader and leder moost famouse of the ordre of prechers" (n. pag.) suggesting perhaps a Dominican origin of this part.

27. Title given by Wynkyn de Worde in his editions of 1508 and 1519. De Worde's 1519 and 1525 edition give the title as *The remedy ayenst the troubles of temptacyons*, with the 1525 edition omitting the initial article. The transcription below is of excerpts from the 1508 early print version.

28. Nicholas Watson, "Despair," in *Cultural Reformations: Medieval and Renaissance Literary History*, ed. Brian Cummings and James Simpson (Oxford, 2010), 345–347.

29. See Watson, "Despair," 345–347, for a discussion of Flete's take on justification by faith.

30. For more on *The remedy ayenst the troubles of temptacyons* and *De remediis contra temptaciones* as well as a detailed discussion of Flete's approaches to despair and predestination in a fascinating comparison to early modern Protestant views on these subjects, see Watson, "Despair," throughout.

In his *The doubting believer*, the Presbyterian Obadiah Sedgwick of the Westminster Assembly, much like John Duncon (even though Duncon was a Laudian and Sedgwick a Calvinist), attempts to provide a degree of assurance and comfort to his fellow Protestants, and counter the accusation of sternness and coldness frequently directed at Calvinist Protestantism. Sedgwick, much like Flete, recommends finding assurance in being religiously curious only along the lines of Scripture, and by avoiding minute considerations of points of faith, as he emphasizes "the dangers of speculation"[31] in matters of faith that were not firmly and unquestionably anchored in Scripture. Sedgwick thus recommends reading Scripture, but also much like Flete cautions to give up the outward, external, and sensual understanding of God ("evil will," p. 347). He advises the reader to remember that the senses should not be the judge of reason and spirit, and methodically goes through the kinds and sources of despair, doubts, and temptations, providing also a neatly described selection of cures and remedies for them. Sedgwick points out that many temptations are a direct result of human error, whereas Flete blames the Devil much more often. Sedgwick also focuses on slightly different kinds of doubt and despair than Flete, as he speaks more of indecisiveness in devotion, and a fear of giving in to God completely, of uncertainty of one's Christian sentiment, and less about doubt of one's salvation or justification, which occupies Flete more. Sedgwick's view of doubt does eventually veer towards a consideration of the precise sources, causes, and remedies for specific kinds of doubts that he structures with much more precision than Flete.

However, ultimately, the two texts tend in the same direction: only through faith and acute self-examination can one achieve solace. *The doubting believer* is thus a very Protestant text in its structure and language, as well as the minute points of doctrine it considers related to doubts. It is also very Protestant in its purpose, to provide a practical manual for Christian self-study. *The remedy ayenst the troubles of temptacyons*, however, does not fall short of this goal. In its structure and argument, Flete's text likewise is a self-examination manual guiding the reader towards assurance, making both texts a fascinating study of approaches, both before and after the Reformation, to despair and to the comforts and remedies suggested to counter it. Theologically, Sedgwick and Flete would have, naturally, disagreed about a number of doctrines, but their approaches to despair indicate that the theological, pastoral, and devotional aspects of spiritual comfort in both periods shared a number of points of contact, even though Sedgwick did not write his text explicitly in relation to Flete's.[32]

31. Tom Webster, "Preaching and Parliament, 1640–1659," in *The Oxford Handbook of the Early Modern Sermon*, ed. Peter McCullough, Hugh Adlington, and Emma Rhatigan (Oxford, 2011), 404–420, at 418.

32. Although it is not impossible he wrote it as a counter to texts like Duncon's, which in turn were, by the Laudian's own admission, styled to resemble pre-Reformation rhetoric.

15a [William Flete,] *The remedy ayenst the troubles of temptacyons*, 1508; unnumbered pages. *STC* 20875.5. **Source** *EEBO*: British Library, London (S100006).

... *The thyrde chapytre*

And than yf it so be ye haue consented and fallen to synne by ony temptacions, than be sory and crye god mercy therof. And yet be ye not dyscomforted, but thynke well on the grete mercy of god, how he for gaue Dauid his grete synnes, Peter, and Magdalene, and not onely them but also all those that haue ben, or now be, or shall be contryte for theyr synnes, and meke them lowly and crye our lorde mercy. And therfore, syster, flee to hym that all mercy is, and aske mercy and ye shall haue it with forgyuenes of all your synnes, and meke you lowly, and take the sacramentes of holy chirche, and than ye ought to byleue faythfully that your synnes be forgyuen and that ye be receyued in to the grace of god. For god sayth hymselfe by his prophete Ezechie,[33] that whan a synfull man soroweth for his synnes he wyll neuer haue mynde therof, and yf a man perceyue in his herte no very sorowe, and though he thynke whan he byddeth his bedes or cryeth to god for mercy that he dooth all ayenst herte, yet therfore sholde he not deme hymselfe graceles, for who so wolde haue very sorowe for his synnes or wold crye god mercy, for them or in his herte wold crye for mercy, he cryeth god mercy truly; for, as I haue sayd, before god taketh hede to mannes wyll and not to his trauayllous fantasyes, it is good that a man take noo hede of suche fantasyes or sterynges that cometh in suche maner. For god hydeth from them the knowleges of suche fantasyes for many causes vnto the proufyte of theyr soules, wherfore suche passyons be not synfull but rather mater of grace and of grete meryte. And soo, good syster, thynke ye alwaye and yf it be soo that temptacyon cease not but were alwaye more and more, be not afrayed, but saye somtyme amonge in the worshyp of god and in the spyte of the fende your crede and knowlege your byleue and hope, and thynke on the wordes of saynt Poule that sayth, Knowlege of mouth is done to the helpe of soules and they shall not be deceyued by the fendes whyles that with a good auysement bothe in worde and wyll withstandeth hym strongly. For there was neuer man deceyued of the fende but by consent of his owne wyll, and that with suche a wyll as the herte consented with the same, for other fantastycall troublous wylles putteth not awaye man from god.

33. Ezechiel.

The fourth chapytre.

And therfore sholde noo man care nor be heuy that he is so troubled more than an other. Syster, alwaye whan I speke of a man in this wrytynge take it bothe for man and woman, for so it is ment in all suche wrytynges, for all is mankynde; and ferther more as touchynge your troubles thynke in all your dyseases what troubles goddes seruauntes hath suffred and what paynes and turmentes they haue had here in this worlde in many sondry maners, and ye shall fynde cause to suffre. Leo the pope sayth, it happeth somtyme that good and ryght wyse soules be styred sharpely by the fende, and somtyme by theyr owne compleccyon to angers, troubles, dredes, and suche other taryenges that it semeth to them theyr lyf a turment in so moche that somtyme for very drede the[34] begyn to dyspayre bothe in lyfe of body and soule, thynkynge they be forsaken of god, whiche dooth it but to assaye and proue his chosen chyldren and frendes by suche temptacyons. For as I afore haue sayd at the begynnynge of this wrytyng, in lyke maner as fyre purgeth golde and as a knyghte is proued good and hardy by batayle, ryght so temptacyons and troubles purgeth a ryght wyse soule; this is proued well by Toby for the aungell Raphaell sayd this to hym, To by for as moche as thou arte ryghtfull to god it is nedefull that temptacyon sholde preue thy wyll, and well it is knowen that sykenes falleth to a man after the dysposycyon of his compleccyon. So, lyke wyse, temptacyon, as Leo the pope sayth. The fende our ghostly enemy aspyeth in euery man what wyse he is dysposed by his compleccyon and by that disposicyon he tempteth hym. For there as he fyndeth a man full of malencoly he tempteth hym moost with ghoostly temptacyons of Ire. But they that wyll attende to withstande it for the loue of god they must shape them to pacyence and saye with Iob, Sythen we haue receyued of god so grete benefaytes why sholde we not receyue and suffre dyseases. And thynke on the grete anguysshes, sorowes, and dyseases that our lorde Ihesu cryste suffred hymselfe here in erth. And also suffred his blyssed moder to haue the same. And thynke that to suffre dysease pacyently is the waye to heuen warde. And that ye may not in this frayle worlde be so free as an aungell that is confermed by grace, but whyle your body and soule be togyder in this lyf they must receyue troubles as well as eases. And thynke not that god hath forsaken you, but mekely abyde the comforte of hym and without doubte, whan it nedeth ye shal not fayle therof. But some men whan they haue drede of saluacyon or be tempted to dyspayre by vysyons or ghostly sterynges of theyr owne frayltye, they wene anone that they haue synned in the synne of the holy ghoost and than the fende putteth in them that they may neuer be saued nor forgyuen of theyr trespaces. Thus speketh the fende wtin them.

34. "They," most likely, was intended here.

So ferynge synne, good creatures that they wene to goo out of theyr myndes. But they that ben thus tempted answere the fende thus agayne that he is false, and a lyer, as his nature is to be. For the synne of the holy ghoost, as clerkes sayth, is infynyte without repentaunce. And that is whan a man wylfully by delyberacyon wyll neuer repente nor aske god mercy ne forgyuenes of his synnes, nor wyll be tourned but wylfully departeth hym from the goodnes of god and in his wretchednes abydeth wylfully with full consent of wyll, he that doth thus synneth in the holy ghoost, whiche may not be forgyuen here nor elles, where for he wyll not trust in the goodnes of the holy ghoost nor aske forgyuenes of his synnes. And therfore he that wyll noo mercy aske noo mercy shall haue, for his synnes be infynyte without repentaunce. But thoughe a man or a woman haue or fele all these vycyous sterynges, and as many moo as ony herte can thynke ayenst theyr owne free wyll, and whan reason cometh to them they be sory therof and flee alwaye hastely to the mercy of god: it is to them but a preuynge or a clensynge of theyr synnes though they be neuer soo ofte in the nyght and the daye, now vp, now downe as wrestelers be; and thoughe ye haue ony tyme fall in ony synne, ghoostly or flesshely, and layne therin wylfully by delyberacyon and full content of herte, ye than ought to be sory and aske god forgyuenes with as grete contrycyon as god wyll gyue you grace, and than thynke fully the goodnes of the holy ghoost surmounteth all synnes that euer was done or euer shall be done, though a man had synned in them all as well in dede as thought; he beynge truly contryte and confessed, mekynge hymselfe lowly to almyghty god and to his sacramentes of holy chyrche, doubte ye not he so askynge mercy shall haue full forgyuenes of all his synnes, for the mercy of god is so grete that it passeth all his werkes. And therfore thoughe ye somtyme here by spekynge, or elles of wrytynge, or redynge in bokes sharpe wordes and harde sentences, yet comforte your selfe and thynke well that all suche harde wordes be sayd and wryten to chastyse the synners and to withdrawe them from euyll, and also to pourge and pure goddes specyall louers as the metall is in the fyre afore rehersed, and in them god wyll make his hous ... .

Moyses ledde the chyldren of Israell ouer the reed see, whiche were goddes people. Moyses wente before them and smote the water with his rodde and therwith the water parted and the chyldren of Israell wente ouer in suertye. And they of egypte that folowed perysshed and were drowned. By Moyses I vnderstonde our lorde Ihesu cryste, and by the yerde or rodde that departed the water I vnderstonde his holy passion, and by the chyldren of Israell that were not perysshed all crysten people, for ryght so our lorde Ihesu cryst came from his faders bosome to the see of trybulacyons and temptacyons to be our guyde and leder, he gooth before vs with his precyous passyon, and smyteth awaye the perylles of our troublous temptacyons so that we shall not perysshe, but it shall brynge vs to suertye of euerlastynge lyf; and therfore gyue we to hym thankynges, louynges, and infynyte praysynges as the chyldren of Israell dyde, for thoughe a crysten man were neuer soo synfull thynkynge hymselfe that he stode in the sentences of the hardest wordes that be wryten, yet sholde he trust faythfully in the mercy of god, for and he wyll forsake his synnes and tourne hym to good and vertuous lyf. He shall haue grace and forgyuenes, and the harde sharpe wordes of dampnacyon sholde tourne hym to mercy and saluacyon. For thus sayth our lord god in holy wryte by his prophete Ieremye, though I make grete thretes I shall repent me of my wordes yf my people wyll repent them of theyr synnes. O beholde the grete goodnes of our lorde and how pyte alwaye constrayneth hym to mercy, worshyp, and thankes be euer to his goodnes, he is so benygne and mercyfull to them that be repentaunt that he frely wyll chaunge his sentences from sharpe vengeaunce to forgyuenes, and of the paynes that they be worthy to suffre gyue them alygeaunce or lyghter payne to suffre. He sayth also by the prophete Isaye, I shall forgyue the synnes of euery man that with very true contrycyon wyll drawe hym to good and vertuous lyfe. ... But for all this thy grete goodnes, god forbede that ony man sholde be the more bolder, to synne or wylfully and wyttyngly, by delyberacyon sholde presume to falle to synne vpon trust of thy mercy. And therfore our lorde is so mercyfull I surely trust that euery true courteys soule wyl be the more lothe to offende his goodnes, and as for you that be tempted ayenst your wyll, and wyll not for all the worlde dysplease god wylfully, but that ye be thus begyled and encombred by the fende with many paynefull thoughtes, be ye not afrayde of the fende nor of his ferefull assawtes for he is full sore dyscomforted whan that he seeth a man or a woman whiche he soo tempteth is not aferde of hym.

Somtyme the fende cometh and tempteth a soule fyersly lyke a dragon, and somtyme he assaylleth hym lyke a rampynge lyon, but and yf a creature strengthynge hymselfe saddely in the passyon of almyghty god, and arme hym with that holy passyon, a thousande suche fendes how someuer that they come shall haue noo more power ouer hym thenne hath as many flyes or gnattes. And therfore strength you all in god and be not abasshed. Soo to strength and arme you in hym, though ye be synfull, for he sayth hymselfe in the gospell, he came for synners. And in an other place of the gospell he saythe that he came for mercy and not for noo vengeaunce, and to be our shelde and strength, and so lette vs humbly with a meke herte take hym. And yf ye fele ony dredes by ymagynacyon or temptacyon, or for wordes that ye haue herde or redde in bookes by the whiche ye doubte of saluacyon, than thynke on the wordes that cryste hymselfe taught to a man that doubted sayenge and askynge of our lorde who sholde be saued, for he thoughte it was to harde to hymselfe for to eschewe all the poyntes that ledde man to pardycyon. ...

Byleue, sayd our lorde Ihesu, that god the fader is almyghty and that no thynge to hym is impossyble, but that he may forgyue all synnes and redresse all wronges and brynge the soules to his blysse, and thynke ferthermore that his myght and power may do all that his wysdome can, and his goodnes wyl, and therfore truste fully that by his goodnes he wyll saue you and brynge you to euerlastynge Ioye whan he seeth best tyme, for he hath bought you full dere with his precyous blode and paynefull deth. And I dare sauely saye that there is none so synfull a caytyf whiche is crystened or wolde be crystened this daye on the erthe all thoughe he were in the syght of god dampnable and in the syght of all creatures also, ye, and yet were Iuged to be dampned by all scrypture and he wolde for sake his synne and be contryte and aske god forgyuenes, he sholde haue mercy and forgyuenes of hym; and yf it were so that he stode in that case or had a good mynde to stonde so in the tyme of deth he sholde be saued; the myght and mercy of god is so grete that it surmounteth all his lawes, Iugementes, and scryptures .... And therfore be ye not doubtefull nor heuy, for it shall neuertourne you to peryll ne daunger but to grete proufyte. For therby ye shall wynne the crowne of glorye and the palme of vyctorye whiche shall be gyuen to you for withstandynge of suche temptacyons, and to the fende it shall tourne to shame and confusion; and though it semeth to you somtyme that ye fele dyscorde bytwene god and you, be not therfore recreaunt ne dyscomforted. ...

The fyfte chapytre

And therfore grutche not agaynst the wyll of god, ne meruayle not of these temptacyons, for the more that a man or a woman be tempted in this maner or in ony other agaynst theyr wyll and they withstande it, that is to saye not wyllyngly consentynge therto but mekely suffreth the same, the more they shall encreace in vertues to the proufyte of theyr soules in the syght of god; thoughe it be hydde from them, for perauenture whan ye be sharpely tempted ye thynke ye be to dull and neglygent in ghoostly excercyse thorughe wyckednes of your spyryte, that is sore trauayled and vexed, wherby ye thynke that ye haue a wyll consented to suche temptacyons as ye be tempted with but it is not so .... Therfore ye good chyldren that sharpely be vexed with suche temptacyons and tribulacions comforte your selfe in your benygne and mercyfull fader that sayth to you by his prophete in holy wryte, my chyldren though ye go in the fyre drede ye not, for the flame therof shall not trouble you. As who sayth ye that be crysten people wyllyngly to do well though ye goo in to the fyre of trybulacyons and temptacyons drede you not, for it shall tourne you to no peryll but thorugh my goodnes and the merytes of my passyon it shall tourne you to grete proufyte and comforte of your soule; the maner of all these temptacyons and the remedyes of the same sheweth our sauyour Iesu cryst to his apostle saynt Peter, as it appereth in the gospel, where he sayth thus, Peter sathanas asketh and desyreth to syfte the as men syfte whete wherby it appereth well that the fende hath no myght, ne power to attempte the seruauntes of almyghty god but by his suffraunce, and that was euydently knowen by the temptacyons of Iob whome the fende besyfted and tempted, for the more that whete is syfted and cast from syde to syde the more clene it is. Ryght so the more that a man or a woman be tempted with the fende ayenst theyr wyll the more clene they be afore god, wherfore it appereth playnly that almyghty god suffreth not his seruauntes to be tempted, but for theyr grete wele and profyte yf they purpose them selfe myghtely to withstande the fendes temptacyon, whiche no man may withstande without the helpe of god. Therfore of his helpe he maketh vs sure lyke as he sayd to peter these wordes, I haue prayed for the that thy fayth fayle the not, and therfore that man whiche pacyently is redy to suffre all troubles and dyseases for the loue of his maker almyghty Ihesu, not takynge hede of all the fendes mocyons and temptacyons, that man thrugh the myght and grace of cryst bereth downe and ouercometh the fende, wherby he may be called a vaynquyssher or ouercomer.

And to suche men may be sayd thus, thou that arte thus tourned to almyghty god by the vertue of pacyence, but yf thou helpe to counseyle and conferme thy bretherne. And teche them to suffre as the grace of god hath taught the, or elles thou arte vnkynde. For Salamon sayth that one brother well counseylled and confermed by an other is a myghty Cyte ayenst the fende, and therfore they that be sharpely trauaylled and tempted whan they haue had the good counseyle of theyr brother, they ought to take comforte to them sayenge with Dauid whiche sayth, O my soule why arte thou so vnstedfast thus to assayle and trouble me; trust onely to almyghty god that is full of benygnyte and mercy whome I onely confesse and knowlege to serue, be I neuer so sore trauaylled ne troubled. And to suche men thus vexed with thoughtes, mocyons, and sterynges is behouefull to take the counseyle and techynge of the wyse and dyscrete persones, fleynge vtterly theyr owne wylde fantasyes whiche often tymes gretely troubleth them. And in eschewynge of suche temptacyons and troubles they must gyue them selfe to good and vertuous occupacyons, as to redynge and sayenge the seruyce of almyghty god, and doynge other vertuous dedes, and euer amonge prayenge to almyghty god they may haue strength in theyr soules to resyste suche mocyons and temptacyons. And though they fynde in them selfe noo maner of swetenes ne sauour in goddes seruyce, yet they ought not to be heuy therfore yf theyr wyll and mynde be to fulfyll the same. For as holy wryte sayth euery good wyl is accepted for the dede. Saynt Barnarde sayth that somtyme god withdraweth deuocyon from prayer to make the prayer more medefull, for he wyll be serued somtyme in bytternes and somtyme in swetenes, whiche bothe two we muste mekely receyue. And therfore Arystotle sayth that with the more dyffyculte and trauayle vertuous ben goten, the more they proufyte and encrease in the soule. ... Ryght so yf a man be in perfyte rest and quyetnes of herte, it is no maystry for hym to serue god. But it is a maystry to hym that is in trauayle and out of quyetnes of herte to serue hym; therfore, that creature that is tempted or vexed in the seruyce of almyghty god and is in wyll to withstande the sayd temptacyons tyll he after be strengthed and comforted by the holy ghost, the fende shall neuer haue power to fere, ne put hym in drede, for though it be longe or he fele comforte yet let not hym drede, for our mercyfull sauyour knoweth what tyme comforte is moost nedefull to hym than he fayleth not to gyue it hym. For somtyme the felynge of swetnes is withdrawen from man or elles he sholde wexe proude and presumtuous, or neglygent and recheles in vertuous lyuynge, and therfore it is withdrawen for the best to the helth of his soule, wherfore hardnes and sharpenes sente to a creature is full proufytable to the soule; as saynt Austyn sayth in techynge vs of the maner of almyghty god, that whan a man is feble and newly tourned to hym he gyueth hym peas and swetnes to the entent to stablysshe hym in his lawe and loue. But whan he is stablysshed and sadly[35] grounded in his loue, than suffreth he hym to be vexed and trauaylled for two reasons, one is to proue hym and to crowne hym the hyer in the blysse of heuen. An other is to pourge hym of his synnes in this worlde, that in noo wyse he be from hym in the euerlastynge worlde.

The syxte chapytre

And for as moche as many men can not, nor wyll not in tyme of temptacion se or perceyue it, but haue a dredefulnes and a sorynes in themselfe by sterynge of theyr compleccyon, therfore to all suche men thre thynges be nedefull and necessarye. The fyrst is that they be not moche alone. The seconde is that they thynke ne study to depely in ony one thynge, but fully ordre them by some dyscrete persone, as afore I sayd and thoughe it come in theyr mynde that they sholde be in Ieopardye or peryll vtterly to be lost; they sholde take no hede of suche sterynges or thoughtes for it neuer may tourne them to daunger of theyr soules. Almyghty god sayth in the gospell, if the entent of a mannes purpose be good the dede is good.

35. Fully, completely, firmly, steadily, steadfastly: *MED* s.v. "sadli".

The thyrde remedye is this that for as moche as the fende laboureth to make a man dredefull and sorye, a man agayne ought to the honour of god and confusyon of the fende to strength hymselfe and be mery though it be ayenst his herte and drede, noo thynge the fendes malyce. For the lesse gladnes that he feleth in hymselfe the more meryte he shall haue whan he so enforceth hymselfe to be mery to the honour of god, and in spyte of his ghoostly enemy the deuyll. For as holy wryte sayth the holy appostles wente awaye mery and gladde whan the Iues, enemyes of god, had shamefully beten them. Also a man ought to be gladde for thre causes whan the fende tempteth and turmenteth hym. The fyrst is that he is troubled by the enemy of god. The seconde is by suche temptacyons and turmentes the fende sheweth playnly that he is his enemye and euery man ought to be gladde that goddes enemy is his enemy. And the thyrde is that by suche turmentes a man is not onely released of the paynes in purgatorye, but also it maketh hym to wynne euerlastynge blysse. Our lorde Ihesu sayth in the gospell, blessyd be they that suffreth persecucyon for ryght wysnes, for they shall haue the kyngdome of heuen. ...

The nynth chapytre

Also though the fende put in you ony thought of dyspayre, or make you to thynke that in the houre of deth ye shall haue suche euyll thoughtes and greuous sterynges, and that ye than shall be but lost; yet for all that byleue hym noo thynge, but answere that ye haue fully put your truste in god, and therfore for all his temptacions by the grete power of almyghty god and merytes of his passyon thynke verayly it shall be to you noo peryll of soule, but tourne to the shame and confusyon of your ghostly enemye and yf ony creature, man or woman, speke to you sharpe or dyscomfortable wordes take it mekely and pacyently, and thynke that perauenture it is done by the temptacyon of the fende to trouble and lette you, or that it is a chastysynge of god for some worde or dede that ye haue done contrarye to his wyll; for our lorde god dooth lyke a kynde moder, for a louynge moder that is wyse and well taught her selfe, she wolde that her chyldren were vertuously and well nurtured; and yf she may knowe ony of theym with a defaute she wyll gyue theym a knocke on the heed, and yf the defaute be more she wyll gyue hym a buffet on the cheke, and yf he doo a grete faute she wyll sharpely lasshe hym with a rode; and thus dooth god that is our louynge fader from whome all vertue and goodnes cometh; he wyll that his specyall chosen chyldren be vertuously and well taught in theyr soules, and yf they doo a defaute he wyll knocke them on theyr hedes with some wordes of dyscomforte and dyspleasure, and yf they doo a greter faute he wyll gyue them a buffet with grete sharpenes in sondry maners after the dyuerse condycyon of the defautes, and yf they doo a moche greter trespas than he chastyseth theym moche more sharpely.

And all this our blessyd lord doth for the specyall loue he hath vnto vs, for as he sayth hymselfe, them that he loueth them he chastyseth. Now truly and we toke good hede of these wordes we wolde be gladder of his chastysynge than of all this worldes cherysshynge, and yf we so dyde, all dysease and trouble sholde tourne vs to comforte and Ioye, but it is full harde thus to doo in the tyme of sharpe heuynes, whan a soule standeth naked from all ghoostly and bodely comforte to take and fynde Ioye in disease; al be it they that be in suche inwarde dures they must seke in all wayes how they may comforte themselfe in god, and thynke and trust fully that god sente neuer suche chastysynge but that he wolde in longe tyme or in shorte sende comforte, wherby they sholde be brought out of these heuynes. For the prophete sayth many be the trybulacyons of ryght wysmen, and all suche god shall delyuer; and though ye fele somtymes sterynges of desyres of suche vnkyndly euyll thoughtes, comforte you euer in the goodnes of god and in the paynefull passyon that his manhode suffreth for you; for the fende tempteth many of the seruauntes of god to dysperacyon and drede of saluacyon as well worldely men as other ghoostly lyuers, puttynge in worldely mennes myndes the greuousnesse of theyr synnes, and to the ghoostly lyuers he putteth drede and strayte conscyence in many more sondry wyses than I can tell; and full gracyously god hathe comforted theym and brought theym out of theyr errours ... . There sholde noo man be dyscomforted nor dyspayre of ony temptacyons, for hardely god wyll comforte hym whan he seeth his tyme, and thoughe he sende not a man comforte shortely, it shall be to his more mede; and therfore thynke alwaye whan ye thynke of ony temptacyons, bodely or ghostly, that ye stande in the blessynges of all holy chyrche, for holy wryte sayth,blessyd be they that suffreth temptacyons. For whan they be well proued they shall haue the crowne of lyf, the whiche almyghty god hath promysed to them that loue hym. ...

15b Obadiah Sedgwick, *The doubting beleever: or, A treatise containing 1. The nature 2. The kinds 3. The springs 4. The remedies of doubtings, incident to weak beleevers. By Obadiah Sedgwick, Bachelor in Divinity, and Minister of Coggeshall in Essex*, 1641, pp. 5–310.[36] *Wing* S2369. **Sources**: Thomas Fisher Rare Book Library, University of Toronto (forbes 00868).

... *CAP. I. The nature of Doubtings*

To understand this, you must know that in the worst part of the soul there are severall qualities, *viz.* 1. Infidelity, which strictly and amongst those which professe

36. The highly elaborate notes on the margins of the original are not included in this transcription.

the Gospel is a positive rejecting of heavenly truths, with their secret goodnesse; herein men forsake their owne mercies by plain dissents and sleightings of the good word of grace: as is evident in the Pharisees, *Luk.* 7:30, who rejected the counsell of God, &c.

2. Despaire, which is a manifest dissent not so much in respect of the thing, or object, (for this is assented unto as true in respect of it selfe, *viz.* That God is mercifull, and Christ did die for sinners) but in respect of the person or subject, wherein the soule gives up it self as lost, as without the compasse and hopefulnesse of the divine proclamation. It is perswaded that there is no possibility for it to recover the shore, and therefore sinks in the depths. My meaning is, That such a soule, though it sees that in God, and that in Christ which can save, and doth save others, yet cuts off it self as not at all capable of any interest in the mercie of God, or bloud of Christ, and so eternally falls under its owne weight, as is evident in *Judas* and *Cain.*

Now Despaire, so farre as it makes assent unto Truths, it is opposed unto Infidelity; and so farre as it dissents from speciall goodnesse in them, it is opposed to Faith; and so farre as it concludes impossibility of that good unto it selfe, it is opposed to Hope.

3. Fearfull opinions, which are positive assents unto Truths, yet raised upon such probable inducements onely, that the soule is left with a suspition, that the contrary may be true. They are like a man upon a weak plank in a great river, there he sits, and there he fears, because he knows not certainly how long he shall sit there.

4. Doubtings, which are the suspensions or inhibitions (the holdings up) of the soule from any determinate inclinations one way or other: they are the pawsings of the mind.

As take a man in a journey, where he meets with two waies, he looks on this, and inclines it may be the right, and then he looks on that, and supposeth that it may be the right, and then he looks upon both, and makes a stand, and goes on in neither: So it is with the soule in doubtings (spiritually). There are two wayes before it, two objects, two works, to beleeve or not to beleeve, and arguments to incline to the one, and to the other, drawing into some equality of strength and weight; just like a paire of scales, answerably ballanced, so that both are at a stand, there is no turning either to the right hand nor to the left.

Therefore, the Schoolmen say well that *Dubitatio est motus supra utramque partem contradictionis, cum formidine determinandi alteram partem ejus.*

That you may yet conceive this clearly, remember:

1. In our minds there are Assentings, which are the adherents of the understanding to truths known. And there are Dissentings, which are the bearings off

from those truths. There the soule positively inclines, here it declines; there it puts out the hand, and here it keeps it in.

2. Doubtings properly stand betweene them both; they are not plainly the one, nor plainly the other. If I may speak freely, I conceive them to have a twang of either; they are a *medium*, a middle thing, as your mixt colours are which you cannot style directly white, or directly black.

The soule hath a desire to joyne unto Truth, it hath a desire to share in that goodnesse which it apprehends; yet it neither fastens, nor yet rejects, but like the fish to the bait, it likes it, and is striking at it, but dares not, and swims about; or like *a wave of the sea* (that is the Apostles comparison, *James* 1:6) thrusting to the shore, and yet drawing back; or like a Meteor hovering in the aire twixt up and downe: Such rowling, reeling actions of the soule are doubtings; they are a recoyling adventuring: The soule sees reason of either side, to draw, and withdraw, to give on, and to give back. It sees Christ and the promises, knowes the goodnesse and bounty in the one and the other, whereupon it is giving on upon them, and putting out the hand, but then instantly it checks it selfe, and is stayed with contrary arguments and feares; I may not be so bold. Perhaps they belong not unto me.

So that the person is hanging betwixt hope and feare: I would, but I may not; I may, but I dare not. It is just with the soul as with those at Chesse, they set out a man, and think to take a King, but then presently they are checked, and draw him back againe. God he is my Lord and my King, nay and yet he is not; He will do me good, yet I feare he will not; He hath pardoned my sins, and yet I fear he hath not; He doth heare my prayer, yet I doubt he doth not; My estate is good and happy, neverthelesse I suspect it is not. Thus doth a man waver, and rowle, and is like a man in the ungrounded places, he no sooner plucks up one leg out of the dirt, but the other inks in: the soule is not determined one way or other.

3. One thing know more, that though the mind doth not pitch or rise unto a determinate action in spirituall doubtings, yet it ever inclines towards a determinate object; That is, though the doubting Christian cannot come yet to quit those uncertaine, and trembling, and shivering motions, and bring them to a stayednesse, and positive fixing, yet his mind hones, it lookes after Christ and the promises; it doth not reject, nor doth it give up all hopes; it keeps in it two things, which Infidelity and Despaire want.

> 1. One is, that it priseth Christ and the promises, though it cannot claspe them.
>
> 2. Another is, that it gives not up the case as desperate and impossible; but though it cannot fixe, yet it will be hovering about them.

Cap. II. The kinds and diversities of them

The second thing respects the sorts of doubtings, and these I must also touch.

I conjecture that there are foure sorts of doubtings.

1. Some are of admiration: in these the mind doth not gainsay simply, no, it doth beleeve, and is onely solicitous about the hidden manner or way of performance, or accomplishment. Such a doubting was that of the Virgin, *Luke 1:34*. ...

2. Others are of confirmation: Where the soule beleeves, but desires something more to secure and settle it, so that it might be put out of all doubt, as was that of *Gedeons, Judg. 6*. Which kindes of doubtings are the cravings of a little more indulgent security from God in matters of extraordinary concernment; not that we properly question the verity of him, but that (in respect of our selves) we might work the more confidently upon clearer evidence and warrant.

3. A third sort are of negation: and this is such a forme of scrupling wherein we plainly suspect God of his good word of truth; and is incident unto evill men in their generall course, and to good men in respect of some particular carriages and businesses, as is evident in *Zacharias, Luke 1:18. Whereby shall I know this?* This question was a question of doubting, and this doubting, no question, was an unbeleeving one: It did not credit the Angels message; so is it expressed, *ver. 20. Thou shalt be dumbe, because thou beleevest not my words.*

4. A fourth sort are of inquietation, where the mind is diversly carried, and is not come to a rest, as when a cause is not come to a sentence, but hangs in suspence. Now of this sort of doubtings wee speak at this time, which againe may be branched

> 1. Into *Reall*, which questions the principles themselves, either for truth or goodnesse, and so they respect matters of faith; or else they question actions touching lawfulnesse or unlawfulnesse, and so they respect matters of fact. In which respect they are more specially styled Scruples of conscience which are nothing else but some grating and painfull doubts about points practicall. Of which see the Casuists.
>
> 2. Into *Personall*; Where not the things in themselves, but in respect of our selves, are questioned, and onely questioned, not peremptorily denyed or rejected *viz.* I know and beleeve that God is a Father, that Christ is a Redeemer, and the Saviour of sinners; I now doubt, Noe whether there be any truth or good in these, for these I yeeld but upon view of my great sinfulnesse and many defects, now onely question (and this is enough) whether my interests be in that truth and goodnesse. What is said here of a case respecting Spiritualls, the same may be said of that other respecting the promises for Temporalls, because that doubting doe extend to both;

3. Again, there are two sorts of personall doubtings.

1. Some are privative, which move all presence of faith, for which see *1 Tim. 2:8.* and *Jam. 1:6.*

2. Some are contrary, which doe *minuere*, but not *negare*; they doe impaire and keep faith low, but not wholly deny or extinguish it, as in our present Text. ...

Cap. IV. Springs, Causes, and Occasions of doubting are or may be these

... 11. An eleventh cause of doubtings may be the suspension of divine favour. When God holds up his countenance, the light of it from shining into the heart so that a Christian doth not enjoy his day as before, his God as before, in the sensible evidences of his loving favour, now the soule may (possibly) fall into singular distrusts and fears. See it in *David, Psal. 30:7. Lord, by thy favour thou hast made my mountaine to stand strong; Thou didst hide thy face and I was troubled.* A Christian's life is, in some respect, like a Courtiers, who is neare his Prince, upon his countenance or forbearance all his comforts or discomforts doe depend. We may say of him what *Mary* spake when she lost Christ, *Luke 2:48. Behold, thy Father and I have sought thee sorrowing, (i.)* with an heavy heart. ...

2. Againe, In these times nothing can comfort the soul or stay it without much difficulty. Our very graces will hardly uphold us. You know that if the King clouds his countenance they are not the dignities conferred which will content us, they are not our revenews and possessions which will cheare us. So is it with us, when God draws up his loving countenance; They are not our riches, or our gifts, or our graces, or our services, which can delight us. These doe it, whiles in them we see God's love shining towards us, but if that draw back these are all put to a strait. All is nothing to *David* whiles hee is under this enquiry, *Will the Lord be favourable no more? Psal. 77:7.*

3. God doth seldome draw up his favour but for some unkindnesse on our part. Our sins (ordinarily) are the clouds which hide his face from us, they are the wall of separation; perhaps some great sin, as *Davids*, perhaps some carelesse esteems of him, speaking in his Ordinances; perhaps some sleight passing by of his secret motions and counsels ... .

How can the soule but be greatly trouled [*sic*] when it hath turned its day into night, and shut up that light which once it injoyed to its great comfort and solace? *Woman, why weepest thou?* (said Christ to *Mary, Joh.* 20:15) *Because* (said she) *they have taken away my Lord, and I know not where they have laid him.* So may we justly weep when our sinnes have taken away our

God from us in his comfortable favour, and we cannot easily regaine him, and find him.

4. These times of suspension ordinarily are times of tryall wherein God leaves the Christian to some notable combats, and to the great exercises of Graces; at which time, corruptions and temptations will stir, and therefore no marvaile if they be times mixt with some feares and doubtings.

12. Another spring of doubtings is the crediting of Satan's testimony touching our estate, when we rest upon his judgement, and see our conditions through his informations.

You know that objects are diversly represented unto the eye. Sometimes from themselves in their proper nature, as when a man sees a green colour as it is; sometimes mediately, by other things, as when a green colour is seen through a red glasse; now it doth not appeare in its native colour, but in the likenesse of that through which it is perceived. So is it with our spirituall estate.

Sometimes it is represented unto us, as it is truly existing; and thus we shall see it, when we look upon it, and judge of it by the word of God: And sometimes it is represented unto us, not as it is, but as it appears in some corrupt and deceiveable testimonies and reports unto us: As *Josephs* chastity appeared to his Master under the nature of abominable uncleannesse, when he took the testimony of it from his filthy wife.

So shall our most innocent and upright frame appeare unto us to be nothing else but basest hypocrisie, if we put the issue of it upon Satan's informations. For as Satan hath an art to colour over the true condition of sinfull bondage, keeping close and in covert the proper image, or (rather) deformity of it. So he hath a delusion, too, in hiding from our eyes the true powers of gracious sincerity, and fetching up to the judgement all our weaknesses and present imperfections, with all former knowne evils, with which he doth so totally possesse the mind, that it can hardly see any thing that good is in it selfe, or if it doth, yet it sees so much corruption and imperfection as that it is ready almost to turne the scale and ballance. And here our crafty enemy ceaseth not, but taking the advantage of a tender conscience, he exaggerates upon us the large distance of this condition in which we now are, from that which God commands and expects, and hath found in some of his righteous servants, in the citation of whose piety he is not very sparing; that by the consideration of their fulnesse and our owne emptinesse, wee might the more easily suspect our condition, and credit his relations. Which if we once doe, *Bone Deus!* into what labyrinths doe we wind our selves? into what fears? into what doubts? We shall never set out to beleeve any Promise, but hee checks us back with the hollownesse of our condition; we shall never set upon any ordinance or duty, but he foyles us with suspicions (at least) that all is in vaine, God will not blesse and prosper his Ordinances unto such; And in those Ordinances, if any matter of bitternesse or uncomfortablenesse be delivered, he brings home that to us, and tels the soule, This is thy portion.

Now where our estate rests upon a deceitfull informer, where we take things as Satan makes them, where we judge of sin as he pleads it, and of God's love to us as he conveys it, and of God's Promises as he interprets them to us, and of our owne Graces, and holy temper as he cleares and evidenceth them unto us, there can be nothing but jealousies, feares, distractions, and daily doubtings in the heart.

13. Another spring may be some new risings of old sinnes after humiliation, and some singular assurance of their pardon. *David* gives a touch at this (I think) *Psal.* 25:7, when he prayes, *Remember not the sins of my youth, nor my transgressions.* So doth *Job,* 13:26. *Thou writest bitter things against me, and makest me possesse the iniquities of my youth.*

It would trouble us to see a man rise up out of his grave, (who hath been buried a long time) and now to haunt us. So these sins which we have long since committed and long since bewailed, and long since renounced, and after long humiliations their discharge hath been obtained; to meet these sins (like an enemy with a sword in his hand) with guilt in their faces and countenances againe, this will amaze the soule, it will appale it, and startle it, and make us more then once to sigh and inquire, Why is it so? Two things will now fall into question.

> 1. The reality of pardon: Where God saith, he *pardons sinne,* there he saith, that he will *remember it no more.* But it seemes he doth remember it, (else how comes it thus upon me as a debt not yet discharged, as a guilt not yet removed?) and if he doth thus remember it against me, I much feare, that as yet the Book is not crossed, this sin is not pardoned. Upon which something else may fall in. If this sinne be not pardoned, perhaps the rest are not; and if this be risen up against me, how can I tel but all the rest may (afresh) set themselves in array, and give a second charge upon my conscience too?
>
> 2. The reality of Repentance. For where God calls for sound repentance, (as *Esay* 1:16. *Wash you, make you cleane, put away the evill of your doings from before mine eyes, cease to doe evill*) there God doth promise, (*ver.* 18) that *Though our sins be as scarlet, yet they shall be as white as snow; and though they be red like crimson, yet they shall be as wooll,* in which words are expressed a plaine change of the sinfull condition; our sins shall not be what and as once they were. ...

These are the springs of Doubtings, which I have enlarged in their opening unto you; it is likely there may be more then these, (I could also deliver you more about the temporall estate; but that is out of our scope and compasse now). It now remains that I descend to the closing up of these springs, to the cures and remedies of these Doubtings, which is the last thing proposed.

CAP. V. The Cures and Remedies of Doubtings

Here lies our next and greatest work. And therefore as Physitians in this part are more cautelous to administer things which are in their qualities most proper, and in their measures most convenient; so must we in the healings and closings of the spirituall distempers of the soule. And therefore that this work may be happily performed, I shall (desiring Gods grace to assist and blesse) prescribe unto you, 1. The particular cures which shall answer all those particular springs of doubtings before mentioned. Then 2. The generall Cures and Remedies which may extend to the help of all, or most of our doubtings, if time and leasure hold out.

The particular Cures

... [3.] 2. Particularly, for the mortifying of remaining Infidelity doe three things:

1. Study exactly the Covenant of Grace, in the Author of it, foundation of it, matters contained in it, and all the adjuncts and termes of graciousnesse, sutablenesse, fulnesse, faithfulnesse, &c. appertaining to it.

2. Study Jesus Christ thoroughly, know him distinctly in the person of a Mediator, and offices, and effects, and works.

Then 3. To much meditation in these abound in Prayer, that God in particular would cause thee by faith to set thy seale unto them. But more of this will follow in answering some other causes of doubtings.

2. The second spring was weaknesse and imperfection in faith. The cure and remedy of which is to perfect and strengthen faith; put more strength, more growth, more ripenesse into faith, and your doubtings will be lesse. The more purely the fire burnes, the lesse smoke it hath; and when the light and heat of the Sunne are greatest, then the clouds and misty vapours are fewest. Faith and Doubtings are like a paire of scales, where the waight of the one beares away the other. The Disciples, I remember, prayed, *Lord, increase our faith;* and so did he of whom you heard in *Mark* 9. *Lord, help my unbeliefe.* You will say, No man can deny, that if his faith had more strength, then his heart should have lesse doubting; But how may that be done? How may faith be strengthened?

I answer,

1. God, who gave faith, can strengthen it; for every grace depends upon him, not onely for birth, but also for complement; his strength must lead us on from strength to strength, from faith to faith; he who is the Author, is also the finisher of it. And therefore if thou wouldst have a strong faith, thou shouldst go to a strong God, and beg of him, *Lord, increase my faith*. My knowledge is dim, lighten that candle, open mine eyes yet more, that I may see thy truths. My assents many times shaking, but do thou establish and comfirm my heart in thy truths. My embracings, applications, very trembling and broken, and interrupted, but doe thou guide mine eye to look upon my Saviour, do thou guide my hand to lay hold on him, doe thou enable my will and affections to embrace all the goodnesse of thy selfe, of thy Christ, of thy Word.

It is God's method to lay in (at the first) weak faith, that we might beg for more faith, and give him the honour of all. Had we it strong at first, he should not heare of us, but he dispenseth it by degrees that in all our gettings, and in all our victories over doubtings, &c. his strength may have the glory. Therefore goe to God, and say, Lord, I would have more faith, thou wouldst have me to perfect it, but all perfection is in thee, and I cannot by my meere strength ripen what thou givest, but thou canst water what thou plantest, though it be sowne a weak body, yet thou canst make it rise a strong body; though faith at first be but as a graine of mustard-seed, yet thou canst cause it to blossome, and to spread it selfe into a high measure. Therefore thou who alone canst doe it, doe it for thy weak servant. Thou must take charge of thine own graces; and if thou givest my faith more strength, my beleeving will bring thee in the more glory, &c.

2. The studying of Christ and the Promises more will bring more strength and perfection to faith. It is with the Christian as it is with the Scholar, let the Scholar study more the objects of knowledge, and then his knowledge will grow to be more large. So, let the Christian study more the matters of faith, and his faith will rise to be more full. ...

If a man studyeth his sins in his own way, in a naturall way, he shall neither rightly see them, nor yet be freed from them. So if men study Christ their owne way, if they will have him to be such a one as their fearfull hearts would make him to be, and not such a Saviour as God hath manifested him to be, then not conceiving of Christ as he is, they shall be and remaine still as they were.

3. Be in the wayes of strength. There are wayes in which God doth reveale his arme; his arme is that which doth strengthen us, and his arme is revealed in his Ordinances, for God doth not call us, nor change us, nor strengthen us, nor save us without meanes. He who is too good for the Ordinances, will ever be too weak in his faith. A child which cannot stand when it is borne, may yet goe by the use of the breasts; but that person who is weake, and wants strength, if he feeds not, will abate more, and ere long want life it selfe. This is a truth: A new Christian is sometimes full, and a full Christian is alwayes weak; for our spirituall life is like unto our naturall life, both of which are within us, yet neither of them do rise, but from something without us. ...

Doth not God love those, whom (out of his meere love) he hath chosen? Doth not God respect the descent and generation of Christ? those who come of his blood? They who come from Christ, and are borne of God, are surely beloved of God. ...

3. The third spring of doubtings was the study of the life of sense. The remedy of which is the keeping of it downe. If you will keep off doubtings, you must keepe down sense and feeling. *Blessed* (saith Christ to *Thomas, Joh.* 20:29) *are they that have not seene, and yet have beleeved.* If a man thinks this, That Christ is not mine, unlesse I handle him; and God is not mine, unlesse I see him; and grace is not mine, unlesse I feele it; he will be for ever full of doubts and feares.

For the helping of which, consider these things.

1. Sense is not a fit Judge of our condition; it cannot report our estate but by what it feeles; but, the spirituall estate is not alwayes under feeling: wee should be good and bad, found and lost, cheerfull and sorrowfull, many times in one day, nay in one houre, if that sense gave sentence on our condition. ...

2. The spirituall course many times goes against our sense, and therefore sense must be kept downe. You know that *Abraham* against hope beleeved in hope, *Rom.* 4:18. Faith and sense are many times at a contradiction; faith will beleeve what sense perceiveth not; and what our sense doth perceive that same our faith will not beleeve, but the contrary. *Though he kill me, yet will I trust in him,* saith *Job*. And *Abraham* beleeved his sons safety, in the sacrificing of him; and we our immortality, notwithstanding our death and corruption. This is very certaine that when we feele corruptions living, faith will beleeve them to be dying; and when we feele our selves in trouble, faith will then beleeve our comforts and deliverances. Faith usually (I doe not say alwayes) beleeves the contraries unto sense. ...

3. Sense or feeling is not *medium credendi*, but *fructus fidei*: *(i.)* It is not the ground of beleeving, but a fruit of faith. *v.g.* Take feeling in the most excellent parts of it, as in assurance, and joy, and peace, these are not Antecedents to faith, but Consequents of it. What is that? That is, a man hath not these first, and then faith for or from these, but he hath faith first, and these afterward. ...

8. An eighth cause of doubtings was weaknesse of judgment about the essentials of salvation, which necessarily doth cause doubtings, both in respect of those suspicions, and errors, and mistakings to which it is subject, as also in respect of that scrupulosity which ever adheres to the conscience, where weaknesse adheres to the judgment.

Now the remedy of this spring consists in these particulars.

1. Get a distinct knowledge of Fundamentals. It is the emptinesse of our minds that we be preposterous in our searches. Many a Christian loseth himselfe in a sea of opinions, before he hath squared himselfe with the first grounds of Religion. ...

2. Get a distinguishing knowledge of Fundamentals from Accessories. Every part of the house is not the cornerstone, or the pillars. A man may take away much, and yet the house may stand. If you take away the painting and musick, or some seelings and annexed posts, yet the house may stand. So may a Christians salvation, though he know not many accessory truths; nay, although hee mistake about them; nay, although he deny them, if this denyall be not accompanied with a proud perversnesse, but arise onely from inevidence and inability. ...

3. Reduce all conjectures and consequent truths unto the first truth. It is the counsell of the Apostle, 1 *Thes.* 5:21. *Prove all things.* And the Prophet *Esaiah, To the Law, and to the testimony. Esa.* 8:20. ...

6. Informe the conscience with the nature of a Christian and saving condition. Some things are required towards salvation, some things unto salvation; some things give a being, other things a comfortable being. Of all which if a person had a speciall and distinct knowledge hee might walke more quietly without feares and doubtings. ...

From all this, the doubtfull heart may perhaps be setled about his estate in grace. Aske him, Dost thou love God? I doe. Serve him with all thy might in all thy wayes? I do. Rest upon Jesus Christ? I do. Combat and war against sin? I doe; and yet I feare all is not right. Why? Because I never had such terrors as others. Now then informe thy weak judgment; If God hath shewn unto thee thy sinfulnesse; If he hath abated thee, and emptied thee of thy self; If sin and thou are now at defiance; If thou hast yeelded unto the receiving of Christ upon his owne termes and conditions, though thy legall preparations were not answerable to others, either for intension of strength and measure, or for extension of length and time, yet thy condition is good and safe. For that humiliation which is accompanied with these issues is assuredly blessed and comfortable. If the physick carries away the humour, though it doe not make the person so sick, yet it is good. And though a man want a storme to drive him to shore, yet is he safe enough if he be landed with a softer gale and tide. ...

Brethren, how exceedingly doe we disturbe our selves with doubtings here? Many people, through a weaknesse (I say no more) of judgement, doe fall out with their estate and condition, molest and afflict their hearts, close up all against themselves, suspect, and foolishly reason and argue the nullity of a gracious condition, from the imperfections which they observe in their graces, from their behindments in faith, and zeale, and sorrow, &c. Ah, ignorant people! who are truly industrious after the great measures of Grace, and will not yet quiet their feares, and still their doubtings with this,

1. That such earnest pantings, and inquietations, and unsatisfiablenesses cannot but spring from truth of grace.

2. Then, that where grace is in truth, though in the lowest measure, there the soule hath interest in Christ, in all the Promises, in God, in heaven, in all.

Remember this, He who hath least in grace, hath not that which he would have; and hee who hath most in grace, hath not that which he should have; and he who hath any truth of grace, hath enough to change his heart, and save his soule. I would beleeve in that fulnesse of assurance and reliance as thou dost, and if I cannot, I will yet beleeve as well as I can. He who said, *O woman, great is thy faith*, said also to another, not so strong, *Thy faith hath saved thee*. No man misseth of heaven for want of measure, but of truth. Our consolation lies much in the comparative degree, but our salvation is in the positive. Much grace will yeeld unto us here our heaven, and any grace, if true, will yeeld us heaven hereafter. ...

Remember this one thing: Upright and beleeving persons have alwayes a favourable God, though they have not alwayes the sense of Gods favour: yea though Satan doe testifie the contrary, which is the next spring of doubtings, and comes in now fitly to be handled.

12. A twelfth spring of doubtings was the crediting of Satan's testimony about our spirituall condition, and interests in God and Christ; to which if any distressed Christian doth hearken and attend, he shal never be freed from inqui-

etations and rowlings of mind, because Satan's testimony is ever directly or obliquely against the truth and comfort of our spirituall estate.

For the remedy and cure of which spring, be pleased seriously to consider of these subsequent conclusions:

1. The finall tryall of our eternall estate doth immediately and solely appertaine to the Court of heaven. Indeed, the disquisitive part belongs to us, but the decisive part belongs to God. We ought to search and prove our selves, but no man hath immediate power to decide his estate, by acquitting or condemning himselfe. This must be done by the voice of God in his revealed Word, which commands and forbids, and therefore absolves or binds. ...

Whence two things arise to informe and direct us, *viz.*:

1. Satan's judgment of our estate is but usurped. It doth not belong to him to sit upon our soules. It is against the Law of Nations that the same party should be witnesse and Judge. And we may say to him truly what the Pharisees proudly objected to Christ, *By what authority doth he these things*? Or as they to *Moses, who made thee a Judge over us*? Assuredly the enemy of our salvation is not to be the Judge of it, he being so maliciously vowed against our happinesse it is most unfit for him to decide it; and, therefore, though he usurps a judgement upon Christians, yet as *David* spake in another case, *Thou Lord wilt not leave the righteous when he is judged.* No assuredly, Satan shall one day be judged for taking upon him the judging of Gods people. And doe you thinke that Satan will give a true judgement unto us of our spirituall condition, who dares give in false evidence before God himselfe of *Job*, and who is said to accuse the brethren before God day and night? ...

CURING SPIRITUAL DISEASE

16a *The dyetary of ghostly helthe* (1523). **16b** John Downame, *Foure treatises, tending to disswade all Christians from foure no lesse hainous then common sinnes* (1613).

Introduction Little is known about the *Dyetary of ghostly helthe.* Much like many works throughout the Middle Ages, from *Ancrene wisse* to Flete's *Remedies,* it was dedicated to a community of religious, probably nuns, and relying on what is known about other such texts it is possible to assume that it was written by the spiritual advisor or confessor of these nuns.[37] Composed "In the begynnynge of this newe yere [1520]" (n. pag.) it was intended as a gift in return for the gifts that the community of sisters presented the author with on the occasion of the New Year.[38] The first printed edition comes from 1520 and there are no known manuscript versions of this text. The 1523 edition includes a portrait (engraved by W. Marshall in the seventeenth century, and added by a later, seventeenth-century reader[39]) of Hildegard of Bingen and a short biographical note about her, in addition to two engravings of a nun, one of her kneeling with rays of light spreading from a figure of God above her heart, and a dove close to her chest, with the nun seated at a writing table. Other editions include similar engravings, and all can be with good reason identified as woodcuts representing Hildegard of Bingen, particularly in light of the 1523 edition. The inclusion of these images in the editions of this text indicates a connection of the text to Hildegard herself, being perhaps a translation of a compilation of excerpts

37. It seems most likely it was their spiritual advisor, much like Walter Hilton was to the nuns to whom he addressed his *Scale of perfection,* as the author of the *Dyetary* says: "It is full vnsemynge to me for to shewe or wryte vnto you of the waye to vertue whiche am not yet all out of the way of wyckednes. Yet a gryndyngston maketh a knyfe bryght and sharpe thoughe it be neuer the sharper it selfe. So I maye moeue you to make you sharpe and quycke to ghostly thynges and to clerenesse of good lyuynge though I my selfe be ryght slowe and dull vnto the same. To teche goodnesse is a thynge that may not be vndone of them that haue cure and rewle of other persones though they do but lytell good themselfe. Cryst sayd of the pharysyes rulers of the people. Do as they saye, but not as they do. Not withstandynge our lorde hathe gyuen me a desyre to do well. I beseche hym I maye haue grace to perfourme my desyre to his pleasure honoure and laude. Therfore though my symple lyuynge can styrre you but lytell. I trust that my good wyll and desyre that I haue to your ghostly profyte shall excyte you bothe to encreace the more in vertu and also to helpe me with your prayers vnto the same" (*Dyetary,* Prologue, n. pag.).

38. T.A. Birrell, "The Printed Books of Dame Margaret Nicollson: A Pre-Reformation Collection," in *Essays on English and American Literature, and a Sheaf of Poems,* ed. Jan Bakker, J.A. Verleun, and J. Vriesenaerde (Amsterdam, 1987), 27–34, at 30.

39. I am grateful to Emily Reiner for help with this.

of some of her works on health, such as *Causae et curae*,[40] for example, or a translation of a short text found in a manuscript compilation containing some of Hildegard's works and wrongly attributed to her authorship, or perhaps a translation, copy, or paraphrase of some of her shorter works or letters addressed to a community of nuns. Alternatively, the portrait of Hildegard might simply indicate a broader indebtedness to Hildegard's work on health, particularly her approach to health as a holistic system including body, soul, mind, and the universe together, if the text itself was not taken directly from her writings. It is also possible that the author simply wished to present Hildegard to his or her readers as an exemplary nun, or that the text was addressed to Benedictine nuns, which seems highly likely.

The text was quite popular throughout the 1520s with editions in 1520, 1521, 1523, and 1527. Fairly short, the *Dyetary* contains tips on how to live a good, holy life, and how to maintain spiritual stamina. Spiritual health is an important goal many wished to reach, making works on the process of achieving this aim a popular, albeit somewhat loosely defined genre. The *Dyetary* is divided, as the author informs his readers, "into .xxiiij consyderacyons as the daye is deuyded into .xxxiiij [*sic*]. hours" (n. pag.) with each point treating a different aspect of godly life. The particular chapters thus speak of a number of topics: remembering that life is a pilgrimage (towards death); the brevity of life; the omnipresence of God; the importance of good deeds and good thoughts; the temptations of the world; the evils of idleness; the importance of activity (so as to avoid idleness) as well as of prayer and "study"; the importance of hearing mass and praying (including how to perform both); and the importance of virginity, meekness, patience, obedience, and of reverence to particular saints. Finally, the text speaks also of the virtue of sadness and moderation (including in speech); temperance in eating and drinking; of proper behaviour around the table and after the meal; of temptation and how to avoid it, particularly recommending meditation. Clearly designed for a religious audience, this text could also serve the laity in that many of the virtues and activities it proposes to nourish spiritual health can easily be accomplished by a devout lay person: a warning against idleness and a commendation of activity, work, prayer, meditation, and reading. It is thus likely that the *Dyetary* was also used by non-religious readers who treated recipes for spiritual health that it contains selectively, as a model to aspire to rather than a strict rule.

The *Foure treatises* is a text that, at first glance, is only loosely connected to the Dyetary, in that it is a work concerned with spiritual embetterment, although closer scrutiny reveals that they share a number of important features. A Westminster Assembly Protestant clergyman, as well as a licensor of the press and public preachers, John Dow-

40. The section on sadness in the *Dyetary* seems to contradict this, though, because Hildegard praised joy over sadness, whereas the *Dyetary* clearly advises its readers to keep themselves in virtuous sadness willingly. It is likely, however, that the *Dyetary* had more than one source and individual sections could belong to a different text, perhaps copied onto the same manuscript, while still being in part inspired by works of Hildegard.

name wrote his *Foure treatises* (including his *Treatise on Anger*, excerpted here) exclusively for a lay audience, and intended his work as a spiritual health manual, but produced a text much different from the *Dyetary* or similar texts of that kind. His *Treatise on Anger* is a treatise not about general spiritual health nor about general directions on how to achieve it, but very specifically about anger as a spiritual problem. The connections between physical and spiritual health[41] will become apparent to the reader after reading texts both from this section and the corresponding one in Part 2 of this book, but in Downame's text itself the connection is already very clear. As the *Dyetary* lists recommendations for the general wellbeing of the soul, so Downame lists them in view of the problems he believes anger poses to the soul, and finds that its source is predominantly physical, "choler," recommending a set of spiritual remedies to counteract it. The text is thus an interesting mixture of spiritual advice and less spiritual considerations of human behaviour, verging on being a treatise on the *sin* of anger as much as on the *emotion* of anger.[42]

Downame first defines what he considers wrath, and lists when it can be good and constructive: it can be theoretically commended since it was created by God, and can be used to convert sinners ("just" anger), but can likewise be misused and lead to evil ("unjust" anger). Among the internal causes of anger, the text then lists sins such as arrogance, pride, covetousness, "luxuriousnesse" (which echoes the capital sins), and curiosity, as well as lack of meditation. "External" causes of anger stem from interactions with others. Following a lengthy description of other "evils" that accompany it, the *Treatise* proceeds to remedies for unjust anger, and in these remedies we find an echo of what the author of the *Dyetary* likewise thought beneficial to spiritual health: the simple Christian virtues of patience (particularly since Downame defines anger as "the disease of impatiencie"[43]), modesty, and chastity, as well as avoiding temptation (or situations

41. For more, see Michael C. Schoenfeldt, *Bodies and Selves in Early Modern England: Physiology and Inwardness in Spenser, Shakespeare, Herbert, and Milton* (Cambridge, 1999).

42. For more on emotions and their relationship to sin in the late medieval and early modern period, see *Early Modern Emotions: An Introduction* (London, 2016), ed. Susan Broomhall, esp. chapters by Danijela Kambaskovic, Stephanie Trigg, R.S. White, Patricia Simons, Hannah Newton, and Aleksondra Hultquist; Barbara Rosenwein, "Theories of Change in the History of Emotions," in *A History of Emotions 1200–1800*, ed. Jonas Liliequist (New York, 2016); *A Cultural History of the Senses in the Renaissance, 1450–1650*, ed. Herman Roodenburg (London, 2014); Barbara Rosenwein, *Anger's Past: The Social Uses of an Emotion in the Middle Ages* (Ithaca, 2011); Morton Bloomfield, *The Seven Deadly Sins: An Introduction to the History of a Religious Concept, With Special Reference to Medieval English Literature* (East Lansing, MI, 1952).

43. From the title of the 1616 edition entitled *Spiritual physicke to cure the diseases of the soule, arising from superfluitie of choller, prescribed out of Gods word. Wherein the chollericke man may see the dangerousnesse of this disease of the soule vniust anger, the preseruatiues to keepe him from the infection thereof, and also fit medicines to restore him to health beeing alreadie subiect to this raging passion. Profitable for all to vse, seeing all are patients in this disease of impatiencie.*

that can awaken anger), moderation in speech as well as drink, thoughtfulness, and trust in God. While very different, then, these two texts share an interest in a holistically defined spiritual health for their readers and share a belief in the efficacy of the remedies they prescribe for spiritual tribulations; while they wish to cure different diseases, their advice indicates shared trust in religion and God as reliable medicine, as much for spiritual temptations as for the "excess of choler." Both also touch upon emotions, or "passions," as they were known, i.e., sadness (*Dyetary*), and anger (*Treatise*).

16a *The dyetary of ghostly helthe*, 1523; unnumbered pages. *STC* 6835. **Source** *EEBO*: Folger Shakespeare Library, Washington, DC (FILM Fo. 291.26).

... *Not onely the body but also the mynde muste be sparred vs from the occasyon of euyll.*

Thynke, though ye sholde be closed vp within. iiij. walles. It is not ynough to haue your bodyes sparred from the occasyons of euyll, where the mynde is wandrynge abrode in carnall pleasure, musynge vpon worldly vanytes, besyde with workes and matters of other persones, and caryenge moche for your frendes and kynnesfolkes, occupyed somtyme with vnlawfull and vnclenly thoughtes and desyres. Therfore ye must close vp also your minde and affeccyon from all suche thynges. And that must be by often and contynuall remembraunce of god as nere as ye maye. Close vp and hyde your loue and mynde in the depe and large woundes of our lorde Iesu cryst by deuoute remembraunce of his pytefull passyon, alway abydynge there for there our enemyes dare not medle, but whyder ye wyll or not, they wyl entre with you into the materyall cloyster: your enemy the flesshe must nedes in the deuyll wyll not be behynde. And as I suppose ye shall haue of hym more force and stronger batayle there than euer ye had before. And that we thynke nowe ryght lytell and easy shal than perchaunce be full harde and greuous to ouercome. Therfore prepayre your selfe manly. Stande fast in fayth and remembre the rewarde of your vyctory, trustynge in god onely for strength. ...

Of the vertue of sadnesse.

Se that ye be of sadde behauour bothe in mynde and outwarde gesture. Kepe your mynde dylygently in sadnes, and gyue it all to spyrytual exercyses, sufferynge no vayne thoughtes to reste therin. And myghtely subdue the concupyscence and passyons of the body, as wrath, carnall loue, bodily and worldly fere, sensual ioy, or dysolate laughyng. For ye can not be wel ordred outwarde but yf these ben ordred and well ruled inwarde, but yet that outwarde behauoure helpeth moche to ouercome these inwarde passyons. And therfore it behoueth to kepe wysely the bodyly. v. wyttes that ye shal se, here, or touche nothynge that sholde styre you to euyll or dysteyne good maners; kepe youre syght close towarde the erthe, consyderynge that the eye is a thefe and wyll betray the soule yf it be not warely kepte. Fyxe not your syght vpon beautyfull thynges and here no vayne ne vycyous comunynge, ferynge leest dethe wyll entre in at your wyndowes and infecte your soules with synne.

Of sadnesse and dyscrecyon in speche and other behauoure.
Moost dylygently refrayne youre tonge and speke not without a reasonable questyon be made vnto you, or elles whan ye be constrayned by euydent nede, and than study to gyue an answere breuely and mekely, spekynge with sad countenaunce, reuerence, and swete fere of god, eschewynge alway talkynge and the occasyons of the same, excepte it be of ghostly maters and with ryght ghostly persones. Speke no thynge but yf it be semynge for the tyme, place, and persone. Myxte your honest myrthe with sadnes bothe in speche, laughynge, and gesture of body without rownynge or castynge the syght towarde ony persone suspectly, without lystynge or mouynge of the heed or ony other membre vnsemyngly. Be gentyl without grutchyng your countenaunce lowly, and cherefull without frownynge, lowrynge, or derysyon. Whan ye speke, laugh, or smyle se it be without scornynge or lowde voyce. Be not to hasty nor to slowe in your goynge. Shewe no sluggysshnes in your restyng. Inquyre not of other persones conuersacyons ne consyder theyr defautes. Refourme that is amys in other persones without ony reprouynge. Neyther prayse ne dysprayse your selfe nor gretly other persone. Speke nothyng to be reputed holy or connynge. Gyue place to yre betymes, and to them that multyply wordes agaynst you, and forgyue shortly theyr errour or neglygence. And thus ye shall kepe the vertu of sadnes and descrecyon, whiche is a greate helpe to charyte and to all other vertues. Wherto saynt Poule moeueth vs sayenge, Let your sadnes be knowen to all men. And so by good ensample ye maye profyte other and meryte very moche. ...

How to ouercome temptacyon.
If he be very fyerce agaynst you with temptacyon or trybulacyon, how soeuer greuous it be, dyspayre not. Thynke, there ben. xii. dyuers houres in the daye, they shall not be alyke vnto you. Some good and some badde. Thynke how oure lorde loketh vpon you to proue youre stedfastnesse and manlynesse, for to gyue you the larger crowne of glory and saye with Tobe, Yf we haue not taken good thynges of the hande of god, why sholde we not take yll. And remembre holy

saytes that haue ben troubled here before. And marke it wel that whom soeuer god wyll vysyte with grace and consolacyons, hym wyll he fyrste proue in the fyre of trybulacyon. Therfore neuer gyue vp to youre aduersary, ne grutche not with the troublous temptacyons, nor loke to moche of that that is layde to you by temptacyon, but goo forwarde aboute your good besynesse as thoughe ye dysdeyned to here of suche thynges. Or elles speke thus in youre mynde, refourmynge youre soule, sayenge. Lo, my soule, lo how the deuyll knocketh at thy gate. Yf thou suffere hym to come in, thy strength shall go from the, and thou shalte perysshe with grete mysery, and thou shalte suffre grete payne and shame before god and man. O thou frayle body, all this wyckednesse precedeth of the. Beware thou be not subiecte vnto the deuyll. Consyder howe that god is present to se how thou shalte fyght with thyne enemy. Crye for helpe vnto heuen that they may assyst vs and put away our aduersaryes. Thou can not se them and therfore the batayle is the more peryllous. Suffer and take vpon the a lytell payne, and thynke howe pleasaunt thy vyctory shall be. And contrary, yf thou folowe the shorte pleasure of thy temptacyon, eternall payne wyll folowe. Therfore, beware, and than fall to prayer, and what soeuer the deuyl speketh in you by temptacyon, thynke it is not your worde nor youre doynge, therfore care not for it, but goo forwarde, trustynge that as after grete stormes cometh fayre weder. So after grete trybulacyon shall folowe ghostly consolacyon.

How study or medytacyon in holy wrytynge profyteth moche agaynst temptacyon.
For this cause I wolde ye sholde alway fere, trustynge nothynge vpon your owne strength but alway suspecte your owne fraylte, and as a dowue that fereth the hawke dothe comunely vse the ryuer syde, and as in a glasse dothe spye in the water the shadowe of the hawke flyenge for to deuoure her, and so is aware of her and saueth herself, so I wolde ye sholde do. The ryuers or waters ben the sentences of holy scrypture, the lyfe of our sauyour Ihesu cryst, and of other holy saytes. Whiche flowynge fro the moost clere fountayne of the dyuyne wysedome dothe shewe and dyscouer the subtyll crafte and false suggestyon of our enemye the deuyll, and techeth vs howe we shall beware of hym for to escape his daunger. Nothynge swageth concupyscence more, nothynge putteth away euyl thoughtes better, than with the study or medytacyon of the worde of god and holy redynge. Vnto the whiche I wolde that ye sholde so accustome your mynde and occupy youre hartes so therupon, that whan ye go to bed ye myght fall on slepe in the thynkynge of some sentence of holy scryptures or saytes lyues and dreame of them in your slepe; that as soone as ye shall wake they maye cleue to your memory. And therfore whan ye be troubled or waked by the crafte or

yllusyon of your enemy, beware of vayne thoughtes, betymes auoydynge al dulnesse of body and mynde. And ocupye you thus or elles in prayers. ...

16b John Downame, *Foure treatises, tending to disswade all Christians from foure no lesse hainous then common sinnes; namely, the abuses of swearing, drunkennesse, whoredome, and bribery. Wherein the greatnesse and odiousnesse of these vices is discouered; and the meanes and remedies, which may either preserue, or weane men from them, are propounded. Whereunto is annexed a treatise of anger. By Iohn Downame Batcheler in Diuinity, and preacher of Gods word*, 1613, pp. 60–67.[44] *STC* 7142. **Source** *EEBO*: The Huntington Library, San Marino, CA (Syn. 7.60. 141).

A Treatise of Anger, wherein the lawfull vse, and the vnlawfull abuse of this affection is shewed out of Gods word
CHAP. VII. The remedies of vniust anger.
... The remedies against anger are of two sorts: first, those which cure anger in our selues; secondly, those which cure it in others; and they both are of two kindes: first, such as preuent anger and preserue vs from falling into it; secondly, such as free vs from it after it hath taken place. For anger is a disease of the minde: as therefore wise Physitions thinke it the better and safer course to preserue health and preuent sicknesse, then to remooue the disease after it hath taken possession of the body; so the best course in ministring spirituall Phisick is to preserue the soule from vice rather then to purge it away after it hath infected it; for *Vitia facilius repelluntur, quam expelluntur*: Vices are more easily kept from entrance then thrust out after they are entred; for as the common prouerbe is, there are but twelue points in the law, and possession is as good as eleauen of them. If therefore anger haue gotten possession, we shall hardly dispossesse it: It is our soules mortall enemy; as therefore we first seeke to keepe the enemy from entring the frontires of our country, but if he be entred, as soone as we can to expell him, so we must first endeauour to repel anger by stopping the passages of our harts, that it may haue no entrance, but if it haue taken place, quickly to expell and remooue it. ...

The first cause of anger is selfe loue; if therefore we would not fall into anger, we must labour to banish selfe loue, and to follow the rule of charitie; *Loue our neighbours as our selues, and doe nothing vnto them, which wee would not haue them do vnto vs.* Before therefore we let the reines loose vnto our anger, let vs set our

44. Marginal notes in the original source were not included in the transcription.

selues in the place of him with whom we are angry, and consider how we would desire to be vsed if we had so offended, and in like manner are we to behaue our selues towards him. So shall we not aggrauate those iniuries which are offered vs, and extenuate those which we offer others, so shall we not haue our iudgement ouer-ballanced with an vnequall affection, so shall we not bee incensed for suffering that which wee haue often offered.

The second cause of anger is pride and hautinesse of spirit; if therefore we would not fall into anger, we are to subdue pride and labour for the contrary grace of humilitie. For they who would bee meeke with our Sauiour Christ must also learne of him the lesson of true humilitie, *Math.* 11:29. *Learne of me, for I am meeke and lowly of hart.* If we would lay aside that arrogant conceit which we haue of our selues, and the ouerweening opinion of our owne excellencies, if we would consider with *Abraham* that we are but *dust and ashes,* and with *Dauid,* that wee *are wormes and no men;* or if we would in sincerity of hart say with *Iob, Vnto corruption, thou art my father, and vnto the worme, thou art my mother, and my sister.* ...

The third cause is Couetousnesse, which vice wee must banish out of our hearts if we would not be ouercome with vniust anger; so shall wee not gape after great preferments, nor expect much; and consequently, we shall not be disturbed with vnquietnesse, nor incensed with anger, when wee come short of our hopes. So shall we not intermeddle with euery domesticall trifle, but commit some thing to the care of Seruants, some thing to Children, and most of all to the Wife, who is a ioynt gouernour in this little commonwealth. And if any thing miscarry vnder any of their hands, we will not so much looke to the meanes, as to the supreame cause, the prouidence of God, considering that if he build not the house they labour in vaine that build it, if he blesse not their labours they cannot prosper.

The fourth cause is luxuriousnesse and curious nicenesse; if therefore we would subdue anger, we must subdue this vice also, and labour to attaine vnto decent homelines the Nurse of good hospitality, and the preseruer of peace and quietnesse; for if with our first parents *Adam* and *Eue* we were clothed with skinnes, that is, with meane attyre, we would not be so easily prouoked to anger if a spotte or wrinckle be found vpon our garments; if with them we did feed vpon roots and hearbs, we would not eate with surfetted and cloyed appetites, and consequently (our meates being saused with hunger) our tastes would not be so wantonly curious, that no ordinary cookery can please them. ...

The fift cause of vniust anger is vaine curiositie in desiring to heare and see all things. If therefore we would auoid anger, we are to abandon this troublesome companion, needlesse curiositie. For many things will neither grieue nor hurt vs if we neuer heare nor see them. Whereas he that busily inquireth what is said against him in euery company, he that listneth at euery doore, and vnder euery wall, he that rippeth vp ill words spoken against him in secret doth both disquiet himselfe with anger, and make his owne faults more publike. ...

The sixt cause is to haue open eares to euery tale-bearer, and credulous hearts to beleeue them. For it is the nature of men to be most desirous of hearing that which most displeaseth them, *Et libenter credere quae inuitè audiunt,* willingly to beleeue those things which they are most sorry to heare. But if we would auoid vniust anger, we must auoyd this vice also: *Multos absoluemus si caeperimus ante iudicare quam irasci,* we shall acquit many, if we will not be angry before we iudge. ...

The last cause of vniust anger is want of meditation concerning humaine infirmities, either those which are common to all mankinde, or those which are more proper and peculiar to our selues. If therefore we would be restrained from anger we must often thinke of this contagious leprosie of originall sinne, which hath so generally infected all the sonnes of *Adam* that there remaineth nothing in vs but pollution and filthines. And then, as one infected with the plague is not offended with him that is subiect to the same infection, As the Lazar doth neither with scorne nor choller, but rather with pittie and compassion behold the sores of his fellow, so the plague and sore of sinne which we see in another will not make vs angry with the party which is infected and visited, but rather in commiseration and pittie to vse all good meanes wherby he may be cured, if we consider that this plague and sore of sinne is so vniuersall that it hath infected all mankinde. When word was brought to Anaxagoras that his sonne was dead, he was not much moued with the news because (as he said) he knew and had considered long before that his sonne was mortall: so if we would consider and meditate on humane frailtie and infirmities, we should not be so much vexed when they shew themselues, because they would not happen beyond our expectation. If he that hyreth a seruant would thinke with himselfe that he hireth one who is not free from faults, if he that choseth a friend would then consider that he hath his wants and imperfections; If he that marrieth a wife would remember that he marrieth a woman, and therefore one subiect to infirmities, neither the small faults of his seruants, nor imperfections of his friends, nor infirmities of his wife would easily prouoke him to choller and fury, seeing he did not come short of his reckoning. ...

CHAP. VIII. The second meanes to subdue anger is to labour for patience.

The second meanes to subdue anger is to labour for the contrary vertue of patience and long suffering. And to this end we are first to consider that nothing happeneth vnto vs without God's all seeing prouidence, who if we be his children will dispose of euery thing for our good. Why therefore should we vexe our selues with anger, seeing God will turne the iniuries of men into blessings? let vs rather when any wrong is offered vs, which we cannot by iust and lawfull meanes auoyde, say with our sauiour Christ, *Iohn.* 18:11. *should not I drinke of the cup which my father hath prouided for me?* should I be angry with the cup because the Phisicke is bitter? or with the hand whereby it is conuaied vnto me? ...

The third meanes to subdue anger by arming vs with patience is to call continually to remembrance the bitter passion and sufferings of Christ for our sinnes. For if we consider how patiently he indured scoffes and reproaches, rayling and reuiling, buffering and scourging, yea death itselfe, and the anger of God more grieuous then death, not for any demerit of his, but for our sakes, we may easily suffer such small iniuries as are offered vnto vs by men, at our sauiour Christ's request, seeing we haue deserued far greater. ...

The fourth meanes to worke patience and repell anger is to consider the necessitie hereof, for if the loue of our brethren be not of more force to restraine vs from reuenge then anger to prouoke vs thereunto, we can haue no assurance that we are the Children of God ... .

17a [Jacobus de Gruytrode,] *The mirroure of golde for the synfull soule* (1506?). **17b** Thomas Brooks, *The silent soul* (1659).

Introduction Originally attributed to Denis the Carthusian, *The mirroure of golde* was in fact a translation of a work by a different Carthusian, Jacobus de Gruytrode, who wrote the original Latin *Speculum aureum* (ca. 1485). It is a work about penance and the temptations and corruptions of the world, with extensive quotations from the Bible and Church Fathers. The author in the prologue states that the text is in fact a compilation of "divers" writings of "doctors of theology" which were gathered so that "the pore synfull soule troubled by the fraude of enmye and oft ouercome, may by holy monicions and auctorites be addressed to the light of iustice and trouth."[45] The work is thus intended as a spiritual edification manual, but its focus is not on remedies to temptations or general directions how to make life holier, but is rather intended as an admonition for sin, described as pestilence and a contagious sickness. The recommendation the text makes is to consider all world as vanity and to withdraw from it, focusing on God, contemplating death, and performing penance frequently. It is thus much more austere than most texts on spiritual health, and much more explicit about sin as a disease that needs to be

45. *The mirroure of golde*, n. pag.

treated firmly and decisively, with sternness and austerity, making it fairly atypical compared to other works in the same genre.

Thomas Brooks, a popular puritan minister and non-conformist, proposed his *Silent soul, with soveraign antidotes against the most miserable exigents* to help souls "bee still, quiet, calm and silent"[46] through offering cures for spiritual afflictions. His work belongs to the genre of texts on practical divinity, a popular puritan genre, but it is, like de Gruytrode's text, fairly atypical, in the sense that in Brooks' view, sin is the one malady that requires full spiritual attention. In describing sin as poison, as worse than any other affliction, and in advising penance as a remedy to afflictions caused by sin, Brooks makes similar points to de Gruytrode, but his focus lies in an objection to sin as means out of a troubling situation, a problem not much discussed in *The mirroure of golde*. Brooks is interested in the avoidance of sin, but not so much through withdrawal from the world, as through reminding his readers that easy solutions to problems are often sinful, and should be well considered before being applied. The *Silent soul* is also interested in sins connected to speech (and conversely, the virtue of silence), swearing, cursing, and other sins of the tongue, while sharing with the *The mirroure of golde* a belief in the efficacy of teaching through admonition. Both texts are therefore concerned with the spiritual health of their audiences and both reach out to them by making their readers aware of the sinfulness of their actions, both being more austere in their discussions of spiritual health than some other texts on the matter, as both are more concerned with admonition than consolation, and with sin as a disease that can be cured by penance.

17a [Jacobus de Gruytrode,] *The mirroure of golde for the synfull soule*, 1506 (?); unnumbered pages. *STC* 6894.5. **Source** *EEBO*: Bodleian Library, Oxford (019510989).

Howe we ought to dispise and hate the worlde

... Firste thou oughtest to consider that the wyse wyllyngly wold departe for the conseruynge and kepynge of their helthe placis corrupte with pestilence, and principally, yf they fele and perceyue sekenes of disposicion daungerous. In this maner is the world, for it is infecte with corrupte pestilence by thabboundaunce[47] of synne. And in so moche as synne is right contagious sekenes: Soo it is to be fled and left. And also the company of wretched synnes, For it is vnsure and vnholsome to them that be hole in all theyr membres to folowe and vse the company of them that be lepris and vnclene. In lyke wyse it can not be thinge sure to man

46. Quotation from the title.

47. The abundance.

that wyll be pure and clene to folowe this synfulle worlde fulfylled with alle vices. To the whiche purpose it is sayd in ecclesiastices is in the .xiii. Chapitour, He that toucheth pitche in berynge therof, shall take somme to wche[48] of fowlnes; And he that is companyed with prowde, shal fynde some apparell or clothinge of pryde.

And to saye the trouth, It is a thynge Inpossible that he abide longe in good werkes that often frequenteth with euyll parsones. And for so moche saith the psalmyste: with the hooly thou shalte fynde the holy, and with the euyll thou shalt fynde the euyll; and soo as euyll conuersacion is noysaunt and hurtefull right so is the good company good and profytable, for he that fyndethe good companye fyndeth helthfull lyfe and haboundaunt in riches. And for a true declaracion, beleue verayly that full seldome it is seen, butte a man becometh good or euyll after the company where he is enterteyned. And as saith Saint Ierome the hartis of chyldren is as it were a cleane pure table, In the whiche noo thinge is paynted, wherfore it is a true lykenes that the workes and condicions that they lerne in youth; be it goode or euyll, they wyll folowe in their aige. Thenne lette vs withdrawe frome this worlde, as frome an euyll neyghbour. For in this worlde is there not a worse neyghbour, nor that so moche maye annoy vs, as the affinite and affeccion of synnes wherwith this worlde is replenysshed.

Secoundly, the wyse of their nature withdrawith and departeh frome the places where they haue doubte to be trayed, solde, or delyuered to the handes of their Enmyes, whiche the world doth from day to daye, wherfore the wordes of Iudas that betrayed his maister is propre to that purpose, whiche saide he that I shalle kysse, take, and holde hym for he is that I shulde delyuer you; suche or resemblable wordes saithe the world to the deuyll, For he that the worlde clippeth, and kysseth, and lyftith vppe in great honour, he betrayeth and geueth them into the handes of their greate Enmye, the deuyll. Wherfore thou oughtest well to note that in this worlde there is noo suertie ne trouth. For as saithe saynt Ierome, the moste greate and manifest signe of dampnacion is to haue and folowe in this corporall lyfe the pleasures, the sportis, and felicities therof, and to be byloued of the worlde. For he erreth and far goeth oute of the way of Iustice that by riches and delitis enforsith hym to please the worlde.

Thyrdly, the wyse withdrawith hym frome that place where he weneth there be perell, certainly soo is the worlde a place right perlious whiche is called a See, as saithe the psalmyst, the worlde is a great see spacious of the whiche, as saithe saint Barnarde, the difficulte of passage and the multitude of passers proueth

48. "Whiche" is most likely intended here.

the daungier, as in the see of marcell if there be .iiii. shyppes oon scarslye can passe withoute perell. Soo is it of the See of this worlde of .iiii. soules one amonge them with payne commeth to saluacion. This worlde is lyke the diluuie[49] where fewe folkes be saued in respecte of them that perisshe. It is as the fournes of Babilon enbraced with the fyre of hell wherfore aboue all thinge man ought to drede and flee it. For by the wynde of, in a lytell worde, man is enbraced to the fyre of Ire. And for the beholdyng of oon woman is enbraced with the fyre of lechery, and for the beholdynge of one precious Iuell is enbraced with the fyre of couetous concupiscence.

Fourthly, we see by experince that man gladly withdrawith and departith frome hym that desyreth hym and principally frome his Capitall Enmye. And oure capitalle Emnyes the deuell, prince of the worlde, that nyght and daye many sseth oure deth, frome whome withdrawe vs when we forsake the world. And for so moche saith Ecclesiastic is in the .ix. chapitour, holde the alway far frome a man that hathe power to slee the, by the whiche man is vnderstande the deuyll that man is ouercomme by; as saithe saint Mathewe in his .xiiii. chapitour, such thinges be doon by the euyll man, vnderstandyng the deuyl, oure gostly Enmye. For whiche cause aboue said we ought to knowe and vnderstonde that the souerayne remedy to ouercome the worlde is to flee and departe therwith. And to this purpose we rede in the lyfe of faders that saint Agryme, beyng resundunt, and dwellyng in the palace of the Emperoure made his Orison to god saynge, lorde, I pray the addresse me in the way of helth, in the whiche Orison makyng came to hym a voice saiynge, Agrym, fle the world and the men therof and thou shalt be saued. And a noon after the hooly man wente in to a deuoute Religion, in the whiche place he prayed semblaby as he had don afore, lorde addresse and shewe to me the way of helth. And agayne a voice answered hym agayne, fle, ouercome, kepe silence and rest the. Thies[50] be the rotes to fle synne by the fleynge is ouercome the concupissence of the flesshe; by kepynge silence, is ouercome pryde by rest; and seassinge the loue and desires of the world, couetise and auaricie is ouercome. Item Isodor, she with vs in this maner to dispraise the world yf thou wilt lyue in rest, take away and put from the all thinges that may noie, or take from the, thy gode purpose be comme to the world as dede, and so the worlde to the nother care for the glory of the world more then thou were deed dispraise in thy lyf; the thinges that thou maist not haue after thy deth, of this mater spekith saint Ierome in this wyse, O lyf of the worlde: not lyf but deth a lyfe false and deceyuable, a lyfe

49. Flood, deluge: *MED* s.v. "dilūvīe".
50. These: *MED* s.v. "thēs(e".

mixed and medled with disters. A lyfe shadowed with lyes nowe as a fresshe floure, and a noon drye a lyfe fragile and caduke. O lyf miserable, to the true lyfe contrary that the more he groweth; the more he mynyssheth, the more he goeth forth, the nygher is the deth. ...

17b Thomas Brooks, *The silent soul, with soveraign antidotes against the most miserable exigents: or, A Christian with an olive-leaf in his mouth, when he is under the greatest afflictions, the sharpest and sorest trials and troubles, the saddest and darkest providences and changes, with answers to divers questions and objections that are of greatest importance, all tending to win and work souls to bee still, quiet, calm and silent under all changes that have, or may pass upon them in this world, &c. By Thomas Brooks preacher of the word at Margarets New Fish-street London, and pastor of the Church of Christ meeting there,* 1659, pp. 103–111.[51] *Wing* B4962. **Source** Houghton Library, Harvard University, Cambridge, MA (004207553).

... Frist [*sic*], Consider, that there is infinitely more evil in the least sin than there is in the greatest miseries and afflictions that can possibly come upon you; yea, there is more evil in the least sin than there is in all the troubles that ever came upon the world; yea, than there is in all the miseries and torments of hell; the least sin is an offence to the great God, it is a wrong to the immortal soul, it is a breach of a righteous Law; it cannot bee wash'd away, but by the blood of Jesus; it can shut the soul out of Heaven, and shut the soul up, a close prisoner in Hell for ever, and ever. The least sin is rather to bee avoided, and prevented, than the greatest sufferings; if this Cockatrice bee not crushed in the Egg, it will soon become a Serpent, the very thought of sin, if not thought on, will break out into action, action into custome, custome into habit, and then both body and soul are lost irrecoverably, to all eternity. The least sin is very dangerous; *Caesar* was stabbed with bodkins, *Herod* was eaten up of Lice, Pope *Adrian* was choaked with a Gnat. A Mouse is but little, yet killeth an Elephant, if hee gets up into his Trunck; a Scorpion is little, yet able to sting a Lion to death; though the Leopard bee great, yet hee is poisoned with a head of Garlick; the least spark may consume the greatest house; and the least leak sink the greatest ship: a whole arm hath been impostumated with the prick of a little finger; A little Postern opened may betray the greatest City; A dram of poison diffuseth it self to all parts, till it strangle the vital spirits, and turn out the soul from the body; if the Serpent can

51. Marginal notes in the original source were not included in the transcription.

but wriggle in his tail, by an evil thought, hee will soon make a surprisal of the soul, as you see in that great instance of *Adam* and *Eve*.

The trees of the forrest (saith one in a Parable) held a solemn Parliament wherein they consulted of the innumerable wrongs which the Axe had done them, therefore made an Act, that no tree should hereafter lend the Axe an helve, on pain of being cut down. The Axe travels up and down the forrest, begs wood of the Cedar, Oak, Ash, Elm, even of the Poplar, not one would lend him a chip. At last hee desired so much as would serve him to cut down the briers and bushes, alledging that such shrubs as they did but suck away the juice of the ground, and hinder the growth, and obscure the glory of the fair and goodly trees; hereupon, they were all content to afford him so much; hee pretends a thorow reformation, but behold a sad deformation; for when hee had got his Helve, down went both Cedar, Oak, Ash, Elm, and all that stood in his way. Such are the subtil reaches of sin, it will promise to remove the Briers and Bushes of afflictions and troubles, that hinder the soul of that juice, sweetnesse, comfort, delight and content that otherwise it might enjoy. Oh do but now yeeld a little to it, and instead of removing your troubles, it will cut down your peace, your hopes, your comforts, yea it will cut down your precious souls. What is the breathing of a vein to the being let blood in the throat, or a scratch on the hand to a stab at the heart? no more are the greatest afflictions to the least sins, and therefore Christians never use sinful shifts to shift your selves out of troubles, but rather bee mute and silent under them, till the Lord shall work out your deliverance from them.

But, Secondly, Consider, it is an impossible thing for any to sin themselves out of their troubles. *Abraham*, *Job*, and *Jonah* attempts it, but could not effect it; the devils have experienced this near this six thousand years, they had not been now in chains, could they but have sinned themselves out of their chains; could the damned sin there would have been none now a roaring in that devouring unquenchable fire. Hell would have no inhabitants could they but sin themselves out of it. Ah, Christians! devils and damned spirits shall as soon sin themselves out of Hell, as you shall bee able to sin your selves out of your afflictions. Christians! you shall as soon stop the Sun from running her course, contract the Sea in a Nut shell, compasse the earth with a span, and raise the dead at your pleasure, as ever you shall be able to sin your selves out of your sufferings and therefore it is better to bee silent and quiet under them than to attempt that which is impossible to accomplish; this second consideration will receive further confirmation by the next particular.

Thirdly, As it is an impossible thing, so it is a very prejudical, a very dangerous thing, to attempt to sin your selves out of your troubles; for by attempting to sin your selves out of one trouble you will sin your selves into many troubles, as *Jonah* and *Jacob* did; and by labouring to sin your selves out of lesse troubles, you will sin your selves into greater troubles, as *Saul* did; and by endeavouring to sin your selves from under outward troubles, you will sin your selves under inward troubles and distresses, which are the sorest and saddest of all troubles.; thus did *Spira, Jerom* of *Prague, Bilney* and others. Some there have been who by labouring to sin themselves out of their present sufferings have sinned themselves under such horrours and terrours of conscience that they could neither eat, nor drink, nor sleep, but have been ready to lay violent hands upon themselves. And *Cyprian,* in his Sermon *de lapsis,* speaks of divers, who forsaking the Faith to avoid sufferings, were given over to bee possessed of evil spirits, and died fearfully. Oh man! thou dost not know what deadly sin, what deadly temptation, what deadly judgement, what deadly stroak thou mayest fall under, who attempts to sin thy self out of troubles: what is it to take *Venice,* and to bee hanged at the gates thereof? It is better to bee silent and mute under thy afflictions, than by using sinful shifts, to sin thy self under greater afflictions.

Fourthly, Consider, it is a very ignoble and unworthy thing to go to sin your selves out of your troubles and straights; it argues a poor, a low, a weak, a dasterdly, and an effeminate spirit, to use base shifts, to shuffle your selves out of your troubles. Men of noble, couragious and magnanimous spirits will disdain and scorn it. As you may see in the three children, *Daniel,* and those worthies, in that 11th of the *Hebrews,* of whom this world was not worthy. *Jerom* writes of a brave woman who being upon the rack bad her persecutors do their worst, for shee was resolved to die, rather than lie. And the Prince of *Conde* being taken prisoner by *Charles* the ninth King of *France,* and put to his choice, whether hee would go to Masse, or bee put to death, or suffer perpetual imprisonment; his noble answer was that by God's help hee would never chuse the first, and for either of the latter hee left to the Kings pleasure, and God's providence. ...

PART 2

Body

WOMEN AND MEN

18a [Guillaume Alexis,] *He* [sic] *begynneth an interlocucyon, with an argument, betwyxt man and woman* (1525). **18b** Cotton Mather, *Ornaments for the daughters of Zion* (1692).

Introduction The differences between men and women, a "battle of the sexes," was one of the defining tropes of Western literature of the Middle Ages and the early modern period. A translation from a French original of ca. 1460 by Guillaume Alexis (1460–1486), the English *Interlocucyon* belongs to the gender debate genre that, while flourishing in print in the sixteenth century, was an established literary trope already in the late Middle Ages, particularly with the writings of such authors as Christine de Pizan (e.g., *Le Livre de la Cité des Dames*, ca. 1400).[1] Alexis' *Interlocucyon* was a popular text, still extant in many manuscript copies, as well as at least seven print editions from before 1530. The work is a dialogue between a man and a woman, and is initially fairly typical of its genre, with the "man" voice posing well-established accusations of avarice, pride, quarrelsomeness, gossip, lying, and deception to the female character. The "woman" then retorts to all these accusations by enumerating female virtues: chastity, mercy, devoutness, caring, and so on. The examples both voices give to further their arguments are strongly biblical in nature, which is characteristic of late medieval works of this kind, though quite rare for later adaptations of this genre. The "man's" accusations come from such biblical stories as that of Eve, Solomon and Sheba, and Samson and Delilah, although there are likewise references to classical literature (e.g., Troy); the "woman" replies with the example of the virtuous Virgin Mary. These are mixed with "social" arguments about female infidelity and fickleness, countered by common-sense and witty responses from the "woman."

1. Anne E.B. Coldiron, *English Printing, Verse Translation, and the Battle of the Sexes, 1476–1557* (New York, 2009). See this book throughout for more on the *Interlocucyon* and the gender-debate genre.

While the text seems to indicate a fairly typical, narrow, anti-woman agenda it is in fact much more complex and resembles a true debate: the male voice, while armed with substantial arguments, is well countered by the female defence, and the final section is given entirely to the female voice. In that lengthy description of male vices the female voice goes from the defensive to the offensive, and since the "woman's" final accusations towards men remain unanswered, the impression is that the "woman" won the debate, although the author at the end of the text clearly calls on the readers to decide for themselves. The work is thus, in the end, fairly unusual compared to sixteenth-century texts and, given that it was originally composed in the fifteenth century but seems to have had a good audience in the early sixteenth century, it remained a popular twist on the genre for early modern readership perhaps precisely due to this atypicality. Its religious focus also makes the *Interlocucyon* an interesting study of how standards of morality drawn from Christian teaching penetrated social norms, of female behaviour in particular.

Cotton Mather, a renowned puritan minister, wrote his *Ornaments for the daughters of Zion* more as an instruction manual than a gender debate text; in fact, there is no disputation or debate in Mather's *Ornaments* at all and the text reads more like a lengthy sermon. Akin to other, more secular books of conduct like Richard Allestree's *Ladies calling* (1673), the *Ornaments* is a manual of good female behaviour (that also provides descriptions of behaviours unfitting to women), and a detailed set of instructions reliant on the Bible and patristic texts on how to behave in order to be an exemplary maid, wife, and widow. While Mather insists that virtuous women are meek, humble, devout, and modest he does not focus on condemning those who are not.[2] Instead, the *Ornaments* praises virtuous women from the Bible as examples proving that women are naturally religious and pure, indicating that Mather, in the perfect world he constructs, believes (good) women are admirable and respectable.

Just as Cotton Mather was a popular preacher and writer, the *Ornaments* was a popular text, edited three times between 1692 and 1741. It starts with a description of the character and happiness of a virtuous woman in general, and is then divided into four parts: virtuous maid, virtuous wife, virtuous mother, and virtuous widow, a classic division of a woman's life according to her marital status, determining proper behaviours, interests, and virtues of women in different social situations. While the *Ornaments* is in many ways different from Alexis' *Interlocucyon* generically, as it is not a debate, not versified, and has an ultimately different purpose and conclusion, the *Ornaments* does also bear similarities that the reader is sure to notice. These include the use of biblical and

2. Unlike many early modern texts participating in the gender-debate, e.g., Joseph Swetnam's 1615 *The arraignment of women.*

classical examples supporting female virtuousness, the ultimately positive conclusions about female character, and the shared use of commonplace and in places stereotypical language about women used for a didactic effect. The texts are thus connected in their use of religious language, examples, and religiously-informed reasoning to discuss the nature of women and their place in society. The secular relevance of texts full of religious examples and vocabulary make both works instances of the vastness of approaches to gender differences in the early modern period, and illustrate the role religious vocabulary played in defining standards of moral and virtuous behaviour.

18a [Guillaume Alexis,] *He* [sic] *begynneth an interlocucyon, with an argument, betwyxt man and woman, and whiche of them could proue to be most excellent*, 1525; unnumbered pages. *STC* 14109. **Source** *EEBO*: British Library, London (Huth.52.).

... *The man.*
The fyrst whiche I herde was the man that sayde
Adam our forfather by woman's shrewde councell
To ete of an apple was pyteously betrayde
Well happy is he that with you dothe not mell.

The woman.
Ihesu of a mayden and vyrgyn his mother
Was incarnated to redeme that man had loste
Set thou this one now agaynst the other
And woman is more excellent in euery coste.

The man.
No women in to aungels neuer was transfformed
But women in to deuyls full ofte hath ben fygurate
For theyr pryde in hell cruelly to be burned
Unhappy is he that hath one to his make.

The woman.
Many aungels to women haue ben transported
More than to men for theyr chastyte
Fyrst our dere lady thaungell exorted
Sayenge the son of god in her conceyued shold be.

The man.
Ioseph by woman was put in pryson
And Urye was slayne by treason cruell
Dauyd an adulterer with woman was become
Well happy is he that with them doth not mell.

The woman.
Mankynde to delyuer out of this worldly payne
And brynge hym to the ioye of the celestyall place
God in his mother toke nature humayne
Who dysprayseth women god sende hym no grace.

The man.
For woman was slayne the worthy prynce Amon
The loue of them causeth moche dyspleasure
By women was dysceyued the sage Salomon
Whiche by the meane of them false ydols dyd adoure.

The woman.
That woman is moost replete with grace
By good reason I shall proue playne
For god in woman fyrst toke his place
Whan into this worlde he came certayne.

The man.
Vyrgyll the sage clerke of great intellygence
Betrayed was by woman as wryten ye may fynde
Trustynge in her grace in euery mannes presence
Was tyed at a wyndowe tyll men dyd hym vnbynde.

The woman.
God to vs by woman paradyse hath restored
That before was loste by our great neglygence
And aboue all payntes hyghly hath honored
Mary, his mother, woman of moost excellence.

The man.
Townes haue be destroyed and cytes many one
Dyuers men for women be dampned depe in hell
More ioyfull vnto man than woman hath be none
Well happy is he that with them doth not mell.
... Pryam, Paris, and Deiphebus
Fyrst by thoccasyon of women was slayne
Also Troylus, Hector, and Helenus
And all Troye hath ben confounded playne.
... Women theyr face and foreheed doth paynt
For to deceyue both yonge and olde
The stronge Sampson Dalyda dyd attaynt
And hym betrayed, his heed when she had polde.

The woman.
Woman is honored in euery place
For quene of erth and of heuen hye
Whiche is petycioner for mannes trespace
To good on theyr soules to haue mercye.

The man.
Some women can flatter and moost can lye
To optayne mannes loue they can fayne well
They wyll neuer leue it vntyll they dye
Well happy is he that with them doth not mell.

The woman.
Woman is called treasure of grace
In heuen our lady it is full suer
For she for mannes soule doth so purchase
That thousandes she saued by her prayer.

The man.
Some that hath be taken for very sage
By womans loue dyd so hym indeuer
That for it he solde all his herytage
And after hath he dyed a myserable begger.

The woman.
Many hath offyces and good wages
By women to lyue ryght prosperately
Benefyces and auauntages
To mayntayne men accordyngly.

The man.
When a yonge pegeon a woman hath gotyn
She wyll make hym at length as stronge as a crane
For surely she wyll neuer forsake hym
Tyll that his croper bone wax very lame.

The woman.
Then loke a cawdell you do gyt
And soone ye loke you a better norce
For I harde say god gaue man wyt
To knowe the better from the worse.

The man
Women wyll speke and contrary say
They wyll nat shame a lye to tell
To scolde and brawle is all theyr play
Well happy is he that with them doth not mell.

The woman.
The commynge of our lorde Ihesu
Many deuout woman dyd prophecye
Sybellys they were that it best knewe
For to dysprayse women ye do now vnwyssye.

The man.
One must them gyue that they desyre
To bete or correcte them they waxen worse
They neuer wyll stynt for to requyre
As longe as a peny is in ones purse.

The woman.
When all thappostles from our lorde flyed
Women tyll his deth styll dyd hym ensue
Neuer woman our lorde denyed
As Peter dyd but euer was true.

The man.
When ye of ony man knowe the intencyon
Whiche coulde be secrete ye publysshe it by and by
Vnto your gosseppys ye make therof mencyon
As soone as ye togyther byb charryng lyke a pye.

The woman.
Chryste after his deth for our consolacyon
Fyrst shewed vnto woman personally
To Mary magdaleyn after his resurreccyon
Whiche for his deth be wayled greuously.

The man.
A Wyfe of her husbande
Wyll haue the audyence
As chyef maystres her tale to tell
She wyll crye and wepe except she haue the peremynence
Wyll happy is he that with them doth not mell.

The woman.
That a man shold a woman or his wyfe byleue
By Abraham is sygnyfyed playne
For god vnto Sara fyrst knowlege dyd gyue
That a chyld shold be procreat bytwyxt them twayne.

The man.
Many cautelous craftes now women they haue
To make them proper and coynte to seme
For proude apparell euer styll they craue
Yet be they moost stynkynge and fylthy within.

The woman.
Of good women haue be founde many one
Whiche haue ben chast and holy vyrgyns pure
And that out of goddes lawes neuer hath gone
Wherfore in heuen now sayntys be they sure.

The man.
But now of euyll there be so many
Theyr kynde encreaseth styll euery day
From euyl in to worse so fast they multyplye
That wolde the deuyll had one to cary thother away.

The woman.
One vyrgyn another for goddis loue hath martyred
By compulsyon of man as scrypture hath exprest
That in a day .xi. thousand dyed
Wherfore to dysprayse women ye do not best.

The man.
Consyderyng the euyll which of women haue com
How false they, be how cursed and cruell
One ought to flye them and from them to ronne
For well happy is he that with them doth not mell.

The woman.
All the nobles of tyme passed
And all the payntes of paradyse
Fyrst all from women they haue proceded
For to dysprayse women in fayth ye be not wyse.

The man.
Do weye your blame and laude in balaunce
To se of them whiche twayne weye moste
And when that ye se there the dyfferaunce
I trowe of your laude ye wyll make small boste.

The woman.
For all the blames and offence
That agaynst vs women ye can laye
Consyder the bounte of our ladyes excellence
And all our euylles her goodnes dothe delaye.

La femme replique.
Now the conclusyon the woman thus began
These infamous men with all theyr polecy
All noble women wolde gladly defame
Were not our goodnes excedynge theyr glory.
For Caym kylled Abell his gentyll brother
And Iudas Ruben his father dyd slay
Nero made open his owne mother
To se the place where that he lay
The men of Iury made god to dye
Iudas scaryot hym solde by false treason
And after hym selfe hanged, this is no lye
Wherfore styll in payne his soule it doth won.
Chrystes Apostles dyd hym denye
Men dyd hym crucefye by great vyolence
And tyrans enraged dyspyte fullye
Ten thousande slewe of Innocence.
Also in a day they dyd confounde
A .xi. thousande vyrgyns vnto theyr deth
Some they heedyd,[3] and some they drownde
Some they smolthered and stopped theyr breth.

Men they had peruerse courage
As ye may se now euydently
To do vnto sayntes suche oultrage
Without offence and no cause why.
Men make warres and dyscencyons
In euery place as ye may se
Theftes, mordres, and traysons
Replete with all iniquyte.

3. Beheaded: *MED* s.v. "heden".

More men there be in pryson
In chaynes bounde for theyr offence
More women come vnto sermon
To lerne goddys lawes with dylygence.
Of euery man in all degre
Mother and norces women hath ben
Of all that are and euer shalbe
Women haue fyrst thautorite clen.
Wherfore of vs ye ought say well
For to myssay ye can not wyn
And ye that hath no grace goodnes to tell
To holde his peace is best for hym.
Do ye say of vs the best
Syns we ye kept When ye were small
For of lytell medlynge cometh moche rest
And god amende the worst of vs all.

The auctor.
Of this argument the hole entent
I marked it effectually
And after I had herde them at this discent
I presed towardes them incontynently
But when they sawe me aproche them to
Lest I wolde repreue theyr argument
Full fast they fledde then bothe me fro
That I ne wyst whyther they went
Wherfore now to iudge whiche is moost excellent
I admyt it vnto this reders prudence
Whyther to man or woman is more conuenyent
The laude to be gyuen and wordly magnyfycence.

18b Cotton Mather, *Ornaments for the daughters of Zion. Or The character and happiness of a vertuous woman: in a discourse which directs the female-sex how to express the fear of God, in every age and state of their life; and obtain both temporal and external blessedness. Written by Cotton Mather*, Cambridge, MA, 1692, pp. 11–28. *Wing*, 2nd ed. M1135. **Source** Houghton Library, Harvard University, Cambridge, MA (006066564).

I. The Character of a Vertuous Woman.
And this Character is both *Negatively* and *Positively* offered. Negatively, 'tis not a *Deceitful Favour* or a *Vain Beauty* that sets her off. Women that have none but those things to Value themselves upon are driven out from *The Temple of Honour*, here. But, Positively, 'tis the *Fear of the Lord* that is her Commendation. 'Tis implyed not only That *Favour* and *Beauty* are poor Things Compar'd with the *Fear of God*, but also that they who have the *Fear of God* will not Value themselves upon their *Favour* and *Beauty* … .

Conclusion. 1.
The *Vertuous Woman* counts the best Female *Favour* to be *Deceitful*, the best Female *Beauty* to be *Vain*.

By *Favour* is meant a Comely Presence, an Handsome Carriage, a Decent Gesture, a Ready Wit agreeably expressing it self, with all other Gracefull Motions, and whatsoever procures *Favour* for a Woman among her Neighbours. The *Virtuous Woman* is willing to have this *Favour*, so far as is consistent with *Vertue*. Shee Counts it a *Favour* of God for one to be graced with it; But still she looks upon it as a *Deceitfull* Thing. She is carefull that She do not hereby *Deceive* her self into proud Imaginations, and into an Humour, *Conceited* of her self, or *Contempteous* towards others. Carefull She likewise is, lest hereby She *Deceive* Unwary men *into* those Amours which bewitching looks and Smiles do often betray the Children of men. …

Conclusion. 2.
There is a *Favour* so particularly *Deceitful* and a *Beauty* so Remarkably *Vain*, as that a *Vertuous Woman* would be loth to be *Deformed* with it.

The *Favour* whereat a *Vertuous Woman* ha's a Particular Distast, is that which *Promiscuous Dancing* is applauded for. The Exercise of *Promiscous Dancing* is that which pretends to be a peece of Breeding which demands the *Favour* of Womankind; but a *Vertuous Woman* esteems them *Deceived* who count it so, nor will She affect such an Exercise … and leave them either to the Pagans whose manner it was to *Dance* in the Worship of *Bacchus,* or to the Monkeyes whom of old they brought forth to *Dance* at the Festival of *Diana.* Some of the more Sober Papists have not stuck to say, *The Dancer breaks the Covenant of God, made it Baptism; he Promis'd to Renounce the Divel, and his pomps but when he enters into a Dance, he goes in the Pompous Procession of the Divel.* They are not a few Silly Scrupulous precesians, by whom these *Dancings* have been Stigmatized .... And the blessed old *Waldenses* testified, *In a Dance one breaks all the Ten Commandments of God.* The most eminent Reformers above an hundred years agoe concurred in witnessing against these *Dances,* as an *unlawfull Recreation;* and among the English *Divines,* yea among the English *Bishops,* they have been decry'd by *A cloud of Witnesses;* they have branded our *Dancers* as the *Capering Goats* that will not be found among the *Sheep* in the Day of the Lord. ...

The *Beauty* whereof a *Vertuous woman* hath a Remarkable Dislike is that which hath *Artificial Painting* in it. The usage of *Artificiall Painting* is practised by many women who think thereby to be valued for a *Beauty* which they are not Really the owners of. But a *Vertuous woman* will not be guilty of such a *Vanity.* There is a wicked Book that pleads for this ungodly practice; but that Good Lady uttered the Language of a *Vertuous Woman* upon Reading such a Book, *O Lord, I thank thee, that thou gavest mee not Wit enough to Write such a Book, unless withal thou hadst given me Grace Enough not to Write it.* Although it be not Unlawful for a Person Transiently to Preserve or to Restore her Native *Complexion* by Convenient Medicines when She is in any special Danger of Loosing it, Yet for a Person to *Paint* her self, that She may make some Ostentation of a Complexion which God ha's not made her the Owner of, is a thing that ha's heard ill among the most Godly Christians; nor will a *Vertuous Woman* Easily be Reconcil'd unto it .... Moreover, Our *Face* is a Seat which ha's much of the Divine *Image* and *Wisdom* appearing in it; and it is a Vile Affront unto God for a Woman to *Deface* the Workmanship of the Almighty there by such an *Inversion* ....

Now, the *Paint* which is laid upon it, not only Disfigures the Face for the present, but also do's Corrupt it and Corrode it, and Poison it, and hasten Wrinkles and Ruines thereupon; it will *Rent the Face,* at the Scripture speaks of it; and I am sure it should *Rent the Heart* of them that use it. Besides, Our Lord Rebuked it, as a base *Hypocrisy* for Persons to *alter their Faces* that they might appear to be *Fasting* when they were so indeed; how much more basely Hypocritical is it for Persons to *alter their Faces* that they might appear to be *Comely* when indeed they are not so? ... The Ancients tell us, That the Divel was the Inventor of this *Hellish Art;* and it can be nothing but either *Lust* or *Pride* (both Brats of the *Divel*) that shall dispose any to the using of it. ... She leave these foul *Paintings* and now the old *Picts* are dead, She would not help to Revive that *Pagan* Generation, or make her self a Sister to the *Squaws* in the Thickets of *America*. ...

Conclusion. 3.

The *Fear of God* is that which the Heart of a *Vertuous Woman* is under the Power of. The *Female Sex* is naturally the *Fearful Sex*; but the *Fear of God* is that which Exceeds (and sometimes Extinguishes) all other *Fears* in the *Vertuous Woman*. To state this matter aright we are to know That the *Fear of God* is an *Old* Testament Expression, as the *Love of God* is a *New* Testament one, for all true *Religion* whatsoever. It may then be said of a *Vertuous Woman*, That she is a *Religious Woman*. She ha's *Bound* her self *again* to that God, whom She had by the Sin and Fall of her *First Mother* departed from. She ha's a *Love* which do's not cast *out the Fear* that is no *Fault*, but confirm and settle her in that *Fear* of God, That all kind of *Piety* and of *Charity* is prevailing in her Disposition. That *Sobriety* and *Righteousness* and *Godliness* are Visible in her whole Behaviour, and That She does *Justice*, loves *Mercy*, and walks *Humbly* with her God.

... The Vertuous Woman in like manner Believes the *Essence* of God; and that thought, *God is*, it raises a Sacred *Fear* of Him in her humble and moved Soul. She sees the *Being* of a God prov'd from the Works of *Creation* .... Even the *Dumb*, the *Mute* Creatures do loudly *speak* this Truth unto her. She Considers That the World had a *Beginning* inasmuch as 'tis *Older* and *Changing* every Day; And that it could not have its *Beginning* from it self; inasmuch as *Nothing* would then be the cause of *Something*. So, She sees, There is a God; and She sees the *Wisdom* of a God, the *Power* of a God, the *Goodness* of a God, throughout the Universe. ... When She sees *Prayers* Extraordinarily Answered, Good men Extraordinarily *Rewarded*, Ill men Extraordinarily *Punished*, She cryes out, *The Finger of a God is here!* She finds her self born with a Notion of a God, wherein She ha's not been by any *Tradition* or *Policy* of others Impos'd upon, and She graciously Cherishes that Notion. ...

Fourthly, A *Vertuous Woman* Labours to *Please* and *Serve* the great God with the greatest of her cares. The *Fear* of *God* is thus described by the Apostle in *Heb.* 12:2, *Let us Serve God Acceptably with Reverence and Godly Fear*. And nothing is more *Acceptable* to the Vertuous Woman than that she may *Acceptably Serve* her God. ... Let her be of never so *Low* Rank, She will not stoop to be a *Servant* of the World, or of the Flesh, or of the Divel; nor can she brook that the Curse of ... being *A Servant of Servants* ever should come upon her. When she Contemplates that Lord who is *A Greater than Solomon*. She crys out, *Happy are thy Servants; Oh that I might be one of them*! And she would alwayes be doing the will of God, in such a manner as may be pleasing to Him. We read of One, *He had this Testimony, that He pleased God*. Now; That is the Testimonial to be given of the Vertuous Woman. She aspires after the Imitation of the Lord Jesus, in *Doing alwayes the things that please the Father*. It is the Name of a Good man, *The man that Pleaseth God*; and whatever Change the Name of this Woman may undergo, still she keeps that Name, *The Woman that pleaseth God*. ...

Fifthly. A *Vertuous Woman* do's attend the *Worship* of God, with an Unwearied and Exemplary Diligence. ... *Prayer* is what She will be *Early* as well as often at, and she is every Morning Jealous, lest like *Origen*, She give the Divel an Advantage, by Omitting of it. She makes not her *Closet* a place for meer Trifles and Pictures, but for *Prayers* with Devoutest *Meditations*. She Retires into her *Closet* every Day, that she may there have a Visit from the Eternal *Bridegroom* of her Soul; and whatever Exercises may be at any time upon her mind, She do's as *Hannah* did: *She Pours out her Soul unto the Lord, that she may be no more sad*. Yea, she is not unacquainted with solemn *Humiliations*, and solemn *Thanksgivings*, upon the Just Occasions of them. She is a Woman whom *Scriptures* and *Sermons* are very dear unto; and it is not every Trifle (as the want of a Garment, or a dread of the Weather) that she will make her Excuse for her Absence from the *means of Grace*. How fain would she be with *Mary*, alwayes hearing the Sweet Admonitions of her Lord, about *The One thing Needful*, and, *The Good part which cannot be taken away!* The *Sabbath* she calls *Her Delight*; nor will she wast the Sacred Hours of it in the *Naughty Superfluities* of Diet and Rayment; but be as often as well she can, in the Congregation of *The People of God*; and there, as her *Voice* makes a sound that shall be no *Base*, for the Musick of the Publick *Psalmes*, thus her *Heart* is an *Altar* from whence, during the whole Solemnity, there ascend unto God *The Sacrifices which He Desires*. ... Although She sometimes counts her self as a *Dog*, yet like that *Syrophenician* Woman, She will ask for some *Crumbs from the Table of the Lord*. Having had her Soul *Purify'd* by *Regeneration*, She brings her *Offerings* to the *Tabernacle*. ...

STRANGERS IN FOREIGN LANDS

19a *Here begynneth a lytell treatyse of the turkes lawe called Alcaron* (1519?). **19b** [Johannes Andreas Maurus,] *The confusion of Muhamed's sect* (1652).

Introduction Encounters between the East and the West have an incredibly long history, from trade relations, through the crusades, to the exchange of science and learning. The appeal of "Saracen" (which meant Arab and Muslim in the Middle Ages) culture, language, literature, knowledge, and religion to medieval audiences was immense,[4] and it only increased with the passing of time. Particularly in the late Middle Ages, after the conclusion of the crusades, after the renaissance of the twelfth century and its popularization of Arabic learning was established among various academic and popular audiences, and after "Saracen" romances popularized the appeal of Arabic culture, trade between the East and the West increased, as did travel, missionary activity, and pilgrimages to the Holy Land. Various travelogues of the late medieval period likewise contributed to the surge in interest in all things Arabic among medieval audiences. The expansion of Islam in the late medieval and early modern period furthered interest, and concerns, about Islam as well.

As there was gradually more knowledge gathered about the Muslim world, interest in its founding book, the Koran, led many to wish to read it, because it "informed a vast, competing, dangerous, and deeply attractive civilization" and "demanded to be read by Christian Europeans across the whole period from the mid-twelfth to the mid-sixteenth century."[5] Indeed, the Koran was translated into Latin at least three times in the Middle Ages, extant in at least forty manuscripts, and there were at least two sixteenth-century print editions of the Latin Koran available.[6] This interest also fed into a body of popular knowledge about Islam that presented Muslims as heretics and sinners, and Muhammad as a necromancer and devil-worshipper. Since the Koran was available in Latin, many medieval and early modern scholars searched its passages to find excerpts that could be refuted, and thus the superiority of Christianity made to shine; popular literature contributed to perpetuating this image of the Muslim Other.[7] There were, however, no translations of the Koran itself into the vernacular: most people treated popular literature,

4. Dorothee Metlitzki, *The Matter of Araby in Medieval England* (New Haven, CT, 2005), 3–4.

5. Thomas E. Burman, *Reading the Qur'an in Latin Christendom, 1140–1560* (Philadelphia, 2007), 1.

6. Burman, *Reading the Qur'an*, 1.

7. For more on this, see Norman Daniel, *Islam and the West: The Making of an Image* (Oxford, 1960).

such as romances (e.g., *The King of Tars*, ca. 1330) and various bits and pieces of Christian polemic as sources of their knowledge on Islam. This gap was filled with early English printed works describing the Koran that, while repeating many of the polemical definitions and quotations from and about Islam, now reached out to a broader, non-academic and non-Latinate audience.

One such text, the first to date of this kind, is the 1519 *Lytell treatyse of the turkes lawe called Alcaron*, a work on the Koran.[8] Its rhetoric about Muhammad represents the standard medieval (and also early modern) understanding of his place in religious history: he stands with the devil – literally, in the engraving that accompanies this edition, as well as, of course, metaphorically and polemically. The text is a short work on what the author considered the "highlights" of Islam, and comprises a useful, brief and succinct "compendium" of knowledge on Muslims and their "Alcaron." Its source was, as was the case with the majority of works on the Koran in pre- and post-Reformation Europe, a Latin translation of the Koran by Robert of Ketton, commissioned by Peter the Venerable in 1142. This remained almost exclusively the one source translation available in Europe until as late as the middle of the seventeenth century; in 1649 the first translation of the Koran into English was published, a translation from French, by Alexander Ross.[9] Robert of Ketton's translation served many post-Reformation authors including Theodorus Bibliander, whose well-known, annotated *Alcoran* (1543),[10] was prefaced by Martin Luther himself. In his preface, "Luther helped frame the image of the Ottoman enemy in sixteenth-century Europe in terms that ensured a remarkable continuity with earlier interpretations."[11]

Through Luther's influence,[12] and in combination with concerns about the spread of the Ottoman empire in the sixteenth and, in particular, the seventeenth century, as well as the printing of earlier works on Islam, post-Reformation Protestant authors and audiences received a well-established tradition of objectifying the Muslim Other. While many texts included new observations by an increasing number of travellers who described their voyages in travelogues, convictions about the "sorcery" of Muslims and

8. In the majority of works on the subjects Englished as Alcoran, from Al-Qur'an.

9. Matthew Birchwood, *Staging Islam in England: Drama and Culture, 1640–1685* (Cambridge, 2007), 64.

10. Bibliander's text resembles closely both the *Lytell treatyse of the turkes* and other similar works because early modern works relied on the standard established by medieval Christian polemicists, and remained largely a paraphrase with commentary of the Koran rather than a faithful translation.

11. Paul T. Levin, *Turkey and the European Union: Christian and Secular Images of Islam* (New York, 2011), 99.

12. For more, see, for example, Adam S. Francisco, *Martin Luther and Islam: A Study in Sixteenth-Century Polemics and Apologetics* (Leiden, 2007).

their secret wish to either destroy Christianity or convert to it[13] remained strong. In many ways, Protestant interest in the Koran and Islam in general, perhaps due to the general tensions of the seventeenth century (particularly wars with the Ottoman Empire), resulted in a surge in the number of texts printed on the subject, including a heightened interest in pre-Reformation works about Islam. *The confusion of Muhamed's sect*, allegedly by an author known as Johannes Andreas Maurus, a medieval Muslim convert to Christianity (d. ca. 1254) who became the administrator of Lucera, a Muslim colony of the Holy Roman Empire in Apulia,[14] is one such text in which an association with a famous medieval Muslim convert adds credibility to the condemnation of Islam, even if Maurus did not, in fact, author this text.[15]

Like many other works written at the time, the *Confusion* represents the peak of concerns about Islam that were pinned onto the broader context of religious tensions in early modern England, including the rhetoric of accusing opponents in intra-Protestant conflicts of being "Mahumetans" or "Turks," as the puritans sometimes were.[16] The text is considerably longer than the *Lytell treatyse of the turkes lawe called Alcoran* but its agenda is largely similar, focusing on the life of Muhammad and his dream vision of heaven and hell (including also a vision of a woman prophesying the falseness of Islam and a mass conversion of Muslims to Christianity). The text then passes on to debunking some "untruths" of the Koran. As a Protestant text, the *Confusion* focuses on the religious foundations of the Koran in much greater detail than the 1519 text, which sees it more as a book of laws. Both works, in the end, represent a traditional Christian approach to Islam and focus on criticizing the Koran, and pointing out its inconsistencies. Both texts argue also for the heretical nature of Islam and the sinfulness of Muhammad. Both also use an approximated version of Arabic to "quote" certain passages, rules, or expressions from the Koran. At the same time, the texts differ in details of their descriptions, and they were printed in slightly different contexts, one as illustrative of general interest in Muslim culture and the other as part of contemporary intra- and inter-religious tensions, thus illus-

13. Nabil Matar, "Muslim Conversion to Christianity in the Early Modern Period: Arabic Texts, European Contexts," in *Mediterranean Identities in the Premodern Era: Entrepôts, Islands, Empires*, ed. John Watkins and Kathryn L. Reyerson (Farnham, Surrey; Burlington, VT, 2014), 211–230, at 214.

14. Geraldine Heng, "An African Saint in Medieval Europe: The Black Saint Maurice and the Enigma of Racial Sanctity," in *Sainthood and Race: Marked Flesh, Holy Flesh*, ed. Molly H. Bassett and Vincent W. Lloyd (London, 2014), 11–44, at 24.

15. Although there is evidence that the 1652 edition of *The confusion of Muhamed's sect* was indeed a translation of a text by Maurus, done by Joshua Nostock (Birchwood, *Staging Islam*, 88; see this chapter throughout for more on the varied approaches to Islam in seventeenth-century England).

16. As, for example, in the 1660 *Dregs of drollery*.

trating the varied pre- and post-Reformation concerns, approaches to, and appropriations of, the Koran and Islam.

19a *Here begynneth a lytell treatyse of the turkes lawe called Alcaron. And also it speketh of Machamet the nygromancer,* 1519 (?); unnumbered pages. *STC* 15084. **Source** *EEBO*: British Library, London (C.25. k.13).

... So wyll I somwhat wryte of the turkes lawes, whiche lawe in many poyntes accordeth with our lawe, and is the lawe of Machomet, the whiche in his lawe vsed a worde *occidite,* That is to saye kylle. So all them that wyll not byleue in theyr lawe, they slee them. And that is agaynst the lawe of oure lorde Ihesu cryst, for he byddeth that we shall loue them that loue not vs, and praye for oure enemys. And the turkes ben charged to theyr byleue. But the crysten people be not soo, but amyably lerned and teched. And whan that the predycante or prechour shal go to preche theyr fals byleue, he hath a naked swerde in his hande as longe as his sermon shall endure and last. Or elles he putteth the sayd swerde in a hyghe place wher as euery body may beholde it that is there, for to fere and threten them therwithall. And we crysten people putteth a crucyfyxe in the myddes of the chyrche on hyghe, for humylyte and not for fere or thretenynge, lyke as the turkes do the forsayd swerde. And so forthe I wyll procede and wryte of theyr lawes and boke the whiche is named comenly Alcaron. And some men dothe call it the boke of Mesaap, and some of them be of dyuers langages and in lyke wyse of dyuers countrees, the whiche boke Machamet made and gaue it vnto them. In the whiche boke this fals nygromancer, Machamet, wrote amonge other thynges as many one hathe redde and sene here before, that they the whiche ben good shall go vnto paradyse and they the whiche ben euyll to helle, and that byleueth all the sarasyns.

And yf a man asketh theym what paradyse meneth they saye it is a place of delyte and Ioye, where a man shall fynde all maner of delytes and fruytes, and all maner of fruytes at all tymes, and the ryuer renneth mylke, wyne, hony, and fresshe water. And they shall haue fayre houses after that they haue deserued them here, and those same houses ben made of precyous stones of golde and syluer, and eche man shall haue ten wyues and all maydens, and also they speke and troweth vpon the vyrgyn Mary and in lyke wyse vpon the Incarnacyon of our lorde Ihesu cryst.

... And they saye that they knowe well that theyr lawe of Machamet shall fayle as dothe the lawe of the Iwes [sic], and that the crysten lawe shall last vnto the worldes ende. And yf a man aske theym wherin they byleue, they saye in god almyghty, maker of heuen and erthe and all other thynges that ben therin and withoute hym is nothynge done nor begonne, and at the day of dome all thynge shall be rewarded after theyr deseruynge, and all thynge is true that cryst sayd by the mouthes of the prophetes. And also Machamet bade in his Alcaron that euery man sholde haue two or thre wyues, and nowe they take ten or twelue or as many lemmans as they may gete. And yf ony of theyr wyues dothe a mysse to theyr husbandes they maye dryue them away and take another but he muste gyue her a parte of his goodes. Also, whan men speketh of the fader, and sone, and holy ghost they saye that they are thre persones and not one god, but they scorne it and speke not therof but of the trynyte. But, they saye that god spake or elles he was dome, and god is a goost, or he were on lyue and saye that goddes haue grete strength, and so saye they in scorne. And the saye also that Abraham and Machamet were well in the grace of god, for they spake with hym dyuers tymes. And they saye in lyke wyse the Machamet was the very messanger of god, and they haue many good artycles of oure fayth and they all vnderstande the scryptures and the prophecyes, for they haue theym wryten in the gospelles and in the byble in theyr langage, and so they knowe moche of the holy scrypture, but they vnderstande it not, but after the lettre of the gospell; and therfore saynt poule sayth thus: *Littera occidit. spiritus viuificat,* That is to saye, the lettre sleeth and the ghost quyckeneth. And the sarasyns saye that the Iwes [sic] kepe not the lawe that Moyses toke vnto them. And also crysten men do not well, bycause that they kepte not the ten commaundementes of the gospell the whiche Ihesu cryst gaue vnto them.

And therfore I shall tell you what the soudan sayde vnto a crysten man vpon a daye in his chambre. He made for to auoyde out of his chambre lordes and ladyes and all that was therin, for he wolde speke with hym in counsayll. And whan all was auoyded he demaunded hym how the crysten men gouerned them, and he sayd ryght well blessyd be god. And the soudan sayd sykerly, naye, for he sayd that our prestes sayd not theyr seruyce as they sholde doo, nor gyue not good example of good lyuynge vnto the people as they ought for to do. And whan the people sholde go for to serue god, they go vnto the tauerne and lyeth there in glotonye all the daye and all the nyghte, and eteth and drynketh as beestes, and wote not whan they haue ynoughe; And he sayd that crysten men enforced them for to fyght togyder and echone to begyle other, and they be soo proude that they wote not how for to clothe them, nor how longe, nor howe shorte, now streyte now wyde, in all maner of guises, and sayd that they sholde be meke, and symple, and sothfast, and do almesse as cryst dyde in whome they byleue. And they be so couetous that for a lytell syluer they sell theyr trouhte and theyr chyldren, and theyr systers, and theyr wyues, that one taketh another mannes wyfe and fewe holdeth theyr trouthe. And therfore, he sayd, for these synnes crysten men haue lost all the landes that we holde; For thoughe synne hathe god put this lande in to oure handes and not thrugh strengthe, but thorughe your synnes and wretchedenes. But we knowe ryght well for a certaynte that whan ye serue well your god that he wyll helpe and socoure you, In suche wyse that no man can withstande agaynst you. And that also we knowe well by oure prophecyes that the crysten men shall wyune these landes agayne whan they serue theyr god well. But whyles that they lyue so synfully and so wretchedly as they do, we haue no drede of them. And thenne he asked the soudan how that he knewe so all the estate of crystendome. And the soudan sayd that he knowe it bothe of lordes and commons, and by his messangers the whiche he sente thorughte all countrees, as they were marchauntes with perles and precyous stones, and dyuers other marchaundyses for to knowe the maner of all countrees. And then the soudan called in the lordes agayne. ... And so the turkes and sarasyns, the whiche sholde be torned to Ihesu cryste by good example, they ben drawen awaye thorughe our synne and wretched lyuynge for they saye so, the wherfore it is grete pyte for to beholde and here the synnes that reygneth now thorughe all crystendome.

But the sarasyns ben true. For they kepe well the lawe or wrytynge of Alcaron that they saye that god sente then by his messanger Machamet, vnto whome they saye that Saynt gabryell spake often with hym and tolde to hym the wyll of oure lorde. And this Machamet was borne in Arabye, and he was fyrste a knaue and kepte the horses in the stable, and he wente after marchantes; So he came ones in to Egypte with a marchaunt. And egypte was the tyme crysten, and there was a chapell besyde Arabye wherin dyde dwelle an hermyte, and whan he entred in to the chapell the whiche was but a lytell hous and a lowe anone, it ganne for to waxe as grete as a palays gate. And the sarasyns sayd that it was the fyrste myracle that Machamet dyde in his yongthe. And afterwarde Machamet beganne for to be ryght wyse. And he was afterwarde a grete astronomyer, and syth he was keper of all the golde of the prynces of Corydan, and he gouerned and kepte it full wysely. And whan that the prynce of Corydan was deed he wedded his wyfe, the lady that men called Quadryge. And this fals Machamet fell often into the fallynge euyll wherfore the lady was wrothe bycause that she hadde taken hym to her husbande. But this Machamet made her to byleue that at euery tyme that he fell soo that the aungell gabryell spake vnto hym and that for the grete bryghtnesse of the aungell he felle downe. This machamet regned in Arabye the yere of our lorde Ihesu cryst. vi. hondreth and twenty. And was of the kynred of Ismael that was Abrahams sone, and he begate hym on Arage his chamberes. And therfore the sarasyns ben calld Ismahelytes and some Agaren, and some of Agar. And some there be that ben called Moabytes and some Amonytys after the two sones of Lothe.

And this fals Machamet loued well an holy man the whiche dwelled in a wyldernesse that was a myle from the mounte of Synay in the vale, as men dothe go fro Arabye vnto Caldas, and it is but a dayes Iourneye fro the see whan marchauntes come from Venis. Machamet went often into that hermytage wherfore his men wexed all angry and wrothe, and forsothe he wolde gladly here the hermyte preche and made his men for to wake all nyght wherfore they wolde gladly haue hadde the hermyte deed. And so it be fell vpon a nyght that Machamet hadde well dronken wyne and fell a slepe, and his men toke his swerde oute of his shethe whyles that he laye and slepte so fast, and slewe therwith this hermyte. And then they put vp his swerde agayne in his shethe all blody and vpon the morowe whan he founde the hermyte deed he was wrothe out of mesure and wolde haue slayne his men. But they with one accorde sayde that he hymselfe hadde slayne hym whan he was dronken. And then they badde hym loke vpon his swerde the whiche was all blody. And whan he behelde it he wende that they had sayde sothe and this is the seconde myracle the Marchmet dyde, and he cursed the wyne and all them that dronke ony wyne. And therfore the sarasyns dare not drynke no wyne, but some drynke it pryuely for, and they drynke good beuerage and nouryshynge, the whiche is made of Camamyle and thereof is the sugre made.

Also it be falleth somtyme that crysten men become sarasyns, eyther thrughe pouerte or throughe wyckednes; and whan that they haue renounced the crysten fayth they lerne hym theyr fals bylyue and maketh hym for to saye thus whan they receyue hym: *La oles ella Machamet roses alla,* That is to saye, there is no god but one, and Machamet is his messenger. &c. Also the turkes byleue is strongly kepte in theyr cyrcumcysyon. And they ben cyrcumcysed whan they be of the aege of .xii. yere, for Ismael, Abrahams fyrst sone, was circumcysed at thyrten yere olde of whome they ben all proceded and comen. And that lawe they kepe styll after the olde maner and theyr byleue is that they may drynke no wyne. And theyr lawe is that they sholde praye and faste moche but they kepe it but lytell. But Machamet knewe not the our lorde Ihesu cryst was god and man. And he sayth also in his Alcaron that the Iewes put not our lorde Ihesu cryst vpon the crosse nor put hym not vnto deth. For the turkes saye that whan they wolde haue taken out[17] lorde they toke Iudas, his traytoure, in his stede. For thy saye

17. "Our" probably intended here.

that our lorde Ihesu cryst hadde altred hymselfe in his lykenesse, and incontynent as he hadde done this he wente into heuen, and Iudas was put vpon the crosse in his stede; this is theyr fals byleue; And shall come again in the end to the worlde and Iuge, and shall dystroye Antecryst. And they saye that suche a grete prophete wolde not deye suche a shamefull dethe. For he dyde, arayse the deed, and in this fals opynyon they accorde with the secte of Manacheen, and they saye that the crosse is a token of the deuyll and that no man sholde worshyp it. And they byleue not that he is arysen from dethe vnto lyfe and they forsake it, Also the seuen sacramentes of holy churche the whiche ben ronne out of his holy fyue woundes, the whiche kepe vs frome all mysbyleue and brynge vs in to euerlastynge Ioye, there as his holy fyue woundes ben bryghter and fayrer than the sonne. Amen.

19b [Johannes Andreas Maurus,] *The confusion of Muhamed's sect, or a confutation of the Turkish Alcoran. Being a discovery of many secret policies and practices in that religion, not till now revealed. Written originally in Spanish, by Johannes Andreas, Maurus, who was one of their bishops and afterwards turned Christian. Translated into English, by I.N.*, 1652, pp. 62–102. *Wing*, 2nd ed. A3315. **Source** *EEBO*: British Library, London (Ames.4(2292)).

CHAP. IIII.

The fourth Chapter of this book handleth certain arguments which may be framed and brought against the Alchoran, *proving that it is false of it self, and not the word of God; And also against* Muhameds Suné, *proving that it is of it self a ridiculous thing, and fit for men of little knowledge and judgment.*

The first argument is from what is said in the second Chapter of the fourth book, which is in *Arabick Ogna Nofigha, &c. (i. e.)*, that at the end of the world a trumpet or horn shall sound, and the Angels in Heaven, and men on earth, shall fall down dead; and afterwards the said trumpet or horn shall sound again, and all aswell Angels as men shall rise again; wherein the *Alchoran* affirmeth that Angels are mortall, and that they must all dye and rise again, the which impugneth divine and humane Law, and is against all naturall reason; and that for severall causes. First, because Angels are spirits, having no body, but spirit onely, and not having bodies they cannot dye, for death is nothing but the separation of the soul from the body, and in regard men are compos'd of body and soul, when the soul is separated from the body and departed, the body becomes a Caryon, and the soul goes whether God pleaseth, according to every mans deserts and works; and because the body is composed of the four Elements, it corrupteth and turneth to earth; but the soul of man after it is created never dyes; how then can it be as the *Alcoran* says, that Angels dye, when humane souls dye not? The second cause is, because *Adam*'s sin was the occasion of his death, by which sinning all his posterity were condemned to dye; whence it follows that if he had not sinned, neither he nor any of his posterity had been subject to death. Now tell me, *O Moore*, what sins have the Angels committed whereby they have deserved death as *Adam*, who incurred it by sin? The third cause or ground is a naturall reason, which gives all men to know and understand that Angels dye not, neither can dye, which is this: *Lucifer* and all the Angels that sinned with him by their pride against God were for this sin deprived of the glory of Heaven and Paradice, and were cast into the bottomless pit for ever, and were not condemned to dye, because they were spirits. And if the devils by reason of their sins were not condemned to dye, how is it that the *Alcoran* sayes that Angels shall dye? So, from these three grounds we may conclude that Angels shall not dye, and that he that says that Angels dye speaks not the truth, and in regard the *Alcoran* says that Angels dye, I say it is not of God, nor the word of God. ...

The third Argument is upon the first Chapter of the third Book, where hee sayes that the Virgin *Mary*, the Mother of Jesus Christ, was the Sister of *Aaron* and *Moses*, and sayes in Arabick thus, *Ogia Mariamu ya ohta Aron, (i. e.)* O *Mary*, O Sister of *Aaron*. Observe, *O Moore*, the great error which the *Alchoran* committeth in this place, and how he takes one person for another, putting the Virgin *Mary* for the Sister of *Moses* and *Aaron*, who was called *Mary* the Prophetess, and there were above 1500. years between them. Now can we call a Scripture which erres in so much time the Word or Scripture of God? And if it were, as some learned *Moores* say, that even as God would and Commanded that *Sarah, Abraham's* Wife should conceive her son *Isaac*, when she was already ninety years old, and was forty years past the time of conception. So also God had preserved this *Mary*, the Sister of *Aaron*, that from her Jesus Christ our Saviour, the Messias should come. This reason is not good, because in the second Chapter of the first Book he relates the conception of the Virgin *Mary*, the Mother of Jesus Christ, and how she was offered in the Temple for the service of God, and that the Priests in those times cast lots which of them should have the tuition of her, and the said Chapter sayes, that the lot fell upon *Zachary*, and that he took charge of her. And in the same chapter sayes further that this *Mary* had communication with the Angels, and talked with them, and that she was fed and nourished with celestiall food, which ye may read thus in the *Arabick, Ogna id calati, &c.* and likewise he sayes in *Arabick, O quullenie da hale, &c. (i. e.)* That the Angell said to *Mary*, O

Mary, certainly God hath chosen, adorned, and exalted thee above the women of all generations; and sayes further, that one day *Zachary* went into *Maries* Oratory (he having the keyes) and there found her eating food which he had not given her, and he said, O *Mary!* whence hadst thou this food, seeing I have the Keyes of the Oratory, and she answered him that God sent it her. The Commentators of the *Alcoran* say upon this place that the food which *Zachary* found *Mary* eating was ripe fruits out of their season. This was the same *Mary* to whom the Angell *Gabriel* came, as appears in the same Chapter, which is called in *Arabick, Sorathe alehamran, (i. e.)*, a Song of the generation of *Joachim*, the Father of the Virgin *Mary*; I have set down this here for the greater demonstration and proof, that this *Mary* was she unto whom the Angel *Gabriel* came with the salutation, saying; *Hayle* Mary *full of grace, the Lord is with thee, and that conceived Jesus Christ of the Holy Ghost.* This salutation is in *Arabick* thus, *Oya Maryemujune, &c.* Wherefore, *O Moore*, I conclude, that this *Mary* was not the Sister of *Aaron*, for the Sister of *Aaron* was not in the time of *Zacharias*, the Father of St *John Baptist*, as this *Mary* was. And *Muhamed* was deceived here by the name of *Moses* father, who in *Arabick* is called *Hembram*, by which name *Joachim* (our Ladye's father) is called in *Arabick*. And thus, *O Moore*, I tell thee, that the reason which the *Moores* give of *Maries* being *Aarons* Sister is invallid, seeing it is proved by the same *Alcoran* that this *Mary*, the Mother of Jesus Christ, lived in the time of *Zacharias*, above 1500. years after the other *Mary*. So that wee must say that *Muhamed* and the *Alcoran* take one person for another, and erre in so long time. A thing which is not sutable to a Prophet, nor to the Scripture of God; and therefore I say, that *Muhamed* was neither a Prophet, nor the *Alcoran* the Scripture of God.

And hence it appears how the Cutlers made him erre, and put one thing for another in the *Alcoran*, and transpose the Histories of the Prophets out of due place, putting the first last, and the last first, as shall hereafter appear; so that it hapned to *Muhamed* with his Cutlers, as the Proverb sayes, When the blind leads the blind, they both fall into the ditch.

The fourth Argument is from what he sayes in the third Chapter of the third Book, the words in *Arabick* are, *O qualacad, &c. (i. e.)*, That God sent the *Alforcan* (which is the same with the *Alcoran*) unto *Moses* and *Aaron* for a Light and admonition to the just. If the *Moores* say that *Alforcan* doth not signifie the *Alcoran*, I will prove the contrary by the same *Alcoran*, which in the second Chapter of the first Book sayes, *Onzele athorata y aliugile y nezele alforcane haleique, (i. e.)*, God inspired the *Thora*, the Gospell, and the *Alforcan* into *Muhamed*; and the same is in the seventh Chapter of the third Book, in *Arabick, Otabaraque, &c. (i.*

e.) blessed be he that caused the *Alforcan* to descend upon his servant *Muhamed* for to admonish the Nations; whence it appears from the *Alcoran* it self that *Alforcan* imports as much as *Alcoran,* and therefore, *O Moore,* I conclude that *Muhamed* and the *Alcoran* erre likewise in this passage, in saying that God sent it to *Moses,* and wee need not wonder if *Muhamed* lay down this error, seeing he sayes further in the *Suné* that *David* read all the *Alcoran* whilst they sadled his Mule; for hee that sayes the one may as well say the other, and he that makes one girdle, may make a hundred. ...

The seventh Argument is upon what he sayes in the eighth Chapter of the fourth book, and in the Chapter of Devils, where he sayes that a Company of Devils came one night to hear *Muhamed* and the *Moores* read the *Alcoran*; and in these two Chapters hee sayes, that the Devils took such delight in the *Alcoran* that they presently beleived in *Muhamed* and became *Moores.* And the words of the *Alcoran* in the Chapter of Devils are thus, *O coluhia, &c. (i. e.)*: O *Muhamed,* tell the *Moores* that a Company of Devils heard the *Alcoran* and said one to another that they had heard the wonderfull *Alcoran* read, and that they beleived it, and were not miscriants against their Creatour. And the words of the eighth Chapter run thus in *Arabick, O guaid Zarafna, &c. (i. e.)*: And when God sent thee a Company of Devils that they might hear the *Alcoran,* when they heard it read, they bad each other be silent, and after they had heard it read, they all went and admonished their people, saying, O our people! know ye, that wee have heard a book read which is inspired since *Moses,* which book shews the right way of Truth, wherefore come yee and obey the Prophet, and beleive in him, and God will pardon your sins, and deliver you from cruell torments, and whosoever will not obey the Prophet and beleive in him, shall not dwell long on earth, and shall have great torments. All this is in the *Arabick verbatim* as in our tongue, and ye may read it in the *Alcoran* in the two fore quoted Chapters, Which is not onely against reason and against divine and humane Law, but is also a great heresy and a horrid blasphemy, being against God, Angels, and men, against all Scripture, and the very *Alcoran* it self. For tell me, *O Moore,* who daily readest the *Alcoran,* doth it not direct thee to apply unto God for defence against evill and cursed Devils? and Commandeth thee that when ever thou takest in hand to read the *Alcoran,* thou must say in *Arabick O ahudu billehi mine Saytani ragini, (i. e.),* Preserve me O God from the wicked and cursed Devill? In divers places the *Alcoran* sayes that ye must resist the Devill, because he is the manifest enemy of men, and yet here the *Alcoran* sayes that they arė become the friends of men, God, *Muhamed,* and the Angels. Doest thou not conceive that this contradicts the Commandement of God, who cursed the Devill and for ever deprived him of his favour; and when he sayes that God pardoned their sins who became *Moores*, he contradicteth and opposeth the very Angels; For all the good Angels fought against the evill Angels, and vanquished them, and drove them out of Paradice, and they fell from their seats for ever; and yet the *Alcoran* sayes that the Devils must goe into Paradise, and be pertakers of glory with the Angels, and return to their first Stations. Doth it not appear unto thee, *O Moore*, to be injustice in God, that the Devils whom he hath for ever rejected should return again into his glory? Behold, *O Moore*, and consider this grosse error which *Muhamed* hath inserted in his *Alchoran*, and thou wilt perceive that it is not the word of God, nor a Law given by him.

The eight Argument is from the eight Chapter of the fifth book, and the Chapter of *Decoquer at* in the fourth book, where he sayes that brutish and irrationall creatures shall rise again at the day of Judgement, and that God shall judge between them; this *Muhamed* sayes in the *Suné*. The words of the *Alcoran* are thus in *Arabick Oguame mindelbetin, &c. (i. e.)* that all the beasts of the earth, and all the foules of the ayre shall rise again in the day of Judgement. And in the *Suné* he sayes, that God shall so doe justice betwixt the creatures, that the beast that hath been gored with a horne shall have satisfaction from the beast that gored it. Likewise, he sayes in the *Suné* that all the sheepe which the *Moores* kill in their feasts or Passeovers shall rise at the day of judgement, and pray for the *Moores* who caused them to bee slain. And sayes further that when the Angell *St Michael* shall weigh the good and bad works of men, these sheep shall come and lye in the ballance of their good works, so that the good works of such a man shall weigh more than his evill works. And for this reason the *Moores* kill many sheep in their feast or passeover, although they are not bound to kill above one. Now tell mee, *O Moore*, who art endowed with reason and discretion, what thinkest thou of this aforesaid, is it not an unreasonable thing and Contrary to all divine and humane Lawes, yea, against the very *Alcoran* it self? because in the second Chapter of the second book of the *Alcoran* he sayes these words in *Arabick, Oinne Sarra, &c. (i. e.)*, that the worst beasts before God are those which are deafe and dumb, which understand nothing; as if he should say, that bruite beasts are deaf without understanding, and dumb without reason and judgement. And in regard they are without reason and judgement, therefore they are not lyable to punishment in this world for any hurt they doe, for these beasts daily kill other beasts, and divers men, but a beast is not to suffer for the death of another beast, nor for the death of a man; as wee often see a bull bayted kill two or three men without being punished for it, because that (as the *Alcoran* sayes) they are deaf without understanding, and dumb without reason and judgement. How is it then, that the *Alcoran* sayes here that beasts shall rise to judgement? If wee say that beasts shall rise to judgement at the last day, wee must also say that those beasts which have done good works shall be rewarded and goe into Paradise, and those which shall have done evill works shall be punished in hell; the which *Muhamed* sayes and affirmes in the *Suné,* though the *Alcoran* say it not. And in the *Suné Muhamed* sayes that the sheep which the *Moores* kill at their Easter shall goe into Paradise. ... In breife, all that the *Moores* beleeve and hold is corporeall and terrene, and not spirituall; aswell in respect of this mundane life and conversation, as in respect of the glory which wee are to have in the world to come. And in *Muhamed's* Law or Religion it is not sufficient to say that men eat and drink in Paradise, but he comes to the impudence as to say that bruit beasts goe, eat and drink in Paradise; and so I conclude that the Law, the Prophet, and Scripture, which treateth and speaketh of such things, is not the Law nor the Prophet, much lesse the scripture of God; for all the premises doe impugne Truth, Reason, Philosophy, Logick, Astrology, and chiefly Theology, but not that Divinity of the *Moores* which speaks not of spirituall things, but of Corporeall and Terrene.

... CHAP. VII.

The seventh Chapter treateth of Muhamed's *wives and Virgins, and how many profered themselves to him without Contract of mariage, by a speciall Law which he made for himself; and of the jarrs, differences, dissentions and offences, which hapned betwixt* Muhamed *and his wives and slaves.*

I Say and prove by the book of *Azar* that *Muhamed* maried fifteen wives, and had eleven wives together, besides slaves, and of all his wives had but two Virgins, and had also four wives who profered themselves to him by vertue of the said speciall Law. And, *O Moore,* if thou dost not know that *Muhamed* had nine wives together, I prove it by a book called *Assamiel,* which is the book of the good customes of *Muhamed,* where praising *Muhamed,* and speaking of his virill strength, it sayes that in one hower *Muhamed* lay with all his wives which were eleaven. The words of the said book, *Assaniel,* are in *Arabick*: Thus, *O guamin, &c.* (Which Text might well have been omitted, and better have been silent of such things than to publish them, for it is unseemly to make a vertue of vice, and to apply carnall and luxurious things to sanctity and good customes, and to say that God was pleased and served with such basenes as which we have already shewn, and shall further shew in this Chapter). And I further prove it by the said book *Azar,* and by a book called *Almazhedi,* which say That when *Muhamed* died, his nine wives were present, which nine wives continued widdowes and so died, by a speciall Law which *Muhamed* made for himself ... .

20a [John Mandeville,] *Here begynneth a lytell treatyse or booke named Johan Maundeuyll* (1499). **20b** Samuel Purchas, *Purchas his pilgrimage* (1614).

Introduction Pre- and post-Reformation knowledge about the East was not restricted to the Muslim world. All lands on the way to, or in the vicinity of, Jerusalem, as well as all countries and lands known via trade routes and missionary activity aroused the curiosity of audiences, who listened to and read stories about the "marvels of the East." This curiosity developed a market for travelogues, a genre of travel diary that served as a window into the East and countries like Ethiopia, China, Japan, India, and Syria, and their cultures, religions, customs, and "curiosities," including information about their inhabitants which, to many, was the most interesting aspect of such texts. While foreigners from the East were not unknown in medieval Europe, most people had only a very vague idea where "Moors" or "Kithayans" came from, and had a keen interest in learning what the peoples of Egypt, Jordan or, later, North America, were like; this interest was both fuelled and satisfied by works like the *Travels of John Mandeville.*

Originally a late medieval travelogue, *The book of John Mandeville* claims it was composed ca. 1356 in England, but in fact the text's origins and authorship are unclear, with no evidence to date that a John Mandeville indeed penned this work, nor travelled to places the text describes, if he travelled at all. Most scholars agree that the text was originally composed in French, with its first manuscript copy reliably dated to 1371, while the original work might have indeed been composed around 1356. Within the first few years of its circulation the text became massively popular, translated into ten languages (including English, Dutch, Czech, and Irish); to date there are as many as 300 manuscript copies surviving. Before 1515 the *Book* was printed in eight languages and went through multiple editions by 1600; in England its popularity was almost unparalleled, there were two print editions in the late fifteenth century, six in the sixteenth century, and ten in the seventeenth century, and a few later as well.

While not a "real" travelogue, the *Book* is a compilation of existing travel narratives,[18] connected by the character of Sir John Mandeville, an English knight, who becomes the narrator and guide for the readers of his work, while the actual accounts of travels are most likely not his own.[19] The popularity of the text can be partially explained by the diversity of sources it uses to describe a wide range of lands and countries, the more fable-like "marvels" (such as humanoids with one large foot instead of two), its description of

18. For a list of the text's sources, see Iain McLeod Higgins, *Writing East: The "Travels" of Sir John Mandeville* (Philadelphia, 1997), 9–13.

19. Higgins, *Writing East*, 6–9.

the famous kingdom of Prester John,[20] and the diversity of its descriptions of a number of geographical regions, peoples, and cultures. While late medieval audiences were interested in all regions of the world, including India, Africa, and America, the excerpt chosen here focuses on Asia, and the land of "Cathay," i.e., China, sometimes blended or confused with Japan and Mongolia,[21] as the late medieval period saw a surge in interest in these regions of the world,[22] an interest continued in the early modern period.[23]

A Church of England clergyman, Samuel Purchas, was another author in the long chain of early modern writers inspired by Mandeville's *Book* and its later print editions. Purchas was, much like the author of the *Book*, not a well-travelled man himself, but a collector of stories that were told to him by sailors and other travelers, which he later compiled into his first book, *Purchas his pilgrimage* (1613). Intended as a Protestant study of the wonders of God's creations,[24] it is a good example of the universality of Mandeville's *Book* as well as the confessional flexibility of its inevitably religious side, which went without saying in medieval scholarship, including the sources for the *Book*. In 1625, Purchas edited the remaining works of Richard Hakluyt, a well-known early modern English author, editor, and translator and chaplain to Robert Cecil, to which works Purchas added his own edition of Mandeville's *Book*; in Purchas' view, Mandeville needed editing because "many things seeme not worthie credit" to him, but he ultimately decided it was a worthy contribution to his compendium of travel narratives, and Mandeville a great world traveler,[25] if in need of certain allowances in specific places of his narrative.[26]

Purchas' 1613 work and its subsequent editions are much longer than the 1499 *Lytell treatyse or booke named Johan Maundeuyll* and are divided according to geographical areas,

20. See, for example, Matteo Salvatore, *The African Prester John and the Birth of Ethiopian-European Relations, 1402–1555* (London, 2017); and Keagan Brewer, *Prester John: The Legend and its Sources* (Farnham, Surrey; Burlington, VT, 2015).

21. See Higgins, *Writing East*, 156–200.

22. See, for example, Fumihiko Kobayashi, "Looking for the Unknown Asia: The Asian Mystique in Early Modern European Textual History," in *Imagining Early Modern Histories*, ed. Allison Kavey and Elizabeth Ketner (New York, 2016), 125–152. See also Susanne Röhl, "Le *Livre de Mandeville* à Paris autour de 1400," in *Patrons, Authors, and Workshops: Books and Book Production in Paris around 1400*, ed. Godfried Croenen and Peter Ainsworth (Leuven, 2006), 279–296.

23. For more on late medieval and early modern interest, knowledge, and "discovery" of Asia see, for example, Rotem Kowner, *From White to Yellow: The Japanese in European Racial Thought 1300–1735* (Montreal, 2014); and *A Vision of China in the English Literature of the Seventeenth and Eighteenth Centuries*, ed. Adrian Hsia (Hong Kong, 1998).

24. Richard Hitchcock, "Samuel Purchas as Editor: A Case Study: Anthony Knyvett's Journal," *The Modern Language Review* 99 (2): 301–312.

25. Stephen Greenblatt, *Marvelous Possessions: The Wonder of the New World* (Chicago, 1991), 30.

26. Higgins, *Writing East*, 8.

much like the *Lytell treatyse.* The 1499 text, as its original, was arranged according to an imagined way to the Holy Land, whereas Purchas' text is divided into regions or continents: Asia, Africa, and so on. Interestingly, Mandeville's text, even though concerned with a pilgrimage, uses "travels" in its title, whereas Purchas' work, concerned with travels, contains "pilgrimage" in its title; perhaps Purchas intended this as an indication of the relationship of his work to the Mandeville text, or maybe to further the religious agenda of his text. Indeed, both works are related in a number of ways: the 1499 edition of Mandeville is an edition of one of many existing copies, and versions, of the original text, which in itself is a compilation of travel narratives; Purchas' text is likewise a compilation of various works on the subject, gathered with a Protestant agenda in mind. In both cases the descriptions of Cathay are interesting as, even though to an extent they rely on similar sources, Purchas' sources are more to-date and wider in scope and number than the ones available to the author of Mandeville's *Book,* making Purchas' text an example as much of continuity with the pre-Reformation tradition of viewing Asia, as a testimony to geographical expansion of Western culture and Christianity in the early modern period. Both texts thus present congruent and similar yet not identical views on the peoples and religions of Asia.

20a [John Mandeville,] *Here begynneth a lytell treatyse or booke named Johan Maundeuyll knyght born in Englonde in the towne of saynt Albone and speketh of the wayes of the holy londe towarde Jherusalem, and of marueyles of Ynde and of other dyuerse countrees,* Westminster, 1499, pp. lxxvii–lxxxv; pages are numbered on every second page. *STC* 17247. **Source** *EEBO*: Cambridge University Library (Inc. 5.J.1.2[3556]).

... *Of the londe named Cathay and the grete rychesses therof. ca. lxvi.*
And from thens men go vpon a ryuer that men calle Ceremosan, and this ryuer gooth thrugh Cathay and doth many tymes harme whan it waxeth grete. Cathay is a fayre countree and ryche, full of goodes and marchaundyses; thyder come marchauntes euery yere for to fetche spyces, and other marchaundyses more comonly than they do in to other countrees. And ye shall vnderstande that marchauntes that come from Denys of[27] fro Geene, or from other places, of Lombardy, or of Romayne, they go by see and londe .xi. monethes and more or they may come to Cathay.

Of a grete cyte named Cadon where in is the grete Chans palays and sege. ca. lxvij.
In the prouynce of Cathay towarde the eest is an olde cyte, and besyde that cyte the Tartarynes haue made an other Cyte that men calle Cadon that hath .xij.

27. Perhaps "or" was intended here.

gates, and euer bytwene two gates is a grete myle so that those two cytees, the olde and the newe, is rounde about .xx. myle. In this cyte is the palays and sege of the grete Chane in a full fayr place and grete, of whiche the walles about is two myle and within that are many fayre places; and in the gardeyne of that palays is a ryght grete hylle on the whiche is an other palays, and it is the fayrest that may be founde in ony place, and all about that hylle are many trees berynge dyuerse fruytes, and about that hylle is a grete dyche, and there nere are many vyuers on eche syde, and in those are many wylde foules that he may take and go not out of the palays. Within the halle of that palays are .xxiiij. pylers of golde, and all the walles are couered with ryche skynnes of beestes that men calle panters. Those are fayr beestes and well smellynge, and of the smelle of the skynnes none euyll smelle may come to the palays; those skynnes are as reed as blood, and they shyne so agayne the sonne that vnethes may men beholde theym; and men prayse those skynnes as moche as it were golde. In myddes of that palays is a place made that they calle the mountour for the grete Chane, that is well made with precyous stones and grete perles hangynge about; and at the four corners of that mountour are four nedders of golde, and vnder that mountour and aboue are conduytes of beuerage that they drynke in thempenrours[28] courte. And the halle of that palays is rychely dyght and well, and fyrste at the ouer ende of the halle is the throne of the Emperour ryght hye, where he sytteth at mete at a table that is well bordured with golde, and that bordure is full of precyous stones and grrete perles, and the greces on whiche he gooth vp are of dyuerse precyous stones bordred with golde. At the lyfte syde of his throne is the sege of his wyf, a degree lower than he sytteth, and that is of Iasper bordured with golde, and the sege of his seconde wyf is a degree lower than the fyrst and thats also of good Iasper bordured with golde, and the sege of the thyrde wyf is a degree lower thanthe seconde for alwaye he hath thre wyues with ym where soeuer he is; besyde thyse wyues on the same syde sytteth other ladyes of his kynne, echone lower than other as they are of degree, and all those that are wedded haue a counterfeet of a mannes foot vpon theyr heedes a cubyte longe, and all made with precyous stones, and aboue are they made with shynynge feders of pecoks or suche other in tokenynge that they are in subgeccyon of man and vnder mannes foot, and they that are not wedded haue none suche.

And on the ryght syde of the Emperour sytteth fyrst his sone that shall be Emperour after hym, and he sytteth also a degree lower than the Emperour in suche maner of seges as the Emperour sytteth, and by hym sytteth other lordes

28. The emperor's.

of his kynne echone lower than other as they are of degree. And themperour hath his table by himself, allone, that is made of golde and precyous stones, or of whyte crystal, or yelowe bordred with golde and echone of his wyues hath a table by herself. And vnder the Emperours table sytteth four clerkes at his feet that wryte all that the Emperour sayth, be it good or ylle. And at grete festes aboue the Emperours table and all other tables in the halle is a vyne made of fyne golde that gooth all about the halle and it hath many braunches of grapes lyke to grapes of the vyne; some are whyte, some are yelowe, some reed, some grene, and some blacke; all the reed[29] are of rubyes, of cremas, or alabaunce; the whyte arte of crystall or byrall, the yelowe are of topaces, thgrene are of emeraudes and crysolytys, and the blackeare of quyches and gerandes; and this vyne is made thus of precyous stones so properly that it semeth as i were a vyne growynge. And before the borde of the Enperour standeth grete lordes and no man is so harde to speke to hym but it be mynstrels for to solace themperour. And all the vessell that is seued in his halle or chambres are of precyous stones, and namely at tables where grete lordes ete, that is to saye of Iasper, crystal, amatyst, or fyne golde, and the cuppes are of emeraudes, saphyres, topaces. And other many maner of stones, and of syluer haue they noo vessell for they prayse syluer but lytell to make vessell of, but they make of syluer greces, pylers, and pauymentes of halles and of chambres. And ye shall vnderstande that my felowe and I was in soudy with hym .xvi. monethes agayne the kyng of Mancy, vpon whom he made warre and the cause was for we had so grete desyre to see the nobley of his courte, yf it were suche as we herde speke of, and forsoth we founde it more rycher and solempne than euer we herde speke of, and we sholde neuer haue byleued it had we not seen it, but ye shall vnderstande that mete and drynke is more honest amonge vs, than it is in those countrees for all the comons ete vpon skynnes of bestes on theyr knees, and ete but flesshe of all maner bestes, and whan they haue all eten they wype theyr hondes on theyr skyrtes, and they ete but ones on the daye, and ete but lytell brede, but the estate of the lordes is full nobley and full rychely.

Wherfore that the Emperour of Cathay is called the grete Chane. ca. lxviij.

And ye shall wete why he is called the grete Chane, ye wote well that all the worlde was destroyed with Noes flood but Noe and his wyf and his childern. Noe had thre sones, Sem, Cham, and Iapheth. Cham was he that sawe his faders balockes naked whan he slepte and scorned it, and therfore was he cursyd, and Iapheth couered it agayne. Thyse thre brethern had all the londe. Cham toke the

29. Copy slightly unclear here.

best parte ecstwarde that is called Asia. Sem toke Affryke, and Iapheth toke Europe. Cham was the myghtyest and rychest of his brethren, and of hym are come the paen folke and dyuers maner of men of the yles, some hedles and other men dysfygured, and for this Cham the Emperour there called hym Cham and lorde of all. But ye shall vnderstande that the Emperour of Cathay is called Chane and Cham, and for this cause it is not longe gone that all Tartary was in subgeccyon and thrall to other nacyons about, and they were made herdemen to kepe beestes; and amonge theym was. vij. lynages or kyndes: the fyrst was called Tartary that is the best, the seconde lynage is called Tanghot, the thyrde Eurace, the fourthe Valayre, the fyfthe Semoth, the sixth Menchy, the seuenth Sobeth. Thyse are all holdynge of the grete Chane of Cathay.

Now it befelle so that in the fyrst lynage was an olde man, and he was not ryche and men calle hym Changyus. This man laye and slept on a nyght in his bedde and there came to hym a knyght all whyte, syttynge vpon a whyte hors, and sayd to hym, Chane slepest thou, god that is almyghty sent me to the and it is his wyll that thou saye to the. vij. lynages that thou shalt Be theyr Emperour, for ye shall conquere all the londes that are about you and they shall be in your subgeccyon, as ye haue be in theyrs. And whan morowe came he rose vp and sayd it to the. vij. lynages and they scorned hym and sayd he was a fole. And the nyght after the same knyght came to the. vij. lynages and badde theym of goddes behalf to make Changyus theyr Emperour, and they sholde be out of all subgeccyon. And on the morowe they chose Changyus to Emperour and dyde hym all worshyp that they myght do, and called hym Chane as the whyte knyght called hym, and they sayd they wolde do as he badde theym. Than he made many statutes and lawes the whiche he called Ysakan. The fyrst statute was that they sholde be obedyent to god almyghty and byleue that he sholde delyuer theym out of thraldom, and that they sholde call on hym in al theyr werkes. An other statute was that all men that myght bere armes sholde be nombred, and to eche. x. sholde be a mayster, and to an hondred a mayster, and to a thousande a mayster. Than he commaunded to all the grettest and pryncypalest of the. vij. lygnages that they sholde forsake all that they hadde in herytage or lordshyp, and that they sholde holde theym payed of that he wolde gyue theym of his grace and they dyde so. And also he badde theym that eche man sholde brynge his eldest sone before hym and slee his owne sone with his owne hondes and smyte of theyr heedes, and as soone they dyde his byddynge. And whan he sawe they made no lettynge of that he badde theym do, than badde he theym folowe his baner, and than he put in subgeccyon all the londes about hym. ...

How the Empyre of the grete Chane is departed in to. xij. prouynces and how that they do cast ensence in the fyre where the grete Chane passeth thorugh the cytees and townes in worshyp of the Emperour. ca. lxxiiij.

The londe of the grete Chane is departed in. xij. prouynces and eche prouynce hath more than two thousande cytees and townes. Also whan themperour rydeth thrugh the countree, and he passeth thrugh cytees and townes, eche man maketh a fyre before his hous and casteth therin ensence and other thynges that gyue good smell to themperour. And yf ony men of relygyon that are crysten dwelle nere as themperour cometh, they mete hym with processyon with a crosse and holy water, and they synge *Veni creator spiritus* with a loude voyce. And whan he see theym come, he commaundeth the lordes that ryde nere hym to make waye that the relygyous men may come to hym, and whan he see the crosse he doth of his hatte that is made of precyous stones and grete perles, and that hatte is so ryche that it is meruayle to telle, and than he enclyned to the crosse. And the prelate of the relygyous men sayth orysons before hym and gyueth hym the benyson with the crosse, and he enclyneth to the benyson full deuoutly, and than the same prelate gyueth hym some fruyte of the nombre of .ix. in a plate of golde, as peres, or apples, or other fruyte, and than the Emperour taketh one therof and the other he gyueth to his lordes, for the maner is suche[30] there that no straunge man shall come before themperour but he gyue hym som, what after the olde lawe that sayth, *Non accedat in spectu me inanis*; That is to saye, No man come in to my syght ydle. And than the Emperour byddeth thyse relygyous men that they shall go forth, so that men of his oost defoule them not. And those relygyous men that dwelle where the Empresse or the Emperours sone cometh do in the same maner.

How that the grete Chane is the myghtyest lorde of all the worlde. ca. lxxv.

This grete Chane is the myghtyest lorde of the worlde, for prester Iohan is not so grete a lorde as he, ne the Soudan of Babylon, ne the Enperour of Persy. In his londe a man hath hondred wyues, and some .xl., some more, some lesse, and they take of theyr kynne to wyues all saue theyr systers of theyr moders, but theyr systers of theyr faders, other wyues they take also, and they take also well theyr stepmoder yf theyr fader be deed, and men and women haue all one maner of clothynge so that they may not be knowen but that women that are wedded bere a token on theyr heedes, and they dwelle not with theyr husbondes but he may lye by whiche that he wyll. They haue plente of all maner of bestes saue swyne,

30. The ink on the "c" in this word has faded away.

and forsoth they wyll none, and they byleue well in god that made all thynge and yet haue they ydols of golde and syluer, and to those ydols they offre theyr fyrst mylke of theyr bestes.

Yet of other maners of this countree. ca. lxxvi.
This Emperour, the grete Chane, hath thre wyues, and the pryncypall wyf was preester Iohans doughter. And the people of this countree begynne to do all theyr thynges in the newe mone, and they worshyp moche the sonne and the mone; those men ryde comonly without spores and they holde it grete synne to breke a bone with an other, and to cast mylke on the erthe or other lycour that men may drynke. And the moost synne that they may do is to pysse in theyr houses Where they dwelle, and he that pysseth in his hous shall be slayne, and of those synnes they shryue theym to theyr preestes, and for theyr penaunce they shall gyue syluer, and the place where men haue pysseth shall be halowed or els may no man come there. And whan they haue do theyr penaunce they shall passe thrugh a fayre fyre or two to wake theym clene of theyr synnes. ... And yf he bydde that ony be slayne he shall be slayne. And they answere all with one voyce, all that ye bydde shall be done. Than sayth themperour,[31] fro now forth my wordes shall cutte as my swerde, and than they sette hym in a chayre and crowne hym, and than all the good townes therabout sende to hym presentes soo moche that he shall haue more than hondred Camels laden with golde and syluer besyde other Iewels that he shall haue of lordes, of precyous stones and golde without nombre, and hors and ryhe clothes of camacas, and tartaryns and suche other.

20b Samuel Purchas, *Purchas his pilgrimage, or, Relations of the world and the religions observed in all ages and places discouered, from the creation unto this present. The second edition, of the first part of fower intended,* 1614, pp. 402–534.[32] *STC* 20506. **Source** Centre for Reformation and Renaissance Studies Rare Book Library, University of Toronto (G159. P976 1614).

The Fourth Booke
CHAP. XI.
Of the Tartarians, and of diuers Nations which they subdued with their Pristine Rites
... To returne to our Frier with whom we beganne, he reporteth that *Cingis*, after his victorie against the *Naimani*, warred vpon the Kythayans but were

31. The emperor.
32. Marginal notes in the original source were not included in the transcription.

ouerthrowne, and all the Nobles, except seuen, slaine. Hauing breathed himselfe a while at home, he inuaded the *Huyri,* a Christian people of the Nestorian Sect, whome they ouercame, and receiued of them letters of which before they were ignorant. After them hee subdued the Saroyur, Karanites, and Hudirat. This done, hee waged warre against the Kythayans or Cathayans, whose Emperour hee shut vp into his chiefe Citie, where *Cingis* besieged him, till that victuall fayling in his Campe, he commaunded that they should eate euery tenth man of the Armie. They of the Citie fought valiantly with Engines, Darts, Arrowes, and when stones wanted, they threw Siluer, especially molten Siluer. But by vndermining the Tartars made way from the Armie into the middest of the Citie, where they issued vp and opened the gates by force, and slew the Citizens. This is the first time that the Emperour of the Kathayans being vanquished, *Cingis Cham* obtained the Empire. The men of Kytay are Pagans, hauing a speciall kinde of writing by themselues, and, as it is reported, the Scriptures of the Old and New Testament. They haue also recorded in Histories the liues of their fore-fathers, and they haue Eremites, and certaine houses made after the maner of our Churches, which, in those daies they greatly resorted vnto. They say that they haue diuers Saints also, and they worship one God. They adore and reuerence Christ Iesus our Lord, and beleeue the Article of eternall life, but are not baptized. They doe also honorably esteeme and reuerence our Scriptures. They loue Christians and bestow much almes, and are a very courteous and gentle people. They haue no beards, and they agree partly with the Mongals in the disposition of their countenance. There are not better Artificers in the world. Their Countrey is exceeding rich in Corne, Wine, Gold, Silke, and other commodities. ...

... CHAP. XII.

A Continuation of the Tartarian Historie, and the question discussed, whether Cathay and China be the same.

Since *Tamor Can* we haue not so continued a Historie of their Empire and Emperours as before, and yet we haue had succeeding testimonies a long time of their State and Magnificence, but neither so diligent obseruers, nor so exact Writers as the former: besides that, their Histories seeme in some things more fabulous. Of this later sort are *Odoricus,* a Frier, which liued three yeares in the Emperours Court, and trauelled as farre as Quinsay, who died in the yeere 1331; *Sir Iohn Mandeuile* our Countryman spent many yeeres in those Countries a few yeares after *Odoricus,* and writ the Historie of his Trauels in the reigne of *Edward* the third of England, *Echiant Can* being then Emperour of the Tartars; in which, if many things seeme not worthie credit, yet are they such as *Odoricus*, or some others, not of the worst Authors, had before committed to writing, and haply be others after his time, in those daies when Printing wanted, foisted into his booke. Once, hee setteth downe the distances and passages of Countries so exactly, as I thinke hee could not then haue learned but by his owne Trauels. After his time *Nicholo di Conti*, a Venetian, trauelled through India and Cathay, after fiue and twentie yeeres returning home; and going to *Eugenius* the fourth, then Pope, to be absolued, because he had denied the Christian Faith to saue his life, his enioyned penance was truly to relate to *Poggius* the Popes Secretarie his long peregrination. This was in the yeere 1444. About the same time *Iosafa Barbaro*, a Venetian, in the yeare 1436, had learned of a Tartarian Embassadour (which had beene at Cambalu, and returning by Tana, was entertained of the said *Iosafa*) some particulars touching the great Cham and Cathay, some part whereof he heard after confirmed by the mouth of *Usun-cassan*, the mightie Persian King, in the yeere 1474. So that from the yeere 1246 thus farre we haue a continued succession of the Cathayan Historie, besides that which an Arabian hath written in his Historie of *Tamerlane*, now extant in English.

I am the more curious in naming these Authors, least any should thinke that which is written of this people to be fabulous (all these, in a manner, concurring in the most substantiall things) or should confound, as diverse lately haue done, the Countries and affaires of China and Cathay. The cause of both these errours is because that in these last hundred yeares and more, in which more of the World then euer before hath beene discouered, yet nothing of moment is found out of this Countrey or People. Whereunto may be answered, That since diuers of the great Tartarian Lords before subiects to the great *Cham*, hauing made themselues absolute Lords of their seuerall States, the way hath not beene so open to passe, being otherwise of it selfe exceedingly both long, difficult, and dangerous; and the adioyning Princes recouering themselues from Tartarian seruitude will neither suffer their owne to goe out, nor others freely to enter their Dominions; as the Muscouite, the King of China, and others. M. *Ant. Ienkinson*, which went as farre thither-ward as Bogharre, could not passe further for warres in those parts. Neither haue any gone thither by Sea. And yet euen in this time we haue not altogether wanted witnesses. *Ludouicus Vertomannus*, a hundred yeares since, in Bengala met with diuerse Christians who affirmed that there were in their Countrey diuers Signiors, Christians, subiect to the great *Cham*. These were white men of a Citie called Sarnau. In M. *Hakluits* painefull labours we may reade of diuerse passages out of Russia and Persia by Carauans into Cathay. *Ramusius* also, in his Annotations before M. *Paulus* telleth of one *Chaggai Memet*, a Persian Marchant, who had beene at Campion and Succuir in Catay (*Damircan* then raigning) and had acquainted him with diuers particulars thereof.

... The greatest obiection against this Historie that distinguisheth Cathay from China is the report of *Iacob Pantogio*, a Iesuit, in a letter dated from Panquin, the Seat Royall of China, in March 1602, in which he blameth a double error of our Mappes, both for making China larger then it is, and for adioyning to the same this questioned Kingdome of Cathay, whereas (saith he) China, or Sina, is Cathay, and this Panquin, where now we liue, is Cambalu. This he proueth by the incredible riches which he here saw, agreeing to that which is commonly reported of Cathay, and by the testimonie of certaine Moores and Mahumetanes whome he found in Panquin, which vsually, euery fifth yeare, resort hither vnder shew of an Embassage, and paying of tribute; indeede for gaine, by way of traffique (their tribute meane-while obtaining sufficient retribution out of the Kings Coffers, who sustaineth them and theirs, all the time of their abode in China, at his owne costs, besides other gifts). Of these Marchants which resorted hither out of Persia and the Countrey of the Mogores, the Iesuits by enquirie learned that this countrey of China was called Cathay, and had no other name in Persia, and among the Mogores, nor did they know any other Countrey so called. And asking further how they called the Citie Panquin, they answered, Cambalu: whereupon the Iesuit concludeth without all scruple, as is said. And againe, in the Chinian Epistles, dated 1607, is reported, That *Benedictus Goes* (sent sixe yeares after of the Iesuites by the way of Mogor to finde out Cathay) remained in the borders of China, in the Prouince of Xanti, from whence he writ, *Anno* 1606., That he could finde no other Catay then the Kingdome of China. This report furthereth *Pantogiaes* opinion.

But if it be not sufficient to oppose the former report of *Xauier* to these of *Pantogia* and *Goes*, and the different qualities of the Chinians and Cathayans (as in their proper places shall follow) both in things priuate and publike, Diuine and Humane; I answere, That the name Cambalu is by *Marcus Paulus* and others interpreted *The Citie of the Prince*, or *Cam*. And *Perera* interpreteth Pachin, or Panquin, where the King of China alwayes resideth, to signifie the Towne of the Kingdome, as hee was there aduertised, the same signification (in manner) remaining to the diuers appellations in differing Languages, as a common name to be applyed to any Citie Royall. This *Perera* was himselfe a long time prisoner there, and accounted it a wonder in one Citie to meete with a few Moores, who were detained in China, hauing come thither twentie yeares before, and were permitted the vse of their Religion; of which they could say almost nothing, but *Mahomet* was a Moore, and their father was a Moore, and I am a Moore, with some other wordes of their Alcoran; wherewithall, and in abstinence from Swines flesh, they liue (sayth he) till the Diuell take them all. And yet the report of *Xauier* telleth vs That the Moores are many and mightie in Cathay; of Iewes I remember not the mention of them in any Chinian relation; of Christians, which (he saith) is the Religion in Cathay, there are not to my knowledge, except some late gleanings of the Iesuits, any reported to be at all in China, but at Xensi at Xucheo, which also were aliens, as appeareth by their complexion, long beards, and the vse of Bells.

And whereas in China theeues and malefactors are seldome executed (and none hath power to execute any without speciall Commission from the King) but either they die by stripes, hunger, or imprisonment; except, some few once in a yeare. *Marcus Paulus* and *Iosafa Barbaro,* from the relation of eye-witnesses, affirme, that in Cambalu was such sudden and rigorous execution of Iustice, that one taking a Iarre of Milke from a womans head, and beginning to drinke, vpon the womans out-cry was apprehended, and presently with a sword cut in sunder, that the bloud and milke issued together, a Tartarian Embassador affirming both this, and that he had seene the like execution vpon another, for taking a piece of Bayes from a woman, so chopped in twaine. But the relation of the Chinian and Cathayan differing Rites will further cleare this point. As for the name of Cathay, ascribed to China by the Moores, I answere, That *William de Rubruquis,* who was in the Court of *Mangu Can* supposeth Cathay to be *Serica Regio,* described by *Ptolomey* farre more Northerly then the Iesuite reporteth China to be, by his own Astrolabicall obseruation. And to these *Seres Ptolomey* ioyneth the *Sina,* or Chinois, on the South, and our later Geographers generally concurre in this opinion. He also which readeth *Ioannes de Plano Carpini* shall finde that the Tartars conquered the Kara-Kitai, or blacke Cathayans, and then the Emperour of Kithai, by vndermining his Citie, as is said, in the dayes of *Cyngis;* and yet a great part of Kitai remained yet vnconquered, and withstood his forces, and namely that part which is neerest the Sea. And this wealthy Countrey of Great Cathaya hath many Prouinces, the more part whereof doe yet withstand the Moals or Tartars (it is the last period in *William de Rubruquis*). I hence gather that the name Kitai was applyed to a great part of the North-east corner of Asia, happily no lesse generall to many Regions on that side, then India to the Southerly parts. And why may not the name of Kathay, as well by the Mogores and Persians, be giuen to the North parts of China (one parcell of the North-east of Asia) as the name of India, not onely to so great a part of Asia, but to America also, which was called India, because the first Discouerers thought they had encountred the Indian Continent? And these parts of China may much fitter retaine the name of Cathay to which Empire it had so long beene subiect, and by the Cathayan conquest was first knowne to our world. ...

But they knew no Countrey else so named. True, for the Lawes of the Cathayans forbidding egresse of the Natiues, and ingresse of Aliens, and a more forcible law of Mountaines and Deserts, wilde beastes, and wilder men; the manifold smaller and more beggerly Segniories betweene euery one challenging their ninth (if not themselues confiscating, or theirs robbing all) now in so long a space may burie euen the name and knowledge of the great *Can*, whereas neither Armes of Princes, nor traffique of Subiects, can open any new, or retaine the old notice of Nations. ...

Euen as in Nature it falleth out that the Sunne shineth there many howers before it ariseth to vs, so in Historie it may happen that there may shine a Tartarian Sunne in Cathay, when as a darke night in this longinquitie of distance hideth him from our eyes. Let euerie Reader iudge as pleaseth him: I am afraid betwixt Cathay and China I shall get a checke for staying longer then becommeth a *Pilgrim*. ...

CHAP. XIII.
Of the Religion of the Tartars, and Cathayans.

... They beleeue that there is one God, the Maker of all things visible and inuisible, the Author of good things and punishments, yet doe they not worship him with prayers, prayses, or any certaine rites. They haue also Idols of Felt, in the fashion of a man, and the same they set on both sides of their Tent-doores, and vnder them they put a thing of Felt fashioned like a Dugge. These they account the keepers of their Cattell, Authors of their Milke and yong store. Others they make of Silke, and doe them much honour. Some place them in a faire Chariot, couered before the doore of their slation, and whosoeuer stealeth any thing out of that Chariot is slaine without all pittie. Their Captains haue one alway in the middest of their Tent. To these Idols they offer the first fruits of their Milke, and the first morsels of their meat, and first draught of their drinke at meales. And when they kill a beast, they offer the heart to their Idoll, leauing it before him till the morning, and then they take and eate it. They make an Idoll also to their Chiefe Emperour, and offer thereunto with great solemnitie as well other creatures as horses, which none after dare ride on till death. They breake not a bone of the beasts which they kill for meate, but burne them with fire. They bend themselues to this Idoll toward the South, as to God. They worship the Sunne, Lights, and Fire, Water also, and the Earth, offering thereunto the first of their meates and drinkes, and in the morning before they eate or drinke. They haue no set rites prescribed by Law, nor doe they compell any to deny their religion; simplie, although in some of their customes they are very rigorous. Thus they martyred *Michael* Duke of Russia, because he refused to doe reuerence to the Image of *Cingis Can,* which had beene their first Emperour, and compelled they yonger brother of *Andrew* Duke of Saruogle in Russia to marrie his said brother's wife, according to their custome, after that they had slaine her former Husband.

They haue certaine traditions according to which they reckon these things following to be sinnes. To thrust a knife into the fire or any way to touch the fire with a knife, or with their knife to take flesh out of the Cauldron, or to hew with an hatchet neere to the fire. For they thinke that they should so cut away the head of the fire. They account it sinne also to leane on the whip wherewith they beate their horses (for they ride not with spurres). Also to touch arrowes with a whip, to take or kill yong Birds, to strike an horse with the raine of their bridle, and to breake one bone against another. Likewise to poure out meate, milke, or any kinde of drinke vpon the ground, or to make water within their Tabernacle, which whosoeuer doth willingly, is slaine, but otherwise he must pay a great summe of money to the Inchanter to bee purified, who causeth the Tabernacle with all things therein to passe betweene two fires. Besides, if any hath a morsell giuen him which hee is not able to swallow, and for that cause casteth it out of his mouth, there is an hole made vnder his Tabernacle, by which he is drawne forth, and slaine without all compassion. Likewise whosoeuer treades vpon the threshold of any of the Duke's Tabernacles hee is put to death. Thus are these *Gnats strayned,* when as hostile inuasions, murther, and such other *Camels* are easily amongst them *swallowed.* They thinke that after death they shall liue in another world, and there multiply there cattell, eate, drinke and doe other actions of life. At a new Moone, or a full Moone, they begin all new enterprises. They call her the great Emperour, and bow their knees and pray thereto. The Sunne they say is the Moones mother, because she hath thence her light.

They are giuen to Diuinations, Auguries, Sooth-sayings, Witchcrafts, Inchantments, and when they receiue answere from the Diuell, they attribute the same vnto God, whom they call *Itoga,* and the Comanians call him *Chan,* that is, Emperor, whom they maruellously feare and reuerence, offering to him many Oblations, and the first fruits of their meate and drinke. According to his answeres they dispose all things. They beleeue that all things are purged by fire; therefore, when any Embassadours, Princes or other Personages whatsoeuer, come vnto them, they and their gifts must passe betweene two fires to be purified, least peraduenture they haue practised some Witchcraft, or haue brought some poison or other mischiefe with them. And if fire fall from heauen vpon men or beasts, which there often hapneth, or if they thinke themselues any way defiled or vncleane, they thus are purified by their Inchanters. If any be sicke, a speare is set vp in his Tent with blacke Felt welted about it, and from thenceforth no stranger entreth therein. For none of them which are present at his death may enter the hord of any Duke or Emperour, till a New-Moone. When he is dead, if he be a chiefe man, he is buried in the field where pleaseth him. And he is buried with his Tent, sitting in the middest thereof, with a Table set before him, and a platter full of meate, and a Cuppe of Mares-milke. There is also buried with him a Mare and Colt, a Horse with bridle and saddle, and they eate another Horse, whose bones the women burne for the soule of the dead, stuffing his hide with straw, setting it aloft on two or foure poles, that hee may haue in the other world a Tabernacle and other things fitting for his vse. They burie his golde and siluer with him, the Chariot or Cart in which he is carried forth is broken, his Tent is destroyed, neither is it lawfull to name his name, till the third generation. ... They are reasonably courteous one to another: their women are chaste; adulterie is seldome heard of, and theft is rare, both punished by death. Drunkennesse common, but without bralls among themselues, or discredit among others. They are proud, greedie, deceitfull. They eate Dogs, Wolues, Foxes, Horses, and in necessitie, mans flesh, Mice, and other filth, and that in as filthy a manner, without Cloathes, and Napkins, (their Bootes and the Grasse can serue to wipe their greasie handes) they haue no Bread, Hearbes, Wine, Meate or Beere, nor doe they wash their dishes. It is a great sinne amongst them to suffer any of their foode to be lost, and therefore they will not bestow a bone on a Dogge, till they haue eaten the marrow.

... Astrologers, or Necromancers, are in their Art maruellous. When the skie is cloudie and threatneth raine, they will ascend the roofe of the Pallace of the *Grand Can* and cause the raine and tempests to fall round about, without touching the said Pallace. These which thus doe are called *Tebeth,* and *Chesmir,* two sorts of Idolaters, which delude the people with opinion of their sanctitie, imputing these workes to their dissembled holinesse, and for this cause they goe in filthy and beastly manner, not caring who seeth them, with dirt on their faces, neuer washing nor combing themselues. And if any be condemned to death, they take, dresse, and eate him; which they doe not if any die naturally. They are also called *Bachsi,* that is of such a Religion or Order, as if one should say a Frier, Preacher, or Minor, and are exceedingly expert in their diuellish Art. They cause that the bottles in the Hall of the great *Can* doe fill the Balls of their owne accord, which also without mans helpe passe tenne paces through the ayre, into the hands of the said *Can,* and when he hath drunke in like sort returne to their place. These

Bachsi sometimes resort vnto the officers, and threaten plagues or other misfortune from their Idols, which to preuent, they desire so many Muttons with blacke heads, and so many pounds of Incense, and *Lignum Aloes* to performe their due sacrifices. Which they accordingly receiue and offer on their Feast-day, sprinkling Broth before their Idols. There be of these great Monasteries which seeme like a small Citie, in some whereof are two thousand Monkes, which shaue their heads and beards, and weare a religious habite, and hallow their Idols feasts with great solemnitie of Hymnes and lights. Some of these may bee married. Other there are called *Sensim*, an order which obserueth great abstinence and strictnesse of life, in all their life eating nothing but Branne, which they put in hot water, and let it stand till all the white of the meale be taken away, and then eate it being thus washed. These worship the Fire, and are condemned of the other for Heretikes, because they worship not their Idols, and will not marry in any case. They are shauen, and weare hempen-garments of blacke or bright yellow, and although they were silke, yet would they not alter the colour. They sleepe on great mats, and liue the austerest life in the world.

... They are great Vsurers, taking tenne in the hundred for a moneth, besides vse vpon vse; insomuch, that a souldier in Georgia which had borrowed fiue hundred peeces of coine called *Yperpera*, retaining the same fiue yeares, was constrained to repay seuen thousand. And a Tartarian Ladie for seuen yeares vse of fiftie sheep demaunded seuen thousand *Yperpera*. They are so couetous that though they abound in cattell, they will scarce allow any to their owne expence, while it is found and good, but if it die, or be sicke. They are addicted to sodomie or buggerie. They eate sometimes for necessity mans flesh, sometimes to delight themselues, and sometimes to terrifie others, reckoning it a great glory to haue slaine many, and that by varietie of crueltie. Their heads they shaue from eare to eare, in manner of a horse-shooe: wearing long lockes at their eares and neckes. There be some of the Tartars which when they see their fathers grow old and diseased, they giue them fatte meates which may choake them. And when they are thus dead, they burne their bodies, reseruing the ashes as a precious jewell, sprinkling their meates with that powder. ...

CHAP. XIIII.

Of the festiuall solemnities, and of the magnificence of the Grand Can.

We haue already spoken of the solemne sacrifice obserued on the eight and twentieth day of August. We reade in our Author *Marcus Paulus* an eye-witnes of these his relations, of other the *Grand Cans* grand solemnities. Of which two are principall: one on his birth-day, which in *Cublai Cans* time was the eight and twentieth of September. On which himselfe was royally clothed in cloth of gold, and twenty thousand of his Barons and souldiers were all apparelled in one colour, and like (excepting the price) to himselfe, euery one hauing a girdle wrought of Gold and Siluer, and a paire of shooes, some of their garments richly set with pearles and jewells, which they weare on the thirteene solemnities, according to the thirteene Moones of the yeare. On this day all the Tartars, and seuerall Princes subiect, present him with rich gifts, and all sects of Religions pray vnto their gods for his health, and long life.

But their chiefe feast is on the first day of their yeare, which they beginne in February, celebrated by the *Grand Can* and all the Countries subiect to him, in which they are all arayed in white, a colour in their estimation portending good lucke. And then he is presented with many clothes and horses of white colour, and other rich presents, in the same religiously obseruing the number of nine, as nine times nine horses, if they be able, and so of peeces of gold, cloth, and the rest. Then also the Elephants (which are about fiue thousand) are brought forth in sumptuous furniture, and Camels couered with silke. And in the morning they present themselues in the Hall as many as can, the rest standing without in their due order. First, those of the Imperiall progenie; next, the Kings, Dukes, and others, in their due place. Then commeth forth a great man or Prelate which cryeth out with a lowd voyce, Bow downe your selues, and worship; which they presently doe, with their faces to the earth. This Prelate addeth, God saue and preserue our Lord long to liue with ioy and gladnesse. They all answere, God grant it. The Prelate againe, God encrease his Dominion, and preserue in peace all his subiects, and prosper all things in all his Countries. Whereunto they answer as before. Thus they doe worship foure times. After this, the said Prelate goeth to an Altar there, richly adorned; on which is a red Table with the name of the Great *Can* written in it, and a Censer with Incense, which he incenseth in stead of them all, with great reuerence performed vnto the Table. This done, they returne to their places, and present their gifts, and after are feasted.

When *Cublai* had ouerthrowne *Naiam* his vncle (as before is said) vnderstanding that the Christians obserued their yearely solemnity of Easter, hee caused them all to come vnto him, and to bring the Booke of the foure Gospels, which he incensed often with great Ceremonies, deuoutly kissing it, and caused his Barons to doe the like. And this he obserueth alway in the principall feasts of the Christians, as *Christmasse* and *Easter*. The like he did in the chiefe feasts of the Saracens, Iewes, and Idolaters. The cause (he said) was because of those foure Prophets, to which all the world doth reuerence: IESVS of the Christians, *Mahomet* of the Saracens, *Moses* of the Iewes, and *Sogomambar Can* the first

Idoll of the Pagans: and I (saith hee) doe honour to them all, and pray him which is the greatest in Heauen, and truest, to helpe me. Yet he had best opinion of the Christian faith, because it contained nothing but goodnesse, and would not suffer the Christians to carrie before them the Crosse on which so great a man as Christ was crucified. He also sent *Nicolo* and *Maffio*, the father and vncle of *Marco Polo* our Author, in Embassage to the Pope, to send him a hundred wise men which might conuince the Idolaters that boasted of those their magicall wonders, whereas the Christians that were there were but simple men, not able to answer them, which if it had beene effected, hee and his Barons would haue beene baptized. ...

CHAP. XV.

Of the alterations of Religion among the Tartars: and of the diuers sorts, sects, and nations of them now remaining

... These three sorts of Tartars which wee haue hitherto mentioned are all, for the most part, Mahumetans. There are some yet (as *Michonius* affirmeth) neere the Caspian Sea which are not Mahumetans, nor shaue their haire of their heads after the Tartarian manner; and therefore they call them *Calmuch* or Pagans.

The fourth are those which in greatnesse are first, namely the Cathayans, called *Carabas* (that is, black-heads) of their Turbants, as the former, *Ieselbas*. But of their Religion, further then that which hath beene before expressed, we can say little. And it seemeth by the relations mentioned in the former Chapters that they are Gentiles or Christians, and not of *Mahomets* errour. *Chaggi Memet*, a Persian Marchant, related (as in part is said before) to *Ramusius*, that he had beene at Campion, *Damir Can* then raigning, and that vnto *Camul*, the Westerly part of Tanguth, they were Idolaters and Ethnikes; from thence Westwards, Musulmans, or Saracens. In the Epistle of *Carualius* the Iesuite it is reported by a Mahumetane Marchant, that they were Christians, happily because of Images which the Idolaters and Pseudo-Christians doe equally worship. ...

The Fift Booke

CHAP. XVI.

A Continuation of the former Discourse touching the Religions of Iapon.

... Touching the Kingdome of Iapan, we cannot set downe the number and order of their Kings in auncient times. It seemeth that these last eight hundred yeares they haue beene much disquieted with ciuill warres; euery one getting as many shires or Kingdomes (which in Iapan are threescore and sixe), as he could.

Nabunanga was a great Prince and *Quabacondonus* a greater; both great Tyrants. This last caused his Nephew to be made *Quabacondono*, contenting himselfe with the title of *Taicosama*, but soone after, iealous of his greatnesse, he forced him (after the Iaponian maner) with his companions, to kill himselfe. He hauing no children but one infant when he was sicke and neere to death, sent for *Gieiaso* the chiefe of the Iaponian Nobles, Lord of eight Kingdomes, and made him administrator of the Kingdome till his sonne should be of age, and further to binde him hereunto, hee made a marriage betwixt *Gieiasoes* Neece, two years old, and this infant of his about the same age, causing the same presently to be consummated. He took an oath of him, and the other nobles for their fealtie to his sonne. ... But after his death there arose great contentions, which *Gieiaso* (now calling himself *Daifusama*) appeased, and after some battells against his aduersaries inuested himself in the Empire, *Anno* 1601. This hee did then in young *Taicosamas* name, but since he hath seized the Empire fully to himselfe. And calling himselfe *Cubo*, since that time (as the later Epistles testifie) hath entitled his owne sonne to the Iaponian Empire. ...

21a *Of the newe landes and of the people founde by the messengers of the kynge of portyngale named Emanuel* (1510?). **21b** Richard Hakluyt, *The principal nauigations, voyages, traffiques and discoueries of the English nation made by sea or ouer-land* (1600).

Introduction Another book published by the Dutch printer John of Doesborowe, *Of the newe landes and of the people founde by the messengers of the kynge of portyngale named Emanuel* is comprised of three sections: the "lands and peoples found by King Emanuel's messengers," in which places like "the lande of Canarien," "Allago," "Maior India" and "Arabia" are described; then in part two "Cristened nations," i.e., Christian nations, and their habitats are described, ending with the third part, comprised of a version of the medieval legend of Prester John. As popular as stories about King Arthur, tales of the Christian king and priest and his country lost among the Muslim and pagan nations somewhere in the East, variously placed in India, through Asia, to Ethiopia, excited the imaginations as well as intellectual efforts of many in the West throughout the Middle Ages. The legend had its beginning sometime in the twelfth century, and its popularity endured at least until the end of the seventeenth century. Many late medieval and early modern travelogues made references to the land of Prester John, as many set out to find it, or claimed they did, and the presence of these stories often connected late medieval and early modern texts otherwise very different from one another.[33] *Of the newe landes* is considered to be one of the first texts in English that speaks of America ("Armenica," n. pag.). One of the most fascinating features of this work is its description of the Pygmies. Known to the Christian West through the writings of Pliny and later travel stories, medieval scholars devoted much intellectual attention to what they believed were imperfectly developed human beings,[34] but to popular audiences the existence of Pygmies was also tangible evidence of the existence of "wonders" and "different" human beings (as opposed to some other humanoids, such as creatures with only one foot, described in the *Book of John Mandeville*).

Richard Hakluyt's *The principal nauigations, voyages, traffiques and discoueries* established him as "perhaps the most significant figure in the history of English travel writing."[35] The text's impressive scope spans all regions of the world reached by Englishmen throughout the history of England (with the first edition also including Mandeville), gathered from both contemporary and medieval authors, including voyages from the Anglo-Saxon period. Just as previous works in this section, Hakluyt's *Principal nauigations* is a compilation of travel narratives of others, edited together in view of the rising interest in North America and other newly "discovered" places.[36] Ordained as Anglican priest in 1583, Hakluyt was a firm believer in the capacity of England to establish a functioning godly "empire" in the newly expanding world,[37] and an accomplished editor and compiler, providing inspiration to such authors as Samuel Purchas. The second edition

33. For example, Edward Webbe's *The rare and most wonderfull things which Edward Webbe and Englishman borne, hath seen and passed in his troublesome travailes* (1590). For more on the history of Prester John, see Brewer, *Prester John*, 1–28, and throughout.

34. Barry Wind, *"A Foul and Pestilent Congregation": Images of "Freaks" in Baroque Art* (Aldershot, Hampshire; Brookfield, VT, 1998), 9. See also John Block Friedman, *The Monstrous Races in Medieval Art and Thought* (New York, 2000), esp. Chapter 9. The view, originating in classical thought, that certain "savage" populations were more akin to apes then humans persisted throughout the later Middle Ages, through the Renaissance, until the eighteenth century (Ian J. McNiven and Lynette Russell, *Appropriated Pasts: Indigenous Peoples and the Colonial Culture of Archeology* [Lanham, MD, 2005], 36).

35. Daniel Carey and Claire Jowitt, "Introduction," in *Richard Hakluyt and Travel Writing in Early Modern Europe*, ed. Daniel Carey and Claire Jowitt (Farnham, Surrey; Burlington, VT, 2012), 1–12, at 1.

36. Carey and Jowitt, "Introduction," 1.

37. *He also firmly believed in the excellence of English culture, hence a lengthy quotation from Chaucer's Prologue to* The Knight's Tale, *prefaced with the following summary: "The verses of Geofrey Chaucer in the knights Prologue, who liuing in the yeere 1402. (as hee writeth himselfe in his Epistle of Cupide) shewed that the English Knights after the losse of Acon, were wont in his time to trauaile into Prussia and Lettowe, and other heathen lands, to aduance the Christian faith against Infidels and miscreants, and to seeke honour by feats of armes" (124).*

of Hakluyt's text, excerpted here, is divided into three volumes, the first one on English travels to "the North and Northeast quarters," the second gathering details of travels to the "South and Southeast quarters of the world," and the third dealing with "some few Places, where they have not been, of Strangers,"[38] each with detailed catalogues of the places and narratives included in each volume. The text is thus a compilation of wondrous tales and actual travel narratives, and features stories ranging from those on the Queen of Sheba to accounts by travellers to Lebanon. In its encyclopaedia-like style the text resembles the 1510 text printed by Doesborowe, but is significantly longer than the fairly short *Of the newe lands*, and distinctly early modern in its acute attention to detail. This reflects Hakluyt's attempts to manifest the superiority of the English at sea and on land, and through that, also of English Protestantism over other confessions and religions, as a faith that inspires the English to greatness. Its descriptions of the peoples and cultures encountered during various voyages of explorers and merchants contrast both with *Of the newe landes* and with the *Book of John Mandeville* (which, after consideration, Hakluyt did not include in this second edition of his *Principal Navigations*) in that the descriptions are more obviously aimed to describe "facts" and not "wonders" (e.g., there are no mentions of griffons, etc.), but at the same time display an affinity with these earlier texts by, for instance, including information on the land of Prester John.

21a *Of the newe landes and of the people founde by the messengers of the kynge of portyngale named Emanuel. Of the. x. dyuers nacyons crystened. Of pope Iohn and his landes, and of the costely keyes and wonders molodyes that in that lande is*, Antwerp, 1510 (?); unnumbered pages. *STC* 7677. **Source** *EEBO*: British Library, *London (G.7106)*.

... *Arabia.*

... And out[39] this kyngdone hath be oon of the thre holy kyngys. Item ther bynde they ther oxe son with Arabie gold about ther hornes and erys; And also goldyn rynges aboute thyr legges. And for gold take they of marchaundes sylkyng kerchers and lynen clothe. Item ther after sewe now .v. ylandes; the fyrst yland named Monsabith; sixty myles from Safalen is leeid the towne Quiola that was founde of the kynges folke of portyngal. And they slewe there moche people and robbed the towne. And there without had there kynge edyfyed on castell that is named seynt Iacobis castell; there in lyeth a .C. bolde and hardy men that lyeth and kepeth it. ...

38. From the title page.
39. "Of" would make sense here.

The thirde nacyon.
They of Indyen hath one prynce and that is pope Iohn,[40] whose myghtynes and rychedome amounteth aboue all prynces of the world, for he hath vnder hym .lxxij. kynges; and as pope Iohn dayely rydeth, he bere a fore hym one crosse of wode for to thynke on at all tymes and remember vpon the passions of Iesu, and to the batayle doth he bere .xij. crosses of golde made and set with precyouse stones, for his baners in this lande is the body of seynt Thomas. ...

The tenthe nacyon.
... They haue in theyr seruyce of god lateyne, as we do. And they be vnder the obeyisaunce of the chyrche of Rome; And the latynes prelates, but in many thynges ben they dyuerse, departed, for also the day hath xxiiij. hours. Also many tymes hymnes and psalmes and other orasouns haue they and very longe. And that that the Latyns rede in the begynnyng of theyr seruyce that rede they in the mydle or in the laste ende. And that sacrament of the auter breketh some of them in .vij. partes, and somc in .x. parties, and these people be very deuoute, and they mareye but ones in theyr lyfe, and as the women hath loste theyr fyrst husbond so dothe they meddle no more with no man but a byde fro thensfourth in chastyte.

For .ij. causes cometh the departynge of the crysten nacyons. The fyrste cause is that men in olde tyme myght the crysten haue only haue generall consilium. Therfore, as the ketters stode vp ayen the crysten belefe, so was there no body turned nor saught counsayll there ayen. The other cause was the ferswynmygnes of the opprest pope of the schole of Rome, that no messengere nor lerned shulde to the krysten thow that were come in seche lodyng, for had they do that they shulde haue be conuerted to the ryght belefe. Thorowsth whiche ryght belefe brynge vs to the hyghest glorye, the fader, the sone, the holy ghoste, thre persones and one god. Amen.

Pope Iohn, by the grace of god the mooste myghty, stekynge a boue all kyngys of the worlde, gyue saluyte the Emperour of Rome and also the kinge of Frannce. Oure wel belouyd frynde, We late you vnderstande and knowe of our lande, and the maner of oure lyuinge, and of our people, beestes, and fowles. And you saye that we beleue not in god and praye not to hym as you do, So late we you vnderstande that we beleue in god the fader, in god the sonne, and in god the

40. There appears to be a macron here, which would give the irregular spelling of Iohnn, but this could also be accidental, or an abbreviation for Iohan or Iohannes. All instances of this word in this text were printed this way, and I am inclined to assume that indeed Iohan or Iohannes is meant here. For this reason, no irregular spelling was marked on the transcription.

holy gooste, The whyche be vnpartyble and one very god, and is allthynge myghty. And also certefye yow with oure lettres sealed, and doo you knowelege of oure folke, or people, and of our lande. And yf there be ony thynge that we kan doo for you, sende vs worde, and we shall it doo with good herte and wyll. And yf it please ony of you to come in our lande, we shall gyue they in gold and syluer to thyr necessite, and make them great lordis, and gyue to them also lande and good to lyue on, and doo to hem worshyp and honor, For the goodnes that we haue, herde say of you. And we do you knowlege that we haue the richeste crowne of the worlde as of golde, and syluer, and of precyous stones in great multitude. And we haue also vnder vs mighty .xlij. kingdomes and al good cristen people, and we kepe also the poure people with our almes, alle that cometh, be it strenger or of oure owne people, thorough the loue of almyghty god oure lorde Ihesu Criste.

Item, Oure lande is parted in .iiij. For the landes of Indien there be two, and in that grettest Indien is the body of seynt Thomas. And this same Indien is partiner of the coste of orient, for it lyeth besyde a toure the whych is caalled babel, and it id[41] not ferre fro Babilonyen. And also that other parte of Indien is aboute Septentryon, and there is great plenty of wyne, bredde, and all maner of vytayle.

Item, aso[42] in our lande be griffons, and it is a greate byrde and a mighty, for he wyll well cary in his neste an oxe, or an horse, for his yonge byrdes to ete. Also in Saxen is a towne whych is called Grounzwyk; ther is one of the clawes that whych is well as great as an horn of an oxe. In our lande be olyphantes, dromedaries, wylde oxes the whyche haue .vij. hornes. Also Beeres, and Lyons of dyuers colours as the redd, grene, blacke, and white. Item, and also be wylde asses the whych haue longe eeres and haue twoo smale hornes. &c.

In our lande be also fowles the whyche that haue the maystery of all birdes of the worlde, and haue a colour lyke the fyer, and his wyngis kyt lyke a rasour. And this byrdes ben called Ilerion, and in alle the worlde is nomore than two; and they lyuen .iij. skore yere and thenne they laye eggis and sytte vpon theym .xl. dayes, and as sone as they haue yonges they flee awaye, fader and moder to the see and ther they drowne theym self. And alle tho byrdes that come ayenst them do them company to the see, and as sone as the be drowned all the other byrdes tourne ayen to the neste, there they yonge byrdes ben lefte and gyue them mete and drinke to the tyme that the can flee and nurter them selfe. &c. Yet ben there other byrdes the whyche ben called Tygris, and they be so stronge that they wyll

41. "Is" probably intended here.

42. "Also" intended here.

bere or cary in theyr neste a man sytting vpon an horse all armyd fro the hede to the fote.

Item, In our lande is also a grete deserte or forest; therin dweleth people, bothe men and wymmen, the whyche haue nomore than one eye afore, and behinde they haue .iij. or .iiij. eyen.

Yet is in oure lande an other maner of people the whiche ete none other than rawe fleshe, and they care not yf it were of man, or woman, or of beestis; the care not of ther owne deth. And as sone as there one of them dyeth the ete theym alle rawe, both there one fader or moeder. And they saye that mans fleyshe is good and naturly to ete rawe, for they saye that they doe it for parte of penaunce for there synnes. And they be also cursed of god, and they be called Gog and Magog. And of them be no more than one maner of people of this worlde, and they shall be dystributed or parted thorough all the world whan Antechryst shall come. And these same were the people or folke the whych that hadde put in prysone or in holde the great kynge Alexander of Macedonien. But for all that he wente his way; And of this people shalbe no iugement at the dredefull day of dome lyke the prophete sayeth, *Nescio quis. &c.* But neuertheles, thonder and lytenynge shall come fro heuen and bourne theym all in poder. And whan that we haue ony enemyes, thanne gyue we theym lycence to put theym downe and ete them that be ayensse vs, and then make we them to tourne ageyne into there owne lande. For if they sholde abyde longe with vs they shuld vndo vs all and ete vs lyke as they do there owne propre folke.

And yet is there another manere of people the whyche hath rownde fete lyke an horse, and also they haue .iiij. sharpe clawes behynde at there Heles. Wherewith they strongely fyght, that there is no manere thyng can stonde ayenste them nether harnayse, yrone nor stele; they passe all thorowth, and this people gyue vnto vs great tribute, and they be also without dowte great labourers.

Yet is there a nother smale lande in a parte of that same forest aforesayde, and it is .xlij. dayes Iourneyes longe. And it is called Feminie the great. And in that same lande there be thre Quenes without all other landes, thowe that holden there been of these quenes forsayde. And whan these quenes shall goo to felde then eche of then hath .iij. hondered .M. wymen, and all in harneyse with out all the other women the whych that caray vytayle with carte, horse, and also with olyfauntes. And these women be very manly in fytynge and hardy. And in this same lande may come no men but .ix. dayes in the yere and no lenger, and than they haue conuersacion and felysshyp with the men and nomore of the hole yere. For if the men there wolde abyde the women shulde them slee all.

And this same lande is closed all aboute with a water called Cyphon comynge out of paradise. And in this same lande may come no man without a great shyp or a great barke.

Of the people named Pygnies.

And yet is there a nother smale lande and also another Ryuer called Pyconye, that is .x. dayes iourneye longe and .vij. brode, and this people of this forsayde lande be not great, but they be lyke chyldren of .vij. yere of age, and they haue horseys as great as a great dogge, and they be good crystened folke, and they haue no warre ayenste noman. But they haue warre ayenste the fowles euery yere, whan they shall haue in there frute and corne. And than the kynge putteth on his harneyse, and than they fyght ayenste the byrdes. And than there be slayn on bothe partyes many on, and also they be great labourers and whan the fylde is don than the byrdes flee a waye fro them.

Also in our lande been the Sagittary, the whyche ben fro the myddel vpward lyke men, and fro the myddell donwarde ben they lyke the halfe neder parte of an horse, and they bere bowes and arowes. And the[43] shute stronger than ony other nacyon of people.

And in our lande be also vnicornes, and they been of the manere with blacke and grene, and these vnicornes slee many Lyons. And the Lyon sleeth the vnicorne with subtylnes. Whan the Vnicorne hath put hym to rest at a tree, and than cometh the Lyon and ronnyth aboute the tree and after hym than ronnyth the vnycorne and wolde fayne sley hym, and than he ronnyth hym selfe into the tree with his horne so harde that he cannot pull it out ageyne. Than com*m*eth the Lyon and hath the mastery vpon the vnicorne.

Item, there is a nother parte of a forest therin dwelleth another maner of folke and this people ben .xx. Cubettes of heythe. But they were in tyme paste to be of the heyth of .xl. Cubettes. And they haue nat the pore to come out of that deserte or foreste and all is thorowe the myghte of almyghty god. For if they sholde come out, by there strength and hardynesse the wolde conquere all the worlde.

... Item, Betwene oure lande and the Turkes lande is a ryuer ronnynge and is called Sydon; it commeth out of paradyse, of the erthe, and is full of precyous stones. And also in oure lande ben ronnyge many smale riuers the whyche that come out of this forsayde riuer, and they also ben fulle of precyous stones, As Ysmaraddus, Iaspis, Saphyris, Scobassus, Dyamant, Topasius, Carbonkel, Rubin,

43. "They" probably intended here.

and yet more other they whyche I not all can reherce. Also in oure lande groweth on herbe and is called Parmanabel, and that same herbe is so myghty euer soo who that same herbe beryth a boute hym he maye coniure the deuyll of helle and do hym saye what so euer he wyl axe of hym, and therfore the deuyll dare not come in to our lande.

... Also ye shall vnderstande that betwene vs and the Iewes ronnyth a great ryuer that is full of precyous stones, and it is so stronge in here ronnyng that noman ther ouer can passe, excepte the saterdaye, and than parted she here and toke with here all that she fyndeth in here waye. And this same lande moste we strongely kepe for oure ennemyes, and vp these costes haue we .xlij. stronge castels, none stronger in the world, and ben well kepte of people. To vnderstande .x.M. knyghtes on horsbacke, .vi.M. Crosse bowes, .xv.M. longe bowes, and .xl.M. othere men on horsbacke well armed, that whyche these Castels haue in kyping by cause that the great kynge of Israhel shall not ther passe with his people, For he is twyes as stronge as I am. And his lande is twyes as grete as all Crystence an turkey. For he hath in his kepynge the seconde parte of the worlde. And the great kynge of Israhel hath vnder hym iij.C. kynges, .iiij.M. princes, duces, erles, baros, knyghtes, squyers without nombre. And all these be subgette to the great kynge of Israhel. But yf he myght passe ouer this forsayde ryuer with his people they sholde slee both crysten and turkes. And ye shall knowe that we all saterdaye late passe .viij.C. or M. men, for beye suche manere good or marchaundyse as they wyll haue, but we late them not come with in the wallis of thys castels. For they bye it with out the walles of thys fortresses, and they paye ther marchaundyses with platis of siluer or of gold, for they haue none other money. and whan they haue don ther besynes they tourne home ayen in theyr owne lande, and these forsayde castels be sete to gyder within a bowe shotte.

And ye shall vnderstande that within a myle of these castels is a great Cite and a fayre, and it is the strongest of all the worlde. The whyche cite is in our kepyng of one of our kyngis, and he receyueth tribute of the great kyng of Israhel. And also gyueth vs euery yere .ij.C. horses laden with golde, syluer, and precyous stones. Except alle charges and costes that men doth in the cyte and in thyse forsayde castels. And whan that we haue warre ayenst them than slee we them alle and late noman alyue, and therfore they wyll kepe no warre ayenste vs; and the wymmen of the Iewes be very fayre, none fayrer in erth nowe a dayes lyuinge. And by this forsayde ryuer is a see; ther noman maye passe but whan the wynde blowyth fro benethe strongely; than parted she here and thanne the passe with great hast, and than they take with hym all maner of precious stones, but they may selle none therof for that wee haue taken therof our chose.

... And ye shall also knowe that there be dyuers of people of fason in oure lande; also there be people that haue the body of a man and the hede lyke a dogge, and they be good takers of fysshe; and they be good to vnderstande of theyre speche, and they wyll goo in to the see a hole daye longe to the tyme that they haue taken suche as they wolde haue, and than the come ayen charged with fysshe, and bere them in to ye houses for they haue there dwellinge places vnder erthe, and thenne take we part of there fysshes that vs beste lyketh ... .

21b Richard Hakluyt, *The principal nauigations, voyages, traffiques and discoueries of the English nation, made by sea or ouer-land, to the remote and farthest distant quarters of the earth, at any time within the compasse of these 1600. yeres: diuided into three seuerall volumes, according to the positions of the regions, whereunto they were directed. The first volume containeth the worthy discoueries, &c. of the English toward the North and Northeast Sea. ... The second volume comprehendeth the principall nauigations, voyages, traffiques, and discoueries of the English. Nation, made by Sea or ouer-land to the south and south-east parts of the world. ... By Richard Hakluyt preacher, and sometime student of Christ-Church in Oxford*, 1600, pp. 331–334.[44] STC *12626a.* **Source** *EEBO*: The Huntington Library, San Marino, CA (3440).

The Second Part of This Second volume containing the principall Nauigations, Voyages, Traffiques, and Discoueries of the English nation, made to the South and South-east quarters of the world without the Straights of Gibraltar, namely to the Ilands of Madera, and of the Canaries, to the kingdome of Barbarie, to the Iles of Capo Verde, to the riuer of Senega, to the coast of Ghinea and Benin, about the cape of Buona Esperansa, and so to Goa in the East Indies, and likewise beyond cape Comori to the Iles of Nicubar, to Sumatra, to the chanell of Sincapura ouer against the city of Malacca, and to diuers other places

... Now therefore I will speake somewhat of the people and their maners, and maner of liuing with an other briefe description of *Africa* also. It is to be vnderstood that the people which now inhabite the reigons of the coast of *Guinea* and the midle parts of *Africa,* as *Libya* the inner, and *Nubia,* with diuers other great and large regions about the same, were in old time called *Aethiopes* and *Nigritae,* which we now call *Moores, Moorens,* or *Negroes,* a people of beastly liuing, with-

44. The pagination is faulty in this part and jumps between 12–13 to 326, to 15, to 328, to 29, to 330 and 331. Marginal notes in the original source were not included in the transcription.

out a God, lawe, religion, or common wealth, and so scorched and vexed with the heat of the sunne that in many places they curse it when it riseth. Of the regions and people about the inner *Libya* (called *Libya interior*) *Gemma Phrysius* writeth thus:

Libya interior is very large and desolate, in the which are many horrible wildernesses and mountaines, replenished with diuers kinds of wilde and monstrous beastes and serpents. First from *Mauritania* or *Barbary* toward the South is *Getulia,* a rough and sauage region, whose inhabitants are wilde and wandering people. After these follow the people called *Melanogetuli* and *Pharusij,* which wander in the wildernesse, carrying with them great gourdes of water. The *Ethiopians* called *Nigritae* occupy a great part of *Africa,* and are extended to the West Ocean. Southward also they reach to the riuer *Nigritis,* whose nature agreeth with the riuer of *Nilus,* forasmuch as it is increased and diminished at the same time, and bringeth forth the like beasts as the *Crocodile.* By reason whereof, I thinke this to be the same riuer which the *Portugals* call *Senega,* For this riuer is also of the same nature. It is furthermore marueilous and very strange that is said of this riuer, And this is, that on the one side thereof, the inhabitants are of high stature and black, and on the other side, of browne or tawnie colour, and low stature, which thing also our men confirme to be true.

There are also other people of *Libya* called *Garamantes,* whose women are common, for they contract no matrimonie, neither haue respect to chastitie. After these are the nations of the people called *Pyrei, Sathiodaphnitae, Odrangi, Mimaces, Lynxamate, Dolopes, Agangine, Leuci Ethiopes, Xilicei Ethiopes, Calcei Ethiopes,* and *Nubi.* These haue the same situation in *Ptolome* that they now giue to the kingdome of *Nubia.* Here are certaine Christians vnder the dominion of the great Emperour of *Aethiopia,* called *Prester Iohn.* From these toward the West is a great nation of people called *Aphricerones,* whose region (as farre as may be gathered by coniecture) is the same that is now called *Regnum Orguene,* confining vpon the East parts of *Guinea.* From hence Westward, and somewhat toward the North, are the kingdoms of *Gambra* and *Budomel,* not farre from the riuer of *Senega.* And from hence toward the inland regions, and along by the sea coast, are the regions of *Ginoia* or *Guinea,* which we commonly call *Ginnee.* On the Westside of these regions toward the Ocean, is the cape or point called *Cabo verde,* or *Caput viride,* (that is) the greene cape, to the which the *Portugals* first direct their course when they saile to *America,* or the land of *Brasile.* Then departing from hence, they turne to the right hand toward the quarter of the winde called *Garbino,* which is betweene the West and the South. But to speake some what more of *Aethiopia,* although there are many nations of people so named, yet is

Aethiopia chiefly diuided into two parts, whereof the one is called *Aethiopia* vnder *Aegypt*, a great and rich region. To this perteineth the Island *Meroe*, imbraced round about with the stremes of the riuer *Nilus*. In this Island women reigned in old time. *Iosephus* writeth, that it was sometime called *Sabea*, and that the Queene of *Saba* came from thence to *Ierusalem*, to heare the wisedom of *Salomon*. From hence toward the East reigneth the said *Christian* Emperor *Prester Iohn*, whom some cal *Papa Iohannes*, and other say that he is called *Pean Iuan* (that is) great *Iohn*, whose Empire reacheth far beyond *Nilus*, and is extended to the coasts of the Red sea and *Indian* sea. The middle of the region is almost in 66. degrees of longitude, and 12. degrees of latitude. About this region inhabite the people called *Clodi, Risophagi, Babylonij, Axiunitae, Molili*, and *Molibae*. After these is the region called *Troglodytica*, whose inhabitants dwel in caues and dennes, for these are their houses, and the flesh of serpents their meat, as writeth *Plinie*, and *Diodorus Siculus*. They haue no speech but rather a grinning and chattering. There are also people without heads, called *Blemines*, hauing their eyes and mouth in their breast. Likewise *Strucophagi*, and naked *Ganphasantes*; *Satyrs* also, which haue nothing of men but onely shape. Moreover *Oripei*, great hunters. *Mennones* also, and the region of *Smyrnophora*, which bringeth foorth myrthe. After these is the region of *Azania*, in the which many Elephants are found. A great part of the other regions of *Africke* that are beyond the *Aequinoctiall* line, are now ascribed to the kingdome of *Melinde*, whose inhabitants are accustomed to trafique with the nations of *Arabia*, and their king is ioyned in friendship with the king of *Portugal*, and payeth tribute to *Prester Iohn*.

... Many things more our men saw and considered in this voyage, woorthy to be noted, whereof I haue thought good to put some in memory, that the reader may aswell take pleasure in the variety of things, as knowledge of the historie. Among other things therefore, touching the maners and nature of the people, this may seeme strange, that their princes and noble men vse to pounce and rase their skinnes with pretie knots in diuers formes, as it were branched damaske, thinking that to be a decent ornament. And albeit they goe in maner all naked, yet are many of them, and especialy their women, in maner laden with collars, bracelets, hoopes, and chaines, either of gold, copper, or iuory.

I my selfe haue one of their brasets of Iuory, weighing two pound and sixe ounces of *Troy* weight, which make eight and thirtie ounces; this one of their women did weare vpon her arme. It is made of one whole piece of the biggest part of the tooth, turned and somewhat carued, with a hole in the midst, wherin they put their hands to weare it on their arme. Some haue on euery arme one, and as many on their legges, wherewith some of them are so galled, that although they are in maner made lame thereby, yet will they by no meanes leaue them off. Some weare also on their legges great shackles of bright copper, which they thinke to bee no lesse comely. They weare also collars, bracelets, garlands, and girdles, of certain blew stones like beads. Likewise some of their women weare on their bare armes certaine foresleeues made of the plates of beaten golde. On their fingers also they weare rings, made of golden wires, with a knot or wreath, like vnto that which children make in a ring of a rush. Among other things of golde that our men bought of them for exchange of their wares, were certaine dogs-chaines and collers.

They are very wary people in their bargaining, and will not lose one sparke of golde of any value. They vse weights and measures, and are very circumspect in occupying the same. They that shall haue to doe with them, must vse them gently, for they will not trafique or bring in any wares if they be euill vsed. At the first voyage that our men had into these parties, it so chanced, that at their departure from the first place where they did trafick, one of them either stole a muske Cat, or tooke her away by force, not mistrusting that that should haue hindered their bargaining in another place whither they intended to goe. But for all the haste they coulde make with full sailes, the fame of their misusage so preuented them, that the people of that place also, offended thereby, would bring in no wares, insomuch that they were inforced either to restore the Cat, or pay for her at their price, before they could trafique there.

Their houses are made of foure postes or trees, and couered with boughes. Their common feeding is of roots, and such fishes as they take, whereof they haue great plenty. There are also such flying fishes as are seene in the sea of the West *Indies*. Our men salted of their fishes, hoping to prouide store thereof, but they would take no salt, and must therfore be eaten forthwith as some say. Howbeit other affirme, that if they be salted immediatly after they be taken, they wil last vncorrupted ten or twelue dayes. But this is more strange that part of such flesh as they caried with them out of *England*, which putrified there, became sweete againe at their returne to the clime of temperate regions.

They vse also a strange making of bread, in this maner: They grinde betweene two stones with their handes as much corne as they thinke may suffice their family, and when they haue thus brought it to floure, they put thereto a certaine quantitie of water, and make thereof very thinne dough, which they sticke vpon some post of their houses, where it is baked by the heate of the Sunne: so that when the master of the house or any of his family will eate thereof, they take it downe and eate it.

... Many things more nught be saide of the maners of the people, and of the wonders and monstrous things that are engendred in *Africke*. But it shall suffice to haue saide thus much of such things as our men partly sawe, and partly brought with them.

Mind

THE EVIL AND IGNORANT MIND

22a *This tretyse is of loue and spekyth of iiij of the most specyall louys that ben in the worlde* (1493). **22b** John Sheffield,[1] *The sinfulnesse of evil thoughts* (1659).

Introduction The author of the *Tretyse of loue* is unknown. It is a fifteenth-century text likely originally composed in French and then translated into English in the late fifteenth century, and printed by Wynkyn de Worde in 1493. It is part of a compilation of ten devotional texts, making it probable that it was originally also included with them in its manuscript version.[2] In itself it is an adaptation of excerpts from *Ancrene wisse* (mainly from Parts IV and VII), an anonymous thirteenth-century manual for anchoresses, and a popular text translated into French; it is likely that from this French translation and expansion the *Tretyse of loue* was compiled, and then translated back into English. Just as *The*

1. In the copy of the text used for the transcription the author's last name is misprinted as "Sheffeild."

2. The postscript to the 1493 printed edition states as follows:

Thus endeth this present boke whiche treateth fyrst of the gloryous passion of our Sauyour and of the compascyon that his blessyd moder had therof, and also sheweth in a nother treatyse folowyng wherfore we ought to loue our sauyour more than ony other thynge.

Also sheweth a nother treatise moche prouffytable for reformacyon of soules defoyled wyth ony of the vij. dedely synnes.

Item a nother treatyse shewynge the signes of goostly loue.

Item a treatise of the vertues and of the braunches of the appultree whiche is expowned morally as is before expressyd.

Also folowing is declared wherby men maye seke the loue of our lorde Ihesu cryst.

And the last treatyse of this forsayd boke spekyth to exhorte the persone to eschewe and haue in contempte all euyll thoughts, and to reduce theymself in all poyntes to good werkes vnder the hope of dyuyne grace.

Whiche boke was lately translated oute of frenshe in to englisshe by a Right well dysposed persone for by cause the sayd persone thoughte it necessary to al deuoute peple to rede or to here it redde. And also caused the sayd boke to be enprynted. (*Tretyse of loue*, final page.)

Chastising of God's children (ca. 1400) with which it was often bound, the *Tretyse of loue* was an expanded version of its source texts that allowed for a wider readership, not only of devout and cloistered women, but a broader, general readership of lay people interested in advice on how to lead a more spiritual life, and catering to a large demand for such books in late medieval England.[3]

The *Tretyse of loue* thus provided an updated study of practical devotion and issues of individual piety pre-Reformation audiences probably struggled with and wished to read about. One of these issues was the concept of evil thoughts. Resting at the very foundations of the Western moral system and a central concept to the Seven Deadly Sins, the eight evil thoughts defined by Evagrius Ponticus were an early medieval attempt at categorizing temptations that led monks away from being devoutly occupied in their minds. In the course of their development these eight thoughts became the familiar heptad.[4] As the late medieval period was characterized by an increased focus on concepts of evil that expanded the traditional heptad (such as the sins of the tongue and the sins of the tavern), the concept of evil thoughts likewise changed from an underlying source of the deadly sins, to one of them. Evil thoughts became another sin or rather a group of sins that emerged from sins like envy or wrath, considered one of the sins that belonged to the Devil,[5] as William Flete warned in his *De remediis* (ca. 1359).

The *Tretyse of loue* in the excerpt below describes evil thoughts and their dangers to the soul, particularly carnal thoughts connected to lust, and warns that the Devil often does not need to act but rather prefers to provoke evil thoughts that lead the soul into sin out of the soul's own free will. The author reminds, as a warning, of the pains of hell awaiting those whose minds are polluted with sin, and recommends prayer as a remedy above all others to direct thoughts onto godly subjects, allowing one to avoid the temptations of an evil mind. The text's focus on other sins, including sloth, likewise connects them to evil thoughts which, as the reader is to understand, lie at the foundation of all sins, an idea that links the text to the original concept of Evagrius Ponticus.

3. Catherine Innes-Parker, "The Legacy of *Ancrene Wisse*: Translations, Adaptations, Influences, and Audience, with Special Attention to Women Readers," in *A Companion to Ancrene Wisse*, ed. Yoko Wada (Cambridge, 2003), 145–174, at 146, 154–156, 164, 170.

4. Richard Newhauser, "Introduction," in *In the Garden Of Evil: The Vices and Culture in the Middle Ages* (Toronto, 2005), x. See also Richard Newhauser, *The Early History of Greed: The Sin of Avarice in Early Medieval Thought and Literature* (Cambridge, 2004), 57; and Morton Bloomfield, *The Seven Deadly Sins: An Introduction to the History of a Religious Concept, With Special Reference to Medieval Literature* (East Lansing, MI, 1952), on the eight evil thoughts.

5. As in, for instance, *Jacob's well* (ca. 1450), where the Devil says that "he hath drunkyn of my crewett of euyll thou3ys, of slepyng, of iangelyng, of ydelnes, of slugnesse, of heuynes, and of lustys. so he hath drunkyn of vj. of my crewettys, and hym I haue full enpoysonyd in slawthe, and I haue wonnyn hym" (*Jacob's well*, 116).

John Sheffield was rector of St Swithin in London and the author of sermons and devotional works, including *A good conscience the strongest hold* (1650), and *The rising sun of righteousness* (1654). He was a non-conformist (affected by the 1662 Great Ejection[6]) preacher and author, although little else is known about his life.[7] His *Sinfulnesse of evil thoughts* (1659) is a good illustration of Protestant engagement with the concept of evil thoughts: while the majority of Protestant texts would not focus exclusively on evil thoughts, most had an interest in them as a separate, and very serious, sin, William Perkins being one of the most influential Protestant preachers who took up that subject.[8] Many Protestant divines had an avid interest in the human mind as they saw it as a source of many trials of the soul, through commission (when the mind caused trouble to the soul by provoking an action, such as lustful thoughts leading to commit the sin of lust) or omission (of an action, such as prayer), and by it being sensitive to external influence (such as temptations of the Devil). In other words, the concept of evil thoughts not only remained an important element of Protestant pastoral interest, and an essential subject in any and all practical divinity texts, but was also developed by Protestant thinkers into a category that treated evil thoughts, and the mind in general, psychologically as much as pastorally, not only as an issue of the soul but also as a thing in itself, in need of pastoral care. *The Sinfulnesse of evil thoughts* discusses carnal thoughts as the most dangerous kind, and in many ways echoes the earlier *Tretyse of loue* (interestingly, also citing two late medieval popes, Sixtus IV and Clement VIII) in suggesting that sin begins in the mind, and only because of thoughts, and through them, do sins become deeds. Sheffield also draws attention to the issue of freedom of thought, and then passes on to discussing remedies which address how to avoid evil thoughts: humility, self-reflection, a focus on good thoughts, and meditation.

6. After the Restoration, in 1662, the English Parliament issued the Act of Uniformity and, as its consequence, many Protestant (particularly puritan) ministers who did not conform to the Book of Common Prayer were ejected from the Church of England and lost their positions. For more on this subject see, for example, David J. Appleby, *Black Bartholomew's Day: Preaching, Polemic and Restoration Nonconformity* (Manchester, 2013), and Martin Sutherland, *Peace, Toleration and Decay: The Ecclesiology of Later Stuart Dissent* (Eugene, OR, 2003).

7. Stephen Wright, "Sheffield [Sheffeild], John (d. 1680), clergyman and ejected minister," in *Oxford Dictionary of National Biography* online (Oxford, 2004), https://doi.org/10.1093/ref:odnb/25296, last updated 3 January 2008.

8. In his 1607 work, *A treatise of mans imaginations Shewing his naturall euill thoughts: His want of good thoughts: The way to reforme them.*

22a *This tretyse is of loue and spekyth of iiij of the most specyall louys that ben in the worlde and shewyth veryly and perfitely bi gret resons and causis, how the meruelous and bounteuous loue that our lord Ihesu cryste had to mannys soule excedyth to ferre alle other loues ... Whiche tretyse was translatid out of frenshe into englyshe, the yere of our lord M cccc lxxxxiij, by a persone that is vnperfight insuche werke ...* , Westminster, 1493; unnumbered pages. *STC* 24234. **Source** *EEBO*: The Huntington Library, San Marino, CA (69688).

How fayth exhorteth the persone to eschewe and haue in contempt all euyl thoughtes and to reduse them self in al poyntes to good werkes vnder the hope of diuyne grace
Grete awayte ought eueri bodi to haue vpon theymself that they retorne not ayen vnto those synnes that they haue ben reconsiled of. For vain is the penaunce that the same offence soyleth ayen. Where resiste wyth al your power from doyng those synnes that ye haue lost soo that they growe not in you ayen. Thenne vnderstonde what ye ben and to what entent ye ben made, for suche as god hath ordeyned you ought ye to be. Haue in you very byleue that ye by one onnly sinne ben many vertues lost. Thenne for the loue of god gyue not your sowle to the power of the flessh, suffre none vnclennes to abyde in you. Resist at the beginnyng of euyll thoughtes and soone may ye thenne surmount the remenaunt. Knowe ye for trouth that by your thoughtes shall ye be Iuged, for the body may not be corrupt till the thought be fyrst corrupt. And whan the wylle therto consenteth, the flesshe is all redy to synne, and therfore torne your wylle from euyll thoughtes and the body shall not synne. Vnderstonde to this that is admonested to you, that ye be not foyled wyth none vnclennes of lecherye, nor that ye be vainquynshed bi fornycacyon. For thise ben grete sinnes among all other. For better is it to dey than to doo fornycacyon, and better to lese your life than be foiled with lecherye. Therfore bewaar, for contynuaunce somtyme makith one to synne. Haa god how chastite atteyneth the blestful reame of heuen, and lechery draweth a man to the derke dongeon of helle. Yf lecheri asayleth you, thynke what turment they suffre that hath be therto habandonned, and horryble ben the paynes of helle; wherfore pray god deuoutly wyth teres both nyght and day, and whan ye awake of your fyrste slepe retorne ye To prayers; for customably oryson surmounteth tharmes of the fende. Oryson is the fyrst vertue agayn thasawtes of all euyll thoughts. Fulfyll not your appetyte by metes, but chastise your bodies by fastyng, for otherwyse it is harde to vaynquyssh the temptacyon of the flessh, but by fastynge and orysons for ouermoche delicacye in mete and drynke enclineth the flesshh to vnclennesse. The eyen ben the fyrst armes of vnclennesse. The sight is the fyrste couetyse of men or wymen. Therfore wythdraw your eyen yf ye

be nighe the serpent, soo that ye be not hurt. For yf ye be nygh the fire though ye were of yren; Yet sholde ye be somtyme warme. For that sinne hurteth gretly suche as ben founden vayn. Therfore ocupye you perfightly in good werkes and gode thoughtes. Chatyse your bodyes by rightful traueyle and soo may ye prouffyte to yourself and to other. And be alwaye humble to all folks. Yf ye kepe humylite ye shall haue glory, for the more humble ye be the more shall ye folow the hienes of glory. Vse not to auaunte you of your gode dedes, so that ye bryng not yourself in pryde. But rather obeye and humble yourself moost whan ye fele your herte meuyd to be rased wyth pryde.

Beware of hye mountynge for fere of ouer lowe descendynge. For pryde casted downe thangels out of heuen and made theim fendes in helle. Remembre ye of the humylite of our lorde whiche was obeysaunt to his fader vnto the dethe. Soo take ye perfightly thensample of hym. Wyll ye be humble, thenne haue alway shame in your hert of the remembraunce of your sinnes. And goo alway wyth humble maners and sobre visage, and by sighyng and weping in your hert, and swete shall be tho teres, for grete sinnes asken grete amendes. Ouer all thynges make you sure of your synnes. For therin shall ye fynde mater ynouh to make you pensif. And in all your other siknesses and trowbles be not sorrowful. But ye ought humbli to yelde god thankynges, that hathe sent theim to you to thentent that ye shold come the more clene before hym. Haue alway attemperance in prosperyte, and pacyence in aduersitee. Refrayne your Ire and ouercome it by suffraunce. Suffre other pacyently whan they doo you wrong. For by pacyence and beyng stylle shall ye soone ouercom the wrathfull. Thinke what payne almyghty god suffred for you, that was perced with nayles and crowned wyth thornes and condempned to be crucified on the crosse. This ought to gyue you a grete comfort to bere wyth pacyence all Iniurye. And be not hasty to stryke theim that haue stryken you. But suffre al suche thynges for the loue of god and he wyll gyue you a grete rewarde. Yf ye haue displeysed ony man, slepe not tyl ye haue accorded him with you again. Yf ony man hath done against you yelde him not after his desert but wyth good herte pardon hym. For wrath departeth man from god. Be of good wyll to all folkes. Yf your enmye haue ony mysauenture ye oughte not to reioyse it. For ye may happe to fall in like peryll. Wyth compleyners pleyne ye wyth theim that wepe, wepe ye. Be of charytable herte to all folkes and care not who prayseth you or blameth you. For none may better know what ye ben than yourselfe. Be simple, and clene, and of dyscrete manere soo that youre demeanyng offende not the voys of other wherby they may falle in sinne. Flee the company of many folkes and specyally of theym that ben lighte to falle in synne. Who desireth and haunteth the companye of wyse folkes is wyse. And a peryllous thyng is it to be conuersaunt amonge theym that ben euyll. ...

Slouth noyeth moche to good werkes. Necligence slaketh the courage and quencheth the light of conmyge.[9] Vyces ouercometh sone the slouthfull persones. Take kepe to this to thentent that ye ben not founden vayn. For yf slouth hath a lityll entree it wyll lightly growe tomoche. Yf ye be good and vertuous, thenne shall ye be gloryfied. Beware whan ye doo ony thyng well that ye coueyte not the preyse of folkes wherby ye may lese the grete rewarde that ye sholde haue of god. Lese noo tyme but that ye do alway some good, nor coueyte not to knowe of other thus that they wolde be lothe ye knewe. Whan folkes speke to you herken them redely and speke by deliberacyon. For in some thynge is thende gretter than the beginnyng; In whiche the speker hathe more grete honour: and better shold be the last worde than the fyrst. Demeane yourselfe to euery body soo thatye offende not the wylle of god. Grete payne shal haue the cruel persones and suche as therto consenten. Wherfore consente ye to noo synne. But whan ye ben moued soone retorne your hertes so that ye be not enuenemyd therwith. Be not ouersharpe to your seruates but doo soo that they haue delite to serue you. In all your werkes oughte to be attemperaunce; For euery ouermesure torneth to vyce as to moche or te lityll. In al your dedes holde descrecyon. For yf ye kepe not dyscrecyon there is noo vertue in noo thyng that ye do, but rather it is vyce. Doo by other as ye wolde they sholde doo by you. ...

22b John Sheffield, *The sinfulnesse of evil thoughts: or, a discourse, wherein, the chambers of imagery are unlocked: the cabinet of the heart opened. The secrets of the inner-man disclosed. In the particular discovery of the numerous evil thoughts, to be found in the most of men, with thei various, and severall kinds, sinful causes, sad effects, and proper remedies or cures. Together with directions how to observe and keep the heart; the highest, hardest, nad most necessary work of him that would be a real Christian. By Jo. Sheffeild Pastor of Swithins London,* 1659, pp. 127–212.[10] *Wing* S3064A. **Source** *EEBO*: British Library, London (E.1863[1]).

CHAP. XVIII. Of carnall thoughts

Besides these, there are a many *Carnall* thoughts to be taken notice of. Dangerous thoughts. Carnall thoughts *of God,* of his *word, worship* and all his *wayes.*

9. Intelligence, knowledge, skill: *MED* s.v. "conningnesse".

10. Marginal notes in the original text were not included in the transcription.

These the *naturall man* is made up of, and they are the best thoughts he hath or can have, till he have another heart and become a *spirituall* person. *He savoureth the things of the flesh. He understandeth not,* doth not receive, perceive, or relish *any thing that is spirituall.* The *wisdome of God is foolishnesse with such.* How contemptuously may you often heare such speak of divine things, of the *spirit,* of the *new birth, of praying by the spirit, living in the spirit, being in the spirit, walking after the spirit?* How grosly do they conceive of many truths and duties laid down in Scripture? *Regeneration* they know not what it is, if it be not *Baptisme; feeding on Christ* they know no other but either *Carnall,* or *Sacramentall.* Oh, what strangers are they to the *life of God,* to the *life of faith,* to *Union with Christ,* to the *power of Godlinesse.* But *to be carnally minded,* the Apostle saith, *is death,* hadst thou no other sins. To be carnally minded is death, *They that are in the flesh cannot please God.* ...

... *CHAP. XXVIII. The first use of confutation of that common error, that thoughts are free*

In the first place to come to the Application, see the vanity and falshood of that common assertion, That *thought is free.* To men and humane judicatories they are, to God they are not.

1. God passeth his judgment on the thoughts, *1 Cor. 4:5.*

2. The word of God is a judge of the thoughts, *Heb. 4:12.*

3. The *Ministers* work is to encounter and demolish the evil thought, *2 Cor. 10:4.*

4. *Conscience's* busiest work is to overlook the thought, *Rom. 2:15.*

Lastly, The true converts humiliation begins at his thoughts, *1 Cor. 14:25.*

Is *Thought nothing*? Did God condemne the old world for nothing? Is *Magus* sentenced to be in the Gall of bitternesse for *nothing?* Was it sin in the Gentiles to be *vain in their imaginations?* and is it no sin in thee? They were impious Atheists who said *our tongues are our own, who is Lord over us?* And is it lesse impiety to say *our hearts are our owne,* who shall hinder us from *paying* it with thinking? This is the *shop* and warehouse of all evil, the devils *strong hold,* the *imagery chambers* wherein the foulest abominations are pourtrayed; into these the Lord lookes most narrowly. We are as those tradesmen for the most of us, who furnish their shops, and lay out their best wares as Pedlars, when the inner roomes, and upper Garrets have little in them; as the Goldsmith whose shop is full of plate, Jewels, Rings, when he hath little within doores for his own use. Their *inward part is very wickednesse Psal. 5.* The Lords eye is upon the heart and thoughts, *Jer. 6:19.* The evil of thoughts how little soever they be thought, are the greatest evils. Satan's sins are onely spirituall wickednesses, not carnall or bodily pollutions, *nihil fecit, nihil operatus est Satanas, solummodo cogitavit,* saith *Bernard,* The devil *wrought* not evil, onely *thought* evil. Look how much *Principalities* and *powers* are above *flesh and blood,* so much do spirituall wickednesses exceed any carnall. These make us more like beasts, but those like Satan; And if we shall divide all the sins of the world into three parts, *Thought, word, deed,* more are the sins of the thoughts for number, and worse for nature, then both the other, and all the sins in the world besides. Instance in the worst of sins we shall find them here:

1. Is *ignorance* a great sin? The Lord *shall come in flaming fire to render vengeance to them who know not God;* This is as bad as drunkennesse, whordom, &c. yet is this onely in the thoughts, and in the heart.

2. Is *Error* any sin, It is counted little in these daies, yet did God shut out the carnall Israelites, and *sware in his wrath they should not enter into his rest, because they erred in their hearts.* They whose plague was in their *head,* were *utterly unclean* above all others, and shut out of the camp. Error is *soul adultery,* and defiles no lesse then bodily fornication, those who go a whoring after it.

3. *Haeresy,* a foule sin, shutting out of Gods Kingdome, is onely in the mind and thoughts.

4. *Infidelity,* that great Gospel sin, and that fearfull *Apollyon* and soul murderer, is onely a sin of the heart and thoughts.

5. The like I might say of *impenitency, hypocrisie, spirituall pride, malice, envy, covetousnesse,* and the worst of sins are all lodged in the heart.

6. Yea, the sin against the *Holy Ghost* is not any outward acting of the most monstrous impiety or abomination, but the fear of it is in the heart, the contagion of it chiefly poisons the *understanding, conscience and will.*

As the *diseases* of the *mind* are worse and more incurable then *bodily. Lunacy* is worse then a feaver, a fit of *Phrensie* worse then of *Stone,* or Gout. The Doctor can say little to these diseases of the mind; so sins of the mind worse then any bodily. *The spirit of a man may sustain any infirmity of body, but the wounded spirit who can beare?*

And as the *Judgments* inflicted on the soul are above all the *heaviest* judgments, as the immediate wrath of God darted into the soul, *That fire not blowen,* horror of conscience, the *seared* conscience, the spirit of *slumber,* or of remorse, *Vile affections, the reprobate mind,* are all such plagues as hell hath no greater, so are *soul sins* worst of sins. The wrath of God is poured usually on the spirits of men, the devils *chaines* are not of *Iron,* but of *darknesse,* the paines of hell take not hold yet of the body, but of the spirit onely.

Yea, as all the *Treasures* of grace and comfort in the Godly are laid up in the *hidden man of the heart,* there is his best, and he is a *thousand times* better in his heart, intention, desire, then he can be in all his holy acts and duties; he would do much more and better still, so the worst wickednesse even in the most wicked is *within,* when he doth most villanously and talketh most impudently, his *heart* is a thousand times worse yet then all his actions, for this as it is the *seat* of *grace* and vertue, so of *all sin* and vice.

Yea, so much *Malignity* is in an evil thought that as one drop of poison may mar a whole cup of wine, so an evil thought spoils the best duty and performance. *The sacrifice of the wicked is an abomination to the Lord, because also* (so some read it) *he bringeth it with a wicked minde. Judas,* his charitable *motion* stank, because of the covetousnesse that was in his heart, and his *kisse* of piety stank worse, because of the horrid treason and war which was in his heart, though his words both times[11] *smoother then oyl.*

... *CHAP. XXIX. The Second use for humiliation*

In the second place, see what cause is here for *Humiliation, universall* and *continuall* humiliation; above all other sins be humbled for thy Thoughts. Whatsoever is *fair* without, thy thoughts are *foul* to be sure, *who can say his heart is clean?* Yea, whatever is *foulest* without, the thoughts are yet *more foul* and filthy. Many men are like the *Egyptian* Temples, rich, fair, beautifull without, when you come in *Cats, mice, serpents, Crocodyles;* fair sepulchers, and painted over, full of stench and rottennesse within; when as the godly soul desires to be like *Solomon's* Temple, which had the lights *narrower without, wider within,* which had nothing but *stone* and *timber* to be seen *without,* within nothing *but gold.*

Alas! have not we many a *wild,* many a *vile* and sinfull Thought to bewaile, not *transient* and *involuntary,* but *deliberate,* fixed and voluntary thoughts? How hard to get the heart in a good frame? how hardly doth a good thought enter? how soon is it turned out of doors? what cold welcome do we give it? But to ill thoughts we set doors wide open, we make room to entertain them, we keep them company, discourse with them with much delight, and never think the time long they stay, and are loth to let them go.

Oh how many forgetfull thoughts have we *of God,* either *no* thoughts, or *low thoughts,* or *hard* thoughts, or *Atheisticall,* or *blasphemous,* or *impious,* at least *dishonourable* and *distrustfull* thoughts of God. Towards thy *neighbour* how many *unkind,* uncharitable, envious, censorious, passionate, malicious, proud, scorn-

11. "Were" seems appropriate between "times" and "smoother."

full, injurious thoughts hast thou had? And for thy *self*, who need tell thee of thy vain, impure, self-deceiving, self-exalting, self-magnifying, self-seeking thoughts? who can number thy carking, caring, plodding, plotting thoughts, thy empty, aery, frothy, endlesse, uselesse, unprofitable, and unsavoury thoughts? Is not thy heart full of carnall reasonings, roving imaginations, motions, yea, of sinfull counsels, devises, purposes?

... Oh, what a piece is this heart of man! Oh, what a piece of carrion, which hath alwaies such a swarm *of flies* humming about, fastening and blowing on it, and what a breed and nest of Vermine that are bred in it, and at last devour it. I have read of a *poor Monk* who rebuking a *rich Prelate* was bidden in scorne, go *kill his lice,* who answered boldly, *My Lord, I have killed mine, but yours will kill you.* The poor man's *lice and Vermine* are not so dangerous to the *body,* as the rich, proud and wicked mans are to his *soul*. ... The *best eye,* having the help of the best *perspective,* upon the fairest *prospect,* and in the *clearest summer's day,* sees much, but not the thousandth part of heaven, or earth; nor we of sin. They say much of the earth is *unknown,* to be sure much of *hell* in thy heart is. If there be any part of an *unknown world* yet undiscovered, I am sure there is a great part of an unknown world yet undiscovered in thy heart. It is long ere a stranger can know all the *streets, lanes, and allies* in the City, but thou wilt never know all the windings and turnings of thy heart. In a great house sometimes at first a stranger looseth himself, but in the heart to the last, it is strange if the owner hath not been lost. *My heart,* saith *Bernard, is like the deep sea, in which are creeping things and that without number.* A *flint* it is, which, though cold, and dark, hath seeds of fire, and a thousand sparks lodged in it; if you strike and break it, the seeds of all sin are there, even of the sin against the holy Ghost. ... None is able to make the hearts Epitaph and to say what lies there, Unlesse we shall write as of Pope *Sixtus* the Fourth: *Hic scelus omne simul clauditur, and vitium.* Or that, like it, of Pope *Clement* the 8th: *Urna brevis vitium claudit, and omne scelus.*

... The great *Volumes* of Arts and sciences have been *Epitomized,* and the whole *body* or summe of Divinity hath been often *contracted* into a narrow compasse or Systeme; but *the body of sin* in the *heart* is not to be contracted or summed up. Some learned men of old and late have made *Catalogues* of the noted *Errors* and *Heresies* that have troubled the whole Church from the beginning, but none dare undertake to enumerate and catalogue the errors and enormities of one poor single heart.

23a Paul Bush, *Here begynneth a lytell treatyse in Englysshe, called the Extripacion of ignorancy* (1526?). **23b** William Gearing, *The arraignment of ignorance* (1659).

Introduction Paul Bush was bishop of Bristol, rector of Winterborn, and an Augustinian friar.[12] Born and educated before the Reformation (born ca. 1490, B.A. 1517), Bush was a pre-Reformation priest who accepted some of the tenets of the early Henrician Reformation, such as the marriage of priests (he was prosecuted for his marriage under Mary Tudor), and became chaplain to Henry VIII. At the same time, though, he remained an orthodox Roman Catholic throughout his later life, particularly in regard to the liturgy, for which he was criticized by such Reformers as John Bale, who lamented that a non-Protestant was granted a bishopric after the Reformation. Bush is thus a good example of the fluidity of confessional identities in late medieval and early Reformation England, as Richard Carpenter, the "confessional chameleon" was in early modern Protestant England.[13] Bush's text, then, is an interesting example of the endurance of the legacy of pre-Reformation thought in the budding ambience of reform in early sixteenth-century England, and also gives testimony to the relevance and reconcilability of aspects of pre-Reformation thought with post-Reformation audiences. Published just under ten years before the Reformation, Bush's verse text was unthreatened by the early Reformist ardour, which mostly targeted monasteries, and was also clearly unaffected by Bush's refusal to accept the Mass in English, his refusal to cease saying paid masses for the dead, the criticism of his work by more ardent Protestants, and his elevation to bishop under

12. J.H. Bettey, "Bush, Paul (1489/90–1558), bishop of Bristol," in *Oxford Dictionary of National Biography* online, https://doi.org/10.1093/ref:odnb/4159, last updated 3 January 2008.

13. Carpenter was religiously "flexible": raised Protestant, he converted to Roman Catholicism (becoming a Benedictine and Jesuit), but converted back to the Church of England (under William Laud) upon his return from the Continent, through a recantation sermon he gave at St Paul's Cathedral in London in 1635. Then, after a brief conflict with both Laudian Protestants and Roman Catholics close to his parish he went back to the Continent, became a Roman Catholic once again, but later came back to England and became a Protestant again. Due to this religious fluidity some Protestants regarded him as suspicious and by around 1650 a certificate was issued against him that barred him from preaching. Carpenter, however, continued to be active as an independent preacher and, following his Catholic apostasy sermon of 1635, he continued to write anti-Catholic texts, even though his reputation as a Protestant was dubious among a number of other Protestants. William E. Burns, "Carpenter, Richard (1604/5–1670?)," in *Oxford National Bibliography* online, https://doi.org/10.1093/ref:odnb/4739. See also Alison Shell, "Multiple Conversion and the Menippean Self: The Case of Richard Carpenter," in *Catholicism and Anti-Catholicism in Early Modern English Texts*, ed. A.F. Marotti (New York, 1999), 154–197; and Richard Newhauser, "'These Seaven Devils': The Capital Vices on the Way to Modernity," in *Sin in Medieval and Early Modern Culture: The Tradition of the Seven Deadly Sins*, ed. Richard G. Newhauser and Susan J. Ridyard (Woodbridge, Suffolk, 2012), 157–188, at 172–173.

Henry VIII (from which he resigned under Mary Tudor). The 1526 text[14] was, in fact, dedicated to Mary Tudor, and is a homiletic work on the importance of fearing and loving God, and fearing and loving the King. The sin of ignorance was a central concept (its source in the Old Testament) to pre-Reformation pastoral care, as ignorance led to other sins: not knowing meant making mistakes, and mistakes could be dangerous to the soul and the body. In other words, the mind (knowledge or lack thereof) was essential to the wellbeing of the spirit, and vices such as blindness, close-mindedness, obstinacy, lack of respect, ingratitude, and "folly" all stemmed from ignorance, as did pride, envy, wrath, and sloth.

Little else is known about the Protestant William Gearing, who in the 1650s served as minister in Lymington, apart from the fact that he was a fairly prolific writer who authored over fifteen books on divinity, meditation, social sins, and an influential compendium *The history of the Church of Great Britain from the birth of Our Saviour, until the year of Our Lord, 1667*. Gearing dedicated his work on ignorance to three puritans: John Button, John Bulkeley, and John Hildesley, with whom he shared a conviction that it was necessary to redeem knowledge and wisdom.[15] By knowledge, Gearing meant the knowledge of God, and by wisdom the wisdom of heaven, as he focused his text on drawing the attention of Christians to the importance of religious observance and the search for truth. Gearing believed that whoever refused, or did not make enough effort, to know God was not only a sinner, but also a fool, in that this kind of spiritual ignorance was a sin both of omission and commission. He condemned ignorance as a vice of the mind and of the soul, a shorthand for sin that prevents the soul from searching for knowledge of God, induces disobedience, and through lack of knowledge leads to sin. Gearing's text is thus, like Bush's, a homiletic work, but is more focused on doctrine and religious observance than *The extripacion of ignorancy*. Both texts focus on ignorance, a feature of thought, as a sin, and thus both combine religion with thought, and knowledge with being Christian.

23a Paul Bush, *Here begynneth a lytell treatyse in Englysshe, called the Extripacion of ignorancy: and it treateth and speketh of the ignorance of people, shewyng them howe they are bounde to feare god, to loue god, and to honour their prince. Which treatise is lately compyled by sir Paule Busshe preest, and bonhome of Edyndon: and dedicate vnto the yong and most hye renomed lady Mary, princes and*

14. Most likely written earlier, as indicated, for instance, by the use of scribal abbreviations and markers, which indicates that it was first written and perhaps copied by hand by a scribe and only then adapted by the printer.

15. Andrew M. Coleby, *Central Government and the Localities: Hampshire 1649–1698* (Cambridge, 1987), 74.

doughter vnto the noble progenytour, our worthy souerayne kyng Henry the eight, kyng of Englande and of Fraunce, and hye defender of ye christenfaithe. &c., 1526 (?); unnumbered pages. *STC* 4186. **Source** *EEBO*: Cambridge University Library (Sel. 5.58).

The prologue generall of Paule Busshe, composytour of this lytell treatyse. Deum timete et regem honorificate. Prima Petri secundi.

... And as I walked alone in mynde thus musyng
I thought to endyte what thyng were necessary
And by long delyberacion I coniectred most sytting
Somwhat to write of mans ingratytude and folly
And to prosecute his demeaner all croked and contrary
To god his maker by lyueng nat commendable
Subdued by vyce and suche maters semblable.

And no great marueyle, ne wonder certayne
Though suche inconuenyence enshewe vs amonge
For wylfully is broken the bridell and the rayne
Whiche shulde gouerne man in euery thronge.
As first drede is expulsed by audacite stronge
And sensualyte ruleth as gouernour principall,
So that Christ is nat dradde ne feared at all.

Also perfyte loue whiche shulde deuout myndes
Sette on fyre in louyng god omnipotent
Is subpeditate by enormytes of sondrie kyndes.
Wherfore I thought it semyng and most conuenyent
As touchyng my purpose for this tyme present
Of these two maters and their circumstaunce chefely
Somwhat to write, to mittygate suche folly.

And also to speke I thought it expedient
Thirdly of ignorance which ledeth people forward
Shewyng them by auctorites and reasons euydent
Howe they are oblygate in especiall regarde
Their prince to honour as capten of their forward
Whose magnanimyte they ought to auaunce
With hertes and goodes after their substaunce.

... What causeth mischefe? what causeth discencion,
Discorde and debate; But onely disobedience
Thus olde hystores and scripture maketh mencion
For it is counted a lyfe brutall, euer saithe sapience
Whan that people lyueng dothe nat their dilygence
God chefly to worship and their prince to honour
As the thyng speciall of their corporall treasour.

What caused cyties and townes to fall to ruyne,
But onely the decayeng of Christes hye honour
Whan the people to vyce them selfe dyd fully enclyne.
Somtyme the Romayns habounded in treasour
But whan christs honor decayed and they fell to error
Than their renome abated, vrged by violence
For their vnstable demeaner to kepe true sylence.

Manyfolde presydentes reduce we may to memory
Cotidially shewed of mannes vnstable dotage
Wauernyg as the wynde laboring right busely
For honour and worship as one of hye linage
Clyming so hye that forgoten is their parentage
The god and his prince and hymselfe also
Whiche after subuerteth his state to sorowe and wo.

Well this set clene aside I shall my wittes auaunce
My purpose to comprice and therto my pen direct
No lengar to remayne by goddes gouernaunce
In maters dependyng nothyng to theffecte
Eschewing wordes superflewe, which oft doth infect
The sentence clere of hystores true and autentycall
Lefte for morall presydentes to people vnyuersall.

But in mynde whan I pondre this prouerbe olde
Who casteth lesse peryls than dothe bayarde[16] blynde
It maketh my hande quake and also my hert colde
And tosseth my wyttes as a ship before the wynde

16. Aimless, heedless, "as blind as a baiard": *MED* s.v. "baiard".

Lest some frowarde persons peruert and vnkynde
Shulde by me reporte wordes somwhat equalent[17]
Sayeng to enterprice suche causes he is insufficient.

Such saying may be verified that dede maketh relacion
Wherfore to my maisters knowyng the quiditice[18]
Of scolasticall actes by practyse and speculacion
I submyt my selfe in most humble wyse
Their due correction in no case to dispyce
But as a discyple leanyng to doctryne
So vnto their tradicions gladly I shall enclyne.
... Commendacion it is none this I knowe certayne
A relygious man to ydelnesse to be obedient
Nor the laude is but small vyle and mundayne
His tyme to contryue in discribing workes insolent
For to suche thynges if he do his mynde frequent
Wysemen shall say deprauyng his fame
This man gothe about to lese his good name.

Therefore my lordes and maisters in generall
Pondre the entent of my enterprise rude
For the thyng that pruoked me to this worke speciall
My study to apply with dilygent solicitude
Was that slouthfull idelnesse shulde nat me illude
And that I maye accomplysshe my purpose and entent
First shall I pray as it is most expedient.

Nowe lorde as thy sapience surmounteth mans estimacion
In rulyng and gouernyng by prouidence incomparable
Heuyn erthe and hell as doctors make relacion
So nowe rule my penne and my wytte variable.

23b William Gearing, *The arraignment of ignorance: or, ignorance. With the causes and kinds of it; the mischiefes and danger of it, together with the cure of ignorance: as also, the excellency, profit, and benefit of heavenly knowledge, largely set*

17. Possibly "equaeualent"; this might be spelled with q with superscript e (text slightly unclear).

18. Possibly meaning "essential nature" or "subtletlies" here.

forth from Hos. 4:6. By W. G. Minister of the word at Lymington in the County of South-hampton, 1659, unnumbered prologue and p. 64.[19] *Wing* G429. **Source** *EEBO*: British Library, London (E.1760(1)).

To the Reader.[20]

These are dayes that abound in the means of saving knowledge, but few partake of it; the most, like brutes, do altogether neglect it, others seek after it, *but not* as for Gold; *and many there be that preferre childish toyes, and trifling knowledge, before that wisdom that is from above. A natural man is apt to affect things more or lesse according to the sense and understanding that he hath of them; now, a natural man cannot understand the things of the spirit, therefore he cannot truly affect them; the excellent knowledge of Christ, the glorious priviledges of the Gospel, are things transcending all created understanding; the love of Christ is a love that* passeth knowledge, *saith the* Apostle; *the* Peace of God, *a peace* that passeth all understanding; *communion with God in the Spirit, and joy in the Holy Ghost, these are things that even the understanding of a spitual man cannot reach unto, but a natural man is in darkenesse, and altogether blinde towards them.* Faith is the evidence of things not seen, *it discovereth to a believing soul things invisible. A carnal man wanteth faith, therefore when the glorious excellencies of the Gospel are presented before him he wanteth an evidence to discover these things unto him; visible things being presented, are to be seen with bodily eyes, but spiritual and invisible things cannot be seen by those that want the eye of Faith.*

... There is a rich price in hand, much means of knowledge, by Preaching, Expounding, Writing, Catechising the things of God excellently and clearly set out to us; but all this while this price is in the hand of a fool, one who (though worldly wise) yet wanteth the light of the Spirit to direct him to true happinesse, and to shew him the worth of Heavenly things, and thereupon it followeth that he hath no heart to it. A similitude taken from a Man that is going to a Town or City where there is some great Mart or Faire, with money in his hand to buy Commodities; but for want of judgement he passeth by the most advantagious Commodities, being ignorant of the goodnesse and profitablenesse of them, and throwes away his money upon toyes and trifles that are of no advantage to him.

So there is a price put into the hands of the sonnes of men, to get Heavenly Wisdom, but the carnal worldling remains a starke foole, he cannot see into the excellency of Heavenly things, and thereupon hath no heart to them but passeth by them, and

19. Marginal notes in the original source were not included in the transcription.

20. The whole of "To the Reader" is italicized in the original text, apart from particular words and expressions, as marked in the transcription.

embraceth a thing of nought instead of them. God is to be sought above all, and may be found of all that will seek after him, and take any paines to know him: but the greatest part of the World have not a minde to know him, and therefore doe not follow on to know him. When man will not use those helpes that God hath left him to search after the saving knowledge of God, God justly suffereth him to fall into divers opinions and grosse conceits, which shut him up in the bottome of a stinking Dungeon, where he findeth nothing but ignorance, errour, and irkesome uncertainties, as filthy vermine, creeping round about him; where the darknesse of ignorance fills the minde, the Prince of darkenesse fills the heart. The Sepia *or* Cuttle-fish, *saith* Tertullian, *when he is in danger to be taken, casteth about him a black inkie matter, wherewith he darkneth the water, that the Fishermen cannot see him: So many people do seek to compasse themselves with the darke cloudes of ignorance, to hide themselves and their wicked practises, which would appeare to be very odious, should they come to be viewed and surveyed by the light of the Word. And for many others that are a little enlightned, they professe wisdome, but they practise folly, and so their knowledge is no better than ignorance.*

... What man can reckon himself a Christian that is ignorant of God? Without the knowledge of God, all that we do is but in a customary or uncertain way; hereby, we know whom we serve, and the great advantages we shall reape by his Service, and are sensible of our estate in Grace, measuring God's gracious presence with us, or his absence and with-drawings from us, and our own strength and weaknesse; it is the earnest of our Heavenly Inheritance, the first fruites of the Beatifick Vision, our acquaintance with his face in this Life, and our Heaven upon Earth.

And now (Reader) if thou art in an ignorant estate, and one who art willing to be brought to the sense of thy ignorance and blindnesse and so to come to him who is the Light of the World; Then say I to thee, as Jehu *to* Jonadab: Give me thy hand, and thou and I shall quickly accord, *and thou shalt be a fit and welcome Reader to this poor Treatise; and I hope I have written that which shall be both for thy satisfaction and comfort.*

... The Arraignment of Ignorance.

... 7. *Ignorance makes a man like a beast.* A man without knowledge is like *Nebuchadnezzar,* who had the heart of a beast in the shape of a man: an ignorant man hath the head and heart of a beast, an ignorant man is a very beast. For what difference between a man and a beast? A beast hath eyes, ears, legs, as well as a man; seeth, heareth, goeth, smelleth, tasteth, as well as a man can do, nay, many beasts can doe these things better then a man can doe; a man, then, differeth only from a beast in *understanding* and *discourse*. Therefore, saith God to his people, *Be not as the horse or mule, that hath no understanding*; as the Poet calleth an ignorant man a *sottish man*, yea, a sottish mule. Ask an ignorant man what *God* is, what *Jesus Christ* is, what his *natures*, what his *offices* are? Ask him what the *Spirit of God* is, what God requireth at his hands, how he should serve him? Ask him how he will get faith? Examine him about the doctrines of *Justification, Adoption, Sanctification*, what *evidences* he can shew for everlasting life and salvation, what marks of Christianity he can shew, what tokens of sound conversion and sincerity in himself; what strange answers shall you receive from an ignorant man? so that the bleating of a sheep, the neighing of an horse, or the lowing of an Oxe is as much to the purpose as his answers are. Is he rich? he is a rich beast; as *Diogenes Cynicus* called a rich man that was unlearned, a *sheep with a golden fleece*. Is he honourable? he is an *honourable* beast, if ignorant; as one said of an ignorant and unlearned King, that he was but a crowned Asse. ...

VICES AND VIRTUES OF THE MIND

24a *The boke of wysdome*, trans. John Larke (1532). **24b** *A discourse of the repugnancy of sin to the principles of universal reason* (1679).

Introduction *The boke of wysdome* derives from a French work, *Chapelet des vertus*, which in turn is a translation of an Italian text, *Fiore di virtù* (attr. to Thommaso Leoni, ca. 1323); the translator of *Chapelet* into English was a secular preacher, John Larke,[21] a friend of Thomas More, executed during the reign of Henry VIII.[22] The *Chapelet* was a popular fourteenth-century text, extant in fourteen manuscript copies and as many as sixteen printed editions before 1550;[23] the English translation went through five editions in the sixteenth century. Being a translation of a translation of a translation, *The boke of wysdome* is in many ways its own work in that it gathered the "residue" of different styles, often defined by the context and time of the translation, and is thus representative as much of the period in which it was translated as it is of the background of the translation.

21. Zsolt Almási, "'Be Not ye of That Sect of Philosophers Called Pirhonici?': Caninius and Pyrhonian Scepticism in Thomas Elyot's *The Defense of Good Women*," in *New Perspectives on Tudor Cultures*, ed. Mike Pincombe and Zsolt Almási (Cambridge, 2012), 20–34, at 32.

22. The Nuns of Tyburn Convent, *The One Hundred and Five Martyrs of Tyburn*, introd. Bede Camm (London, 1917), 32.

23. Mary A. Rouse and Richard H. Rouse, "Prudence, Mother of Virtues: The *Chapelet des vertus* and Christine de Pizan," *Viator* 39 (2008): 185–228, at 185.

John Larke decided that the philosophical and moral contents of the *Chapelet* were desirable and interesting to his English audience, and anchored in "traditional religion."[24] The focus of the text is on prudence as a virtue of the mind, and it organizes its contents, a compilation of philosophical, biblical, and patristic quotations and thought, along an ordered framework of about forty vices and virtues. Prudence was considered by such late medieval thinkers as John Gerson to be the most important virtue of all, and the root of all others.[25] To Larke, prudence meant the application of reason to make good judgements, which in turn were a defence against vices; it was "good wysdome"[26] which consisted of memory, rationality (a sense of duty and the ability to tell good from evil), and planning ("prouysion"[27]). The virtues are presented in the classic psychomachic style (i.e., the personification of abstract concepts; in this case featuring the characters Dame Prudence, Dame Sapyence, and so on). To each virtue its contrary vice is given, including the sins of the heptad expanded with such vices as melancholy, fear, or "distemperance." The contrary of prudence, folly, along with other virtues and their contrary vices are explained with the use of evidence from ancient, biblical, and patristic sources. The text speaks of reason as a virtue of the mind and soul: reason signifies a spiritual state of mental balance, and is thus a virtue achievable exclusively by the exercise of the mind.

The anonymous *Discourse of the repugnancy of sin to the principles of universal reason*[28] is a treatise on sin, possibly originally preached as a sermon and then expanded before being put to print, although it is also possible it belongs to the genre of fairly short anonymous works on religious matters, such as the *Nine mortal weapons* (1650) (albeit considerably longer). Its detailed focus is on equating reason with virtue, proving through examples and biblically-supported argumentation that since the natural state of reason is being sin-free, sin must naturally be contrary to reason. Through the use of such words as wisdom, wit, reason, and folly, the text makes use of the discourse of virtues and vices of the mind. It goes further than Larke's text, however, in that it actively persuades its readers that they are reasonable creatures by God's design, but that reasonableness, by virtue of coming from God, includes finding sin irrational and in conflict with all that the mind and soul stand for. So while Larke focuses on describing the general vices of a fool-

24. Eamon Duffy, *The Stripping of the Altars: Traditional Religion in England, 1400–1580* (New Haven, 1992), throughout.

25. Jean Gerson, *Harangue faicte au nom de l'Université de Paris devant le Roy Charles sixiesme ... 1405*, ed. A.M.H. Boulard (Paris, 1824), 26–32, as quoted by Rouse and Rouse, "Prudence, Mother of Virtues," 200.

26. *The boke of wysdome*, 1532, n. pag. See excerpt below.

27. *The boke of wysdome*, 1532, n. pag. See excerpt below.

28. In one source the text is attributed to John Jeffrey, a Protestant minister; C. Wilkins-Jones, "Norwich City Library and Its Intellectual Milieu; 1608–1825" (PhD diss., University of East Anglia, 2000), 235–237.

ish mind and the virtues of a wise mind, the *Discourse of the repugnancy of sin to the principles of universal reason* narrows in on foolishness as sin, and sin as the unnatural and irrational rebellion against God and the God-given faculty of reason. The text argues that in order to strive for living a more reasonable (i.e., godly and virtuous) life, not so much mental exercise as faith and a humble understanding of God's intentions in creating the human mind are required.

While Larke discusses virtue as achievable via mental effort, this text is clearly a Protestant work through the emphasis it gives to the omnipotence of God the creator, and in its recommendation of faith and trust in God as the path to reason and wisdom. At the same time, both texts illustrate a conflation of ideas on the mind with those on vices and virtues, with praise of prudence or reason conflated with the praise of virtue and religious obedience, and the condemnation of folly presented as a condemnation of vice and sin. The texts also illustrate the development of thought on the relationship between the mind and the virtues and vices over the late medieval and early modern periods. Folly, perhaps echoing the Erasmian notions of folly,[29] is the primary vice in both texts, as it stands in opposition to prudence or reason, and is the cause of sin. The inclusion of folly as the primary vice also contextualizes Larke's translation of the medieval original by showing that, likely, Larke modernized some of the discussion in the original work to reflect more contemporary interests in folly. Both texts, then, are religiously-phrased studies of the vices of the mind, and though perhaps they differ generically, and were not written in direct relationship to one another, are good indications of the enduring legacy of pre-Reformation influences on post-Reformation texts on reason and folly.

24a *The boke of wysdome, folowynge the auctoryties of auncyent phylosophers, dyuydynge, and spekyng of vyces and vertues, wherby a man may be praysed, or dyspraysed, with the maner to speke alwayes well and wysely to all folkes, of what estate so euer they be*, trans. John Larke, 1532; unnumbered pages. *STC* 3357. **Source** *EEBO*: The Huntington Library, San Marino, CA (990005).

... *Howe Prudence is the chyef buckeser*[30] *and defence of all vertues. And of the great goodnesse that maye come of the same to all persones, after the auncyent Phylosophers.* Prudence, called good wysdome, dyscrecyon, and sagenesse, be in thre maners, and forter after the sayenge of Iusse. The fyrste is memory, that is to say remembraunce of thynges passed. The seconde is to know that thynge that a man hathe to do, the good from the euyll, and the treuthe from the falshed. The thyrde is

29. *The praise of folly*, printed in 1509, is an essay against superstition, and a satyrical work on many human vices (such as forgetfulness or intemperance).

30. Probably "buckler" (i.e., a small shield).

prouydence or prouysion, that is to say for the tyme to com of that thynge that a man hathe to do. And these thre vertues be formed and rewled by two other, that is to say counceyll and dylygence. Arystotell sayth that counceyll is a certayne inquysycyon, procedynge from one thynge to another, dylygence is to haue care and regarde vnto that thynge that a man hathe to do. ... Dauid sayth that the begynnynge of wysdome is to fere and drede god. Salomon sayth that wysdom is better and more worth than all the rychesse of the worlde, for no rychesse maye be comparyd to sagenesse and wysdome. ...

Boetius sayth that it is not suffycyent to know the thynges as a man dothe se them before hym, but Prudence is that whiche doth mesure the ende of all thynges; it was demaunded of a wyse man howe a man shulde behaue hym selfe and what he shuld do that he shulde not haue nede ot another man. And he answerrd that yf a man be ryche, let hym lyue measurably and temperatlye. And yf he be poore let hym laboure dylygentlye. And so he shall lyue without daunger, for dylygence is the mother of rychesse; And sayth that he ought not to be called ryche whiche gatheryth moche rychesse and goodes togyther, but he whiche doth spende them with reason. And sayth also that there is no greatter treasoure in the worlde then wytte and dyscrecyon.

Socrates sayth that scyence is gotten by dylygence of man, but prudence and wysdom is the gyfte of god, and amonges all other gyftes the moste excellent. Hermes sayth also that there is no greatter treasoure in the worlde then wytte and dyscrecyon, nor greatter pouertye then ignoraunce, nor better frendes then to haue good custome and manners. ... There came ones to a wyse man a kynsman of his and prayed hym that it wold please hym to lene hym a certayne summe of money, the whiche wyse man answeryd, trewely my frende, I shall not be so euyll content with the yf I do not lene the, as I shall be yf I lene the, for afterwade I wolde recouer it of the, and preaunetrue I can not.

Plato sayth that prudence and wysdom doth decorate and aorne the rychesse of man. And sayth also that the prudent and wyse man doth not fere deth, for prudence gouerneth his vnderstandynge; his tonge is the voyce of treweth, his herte is good wyll, pyte and mercy be his armures. And also to seche the wyse man is wysdom and prudence his power and auctoryte is iustyce, his reygne is mesure, his laude and prayse is peas, his werkes be saluacuon, his chyualrye or knyghtode is the counceyll of wyse men, his apparel is pacyence, his treasoure is dyscyplyne or doctrine, the company of good persones is his loue. And all hys desyre is to flye from synne and to serue god, and to haue his fayth and truste in hym, for without that no man can not please god, as sayth saynt Paule.

... How Folye is contrary to Prudence. And howe Folye is dyuyed into many partes of the man. Also the maner to knowe the Fole by his dedes. And the wyse man by his workes.

Folye is a vyce contrary to the vertue of prudence, As sayth Plato, of the whiche Folye there is dyuerse and many sortes and maners. There is Folye accustomed, as those persones whiche be foles from theyr natyuyte and byrthe. And other there be whiche be Lunatyke or frantyke for a certayne space. And yet there is another maner of Folye whiche is lesse then the other aboue sayde, as of those persones whiche hathe loste ther wytte. And this Folye maye be deuyded in foure maners. The fyrst is of those persones whiche do not regarde nor thynke besely vpon those matters that they haue to do, but do all thynges ...[31] without any maner of consyderacyon and reason. The seconde maner of folye is of them that do not consyder nor regarde the ende that maye happe and come of the maters, that they haue enterprysed but do all thinges sodeynly, as it commeth in theyr mynde and wyll. The thyrd maner of folye is to be to hasty to do that thyng that a man hath to do. The fourth maner of folye is to be neclygent and slouthfull in that thynge that a man hathe to do, and to haue no thought nor care of the same but rather neclygently to lette it passe, and can not fynde the maner to begyn any thynge. And yf another man begyn yet can not he folowe, and yf a man pursewe and folow, yet can not he fynde the maner to make an ende; knowe ye that neclygence is mother and nowryhe of pouerte. And so that man whiche is neclygent may be reputed for a fol.

Salamon sayth, medle not but as lyttel as thou may with a fole, for he wyll not regarde thy wordes, excepte they be after his pleasure. Senec sayth that a fole maye be comparyd to the Moldewarpe, whiche heryth but vnderstandeth not. And sayth that the fole lyghtly byleueth the good that a man speketh of hym. And heryth verye gladlye the euyll spoken of another man. And saythe also that the wyse man dothe folowe the domages and harmes, and gothe not aboute to fynde them, but the fole taketh great payne to fynde them. And sayth yf thou wyll haue the loue of a fole fulfill his wyll and pleasure in all thynges. And sayth that the loue of a fole shall be greater domage vnto the then his euyll wyll. And yf it chaunce that he be ryche he shalbe proude and presumptuous, and yf he be pore he wyll despayre of the goodnes of god. And yf a man gyue hym any thyng he wyll neuer thanke hym for it; yf a man tell hym any secrete mater he wyll shewe it incontynent to another; yf he speke he wyll be herde and wyll haue audyence aboue all men. And yf other men speake he wyll not heare nor gyue audyence vnto them; he ys sodeynly mery and full of ioye without any measure and rea-

31. Text unclear, but the 1565 and 1575 editions have "at auenture" here.

son. And sodeynly also he is full of Yre, melancoly, and angry without reason, yf a man praye hym to pardone and forgyue any man, he wyll answere that in no maner of wyse he wyll so do: he loueth better warre and dyscencion then peace, and falsheed and lyenge then trewth; no man can brynge hym out of his opynyon. And commonly he is couetous in all his besynes, yf he talke wyth a wyse man he wyll neuer humylat hym selfe, nor skarsly gyue hym herynge; yf thou be ryche he wyll say thou art an vsurer, yf thou be poore, he wyl speke to the with vyle wordes, yf thou do well and vse to do many good dedes he wyll say that thou arte an Ypocryte, yf thou do euyll, he wyll dyffame the; yf perauenture he do accorde hym self to trewth in any maner of thynge that dothe please hym, he wyll prayse it greatly, but yf it be contrary to his pleasure and wyll, he wyll dysprayse it.

But the wyse man is of the contrary opynyon, for he hath contynuance in iustyce, humylyte, and pardon; he can speake well, and also holde his peace when place and tyme is; he hathe measure in his power, he is lyberall to the demaunders, and also he is a fayre speaker and a fayre gyuer of answere, he that sheweth him his counseill he doth kepe it secrete, yf he gyue any thynge, he gyueth it merely and wyth a good herte, and without any reproche; he dothe none other wyse to any man, but as he wolde were done vnto hym.

Yf he be ryche he wyll neuer be the prouder therefore, yf he be poore yet therfore wyll not he leue and forsake to serue god; he is not angry nor dyspleasyd to se another man better then he, nor he wyll not dysprayse a worse man then hymself; he demaundeth nor claymeth no thynge there where he hathe no ryght, he is agreable and pleasaunt in all his answeres; And sayth no thyng but that he knoweth well; he doth not hyde his scyence, he constrayneth and accordeth his wyl by force to trewthe and ryght, and he causeth hym selfe to be loued of euery man; yf he bere wytnesse yt shall be trewe, yf he judge yt shall be ryght. And shall neuer prolonge the causes of any man; he doth repute hym selfe a straunger in this worlde and thynketh alwayes to departe from it; he dothe well, and gyueth good example to other to do well; he forbyddeth the euyll and dothe kepe hym from it to his power, all his dedes and his sayenges be acordable, and very pacyently doth sufre and endure the enuymys and opprobryous wordes spoken agaynste hym, without takynge any venegeaunce. The wyseman is al wayes in one mynde and courage, he is not in dyuers opynyons, he wyll not be letted for no maner of thynge to tell the trewth.

24b *A discourse of the repugnancy of sin to the principles of universal reason. Being a dissuasive from a sinful life from principles of common wisdom, currant amongst all mankind, save onely in the concerns of their souls*, 1679, pp. 91–116. *Wing*

D1608. **Source** Houghton Rare Book Library, Harvard University, Cambridge, MA (004211661).

SECT. VII.

To continue a sinful life is to practise contradiction to that self-evident principle and dictate of the common Reason of Man. *That the greatest honour and first place in our account, intention, and endeavours, doth of right belong to the greatest good.* All the doubt to a wise man when he is permitted his choice, is not whether the best is to be chosen, but which is the best; and when the disparity is evident he ceases to doubt. We leave it to children to chuse a beautiful Apple before as much Gold as will buy the whole Plantation where it grew, but we cannot allow our selves such a childish election, but in the choice of the pleasures of Sin, we continue the same folly to grey hairs, and make all our days a choice that we would blush to own in any besides eternal concerns; for which the truest excuse that can be made, is this sad one, that it is but in the case of our souls, wherein onely it seems pardonable not to do wisely, not (I hope) for this reason, that all eternity will be long enough to repent in. To make choice of Sin, a thing inconsistent with our eternal hopes, is to say to a work of darkness, *Sit thou there in a place of honour*; and to say to the joys of Heaven, *Stand ye there behind my back, or lie you there below my footstool.* If we do allow to the heavenly Kingdom an excellency surpassing all earthly good, and that the wisdom of our Creator hath done it but right in placing it above the earth we tread on, then what our Lord gave us in command becomes a peremptory dictate of our own reason, namely, *first to seek the Kingdom of God*, St *Matth.* 6:33.

The possibility of the attainment thereof being added to its universally acknowledged excellency to seek any thing before it, and thereby in our account to displace the Creation, is so grosly unreasonable that the most foolish actions that are to be found in the History of all the Lives in the World are very unequal to that folly, and the man who in sacred Records sold his birthright to allay his present hunger, and the Prince who in prophane Story gave away his Kingdom to quench his thirst, may make a far better defence against the shame of their choice than the prophane Sinner who quits a comfortable prospect to Heaven in exchange for his Sin; for to retain his sins is to make such a foolish exchange. In things not greatly material, or of no greatly different worth, we allow for the *peculiarity* of every mans fansie and easily pardon a mistake which it is easie to commit; but in things of great importance, and where the *disparity* is apparent, to make a wrong choice is infamous, and speaks him that makes it to be a Fool or Brute; onely Custom, which is able to do strange things, hath obtained that in all cases pertaining to the World to come we may do the most unreasonable, that is, the most shameful things with little shame, and in case of eternity not much endanger our reputation for wisdom by the most foolish choice. For though Wisdom can justifie it self by the best arguments, yet Folly is defended by the greatest numbers, but it cannot but be it self still, a shameful thing, though it have so mighty numbers on its side as were able to drie up Rivers with the soles of their feet; and Wisdom, though left alone in the person of one single *Eliah*, (as he once supposed) though her children that do justifie her be never so few in number; yet is its own justification. For Wisdom and Folly in the choice before us are as evident as the light, and as discernible one from the other as light from darkness, to distinguish which there is no need of any great skill, and it is onely requisite not to be blind; for there is no just comparison at all between the things in competition for our choice, so that it is necessary not to know or to forget the Heavenly blessedness to take advantage of its distance and invisibility to be able to neglect it, and to make our choice without comparing the things to be chosen, for what comparison is there between a day and a thousand years, yea, ten thousand Ages, between light which glimmers in a coal which is but bright enough to make it self discernible, and light which shines in the Sun and clears all the World? What comparison between a little dead Water in a Cistern, and a spring of living Water that ever flows without either cessation or end? Such, nay, less than such, is the comparison between Earth and Heaven; between either lawful or unlawful pleasures here, and *those rivers of pleasure and life which flow at the right hand, and from the throne of God and of the Lamb for evermore.* (*Psal.* 16:11, *Rev.* 22:1.) How can the pleasures of Sin, which are but for a season, abide a comparison with the eternal joys and *glory to be revealead?* Is it not beyond all difficulty and doubt better to rejoice eternally for great and substantial causes, and most satisfactory reasons, than to laugh on now a little time, and with as little reason in a forced Mirth, and with the Conscience that there is no such cause of joy, but rather to mourn and to lament, and with many a misgiving thought accusing the Sinner for rejoicing unjustly?

We shall more evidently discover the inequality of the comparison, and more fully convince the Sinner of the folly and shame of such an unreasonable choice if we consider distinctly the things in competition, taking into examination what is to be known of the blessedness to come, and what may be pleaded and alledged in favour, defence, or excuse of a sinful life; and having placed both in our open view we may desire the Sinner to ask himself whether in reason that blessed state ought to be slighted, or the pleasures of Sin doth not cost too dear at the price of so much blessedness slighted and put away from him for their sakes? ...

It hath been the opinion of wise men that if Vertue were equally discernible with sensible excellencies it would appear to be far more beautiful; and if from a composure of colours laid over a little mass of flesh, with organs and parts diversified in a due proportion by a divine skill there results so much beauty as is able to detain the eyes of Monarchs and Conquerors, and endangers beholders to betray their reason to its charms; what wonders of beauty are there to be seen in the infinite wisdom, goodness, and holiness, and all the divine excellencies evidently conspicuous in the *beatifical vision*, when we shall see God as he is! for let us conceive all the diffused ways of beauty scattered over all the Creation to be united in one most lovely object, and all the scattered particles of good united in one common center of goodness; and all the scattered excellencies over all the World abstracted from the imperfections which adhere to them, and gathered together in one, in the greatest purity and perfection; and yet, then we come short of a just resemblance of the infinitly more transcending beauty, goodness, and excellency that shine in their full glory in the face of God, who is the original and fountain of all that is worthy to be desired and worthy to be loved, from whom it first sprung, and where it still is in its greatest eminency.

25a *Here foloweth a notable treatyse and full necessary to an crysten men for to knowe and it is named the Ordynarye of crystyanyte or of crysten men*, trans. Andrew Chertsey (1502).
25b [Levinus Lemnius,] *The touchstone of complexions*, trans. Thomas Newton (1633).

Introduction Andrew Chertsey was a translator active in the late fifteenth and early sixteenth centuries, and often worked for Wynkyn de Worde and other printers. He translated from French, and specialized in devotional works. Not much is known about him apart from the fact that he is called a "gentleman"[32] and Robert Copland praised him in a prologue to the 1521 edition of *The passion of our lorde Jesu cryst* as a "prudent wytted" man.[33] The original version of the *Ordynarye of crysten men* is a fifteenth-century French text, *L'ordinaire des chrestiens* (1491?),[34] a very popular text printed a number of times in

32. Julia Boffey, "Chertsey [Chertesey], Andrew (fl. 1502–1527), translator," in *Oxford Dictionary of National Biography* online, https://doi.org/10.1093/ref:odnb/5225.

33. Thomas Warton, *History of English Poetry, from the Twelfth to the Close of the Sixteenth Century* (London, 1871), 4: 75.

34. This is the date of the first printed edition, but the 1502 edition suggests that the year of composition was closer to 1467: "for to satysfye vnto these clerkes and for the more parfectly to conferme that the whiche is wryten in englysshe as also for to eschewe and detraccion of lytell vnderstandynge of symple people I put in the heed of this boke in many passages these auctorytees

late fifteenth- and early sixteenth-century France, and equally popular in England in translation.[35] It is a vernacular pastoral manual intended to be read to and by laity (though not excluding a clerical audience),[36] which gathers the basic tenets of Christianity, thus serving a catechising purpose. It provides basic moral instruction, catering to its pastoral function and to potential interest among clerical readership. The text starts with a prologue followed by five parts: on baptism (including exorcism with the use of salt) and the twelve articles of faith, on the Ten Commandments, on the works of mercy, on confession, on the pains of hell and the joys of paradise.

The *Ordynarye* is thus akin to John Mirk's *Festial* (ca. 1400), or the 1486 *Doctrinal of sapience* in that, instead of repeating the content of such works as *The articles of oure faith* (1509) or even Caxton's *Royal book* (1485), which give detailed descriptions of the Seven Deadly Sins or the gifts of the Holy Ghost, it repeats only selected aspects of doctrine. It is more interested in translating these tenets into practice, making them as useful as the commandments of the Church in leading to thoughtful reflection on the nature and matter of the surrounding world. In other words, this is a manual for meditation, encouraging interest and curiosity about the world and an honest examination of one's gifts and sins, and useful also to the clergy who could have used it as a source for sermons. The underlying characteristic of the *Ordynarye* is its focus on the mind (including understanding and will) as the ultimate judge of right and wrong, the most cherished gift of God and thus a "gift" the abuse of which should be mercilessly punished by eternal suffering in hell. As the text suggests, the greater the gift, the greater the "treason" of its abuse, and the greater the punishment ought to be for such abuse. From establishing the mind as the distinguishing feature of human beings that truly makes them in the likeness of God, the text goes on to categorize all matter and spirit in the world accordingly, and ventures to explain various personalities, or gifts, of various people: the gifts of the Holy Ghost. However, the focus is here on virtue and the ability to fight the Devil rather than on "humours," which we will see in later, early modern texts.

The Touchstone of complexions, a work originally in Latin by the Dutch physician Levinus Lemnius, and translated into English by Thomas Newton, an Anglican clergy-

---

conuocacions and allegacions the whiche be made in latyn excepte the texte of the vowe of baptyme the whiche I haue wyll to put worde by worde in this wrytynge for to shewe the charyte ruyne of crysten people in all estates in the whiche they lyuen at this daye. That is to wyte the .xiiij. daye of January the yere of our lorde. M. CCCC. lxvij. after the Natyuyte of our lorde Jhesu cryste after dyuers cronycles and maner of nombre the yeres. In the whiche yere and daye this present boke hath be fyrst begonne to be wryten" (*Ordynarye of crysten men*, 1502, Prologue, n. pag.).

35. Ashley Null, *Thomas Cranmer's Doctrine of Repentance: Renewing the Power to Love* (Oxford), 2000, 33.

36. Duffy, *Stripping of the Altars*, 56.

man (with three English editions, in 1576, 1581, and 1633), is an example of such a text. It is a work focused on the theory of the humours and on the Galenic theory of psychological constitution.[37] While in itself a medical work and thus, at first glance, perhaps offering little in common with the *Ordynarye*, Lemnius' work is, in fact, also a moral text, which is perhaps why an Anglican minister decided to translate it into English.[38] It is representative of "moral science," that is, a genre of texts in which theological and devotional vocabulary and ideas mix with scientific reasoning and subject matter, represented, for instance, by the 1608 anonymous *Two guides to a good life. The anathomy of sinne. And the genealogie of vertue*. In Lemnius' work, the "ideal" complexion is that of exemplary morality, although Lemnius is clear in stating that the ideal, embodied by Christ only, is not attainable by human beings, but needs nevertheless to be sought. He further recommends temperance (a virtue) as the most desired trait of a moral human being, as temperance allows the mind to fully appreciate God's gifts, as opposed to a "distemperate" personality that rejects divine magnanimity; to Lemnius, similar to the *Ordynarye*, this indicates damnable ingratitude, such as leads to unhappiness and melancholy, which could easily become vices.[39]

The Touchstone of complexions is also a work on the nature of matter and the human mind, but in its understanding of nature, it cautions its readers not to stop at admiring nature only, but to remember that all things, nature as much as the human mind, come from God the Creator, and are to be treated with the reverence due to Him who made them be. In his understanding of disease, Lemnius concludes that while no disease could be attributed to evil spirits alone, as sickness is caused by imbalance in the humours or other physiological reasons, yet evil spirits did participate in disease by aggravating the sick person's condition,[40] thus aligning his understanding of the interconnectedness of the mind and the body with the spiritual world of God and the Devil. This immensely rich work's focus is, ultimately, the health of the mind, and in the excerpt below, it first encour-

37. See also the description of the 1576 edition of this work in *The Memory Arts in Renaissance England, A Critical Anthology*, ed. William E. Engel, Rory Loughnane, and Grant Williams (Cambridge, 2016), 156–157, for more on the general contents of the text.

38. Physicians in both pre- and post-Reformation England were often divided into physicians of the body and of the soul (doctors and ministers). Newton also translated other works by Lemnius, including another medical-moral text, *An herbal for the Bible, containing a plaine and familiar exposition of such similitudes, parables, and metaphors, both in the olde Testamente and the newe* (1587).

39. See Stephanie Shirilan, *Robert Burton and the Transformative Powers of Melancholy* (Farnham, Surrey; Burlington, VT, 2015), 89–90, for more on Lemnius' moral thought and its congruence, in translation, to the Church of England's *Thirty-Nine Articles* (1563).

40. David B. Ruderman, *Kabbalah, Magic, and Science: The Cultural Universe of a Sixteenth-century Jewish Physician* (Cambridge, 1988), 51.

ages its readers to examine their own minds in order to identify the kind of "spirit" that governs their mind, so that they can identify their propensity both to certain vices and virtues, and so that they are able to better govern their behaviour. In other words, *The Touchstone of complexions* describes human nature as related to the spirit inseparably tied to nature and God, with the mind as a scale on which good and bad judgement, and virtues and vices, are weighed according to the mind's predispositions, gifts, and its capacity to make use of reason. In that, the text mixes moral instruction with medical knowledge, and develops topics that seem to be of similar interest to Chertsey's translation, but does not mention punishment for the abuse of "gifts," which occupies a significant part of Chertsey's work.

25a *Here foloweth a notable treatyse and full necessary to an crysten men for to knowe and it is named the Ordynarye of crystyanyte or of crysten men*, trans. Andrew Chertsey, 1502; unnumbered pages. *STC* 5198. **Source** *EEBO*: Cambridge University Library (Sel. 5.47).

[Part I] Here foloweth euery artycle in partyculer and of the werke for to answere ...

... Here foloweth the .viij. artycle.

Credo in spiritum sanctum. That is to saye I byleue in the holy goost. ... Also euery thynge corpprall hath thre thynges, that is the length, the largenes, and the depnes. Also in all the worlde there is but thre maner thynges. The fyrst ben spirytuell all oonly, that is nature angelyke. The seconde ben corporell all oonly, as the foure elementes. The thyrde ben thynges spirytuall and corporall togyder, that is man and woman. Also in the soule the whiche is vnto the ymage of the blessyd trynyte hath thre myghtes. That is to knowe, mynde, vnderstandynge, and wyll, and is not but one soule in the trynyte and the trynyte in vnyte. I byleue than euery crysten man the persone of the holy goost to be one dyuynyte, one puyssaunce, one maieste, with these persones of the fader, and of the sone, and that that make the one of these thre persones as in regarde of the creacyon and of the gouernynge of all the worlde, and to glorifye the good and to dampne the euyll, is made of all these thre without dyfference. The werke of this artycle as vnto the moralyte is for to meruayll. For as sayth saynt Poule, they in whome the holy goost enhabyted by grace, habunden in dyuers gyftes. Some haue grace to speke well and wysely, some other haue vnderstandynge and knowlege of many thynges that man may not knowe but by the gyfte of the holy goost and of prophecye. Some other do miracles, some other suche merytes and vertues by humylyte, charyte, and mercy in the vertue of the holy goost the whiche conuerted, moued, and teched, and enbrached in loue these humayne bodyes the whiche dyspose them to receyue it, and them gyued spirytuall lyf by the whiche they profyte in good werkes; they fyght, and resyste the worlde and the deuyll and vnto theyr inclynacyons sensualles. ...

Here foloweth the fyfth and finall partie of this boke in the whiche is made mencyon of the paynes of helle and of the Joyes of paradyse and fyrste of the paynes of helle

... *Here foloweth the chapytre of the causes and reasons wherfore the paynes of helle sholde be eternall.*
Notwithstondynge that some thynge hath ben touched of the eternyte of paynes and tormentes of them reproued yet for the more greater admyracyon and also for to mete with folysshe sentences and oppynyons that the deuyll soweth amonge the hertes of many worldly people blynded and dowed in theyr synnes. Here folowen many causes and reasons by the whiche it is euydently shewed that the sayd paynes ought to be eternalles without euer there to haue releasynge, and pryncypally for thre reasons generalles. The fyrste is vnto the regarde of that condycyon of mortall synne. The seconde vnto the regarde of the creatour the whiche is gloryous and eternall. The thyrde is the consyderacyon of the vnyuersall worlde.

As vnto the fyrste that is of the consyderacyon of synne it is to vnderstonde that for four reasons Justyce dyuyne requyreth that synne be punysshed in eternyte. The fyrste is for that that after all Jugement of reason the offence of synne ought to be weyed and punysshed after the dygnyte, grete, lytell, or meane of hym the whiche is offended; for none ne may ymagen that it were no grete offence to stryke vniustely a bysshop than a symple chapelayne or that souerayn bysshop that is the pope than another man of the chirche in lesse dygnyte. Now is it soo that by euery synne mortall god is offended soueraynly and as moche greuously as his maieste is dygne and infynyte. By the whiche it foloweth that Justyce requyreth payne who answereth, and by the consequent infynyte for euery mortall synne. The seconde reason is for as moche that by mortall synne euery creature is depryued from welth eternall the whiche is god and by suche wyse he hym submytteth vnto his oposyte that is dampnacyon eternall. The thyrde reason is for asmoche that mortall synne depryueth the creature from welth paste, present, and to come. The welth paste that is the passyon of the blyssed Jhesu cryste without the whiche it were vnpossyble vnto all the worlde to mowe euade the bondes of the deuyll and euer more by mortall synne a man hym depryueth from suche benefyce. The good present that is the meryte of holy chirche from the whiche the synner beynge as a synner is depryued and seueryd. The goodes to come that ben the goodes of glorye the whiche by good Justyce sholde not be gyuen in ony wyse vnto those the whiche ben enemyes and aduersaryes vnto the creatoure as ben all those the whiche fynally abyden in mortall synne. The fourth reason is for asmoche that mortall synne of his propre condycyon destroyeth all the good dedes of the creature the whiche he commytted for euery thynge destroyeth his contrary in as moche as is in hym, as it appereth of fyre and of water, of lyght, and of derkenes, and so of other thynges contraryes. Now is it ynough certayne that there is nothynge contraryous vnto the wyll dyuyne but oonly synne, and by the consequent synne destroyeth and putteth vnto nought as moche as is in hym the wyll dyuyne and so putteth all that blyssed Trynyte vnto nothynge and in suche wyse he destroyeth all the worlde as well the holy men and women of paradyse as also all these other creatures; for it is Impossyble that creature may be to haue enduryd but in that that god hym holdeth and conserueth and yf god be dystroyed by synne the whiche aloonly vnto hym is contrary euery creature is deed and destroyed in the deth of the creatour. But it is a thynge impossyble that god may not be, or to dye, by the whiche it foloweth and behoueth that synne be punysshed after the puyssaunce, sapyence, and eternyte of his contrary, that is god, and yf it were not done there sholde be defaute of Justyce, and yf Justyce dyuyne and infynyte defayle god shold defayle. Also the synner the whiche dyeth in mortall synne synneth in eternyte, for yf he alwayes hadde lyued alwayes he hadde synned. And in as moche as that he endureth in synne he oughte to endure punycyon. Also yf the synne the whiche euer endureth were not for euer punysshed, the Justyce penytyue sholde be to moche vnlawfully dyuynysshed and all trouth dyuyne defraudyd ye anoyntyd the whiche ben thynges to moche impossybles. Also as moche grete is the transgressyon as that grete oblygacyon. Now is it trouth that euery creature is bounde to serue and honoure his creatour the whiche thynge he may not do the whiche is in dedely synne, but more sooner doth the contrary that is to knowe to blaspheme and to dyshonoure god. By the whiche he is the transgressour of the lawe dyuyne and of nature the whiche ben lawes eternal les. By the whiche it foloweth that suche transgressyon ought to be punysshed eternally.

As vnto the seconde poynt the whiche is in the comparyson of the synne and of the creature agayne whome it is done, it is to vnderstonde that for foure reasons he ought to be punysshed eternally. The fyrste is for the grace that god hath done vnto the creature humayne. For of as moche as the grace or the benefyce done vnto ony is grete, of as moche is greter the offence, or the forfayte of hym the whiche is redeuable or shall yelde accompte before hym whome he ought to serue and honoure. As for an example: The kynge gyueth a thousande pounde of rente vnto one knyght and vnto another an hundreth thousands pounde, both tweyne offende and commytte treason agayne the kynge. Than it shall be Jugyd that the treason of hym the whiche hadde an hundreth thousande pounde is more greuous thanne is that of hym the whiche hadde not but aloonly a thousande pounde and therfore for as moche that an hundreth thousande pounde is more greater thynge thenne a thousande pounde aloonly. And vnto the purpose, god vnto vs hath gyuen the body and the soule the whiche ben also as the two knyghtes, vnto the body he hath gyuen sight, tastynge, smellynge, and herynge and so of other gyftes corporalles, but vnto the soule he hath gyuen vnderstondynge mynde, and in creatynge her vnto his ymage and vnto his semblaunce in gyuynge vnto her hym, the whiche is the good and tresour infynyte, and not withstondynge that she it forfayteth and commytteth treason, as many tymes and as often as whan she her consenteth vnto dedely synne. For she withdraweth the honoure, the obedience, and the glory that she oweth vnto her creatoure by the whiche it behoueth to saye that as is moch grete the offence as was grete the benefice, and for as moche that he was infynyte also is the transgressyon and punycyon infynyte, by so ryght Justyce that ony creature nedeth to doubte. …

25b [Levinus Lemnius,] *The touchstone of complexions: expedient and profitable for all such as bee desirous and carefull of their bodily health: containing most ready tokens, whereby every one may perfectly try, and thorowly know, as well the exact state, habit, disposition, and constitution of his body outwardl: as also the inclinations, affections, motions and desires of his minde inwardly. Written in Latine by Levine Lemnie, and now Englished by T.N.*, trans. Thomas Newton, 1633, pp. 21–25.[41] *STC* 15458. **Source** Centre for Reformation and Renaissance Studies Rare Book Library, University of Toronto (R128.6 .L45 1633).

Of the nature and differences of spirits, what they worke in mans body, and what affections they cause. The Second Chapter.

… But to know how to qualifie, bridle, and subdue those great affections and motions of the minde that are engendred by great heat of the spirits, I judge it not amisse for euery man to search out by what kinde of spirit he is most led, to what

41. Apart from the Biblical citation below, marginal notes in this text were not included in the transcription.

motions in dealings hee findeth himselfe most endangered, how fervent or how remisse the agitacions of his minde be.

For by this meanes may those things that consist without mediocrity be reduced and brought to temperatenesse and moderation. Now, this diversity of spirits, out of which springeth such and so great diversities of natures and maners, conceive and take sundry alterations at the humours. Thus the soule, although it be singular, and as *Cicero* termeth it *Vnigena*, yet bringeth forth sundry and manifold actions, according to the nature of the spirits, and differences of the instruments. Hence commeth such and so great variety and diversity in the thoughts, desiers, affections, actions, and perturbations in men's mindes, insomuch that reason and discretion without a speciall assistance of heavenly grace can scarcely tame and represse the same.

For when the naturall and vitall faculty together wyth the naturall and inward spirits waxe somewhat strong, and partly by abundaunce, partly by the quality of meat and nourishment, have attained strength and power, they reject and cast away the bridle of reason, and draw the spirit animal also (for they be all derived out of one fountaine) into their faction and disordered rebellion. Wherby it hapneth that when any lewde device or wilfull thought ariseth in the minde of man, he is prone enough to run into dissolute riot, libidinous lust, filthy and shamefull pleasures; and if he fortune to espy any pretty Wench or beautifull Damsell that liketh his fantasie, his minde is straightwaies enflamed and set on fire with unlawfull desire of her person, for the satisfying of his unbridled concupiscence; and by reason of the store of humours and concourse of spirits resorting thither from every part of his body, his privities undecently swel, and his member of generation becometh stiffe; so that many times it hapneth, man's minde to be overcome and drowned in fleshly concupiscence, unlesse by the speciall grace of Almighty God, and by meditating upon the wholsome Precepts expressed in his sacred Word, hee stoutly withstand the summons of such naughty desires. This promptnesse and inclination to evill is naturally ingrafted in man. *The imaginations and thoughts of mans heart (saith Moses) are onely evill and prone to wickednesse, even from their youth and first beginnings* [Gen. 6 and 8]. But the blessed and most comfortable comming of Christ tooke away this blemish, who by his precious death and glorious resurrection abolished the calamity, and cancelled the bonds of that misery, whereto *Adam's* transgression had brought us.

The consideration wherof ought in the mindes of all men to worke thus much, that because their spirits are provokers and prickers forward both to vices and vertues, every one should with more carefull consideracion and heed attend and looke to conserve and governe them orderly.

And although the Animall Spirit be more excellent then the other, and before the rest in dignity, yet in order is it the later. For out of the naturall, which resembleth vapour and proceedeth by vertue of the liver, from blood, it produceth the vitall which is of Aery nature, and ministreth unto it nourishment; And the vitall doth procreate the Animall, which by reason of his thinnesse and subtility is airy. For it being laboured, prepared and made in the contexed net, cells, and cornery ventricles of the braine, is greatly with sweet smells nourished, and with fragrant things refreshed and cherished. From it is fetched and derived all the power and faculty which the soule hath, and from it doe all actions issue and proceed, making the same appliable to all functions. Well worthy therefore is this animal spirit deemed the proper instrument of the soule to all the sences, for maintenance of moving and nimblenesse, and for preservation of the strength, and firmity of Muscles and Sinewes: for it transporteth and diffuseth his vertues and powers (as the worke-masters of actions) into the Sinewes that have the power of feeling and moving.

All the instruments therfore of the Senses, indued with this power and vertue of the Spirit animall attaine thereby stablenesse, for the atchievement of their functions and charges: as for example, If the wayes and passages whereby this spirit ought to goe and have passage, be stopped and affected, the power of moving and feeling is taken away, as we evidently note and see to happen in the Apoplexie, Palsey, Tetanus, and many diseases moe. And this spirit animall is conveighed into the Sinewes, even like the beames of the Sunne thorow a cleare shining glasse. And even as a fiery heat pearceth and entreth into a glowing hot iron that is very hard, insomuch that the same therewith becommeth soft and tractable; so doth the spirit that is finest and thinnest slylie slide into the Sinewes. All things therefore that need feeling, moving, and agility, require the force, ayde, and power of the spirit animall. As those that by nourishment are to be maintained, continued, and kept, require the naturall and vitall faculties and spirits. He therefore that would preserve his spirits undemnified, and them make most sincere and perfect, must endeuour at any hand to keepe his body in right good plight and order. ...

Health

PREVENTING DISEASE

26a [John of Burgundy,] *In this tretyse that is cleped Gouernayle of helthe* (1490?).
26b Humphrey Brooke, *YTIEINH [HYGIEINE]. Or A conservatory of health* (1650).

Introduction The origin of the *Gouernayle of helthe* is unknown, though the most popular and most comprehensive edition of this text to date, by William Blades (1858), suggests that it is a translation of an original first composed in Latin in the fourteenth century (possibly 1350)[1] and, relying on one of its hundred manuscript copies,[2] gives Joannes de Burgundia[3] as the author. Caxton's printed edition of the *Gouernayle*, according to Blades, contains only a part of the original text, which in Latin was much longer than in its English translation, and omits a detailed study of herbs.[4] The text's English translation was probably finished in the early fifteenth century, and circulated in manuscript version until Caxton printed it in 1490 or 1491. Wynkyn de Worde reprinted it in exactly the same form as the 1490/1491 edition in 1506. Both editions, along with, in all likelihood, the manuscript Caxton's volume originally came from, have a small poetic treatise, *Medicina stomaci*, added to their final pages; this text was attributed to John Lydgate, though according to William Blades his authorship is unlikely.[5] Originally two

1. Joseph Patrick Byrne, *Daily Life During the Black Death* (Westport, CT, 2006), 212.
2. Joseph Patrick Byrne, *Encyclopedia of the Black Death* (Santa Barbara, CA, 2012), 197.
3. Also known as John of Burgundy, John of Bordeaux, John de la Barbe, and even John Mandeville. There were no printed editions of this text, but there were multiple translations. Thomas Moulton's adaptation of this text became immensely popular in the sixteenth century, replacing the John of Burgundy text extant in many manuscripts with its own multiple printed editions (George R. Keiser, "Two Medieval Plague Treatises and Their Afterlife in Early Modern England," *Journal of the History of Medicine and Allied Sciences* 58.3 [2003]: 292–324, at 299, 310).
4. William Blades, *The Gouernayle of Helthe: With The Medecyne of ye Stomacke, Reprinted from Caxton's edition (circa m. cccc. xci.) With Introductory Remarks and Notes, By William Blades* (London, 1858), 12–28.
5. See Blades, *The Gouernayle of Helthe*, for more on this subject.

separate works, the *Gouernale* and the *Medicina stomaci* became one text for early modern audiences.

The main theme of this work is temperance, as it gives directions on how to lead a healthy life, with a healthy body and mind: the key is moderation in food and drink, exercise, virtuous sadness,[6] and understanding one's "humoral complexion" (which determined character) in order to follow a good and healthy diet. The work thus relies on standard Galenic medicine, and is considered the earliest printed book on medicine in England.[7] The excerpt below focuses on daily routines that are to aid in the maintenance of good health, including a fairly detailed description of daily exercise. The text, in other words, speaks on preventing disease by using physical countermeasures, but does not refrain from using the vocabulary of evil to describe illness, and its full title (in Caxton's version) invokes the aid of Christ for the successful maintenance of health. Christ as the physician of the soul was a common Christian motif throughout the Middle Ages and in the early modern period, and this metaphor was often extended to medical texts in which, while no religious agenda was intended, spiritual considerations and doctrines mixed with custom and scientific discourse ensured that all meditations on bodily health were, to a degree, anchored in religious vocabulary and doctrine.

The text by Humphrey Brooke is a good example of a text with a strong religious and medical background. Brooke was a physician and a radical non-conformist. His *Conservatory of health* is a late early modern health advice book, or a book on regimen, which like many of its kind promotes moderation in everything as the best way to maintain good health. Like many Protestant authors of this kind of text before him, Brooke makes little distinction between medical advice and moral instruction, especially in describing excess, such as drunkenness: to him, the causes for many afflictions are sins ("Every Vice hath its Sting"). In a way, then, Brooke's text goes further into the use of religious discourse when writing on health and medicine than the *Gouernayle,* though both share praise of temperance (or moderation, which Brooke describes more elaborately[8]) and exercise as sure ways of achieving and maintaining health. The *Conservatory of health* was written to remedy a perceived shortage of such texts, reaching out to a broad and non-specialized audi-

6. Echoing the *Dyetary of ghostly helth* (1510).

7. Blades, *The Gouernayle of Helthe,* 28. See the subsequent section of Blades' edition for a general description of "The Theory on which the Medical Precepts of the *Gouernayle* are founded," 22.

8. But not named: Brooke decided not to include a discussion of temperance as such, as it was, as he noted, already well described in two very popular medical works at the time, by Alvise Cornaro and Leonardo Lessius (see Tessa Storey, "English and Italian Health Advice: Protestant and Catholic Bodies," in *Conserving Health in Early Modern Culture: Bodies and Environments in Italy and England,* ed. Sandra Cavallo and Tessa Storey [Manchester, 2017], 210–234, at 223–224).

ence rather than to medical doctors, but it witnessed a decline of popularity of the health advice genre in England.[9] Both texts, then, are medical works whose central elements are woven around the discourse of virtues, and both consider keeping healthy in body as directly related to keeping healthy spiritually.

26a [John of Burgundy,] *In this tretyse that is cleped Gouernayle of helthe: what is to be sayd wyth crystis helpe of some thynges that longen to bodily helthe*, Westminster, 1490 (?); unnumbered pages. *STC* 12138. **Source** *EEBO*: Bodleian Library, Oxford (01642346).

In this tretyse that is cleped Gouernayle of helthe: What is to be sayd wyth crystis helpe of some thynges that longen to bodily helthe hadde and to be kept, or to bodily helthe lost and to be recouered and is departed in viij. Chapytures, that is to saye: In the fyrste chapytre of the profytte of goode Gouernayle of helth, In the ij. chapytre what is first on morow to be donn; In the iij. chapitre of bodyly excersyce that is to saye, besynes and his profyte; In the fourth chapytre of spyces of excersice; In the fyfthe chapiytre how a man holde haue hym in mete, in etyng his metes. In the vj. chapitre how a man shold haue hym in drynkyng of his drynkes; In the vij. chapytre what sholde be done after mete; In the viij chapytre of the noyse of euyll gouernaunce.

It nedyth hym that woll haue longe lyff to knowe the crafte of holsome gouerneyle, And so for to kepe contynuelly the helthe of his body, for els he maye not com to his naturell ende, but he shall dye or his kyndeli tyme come; and therfore thus sayeth Galyen the connynge: He, sayth, of holsome gouernaunce is meruelous, for it maketh a man to lyue tylle he be olde, And wythoute sikenes in to the laste of his elde and age. Therfore, the same Galyen after that he knewe the crafte of holsome gouernaumce came neuer into no sikenese; but seelde that was in to a fymeram, that is to saye a sharpe feuer. And that was for trauayll in vysityng of his frendys a boute the comyn profyte. For thus he sayth: I take god to recorde and his angels assygned to kepe me that who that wylfully and besily wyl studye in the treatyse of holsom gouernaunce and woll kepe alhole the doctryne therof, he shal neuer dye but on and vpon kyndly deth, whiche deth is swete and softe wythoute grete payn; as the same Galyen wytnesseth in the dyfference of feuerys.[10] But vnderstonde that holsome gouernaunce may no man duely kepe that most nedys be occupyed, wyl hym or nyl hym, and may not

9. Ken Albala, *Eating Right in the Renaissance* (Los Angeles, 2002), 48.

10. A reference to a work by Galen, *De differentiis febrium*. I am grateful to Winston Black for drawing my attention to this.

when hym nedeth leue of, for thy it nedeth hym that he haue that nedeth hym to his lyf wythoute trauayle and pencyfull, and in alle thyngys that he be of fre condycyon.

Ferthermore, it is to wete that viij. thynges at the leste ben nedefull in holsome gouernayle, of whiche the fyrste is a dyscrete chors of thoo thynges that shall be eten or dronken. The seconde is wylfull bodyli exersice to fore mete and that tyl the swetyng begynne, or namely tyll his wynde chaunge fro sloughe to swyftnes. The thirde is well profytable and wel nedeful that all that shall be etyn be wele and smale chewed. The fourth is that thou ete while thou hast talent to ete; the v. is that thou slepe on morow tyl thou wake be thyne owne wyll. For as arystotle sayth, not only in metys and drynkys be we noryshed and fostred, but also in slepe. The vj. is that thou take no mete and drynk in sorow ne in care but in Joye as moche as thou maye. The vij. is that thou haue ne holde no colde in wynter ne in somer after bloodletynge. The viij. is that thou vse saffron in thy mete, for it quycneth kyndely hete and comforteth thy dygestyon, and taryeth thyne elde or age, and bryngeth in gladness, and letteth thyne humors fro rotynge and driynge.

It is in storyes of our elders that on a tyme a myghty kyng brought togyder thre of the best leches that myght be, of Inde, of Mede, and of Grece, and he commaunded hem that eche of theym sholde studye to assygne the beste medycyne, whiche yf a man wolde vse sholde profyte hym to helpe of bodye and hym sholde nede none other medycyn. Truly, the leche of Grece assygned and sayd that euery daye a man to take twys his mouthe full of hote water sholde make a man soo hole that hym sholde nede none other medycyn; and the leche of Mede assygned and sayd that it sholde profyte moche euery daye fastynge to tak gromel seyd. And I saye, sayd arystotle, that he that that slepeth so moche that he haue noo heuynes in his wombe of mete that he tok to fore hym dare not drede of any grete sikenes ne of the goute. Also who that eteth euery daye erly vij. dragmes that is to saye xxj. peny weyght of swete reisyns he dare not drede of flewmy sikenes, and his mynde shalbe amended and his vnderstondyng shall be clere, and who that vseth it in tyme accordynge to his complexion maye be sure and drede not of the Feuer quarteyn. Also who that eteth nottes and fyges wyth a fewe leues of Yewe that daye shall no venym hym noye. It was axed of Galien what medicyn were meoste profytable, and he ansuerd: abstinence. And constantyne seyth in his book that hight vyatyk[11] that who so well kepe his contynuell helthe, kepe his stomak soo that when hym nede the mete leue it not ne take no mere therof than hym nedeth, and the same vnderstond of drynke, also in holsom gouernaunce

11. *Viaticum* of Constantinus Africanus. I am grateful to Winston Black for drawing my attention to this.

sle wrath, grete thought heuynes, angre, and suche other. For all ghostly accydentes that ys to saye sodeyn fallyng in to a mannys mynde outaken Ioye, alonly dryen, and that moysteth.

Netheles, some hetyn, as wrath, for thy wrath profyteth to flewmatyk men and hit harmeth coleryk men. Morouer, it ys to wete that in sente[12] season, that is to saye in veer[13] and in the begynnyng of somer, children ben wele atte ease after the liknes of tempred qualitees. But other ages ben wele at ease in contraryous tymes, as olde men in somer and yonge men in winter; also, in holsom gouernaunce kepe thys reule yf thou wolt be hoole and sounde: flee heuy charges, be not wooth,[14] soupe not to late, and fle vnder mele slepe, wake after mete, and eschew and spare stronge drynkes, and namely of wyne. Hold not thy pysse ne constrayn the not to siege; kepe well these thre thynges: Gladnes in mynde, traueyll in mesure, and reule of mete and drynke as moche as thou wold ete, boldly in wynter and in veer skarsly, and in somer mesure welthy metes and flee, nameli frutes of auguste; arystotle, wrytyng to gret Alexandre sayd, syth man is a brityl body, me semeth I shold wryte to the some profytable thynge of lechecrafte yf thou wolte, he sayd, besily behold thensample of holsom gouernaunce and lyue after thys precyous ordre of dyet, ye shall nede no leche, oute take accydentes of batayll and suche other.

What is fyrst on morow to be done.

After that a man hath wele and prafible[15] fulfylled his slepe, loke he ryse and cloth hym self wyth goode clothe, and swete yf he haue them, then he oweth to walk a lytil euenli to stretche oute his lymmes and kembe his hed, for whi kembyng draweth out the vapours the[16] comyn from the stomake to the hed in tyme of slepe. And therwyth loke that ye be besie to put oute the superfluytees of the body in siegyng, pyssyng, koughyng, and spyttyng. Then loke be wesshe his handes and his face, in somer wyth colde water, and in wynter wyth hoote water. Then loke he praye and preyse his lorde after the doctryne of his lawe, and vysite the pore in god. Then, yf it lyke hym, he sholde studye, or rede, dispute, or talke, and wyse mennys counceyl and seyeng besily here, and in mesure be mery and flee vtterly wrath and sorow in as moche as he maye, and vse hym selfe measur-

12. Probably transitory weather, change of seasons.

13. Spring: *MED* s.v. "vēr".

14. Risky, inviting danger: *MED* s.v. "wōth".

15. Profitably.

16. The text has a thorn with a superscript e, probably in error; "that" most likely was intended here.

able; trauayl, as walkyng, or ridyng, and in clene highe places fro myer and marrys, for this profyteth moche, for it breketh wynde in a manys body and strenghyth and lyghteth his lymmes and comforteth the heete of the stomak, and strengyth his ioyntes, and melteth euil humors. ...

The spyces of exercyse

Spyces of exercyse ben ther wel many, as ther be dyuerse statys of persones, some be stronge and some be feble, som ryche and some pore, some prelates and at the large, and some subgettes and enclosed. And somtime weder is fayr and clere, and somtyme not so, but derke and reyn. And therfor it nedeth to haue spyces of exercyse for whithe beste spyce, and the fyrste ys to walke to fore mete in hihe places and clene. Another spyce is to ryde, and that is for ryche men, but grete prelates moste haue other maners of exercise, for whithin chambre shall be a grete corde knytted in the ende and hanged vp, and take that corde wyth both handes and stonde vpryght soo that thou touche not the erche and stonde a goode, while thenne runne as moche as thou mayst heder and theder wyth that corde and otherwhile skyppe, and yf this please the not, bane a stone of xxx. li. weyghte or therabout, and yf thou wolt haue helthe therin ofte bere that ston fro that on side of that house to that other side, or a longe whyle holde vp that ston or thou let it doun or bere it a bonte thy necke or bytwene thy handes, and so of other maners tyl thou feynt, or thus holde a staffe in thy hand and lete a nother take hit from the yf he maye wyth euyn draughte, or thus close a peny in thyn hand and lete a nother take it yf he maye, or thus holde thy breth as longe as thou maist and thenne puffe it oute as hard as thou maist do. And this maner of exercyse is full profytable to put oute noyos superfluytees, for why many superfluytees in slepe ben wythholde. Therfore yf thou haue non other maner of exercyse holdyng of breth helpeth it moche. Yet ther ben other maners of exercyse for yonge men that ben lusty, as to renne, to wrestle, to lepe, to caste the stone and so of other playes, also tempred fleshly companyng wyth a yong broun woman is goode in winter, and wyth a yonge white woman ys goode in somer is also goode, and helpyng in gouernyng of helthe to body but not to soule, excepte to hem then that mowen haue it by goddes lawes so netheles, that thee be so moche tym bytwene that he fele hym selfe eased and lyghtened in his body, and that he ete the better and slepe thebetter. But therwyth vnderstonde that as moche as helpyth tempred companyenge, so moche noyeth dystempred companyeng, and namely to moche, for it coleth him, wasteth hym, and kelleth him. For why mannys kynde is made of the beste bloode and beste defyed, that hastely maye torne into mannys lymmes. And for whi whenne a man casteth oute that noble humors to moche he is hugely discolored, and his body moche febled, more then he lete foure sithes so moche bloode oute of his body; also who that moche deleth or companyeth fleshly wyth a woman lyghtly kacheth the palsey wyth more euyll.

26b Humphrey Brooke, *ΥΓΙΕΙΝΗ [HYGIEINE]. Or A conservatory of health. Comprized in a plain and practicall discourse upon the six particulars necessary to mans life, viz. 1. Aire. 2. Meat and drink. 3. Motion and rest. 4. Sleep and wakefulness. 5. The excrements. 6. The passions of the mind. With the discussion of divers questions pertinent thereunto. Compiled and published for the prevention of sickness, and prolongation of life. By H. Brooke. M.B.*, 1650, pp. 143–173.[17] *Wing*, 2nd ed. B4905. **Source** *EEBO*: British Library, London (E.1404[1]).

Of Motion and Rest.
The Commodities of Moderate Motion, or Exercise, are many; principally three.

1. *The Increase of Natural Heat and Spirit.*
2. *The Agility and Firmness of the Body.*
3. *An easy bearing of external accidents.*

To which may be added, *That it assists the Distribution of our Nourishment, and so augments our Growth, that it discusses Vapors and fuliginous excrements* by the Pores or Spiracles of the skin, *Facilitates the Birth, adds Color and Vivacity to the whole Body.*

The Discommodities of too much Rest and Sitting, are:

1. That it makes our Bodies loose and flabby, easily yielding to all external accidents; it begets Multiplication of Humors and excrements, and consequently that they are seldom well at ease, and void of Infirmities. This is especially the unhappiness of *Women* who, mostly leading *a Sedentary Life*, lose their Colours and the vivacity of their Countenances, and are thereby forced to use paintings, whence (being unskilfully administred) they contract Head-aches, pains and blackness in the Teeth, and derive many other Maladies both to themselves and their Posterities. Hence, it is that they are unavoidably in *Continual Physick*, have need of Issues and other artificial Helps, for the evacuation and exiccation of those Superfluous Moistures that might more safely, Naturally, and with infinite less trouble to them, be consumed by easy and constant Labor or Exercise; So that the Indigent People have this recompence to their Poverty that their necessitated Labors keeps them much in Health, and without the need, trouble, and charge of Physick.

17. Marginal notes on the original copy were not included in the transcription.

... When the Body is *very foul* and *replete* with *ill humors,* exercise must be forborn till it be conveniently *cleansed,* for that otherwise it will work and disperse them into the Habit of the Body it Self, and occasion thereby some long and hardly curable Disease. In this case 'tis best to avoid fool-hardiness and *venienti occurrere Morbo,* remember that to prevent is far easier then to Cure.

They that are Lean should exercise only *ad Ruborem,* till the Body and Spirits are gently heated, for that will help to *fatten* them. They that are fat may Exercise *ad Sudorem,* till they Sweat, and that will *extenuate* them.

Exercise is best *before Meals,* for it clears the Stomack and prepares the Appetite, but a little time must be allowed again to settle the body before we eat.

Too *soon after meals* 'tis very bad, for it subverts the Stomack and forces the Victuals thence raw and indigested, and so disperses it into the Veins and Habit of the Body, whereby putrid Feavours, Head-aches, Weakness of the Eyes, and a general Cacochymy[18] or depraved Constitution is engendred.

Avoid exercising in *damp and noysom places,* for that the Lungs being opened and Respiration encreased, much aire is drawn in and the brain thereby filled, and the Lungs corrupted. This Caution is to be observed by all, but especially by those that are *Pthisical and Rheumatick.*

Lastly, too Violent Exercise is very bad, for it too much dries the Body, it engenders the *Stone,* and *Gout,* especially towards old age, when it is discontinued. Let not therefore Pleasure and a too earnest Intention at our sports make us so much our own Enemies, as to convert that which ought to be used only to refresh the Mind, to Strengthen and keep healthfull the Body, into the means of its Infirmity, Sickness and decay, especially knowing that exercise is then only pleasant when the Body is fresh, Vigorous and very well able, and without toil and pain to undergo the same.

Besides that, too *constant a use and intention upon Sports* corrupts the Mind, and distracts it in the midst of all affairs and business and begets a Dotage thereupon, wherein there is not *true Pleasure* and *contentment,* but a *wearish and impotent giving up of the Spirits and Faculties thereunto;* a convenient *mixture of Labor and Exercise* is best, so as that the first do far exceed the last, and that the last be indeed but as a Refreshment and quickning of the Spirit and Body, for the better and more Pleasant undergoing of the first. Lastly, If it be too much or too violent, it is no friend to Prolongation of Life, for it over-heats the Spirits, and renders them easily evaporable. 2. It consumes too much the Moisture of the Body. 3. It wasts the inward Parts which delight most in, and are conserved best, by Rest. We

18. Depraved habit of the body.

see by this the inconveniences of Excess and Defect: *Via Media, via Tuta*; the middle way is best and wholsomest.

A usual error is *the drinking cold beere after Violent Exercise*, and in our Sweat, to which Heat and Thirst intises us; but, the effects are:

1. Damping and almost exstinguishing the small remainder of heat that is left in the inward parts.

2. Surfetting the Body by Mixing cold Drink with the fat, which is at that time melted and floating in the Body. Let that inconvenient custom be therefore carefully left. Another is to *Drink Sack* or *Strong-Water* when we have spent and wearied our selves with hard Labor or Exercise, which is done as for avoiding the former inconvenience, not seeing that thereby we incur another, which *is the over-heating and drying our bodies*, which were *too much heated and dryed before*. To avoid both, and to refresh the body withall, the best way is first to rest a while warm, if conveniently we may, but however to drink a good draught of Cawdle, Mace-Ale, Hot Beer and Sugar, or of some other Supping whose Warmth is not Scorching, but analogous to that of our Bodies, so will the Spirits soon settle and be refreshed, and the Limbs after rest be enabled with ease to undergo new Labor.

For the kinds of Labor some stir the whole *Body*, the best whereof are, *Dancing, Running, Leaping, Bowling, Walking. Tennis* is too Violent, and to be used only upon extraordinary occasions, with convenient Rubbings, Sweating in Bed, and other accommodations after it. *Fencing* hath too many inconveniences attending it, and is best to be learned as necessary for safeguard and Defence, and not used as a customary exercise. There are also Exercises *appropriated to certain parts*, as *lifting great Weights* and *the Pike* to the *Back and Loins. Riding* is availful for the *Stomack*, the *Kidnies* and *Hips. Navigation* for those that are *Pthisical, Ball* and *Bowls* for the *Reins*. The *Breast* and *Lungs* are opened and cleared by *Shooting, Hollowing, Singing, Sawing, Blowing the Horn, or Wind Instruments, Drawing a Rope too and again about a Post or Table, Swinging, Lifting the Poyse or Plummets on high, and letting them down again*. And last of all, the use of *Frications or Rubbings* which hath been much in use but is now grown obsolete, is very convenient for whatsoever part we please. *Gentle Rubbings*, with warm soft Cloths, softens the Parts, attenuates the Humors, and opens the Pores. But, *Strong Rubbings*, with hot and course Cloths used long do Dry and Harden. The Ancients had two *kinds of Frications*, the one which they called *Praeparatorium*, which they used *before Exercise*, to render the Limbs agile and apt to Motion, the other *Recreatorium*, which was used *after Exercise*, and was performed with *sweet* and *Mollifying Oyles*, to Moysten and refresh the Body dryed and wasted with toil.

Nature's great Explorator, in his Centuries, much commends the use of *Frictions* as a *Furtherance* of *Nourishment* and *Augmentation*; he instances in *Horses,* whom for that end we constantly *Rub.* His reasons are for that it draws a great quantity of Spirits and blood to the Parts (*it ought not therefore to be used upon a full Stomack*), and again because it relaxes the Pores, and so makes passage for the Aliment, and dissipates the excrementitious Moistures. He *prefers it before Exercise,* for *Impinguation* or *Fatning* the Body, because in *Frictions* the *outward* parts only are moved, and the *inward* at Rest. Hence, saies he, Gally slaves are Fat and Fleshy, because they stir the Limbs more, and the Inward parts less.

I shall not say more hereof, but only commend its use to good Women that they *gently, and by a warm fire,* either themselves, their Maids, or Nurses, *every night rub the Sides, Back, Shoulders and Hips of their Children,* as very *necessary to prevent obstructions and the Rickets,* and to *further their growth and agility, and also to keep streight and strong the Limbs of their Children.*

27a *The grete herball* (1526). **27b** Thomas Cogan, *The haven of health* (1636).

Introduction *The grete herball* is a printed version of an English translation of a French rendering of Matthaeus Platearius's *Circa instans* (*Circa instans negotium in simplicibus medicinis*), dating back to the middle of the twelfth century.[19] *Circa instans,* as its name suggests, is concerned with "simple" medicines that contain only one active ingredient rather than a combination of components; the text contains descriptions of over 270 of such "simples," considered effective and practical.[20] It was translated into a number of vernacular languages, with various additions and compilation variations with other texts, amounting to as many as two hundred manuscript versions.[21] It was immensely popular throughout the Middle Ages and the early modern period, with its popularity waning only during the Augustan Age.[22] A version of the French translation, *Livre des*

19. Tony Hunt, *Popular Medicine in Thirteenth-Century England: Introduction and Texts* (Woodbridge, Suffolk, 1990), 15. Frank J. Anderson, in his *An Illustrated History of the Herbals* (New York, 1912), at 98, suggests that the probable date of composition is between 1130 and 1150.

20. Jean A. Givens, "Reading and Writing the Illustrated *Tractatus de herbis,* 1280–1526," in *Visualizing Medieval Medicine and Natural History, 1200–1550,* ed. Jean Ann Givens, Karen Reeds, and Alain Touwaide (Aldershot, Hampshire; Burlington, VT, 2006), 115–146, at 118.

21. Hunt, *Popular Medicine,* 15.

22. George R. Keiser, "Vernacular Herbals: A Growth Industry in Late Medieval England," in *Design and Distribution of Late Medieval Manuscripts in England,* ed. Margaret Connolly and Linne R. Mooney (York, 2008), 292–308, at 303.

simples médecines,[23] was printed in England under the title *Arbolayre* around 1485 or 1486. Later French editions of *Circa Instans* were titled *Le grand herbier* (ca. 1498), and it is *Le grant herbier* that the *Grete herball* is a direct translation of, although it was also influenced by the German *Gard der gesundheit* and the 1485 *Hortus sanitatis,*[24] including its woodcuts.[25]

The *Grete herball* was the first illustrated herbal in English, and went through at least five printed editions between 1526 and 1561. Its chapters are organized thematically, according to the names of plants and substances, as well as a separate list of illnesses to which cures could be found in the text, with numbers assigned to each chapter and an index to facilitate finding relevant information; the English translation expanded that list of entries to over four hundred (including plants native to England). Just as the original *Circa instans* and its earlier vernacular versions from which the *Grete herball* was derived, it is interested in the properties and medicinal uses of plants and substances much more than in their systematic description. It gathers practical knowledge (such as what a given plant looks like, where to find it, but primarily how to use it and for what) intended for use by non-Latinate audiences and practitioners. Religious undertones in the text, such as references to God's law or every person's hour of death appointed by God, are slight, but present.

Thomas Cogan was a conformist Protestant supportive of the establishment and the Privy Council's policies.[26] *The haven of health* (orig. published 1584) was "one of the most popular health manuals in early modern England."[27] Like the *Grete herbal,* the *Haven of health* was intended for practical use. It went through nine editions in the sixteenth and seventeenth centuries, and is focused almost exclusively, as its "To the Reader" suggests, on "the dyet of our English nation."[28] Cogan was an educated and practicing physician, and later also an educator, as master of the Manchester grammar school;[29] he authored medical as well as devotional texts (such as the *The well of wisedome,* 1577).

23. There were multiple versions of the French translation (Givens, "Reading and Writing," 136).

24. Which was translated into English in 1597.

25. Stanley H. Johnston, Jr, *The Cleveland Herbal, Botanical, and Horticultural Collections* (Kent, OH, 1992), 33.

26. Margaret Healy, *Fictions of Disease in Early Modern England: Bodies, Plagues and Politics* (New York, 2001), 54.

27. Stephen Pender, "Between Medicine and Rhetoric," in *Rhetoric and Medicine in Early Modern Europe,* ed. Stephen Pender and Nancy Struever (New York, 2012), 37–61, at 54.

28. Thomas Cogan, *The haven of health,* "To the Reader," n. pag.

29. Anon., revised by Rachel E. Davies, "Cogan, Thomas (c. 1545–1607), physician," in *Oxford Dictionary of National Biography* online (Oxford, 2004), https://doi.org/10.1093/ref:odnb/5812.

Cogan placed emphasis on the virtues of labour and exercise, believing that the body needs physical exercise and the mind, which is a part of the soul, mental exercise (study), but his work was primarily concerned with a healthy diet as, he affirmed, it is better to prevent disease than to cure it. Cogan's ideas on healthy living, while obviously founded on his medical training, are pervaded with religious thought, making the text a manual for an "essential Protestant regimen" relying on Scripture, philosophy, common sense, and other medical texts as sources.[30] Cogan admitted at the end of "To the Reader" that he relied most heavily on two sources: Thomas Elyot's *Castel of helth* (1536) and on what he calls *Schola Salerni*: "I confesse that I have taken *Verbatim* out of others wher it served for my purpose, and especially out of *Schola Salerni*" imploring his readers that "If they finde whole sentences taken out of Master *Eliot* his Castle of Health, or out of *Schola Salerni*, or any other author whatsoever, that they will not condemne me of vaine glory."[31] The *Schola Salerni* refers to the Schola Medica Salernitana, that is the works of medical authors from a centre of medicine in southern Italy (Salerno and Montecassino)[32] founded in the ninth century, that was the home of Matthaeus Platearius, the author of *Circa Instans*, as well as, possibly,[33] to the anonymous author of the *Regimen sanitatis Salernitanum* (dated to the twelfth or thirteenth century). The *Regimen* is a verse medical advisory (or regimen of health) concerned with daily practices to maintain health, including a good diet, which was expanded in the fourteenth and fifteenth centuries[34] to create a multi-version compendium, before one of its renderings was translated into English by Thomas Paynell and printed in 1528. This 1528 book is most likely the source Cogan referred to as the *Schola Salerni*, as there were at least seven editions of this text before he wrote his *Haven*, but it is also possible that he read one of the versions of the translations of *Circa instans* (especially as he makes references to a "*Matthiolus*"[35]).

30. Healy, *Fictions of Disease*, 2.

31. Cogan, *The haven of health*, "To the Reader," n. pag.

32. See Paul Oskar Kristeller, "The School of Salerno: Its Development and its Contribution to the History of Learning", *Bulletin of the History of Medicine* 17.2 (1945): 138–194; and *Practical Medicine from Salerno to the Black Death*, ed. Luis Garcia-Ballester, et al. (Cambridge, 1994), 1–30, for more on this subject.

33. See *The School of Salernum. Regimen Sanitatis Salernitanum. The English Version by Sir John Harington. History of the School of Salernum by Francis R. Packard, M.D., and a Note on the Prehistory of the Regimen Sanitatis by Fielding H. Garrison, M.D.* (New York, 1920), 53–67, for a short discussion of the potential origins of this text.

34. Melitta Weiss-Adamson, "Regimen Sanitatis," in *Medieval Science, Technology, and Medicine: An Encyclopedia*, ed. Thomas Glick, Steven J. Livesey, and Faith Wallis (New York, 2005), 438.

35. For instance, "And touching the choice of Wheat, which is best to make bread withall, *Matthiolus* perfectly describeth [*Lib.* 2. *Dios.* 1. *cap* 78.] *Triticum ex quo omnium optimus fit panis,*

It is thus likely that both the *Grete herball* and *The haven of health* are related to the same source, although the *Grete herbal* much more directly than Cogan's text. The relation of Cogan's work to the *Grete herball* indicates a progression of religious and moralistic interest even from texts that did not originally have a straightforwardly religious agenda. The excerpts from *The haven of health* below focus on descriptions of the properties of plants, substances, and prescriptions for various diseases, but the whole of Cogan's work "is characterized ... by constant moral and religious exhortation and a rigorous concern to illustrate medical maxims through scriptural texts."[36] Both works, then, are related to the same source, and both display mixing of religious and medical language, as well as concepts of human health and the properties of nature. Due to the shared source of both texts, albeit mediated by various versions of adaptations and translations, these excerpts illustrate the progression of aspects of medical thought between late medieval and seventeenth-century England.

27a *The grete herball whiche geueth parfyt knowlege and vnderstandyng of all maner of herbes and there gracyous vertues whiche god hath ordeyned for our prosperous welfare and helth, for they hele and cure all maner of dyseases and sekenesses that fall or mysfortune to all maner of creatoures of god created, practysed by many expert and wyse maysters, as Auicenna and other. &c. Also it geueth full parfyte vnderstandynge of the booke lately prentyd by me (Peter treueris) named the noble experiens of the vertuous handwarke of surgery*, 1526; unnumbered pages. *STC* 13176. **Source** *EEBO*: British Library, London (C.27.1.1.).

Aqua. Water. Ca. liiii

Aqua, water, the grekes call it *ydros*, the arabytes call it *squigihill*. Mayster ypocras, in his boke named de aere and aqua,[37] sayth that a man ought to haue grete concyderacyon of waters that ben vsed in meates and drynkes; suche waters ought to be of good sauour, lyght in weight, and clere in colour. For he that drynketh troubled and heuy water comyely, all his body swelleth, from the heed to the fete, and specyally it corupteth the mylte,[38] and maketh yl humours in the body; and,

eligi debet fractu contumax, densum· grave, colore aureum, lucidum· leve, trium mensium, maturum, mundum, pinguique terra ortum," Cogan, *The haven of health*, 25, and "For thus writeth *Matthiolus* [*Lib.* 2. *Dios. c.* 88] *Sunt qui Orisam quoque dicunt genitale augere semen, in bubulo lacte decoctam, additis Saccaro et Cinamomo,"* Cogan, *The haven of health*, 34, etc.

36. Healy, *Fictions of Disease*, 32.

37. This work was known under at least two Latin titles: *De Aere, Aqua, et Locis* and *Liber de Aere, et Aqua, et Regionibus*.

38. Spleen: *MED* s.v. "milt(e)".

therfore, whan water must be vsed in ony medycyne, grete consyderacyon is to be had yf the water be good obadde. The maysters say that water is not good to be drunken, and specyally to them that ben of colde nature, for water bredeth in them many accydentall sekenesses and flux in the body, as feuers and many other procedynge of moystenesse. Also, women that ben with chylde and drynke water ben delyuered with grete payne. Women that drynke moche water ben many tymes letted of theyr floures[39] in theyr tyme, and somtyme causeth them to renne ouer moche, wherfore theyr bodyes ben weyked and theyr heedes shake, for drynkyng of water cooleth the brayne. And, therfore, mayster Isaac sayth that it is vnpossyble for them that drynketh ouermoche water in theyr youth to come to the aege that god hath ordyned them. Also Ipocras sayth that rayne water rotteth lyghtly and geteth a noughty sent,[40] bycause many waters ben medled togider aboue in the eyre; also, the water that cometh of yse or snowe is nought, for if water be ones[41] frozen or tourned to snowe it wyll neuer retourne into the fyrst nature or kynde, nor be so clere as was afore.

Auicen in his fourth cura febrium sayth that water may be gyuen to drynke to them that haue the colde fiuers; yf the feuer cote of the gallen, it behoueth to gyue hym one onely water in due tyme whan the feuers hath left hym, that he neyther feleth colde nor hete; that is, whan he rested. Yf he be hote or colde gyue hym neyther water nor wyne, for the feuer sholde be nourysshed therwith. Auicen sayth in the same boke that hote water freseth sooner than colde. Also he sayth that colde water consumeth an humour comynge fro the galle named humour coleryke. And he sayth that water nouryssheth not, and that colde water ought not to be gyuen to a seke persone whan the humours cesseth, and ben grosse and vndygested. Also he sayth that mannes foode can not be arayed and dressed without water, and he sayth that water of sprynges and rennynge ryuers ben best, and the ferder from the spryng the better and he sayth that the waters that ben hoote in wynter and colde in somer be the best of all, and soden water sonest enereth[42] in to the body. And he sayth in his Fyrste boke, *feu.*,[43] in the fyrst doctryne of the xiii. chapytre, that water may well be dronken whan the mater is dygested and the nature stronge. And he sayth in the same boke that warme water is good to

39. Menstrual period: *MED* s.v. "flŏur".

40. "Scent" was probably intended here.

41. Once: *MED* s.v. "ǒnes".

42. "Entereth" was probably intended here.

43. Should be "fen.," the Arabic name for the chapters of Avicenna's books. This should be followed by a number, but the text does not give one after "fen.," neither in this edition, nor in the 1526, 1529, 1539, or 1561 editions.

be vsed for colyke, passyon, and for swellynge of the mylte, and warme water letreth the dysgestyon and swageth not the thyrst. And he sayth that standynge water, and not currant, noyreth[44] the stomake. Also, he sayth that rayne water that is gadred in somer whan it thondreth and is boystous wether is best to be vsed in medycyne, and rayne water gadred and kept in other seasons letteth the Voyce, and stoppeth the brest.

Galien sayth in the seuenth boke called Terapeutyke, in the seconde chapytre, sayth that colde water dronken noyeth the body, and prouoketh inwarde sekenesse, and therfore it is good to be eschewed; and also he sayth in the fyrst bok, and fyrst chapytre named De morte, that many folke that hath bathed them in colde wa[45] haue dyed or they came home.[46]

Diascorides sayth that water soden with barly or malt is profytable to mannes body, and at some tyme is good in medycyne, and therfore in all sekenesses that cometh of hete, soden water is good and agaynst feuer tercyen. And he sayth that amonge all waters, rayne water is best bycause it is lyghtly dygested of his kynde, and is soone hote and soone colde of his nature. And of all renuynge sprynges those that sprynge agaynst eest and south ben best, but those that sprynge agaynst the west ben the worst, and in lykewyse is many occydentall sekenesses; and, he sayth in his boke de aqua that all waters in theyr kynde ben colde and moyst. ...

De cinamomo. Cynamome or canell. Ca. xcvii.

Cynamome is canell. It is hote and in the thyrde degre, and it is drye in the seconde. There be two maners of it: The one is thycke and is somwhat holowe and grosse or cours, and is the barke of a tre; The other is fyner and is al holowe, and not so thycke, and some say that it is the barke of a lytel tree. They be founde bothe in Inde and in Europe; that which is cours ought to be put in medycynes vomytyues, and the fyner in other medycyns; That is to be chosen that is fyne and smal, with a sharpe taste, swete smell, and gray of colour. This canell is called Cynamomum alichimos and alichimum. That whiche is whytysshe or blacke is nought; yf ye wyll chuse it or knowe by the mouth or taste, whiche is good, clense your mouth fro water, or spattyll, or of slyme that is therin. For by suche moystnesse some a thynge is Iuged to be good that is nought. It is kept .x. yeres, and hath vertue to comfort the brayne by good odoure; by the glutynesyte therof it

44. To harm, injure: *MED* s.v. "noien".
45. "Water" clearly intended here.
46. Meaning unclear.

reioyneth, and dyssolueth, and conforteth dygestyon. It is put in sawces to cause appetyte: this wise medle powdre of canell with percely, sawge, and vyneygre, and make sawce therof.

For the brethe.
To haue a swete brethe chawe canell, for it maketh a good odour in the mouthe.

For the gommes.
Agaynst corrupcyon and rottennesse of the goumes fyrst wasshe them with salt water, and rubbe them tyll they blede and tyll the rotten moystures come out; and than wasshe them with wyne that canell was soden in, and that done, lay on them two partes of powdre of the grete consolyda that is camfery, and the thyrde parte of canell, and it wyll helpe and ease merueylously.

For chyppynge
For newe clyftes or chyppynge of the lyppes and to other sores and woundes lay the powdre of canell in the clyftes and than bynde them wel togyder, or sowe them.

Agaynst passyon of the hert and swownynge
take powdre of canell with the powdre of the leues of gylofres. The cours canell is put in medycynes of vomyte bycause it reprymeth, abateth and demynysshed the vyolence of other medycyns as of tapsus and suche other; also comforteth the stomake and thus it dooth two profytes in the sayde medycyns. ...

De rore marino. Rosmary. Ca. CCC.lxx.
Rosmary is hote and drye; But the auctours tel not in what degre. It is a herbe that groweth in maner of a tree. And, it is not proprely called rosmary, but ros marinus, as it were, dewe of the see, for comynly it groweth in places by the see syde. The floures and the leues be good in medycyne. And the floures ought to be dryed a lytell in the sonne whan they be gadred, and they may be kept a yere; and the leues lyke wyse. The floure of rosmary is called anthos and of it an electuary is named dynythos. The herbe therof is called libramondos or dendrolibanas. Some call it liantis, other ycterycon, and other luim. Whan anthos or rosmary is founde in receptes, it is the floure, and yf ye fynde libramandos or dendrolybanos, it is the leues. Rosmary hath vertue to conforte by the good odoure, And to waste and clense humours, and to put them out by subtyll vapour.

For the herte.
Agaynst dysease of the herte and dysposycyon to fall in swowne. Take the electuary dyanthos with wyne, Or elles sethe the floures of Rosmary in wyne or rose water, and gyue it to the pacyent. Another remedy is, make iuce of rosmary leues medled with rose water with a lytell iuce of panace, and make a syrope therof, whiche shall be good yf some of the bone in the herte of an harre be put therto.

For weykenesse of the brayne.
Agaynst weykenesse of the brayne and coldenesse therof. Sethe rosmarin in wyne and lete the pacyent receyue the smoke at his nose, and kepe his heed warme.

For the throte.
The wyne that rosmary is soden in dryeth the moystnesse of the throte yf gargarysme[47] be made therof.

For the stomake.
Agaynst coldnesse of the stomake and to conforte dygestyon, Take dyanthes or the wyne that rosmary or mastyke is soden in

For the wombe.
Agaynst ache of the wombe causeth of wynde, Take the wyne that rosmary and comyn is soden in.

For the vryne.
Agaynst lette of the vryne, Sethe the leues and floures in wyne and lay to the share.

For the matryce.[48]
To clense the matryce and to helpe concepcyon make bathes in the nether partes with water that rosmary is soden in. Some women sethe the floures in oyle and vse it benethe. ...

27b Thomas Cogan, *The haven of health. Chiefely gathered for the comfort of Students, and consequently of all those that have a care of their health, amplified upon five words of Hippocrates, written Epid. 6. Labor, cibus, potio, somnus,*

47. A gargle: *MED* s.v. "gargarisme".
48. Uterus, womb: MED s.v. "mātrīs".

Venus. Hereunto is added a preseruation from the Pestilence, with a short censure of the late sicknes at Oxford. By Thomas Coghan Master of Arts, and Bacheler of Physicke, 1636, pp. 36–38, 125–126, 234–237.[49] *STC* 5483.7. **Source** *EEBO*: British Library, London (S108449).

CHAP. 12. Of Rosemary.
Next in vertue to Sage is Rosemary, and of much like qualitie. For it is both hot and drie. *Fernelius* saith, *Vna cum cerebro et nervis, cor, sensus omnes et memoriam confirmat, tremori atque paralysi salutaris,* and therefore excellent good for students, any way used. Beside that (as saith *Matthiolus*) *Visum acuit, si toto tempore quo floret, quispiam jeiunus flores una cum circumstantibus foliis cum pane et sale quotidie voraverit. Praestat etiam ad frigidos ventriculi affectus, ad coliacas passiones et vomitum cibi, sicum pane devoretur, aut bibatur in pulverem contritum ex meraco.* The use of Rosemary in Kitchin is well knowne to all men. I would the hearbe were as plentifull among us in England, as it is in that part of France which is named Provance, where it groweth of it selfe without setting, and is used for a common fuell.

Such as have not the Herbe, may yet have the flowers preserved of the Apothecaries, called *Conserva Anthos*, like in operation to the Herb, which I wish to be often used of students. Such as have the Herbe, may use it now and then, as *Alexis* prescribeth, to cleanse and comfort the stomacke, and to make a sweet breath, in this manner: Take Rosemary, with the flowers or without, a handfull or more, seeth it in white Wine a good space, and put thereto, if you may, a little Cinamon; then drinke it, and wash your mouth therewith. The same Wine without Cinamon is good to wash the face and hands, for it maketh a very cleare skinne. I was wont to put a handfull of Rosemary in a quart of white Wine, and to suffer it to boyle in the quart untill it were ready to be burned, and then to use it; or, halfe a handfull in a pint of Wine, and sometimes a few Cloves withall. Which drinke by experience I found greatly to comfort both my stomacke and braine. Or, if you like not to be at the cost of Wine, seeth it in Ale, or pound it and straine it with Ale or Wine. For being so drunke, it is very good to open the obstructions of the Liver and spleene, which is a speciall way to preserve health. Good therefore to be used at the spring or fall of the leafe, for a weeke together. And so I was wont to use *Agrimony* to prevent a dropsie.

If any man list to make a perfect Electuary of Sage and Rosemary to comfort the stomacke and braine, and to make a sweet breath, hee may compound it,

49. Marginal notes in this text were not included in the transcription, except for one, marked with square brackets.

after *Alexis,* in this manner: Take of Sage two ounces, of Rosemary flowers halfe an ounce, of Cloves five drammes, of Cinamon one dramme and a halfe, of Nutmegges one scruple, bray every thing, and with honey or Sugar make an Electuary, and give thereof in the morning halfe a spoonful; then drinke a little red Wine wherein is boyled a little Sage, and this doe every day untill you have your purpose. ...

CHAP. 127. Of Cinnamom.
Cinnamom is hot and dry in the third degree: that which we have is the barke or rinde of a certaine tree growing in the Indies, and is the right Cassia, as *Mathio.* Thinketh [*Lib.* 1. *Dios.* Ca. 13]. The use thereof is great, as well in meats as in medicines, and found to be very comfortable to the stomacke and principall parts of the bodie, insomuch that I have read in an old Authour of Physicke this meeter following, *Cur moriatur homo, qui sumit de Cinamomo?*

There is made a water with Cinamom, very good for many purposes, in this manner. Take a pound of good Cinamom and beat it grosse, then take a pottle of perfect rose-water, and as much of good wine, sacke or Canary wine, or else take a galon of the wine onely without rose-water, steepe all together close covered in some cleane vessell the space of foure and twenty houres, then still it in a Limbecke, you may keepe that which commeth first if you list by it selfe about a pint, for the later will be weaker. Some put a pound of Sugar Candie to steepe with the Cinamom, and so they make it very pleasant. And I have proved the best way to be to take a gallon of Sacke, a pound of Cinamom grosse beaten, and a pound of sugar candie, and to steepe all together, and so distill them. This water hath innumerable vertues, but especially to restore and preserve the debility of nature. And as *Matthiolus* saith in the Chapter aforesaid, *Ventriculum, iecur, lienem, cerebrum, nervosque iuvat, et roborat.* Wherefore, I reckon it a great treasure for a student to have by him in his closet, to take now and then a spoonefull. ...

CHAP. 216. Of Water.
Water is the chiefest of all liquors, not onely because it is one of the foure Elements, but also for that it was the very naturall and first drinke appointed by God to all manner of creatures. And as it appeareth by the holy Scriptures in *Genesis,* there was none other drinke used nor knowne but water, from the creation of the world until *Noah* his floud, during which time men lived eight or nine hundred yeares. Also, after the floud of *Noah,* both Princes and people in all ages dranke water, especially in Asia and the East Countries, as appeareth by the his-

tory of *Moses,* and the children of Israel in *Exodus.* And in Greece likewise it was used for a common drinke, as *Galen* declareth in diverse places of his works, but especially in the first booke, where he affirmeth: *Aquam puram omni aetati utilissimam esse.* And that water to be best, *cujus ad orientem solem fons erumpit, quaeque permeatu aliquem mundus, aut puram colatur terram, eademque calefit ac refrigeratur ocyssime.* But leaving Asia and Grecia aside, and returning home to England, if any shall demand whether or no it bee as wholsome for English men to drinke water as for them that dwell in other Countries, M. *Eliot* in his *Castill* saith that if men from their infancy were accustomed to none other drink but water, onely moderately used, it should bee sufficient to keepe naturall moysture, and to cause the meat that is eaten to pierce and descend into the places of digestion, which are the purposes which drinke serveth for. As in Cornewall, although that the country be in a very cold quarter, yet many of the poorer sort which never or very seldome drinke other drink than pure water, be notwithstanding strong of body, and live and like well untill they be of great age. *Adeo a teneris assuescere multum est.* But otherwise except the custome of drinking of water, I thinke I thinke as it is in *S. Sal.*: *Potut aquae sumptus comedenti incommoda praestat. Hinc friget stomachus, crudus et inde cibus.* That is to say, the drinking of water with meate cooleth the stomacke over much, and so letteth digestion, and maketh the meat that is eaten to bee raw. The like effect it hath if it be drunken after meat, except it bee after a great surfet, or when thirst happeneth after drinking of much wine. For in these cases, cold water drunken is a generall remedy, and I have knowne many by drinking a good draught of cold water to bedward have thereby had quiet rest all night after, and in the morning also it is right wholsome for him that dranke too much overnight, to drinke fasting a cup of cold water, especially if hee bee thirsty, for that will cleanse the stomack, and represse the vapours and fumes, and dispose it to reteine new sustenance.

Some also have I knowne that would oftentimes in a morning fasting drinke a draught of cold water with a little white Sugar, of purpose to cleare and coole the stomacke, and have by that meanes (as they thought) avoided much flegme. But herein alway respect must bee had to him that drinketh it, for to young folks and them that bee hot of complection it doth lesse harme, and sometime it profiteth. But to them that are feeble, old, flegmaticke or melancholy, it is not convenient, for it destroyeth naturall heat, it grieveth the brest, and taketh away the appetite of the stomack, and is very hurtfull to all the sinewy members; and this caveat I will give to all such as be thirsty through great labour and travaile that they drinke not much cold water in their heat or thirst, for thereby I have knowne many fall into sickenesse, and I thinke it better to drinke a draught of Sacke or good wine, or as they use in Lankashire, a hot posset at such times, than small drinke or cold water. For though small drink or cold water seeme to quench thirst better than wine because it moystneth and cooleth more, yet wine being more agreeable with nature, and of more subtile substance and operation, is sooner drawne off the members, and consequently sooner satisfies and fils the veines, and so quencheth thirst without any great alteration of the body, whereas water or small drinke by the great coldnesse thereof sodainely changeth the body from heat to cold, which is a dangerous thing.

DISEASE

28a [Johannes Jacobi,] *A passing gode lityll boke necessarye and behouefull agenst the pestilence* (ca. 1485). **28b** Stephen Hobbes, *A new treatise of the pestilence* (1603).

Introduction Johannes Jacobi (fl. 1364?–1384), also known as Jean Jacme or Jaume, was Chancellor of Montpellier's Medical School, and physician to the king of France and to the pope at Avignon. His Latin work, originally titled *De pestilencia*,[50] was copied a number of times, and around 1450 probably went through an edition by a Scandinavian bishop, Bengt Knutsson of Västerås or Knud Mikkelsen of Viborg, with whom it subsequently became associated, and via this route reached England.[51] It is unclear whether English printed editions of Jacobi's work were all based on manuscript copies of the work attributed to Knutsson (or Mikkelsen), or on other European printed copies that attributed the work to Knutsson (the work was reprinted twenty-one times before 1500[52]), or whether some of them relied on copies unrelated to him.[53] Most of the eight English printed editions, however (not including Thomas Paynell's translation under a different title[54]), attributed the original work to "a bishop and doctor of physicke from Denmark."[55]

50. There are also two French works that seem to be translations of *De pestilencia*: *Régime de l'épidémie* and *Traité de la peste*; it is possible, though perhaps unlikely, that Knutsson (or Mikkelsen) translated either of these versions.

51. Byrne, *Encyclopedia of the Black Death*, 67.

52. Ibid.

53. Kari Anne Rand, *The Index of Middle English Prose, Handlist XVIII* (Cambridge, 2006), 52.

54. *A moche profitable treatise against the pestilence translated into Eglyshe by Thomas Paynel Chanon of Martin Abbey* (1534).

55. From the first page of the 1485 edition: " ... I the Bisshop of Arusiens doctour of Phisike wille write by the most expert and famous doctours auctorised in Phisike somme thinges of the infirmite of Pestilence." From the title page of the 1536 edition: " ... made by a Bysshop, and doctor of Phisick of Denmarke," etc.

The text itself is a short record of the characteristics of the plague that Jacobi was commissioned to write by his superiors in order to provide new information about the disease, which was raging in Europe at the time and for which, in the view of many (as stated in the text itself), the "ancients" did not provide a viable cure as, according to the writer, they had no experience of the disease.[56] The English text thus opens with a list of "tokens" typically announcing the plague: south winds, morning rains, falling stars, etc. It then suggests that these cause a corruption of air (visible also through the multiplication of flies) which in turn enters the body, as poison, through the pores of the skin. The text is rich in suggestions on how to defend against this poisonous air, which included polluted air coming out of the sores of those already infected, such as washing in vinegar (which was also recommended to be poured onto the floors of houses), avoiding large groups of people, as well as opening windows to the north and east, bathing, and burning pleasantly smelling herbs, which served to balance the humours and prevent the plague.[57]

Stephen Hobbes' *A new treatise of the pestilence* was written in the context of a more "local" outbreak of the plague, in 1603, mainly concentrated in London. The author presents himself as knowledgeable in the field of medicine and, although very little is known of him, on the basis of his at least five other publications, which were all concerned with medical issues, it can be surmised that he was indeed a physician or surgeon. One of his works was concerned with the "Schoole of Salerne," indicating that he was also familiar with the work of thinkers from the Schola Medica Salernitana, including Matthaeus Platearius and John of Milan[58] (or at least with works attributed to him) and, while these texts would not necessarily have helped Hobbes write his *New treatise of the pestilence*, his familiarity with the broader medical discourse of the early modern period made it likely he was also familiar with some versions of Jacobi's text, which was popular both in manuscript and print form throughout the sixteenth century. In his text, Hobbes first provides a brief description of what pestilence is, then its causes, then symptoms, and finally "precautions and remedies against the same" (n. pag.). The first cause, according to Hobbes, is "supernatural," i.e., God punishing people for sin, regarding which he cites Deuteronomy 2:15; the second cause is astronomical and is related to the placement of

56. Samuel Cohn, Jr, "Patterns of Plague in Late Medieval and Early Modern Europe," in *The Routledge History of Disease*, ed. Mark Jackson (New York, 2017), 165–183, at 175.

57. For more on this text see Joseph Pickett, "A Translation of the *Canutus* Plague Treatise," in *Popular and Practical Science of Medieval England*, ed. Lister Matheson (East Lansing, MI, 1994), 263–282.

58. Hobbes was the translator of a few such tracts, including the famous anonymous treatise attributed to John of Milan, translated in 1617 as *The English mans doctor. Or the schoole of Salerne. Or physicall obseruations for the perfect preseruing of the bodie of man in continuall health. Whereunto is adioyned precepts for the preseruation of health.*

celestial bodies; the third is related to corrupted air; and the fourth to an imbalance in bodily humours. In other words, Hobbes goes from general to specific imbalances in the microcosm.[59]

Little else is known of this work and its author; the text is one of a few printed in 1603 on the subject, and indicates that the Black Death was still alive in cultural memory, as some references to "auncient" practices of incising the sores (suggested by Hobbes as one of the remedies) originate in fourteenth-century treatments of the disease; this can also suggest some knowledge of the contents of Jacobi's text, although apart from familiarity with fourteenth-century treatments there is little in Hobbes' work to suggest he modelled his *New treatise of the pestilence* on a specific earlier text. Interestingly, Hobbes' work is in many ways more religious in tone than Jacobi's, even though what little is known about Hobbes does not suggest he was a clergyman of any sort, whereas Jacobi had strong ties to the Avignon papacy. Both works indicate an interest in the historical study of cures for pestilence and a dissatisfaction with such remedies as had passed on into historical records, and both attempt to provide a comprehensive study of the plague that would explain to their readers the causes and cures for the disease as well as, perhaps more importantly, offering suggestions on how to avoid it altogether. The early modern work is, very clearly, interested in a religious explanation of the plague and illustrates a religiously-founded holistic understanding of disease, something that it shares with Jacobi's text.

28a [Johannes Jacobi,] *A passing gode lityll boke necessarye and behouefull aȝenst the Pestilence*, ca. 1485; unnumbered pages. *STC* 4591. **Source** *EEBO*: British Library, London (IA.55478.).

... Fyrst I sayde the tokens of this infirmite; .vii. thynges ought to be noted in the same.

The firste is whan in a sommers daye the weder often times chaungeth, as in the morning the wedyr appereth to rayne, afterward it apperyth cloudy, and ate last windy in the southe.

The second token ys wane in sommer the dayes apperyth all derke and like to rayne, and yett hit rayneth not, And of many dayes so continue, it is to drede of grete Pestilence.

The thirde tokyn is whan grete multitude of flyes ben vpon the eerthe; then it is signe the ayer is venomous and enfecte.

59. Anthony Ellis, *Old Age, Masculinity, and Early Modern Drama: Comic Elders on the Italian and Shakespearean Stage* (Farnham, Surrey; Burlington, VT, 2009), 138 n3.

The fourthe tokyn ys whan the sterres semen ofte tymes to falle, then hit is token that the ayer is enfecte with moche venomous vapours.

The v. token is whan à blasyng stere is seen in the element, thenne hit sholde fortune sone after to be grete manslaghter in bataylle.

The vi. token is whanne there is grete lyghtnynge and thunder, namely out of the southe.

The vii. token is whanne grete wyndes passen out of the southe; they be foule and vnclene, therefore whan these tokens appere it is to drede grete Pestilence, but god of hys mercy wil remeue it.

These thinges folowyng be the causes of Pestileuce.

The Pestilence cometh of thre thinges. Som time it cometh fro the rote[60] bynethe, otherwhese fro the rote aboue, so that we may fole sensibly howe the chaunge of the ayer appereth vnto vs. And sometyme it cometh of bothe to gydere, as wele fro the rote aboue as fro the rote bynethe. As we see a sege or preuy next to a chamber or of any other particuler thyng whiche corrupteth the ayer in his substance and qualite, whiche is a thing maye happe euery daye, And thereof cometh the Ague of Pestilence. And aboute the same many Phisicions be deceyued, not supposing this axes to be a Pestilence; somtime it cometh of dede careyn or corrupcion of standyng waters in diches or slouhes and other corrupt places; athese thynges somtyme be vniuersall and somtime particuler; fro the route aboue it fortuneth the causes of the bodyes aboue in the auer, by whome the spyryte of lyfe ys corrupte in a man or in a beste. In like wyse, as Auycenne sayth in his fourthe boke, by the forme of thayer aboue the Body es bene the lightly be infecte. For thynprisyons[61] aboue corrupteth the ayer and soo the spirytes of a man ben corrupte. This infirmite cometh also from the rote aboue and bynethe, Whanne of thynprisions aboue the ayer is corrupt, and of the putrefaction or rotyn careyn of the vyle places bynethe an infirmite is caused in a man. And suche an infirmite somtime is an axes, somtime a perfume or a swellyng, and that Be in many thinges. Also the ayer inspired somtime is venemous and corrupt, hurting the herte; that nature many wayes ys greued, so that he perceyueth not hys harme. For the vryne appereth fayer and sheweth gode digestion, yet neuerthelesse the pacyent ys lyke to dye, wherefore many Phisycions seyng the vryn of their pacyents they speke superficially, and be desceuyed. Ther fore it is nede that euery patient prouyde to hym selfe a gode and expert Phisycion.

60. Reason, source: *MED* s.v. "rǫte".

61. The impressions.

These thynges wryton before are the causes of Pestilence, but aboute these thinges ij. questions be meoued. The fyrst is wherfore one dyeth and another dyeth not in a town, Where men be dede in one hous and in another hous ther dyeth none. The second question is Whether Pestilence sores be contagious. To the firste questyon I saye it may happe to be of ii. causes, That is to saye of that thyng that doth and of that thyng that syffreth. An ensample of that thuyng that doth, the Influence of the bodyes aboue beholdeth that place, or that place more than this place, or this place, And the pacient ys more dysposed to dye than another. Therfore, it is to be noted that bodyes be more hote disposed of oopyn poorys than bodyes in fect hauying the poores stopped with many humours, where bodyes be of resolution or opening, as men whiche abusen them selfe with wymmen or vsen often times bathis, or men that be hote with labour or grete angre, they haue their bodies more disposed to this grete sekenes.

To the second question I saye that Pestelence sores be contagious by cause of enfecte humours, bodyes, and the reek or smoke of suche sores ys venomous and corrupte the ayer. And therefore it is to flee fro suche persons as bee infecte. In pestilence time no body sholde stande in grete preue of people be cause som man of them may be infecte. Therfore wyse Phisicions in visityng seke folkes stande ferre fro the patient, holdyng their face toward the doore or wyndowe. And so sholde the seruaunts of seke folke stande. Also it is gode to a patient euery daye for to chaunge his chambre, and often times to haue the wyndowes opene ayenst the North and Eest, and to spere the wyndowes ayents the South. For the South wynde hath .ii. causes of putrification. The first ys it maketh a man, beyng hole or seke, feble in their bodyes. The seconde cause is, as it is writton in the .iii. of Amphorysmys, the south winde greuyth the heering and hurteth the herte, by cause it openeth the poores of man and entreth into the herte; wher fore it is gode to an hole man in tyme of Pestilence, whan the winde is in the south, to bee within the hous alle the daye. And yf hit shal be nede a man to goo oute yet lette hym abide in hys hous tyl the sonne be vppe in the Eest, passing southward.

28b Stephen Hobbes, *A new treatise of the pestilence, containing the causes, signes, preseruatiues and cure thereof. The like not before this time pubished. And therefore necessarie for all manner of persons, in this time of contagion. S. H. Studious in phisicke*, 1603; unnumbered pages. *STC* 12577. **Source** *EEBO*: British Library, London (C.31.E.16.).

A Treatise of the Pestilence.

Hauing an intent to write certaine Precautions and preseruatiues against the pestilence I thinke not necessarie to be ouer tedious, or so precise as those that write exquisitly and perfectly of the same disease; onely, I am determined to set downe such things as shall be necessary for to be knowne by those which in this case shall haue neede.

And first, I will make a true description of the pestilence, what it is. Secondly, the causes, then the Signes, and lastly, precautions and remedies against the same.

The pestilence is nothing else then a rotten or pestilent feuer which, being ingendred by a rotten and corrupt ayre by a hidden and secret propertie which it hath, doth kill and destroy mortal creatures.

The causes are said to be foure fold, as the first and chiefest cause is supernaturall, as being immediately sent from God for the punishment of sinne and disobedience of mankind, as doth appeare in *Deut. 2:15. If thou wilt not obey the voice of the Lord thy God to keepe and to doe all his commandements and his ordinances which I command thee this day: then all these curses shall come vpon thee, and ouertake thee. Cursed shalt thou be in the towne, and cursed in the field, &c. The Lord shal make the pestilence cleaue vnto thee vntill he haue consumed thee from the Land which thou goest to possesse, &c.* Moreouer we reade that the sinne of *Dauid* was the cause that the Lord sent his Angell which did kill the pestilence in a small time threescore and ten thousand soules.

Now this may be proofe sufficient that sinne is the originall and chiefe cause of this most cruell disease of the pestilence.

The second cause is attributed to an euill constellation, which Astronomers affirme to proceede by the placing of the Sunne, Moone, and Stars, being in the firmament or circles of the heauens by their coniunctions, oppositions, and other Aspects, the one to the other.

The third cause is attributed to the corruption of the ayre, which being corrupted is apt for infection of mans body, for all liuing creatures drawe their breath from the ayre that is round about them, which if it be stinking, wenomous, and corrupt, the bodie of man liuing therein is in danger to be corrupted, whereby often times the pestilence is ingendred.

The fourth cause is the aptnesse of the body of man, through corrupt and rotten humours fitte to receiue the effects of a venomous ayre, putrifying and corrupting the body whereby the pestilence is ingendred. And this aptnsse[62] to infection proceedeth by the abuse of the six things, which are called by the Phisitions not naturall, which are:

1. *Ayre.*
2. *Meate and drinke.*
3. *Sleepe and watch.*

62. "Aptnesse" was likely intended here.

4. Exercise and rest.
5. Emptinesse and repletion.
6. The perturbations and affections of the minde.

Now as the true vse of these things that are called not naturall doth maintaine and cherish health, so the abuse thereof is the occasion of disease and sickenesse. For which cause I counsell all manner of persons in this time of contagion to flie surfeting, gurmandizing, and other vnseasonable banketings, whereby the health of the body is at all times impaired; for who knoweth not that great and often feeding breedeth cruditie and rawe watrish humours in the body, which cruditie is a fitte sediment or subiect for the venomous and corrupt ayre to worke on. For which cause the learned Phisitions, as well Auncient as moderne, giue counsell that in the time of pestilence and contagion those bodies that are humid and moyst must bee by all manner of meanes made drie, and those that are dry to be kept and preserued in their drinesse; for, by obseruation, it is very well knowne that the Phlegmaticke and sanguine body is sooner subiect to infection then the Choloricke or Melancholike, and experience doth dayly teach vs when for the most part women, children, and men of yoong yeares are those that die in this disease of the pestilence, as those bodies that are hot and moyst and thereby fittest to receiue putrification.

But for as much as I promised in the beginning not to be ouer-tedious as those that make a long discourse, I purpose to proceede briefly vnto the signes whereby a man may know and perceiue when the contagion hath taken hold of him, and thereby run speedily vnto such meanes and helps as by the rules of Phisicke shall be to him discribed.

The signes to know when the body is infected are for the most part an Apostum or tumor about the eare, necke, vnder the arme holes, or flancke, with a feuer, and sometimes there ariseth in some other parts of the body a darke greene or euill coloured sore. These signes for the most port doth appeare, but not alwaies. But for the more certainty, we must consider these symtomes or signes that follow: there hapneth after infection a great pricking and shooting in the body, and especially in the necke, armeholes, and flanckes, also extreame heate within the body, and in the hands, knees, and feete very cold, so that there is ioyned with the same a shiuering as in a feuer; Also, ther is heauines of the head, drynesse of the mouth with extreame thirst; also, a drowsinesse and great desire to sleepe; some againe are so watchfull that they cannot sleepe, so that they rave as thought they were in a phrense; there happeneth also great paine in the head, faintnesse, sluggishnesse, weakenesse of the lymmee, pensiuenesse, no desire of meat with often vomiting, the matter being bitter and of diuers colours, the vrine troubled, thicke and stinking, and for the most part without residence.

These are the principall signes of infection and yet not certaine, for sometimes a man may be infected and yet none of these signes apparant. And in like maner a man may haue these signes, and yet free from infection. Some Phisitions are of opinion that there is scarsely any disease where the Pestilence raigneth, but that it is either of the nature of the pestilence, or apt to be turned into the same.

CURING DISEASE

29a Thomas Moulton, *This is the myrour or glasse of helth, necessary and nedefull for euery person to loke in* (1531). **29b** [Joseph du Chesne,] *The practise of chymicall, and hermeticall physicke,* trans. Thomas Tymme (1605).

Introduction Thomas Moulton was a Dominican friar, later referred to in printed versions of his work as "Doctor of Divinity," but little is known about him otherwise. The *Myrour or glasse of helth* is a printed version of a text originally found in a late medieval manuscript miscellany known as a leechbook,[63] i.e., a compilation of texts containing descriptions of and remedies for illnesses of various kinds, intended for practical lay use. The original of the *Myrour* can be dated on the basis of the hand used in its earliest found manuscript copy, as well as references made in the text to an outbreak of plague dated to the second half of the fifteenth century, placing the earliest manuscript of the *Myrour* as composed between the 1460s and 1490s, most likely in 1475.[64] The miscellany also includes other medieval texts such as the *Awyntyrs off Arthure* (ca. 1400?) and *Agnus castus* (ca. 1450?).[65] The text of the *Myrour or glasse of helth* comes from one of the versions of John of Burgundy's plague treatise (1490) (excerpted above, in yet another translation), though Moulton's version contains significant departures from the original text, the most important of them being that Moulton's work is in many ways primarily a moral text, explaining the plague and the movement of planets causing it as divine will and pun-

63. Keiser, "Two Medieval Plague Treatises," 306–307.

64. Keiser, "Two Medieval Plague Treatises," 302.

65. Keiser, "Two Medieval Plague Treatises," 295–297, 302. See pp. 295 and 296 for a full list of the contents. Another part of this miscellany, the recipes by Brother Rufinus, is an adaptation of excerpts of *Circa Instans* (George R. Keiser, "Rosemary: Not Just for Remembrance," in *Health and Healing from the Medieval Garden*, ed. Peter Dendle and Alain Touwaide [Woodbridge, Suffolk, 2008], 180–204, at 182). For more on *Agnus Castus*, see George R. Keiser, "A Middle English Rosemary Treatise in Verse in Prose," *ANQ: A Quarterly Journal of Short Articles, Notes and Reviews* 18 (2005): 9–18.

ishment for sin. Even though such an approach was not present in John of Burgundy's original text, it was a fairly typical understanding of the causes of the plague during the time of the Black Death in the fourteenth century, which Moulton repeats with force in his *Myrour*.[66] He also disregards much of the more academic language of John of Burgundy's original text in order to make it accessible to a lay audience. The text was extremely popular in the sixteenth century, printed at least twenty-one times between 1530 and 1580, and considered not only one of the bestselling books of the sixteenth century but also a work that exerted significant influence on later medical treatises of the early modern period: "this treatise originates in the second half of the fifteenth century and is not a creation of sixteenth century thought, [but] we can recognize that the response to the plague in early modern medicine, although different in some important respects, does continue traditions established before 1500."[67]

Joseph du Chesne (or Duchesne, known also as Quercetanus), a Calvinist Paracelsian,[68] was physician to King Henry IV of France and was considered a leading authority on the "new chemical medicines in Europe."[69] Two of his Latin works were translated by a Church of England minister, Thomas Tymme, an author, translator, and clergyman with distinctly puritan views.[70] Tymme fused two works by du Chesne into one,[71] resulting in *The practise of chymicall, and hermeticall physicke*, whose main theme was Paracelsian theory[72] mixed with medical science and, finally, also the Bible.[73] Tymme took inter-

66. Byrne, *Daily Life During the Black Death*, 212.

67. Keiser, "Two Medieval Plague Treatises," 317. For a comprehensive discussion of medical books printed in England between 1486 and 1605, see Paul Slack, "Mirrours of Health and Treasures of Poor Men: The Uses of the Vernacular Medical Literature of Tudor England," in *Health, Medicine and Mortality in the Sixteenth Century*, ed. Charles Webster (Cambridge, 1979), 237–274.

68. Peter J. Forshaw, "Vitriolic Reactions: Orthodox Responses to the Alchemical Exegesis of Genesis," in *The Word and the World, Biblical Exegesis and Early Modern Science*, ed. Kevin Killeen and Peter J. Forshaw (New York, 2007), 111–137, at 114.

69. Anna Marie Roos, *The Salt of the Earth: Natural Philosophy, Medicine, and Chymistry in England, 1650–1750* (Leiden, 2007), 12.

70. Richard L. Greaves, *Society and Religion in Elizabethan England* (Minneapolis, 1981), 234.

71. *Libert de Priscorum Philosophorum verae medicinae material* (1603) and *Ad Veritatem Hermeticae Medicinae ex Hippocratis vertumque decretis ac Therapeusi* (1604); cited in Roos, *The Salt of the Earth*, 12.

72. Roos, *The Salt of the Earth*, 13.

73. Georgiana D. Hedesan, *An Alchemical Quest for Universal Knowledge: The "Christian Philosophy" of Jan Baptist Van Helmont (1579–1644)* (New York, 2016).

est in the work of du Chesne because he saw potential there to produce a work in English that would be uncorrupted by "pagan" influences and thus of value to his largely religiously conservative audience, a godly work on nature and God that revealed the marvels of God's creations with due reverence.[74] The text Tymme produced is, in many ways, also his own as it is a free adaptation of two works, with a selection of excerpts most fitting to what Tymme deemed useful as well as spiritually beneficial to his readers. In the foreword to the reader, Tymme points out that divisions between various religious groups (both intra-Protestant and intra-Catholic rifts), the influence of other religions ("the false worship of *Turkes, Affricans, Tartars, Persians, Cataians,* and *Indians*"), as well as the influence of various schools of thought contribute to confusion and dissent from "sound and vpright iudgement," and that it is his intention that the reader "mayest procure to thy selfe, but one scruple of knowledge more than before thou haddest, and in time of neede, one dramme of health, it is that which I seeke, wishing thee thy full contentment in all the gifts and graces of God, to thy further profite, and to Gods glorie: to whose protection, I now leaue thee."[75]

The first part of the work (chapters I–XVIII) is concerned with "chemical physicke," the second part with the practice of "hermeticall physike" (I–VII chapters), and the third part is a treatise on the "seals and impressions of things" in which recipes for cures and remedies are included. Tymme proudly ends his book by saying "Thus courteous Reader, I haue shewed thee such secrets in this Art, as neither *Quersitanus, Isacus, Hollandus,* nor any other Phylosopher haue before published in print to my knowledge," presenting himself, the translator, as revealing more than the author of the work he translated intended about the "secrets" of medicine. The work is thus to Tymme a way to propagate godly (i.e., Protestant) learning, void of the paganism of Aristotle, Plato, or Arabic influences. The excerpt below focuses on cures and remedies for illnesses, and provides an interesting comparison, and contrast, to Moulton's views on curing disease in a number of ways, its lack of moral admonition for sin as the cause of disease most prominently among them (although the excerpts of Moulton's work below likewise do not make many references to spiritual matters but rather focus on recipes for remedies). Both works, then, were authored (and translated, in the case of the latter text) by religious men, a friar and a minister, and both, again, treat the nature of disease as connected to spirituality, although in the latter text much less explicitly.

74. Allen G. Debus, "The Chemical Philosophy and the Scientific Revolution," in *The Scientific Revolution: The Essential Readings,* ed. Marcus Hellyer (London, 2003), 159–177, at 171.

75. All three quotations from Joseph du Chesne, *The practise of chymicall, and hermeticall physicke,* trans. Thomas Tymme, "The Fore-Speech to the Reader," n. pag.

29a Thomas Moulton, *This is the myrour or glasse of helth, necessary and nedefull for euery person to loke in, that wyll kepe their bodye from the syckenes of the pestylence: and it sheweth how the planettes raygne, in euery houre of the daye and nyght: with the natures and exposicions of the .xii. sygnes, deuided by the .xii. monethes of the yere. And sheweth the remedyes for manye diuers infyrmytes and diseases, that hurteth the bodye of man,* 1531; unnumbered pages. *STC* 18214a. **Source** *EEBO*: Bodleian Library, Oxford (016415056).

For the head ache. Cap.vii.
Take hemlocke and sethe theim till they be softe as pappe, then laye them to the head there the paine is, and let them lye all nyghte, and on the mornyng laye another hote playster of the same, and do so two or three tymes, and he shall be hole.

For akyng of the head. Cap.viii.
Take and make lye of Veruayne or els of Betayne, or of wormewode, and therewith washe thy head thryse in the weke, and it shall do the good and take a way the ache.

For to spourge the head. Ca.ix.
Take the sede of Stauyscre, and bete it small to pouder, and whan it is beten small, take a fyne lynnem cloth and put the pouder therein, and make there of a lyttel ball, the quantytie of a great hasell nut, and putte it in thy mouthe, and rol to and fro, betwyxt thy tethe chawyng, holdyng downe thy head the space of an houre, and it wil spourge thy head and thy gumes, and kepe thy tethe from akyng.

Also for to spourge the head. Cap. x.
Take the rote of pelater of spain and chewe it betwixt thy tethe, to and fro, a good whyle, and it wyll spourge well thy head, and also fasten thy tethe and spourge thy gumes. ...

For the stomake that is hote and swolen. Cap. xxviii.
For the stomaste that is hote and swolen, take the roote of smalage and stampe it, and put it in swete wyne or in other good wyne all a day and a nyght, and then lette it be passed through a a fayre lynen cloth, and put it in a clene vessell, and vse to drynke a curtesy therof euery day, fasting, .viii. or nyne dayes, and he shalbe hole.

For the stomake that aketh, that commeth of colde. Cap. xxix.
For the stomake that aketh, that commeth of cold, take an herbe that is caled Poleo and drye benes, an handful of syngryn, and as much of this poleo, and put it in a vessell with fayre water, and let it sethe there on the fyer, tyll the thyrd part of the water be soden away; and put therto suger of stone, and a curtesy of hony, and drinke it .vi. dayes fastyng, and he shall be hole.

For to force the stomake. Ca. xxx.
To force the stomake, take canell thre poys, and one poys of mastyke, and one poys of the parynges of Pome garnades, and half a poys of galyngale, and stampe al these together and timper it with hony that hathe bene boyled of the fier, and wel scommed, and use of this asmuch as a nut, euery day duryng .x. dayes fastyng, and he shalbe hole.

For the stomake and the bely that aketh. Capitulo xxxi.
For the stomake and the bely that aketh, take the floure of an herbe that is called Nemaham, that is lyke to Mynte, and it hath a good sauoure; take foure poys of Cosmer, and seuen poys of water, and sethe al together to the third part, and with suger drinke this fyue dayes fastyng, in the mornyng, and he shalbe hole.

And if a man be syke at the stomake or in the bely, or at the hart or head, or were bytten with any euil venemous beast, or poysoned. Ca. xxxii.
And a man were by the waye trauaylyng, or in his house, and he had all these syckenesse, and he had with him a Lectuary that is made of fyue thinges he eate therof, or drinke therof; in water thre poys or .iiii., he shuld be hole, and he vse it fyftene dayes fastyng, and whan he goeth to bedde last he should be hole of all the sickenes in his body, and he drinke euery time two poys; and these thinges they bee Scorlogio, Morre, Genciana, grandorer, and ȝataont, as much of one as of another, and stampe them, and strayne them, and medle them with hony that hath ben wel boyled on the fyer and scummed faire and clene, for this is called the lectuary of lyfe.

A good medecyne for rising vnder the stomake. Capitulo xxxiii.
Take peper, long peper, graynes, saffron, gynger, annyes, licoris, and suger, sethe all these in good ale tyl it be thicke, and geue it the sicke to drinke, and he shalbe hole.

Also a good playster for rising vnder the stomake. Cap. xxxiiii.
Take yerowe, other wyse called mylfoly, reed fenell, reed myntes, borage, rue, fetherfoye, clotes leues, perytory, Egrymonye, of eueryche a lyke much and the

grece of a narow hogge for a man, and for a woman of a yelke hogge, that is of a sowe kynde, and sethe them altogether in good ale, and make a playster thereof, and lay it to the stomake as hote as it may be suffred, .ii. or .iii. times, and he shalbe hole.

... For a dysease at the hart. Cap. xxxix.

Take Sentuary and sethe it in stale ale, and whan it is well sodon stampe it in a morter, and sethe it agayne with the same licour, and than clense it through a cloth and proporcion the ioyce, put ther to thre sponefull of clarified hony and boyle it wel together agayne, and put it in a boxe, and geue it to the pacient euery daye a thre sponefull fastyng tyll he be hole, and this shall do away the glut from his harte, and make him to talent[76] to mete.

For wekenes of the halte.[77] Cap. xl.

Take rose water, and Perles beten small to pouder, and medle it with suger, and drynke it two or thre daies.

... For the palsey. Cap. cxvii.

Take the galle of an oxe, or of a bull of one colour if it may be gotten, and iii. or .iiii. read onions, and roste them tyll they be tender, and than stampe them well in a boule dysshe, and mynge the gall and them together, and looke there be foure tymes as muche of the gal as the onyons, and there with anoynte wel the place that is greued, tyl it be dronke in; and than take a soft shete new wasshen, and warme it agayne the fyer, and wrappe the sycke body therein, and this must be vsed at nyght, to bedwarde, and within .ix. nyghtes it wil amende and make the fleshe growe though it be much awaye, and if the skynee be waxen thicke by vanysshyng away of the flesshe, take read netles roppes and rubbe wel the skin, and this oyntment wyl better drinke in; and this oyntment is good for all maner aches for euery body.

76. Desire, be inclined: *MED* s.v. "talent".

77. "Harte" was most likely intended here.

29b [Joseph du Chesne,] *The practise of chymicall, and hermeticall physicke, for the preseruation of health. Written in Latin by Iosephus Quersitanus, Doctor of Physicke. And translated into English, by Thomas Timme, minister,* trans. Thomas Tymme, 1605; unnumbered pages. *STC* 7276. **Source** The Library of Congress, Washington, DC (R128.6 .D85 Toner Coll).

... *A* Treacle-water *for the head, helping all paines of the same, proper for the Apoplexie, Epilepsie, Palsey, and such like.*
Take of the rootes of Peony, of Misselto, of common Acorns or Cane, of each three ounces. Of ripe Juniparberryes, and of the seeds of Peony, of each, one ounce. Of Cloues and Maces, of each 6. drachmes. Of Castoreum, halfe an ounce. Of the flowers of Stechados, Mary-gold, Rosemary, Sage, Lillyes conually, of the Linden tree, of each, two grypes with two fingers and the thumbe. Cut that which is to bee cut, and beate that which is to bee beaten, and infuse them by the space of 3. dayes, by the heat of a hote Balne, in white wine of the best, 2. pound, and with the waters of Peony, Sage, and of Mary-goldes, of each one pound.

Then, straning them hard, To this liquor adde of Treacle of Alexandria, ounces 4. Of *Anacardine confectionem Mesu.*[78] one ounce and a halfe, of *Diamosth,* and *Aromatici Gabriel,* of each halfe an ounce. Steepe or infuse these againe, by the space of two or three dayes, at the fire gentle of *Blan. M.*[79] Then straine them againe, and distil them vpon ashes to drinesse, and thereof a Treacle-water will bee made. A very smal spoonefull of this is sufficient to be giuen at once against the diseases before expressed.

Another Treacle-water cordiall, and comfortable for the heart, very good against al pestiferous effects therof vsed, with great profite.
Take of the rootes of *Angelica,* of Cloues, of Goates beard, of Tormentil or Set-foyle, of Bifolium, or two-blades of Enula campans, of each two ounces. Of yealow Sanders, and of the barke of the same, of each one ounce and a halfe. Of white Diptani, of Scabiose, of Rus, of Goates beard, otherwise called Meedwoort, of each one handfull. Of the Flowers of the lesse Centaure, of S. *Iohns-woort,* of Broome, of Violets, of Borage, of Buglosse, of Water-Lyllie, of Red Roses, of each, a three finger gripe. Put these into 3. pound of Malmesie infused by the space of 4. dayes, set vpon the fire of *Baln M.* and the Juice of Lemons, the water Melissa,

78. Measure.

79. Most likely a bain-marie (I am grateful to Winston Black for checking the Latin version of this text and for this suggestion). Subsequent instances of this or similar spelling, likewise, most likely refer to a bain-marie.

Acetouse, and of Roses mingled with the sayd Wine, of each one pound. Then strayne them.

In the liqnor distrained, put of Treacle ounces three, of the confection of Hiacinth, one ounce. Of the confection Alchermes, 6. drachmes. Of Diamargarit friged, Diatria Santali, of each 3. drachmes; of Diambre, and Diacoral, of each two drachmes, of Saffron, and Myrrhe, of each halfe a drachme. Infuse them againe, by the space of two or three dayes, at the same fire of *Baln. M.* Then distil them to drinesse by fire of ashes, and it will be a Treacle water. But to make it the more effectuall, the Salt must be extracted out of the feces which remaine, according to arte, and then mingeled with the foresaid water. ...

Principall Remedies to ease the torments and extreame paines of the Goute.

Take of the leaues of Missel, which groweth on the Apple-tree, cut or shred very smal, halfe a pound; the flowers of white Mulline, of Chamomil, of Lyllies, of Wall-woort, or Danewoort, all the kindes of Poppey, with their cases which containe the seed, new gathered, and before they be full ripe, of each one gripe of the 2. fingers and the thumbe; of greene Frogs, or in steed of them, the Ielly or sperme of Frogges, which is to be found in standing waters in the Moneth of Marth, one pound; the seed of white Poppey, brused, 4. ounces, of Crabbes or Crafishes shelles, and all beaten or crushed together, 20. in number; of red Snailes, and Earth-wormes, both wel washed in good white wine, of each 4. Ounces; of Badgers grease 6xe ounces; of Sperma Ceti, 4. ounces; of the oyle of violets or water Lilly, newly made, 6 pound: or if you wil, in steede of these oyles, take so much of oyle Oliue.

Put these into a glasse vessel, for that purpose conuenient, and close stopt, set it in horse dung by the space of 7. or 8. dayes. But if need require more haste let them boyle in a Copper vessel ouer the fire, by the space of two houres, and then straine them strongly. The which also you shalt doe if they stand in Horse dung to be digested.

Thou then shalt seperate the oyle from the watery part thereof according to arte, to the which oyle thou shalt adde of Saffron 2. ounces, of Camphyre hale[80] an ounce. Put all these into a glasse vessel, and set them againe in Horse dung, or in Balneo, or in the Sunne, by the space of 5. dayes, and thou shalt haue a most excellent Balsam to asswage and qualifie all paines of the Goute and in the ioynts.

I wish that all Apothecaries would prepare this, to be reary[81] at al times for present vse, for that they cannot appoint themselues of any thing better than this, which my selfe haue found true by experience.

80. "Halfe" most likely intended here.

81. "Ready" most likely intended here.

A plaister to helpe and easie all paines of the Goute.
Take the marrow or pulpe of Cassla foure ounces, of new Treacle, the newer the better, halfe an ounce. The meale of Barley and Oates, of each three ounces. The crumbes of white breade foure ounces; of Cowe-milke, two or three pound.

Let al these be sodden in the forme of a Cataplasme; which thou shalt apply warme to the grieued parts. It thou shalt adde one ounce of Vitriol calcined, and beaten into the pouder, thou shall make it much better. ...

Further Reading

This section supplements the bibliography for each text and expands the historical and academic scope of texts compiled in Parts 1 and 2 in order to further contextualize each section and subsection, and to provide suggestions for more general secondary source readings relevant to them. For both Parts 1 and 2 recommended primary sources are given, to be read alongside the texts paired in each part and to supplement their reading by giving examples of other primary sources that touch upon the same subject, but often provide different angles, or represent points of view on given matters that differ, confirm, or contradict the texts anthologized here. Secondary sources for each section and subsection provide additional historical and theoretical context. These sources provide both works of a more general interest in relation to each Part's subject matter, and a few more specific studies that should prove helpful in reading both the anthologized primary sources and those listed here. Titles of primary sources (particularly early modern works) are given in shortened versions.

PART 1

Soul

Seven Deadly Sins

Alcock, John. *Mons perfectionis*. 1497.

Ames, William. *The marrow of sacred divinity*. 1642.

Andrewes, Lancelot. *The morall law expounded*. 1642.

Bayly, Lewis. *The practice of pietie*. 1613.

Carpenter, Richard. *The last, and highest appeal. Or, An appeal to God, against the new-religion-makers, dresters, menders, or venders amongst us*. 1656.

Chertsey, Andrew, trans. *Ihesus, The floure of the commaundementes of god*. 1521.

Jacob's well. ca. 1450.

Laurent d'Orléans. *Livre des vices et des vertus*. ca. 1279.

Mannyng, Robert. *Handlyng synne*. 1303.

Narne, William. *The pearle of prayer most pretious and powerfull.* 1630.

New English primer. 1687.

Reynolds, Edward. *Sinfulness of sin.* 1634.

Sheffeild, John. *The hypocrites ladder, or looking-glasse. Or A discourse of the dangerous and destructive nature of hypocrisie.* 1657.

Weye of paradys. ca. 1400.

Sins of the Tongue and Mouth

Baxter, Richard. *The vain religion of the formal hypocrite, and the mischief of an unbridled tongue.* 1660.

Bicknoll, Edmond. *A sword against swearers and blasphemers.* 1609.

Fisher, Samuel. *One antidote more, against that provoking sin of swearing.* 1660.

Hammond, Samuel. *Gods judgements upon drunkards, swearers, and sabbath-breakers.* 1659.

Mather, Increase. *Wo to drunkards. Two sermons testifying against the sin of drunkenness.* 1673.

Secondary sources:

Bejczy, István Pieter. *The Cardinal Virtues in the Middle Ages: A Study in Moral Thought from the Fourth to the Fourteenth Century.* Leiden: Brill, 2011.

Bloomfield, Morton W. *The Seven Deadly Sins.* Michigan: Michigan State College Press, 1952.

Bodden, M. C. *Language as the Site of Revolt in Medieval and Early Modern England.* New York: Palgrave Macmillan, 2011.

Craun, Edwin David. *Lies, Slander and Obscenity in Medieval English Literature. Pastoral Rhetoric and the Deviant Speaker.* Cambridge: Cambridge University Press, 1997.

Herdt, Jennifer A. *Putting on Virtue: the Legacy of the Splendid Vices.* Chicago: Chicago University Press, 2008.

Kamensky, Jane. *Governing the Tongue: The Politics of Speech in Early New England.* New York: Oxford University Press, 1997.

Newhauser, Richard. *The Early History of Greed: The Sin of Avarice in Early Medieval Thought and Literature.* Cambridge: Cambridge University Press, 2000.

—. *In the Garden of Evil. The Vices and Culture in the Middle Ages.* Toronto: Pontifical Institute of Mediaeval Studies, 2005.

—. *The Treatise on Vices and Virtues in Latin and the Vernacular.* Turnhout: Brepols, 1993.

—, and John A. Alford, eds. *Literature and Religion in the Later Middle Ages. Philological Studies in Honor of Siegfried Wenzel.* Binghamton: Medieval & Renaissance Texts & Studies, 1995.

Wenzel, Siegfried. *The Sin of Sloth: Acedia in Medieval Thought and Literature*. Chapel Hill: University of North Carolina Press, 1967.

Emotion

Fear of the Wrath of God, the End of Days, and the Devil

Beard, Thomas, trans. *The theatre of Gods iudgements: or, a collection of histories out of sacred, ecclesiasticall, and prophane authours*. 1597.

A Briefe explanation of the XX chapter of the revelation of Saint John wherein is contained the binding of the dragon for a thousand years. 1641.

Brightman, Thomas. *A revelation of the Apocalyps, that is, the Apocalyps of S. Iohn illustrated with an analysis and scolions*. 1611.

Danforth, Samuel. *The cry of Sodom enquired into; upon occasion of the arraignment and condemnation of Benjamin Goad*. 1674.

Frith, John. *A pistle to the Christen reader. The revelation of Antichrist*. 1529.

Goodwin, Thomas. *A discourse of the punishment of sin in hell; demonstrating the wrath of God to be the immediate cause thereof*. 1680.

Mather, Increase. *An essay for the recording of illustrious providences*. 1684.

Rogers, Nathaniel. *A letter discovering the cause of Gods continuing wrath against the nation notwithstanding the present endeavors of reformation*. 1644.

Smyth, John. *The character of the beast: or, The false constitution of the church*. 1609.

Death, Anxiety, and Sorrow

Bates, William. *The four last things: viz. death, judgment, heaven, hell, practically considered and applied, in several discourses*. 1691.

Bunyan, John. *One thing is needful: or, Serious meditations upon the four last things*. 1680.

Chertsey, Andrew, trans. *The crafte to lyue well and to dye well*. 1505.

Death's universal summons: or, A general call, to all mankind, to the grave. 1650.

The Doctrynalle of dethe. 1498.

Gardiner, Samuel. *The deuotions of the dying man, that desireth to die well*. 1627.

Longland, Thomas. *Quatuor novissma: or, Meditations upon the four last things, delivered in four common-place discourses*. 1657.

Sutton, Christopher. *Disce mori. Learne to die*. 1600.

Threnoikos, the house of mourning. 1640.

Secondary sources:

Daniel, Christopher. *Death and Burial in Medieval England*. London: Routledge, 1997.

Emmerson, Richard and Bernard McGinn, eds. *The Apocalypse in the Middle Ages.* Ithaca: Cornell University Press, 1992.

Ferreiro, Alberto. *The Devil, Heresy, and Witchcraft in the Middle Ages: Essays in Honor of Jeffrey B. Russell.* Leiden: Brill, 1998.

Gordon, Bruce and Peter Marshall, eds. *The Place of the Dead: Death and Remembrance in Medieval and Early Modern Europe.* Cambridge: Cambridge University Press, 2000.

Hall, David D. *Worlds of Wonder, Days of Judgement. Popular Religious Belief in Early New England.* Cambridge: Harvard University Press, 1990.

Hammond, Jeffrey A. *The American Puritan Elegy: A Literary and Cultural Study.* Cambridge: Cambridge University Press, 2004.

Ingebretsen, Edward J. *Maps of Heaven, Maps of Hell.* Armonk, NY: M.E. Sharpe, 1996.

McGinn, Bernard. *Visions of the End: Apocalyptic Traditions in the Middle Ages.* New York: Columbia University Press, 1979.

Stannard, David E. *The Puritan Way of Death: A Study in Religion, Culture, and Social Change.* Oxford: Oxford University Press, 1979.

Walker Bynum, Caroline and Paul Freedman, eds. *Last Things: Death and the Apocalypse in the Middle Ages.* Philadelphia: University of Pennsylvania Press, 2000.

Whalen, Brett Edward. *Dominion of God: Christendom and the Apocalypse in the Middle Ages.* Cambridge: Harvard University Press, 2009.

Spiritual Health

Confession and Contrition

Caryl, Joseph. *Confession of sin.* 1645.

The complaynt of the soule. 1532.

Goodwin, Thomas. *Certaine select cases resolved: specially tending to the comfort of beleevers, in their chief and usuall temptations.* 1651.

Hooker, Thomas. *The soules humiliation.* 1640.

Perkins, William. *The whole treatise of the cases of conscience.* 1608.

Prick of conscience. ca. 1430.

The rote or myrour of consolacyon and conforte. 1496.

"Sinner's lament." ca.1450.

Comfort and Consolation

[Bonaventure.] *Stimulus diuini amoris: that is, the goade of divine love.* 1642.

The clensyng of mannes sowle. ca. 1400.

Hooker, Thomas. *The application of redemption, by the effectual work of the word, and spirit of Christ, for the bringing home of lost sinners to God.* 1656.

Rolle, Richard. *Incendium amoris.* ca.1330.

This tretyse is of loue and spekyth of iiij of the most specyall louys that ben in the worlde. 1493.

Curing Spiritual Disease

Adams, Thomas. *Diseases of the soule: a discourse diuine, morall, and physicall.* 1616.

Andrewes, John. *A soueraigne salue to cure a sicke soule, infected with the poyson of sinne.* 1624.

Brooks, Thomas. *Precious remedies against Satans devices.* 1656.

Love, Christopher. *The dejected soules cure: tending to support poor drooping sinners. With rules, comforts, and cautions in severall cases.* 1657.

Younge, Richard. *A counterpoyson: or, Soverain antidote against all griefe.* 1641.

Secondary sources:

Biller, Peter and A.J. Minnis, eds. *Handling Sin: Confession in the Middle Ages.* York: York Medieval Press, 1998.

Boda, Mark J. and Gordon T. Smith, eds. *Repentance in Christian Theology.* Collegeville, MN: Liturgical Press, 2006.

Brantley, Jessica. *Reading in the Wilderness. Private Devotion and Public Performance in Late Medieval England.* Chicago: University of Chicago Press, 2007.

Bryan, Jennifer. *Looking Inward: Devotional Reading and the Private Self in Late Medieval England.* Philadelphia: University of Pennsylvania Press, 2008.

Cefalụ, Paul. *Moral Identity in Early Modern English Literature.* New York: Cambridge University Press, 2004.

Firey, Abigail, ed. *A New History of Penance.* Leiden: Brill, 2008.

Jolliffe, P.S. *A Check-List of Middle English Prose Writings of Spiritual Guidance.* Subsidia mediaevalia 2. Toronto: Pontifical Institute of Mediaeval Studies, 1974.

PART 2

Body

Women and Men

Allestree, Richard. *The ladies calling.* 1673.

Brathwaite, Richard. *The English gentleman; and the English gentlewoman: both in one volume couched, and in one model portrayed.* 1641.

The cuckholds petition to the parliament of women. 1684.

A description of wanton women. 1674–1679 (according to the English Short Title Catalogue, http://estc.bl.uk; *EEBO*, however, gives 1690).

[Landry de La Tour, Geoffroy.] *Here begynneth the booke which the knyght of the toure made and speketh of many fayre ensamples and thensygnementys and techyng of his daughters.* 1484.

[Roeslin, Eucharius.] *The byrth of mankynde, newly translated out of Laten into Englysshe.* 1540.

Sowernam, Ester. *Ester hath hang'd Haman: or An answere to a lewd pamphlet, entituled, The arraignment of women.* 1617.

Swetnam, Joseph. *The arraignment of lewd, idle, froward, and vnconstant women,* 1615.

Watson, Henry, trans. *The gospelles of dystaues.* 1510.

Strangers in Foreign Lands

[Bartholomaeus Anglicus.] *Batman vppon Bartholome, his booke De proprietatibus rerum.* 1582.

Carr, Ralph, trans. *The Mahumetane or Turkish historie.* 1600.

Cartwright, John. *The preachers trauels. Wherein is set downe a true iournall to the confines of the East Indies, through the great countreyes of Syria, Mesopotamia, Armenia, Media, Hircania and Parthia.* 1611.

Here after foloweth a lytell treatyse agaynst Mahumet and his cursed secte and fyrst foloweth the introduccyon. 1530.

Parry, William. *A new and large discourse of the trauels of sir Anthony Sherley Knight, by sea, and ouer land, to the Persian Empire ... and also, the description and conditions of those countries and people he passed by: with his returne into Christendome.* 1601.

[Polo, Marco.] *The most noble and famous trauels of Marcus Paulus, one of the nobilitie of the state of Venice, into the east partes of the world.* 1579.

This is the begynnynge, and contynuaunce of the pylgrymage of Sir Richarde Guylforde Knyght, and controuler vnto our late soueraygne lorde kynge Henry the. vij. And howe he went with his seruauntz and company towardes Iherusalem. 1511.

Secondary sources:

Bardsley, Sandy. *Women's Roles in the Middle Ages.* Westport, CT: Greenwood, 2007.

Barr, Beth Allison. *The Pastoral Care of Women in Late Medieval England.* Woodbridge, UK: Boydell, 2008.

Cohen, Jeffrey Jerome. *Hybridity, Identity, and Monstrosity in Medieval Britain: On Difficult Middles.* New York: Palgrave Macmillan, 2006.

—, ed. *The Postcolonial Middle Ages.* New York: Palgrave Macmillan, 2001.

Erler, Mary and Maryanne Kowaleski, eds. *Women and Power in the Middle Ages.* Georgia: University of Georgia Press, 1988.

Hallam, Elizabeth and Brian V. Street, eds. *Cultural Encounters: Representing Otherness.* Oxford: Routledge, 2000.

Kay, Sarah and Miri Rubin, eds. *Framing Medieval Bodies.* Manchester: Manchester University Press, 1996.

Ross, Jill and Suzanne Conklin Akabari, eds. *The Ends of the Body: Identity and Community in Medieval Culture.* Toronto: University of Toronto Press, 2013.

Mind

The Evil and Ignorant Mind

[Bernard of Clairvaux.] *A compendius and a moche fruytefull treatyse of well liuynge, contaynyng the hole summe and effect of al vertue. Wrytten by S. Bernard and translated by Thomas Paynell.* 1545.

Perkins, William. *The first part of The cases of conscience.* 1604.

Roye, Gui de. *Thus endeth the doctrinal of sapyence the whyche is ryght vtile and prouffytable to alle crysten men.* 1489.

Rycharde Rolle hermyte of Hampull in his contemplacyons of the drede and loue of god. 1506.

Withford, Richard. *Here followeth dyuers holy instrucyons and teachynges very necessarye for the helth of mannes soule.* 1541.

Vices and Virtues of the Mind

Adams, Thomas. *Mystical bedlam, or the world of mad-men.* 1615.

Betson, Thomas. *Here begynneth a ryght profytable treatyse compendiously drawen out of many and dyuers wrytynges of holy men, to dyspose men to be vertuously occupyed in theyr myndes and prayers.* 1500.

Burton, Robert. *The anatomy of melancholy.* 1621.

Davies, John. *Wits bedlam, – where is had, whipping-cheer, to cure the mad.* 1617.

Elyot, Thomas. *Of the knowledeg whiche maketh a wise man.* 1533.

Mosley, Nicholas. *Psychosophia: or, Natural and divine contemplations of the passions and faculties of the soul of man.* 1653.

Universall madnesse: or, A new merry letany. 1647.

Secondary sources:

Corneanu, Sorana. *Regimens of the Mind: Boyle, Locke, and the Early Modern* Cultura Animi *Tradition.* Chicago: University of Chicago Press, 2011.

Ebbersmeyer, Sabrina, ed. *Emotional Minds: The Passions and the Limits of Pure Inquiry in Early Modern Philosophy.* Berlin: De Gruyter, 2012.

Lund, Mary Anne. *Melancholy, Medicine, and Religion in Early Modern England. Reading the "Anatomy of Melancholy."* Cambridge: Cambridge University Press, 2010.

Schmidt, Jeremy. *Melancholy and the Care of the Soul. Religion, Moral Philosophy and Madness in Early Modern England.* Aldershot, UK: Ashgate, 2007.

Vidal, Fernando. *The Sciences of the Soul. The Early Modern Origins of Psychology.* Chicago: Chicago University Press, 2011.

Waldow, Anik, ed. *Sensibility in the Early Modern Era: From Living Machines to Affective Morality.* New York: Routledge, 2016.

Health

Preventing Disease

Allen, James. *Serious advice to delivered ones from sickness, or any other dangers threatning death.* 1679.

Elyot, Thomas. *The castel of helth.* 1545.

The graces folowyng be graunted to al the bretherne and systers benefactours and good doers ... that they shal neuer be infecte not greued with the stroke of the pestilence. 1522.

Vaughan, William. *Directions for health, naturall and artificiall: derived from the best physicians, as well moderne as antient.* 1633.

Disease

Greaves, Edward. *Morbus epidemius anni 1643. Or, The new disease with the signes, causes, remedies, &c.* 1643.

J.T. of Westminster. *The hunting of the pox: a pleasant discourse betweene the authour, and pild-garlicke. Wherein is declared the nature of the dissease, how it came, and how it may bee cured.* 1619.

A moche profitable treatise against the pestilence translated into Eglyshe by Thomas Paynel Chanon of Martin Abbey. 1534.

Sadler, John. *The sicke womans private looking-glasse wherein methodically are handled all uterine affects, or diseases arising from the wombe.* 1636.

Swadlin, Thomas. *Sermons, meditations, and prayers, upon the plague.* 1637.

Curing Disease

Boorde, Andrew. *The breuiary of helthe, for all maner of syckenesses and diseases.* 1547.

Bunworth, Richard. *Homotropia naturae. A physical discourse, exhibiting the cure of diseases by signature.* 1656.

[Osiander, Andreas.] *How and whither a Christen man ought to flye the horrible plage of the pestilence. A sermon.* 1537.

Proprytees and medicynes of hors. 1497 or 1498.

Secondary sources:

Dobson, Mary J. *Contours of Death and Disease in Early Modern England*. Cambridge: Cambridge University Press, 1997.

Grigsby, Byron Lee. *Pestilence in Medieval and Early Modern English Literature*. London: Routledge, 2004.

Langum, Virginia. *Medicine and the Seven Deadly Sins in Late Medieval Literature and Culture*. New York: Palgrave Macmillan, 2016.

Lindemann, Mary. *Medicine and Society in Early Modern Europe*. Cambridge: Cambridge University Press, 2010.

Pender, Stephen and Nancy Struever, eds. *Rhetoric and Medicine in Early Modern Europe*. Oxford: Routledge, 2012.

Siena, Kevin, ed. *Sins of the Flesh: Responding to Sexual Disease in Early Modern Europe*. Toronto: Centre for Reformation and Renaissance Studies, 2005.

Siraisi, Nancy. *Medieval and Early Renaissance Medicine: An Introduction to Knowledge and Practice*. Chicago: University of Chicago Press, 1990.

Vaught, Jennifer C. *Rhetorics of Bodily Disease and Health in Medieval and Early Modern England*. New York: Routledge, 2016.

Yoshikawa, Naoë Kukita, ed. *Medicine, Religion, and Gender in Medieval Culture*. Cambridge: D.S. Brewer, 2015.